New York Institute of Finance
Guide to
MUTUAL
FUNDS
1999

Kirk Kazanjian

NEW YORK INSTITUTE OF FINANCE

NEW YORK • TORONTO • SYDNEY • TOKYO • SINGAPORE

Library of Congress Cataloging in Publication Data

Kazanjian, Kirk.
   Guide to mutual funds, 1999 / Kirk Kazanjian ; foreword by Stephen
Savage.
      p.   cm.
   At head of title: New York Institute of Finance.
   Includes index.
   ISBN 0-7352-0074-2
   1. Mutual funds—United States—Directories. I. New York
Institute of Finance. II. Title.
HG4930.K393   1998
332.63'27—dc21   98-38867
                                                    CIP

Printed in the United States of America

10 9 8 7 6 5 4 3 2 1

This publication is designed to provide accurate and authoritative information in regard to the
subject matter covered. It is sold with the understanding that the publisher is not engaged in
rendering legal, accounting, or other professional service. If legal advice or other expert
assistance is required, the services of a competent professional person should be sought.

> *. . . From the Declaration of Principles jointly adopted by a Committee of the
> American Bar Association and a Committee of Publishers and Associations.*

Although the information and data in this book was obtained from sources believed to be
reliable, neither the author, publishers, nor Value Line assumes the responsibility for its
accuracy. Under no circumstances does the information in this book represent a
recommendation to buy or sell stocks or funds.

All charts and data are copyrighted by Value Line Publishing, Inc.

ISBN 0-7352-0074-2

ATTENTION: CORPORATIONS AND SCHOOLS
Prentice Hall books are available at quantity discounts with bulk purchase for
educational, business, or sales promotional use. For information, please write to:
Prentice Hall Special Sales, 240 Frisch Court, Paramus, New Jersey 07652. Please
supply: title of book, ISBN, quantity, how the book will be used, date needed.

New York Institute of Finance
An Imprint of Prentice Hall Press
Paramus, NJ 07652
A Simon & Schuster Company

Prentice Hall International (UK) Limited, *London*
Prentice Hall of Australia Pty. Limited, *Sydney*
Prentice Hall Canada, Inc., *Toronto*
Prentice Hall Hispanoamericana, S.A., *Mexico*
Prentice Hall of India Private Limited, *New Delhi*
Prentice Hall of Japan, Inc., *Tokyo*
Simon & Schuster Asia Pte. Ltd., *Singapore*
Editora Prentice Hall do Brasil, Ltda., *Rio de Janeiro*

To my mom and dad,
with love and admiration.

CONTENTS

Chapter 7

Putting Your Portfolio Together 260

Chapter 8

The 25 Best Internet Sites for Mutual Fund Investors 277

Chapter 9

Value Line Performance Data for Some 8,000 Funds 286

FOREWORD

Mutual fund investing just isn't fair. Sure, funds are great vehicles, offering convenience, a range of opportunities, and the best set of safeguards for investors on earth. Yet, despite all the readily available information out there, all the work put into researching and selecting funds, and all the amazing track records we read about, American investors as a group still perform relatively poorly. A recent study compared the actual returns investors received to those of the funds they were invested in. It found that the average investor only made about half the funds' posted returns. How is this possible? Bad timing and a lack of discipline leads most investors to run into funds after they rack up big gains, and then causes them to sell after periods of weakness.

What should you do? Clearly you must have access to good research. The *New York Institute of Finance Guide to Mutual Funds* contains a wealth of information and data that can help you succeed. But you also need a broader context as you evaluate this information, so here are some key points to keep in mind:

- First, consider your overall goals and risk tolerance when putting your portfolio together. This point is admittedly such a cliché that investors don't seem to take it seriously. But to be successful, you must understand your overall objectives and determine what mix of investments makes the most sense for you. It should be a mix that's not likely to lose more than you can stand, while at the same time earning the best possible return. Your time horizon definitely affects the amount of risk you can tolerate.

- Next, you've got to have some basis for choosing a set of investments. You can't just pick the one that's *likely* to make the most money, because you *don't* know, and *can't* know, the answer to that. You are dealing with probabilities and trying to offset the inherent uncertainties involved in investing. This is what the next step, *diversification,* is all about.

- Diversification is the spreading of your investments across different types of assets. It's important because if any one asset class gets hammered, the others will normally pull the slack. Most investors underperform the market because they load up their portfolios with today's hot performers. What they don't realize is that all of these funds are doing well, by and large, because they own the same types of investments. And when the market cycle that put them on top of the charts inevitably shifts, the investor sees his or her entire portfolio go with it.

- Once you've determined a suitable mix of investments, or asset allocation, you need to select funds within those groups. A major benefit of asset allocation is that the process of picking funds becomes immeasurably easier. Since you no longer face the daunting task of trying to select the best fund from a list of nearly 9,000 names, you can concentrate on finding specific funds within far narrower groups. Comparisons now become much easier, since potential holdings are being stacked up only against like funds.

- You should look for funds with consistent track records. Ask some questions as you peer through the data. Does the fund really belong in its class? Does it consistently follow the style for which you are purchasing it? Sometimes the best performers in certain asset classes got there by investing outside their normal area of focus. Also find out if the manager responsible for the strong long-term track record is still running the fund. Manager turnover is common.

- Given all of the uncertainty in investing, it pays to have an edge in the few areas that are certain, such as fixed costs. Pay attention to expense ratios and sales charges, and compare them to similar funds. This is especially true on the bond side, where a few tenths of a percent in expenses can mean the difference between a fund that is near the top or bottom of its peer group.

- Once you have compiled a short list of fund candidates (the *Guide's* 100 Powerhouse Performers is a good place to start), don't be a chicken. Choose your funds, make your investments, and get on with it. Inaction is a greater threat to your financial future than not picking a perfect fund every time. The funds you buy are going to perform, to a greater or lesser extent, like the broader classes they represent. So don't worry. If you've constructed your overall portfolio carefully, you won't have to be overly concerned about any one selection.

- If you are afraid we might be close to a market top, and have a large lump sum to invest, split it up and invest it in equal monthly or quarterly installments over a period of time (say, the next six to twelve months). This technique is known as dollar cost averaging. Continue to add to your investment portfolio in regular increments—that way you will buy more shares when prices are low and fewer shares when they are high. And don't forget your target allocations.

- Finally, if you take away only one thing about building a portfolio from this discussion, remember this: Any time you add a fund, you've got to consider not only its independent characteristics, but also how it reacts with the rest of your holdings. Some funds may add risk with only little added return potential. Meanwhile, sometimes a volatile fund can bring down your portfolio's overall risk, because it behaves so differently from your other holdings.

Without question, you'll need to shift money around periodically to keep your target allocations in balance. And as time marches on, you'll want to gradually shift your mix toward a more conservative bent, to maintain the wealth you earned through a smart, patient, disciplined approach—an approach which may just have begun with the help of this book.

Stephen Savage

INTRODUCTION

Welcome to the first edition of the *New York Institute of Finance Guide to Mutual Funds 1999*. This new, annually updated book contains everything you need for making smart decisions about investing in funds, whether you're a seasoned pro or just starting out. You'll find plenty of helpful advice for putting together a winning investment plan: specific recommendations, model portfolios, and comprehensive performance data from the *Value Line Mutual Fund Survey*. (You won't find this information in any other book on the market today.) Besides getting an inside look at what it's like to manage a fund, from one of the industry's top pros, you'll discover 25 must-see Internet sites for investors loaded with information you can access absolutely free. It's like having the services of a trusted investment adviser at your fingertips all year long. I'll also reveal the names of the 100 most promising funds for 1999 for virtually every investment objective. I call them my "Powerhouse Performers." Each one is written up in a research report that includes historical graphs and a multitude of performance data. I can tell you that when it comes to funds, there are plenty of dogs out there. Fortunately, I have done all the homework for you to uncover the real gems.

Without question, mutual funds are *the* investment of choice among today's smart consumers. In fact, figures from the Investment Company Institute, the fund industry trade association, show that one in three Americans now own shares in at least one fund. Many books have been written on the subject of fund investing, but none contain the kind of specific and timely information found in this *Guide*. It will give you all the tools you need to build a comfortable financial future for yourself and your family. By the time you have finished reading this book, you will know:

- Precisely how mutual funds work,
- What to look for when choosing them,
- Which specific funds should do best in the year ahead,

- How to construct your own personal portfolio plan,
- Ways to make even more money using your computer.

Exhaustive performance data are given for some 8,000 stock and bond funds, along with a glossary of commonly used investment terms that all fund investors should know. You'll want to refer to this valuable information again and again.

HOW TO USE THIS BOOK

If you're brand new to fund investing, you'll want to start with Chapter 1 and work your way through the book from the beginning. Along the way, you'll learn all about how funds work, find out exactly what a portfolio manager does, determine whether you are better off in index or actively managed funds, discover the many ways to buy and sell funds, and get all of the tools you need to put together a winning investment plan. If, on the other hand, you are a more advanced fund investor, you might want to skip around a bit. Perhaps you can start off by reading my exclusive interview with Brian Posner in Chapter 2, to uncover some of the industry's top secrets. Then you can turn to Chapter 5, to learn about the only free lunch you'll find on Wall Street. (Hint: It's available only to fund investors.) After that, you can look through my "100 Powerhouse Performers" in Chapter 6, to uncover new ideas for your portfolio, and be sure to check out my list of the best Internet sites for fund investors in Chapter 8. Finally, everyone should spend some time going through the exhaustive list of Value Line data in Chapter 9. This wealth of information, found in no other book, will give you historical performance information on virtually every fund imaginable. That way you can compare what you own now with the many other choices available out there.

I will be updating this book each year, complete with new fund recommendations, model portfolios, Internet sites, fund manager interviews, performance data, and much more. Be on the lookout for the *New York Institute of Finance Guide to Mutual Funds 2000* at a bookstore near you!

For now let's get started on the road to developing a mutual fund investment plan for the coming year that you can profit from for decades to come.

1

MUTUAL FUNDS—
TODAY'S INVESTMENT
OF CHOICE

Access to the world's leading investment luminaries used to be reserved exclusively for the chosen few—those wealthy individuals with $1 million-plus portfolios. Even plain vanilla index funds, which have lately become all the rage, were off limits to all but the largest institutions. Anyone else who wanted to participate in the fortunes of the stock market had to rely on tips from a commission-based broker, who was likely schooled in salesmanship, not investing. The only alternative was to put money in a bank, where it earned a comparatively inferior amount of interest.

How times have changed! Now, someone with just $1,000 to invest can tap into the same expertise that is available to a corporate CEO with a $20 million portfolio. This is made possible through arguably the greatest invention ever created for individual investors—mutual funds. Virtually every noted Wall Street money pro now either runs a fund of his or her own or is involved in the management of one. Therefore, it's possible for almost everyone to hire the leading brainpower in the business for a very small fee. In fact, owning funds is much cheaper than buying stocks for most investors.

THE EXPLOSION OF MUTUAL FUNDS:
A BRIEF HISTORY

Investors around the world have been pouring money into funds at a record pace since 1995, but these investment vehicles have been around

1

much longer. The mutual fund industry traces its roots back to 1868, when the Foreign and Colonial Government Trust ("the Trust") was formed in London. This British investment company, which issued a fixed number of shares, spread its portfolio across a number of different stocks. The Trust resembled today's closed-end funds: the daily price was determined by supply and demand, instead of by the actual underlying net asset value of the securities. (Closed-end funds trade on one of the stock exchanges and must be purchased and sold through a broker.)

The first open-end fund—the kind we will be focusing on in this book—was launched in 1924, when the Massachusetts Investors Trust opened for business. It began with a $50,000 portfolio containing 45 stocks. In an open-end fund, new shares are continuously offered to the public. Shares can be sold at any time, and their prices are based on the current net asset value of the portfolio's underlying holdings. It's pretty simple to calculate a fund's net asset value (see Figure 1.1). Simply add up the value of every security in the portfolio, based on the closing market price, and divide that result by the number of outstanding shares. In other words, if you have a portfolio worth $100 and you own a total of 100 shares, the net asset value per share would be $1.

TOUGH BEGINNINGS

The mutual fund industry got off to a rocky start in the United States. The 1929 stock market crash, and the resulting Great Depression, scared many investors away from equities in general. These events also caused Congress to enact a series of laws regulating the securities and financial markets, in an effort to protect investors. The Securities Act of 1933, for example, required every fund sponsor to issue a prospectus describing how the portfolio would be invested. The most important law for fund investors is the Investment Company Act of 1940, which mandates that funds are priced based on the day's closing market value. It also prohibits transactions between a fund and its manager, sets up a statutory system of independent

---

FIGURE 1.1   WHAT IS NET ASSET VALUE?

$$\text{Net Asset Value} = \frac{\text{Total Assets} - \text{Liabilities}}{\text{Number of Shares Outstanding}}$$

fund directors, requires funds to redeem shares upon demand, and sets out a series of rules that must be followed in the area of bookkeeping.

Mutual funds began to catch on with the American public during the 1940s and 1950s. In 1940, there were fewer than 80 funds, and their total assets were around $500 million. Two decades later, there were 160 funds with collective assets of $17 billion! Almost all of these early funds had a front-end sales load and were peddled exclusively through stockbrokers. The "load" averaged around 8 percent and served as a commission taken right off the top to compensate the broker. If you invested $100 in a fund with an 8 percent load, $8 immediately went into the broker's pocket, effectively putting only $92 to work. Even behemoth Fidelity Investments, which was formed in the 1930s, distributed its funds through brokers. That policy was changed after the brutal 1973–1974 bear market, which once again soured the public's appetite for mutual funds. In an effort to create new business, Ned Johnson, Fidelity's founder, came up with a unique idea. He introduced the first money market fund with a check-writing feature. These investments were touted as safe vehicles that offered investors easy access to their money. To keep the fund's yield as high as possible, Johnson decided to try selling it directly to the public by advertising a toll-free number in the newspapers. The strategy was so successful that he soon converted many of his stock and bond funds to "no-loads" and began offering them through this channel as well.

There are now some 9,000 mutual funds in the United States alone—more than the number of available individual stocks. These funds' combined assets are close to $5 trillion. This amount is even more staggering when we realize that less than one decade ago, total fund assets stood at a mere $1 trillion. Throughout the mid-1990s, money from individual investors flowed into funds at a feverish pace. Most of this cash landed in stock funds, which showered investors with incredible returns, thanks to a roaring bull market. Without question, this constant stream of new money fueled the market's rise. At year end 1997, 53 percent of total fund assets were in stocks, 23 percent were in bonds, and 24 percent were in money market funds (Figure 1.2).

FUNDS ARE HOT

One reason funds have become so popular is that Americans are now being forced to invest. A generation ago, a recent graduate would go to work for a large company that promised to pay a sizable monthly pension

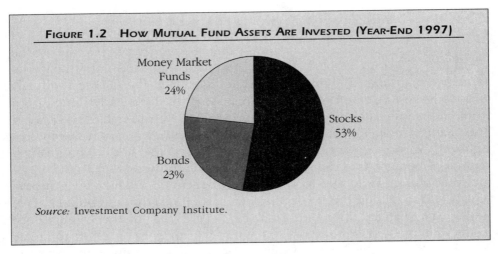

FIGURE 1.2   HOW MUTUAL FUND ASSETS ARE INVESTED (YEAR-END 1997)

Money Market Funds 24%

Stocks 53%

Bonds 23%

Source: Investment Company Institute.

after retirement. That pension, combined with a Social Security check, would surely provide enough income to live comfortably in the sunset years, or so people thought. For better or worse, things are much different now. Most companies, especially smaller ones, don't even offer pensions. Instead, employees may be offered a chance to contribute to a retirement program such as a 401(k) or SEP-IRA, in which workers have a certain percentage of their income deducted and usually placed into a portfolio of funds. It's up to each employee to figure out how that money is to be invested, be it in stocks, bonds, or money market instruments. Therefore, millions of everyday folks have had to bone up on investing, since they are required to make these integral decisions about how to save for their financial future. The other changing dynamic is that most younger Americans don't believe Social Security will be around when they need it, despite the federal government's assurances. Therefore, in addition to contributing to employer-sponsored retirement plans, wise individuals are setting up investment portfolios on their own, both regular and IRAs (individual retirement accounts), to make sure they are taken care of financially when they ultimately decide to leave the workforce. The *really* smart ones invest their money through carefully selected mutual funds.

WHY YOU SHOULD INVEST IN FUNDS

≡ There are a number of reasons why funds make so much sense for most investors. I'll begin with a few of the obvious ones: diversification, low costs, professional management, ease of buying and selling, convenience, and a mix of asset classes.

Diversification

One of the first rules of investing is: Don't put all of your eggs in one basket. That's especially true with the stock market. In today's volatile trading environment, a small disappointment from even a blue-chip company can cause its stock to get hammered severely. What's more, a constant sector rotation is going on in the market. Financial stocks may do well this quarter, but technology companies may find favor with investors in the next quarter, followed by the pharmaceuticals, and so on. If you own a well-rounded list of stocks, you increase the odds that at least a portion of the list will always be in the right place at the right time. Having a large list of holdings also reduces your "specific stock risk"—the danger that a company you own will see its share price get sliced as a result of some unforeseen bad news. When you buy into a stock fund, you instantly tap into a portfolio that likely owns shares in dozens of different companies. Even the most concentrated funds usually list at least 20 names. The same is true for bond and money market funds, which can spread their portfolios across a broad range of companies and maturities to smooth out volatility and increase overall returns. Unless you have at least a six-figure amount to invest, it would be cost-prohibitive to buy a basket of individual securities on your own. The commissions alone would kill you. When you invest in a fund, you instantly benefit from the economies of scale enjoyed by spreading these costs among a large base of shareholders.

Low Costs

Every mutual fund, whether it has a sales load or not, comes with underlying management fees. These charges, expressed in the form of expense ratios, can be found near the front of every prospectus. The average expense ratio for stock funds is around 1.40 percent; for fixed-income portfolios, it is under 1 percent. If you have $1,000 in a stock fund with an expense ratio of 1.40 percent, you would pay the fund $14 a year for managing your money. The fund never sends you a bill for this charge. Instead, the fee is automatically deducted from the net asset value each day. Just think: for $14 a year (give or take a few bucks, depending on the particular fund you choose and the amount you invest), you can hire a highly educated investment pro, backed up by a team of equally smart research analysts, to make buy-and-sell decisions on your behalf. As fund manager Brian Posner argues in Chapter 2, that's one of the best values available in America today.

Incidentally, I recommend that you always stick with no-load funds, especially if you're making your own investment decisions. In the pages that follow, you will be given an enormous amount of information you can use to put together a winning fund portfolio, including my list, in Chapter 6, of the year's "100 Powerhouse Performers." I chose these hand-selected favorites for 1999 after doing an exhaustive amount of proprietary research. You'll notice that every one of these funds is offered on a no-load basis. You won't pay a penny to buy or sell them, so every cent of your investment dollar can work for you.

PROFESSIONAL MANAGEMENT

When you buy shares in a fund, you truly gain access to some of the sharpest minds on Wall Street. A few decades ago, this simply wasn't possible unless an investor placed a ton of money into an individually managed account. The expertise is similar, by the way, whether we're talking about actively managed funds (run by a human) or passive funds (index funds or similar offerings run solely by a computer). After all, it takes a high degree of intelligence to program a computer to properly replicate a given index in the first place. I have been struck, over the past couple of years, by the number of people who are convinced that they could do just as well, if not better, by choosing individual stocks on their own rather than using a fund. This belief has been exacerbated by the abnormally high returns offered by index funds, which have led to a media storm of bashing active managers. If your attitude is "If these highly paid fund managers can't beat the market, I might as well do the stock picking on my own," think about what you're saying. You're contending that you have more brilliance and savvy than managers who spend 16 hours a day researching and watching the market. In an occasional streak of good luck, you might pick a stock that doubles or triples in a short period of time. But, as market veterans say, "Don't confuse brains with a bull market." When you make individual stock selections on your own, you are competing against career experts who have much more experience and clout than you do.

MUTUAL FUND FEES AND EXPENSES

Two types of costs are involved in running a fund: (1) shareholder transaction expenses and (2) annual operating expenses.

1. **Shareholder transaction expenses** are fees charged directly to the investor for purchases, redemptions, or exchanges. For the most part, these expenses apply only to load funds. However, some no-load funds charge fees for early redemption, to discourage short-term trading. The following expenses can be expected:

   - *Front-end sales load.* This fee, charged at the time of purchase, compensates financial professionals for selling the fund to you. By law, this fee may not exceed 8.5 percent of the initial investment.

   - *Deferred sales charge.* Also called a "back-end load," this fee is charged at the time you sell shares in a fund. It is normally used as an alternative to a front-end load. In many funds, the deferred sales charge is reduced or eliminated over time.

   - *Redemption fee.* This is another type of back-end charge imposed for redeeming shares. It can be expressed as either a dollar amount or a percentage of the redemption price. It is occasionally imposed by no-load funds as a way of deterring short-term trading.

   - *Exchange fee.* This charge is imposed on shareholders when transferring money from one fund to another within the same family.

2. **Annual operating expenses** are the normal costs involved in operating a fund (i.e., for research, management, and equipment). Unlike transaction fees, these expenses are deducted directly from fund assets on a daily basis, instead of being billed to the investor. They are expressed as a percentage of the total net worth of the investment.

   - *Management fees.* This is what the fund's investment adviser charges for running the fund. Management fees are typically between 0.5 percent and 1 percent of assets, and ideally are reduced as the asset base increases.

   - *12b-1 fees.* This expense, named for the SEC rule that created it, is being charged by an increasing number of funds. It is used to pay for marketing, advertising, or sales costs. By law, 12b-1 fees cannot exceed 0.75 percent of net assets.

   - *Other expenses.* These include special charges for transfer agency and for accounting costs that are not included in any of the above expenses.

EASE OF BUYING AND SELLING

Mutual fund shares are highly liquid. With a single phone call, you can buy or sell as many shares as you want, and get a check for your proceeds in as little time as one day (especially if you place your transaction through a discount broker). All shares are either purchased or redeemed at their net asset value at the close of business on the day you place your order. It's true that most individual stocks and bonds are equally liquid, but you have to pay a commission when you convert these other instruments into cash. When you buy no-load funds, there is no fee on the way in or out.

CONVENIENCE

Mutual funds provide a clear element of convenience. Chances are you have a day job that doesn't involve selecting and monitoring investments. Maybe you're retired and spend your days improving your golf score or enjoying the great outdoors. In either case, you probably don't have a lot of time to research new investment ideas, follow the market, and continually analyze every one of your holdings. Investing truly is a full-time job, and an array of recordkeeping is involved when purchasing individual securities. When you buy a fund, the fund family or discount broker reduces your work to a minimum by doing most of this recordkeeping for you. Then, at tax-filing time, you only have to deal with a single 1099 form that gives you all the information you need to keep Uncle Sam satisfied. Most funds will gladly reinvest your dividends and capital gains distributions automatically, allowing you to profit from the magic of compounding. Often, you can get check-writing privileges and the ability to make exchanges from one fund to another.

MIX OF ASSET CLASSES

Finally, funds allow you to easily target specific asset classes, which is increasingly important in the current market environment. Here's what I mean: In a broad sense, you have various types of securities—stocks, bonds, and cash—available for investment. But there are subcategories within each of these classes. On the equity side, for example, you have small caps, mid caps, large caps, and international securities. Informed investors have exposure to all of these areas in their portfolios. In fact, research has shown that having the right asset-class mix is even more

---

WHAT'S A MARKET CAP?

A stock's market capitalization is calculated by multiplying the number of out-standing shares by the price per share. For example, a stock trading for $1 with 10 million shares outstanding would have a market capitalization, or market cap, of $10 million. Stocks are categorized into four primary classes and have the following general guidelines:

1. **Micro Cap.** Stocks with market capitalizations of $0 to $300 million.
2. **Small Cap.** Stocks with market capitalizations of $300 million to $1 billion.
3. **Mid Cap.** Stocks with market capitalizations of $1 billion to $5 billion.
4. **Large Cap.** Stocks with market capitalizations of $5 billion or more.

---

important than security selection in determining long-term investment performance. It's virtually impossible to target specific asset classes like this through individual security selection. We'll delve deeper into the subject of asset allocation, and the categories that should be represented in your portfolio, in Chapter 7.

THE DRAWBACKS

Nothing in life is perfect, and that includes mutual funds. As wonderful as they are, funds do have a few shortfalls. For example, despite being closely regulated, funds still aren't held to high standards for disclosure. They don't have to tell you how much fund managers make, and only twice a year must they give you a list of the securities they own. Similarly, because you are hiring a manager to make all of your investment decisions, you have no say as to which stocks or bonds you own. (Some people hate letting go of that control.) Furthermore, although diversification is designed to give you smooth and respectable returns over the long haul, it prevents you from scoring any phenomenal home runs. If you own only one stock and it goes up 1,000 percent, you will become rich. But if you have a portfolio of 200 names and that same stock goes up 1,000 percent, it won't have much of an impact. Keep in mind that stocks have the same chance of falling 100 percent as they do of rising 1,000 percent. This is why diversification makes so much sense. Even with modest returns of 8 to 10 percent a year, if you start early, save religiously, and use excellent funds, I'm confident you will wind up with more money than you know what to do with.

The *biggest* disadvantage to owning funds rather than individual securities relates to taxes. By law, funds must pay out a majority of their built-in investment profits to shareholders at the end of each year. These profits are distributed in the form of dividends and capital gains. When you own individual securities, you don't have to pay taxes on any capital gains until you redeem your shares. With funds, you may incur a tax liability even if you hold on. This drawback has received a great deal of attention since Congress lowered the maximum rate for long-term gains to 20 percent. With funds, you don't always know in advance what percentage of your gains will be counted as long- or short-term, because some portfolio managers trade more frequently than others.

I look at the whole issue of taxation in two ways. First, there are steps you can take to reduce your tax liability. One remedy is to look for tax-efficient funds and those with low turnover. You can find out how tax-efficient a fund is by examining its past distribution record. Its annual turnover rate will be in the prospectus. Low-turnover funds generally hold on to their positions longer, allowing the gains to be carried on for years. Funds don't have to distribute gains to you until they have been realized, so low turnover usually, but not always, translates into greater tax efficiency. You can also buy index funds, which are inherently tax-efficient because they rarely do any trading among positions.

Second, you will eventually have to pay taxes on your gains anyway. Holding on and building them up only delays the inevitable. You get to add any fund distributions to the cost basis of your shares, which will reduce your capital gains liability when you finally sell out. So, although I would rather not share my profits with the IRS until I absolutely have to, I don't think the potential tax consequences should prevent investors from getting involved with funds. Taxes are a major issue in roaring bull markets, but, even then, they can be kept under control with proper planning and good fund selection.

SOME NOTES ON TAXES

Gains are typically paid out at the end of each calendar year, so you should avoid purchasing shares in a fund in December, until it has paid out its annual distribution. Otherwise, you will be taxed on the entire gain, even though you might have owned the fund for only a few weeks. Also, statistics show that 70 percent of all fund assets are in tax-deferred retirement accounts anyway, which means taxes are of no concern whatsoever. (You don't have to worry about taxes until you make withdrawals from such accounts.) Therefore, in most cases, the one major argument against fund ownership doesn't even apply. For more information on the taxation of mutual funds, request Publications 550 (Investment Income and Expenses), 551 (Basis of Assets), and 564 (Mutual Fund Distributions) from the Internal Revenue Service call: (800) TAX-FORM.

MAKING YOUR INITIAL INVESTMENT

In Chapter 4, I will give you guidance on selecting individual funds. For now, let's assume you already have your list of fund choices from Chapter 6 and are ready to make an investment. Where do you go from here? Your first step is to order a prospectus, annual report, and application from the fund. Simply dial the toll-free number listed for the fund in Chapters 6 and 9, and ask for the information you need. Once you have the prospectus and report in hand, be sure to look it over, paying close attention to what really matters. For example, in the prospectus, you'll want to find out what the fund's expense ratio is. (See the box for more on the various fees and expenses charged by funds.) You'll also want to read about the manager's background, how long he or she has been at the fund, the types of investments he or she is allowed to buy, and the minimum amount required for initial and subsequent investments. Prospectuses are typically thick documents, full of incomprehensible legalese, but the Securities and Exchange Commission (SEC) passed a "plain English" rule in 1998, requiring fund companies to use, whenever possible, common words, short sentences, and tables or bullet lists for complex material. They also must refrain from using highly technical legal jargon and multiple negatives.

Next, look through the annual report and read the list of specific securities in the portfolio. Examine whether the fund is properly diversified and whether it owns the kinds of investments you would expect it to. For example, if it's a small-cap fund and you find IBM among its list of holdings, you know something is wrong. By the same token, if it's supposed to be a large-cap, blue-chip fund, and you've never heard of any of the holdings, that should also trigger an alarm. This caution also applies if you are trying to determine how to invest your 401(k) money. You are normally

---

UNDERSTANDING THE EXPENSE RATIO

The following table is similar to an outline of a fund's various expenses, found in every fund prospectus:

Annual Portfolio Operating Expenses:

Management and Administrative Expenses	0.50%
Investment Advisory Expenses	0.25%
12b-1 Marketing Fees	0.25%
Other Expenses	None
Total Operating Expenses (Expense Ratio)	**1.00%**

The operating expenses for each fund will be different. In this example, the fund's total expense ratio is 1%, or $10 per $1,000 of assets.

---

given a list of at least a dozen funds to choose from. Demand a prospectus and report for each one, so you can make an informed decision about where to put your money.

After you have this information and can determine whether a particular fund is right for you (more help with this is on the way), you are then ready to make an investment. You can do it the traditional way: fill out the application that comes with your material, and mail a check directly to the fund. Or, you can purchase your shares through one of the major discount brokers, including Charles Schwab, Jack White & Co., Fidelity Investments, and Waterhouse Securities. I highly recommend the latter method, especially if the funds you are considering are part of the broker's no-load, no-transaction-fee (NTF) programs. Chapter 5, which is devoted to these virtual fund supermarkets, will show you how to use them most effectively.

KEEPING TRACK OF YOUR HOLDINGS

≡ After buying your funds, you'll want to keep track of how they perform on a regular basis. Notice I said *regular,* not *daily.* I would argue that once a quarter will suffice. What you are looking for is how your funds compare to their peers. In other words, *don't* judge a bond fund next to the S&P 500. *Do* compare a small-cap fund to the Russell 2000 index,

HOW TO READ THE NEWSPAPER FUND TABLES

Mutual Funds

Name	NAV	Net Chg	YTD % Ret
WonderFund	7.24	−.03	+2.3
BestFund	10.04	+.13	+5.8
TechFund	8.54	−.01	+7.8
BondFund	3.32	+.22	+1.5

1. This is the name of the fund. In some papers, the listing begins with the name of the fund family in bold, with each individual fund printed below it.

2. This is the fund's net asset value (NAV).

3. This is the difference between the closing NAV price today versus yesterday.

4. This is the fund's year-to-date total return, expressed as a percentage.

which is the benchmark for small-cap stocks. Find out whether your funds are keeping up with the averages. Ideally, your funds should be running ahead of them. If not, you must find out why. Is the manager just having a bad quarter? Is the fund overconcentrated in a lagging sector? Has the fund's manager changed? Have assets bloated the portfolio to the point where the fund is no longer nimble? Once you've answered these questions, you can determine whether to hang on or move on. I don't recommend selling a fund unless it has underperformed for at least 18 months. I've chosen this particular time line for two reasons: (1) you will be able to take advantage of the maximum 20 percent capital gain rule when you sell out, and (2) more important, all managers underperform at one point or another. Funds are designed to be a long-term investment. What's 18 months when your time horizon might be 20, 30, or even 40 years or more? Giving a good manager 18 months to get back into shape is often a wise investment decision.

INSIDE THE MIND
OF A FUND MANAGER

What exactly happens to your hard-earned money after you send it to your favorite fund? To whom are you entrusting your financial future, and what do these folks do with your money? Beyond that, what does it take to become a fund manager? Brains, good looks, financial savvy, luck, good genes, an Ivy League education, or all of the above?

The truth is, characteristics and decisions vary from fund to fund. When most funds get your money, they first place it with a custodian, like a bank, for safekeeping. Then the fund manager uses it to buy additional securities for the portfolio, based on the rules of the prospectus. (In other words, if it's a stock portfolio, the manager will buy stocks. If it's a fixed-income fund, bonds will most likely be added.) The background of each fund manager is also quite different. Some received degrees from prestigious universities, earned MBAs, and have a family pedigree of investment genius. Others are high school graduates who happened to be in the right place at the right time. I have found that no one trait tells you up front whether a fund manager is going to be a brilliant stock picker, but it is certainly encouraging to come across someone with good educational credentials and a pristine performance record to boot.

AN UP-CLOSE LOOK

To more clearly understand what a fund manager does, let's meet and spend a workday with Brian Posner. Posner racked up great numbers at Fidelity Investments before joining Warburg Pincus to run the firm's Growth

Figure 2.1   Brian Posner, Manager of the Warburg Pincus Growth & Income Fund

& Income fund (one of my "100 Powerhouse Performers") in January 1997. Posner grew up in New York and went to Northwestern University, where he earned an undergraduate degree in history. He once had dreams of becoming a doctor. "My dad is an orthopedic surgeon, so I figured that was the only thing there was for me to do," he says. "But that dream only lasted as long as my first class in organic chemistry. I realized I enjoyed reading about history more and decided to change majors."

During summer breaks at Northwestern, Posner worked part-time on the foreign exchange trading desk at Bank Leumi in Chicago. "I got my first taste of the markets there," he recalls. "It was a strange situation. I was hired as a gopher. But the stars and the moon aligned themselves in such a way that they needed someone on the phone. So I learned to be a trader." How did he like his new role? "I hated it," he admits. "Being a trader taught me that I really wanted to become an investor. I certainly didn't want to stare at monitors and scream into the phones all day long. However, it did make me realize that I wanted to do something in finance." He didn't change his major to business; he figured (correctly) that a liberal arts background would be sufficient until he eventually decided to get an MBA.

When he graduated from Northwestern, Posner had two job offers: one from *Crain's* Chicago, working as a business reporter, and the other from Feldman Securities, a small Chicago money manager. He opted to go with the latter. "I did a little bit of everything there, including trading, portfolio construction, and analysis. At the time, there were only four of us at the firm. It eventually grew to a staff of 30. This experience really got me involved in the business of managing money."

After two years at Feldman, Posner quit and went back to school, this time to the University of Chicago, for an MBA. "I figured that, as a history guy, I should go to one of the most quantitative programs around, to see if I could actually add and subtract," he quips. "I went to school full-time, since I felt I needed to be in an intense environment for a couple of years, not only to refine my analytical and accounting skills, but also to become immersed in financial theory. I think you can still get there without business school, although it takes longer. In retrospect, I'm convinced the ability to be in an environment where I could challenge myself, my colleagues, and my professors without costing anyone money, other than what I was paying in tuition, was a fortunate experience. I'm very pro business school."

GETTING INTO FIDELITY

After completing his MBA degree in early 1987, Posner decided there was only one company he wanted to work for—Fidelity Investments. "I perceived it to be, and it is, the most aggressive and creative investment management firm in the industry," he says. Most of his classmates wanted to work on the sales and trading side of the investment banking business; very few yearned to get into portfolio management. Still, the competition for every available opening at Fidelity was keen, and Posner had several strikes against him. "For one thing, Fidelity didn't recruit west of Pennsylvania," he notes. "In fact, I was the first person they ever hired on the equity side who had gone through the University of Chicago business program." Given those odds, how did he get in the door? By being an admitted nudge. "I somehow got hold of the number to Peter Lynch's office and decided to call him on a Saturday morning, figuring he'd be at his desk," Posner reveals. "He answered the phone and put me in touch with the director of research. After innumerable phone calls and harassing on my part, he finally agreed to give me an interview. That got me in the door."

Posner spent three years at Fidelity as a financial services analyst, covering insurance and other nonbank financial companies. "It was a very aggressive and intense environment," he says. "I use those two words in a favorable sense. Everything was performance-driven. And being able to work with fund managers like Peter Lynch [who was still running Magellan] made for some exciting times." Eventually, Posner worked closely with Lynch. "Once you were part of the Fidelity team, Peter wouldn't let you go," he says. "Peter would call all the time and ask what you thought about stuff, just to make sure you were always worrying. It was a very interactive environment, in which all of the fund managers were constantly challenging, questioning, prodding, and pushing."

During his tenure as an analyst, Posner also had a chance to work as an assistant manager on a couple of funds. "It was clear from my experience working on the Fidelity Value fund that my approach and style were value-based," he maintains. "I even wrote a proposal recommending the launch of a second value-oriented fund, because Fidelity Value wasn't being managed as a pure value portfolio at the time." Instead, the company turned Fidelity Value over to Posner in September 1990, giving him his first shot at running a pool of money solo. He managed Fidelity Value until April 1992, during which time assets increased from $88 to $350 million. He was then reassigned to the $880 million Fidelity Equity Income II. "When I left that fund at the end of November 1996, it had swelled to just under $16 billion," he points out.

To most of us, that's an incomprehensible amount of money. Yet, in the mutual fund world, it's really no big deal. I must tell you, however, that I am convinced smaller funds perform better over time because they can be more nimble, and Posner backs up my belief. He was able to grow with Equity Income II, which gave him a chance to deal with gradually increasing assets, but admits that after the fund surpassed the $8 billion mark, many strategic and tactical issues began to emerge. "There may have been a security I owned that I wanted more of but couldn't buy because of liquidity issues," he concedes. "It also depends on what kind of fund you run. If you have a portfolio with high turnover, a few hundred million dollars may prove to be problematic. The smaller the stocks you buy, the more a big asset base can hurt you."

TREKKING TO WARBURG PINCUS

Posner was happy managing Equity Income II and had no plans to leave Fidelity. Then he got an offer to join Warburg Pincus, a much smaller investment firm. "They gave me a chance to not only run a fund, but also to get involved with the entire investment process," he says. "It was an opportunity I couldn't turn down. Plus, I perceived it to be an organization with a desire to grow much larger. It reminded me of where Fidelity was when I started there in 1987." Warburg Pincus wanted Posner to revitalize its Growth & Income fund, which, after a short period of great performance, had turned into a dog. Assets were flowing out, and the firm realized it needed a new skipper to turn the portfolio around. "When I got here, I spent a lot of time with the major shareholders and advisers to see what sort of fund they wanted," he says. "They asked for exactly what I had at Fidelity—a very conservative all-equity fund. To get there, I had to completely restructure and reposition the portfolio."

Growth & Income is one of those categories that means different things to different people. The name seems to connote that there are fixed-income instruments in the mix, but that's normally not true. Most of the "income" generally comes from stock dividends. That's precisely the case with Posner's fund. The majority of his companies have a dividend yield that approximates the S&P 500 index.

THE INVESTMENT PROCESS

Posner now has a much smaller research department than the one at Fidelity, but he says it works the same way. "It is centralized and totally interactive. The fund managers query the analysts about different ideas, and they also bring their own suggestions to the managers directly. We've got a team of about 20 here, and the analysts are really focused." Posner guesses he personally generates about half of the stock ideas for his portfolio; his analysts alert him to the rest. The hunt for promising names is an ongoing process. "It's a function of always revisiting companies I know. Some I haven't invested in for many years, and others I have been watching but never bought," he explains. "I do run screens, although I don't find them to be particularly helpful. I maintain what I refer to as an 'inventory of ideas.' These are companies that, for whatever reason, are depressed because of past sins or recent disappointments. Maybe they're undergoing some sort of significant fundamental or managerial change that I want to understand better. What I try to do is look at every company on the basis of the conditions under which it becomes a buy. It is a function of the fundamentals improving materially and the stock coming down to the price I want to pay for it."

Given his past as a value investor, it follows that Posner runs Warburg Pincus Growth & Income with an eye to buying his stocks when they are on sale. "However, I try not to fall into the trap of investing in bad companies just because they are inexpensive," he insists. "I go beyond market price and such measures as price-to-earnings or price-to-book ratios, since they don't necessarily alert you to the underlying quality of a company. Rather, I look at every company as though there is only one share outstanding. I evaluate it with the thought that, as the sole owner, would I want to purchase the whole company based on the returns it is generating, its free cash flows, sales growth, and those sorts of things? I also estimate what kind of return I can expect to earn from the stock, taking into account the volatility of the business and quality of the balance sheet."

Posner's sell discipline is equally focused. "When the valuation is no longer supported by the fundamentals, or it doesn't appear likely the company will give me the appreciation I need as an owner, I'll get rid of it," he says. "I do set target prices, but I allow them to evolve. If I've found a company that's truly undergoing massive change, the valuation metrics I apply on day one may not be appropriate a year or two later. So, what I do is set the target on day one. As the fundamentals evolve and the stock appreciates, I make allowances for it to move up. That way, I don't wind up buying something at 12 times earnings because it's depressed, then selling it at 14 times earnings, missing the fact that it has gone up eightfold and still remains within my parameters because it is making more money."

STICKING TO A DISCIPLINE

Earlier, I expressed my belief that no single trait virtually ensures that a fund manager is an excellent stock picker. I have, however, found one trait in all the successful managers I know: faithfulness to their discipline. Take, for example, Brian Posner, a self-proclaimed value-oriented manager. Working from a list of criteria he uses to determine whether a company is selling for a fair price, he sets a target going in, and he knows the precise conditions under which he is willing to sell. Even though this means he will likely underperform in a roaring bull market, when growth or momentum stocks may be in greater favor, he stays with his strategy, because it's what he knows best. Others might be more oriented toward small-cap growth stocks, for example, or a contrarian approach. Their preferences don't matter; many different investment styles work just fine over time. The key is to avoid the temptation to stray from what you know best, even when overall market conditions might tempt you to do so. Among the fund managers I have seen, the biggest reason for failure is making investment decisions that are not consistent with their discipline.

Fund managers develop their discipline over time, in various ways. Some are taught specific strategies in school, and they adhere to them throughout their professional careers. Others learn from trial and error. From his various life experiences, Posner concluded that this was the way he was most comfortable investing. "I have a real focus on risk management and am naturally conservative," he says. "I believe my role is to provide people with a conservative all-equity option. By that I mean giving them superior absolute performance, ideally beating the market, but doing it in a way that controls their downside."

Posner admits that value investing isn't easy from an emotional perspective because it usually means buying and selling out of sync with the rest of Wall Street. Nevertheless, his experience has convinced him that it's the best way to go. "When I was a trader, and gold was going through $800 an ounce, the market was incredibly volatile," he reflects. "When I joined Fidelity as an analyst, the market crashed a few months later and I was put on SWAT team duty to help any brokers unable to clear their trades. In 1990–1991, I was deeply involved in analyzing which banks appeared to be in significant trouble. So, even though I'm pretty young, and my career has been relatively short, in the grand scheme of things, I've lived through and experienced some major events that have taught me the importance of focusing on the downside while trying to achieve as much upside as possible."

At 36, Posner is no longer the new kid on the block. Plenty of fund managers with multimillion-dollar portfolios are still in their 20s. That fact has prompted many experienced veterans to question how these Generation Xers will react during the next bear market, since they've only been investing in a bullish environment where virtually all stocks have gone straight up. "I think that's a red herring argument," Posner insists. "Everyone used to point their finger at me when they said this, until I got past 35. I don't think it matters how old you are. We've all lived through trying times, like October 1997 and August 1996, in which the market quickly and precipitously lost a lot of ground and was surrounded by fear. It didn't matter whether you were 25 or 55. Everyone was impacted by their emotions. We're all human. How one will respond in trying times is something you'll never know until it happens. I try to remain focused on where I think the floor is, and where the values are, without worrying too much about what the market in aggregate is doing."

A DAY IN THE LIFE OF A FUND MANAGER

≡ Now that you know about Posner's background and investment philosophy, let's take a look at how he spends his days and, more importantly, what exactly he does with his shareholders' money. "I usually get in around 7 A.M.," he reveals. "I start by entering whatever trades I want to make for the day. I get my orders to the trading desk first thing in the morning, so they can worry about it. I decide what I want to buy and how much, and let them consider the conditions under which to execute the trade." Posner usually buys tens or hundreds of thousands of shares of each stock. Because he deals mostly with larger companies, that's generally not much of a problem. "If I'm looking at a company that is somewhat illiquid, or where I want to be a bit more sensitive to price, I'll let the traders know up front how I want to approach it," he adds. Once the traders have his orders, they go hunting for the stocks. They either buy them from various brokers or go right to the floor of the exchanges.

At 8:30 A.M., Posner and his fellow Warburg Pincus portfolio managers gather for a 15-minute morning meeting. "Then I'm normally on the phone talking to companies for the rest of the day," Posner says. "I analyze stocks both with my analysts and on my own. I also prepare financial models and try to work on new ideas. In some cases, I may have to do some maintenance on existing positions."

During the day, Posner is alerted to where the flows in and out of his fund stand. This helps him decide whether he needs to plan on buying more stock or, instead, raise cash to meet redemptions. (As you know by now, fund shares are highly liquid and can be sold out at any time. Fund managers always have to keep an eye on their cash level, to make sure they can meet the demand from shareholders who want their money back. This usually isn't a problem because fund inflows and outflows tend to remain consistent. The one time this isn't true is when the market is in free-fall and the amount of sell orders is abnormally high. Alternatively, if a fund gets a good write-up in the media, it can cause new cash to flood in.) "I've found that you can relate flows to how the market is doing and the performance of the fund," Posner observes.

When the exchanges close at 4 P.M., Posner takes a deep breath. "Before I leave at 6 P.M. or 7 P.M., I usually go through the foot and a half of mail I get every day from companies and Wall Street," he adds. "I keep what's relevant and throw out the rest." Then he's off for an hour-long train ride to his home in Connecticut. Posner also works on weekends. "I don't come into New York on Saturday and Sunday, but I can tap into our computers from my home," he says. Saturday is normally reserved for spending time with his wife and two small kids. On Sunday, he begins planning for the week ahead. "That's when I start obsessing," he confesses. "During the week, I am very focused and calm. I never yell and scream like those guys in the movies. When things get wacky in the market, I put on my tunnel vision. It reminds me of when I played sports in high school. You don't see anything other than the numbers you're looking at on the screen. It's late at night and on weekends that you start to question whether you've done the right thing. The market is closed and all you can look at are these static numbers on a screen."

PUTTING YOUR MONEY TO WORK

I still haven't answered the question I'm sure you're wondering about: What happens to the money that's sent in to be invested in a fund? Let's say you send $1,000 to Warburg Pincus Growth & Income. What does Posner do with it? "In the stylized world, which doesn't exist, I would push a button and that $1,000 would be invested across the entire portfolio in proportion to my current investments," he says. "On a stylized basis, you would say that makes sense because I presumably like everything I own and am willing to buy more of it. In the real world, however, there are times when it's appropriate to buy a little more of one stock than another.

"So, based on the day-to-day flows, I will respond to where the opportunities are in a manner that doesn't materially change the nature of the fund, in terms of the overall holdings. For instance, if Chrysler is the fiftieth largest position in the fund, I won't necessarily buy more of it to force it up higher on the list. I'll only buy more if I think it's appropriate. I look at where the opportunities are each day. There may also be times when it's appropriate for me to realize a loss in the fund to offset previously realized gains. If there were a redemption on day X, and I needed to raise a little cash, rather than sell across the board, I might unload a position I'm no longer happy with. I feel very strongly that I am called a *portfolio manager* for a reason. I'm not just a stock picker. I manage this portfolio with a certain purpose in mind: to create a set of returns and circumstances on behalf of my shareholders. I'm not simply putting together an ad hoc collection of stocks that I think are cheap."

WHY FUNDS MAKE SENSE

It should come as no surprise that Posner believes mutual funds are the preferred way for individual investors to tap into the equity markets. "I tell my dad I'm the best bargain in America," he says. "For 1 percent of assets [Growth & Income's management fee], you get me worrying on your behalf for 16 hours a day. If people have a strong feeling about a certain company and can do the analysis on their own, I have no problem with their taking advantage of that and buying a stock here and there. I agree with Peter Lynch about that. But the beauty of mutual funds is that they give you the ability to buy broad diversification without worrying about any one security."

But what about index funds, which we'll discuss in greater length in the next chapter? Many personal finance magazines have been touting the benefits of indexing, claiming they consistently beat active managers at less cost. If that's the case, why pay someone like Posner *anything* to manage your portfolio? "If your objective is to achieve market returns and incur market risk, I have nothing against index funds," he concedes. "But what's being lost in this whole index fund debate is that, for most people,

---

WARBURG PINCUS GROWTH & INCOME'S TOP 10 HOLDINGS

(as of June 30, 1998)

PMI Group	Chrysler
British Petroleum	IBM
Citicorp	Merck
Federated Department Stores	Raytheon
Compaq Computer	Polaroid

market risk and market returns are inappropriate. For many investors, it's appropriate to be more aggressive. For others, the opposite is true. People need to spend more time focusing on their objectives and risk profiles. It's easy to stay in an index fund when the market is appreciating at 30 percent a year. However, when the market blips, investors may realize that risk management is an appropriate concept. This doesn't necessarily mean low risk. It means being compensated for the level of risk you take. So whether you are aggressive or conservative, you need to determine where you want to be on the spectrum of risk. Then you must make sure you are investing in a fund that is achieving those objectives."

THE PRESSURE OF PERFORMANCE

Even if fund managers won't admit it, the pressure is always on them to at least keep up with, if not outperform, the indexes. That typically means the S&P 500, although funds are starting to concentrate more on comparing themselves with peer indexes because the S&P 500 has been so hard to beat of late. However, what Posner focuses on, more than the market, is his shareholders, who have entrusted him with their financial futures. "I think about them every day," he claims. "It's the best and worst part of this job. It's the best part because it's an incredible responsibility that I'm glad to take on. It's the worst part because I obsess about it constantly. There are always periods of self-doubt, when you wonder what you could have done better. I spend a lot of time analyzing my past performance and portfolio construction to see where I erred. I go to bed comfortable that, over long cycles, I can provide my shareholders with superior outperformance. If I didn't feel that way, I couldn't stay at this job."

A SHINING STAR

One relatively recent phenomenon in the mutual fund world is the star manager. With the proliferation of personal finance magazines and TV shows, top-performing fund managers, like Posner, are becoming as familiar in our homes as any Hollywood celebrity. Posner has been featured in numerous magazine and newspaper spreads over the years. And after speaking at a recent investor conference in Chicago, he was mobbed by a throng of admirers seeking his autograph. Some Wall Street types might let this notoriety go to their head. Posner insists he takes it all in stride. "I don't feel like a superstar," he says. "That mentality has become more prevalent in the past 15 years, and it's not necessarily a good thing. I'm just a working guy who doesn't get his pants dirty. I don't think I have the ability to do manual labor, so I'm very lucky in that respect. I work hard in a serious business. I guess you could say I'm not much different from my shareholders."

3

INDEX FUNDS—
BETTER THAN
ACTIVE MANAGEMENT?

Once considered inferior investments suitable only for those who didn't know any better, index funds are now among the darlings of the mutual fund industry. Index funds used to be publicly berated by mainstream money managers and stock brokerage houses alike. In fact, for almost two decades, the Vanguard Group was the only major fund company that even offered index funds to the public.

How things have changed! Index funds began to find big-time favor with both Main Street and Wall Street beginning in 1995. That's when investors started to realize what had been true all along: Index funds tend to outperform actively managed funds some 70 percent of the time. In 1996 and 1997, the percentage of outperformance, as measured by the Standard & Poor's 500 index, was closer to 90 percent.

Once this fact became evident a few years ago, index funds got hotter than ever. They were soon touted on the covers of one personal finance magazine after another. Even the mainstream magazines—*Time, Newsweek,* and *Esquire*—began to tell how wonderful index funds were. And, in a startling development, major actively managed fund sponsors, including Fidelity, T. Rowe Price, and Dean Witter, began to roll out and tout index fund offerings of their own. To show you how much favor index funds have found among investors, Vanguard's Index 500 Portfolio is now the second largest fund in the country, just behind the giant Fidelity Magellan.

WHAT ARE INDEX FUNDS ANYWAY?

═══ Many people are talking about them, but I'll bet that most investors have no idea what index funds are, nor do they understand exactly how they work. They may know that their fund is tied to a benchmark like the Standard & Poor's 500 index (S&P 500, for short). But what does that mean? I'll explain in a moment.

First, it's important to realize that index funds are referred to in the industry as "passively managed" investments. In other words, they are based solely on computer models set up to replicate a given index. And there are plenty of indexes to choose from. On the stock side, some choices are: S&P 500; Dow Jones Industrial Average; Russell 2000; Wilshire 4500; Wilshire 5000; Morgan Stanley International; and Europe, Australasia, and Far East (EAFE) index. The list goes on and on. (Incidentally, the vast majority of stock funds today are tied to the S&P 500.) Fixed-income investors also have several indexes to choose from, most notably the Lehman Brothers Aggregate Bond index.

An index fund is comprised of either a complete or a representative sample of the stocks or bonds found in the underlying index. For example, the ideal S&P 500 fund would hold proper weightings of each of the 500 funds found in the index.

A LOOK INSIDE THE INDEXES

You're probably wondering which stocks are found within the various indexes. As I mentioned, there are many different benchmarks. What follows are brief descriptions of the major indexes.

S&P 500

By far the most common index used in the fund industry, the S&P 500 holds a basket of 500 stocks. It is designed to mirror the large-capitalization sector of the U.S. equity market. The S&P 500 represents about 70 percent of the value of the entire market. But it's not necessarily composed of the 500 largest companies. Instead, an eight-member panel selected by Standard & Poor's is responsible for hand-picking which companies are listed in the index, and the list does change from time to time. The committee makes its selections based on market value, company financial conditions, and trading liquidity; it isn't looking for the next hot stock. The goal is to have the index properly represent the country's leading industries. At last check, the S&P 500 was comprised of about 380 industrial, 70 financial, 40 utility, and 10 transportation issues. The S&P 500 is a market-weighted index: the higher a company's market valuation, the more emphasis it is given in the index. Therefore, the stocks of the biggest companies are weighted more heavily and drive a large portion of the index's performance. Among the companies with the most substantial weightings in the S&P 500 are:

General Electric	(3 percent)
Coca-Cola	(2.4 percent)
Exxon	(2.1 percent)
Microsoft	(2.1 percent)
Merck	(1.7 percent)
Royal Dutch	(1.6 percent)
Intel	(1.6 percent)
Philip Morris	(1.5 percent)
Procter & Gamble	(1.4 percent)
IBM	(1.3 percent)

The largest 60 stocks make up about half of the value of the index. Therefore, if these 60 stocks were all down 20 percent for the year, and the remaining 440 were up 20 percent, the S&P 500 would merely break even.

DOW JONES INDUSTRIAL AVERAGE

The Dow Jones Industrial Average (DJIA, or "The Dow"), by contrast, is a price-weighted index. This means that the higher the share price of a stock in the index, the greater the influence it has. Accordingly, a big change in a single company can give a false reading for how the overall market is behaving. The Dow is the most often quoted index in the media today. It was born in 1884, when a journalist named Charles Dow compiled a list of 11 companies and tracked their performance. Two years later, he increased the number of stocks to 12 and began publishing their performance in the pages of a publication he called *The Wall Street Journal*. He wanted readers to get a better feel for what was going on in the stock market. Back then, most of the DJIA's representative companies were in the railroad industry. By 1916, the number of stocks in the DJIA had grown to 20, before leaping to 30 (the current number) in 1928. The 30 stocks listed have changed over the years, either to align with the economy or in response to acquisitions and other events that make previous choices all but irrelevant. As just one example, the DJIA now includes a number of technology companies, reflecting our evolution from a manufacturing-based to a technology-based economy. The DJIA's most recent changes came in March 1997, when Travelers, Hewlett-Packard, Johnson & Johnson, and Wal-Mart replaced Westinghouse, Texaco, Bethlehem Steel, and Woolworth.

RUSSELL 2000

This index is made up of the stocks of small, unseasoned U.S. companies. It is generally considered the best indicator of how the NASDAQ market, and small-cap stocks in general, are doing. NASDAQ stands for National Association of Securities Dealers Automated Quotation System. (You can see why they just call it NASDAQ.) This index is weighted by market value and represents domestic companies that are traded over-the-counter.

WILSHIRE 5000

Despite its name, the Wilshire 5000 tracks more than 6,000 publicly traded securities. It is therefore the most accurate measure of the health of the overall market, and the most diversified index available. Roughly 70 percent of the stocks in the Wilshire 5000 are large caps; the remaining 30 percent are mid and small caps. This benchmark's cousin, the Wilshire 4500, tracks 4,500 stocks that are not part of the S&P 500.

A BRIEF HISTORY OF INDEX FUNDS

The formation of index funds can be traced back to July 1971, when Wells Fargo Bank launched a $6 million fund to manage the pension assets of luggage-maker Samsonite. This fund held an equal amount of every company listed on the New York Stock Exchange. Two years later, Wells Fargo began the first index fund tied to the S&P 500. Both funds were the creation of William Fouse, a West Virginian jazz saxophonist-turned-banker. Fouse initially developed this technology-driven strategy for picking stocks while working at the Pittsburgh-based Mellon Bank in the late 1960s. But when he suggested that Mellon should start a fund run entirely by computer, without analysis by a human manager, he was asked to leave. Ironically, Fouse has since returned to Mellon, which now runs a number of index funds of its own.

As retail investors, you and I, and millions of others, were given our first chance to invest in index funds in 1976, when Vanguard launched the First Index Investment Trust, which was tied to the S&P 500. This fund was originally sold exclusively through brokers and carried a hefty 6 percent load. One year later, at the urging of Vanguard founder John Bogle, the fund became a no-load. Because of the Trust's limited assets in the beginning, the initial portfolio contained only 280 stocks—the 200 largest, plus 80 selected by various optimization models designed to roughly match the remaining companies in the index.

Bogle's timing couldn't have been worse. After outperforming nearly 70 percent of all equity funds from 1972 to 1976, index funds *underperformed* 75 percent of active managers from 1977 to 1979. "This sort of reversal in form, which seems to plague all new fund concepts, is hardly surprising," Bogle says in retrospect. By 1982, the Trust had $100 million in assets, but only because it merged with another fund. Fortunately for Vanguard, this was right at the start of a boom in the stock market that has continued to this day. Index funds soon bounced back to the top of the rankings. By 1990, there were 43 registered index funds, including two from Fidelity, which, before, touted nothing but the advantages of active management.

Still, index funds never quite caught on with the public until around 1995. By then, they had racked up a string of stellar returns. From 1994 to 1996, index funds tied to the S&P 500 outpaced 91 percent of all actively managed offerings. As usual, money followed performance. When this fact was noticed by the media, one story after another began proclaiming how index funds were the next best thing to nirvana. Suddenly, Vanguard's Bogle was a hero, even though he had been preaching the merits of indexing for several decades. And, as index funds rose in notoriety, so did the number of available funds. Today, there are dozens of index funds, tracking virtually every benchmark you can think of.

Index fund investing is predicated on two beliefs: (1) the market is too efficient to beat, and (2) investors can do no better than the market because they *are* the market. This idea was further popularized in a 1973 book, *A Random Walk Down Wall Street,* by Princeton University Professor Burton S. Malkiel, who has long been a strong advocate of index funds.

WHY BUY INDEX FUNDS?

===== Will the dazzling returns provided by index funds continue in the future? Millions of investors are banking on continuation, but the odds are against them. Traditionally, "hot" investment fads don't last forever. There is already evidence that the brilliant outperformance enjoyed by index funds of late is starting to fade. But index funds will always remain excellent investments.

There are several reasons why you might want to include index funds in your portfolio. For one thing, most index funds operate at bare-bones expenses. Vanguard's Index 500 charges just .20 percent of assets. The USAA index fund charges slightly less, at .18 percent. That's more than 1 percent you would pay to own the average actively managed stock fund. The reason index funds are cheaper is simple—a computer runs the show. Fund companies don't have to pay computers the seven-figure salaries that good human managers pull down. As a result, index funds normally are given a huge 1 percent head start right at the beginning.

Second, index funds are generally highly tax-efficient. I mentioned earlier that funds have to distribute all of their capital gains and dividends to shareholders at the end of each year. If your money is not in a tax-deferred account, this can add a significant bite to your tax bill. Index funds, on the other hand, rarely experience any gains because their portfolio turnover is so low. (Managers sell a stock only when they must meet redemptions or make necessary adjustments to stay in line with the index.) Therefore, if you are looking to keep your year-end distributions to an absolute minimum, index funds make a lot of sense.

Third, I have long emphasized the importance of "choosing *managers, not funds.*" (More on this in the next chapter.) Unfortunately, fund managers change jobs with the speed of a Texas tornado these days. With an index fund, the manager is not as important because the fund is run entirely by a computer. Therefore, if you want to buy and hold and forget about your investment until you're ready to touch the money years down the line, index funds may be right for you.

Because you aren't paying for management expertise, a low expense ratio should be your number-one concern when selecting an index fund. All other things being equal, go with the fund that offers the lowest expenses for the benchmark you are trying to track. Index funds from the Vanguard Group are often very cost-efficient, although several other companies have been lowering their expenses to become more competitive. And *never* pay a sales load to buy an index fund. A number of these "deals" are out there, so beware.

THE DOWNSIDE OF INDEX FUNDS

We've talked about the good features. Now it's only fair that we discuss some of the arguments *against* owning funds. For one thing, by definition, you will never be able to outperform the index you are tracking. By contrast, actively managed funds always have a shot at earning more. Granted, a lot of lousy managed funds will severely underperform these passively managed indexes. I've already told you that just choosing the "100 Powerhouse Performers" for this book, from a list of more than 9,000 candidates, was quite a task. However, a number of brilliant stock pickers consistently manage to outperform the indexes. If you're willing to do the work to find them (this book will be an enormous help in that pursuit), I am confident that, over time, you can outperform index funds by a respectable margin. (Even a percentage or two, in the long term, can add significantly to your portfolio.)

Next, index funds have taken in hundreds of millions of dollars in the past few years alone. If their winning streak comes to an end, investors are likely to begin fleeing these investments in favor of actively managed funds. As they say: "What goes up usually comes down much faster." Unfortunately, investors today (both novices and professionals) have very short attention spans and time horizons. The long term, for them, means "as long as the fund is performing as well as it was when I bought it." Once the personal finance magazines and newspapers start writing that "index funds are no longer the great investments we once told you they were"—and I can guarantee you, they eventually will—expect index fund investors to run for the exits. That, of course, would severely hurt the prices of the stocks in these indexes, while creating significant capital gains distributions for those shareholders who stick with the funds.

Finally, you may be interested to know that Warren Buffett, who is generally regarded as the most talented equity investor the world has ever known, once called index investing "unilateral disarmament." In other words, it is an approach that makes no effort to be better than average. Unlike Buffett, those who follow an index fund approach rely on no research or analysis. They bet on "the market" rather than on individual companies.

ENHANCED INDEX FUNDS

Some fund families have come up with a compromise between the active and passive approaches. They have introduced so-called "enhanced index" funds. In essence, such funds mirror most aspects of the index but try to do something different in an effort to produce superior returns. (Remember, true index funds can never outperform their benchmark.) The most common technique used by such funds is complicated and exotic: they buy futures contracts as a way of arbitraging the index. "An S&P 500 enhanced index fund might, for example, invest in the S&P 500 stocks and then switch the portfolio into S&P 500 futures contracts when those contracts are undervalued relative to the stocks," notes a study prepared by Ibbotson Associates, a fund consulting group in Chicago. The study is entitled "Are Enhanced Index Mutual Funds Worthy of Their Name?" Its conclusion? "No, most of them are not worthy." As the Ibbotson study also points out, an enhanced index fund is really actively managed. If you're not replicating the stated benchmark exactly, you're not really running an index fund. As for returns, Ibbotson found that a majority of the enhanced funds it examined *underperformed* their respective indexes—in some cases, by a considerable margin.

FINAL THOUGHTS ABOUT INDEXING

Is indexing right for you? That, of course, is a personal decision only you can make. By now, you should have a good feel for what indexing is, how it works, what kinds of stocks are in the various indexes, and the pros and cons of this approach. Before I end this chapter, let me leave you with some additional thoughts.

For starters, I believe that index funds, particularly those tied to the U.S. market, will remain admirable performers in the future. This belief, in large part, is based on my conviction that the U.S. stock market will continue to rise over time, and those willing to take the risk of investing in equities will be richly rewarded. As a result, I have no problem with your holding an S&P 500 index fund as a core position in your portfolio. It's a fine substitute for almost any large-cap mutual fund you will come across, and it has produced an average annualized return of 16 percent since 1978. That's impressive by any measure. For small-cap and foreign investing, however, I think you are better off with actively managed funds. History backs me up on this. Over the past 10 years, more than half of all diversified international stock funds have whipped the performance of the Morgan Stanley Capital International Europe, Australasia, Far East (EAFE) index. And U.S. small caps are much less efficient than their large-cap brethren, making it possible for active managers to shoot the lights out with selected issues.

If you want a truly passive approach that will allow you to participate in the rise of the market without doing any research to uncover the most promising funds available, indexing may be right for you. Think of it as a lazy person's approach to stock market investing. Should you opt to go this route, however, I would offer a suggestion: If you're going to buy only one fund, I strongly encourage you to purchase one that tracks the Wilshire 5000, instead of the S&P 500. In that way, you'll get exposure to all areas of the market, not just large-cap stocks. The Wilshire 5000 is also much more diversified because the biggest companies are not weighted as heavily. The best fund in this category is Vanguard Total Stock Market, one of my "100 Powerhouse Performers." As I note in the profile for this fund in Chapter 6, I have no problem recommending this fund as the sole holding for the U.S. equity portion of your portfolio, especially if you have a relatively modest amount of money to invest.

I truly believe that, with a little work on your part and with the help of this book, you can beat the indexes by investing in outstanding funds run by the best stock pickers in the business. A study compiled by a financial consulting firm, Evaluation Associates, affirms this. It found that the S&P 500, the index against which most funds are measured, beat less than half of all actively managed large-cap funds during rolling five-year periods from 1981 to 1996. Again, it makes good sense to consider putting a core position of your portfolio in an index fund, to ensure that you'll never significantly underperform the market. But I am convinced that a more active approach to investing is not only more fun but can also produce greater results over the long haul.

FINDING THE FUND
THAT'S RIGHT FOR YOU

Given that some 9,000 stock, bond, and money market funds are currently available, finding the true gems in this enormous mix is a daunting task. After all, funds now outnumber stocks on all of the major exchanges combined. Not to worry. This chapter will give you some guidelines to help you narrow down the field of choices and make smart decisions about which funds are best for you.

This chapter offers several tips to keep in mind when you are scouring the field of contenders. These are the principles I adhere to with my own portfolio, and they were the basis for my Powerhouse Performers selections. I have broken down the characteristics to look for in each asset class—namely, stocks, bonds, and mutual funds. Traits you *must* find in stock funds don't apply for bond funds, and vice versa.

ALWAYS REMEMBER: GO NO-LOAD

The overriding rule you should adhere to, regardless of which type of fund you buy, is: *Always* stick with no-loads. There is no reason, in my opinion, to ever pay a sales commission to purchase or sell a fund you have selected on your own. I have nothing against the folks who peddle load funds. They're entitled to make a living. But that commission comes out of your pocket and goes into theirs. If you're making the selections on your own, there is no reason to pay them. Besides, research by several independent organizations shows that load funds actually perform *worse* than their no-load counterparts. When you buy a load fund, not only is some of your principal immediately wiped away, but you risk poor performance to boot.

Without question, there are some fantastic load funds. Among my good friends are several pristine managers who run only funds that carry sales charges. Nevertheless, for every terrific load fund they might show me, I can almost always point to an equally fine no-load alternative.

So, repeat after me: "I will *never* pay a load to buy or sell a fund that I have selected on my own." By following this rule, you may cut in half the total number of funds you have to sift through. See how much easier the job of analyzing funds can be—and we haven't even delved into the good stuff yet!

STOCK FUND SELECTION

Let's begin with the process of finding equity funds. This is the asset class that requires the most analytical work on your part, because there are so many variables to consider. Remember, a mutual fund is nothing more than one large portfolio with the collective assets (stocks and other securities) of hundreds or even thousands of shareholders, as selected by a fund manager. You are paying for the manager's expertise in selecting the right investments for the portfolio. Therefore, the first thing to keep in mind when hunting for a stock fund is that the manager is everything.

PROVEN MANAGEMENT

In my opinion, you want a manager with a proven track record of beating his or her peers for at least five years—the longer the better. The manager doesn't necessarily have to be at a particular fund for five years. Some of the best investments available are new funds run by experienced managers who have a long history of outperformance. Tom Marsico is a good example. His Marsico Focus Fund, one my "100 Powerhouse Performers," has been around only since the beginning of 1998. However, Marsico spent almost a decade running the Janus Twenty fund, and he racked up a tremendous record. The Marsico Focus Fund has done even better, partly because it is a smaller portfolio. I can't go back five years to see how Marsico Focus Fund has performed, but I can evaluate manager Tom Marsico's record for a much longer period.

Some people fall into the trap of buying funds after reading an ad or doing some skimming research, without checking whether the manager who posted the touted numbers is still in place. In many cases, the manager has moved on. Make sure the manager of a fund you are considering has at least a five-year track record. If necessary, call and ask the fund. If you're told the manager has been at the fund for a shorter period of time, ask which fund he or she managed before that. If the answer is "only private accounts," demand to see the manager's performance record going back as far as possible. If you're told the manager just got out of school, move on to another selection.

A RECORD OF OUTPERFORMANCE

A famous line appears in every fund advertisement and prospectus: "Past performance is no guarantee of future results." This is absolutely true. Just because a manager has been beating the market for the past five years doesn't mean he or she will continue to do so during the next five. But past performance is the only indicator of what the future might hold. It tells you what kind of ability a manager has. If the record shows his or her fund continually lags the market, there is no reason to believe that pattern will change anytime soon. On the other hand, if you find a manager who hits the lights out year after year, you know something is going right. Performance in sports is similar. If a certain player can be relied on for continual scoring, you expect that level of play during every game. Steady performance sets other standards as well. If you're a good driver with a track record of avoiding accidents, your insurance company will reduce the amount of your premium. If you're applying for a loan and have a clean credit report, you'll probably be approved. The lender will check your previous credit history to evaluate whether you're a good risk for the future. So, despite what the SEC-mandated warning tells us, a manager's past performance is our only indication of the future results we can expect. The returns from each fund vary, but we can determine that the manager has a demonstrated trend of outperformance.

When I started telling you how to evaluate managers, I said to make sure they had a record of besting *their peers*. I didn't say besting *the S&P 500 index*, which is the benchmark most media sources and investment advisers refer to. The reason they like it is this: The S&P 500 is a market-weighted index composed primarily of large-cap stocks. Broad market conditions affect all stocks (i.e., when one index goes up, the rest usually follow), but, during certain periods, small caps and mid caps can perform much differently than their large-cap brethren. Consider what's been going on with U.S. stocks since 1995. Large-cap stocks, as a group, have far outshined small caps. Therefore, if you compared a small-cap fund to the S&P 500, you might conclude that the manager fell asleep at the wheel. Instead, you must stack like against like. Large-cap funds should be evaluated next to the S&P 500, which is an appropriate benchmark. Small-cap funds, however, are better compared to the Russell 2000. You also need to check how funds compare to their peers in the same category. Lipper Analytical maintains "category" indexes that are published regularly in the mutual fund section of *The Wall Street Journal*. For a quick feel for how a fund has stacked up against its peers, look at its overall Value Line rank, included as part of the performance data in Chapter 9. This number takes both performance and risk into consideration. On a scale of 1 through 5, look for a fund ranked 1 or 2. A higher number may mean something is wrong. (The Value Line rank is based on performance over a five-year period, so make sure the manager who achieved it is still at the helm. If not, every performance statistic available, including Value Line's, is worthless as a predictor for how the fund might do in the future.)

REASONABLE EXPENSE RATIO

Up to this point, we have talked exclusively about evaluating actively managed funds. Let's review the parameters for selecting stock index funds. Because these investments are run by a computer, issues concerning management and performance are less important. After all, an index fund, by definition, can't beat its benchmark. Therefore, the key factor to look for in an index fund is its expense ratio. The lower, the better. The two Vanguard index funds in my "100 Powerhouse Performers" have expense ratios that are among the lowest in the industry. As a result, they have managed to slightly outperform the competition. All other things being equal, a low expense ratio is the first thing to consider when searching for index funds.

Now let's turn to actively managed funds. I prefer low expense ratios, but I'm really paying for performance. If a manager makes money for me, I'm not going to quibble over the expense ratio. Plenty of funds have low expense ratios and horrible track records. I don't want to own any of them! On the other hand, there are funds with above-average costs that whip the socks off the competition. My general rule is: Look for stock funds with expense ratios of less than 1.5 percent. If we're talking about large-cap U.S. stocks, that number should be even lower. When the topic is international equity funds, the expense ratio often reaches toward 2 percent, because of the added cost of researching foreign securities. The lower, the better; but don't avoid a quality manager because of expenses alone.

LOW TURNOVER

Earlier, we discussed how low turnover often helps to reduce year-end capital gains distributions and keeps your tax liability down. But there's another reason to favor low-turnover funds. Each time a manager buys or sells a stock in the portfolio, a trading commission must be paid, and that fee is *not* reflected in the fund's expense ratio. Excessive trading can shave several percentage points off a fund's annual performance.

I have also found that low-turnover funds tend to do better over time because buy-and-hold investors usually make more money in stocks than do frequent traders. If you don't believe me, just ask a guy named Warren Buffett. One of the most successful funds in history is the Sequoia Fund, which has a mere 4 percent annual turnover. Sequoia manager Bill Ruane adheres to Buffett's teachings in running the portfolio, and the fund's largest holding is Buffett's Berkshire Hathaway. Unfortunately, Sequoia has long been closed to new investors, which is why it's not one of my "100 Powerhouse Performers." Contrast Sequoia with one of the worst performing funds over the past five years, American Heritage, which checks in with an annualized return of −8.87 percent (compared to 23.06 percent for the S&P 500). American Heritage manager Heiko Theime turns over his portfolio 470 percent a year. This doesn't mean all high-turnover funds are bad, but less frequent trading seems to be a huge advantage.

MANAGEABLE ASSET BASE

Is it possible for a mutual fund portfolio to grow too large? That's a debatable question that still hasn't been decisively answered. There are plenty of tiny funds (in terms of asset size) that have been dismal performers for years. At the same time, a number of very large funds offer excellent returns. At some point, size does seem to become an issue for funds, especially those investing in small-cap stocks. Several reasons can be offered. To begin with, the more money a fund attracts, the more stocks a manager normally has to buy. Each time another name is added, the performance punch provided by the biggest winners is diluted. As a portfolio grows in size, the research efforts get severely squeezed. I don't know any managers who can intimately know hundreds of different companies, while staying on top of every new development. It isn't humanly possible.

An even greater problem for small-cap funds is liquidity. Many companies in this universe have market capitalizations (market price multiplied by the number of shares outstanding) of less than $100 million. Diversified funds, by law, cannot have an ownership position of more than 5 percent in any one company, so a $1 billion small-cap fund will have to own a large number of names to meet this requirement. In addition, small-cap stocks tend to be less liquid than their larger counterparts. If a fund manager holds a significant position in any one company, it may be difficult for the fund to get out without severely lowering the share price—if buyers can even be found. Fidelity Investments, the fund giant, apparently concurs that, at some point, fund size is an issue. In 1997, the company closed its $60 billion flagship Magellan Fund to new investors, after years of subpar performance. Then, in 1998, Fidelity shut the doors to its Contrafund and Low-Priced Stock funds, which also began to experience floundering returns after reaching assets of $30 billion and $10 billion, respectively.

My belief is that large-cap funds start to lose their ability to be effective after hitting around $5 billion in assets. However, for small-cap funds, that cutoff amount is much less. I grow uncomfortable when a small-cap fund gets larger than $500 million. I put it on close watch after it hits the $1 billion mark, and I almost always sell it by the time it gets up to $2 billion. I am convinced that small-cap funds with assets greater than $1 billion, and certainly above $2 billion, can provide shareholders with little more than average performance at best, because of the severe limitations placed on the manager. Almost every small-cap fund I have analyzed that is larger than $2 billion has been forced to change its focus from small-cap companies to either mid-cap or large-cap companies, which defeats the purpose of buying the fund in the first place.

Below small caps is a relatively new category called micro caps. In terms of market capitalization, these are the tiniest stocks available to investors. Some of these companies could have capitalizations as low as $10 million. I would avoid any micro-cap fund larger than $300 million in assets; the smaller the better. As for mid-cap funds, I think the $2 billion mark is about as high as I would want a fund in this category to go because, again, there are liquidity issues.

TAX-EFFICIENCY

I won't go over the whole issue of mutual funds and taxes again, other than to remind you that funds distribute taxable gains at the end of each year. You should favor funds that try to keep distributions to an absolute minimum when investing for a taxable account. In retirement plans, this isn't an issue because all distributions are tax-deferred anyway. Low-turnover funds generally have the highest tax efficiency.

AFFORDABLE INVESTMENT REQUIREMENT

The final item to check, when evaluating stock funds, is the minimum investment amount needed to open an account. Although the average fund requires around $2,500, some let you in for as little as $100, and others make you pony up at least $1 million. You should also check the fund's minimum amount for additional contributions, especially if you want to set up a dollar-cost averaging program. Dollar-cost averaging calls for adding a set amount of money to your favorite funds on a regular basis, which enables you to take advantage of market fluctuations. I'll tell you more about this technique in Chapter 7, when we discuss how to structure your personal portfolio.

BOND FUNDS

What should you look for when choosing a bond or fixed-income fund? Think of buying bonds as being the same as lending money to a company or a government. As a lender, you are paid a set interest rate, usually between 3 and 10 percent, depending on the credit quality of the issuer. Short-term bonds are safer and fluctuate less, but they come with a lower yield. Long-term bonds pay more but are highly volatile, especially in times of rising interest rates. Bonds are most suitable for investors seeking to generate income in their portfolios. They can also serve as an added form of diversification, if you want to move away from stocks. When you're evaluating bond funds, look for low expense ratios, credit quality, and favorable maturities.

LOW EXPENSE RATIOS

Choosing bonds for a portfolio doesn't take nearly as much analysis as is required for stocks. Therefore, you should expect to pay the manager of a bond fund less than a manager who picks stocks. As a result, all other things being equal, favor bond funds with the lowest expense ratios.

Yields are relatively low to begin with, and high management fees can quickly eat up your overall returns. If you're investing in short-term Treasuries, for example, the portfolio might be expected to throw off 6 percent a year in dividends and appreciation. If you're paying 1 percent of that for expenses, your return instantly drops to 5 percent. Look for bond funds with annual expenses below 0.5 percent and never pay higher than 1 percent of assets. Depending on your needs, you might also consider buying bonds directly from a discount broker, especially if you plan to hold on through maturity. In that way, you'll avoid paying management fees altogether. (The one exception, which I am about to get to, is high-yield or "junk" bonds. Because these are so risky, I think you're better off buying them through a fund.)

CREDIT QUALITY

It's pretty much a given that the higher the yield offered by a bond fund, the lower the credit quality of the securities in the portfolio. This stands to reason; high-risk companies are forced to pay a premium to borrow money. If you're determined to invest in high-yield bonds, the best way to do it is through a fund. Diversify widely in this area of the market, especially if it looks like the economy could be slowing down or even heading into a recession. Just know, before getting in, that if you buy a portfolio of low credit quality, you can expect a heightened degree of volatility, similar to what you would get from a typical stock fund.

FAVORABLE MATURITIES

Bond funds have an inverse relationship to interest rates. As rates rise, bond prices fall. The opposite is also true. If this doesn't make sense at first glance, let me illustrate why this relationship exists. If you buy a bond today at par, or $1,000, offering a 6 percent yield, and tomorrow interest rates rise to 6.2 percent, I'm certainly not going to pay you $1,000 to buy that 6 percent bond. The value of the bond must fall, to compensate for the higher rate I can get on new issues. If I give you only $950 for that $1,000 bond, the 6 percent yield is suddenly worth more: I'm earning 6 percent annually on $950, which translates into an effective yield of 6.3 percent. The point here is: The longer you'll be holding a bond or bond fund, the more interest rate risk you take. If you'll need your money in less than two years, by all means buy only short-term bond funds. In today's low-interest-rate environment, where the chances are that rates will go up before they go down much more, I think it makes sense to favor short-term and intermediate-term maturities, even if your investment goals are years in the future. In addition to short-term bond and Treasury funds, you might also consider Ginnie Maes (GNMAs, or Government National Mortgage Association bonds), which are mortgage-backed securities with intermediate-term maturities.

MONEY MARKET FUNDS

With bank certificates of deposit and savings passbooks offering such paltry interest rates these days, you would be wise to consider putting your liquid cash into a carefully selected money market fund. Almost every major fund family, broker, and bank has at least one to choose from. You can select from regular taxable funds, U.S. government funds (which are often exempt from state taxes), and municipal funds (which may be exempt from both state and federal taxes but offer a much lower yield). Money market portfolios are comprised primarily of short-term bonds and other cash-equivalent instruments, and are designed to offer higher returns while maintaining a steady per-share net asset value of $1. Current yields range from around 2 percent for municipal funds to 5.5 percent for taxable accounts. Unlike a traditional bank account, these funds are not insured by the government, but they have historically been just as safe. How do you choose a money market fund?

QUALITY COMPANIES

Because money market deposits aren't insured, invest in funds sponsored by companies of integrity. You probably can't go wrong with any of the major brokers or recognized fund families. The reason those choices are important is this: Only twice in recent memory have credit defaults threatened to push a money market fund's net asset value below the magic $1 level. In both cases, the fund management company stepped in and made up the difference, preventing this from happening. Big firms know that letting their money market funds dip under $1 would do irreparable harm;

clients would fear for the safety of the entire organization. They simply won't let it happen.

HIGH YIELD

Do some research to find the fund with the highest yield. Because there isn't much wiggle room with the securities in a portfolio, funds with the lowest operating expenses almost always have the highest yields. Funds at the top of the yield list often waive some or all of their management fees to attract new assets. It's up to you to keep an eye on the date when those fees kick back in, so you can move to another fund if the yield becomes less competitive. You can find the highest yielding funds on a regular basis in publications like *The Wall Street Journal* or *Barron's,* and by visiting the IBC Financial Data Internet site at www.ibcdata.com (a profile of the IBC site is given in Chapter 8).

CONVENIENCE

Because money market funds are generally used as short-term parking places, you want those that give you easy access. Most funds offer some kind of check-writing feature, but look at the rules for this very closely. A few funds cap the number of checks you can write each month; others impose a minimum amount ($500 or more) on each check. Some funds offer ATM card access to your account and other perks that make them more like regular bank checking accounts. You'll normally find that the more perks you are offered, the lower the yield. But that's not always the case, so be sure to shop around.

SELL STRATEGY

Up to this point, the sole focus of this chapter has been on what to look for when deciding to *buy* a fund. It's equally important to know when to *sell*. Here are several good reasons for getting rid of one fund and replacing it with another.

- **A new manager arrives.** If the manager of a fund you own moves on, you should too, unless he or she is replaced by someone whose track record you admire just as much.

- **A better fund comes along**. If you stumble across a fund that's even more attractive than the one you currently own, it might make sense to switch, especially if the new fund is run by a seasoned manager.

- **You need the money**. This is a no-brainer reason. If you're saving money for a long-term goal such as retirement, you will have to sell your fund when your day of need ultimately arrives.

- **Expenses are too high**. Occasionally, funds will actually *raise* the expense ratio, usually for a nonsensical reason. If that happens with your fund, get out.

- **You spot underperformance**. Every manager goes through bad periods. I think it's reasonable to give managers 18 months to get their acts together. If they are still underperforming their peers and comparative benchmarks after that, they probably should get the boot.

- **Tax efficiency is missing**. If you're investing your money in a taxable account and the year-end distributions are unreasonably high, it might be wise to switch into a more tax-efficient fund.

- **Asset allocation is skewed**. We'll get into asset allocation in Chapter 7. Suffice it to say, if the particular fund you own no longer fits your desired asset mix, it's time to move on. (In other words, if you decide to reduce your overall exposure to stocks, you may have to trade a stock fund for a bond fund to get things into balance.)

- **Style drifts occur**. If you bought a small-cap fund that has grown so large it now concentrates on mid-cap stocks, you may want to replace it with a true small-cap offering. Alternatively, if a manager who used to concentrate on value stocks suddenly turns into a growth investor, see the move as a red flag that something's wrong.

- **The fund has become too big**. As a general rule, funds with comparatively tiny asset bases have the potential to perform better than larger ones. This is especially true in the small-cap area. You should consider selling micro-cap funds if assets grow much past $300 million, small caps after $1 billion, mid caps after $2 billion, and *any* fund bigger than $5 billion. There are always exceptions to this rule, but these are good guidelines.

- **You own too many funds**. If you have a tendency to fall in love with funds, you might want to do some housecleaning. No matter how much money you have to invest, you probably don't need to own more than 10 to 15 funds. If you're above that limit, think about cutting back.

THE SEVEN DEADLY SINS
OF MUTUAL FUND INVESTING

1. BUYING LAST YEAR'S HOT PERFORMER

Many investors falsely believe that buying the fund that did best during the previous year is a smart move. They figure the manager will continue to post the same incredible numbers, and they don't want to miss the ride. The sad truth is: Time and time again, one year's winner turns into the next year's dog. Among the many reasons for this reversal, a "star of the year" manager tends to get inundated with new cash, which can disrupt the portfolio and hurt existing shareholders.

2. TIMING THE MARKET

This is clearly a loser's game. I personally know many of the top names on Wall Street, and I can tell you that *no one* is able to *consistently* forecast the direction of the market. That's why it pays to stick with your strategy and stay fully invested at all times. In the 1980s, the annual return on stocks in the S&P 500 index was 17.6 percent. During that period, if you were in cash on the top ten trading days, your return dropped to 12.6 percent. Had you been on the sidelines for the 20 best days, you earned only 9.3 percent. And if you missed the 30 biggest advancing sessions, your return plummeted to 6.5 percent. Especially when it comes to stocks, not being fully invested is costly. It would be great to avoid major market declines and bear markets. Unfortunately, this cannot be done with any degree of accuracy.

3. BLINDLY FOLLOWING THE STARS

Based on all of the fund advertising that's out there today, you might think a fund with four or five stars from a rating service like Morningstar is a surefire winner. The truth is, even the president of Morningstar will tell you that the company's rating system is far from perfect, and that picking a fund solely because of the number of stars it has been given is a loser's game. The Morningstar system is based on risk-adjusted past performance, which has very little predictive value. The manager who earned the stars may no longer be there. Think in terms of buying *managers,* not *funds,* and never rely exclusively on a simplistic rating system for advice, especially without doing further research on your own. You might build a lousy portfolio by buying only five-star funds.

4. PURCHASING FUNDS, NOT MANAGERS

Looking at a fund's track record is not enough. Some of the best-performing funds are those that have been around for just a few years but are spearheaded by veteran managers who have outstanding long-term records. New funds run by seasoned talent are some of my favorites. I am always on the lookout for them. Good managers tend to get a lot of money sent their way, which can bloat their portfolios and hamper performance. When these luminaries launch a new fund, they're able to start with a clean slate. Take advantage of their talents while the fund is still small and nimble.

5. FALLING FOR THE MEDIA'S "FUND DARLING OF THE MONTH"

Members of the media are extremely oriented to the short term. I should know. I used to be a television news reporter. The truth is, the mainstream press usually won't feature a fund until it is poised to underperform. Here's why. They wait until a fund builds a hot short-term performance record, then they do a big write-up on it. Fresh money flows in, and the portfolio manager gets overwhelmed with new cash and underwhelmed with places to put it. As a result, performance usually plummets. It can take years for that situation to reverse itself.

6. FOCUSING ON QUANTITY INSTEAD OF QUALITY

It's a common belief that by simply owning eight or ten different funds, an investor is properly diversified. Unfortunately, that kind of portfolio may not be diversified at all. The reason: Funds with similar investment objectives often hold the same stocks. For example, suppose you own ten different aggressive growth funds. Your diversification is very limited because you are exposed to only one area of the market. Without question, asset allocation decisions are a critical starting point for constructing a well-rounded investment plan.

7. Taking Your Eye Off the Ball

Investors often think they can buy a great fund and never look at it again. There are many flaws with that kind of logic. The fund industry is constantly changing, and you need to keep up with it. The manager running a fund when you bought it may move on and be replaced by a lesser practitioner. That's one of several good reasons to get out. Or, as we've already discussed, funds may grow too large for their own good. Some managers lose their focus or change their investment strategy, which often leads to abysmal results. You should always keep an eye on your fund and be ready to pull the trigger if necessary.

5

SHOPPING AT THE FUND SUPERMARKETS

We learn early that there's no such thing as a free lunch. But when it comes to buying mutual funds, America's leading discount brokers are trying to break this perennial rule.

You already know that one way to purchase shares in a fund is by calling the fund directly, ordering a prospectus and application, completing the necessary paperwork, and sending it all back to the fund with your initial investment to get the ball rolling. When you decide to redeem your shares, you once again have to phone the fund and then wait for your check to arrive. If you want to switch from one fund to another in a different family, you have to order the prospectus and application for the new fund, request a redemption from your old one, fill out a new set of paperwork, cash the check your old fund sends you, and write out a check for the new fund. This is not only a hassle, but valuable time is being consumed. Because transferring from one fund to another can take days or weeks, you risk missing out on gains in the market during the interim.

Now, however, this way of doing business with your favorite funds is becoming a thing of the past. Top discount brokers, including Charles Schwab, Jack White & Co., Fidelity, and Waterhouse Securities, have created what I call virtual "no-load, no-transaction-fee supermarkets." Their programs enable you to buy and sell hundreds of funds in a single account without paying a penny in commissions. The programs are convenient, cost-effective, and, arguably, the most important new development for fund investors in recent memory.

THE START OF SOMETHING BIG

In 1984, San Diego (California) discount broker Jack White & Co. was the first to start selling no-load funds to clients. Rival Charles Schwab quickly did the same. Each offered about 150 funds that could be traded for a minimal transaction fee, similar to the commission charged on stocks.

Both brokers threw in a variety of services that were never before available to those dealing with no-loads—for example, statement consolidation and the ability to purchase shares without having to mail in an order form. However, initial public reaction to the concept, even with the small fee, was disappointing. Schwab soon realized that the transaction fee was a stumbling block; people could still invest free by calling the funds directly. It was apparent that, for many clients, the convenience factor alone wasn't enough to overcome the $30 to $50 transaction fee they were being charged.

In 1990, Charles Schwab himself began working on a plan to get the fund companies to pay the transaction fee on behalf of his clients. He knew that in selling funds he was on to something big, but he understood that investors wouldn't welcome the idea until he completely got rid of the commission. What's now known as Schwab's OneSource program was born in 1992. Just as he had transformed the way people bought stocks 17 years earlier, Schwab dramatically changed the distribution channel for no-load funds with the birth of this program.

ONE-STOP SHOPPING

From the start, OneSource allowed clients to purchase and sell shares from a handful of large fund companies free of charge. How? By charging the participating fund companies anywhere from $.25 to $.35 for every $100 in assets that Schwab brought in. This was considered to be a marketing and distribution fee. Because the funds saved the cost of performing these functions on their own, Schwab argued that it was a good deal for them. Initially, the idea ran into resistance. Many fund families approached it with a "wait-and-see" attitude. They wanted to see how the competition reacted before taking the plunge themselves.

Jack White & Co. soon introduced a similar program, although founder and president Jack White had some doubts that it would ever take off. He knew many fund managers personally, and he figured they would resist paying to be part of a program that made it so easy for investors to buy and sell their shares. Fund companies, as a rule, hate traders and market timers because frequent buying and selling disrupts the normal flow of funds. Just to meet redemptions, managers may have to sell positions they like, thus hurting other shareholders.

As it turned out, the concept caught on and spread like wildfire. One fund family after another started courting Schwab and Jack White to sign up. Before long, fund behemoth Fidelity Investments joined the party with a fund supermarket of its own and was closely followed by almost all of the other major discount brokers, including Muriel Siebert and Waterhouse Securities.

WIDE AVAILABILITY

Today, no-load, no-transaction-fee (NTF) programs have amassed some $200 billion in assets. Almost all of the major no-load fund families participate, as do a number of smaller boutique funds that were formerly available only to high-net-worth institutional investors.

Noticeably absent from the current list of available offerings are funds from giants T. Rowe Price and Vanguard, which maintain that the cost of participation is simply too high. (Funds from these families can still be purchased from the brokers, although a small commission is charged for each transaction.) Even full-service brokers like Merrill Lynch and Smith Barney, once famous for bad-mouthing no-loads, are joining the NTF fund bandwagon to stem the flow of lost assets.

THE WAVE OF THE FUTURE

Some industry analysts predict that funds and brokers that refuse to join these programs will struggle to survive as NTF supermarkets become more popular. Many of the participating funds already get more than half of their assets from them. In fact, most start-up money managers are designing their new funds specifically around the supermarkets, to make sure they can get in right away.

THE ADVANTAGES

It seems inevitable that NTF supermarkets would gain such widespread acceptance. After all, with one phone call, clients can buy and sell hundreds of high-quality funds from dozens of different families, and all of their holdings are consolidated on one monthly statement. In addition, the brokers keep track of pertinent tax information, leaving the client to contend with only one 1099 form at the end of the year. Other advantages include fee-free IRAs and SEP retirement plans, which are perfect for small business owners; no-cost reinvestment of dividends and capital gains; around-the-clock account access by phone and computer; free check writing; and, in some cases, the ability to trade on margin.

THE DRAWBACKS

There are a few drawbacks. When you buy shares through an NTF supermarket, the fund companies won't know you exist. Your investment gets lumped into one omnibus account registered in the name of your broker, so don't expect to get much promotional mail touting your fund companies' new products and services. Your annual reports and other information will likely arrive a few days later than normal, because everything must be sent through each discount broker's third-party mailing center.

In addition, most brokers have short-term trading rules, which require payment of a transaction fee if a fund position is sold before a given time period (usually, 90 days). The rules are designed to discourage frequent switching around. (That's probably a good thing; such regular trading usually leads to lower returns anyway.) All in all, the downside is relatively minor.

GETTING STARTED

How can you take advantage of this first free lunch on Wall Street? Begin by opening an account with the broker of your choice. It usually takes at least $5,000 to get started, and the extra perks begin to kick in at around the $10,000 level.

Which broker is best for you is a very personal decision. Your choice depends on your own needs and preferences. Let's say you want to do most of your trading online. Every broker offers a computerized trading program and/or Internet site, but Schwab and Fidelity currently have the most sophisticated products. If you desire personal face-to-face service, Schwab and Fidelity are the only two firms with branch offices located across the country. Jack White has none. (Keep in mind that it's possible to conduct all of your business over the phone or by computer, so not having a branch office is no big deal.) Jack White offers the most funds, but Fidelity, Waterhouse, and Schwab aren't far behind.

You may want to look at some of the smaller details. For example, Fidelity has by far the best-looking and most comprehensive monthly account statements. Waterhouse and Fidelity are the only brokers that don't charge for using the ATM debit card that comes with your money market account. (Everyone else charges up to $2 per ATM transaction.) Don't be surprised if the programs offered by Jack White & Co. and Waterhouse start looking more alike in the coming months. Waterhouse recently bought out Jack White.

YOUR ONE-STOP BANK, TOO

When you open a brokerage account, you establish an entire cash management program that not only links all of your funds and other investments (including stocks and bonds), but also gives you easy access to an interest-bearing money market account. All of your available cash is automatically swept into this account at the end of each day. You can then write as many checks as your account balance allows, or use a debit card to get cash from automated teller machines (ATMs) around the world. For all intents and purposes, you could make this your primary checking account, and would be well advised to do so. You'll earn a much higher rate of interest than you'll ever get at your local bank, and this option makes it easy for you to invest in your favorite funds on a regular basis.

The beauty of these programs is that they cost you nothing, and the fact that you're getting a lot of free services should be an important consideration. At Fidelity, for example, your account is charged a $12 annual fee for each fund that has a balance below $2,500. If you can't keep your balance that high, look elsewhere. On the other hand, Fidelity waives IRA and Self-Employed Retirement Plan (SEP) fees for balances above $2,500. Jack White and Schwab require a $10,000 balance for this waiver. Waterhouse doesn't charge for IRAs, regardless of your balance.

CHOOSING YOUR BROKER

▆▆▆ Here's the best plan of action for deciding which broker is right for you: Call or visit each one and ask for more information and an application. (Figure 5.1 gives a list of names, toll-free numbers, and Internet

**10 Reasons to Buy Your Mutual Funds
Through the NTF Fund Supermarkets**

1. Purchase hundreds of top-performing no-load funds from more than 90 different families without paying any commissions or transaction costs.

2. Have all of your investment holdings (stocks, bonds, cash, and funds) consolidated on one easy-to-read monthly statement.

3. Gain entry into exclusive funds once available only to high-net-worth institutional investors.

4. Get 24-hour-a-day access to your portfolio holdings and values by phone and computer, allowing you to keep constant tabs on your investments.

5. Buy into funds that have minimum investment requirements of up to $1 million for as little as $1,000.

6. Receive a fee-free retirement account (IRA, SEP, Keogh, etc.) for yourself and your employees, while choosing from a plethora of no-load funds to build your wealth.

7. Enjoy same-day order execution of your fund transactions, and avoid having to rely on mail delivery and signature guarantees to redeem your shares.

8. Let your discount broker keep track of all fund gains and losses, making tax time a breeze.

9. Get a free high-interest-bearing checking account linked directly to your investment portfolio.

10. Keep more money in your pocket by avoiding "loaded" funds, and benefit from the many services provided by America's top discount brokers.

Figure 5.1   NTF Discount Brokers

Broker	Telephone	Internet Address
Charles Schwab & Co.	(800) 845-1714	www.schwab.com
Fidelity Investments	(800) 544-9697	www.fidelity.com
Jack White & Co.	(800) 233-3411	www.jackwhiteco.com
Muriel Siebert & Co.	(800) 872-0711	www.msiebert.com
Waterhouse Securities	(800) 934-4443	www.waterhouse.com

addresses.) Then, on paper, map out the products and services you are seeking. Next, determine which broker(s) offer most of the things on your list. Some of the more popular features include free IRAs and SEPs, large availability of NTF funds, strong computerized trading programs, and all-in-one asset management accounts. I also recommend checking out each broker's Internet site. If you plan to use your computer to keep track of your investments, see what each broker offers via online technology.

Regardless of which broker you ultimately choose, you're sure to find NTF supermarkets a convenient and less expensive way to buy no-load funds in the future. As for the free lunch, the fund families are picking up the tab so eat and enjoy. Deals like this don't come along very often.

6

100 POWERHOUSE
PERFORMERS FOR 1999

I have given you the tools you need to effectively select your own funds, but there are some 9,000 names to sift through and analyze, and the number keeps growing each day. I'm assuming you bought this book to make your investment life easier, and that's exactly what I'm going to do in this chapter. I have performed exhaustive research to uncover the 100 most attractive no-load stock and fixed-income funds for the year ahead. All have brilliant track records and are spearheaded by seasoned managers with a proven talent for picking winning investments. I call these funds my "Powerhouse Performers."

Every Powerhouse Performer is profiled in a two-page report that starts with the fund's name, objective, and manager. Here is a breakdown of the various objectives:

1–16	Large-Cap Growth Funds
17–27	Large-Cap Value Funds
28–34	Mid-Cap Growth Funds
35–45	Mid-Cap Value Funds
46–54	Small-Cap Growth Funds
55–62	Small-Cap Value Funds
63–64	Equity Income Funds
65–72	Growth and Income Funds
73–76	Index Funds
77–81	Balanced Funds
82–87	International Funds

88–91	Global Funds
92–93	Corporate Bond (Intermediate) Funds
94–95	Mortgage-Backed Securities (Intermediate) Funds
96	General Government Bond Funds
97	Federal Municipal Bond Funds
98–100	High-Yield Corporate Funds

Within each group, the funds are arranged alphabetically by the first word of their name. Entries 1 through 91 represent the equity side; entries 92 through 100 represent the fixed-income side.

I have described each fund's style as precisely as possible, based on the manager's most recent portfolio composition. Style refers to the kinds of securities a fund holds. This information tells you whether a given fund will add an element of diversity to your portfolio. Having exposure to many different styles will help you to weather the market's constant fluctuations and sector rotations. You can find definitions for each of these investment styles in the Glossary in the back of the book.

Generally speaking, growth fund managers look for companies experiencing rapid earnings and/or sales growth. Shares in these companies often trade at a premium to the overall stock market. Value fund managers hunt for bargains, often buying slower growing or troubled businesses that are available at depressed prices.

Each Powerhouse Performer's report contains a brief overview of the fund, a description of how the manager invests the portfolio, and why the fund made my list. The accompanying tables show various returns and rankings. You'll find each fund's annualized return over the past one-, three-, and five-year periods (through June 30, 1998) where applicable.

Next come the fund's overall and risk rankings, according to Value Line. The overall ranking takes into account how a given fund has performed compared to its peers. Ranking is on a scale of 1 through 5, with 1 being best. The risk ranking gives you a feel for how volatile the portfolio is. On a scale of 1 through 5, 5 is the riskiest.

Also included are a handful of useful statistics, including the fund's annual turnover rate, expense ratio, 12b-1 fee, maximum sales load, and three-year beta coefficient. Beta is a measure of a fund's volatility in relation to its benchmark index (usually the S&P 500, for stocks). The S&P 500 has a beta of 1. Funds with a beta lower than 1 fluctuate less than the overall market; funds with a beta above 1 are more volatile. If you are conservative and seek to temper your market risk, you need to favor funds with low betas.

For each fund, I give the minimum investment requirements for both regular and IRA accounts, the toll-free telephone number, and the Internet address (where applicable). You can use this information to get a prospectus and/or more information, such as a listing of which discount brokers (if any) carry the fund through their NTF supermarket.

On the second page of every report are two graphs (courtesy of Value Line). The first graph shows how the return on a $10,000 investment in the fund over a period of years compared to its benchmark index. The second graph is a measure of individual annual performance, illustrating, year by year, what kind of returns the fund has generated since its inception or since 1978, whichever is longer. (For some of the newer funds, this information is not available.) Finally, there is a box showing the fund's most recent top 10 portfolio holdings.

In Chapter 7, I will help you put together a portfolio tailored to your individual needs, drawing from my lineup of Powerhouse Performers. For now, let's take a look at some of the most deserving candidates for your investment consideration in 1999.

DREYFUS APPRECIATION

OBJECTIVE:	*Large-Cap Growth*	**1**
MANAGER:	*Fayez Sarofim*	

FUND OVERVIEW:

Since taking over management of Dreyfus Appreciation in 1990, manager Fayez Sarofim has turned this fund into a growth-oriented portfolio full of large-cap global names. Sarofim is no rookie to the investment scene. He founded his firm, Fayez Sarofim & Co., in 1958. It serves as the fund's subadviser and manages some $33.4 billion in assets. Sarofim and his comanager, Russell Hawkins, are convinced that overseas exposure by dominant blue-chip companies will give them an impressive earnings boost over the long run. That's why they are banking on such stocks. Because the top 20 names in the portfolio often account for 60 percent of assets, this can be a more volatile fund than others in the category.

Dreyfus Appreciation's emphasis is on U.S.-based companies that are easily recognized and get at least 35 to 40 percent of their income from international markets. Visibility of earnings is also important. Sarofim will occasionally buy American Depositary Receipts (ADRs) when he feels purchasing them is appropriate. The visibility of a company's future earnings growth is an important consideration, because Sarofim tends to stick with a buy-and-hold strategy.

ANNUALIZED RETURNS		PORTFOLIO STATISTICS	
1-Year	28.33%	**Beta**	0.95
3-Year	31.05%	**Turnover**	0.76
5-Year	24.14%	**12-Month Yield**	0.63%
Overall Rank	1	**12b-1 Fee**	0.25%
Risk Rank	3	**Expense Ratio**	0.88%
MINIMUM INVESTMENT		**CONTACT INFORMATION**	
Regular	$2,500	*Dreyfus Appreciation Fund*	
IRA	$750	*Telephone: (800) 782-6620*	
		www.dreyfus.com	

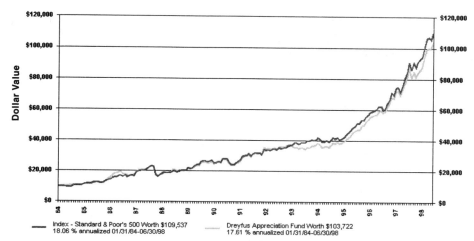

Index - Standard & Poor's 500 Worth $109,537
18.06 % annualized 01/31/84-06/30/98

Dreyfus Appreciation Fund Worth $103,722
17.61 % annualized 01/31/84-06/30/98

GROWTH OF $10,000

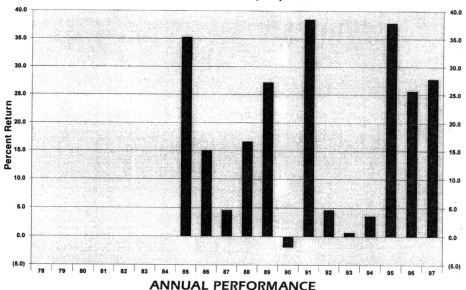

ANNUAL PERFORMANCE

TOP 10 HOLDINGS	
Pfizer	Johnson & Johnson
Coca-Cola	Procter & Gamble
Merck & Co.	General Electric
Intel	Citicorp
Philip Morris	Ford Motor Co.

DREYFUS DISCIPLINED STOCK

OBJECTIVE: *Large-Cap Growth*
MANAGER: *Bert Mullins*

2

FUND OVERVIEW:

Dreyfus Disciplined Stock manager Bert Mullins says his goal is to beat the S&P 500 with less volatility. So far, he's managed to achieve this objective. Mullins gathers information from a diverse group of sources to construct computerized valuation models that rank stocks as being either over- or undervalued. The models measure such things as actual and estimated earnings changes, along with price-to-book, price-to-earnings, and return-on-equity ratios. There are 15 different screens in all. The computer then categorizes each individual stock in various industries according to relative attractiveness. That's when Mullins sends his analysts out to do additional fundamental research. They determine which companies are truly most attractive, and, conversely, which should be sold.

How can Mullins run a portfolio that's less volatile than the S&P 500? By doing good security selection and making sure the fund isn't over-weighted in any one sector or industry. To keep his computer models up-to-date, the screening criteria get updated every two weeks. Mullins remains fully invested most of the time, although he's allowed to keep up to 20 percent in cash if necessary.

ANNUALIZED RETURNS		PORTFOLIO STATISTICS	
1-Year	31.44%	Beta	1.03
3-Year	30.64%	Turnover	68.87%
5-Year	22.57%	12-Month Yield	0.42%
Overall Rank	1	12b-1 Fee	0.10%
Risk Rank	3	Expense Ratio	1.14%
MINIMUM INVESTMENT		**CONTACT INFORMATION**	
Regular	$2,500	*Dreyfus Disciplined Stock Fund*	
IRA	$750	*Telephone: (800) 782-6620*	
		www.dreyfus.com	

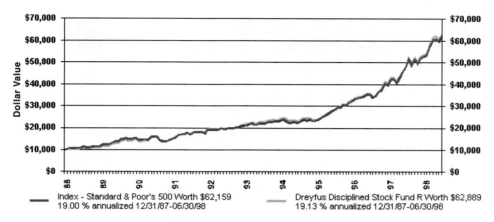

Index - Standard & Poor's 500 Worth $62,159
19.00 % annualized 12/31/87-06/30/98

Dreyfus Disciplined Stock Fund R Worth $62,889
19.13 % annualized 12/31/87-06/30/98

GROWTH OF $10,000

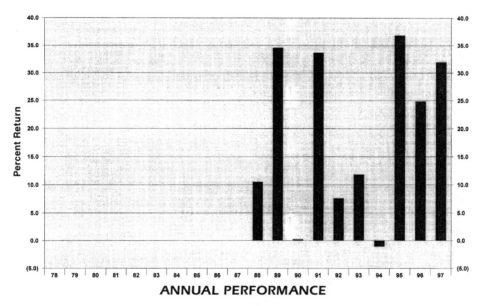

ANNUAL PERFORMANCE

TOP 10 HOLDINGS	
General Electric	IBM
Microsoft	Eli Lilly & Co.
Intel	BankAmerica
Procter & Gamble	Coca-Cola
Exxon	Chase Manhattan

GABELLI GROWTH

OBJECTIVE:	*Large-Cap Growth*	*3*
MANAGER:	*Howard Ward*	

FUND OVERVIEW:

Gabelli Growth manager Howard Ward invests in a diversified portfolio of large, seasoned, well-managed companies that he believes have favorable earnings dynamics and price appreciation potential. His companies normally boast above-average or expanding market shares, high profit margins, and respectable returns on equity. Ward does a lot of hands-on research. He especially likes businesses with a demonstrated competitive advantage that benefit from one or more secular trends, such as the technology revolution, aging of the population, and globalization. He also focuses on valuation, hoping to buy these growers at attractive prices.

The fund's largest weightings are in the financial services, drug, technology, newspaper, and broadcasting sectors. "Virtually all of our companies occupy leading positions in their fields," Ward explains. "We should do well when large growth company stocks do well, and less well when they periodically stall." Ward is a strong advocate of diversification, but he doesn't believe in being spread out more than necessary. He expects to keep his portfolio at around 50 to 70 names, to prevent his best ideas from being unfairly diluted.

ANNUALIZED RETURNS		PORTFOLIO STATISTICS	
1-Year	37.15%	**Beta**	1.07
3-Year	31.12%	**Turnover**	83.40%
5-Year	22.85%	**12-Month Yield**	0.05%
Overall Rank	2	**12b-1 Fee**	0.25%
Risk Rank	3	**Expense Ratio**	1.42%

MINIMUM INVESTMENT		CONTACT INFORMATION
Regular	$1,000	*Gabelli Growth Fund*
IRA	$1,000	*Telephone: (800) 422-3554*
		www.gabelli.com

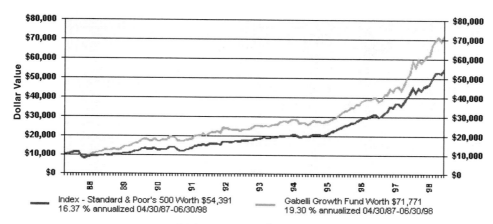

GROWTH OF $10,000

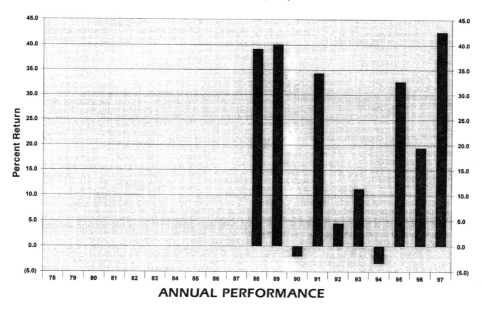

ANNUAL PERFORMANCE

TOP 10 HOLDINGS	
Northern Trust	Schlumberger
Home Depot	Marsh & McLennan
First Data	Merck & Co.
Mellon Bank	Merrill Lynch
Gillette	Gannett

HARBOR CAPITAL APPRECIATION

OBJECTIVE:	*Large-Cap Growth*	*4*
MANAGER:	*Spiros Segalas*	

FUND OVERVIEW:

Harbor Capital Appreciation is one of the more aggressive large-cap growth funds you will come across. Although Spiros Segalas fills his portfolio with blue-chip household names, he's not afraid to trade around his positions with frequency and will concentrate in specific sectors if he thinks that's the best course of action. Segalas is an admitted momentum player. If one of his companies fails to achieve or exceed his expected earnings target, he'll get rid of it, although he doesn't try to time the market itself.

Segalas's bottom-up management style seeks out growth at a reasonable price. He prefers companies with market capitalizations of at least $1 billion and with track records of superior sales growth, high returns on equity, and solid balance sheets. Earnings numbers are also critical, and he is constantly reevaluating his expectations.

Harbor Capital Appreciation has been a stellar performer since Segalas took over in 1990. It has an extremely low expense ratio for a fund of this nature. Clearly, you can expect it to be volatile. But if you can stand these more frequent fluctuations, you will likely be rewarded.

ANNUALIZED RETURNS		PORTFOLIO STATISTICS	
1-Year	34.89%	Beta	1.20
3-Year	27.26%	Turnover	72.80%
5-Year	24.67%	12-Month Yield	0.16%
Overall Rank	2	12b-1 Fee	0.00%
Risk Rank	4	Expense Ratio	0.69%
MINIMUM INVESTMENT		**CONTACT INFORMATION**	
Regular	$2,000	*Harbor Capital Appreciation*	
IRA	$500	*Telephone: (800) 422-1050*	

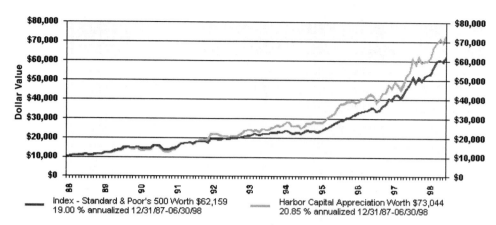

Index - Standard & Poor's 500 Worth $62,159
19.00 % annualized 12/31/87-06/30/98

Harbor Capital Appreciation Worth $73,044
20.85 % annualized 12/31/87-06/30/98

GROWTH OF $10,000

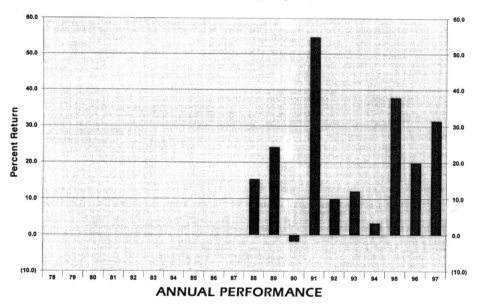

ANNUAL PERFORMANCE

TOP 10 HOLDINGS	
Pfizer	SmithKline Beecham
Cisco Systems	Washington Mutual
Chase Manhattan	Compaq Computer
Schlumberger	Citicorp
Hewlett-Packard	Monsanto

MARSICO FOCUS

| OBJECTIVE: | *Large-Cap Growth* | **5** |
| MANAGER: | *Tom Marsico* | |

FUND OVERVIEW:

Tom Marsico built a stellar record at the Janus Twenty fund, steering it to a 22.38 percent annualized return from January 31, 1988, to August 7,1997. (That compared favorably to an 18.20 percent return for the S&P 500.) He left Janus in late 1997 to start his own shop, and he launched Marsico Focus at the beginning of 1998. However, the portfolio looks almost identical to the old Janus Twenty, only better because he is working with a smaller asset base. Marsico Focus holds this proven manager's 20 to 30 favorite stocks. This added concentration increases both the fund's potential risks and rewards.

Marsico considers this to be a global portfolio, meaning he can invest in both U.S. and foreign securities. He prides himself in being an out-of-the-box thinker who looks for variables that aren't obvious from examining conventional financial analyses. He spends a lot of time talking with the management, suppliers, customers, competitors, and critics of the companies he owns. Among the characteristics he looks for in his high-growth, large-cap businesses are: an element of change, a strong franchise, products with a global reach, and the potential to benefit from a positive emerging social or economic theme.

ANNUALIZED RETURNS		PORTFOLIO STATISTICS	
1-Year	N/A	Beta	N/A
3-Year	N/A	Turnover	N/A
5-Year	N/A	12-Month Yield	N/A
Overall Rank	N/A	12b-1 Fee	0.25%
Risk Rank	N/A	Expense Ratio	N/A
MINIMUM INVESTMENT		**CONTACT INFORMATION**	
Regular	$2,500	*Marsico Focus Fund*	
IRA	$1,000	*Telephone: (888) 860-8686*	
		www.marsicofunds.com	

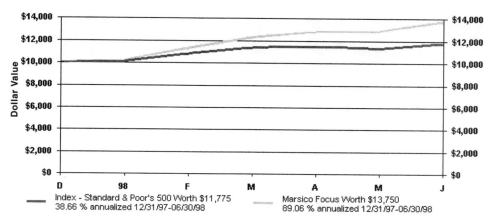

GROWTH OF $10,000

TOP 10 HOLDINGS	
Ford Motor Co.	Merrill Lynch
Dell Computer	Delta & Pine Land
Pfizer	Time Warner
Warner-Lambert	Volkswagen
Citicorp	Northern Telecom

MONTAG & CALDWELL GROWTH

OBJECTIVE:	*Large-Cap Growth*	**6**
MANAGER:	*Ronald E. Canakaris*	

FUND OVERVIEW:

Montag & Caldwell Growth manager Ronald Canakaris seeks to generate long-term capital appreciation by investing in a relatively concentrated portfolio of equities. He buys companies that he believes are undervalued based on both current earning power and ability to generate strong earnings growth over the next 12 to 18 months. Many of the names in the portfolio are established brands with long histories.

"We continue to be quite positive on the outlook for the shares of high-quality growth companies," Canakaris says. "Because we expect more moderate growth in the U.S. economy and corporate profits in the future, the superior and consistent earnings growth rates of these companies should become increasingly attractive." Many of his companies do business around the world, which Canakaris feels gives them a tremendous advantage. "With the U.S. economy already operating at a high level of activity, the multinational consumer, healthcare, and technology companies in the fund are particularly well positioned to benefit from the greater growth opportunities that exist in global markets," he adds.

ANNUALIZED RETURNS		PORTFOLIO STATISTICS	
1-Year	32.56%	Beta	1.07
3-Year	33.42%	Turnover	18.65%
5-Year	N/A	12-Month Yield	N/A
Overall Rank	2	12b-1 Fee	0.25%
Risk Rank	4	Expense Ratio	1.22%

MINIMUM INVESTMENT		CONTACT INFORMATION
Regular	$2,500	*Montag & Caldwell Growth Fund*
IRA	$500	*Telephone: (800) 992-8151*
		www.alleghanyfunds.chicago-rust.com

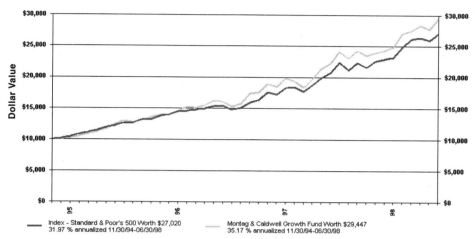

GROWTH OF $10,000

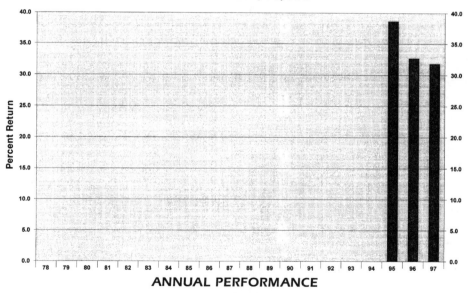

ANNUAL PERFORMANCE

TOP 10 HOLDINGS

Coca-Cola	McDonald's
Gillette	Eli Lilly
Johnson & Johnson	Walt Disney
Procter & Gamble	Schlumberger
Bristol-Myers Squibb	American Intl. Group

PAPP AMERICA ABROAD

		7
OBJECTIVE:	*Large-Cap Growth*	
MANAGER:	*Roy Papp and Rosellen Papp*	

FUND OVERVIEW:

Roy Papp knows there's a world of opportunity out there for investors. He's seen much of it with his own eyes, having traveled around the globe throughout his life. But he's too scared to trust any of his own money to one of the foreign stock exchanges. That's why he started a fund designed to profit from global growth through buying domestically domiciled companies. Papp America Abroad invests primarily in U.S. multinationals, most of which do more than half of their business overseas. Among the many dangers of investing directly in foreign soil, Papp cites currency risk, varying accounting standards, higher transaction costs, political instability, and the loss of SEC protection. He also notes that U.S. companies tend to be more technologically advanced and competitive than their international counterparts, which means their profit potential is greater.

In addition to the international business component, Papp's ideal company is an industry leader—better yet, a monopoly. It is also growing at a rate of 20 to 25 percent a year, and trades at or near a market multiple at the time of initial purchase.

ANNUALIZED RETURNS		PORTFOLIO STATISTICS	
1-Year	14.08%	Beta	0.98%
3-Year	27.82%	Turnover	6.12%
5-Year	24.43%	12-Month Yield	0.06%
Overall Rank	3	**12b-1 Fee**	0.00%
Risk Rank	3	**Expense Ratio**	1.21%
MINIMUM INVESTMENT		**CONTACT INFORMATION**	
Regular	$5,000	*Papp America Abroad Fund*	
IRA	$1,000	*Telephone: (800) 421-4004*	
		www.roypapp.com	

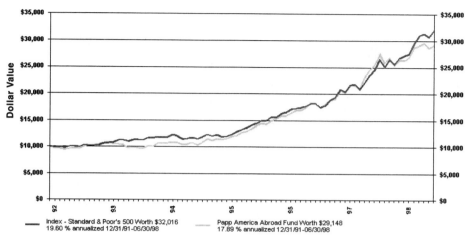

Index - Standard & Poor's 500 Worth $32,016
19.60 % annualized 12/31/91 -06/30/98

Papp America Abroad Fund Worth $29,148
17.89 % annualized 12/31/91 -06/30/98

GROWTH OF $10,000

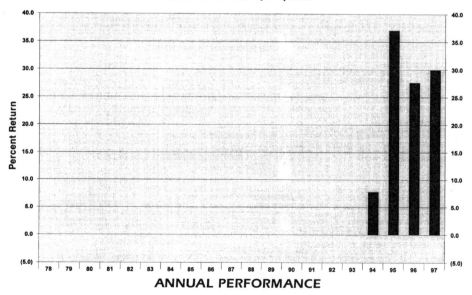

ANNUAL PERFORMANCE

TOP 10 HOLDINGS	
State Street	Hewlett-Packard
Viking Office Products	Service Corp.
Intel	Merck & Co.
Interpublic Group	Air Express Intl.
Manpower	McDonald's

RAINIER CORE EQUITY

OBJECTIVE:	*Large-Cap Growth*	*8*
MANAGER:	*James R. Margard*	

FUND OVERVIEW:

Although the Rainier Core Equity portfolio is composed primarily of companies in the S&P 500 index, manager James Margard can invest in stocks of all sizes. His highly diversified portfolio is spread across a broad range of industries. To reduce risk, he purposely makes sure not to over-weight any single industry. Margard adheres to a "growth at a reasonable price" philosophy, believing it allows him to generate competitive returns in all market environments.

When evaluating individual securities, Margard emphasizes companies likely to experience superior earnings growth, relative to their peers. He also favors businesses with a competitive advantage operating in a favorable regulatory environment, and he wants them at the right price. Strong management, insider ownership, and financial integrity are other requirements. Stocks are sold when they reach a predetermined target price, or if Margard finds a more attractive idea and needs the money to purchase it. Even though the minimum investment requirement is a steep $25,000, you can get in for much less through one of the NTF programs (see Chapter 5).

ANNUALIZED RETURNS		PORTFOLIO STATISTICS	
1-Year	28.69%	**Beta**	0.93%
3-Year	30.10%	**Turnover**	78.00%
5-Year	N/A	**12-Month Yield**	0.26%
Overall Rank	1	**12b-1 Fee**	0.25%
Risk Rank	3	**Expense Ratio**	1.14%
MINIMUM INVESTMENT		**CONTACT INFORMATION**	
Regular	$25,000	*Rainier Core Equity Portfolio*	
IRA	$25,000	*Telephone: (800) 248-6314*	

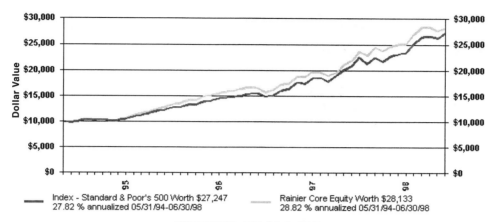

GROWTH OF $10,000

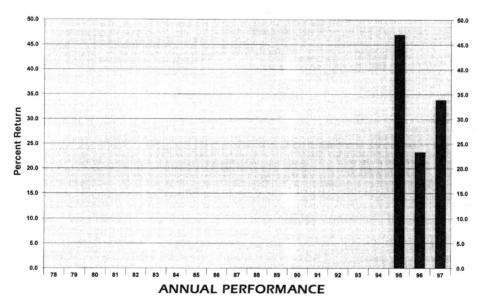

ANNUAL PERFORMANCE

TOP 10 HOLDINGS	
Microsoft	March & McLennan
Merck & Co.	PepsiCo
Mobil	Bristol-Myers Squibb
Household International	Phillips Petroleum
Bell Atlantic	SmithKline Beecham

SPECTRA

OBJECTIVE:	*Large-Cap Growth*	
MANAGER:	*David Alger*	*9*

FUND OVERVIEW:

Although I have placed Spectra in the large-cap growth category, it is technically an "all-cap" portfolio. Manager David Alger will buy anything if it meets his criteria. Specifically, he looks for companies experiencing rapid change caused by high unit-volume growth and positive changes in the product life cycle. He and his staff follow 1,400 companies in their database, and like to marry research talent and technology when evaluating potential ideas. Alger refers to his investment style as being an "hourglass method," because he uses both bottom-up and top-down analysis to run this highly concentrated portfolio.

Spectra has been around since 1968, but it was a closed-end fund until February, 1996. This means it was a fixed portfolio traded on the stock exchange. It had a relatively small shareholder base, comprised mostly of members of the Alger family. David Alger has an excellent track record. Unfortunately, the rest of the funds he manages carry steep front-end sales loads. Spectra was converted into a no-load a few years ago, giving investors a chance to tap into Alger's talent without paying a commission. The fund's expense ratio is higher than normal, but it has been justified by stellar performance.

ANNUALIZED RETURNS		PORTFOLIO STATISTICS	
1-Year	32.28%	Beta	1.12%
3-Year	26.39%	Turnover	133.98%
5-Year	29.29%	12-Month Yield	0.00%
Overall Rank	3	12b-1 Fee	0.00%
Risk Rank	4	Expense Ratio	2.12%
MINIMUM INVESTMENT		**CONTACT INFORMATION**	
Regular	$1,000	*Spectra Fund*	
IRA	$250	*Telephone: (800) 711-6141*	

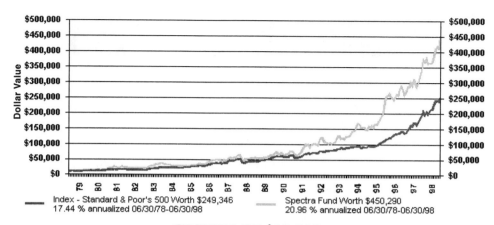

Index - Standard & Poor's 500 Worth $249,346
17.44 % annualized 06/30/78-06/30/98

Spectra Fund Worth $450,290
20.96 % annualized 06/30/78-06/30/98

GROWTH OF $10,000

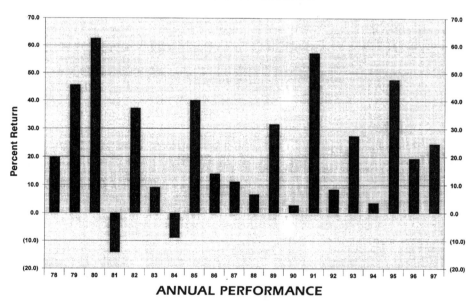

ANNUAL PERFORMANCE

TOP 10 HOLDINGS

Guidant Corp.	Sunbeam
Microsoft	Schering-Plough
Tyco Intl.	Diamond Offshore
Bristol-Myers Squibb	Linear Technology
Electronics for Imaging	Wal-Mart Stores

STEIN ROE YOUNG INVESTOR

OBJECTIVE:	*Large-Cap Growth*	**10**
MANAGER:	*Erik Gustafson and David Brady*	

FUND OVERVIEW:

Even though Stein Roe Young Investor does buy companies of interest to children, the fund's performance has been anything but kid stuff. It has handily outperformed the S&P 500 since inception in 1994, while maintaining a well-diversified portfolio of between 50 and 70 holdings. Although it can invest in both large and small companies, most of the stocks are established blue-chip names. This fund is primarily marketed as a vehicle for growing savings to pay for a young person's college education. However, it is open to all investors.

One reason I like this fund is that Stein Roe writes all shareholder material with its young audience in mind. Big type and graphics are features of every annual report, to make sure children understand how their money is being managed. As a result, the fund gives kids an educational experience while it helps to grow their portfolios. The fund even has its own quarterly newsletter for shareholders, *Dollar Digest,* and asks shareholders to send in their own investment ideas for future consideration. If you agree to add at least $50 per month to the fund, you can get in for a minimum initial investment of only $100.

ANNUALIZED RETURNS		PORTFOLIO STATISTICS	
1-Year	31.16%	Beta	0.96
3-Year	32.84%	Turnover	22.00%
5-Year	N/A	12-Month Yield	0.00%
Overall Rank	2	12b-1 Fee	0.00%
Risk Rank	3	Expense Ratio	1.42%
MINIMUM INVESTMENT		**CONTACT INFORMATION**	
Regular	$2,500	*Stein Roe Young Investor Fund*	
IRA	$500	*Telephone: (800) 338-2550*	
		www.steinroe.com	

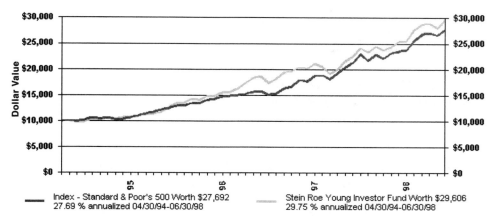

Index - Standard & Poor's 500 Worth $27,692
27.69 % annualized 04/30/94-06/30/98

Stein Roe Young Investor Fund Worth $29,606
29.75 % annualized 04/30/94-06/30/98

GROWTH OF $10,000

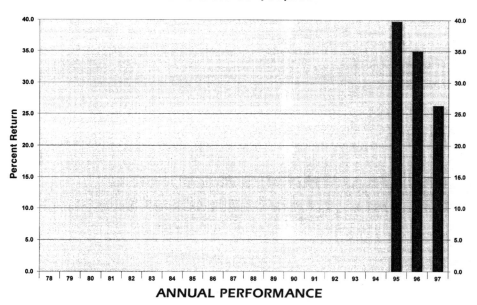

ANNUAL PERFORMANCE

TOP 10 HOLDINGS	
Intel	AT&T
Cendant	MGIC Investment
Mattel	Texas Regal Bancshares
Household International	Associated Group
WM Wrigley	Federal Natl. Mtg. Assn.

U.S. GLOBAL LEADERS GROWTH

OBJECTIVE: *Large-Cap Growth*
MANAGER: *George M. Yeager*

11

FUND OVERVIEW:

George Yeager sounds a lot like Roy Papp (who manages the Papp America Abroad fund I described earlier). Yeager is also a big believer in the growth prospects for both the developed and emerging markets overseas. However, he's convinced the best way to profit from this potential is by investing in U.S. companies that have a commanding overseas presence. Thus, his U.S. Global Leaders Growth Fund looks to make money from consumers around the planet by staying here at home. Surprisingly, there is little overlap between Papp America Abroad and this fund. Yeager is slightly more concentrated and has a smaller asset base. He also only manages this one fund, while Papp runs several. Which is better? U.S. Global Leaders has performed slightly better of late, but it would be perfectly acceptable to have both in your portfolio.

Yeager looks for the fastest-growing, best-valued, and most well-established companies in the United States. He also demands that they get a significant portion of their earnings from the rapid-growing markets of Asia, Latin America, and Eastern Europe. This fund is pretty new, but Yeager has been managing money for some 40 years. He clearly knows what he's doing.

ANNUALIZED RETURNS		PORTFOLIO STATISTICS	
1-Year	37.20%	Beta	N/A
3-Year	N/A	Turnover	21.49%
5-Year	N/A	12-Month Yield	0.00%
Overall Rank	N/A	12b-1 Fee	0.00%
Risk Rank	N/A	Expense Ratio	1.47%
MINIMUM INVESTMENT		**CONTACT INFORMATION**	
Regular	$2,500	*U.S. Global Leaders Growth Fund*	
IRA	$2,500	*Telephone: (800) 282-2340*	

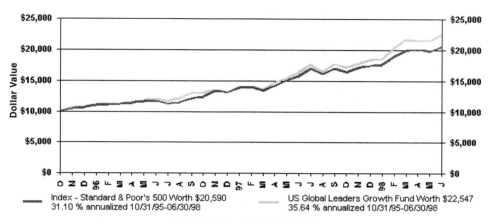

GROWTH OF $10,000

Index - Standard & Poor's 500 Worth $20,590
31.10 % annualized 10/31/95-06/30/98

US Global Leaders Growth Fund Worth $22,547
35.64 % annualized 10/31/95-06/30/98

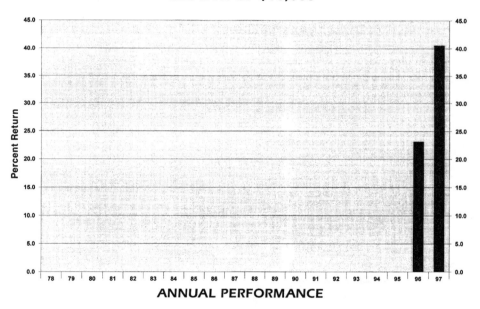

ANNUAL PERFORMANCE

TOP 10 HOLDINGS	
Cendant	Wal-Mart Stores
Pfizer	McDonald's
Tiffany	ALZA
Staples	Starbucks
Home Depot	Schlumberger

VANGUARD U.S. GROWTH

OBJECTIVE:	*Large-Cap Growth*	*12*
MANAGER:	*J. Parker Hall III and David Fowler*	

FUND OVERVIEW:

To make it into the Vanguard U.S. Growth portfolio, a company must be attractively priced, financially strong, have an excellent earnings record, enjoy a dominant position in its market, offer above-average prospects for continued growth, and be big in size. To identify such companies, managers J. Parker Hall and David Fowler rigorously research the 200 or so names that meet their initial screening criteria, which include market capitalizations above $1 billion, strong performance records, relatively low sensitivity to changing economic conditions, and a favorable outlook for continued growth. In the end, fewer than 60 companies usually survive this inspection and ultimately find their way into the portfolio.

The kinds of companies that meet the managers' stringent standards include market leaders from a broad spectrum of industries. You'll normally find such household names as Coca-Cola, AT&T, Cisco Systems, Johnson & Johnson, and Procter & Gamble among the list of top holdings. The fund doesn't tend to do much trading around, and it boasts an annual turnover rate over the past five years of less than 40 percent.

ANNUALIZED RETURNS		PORTFOLIO STATISTICS	
1-Year	32.90%	Beta	0.98%
3-Year	31.12%	Turnover	35.00%
5-Year	24.07%	12-Month Yield	0.74%
Overall Rank	1	12b-1 Fee	0.00%
Risk Rank	3	Expense Ratio	0.41%
MINIMUM INVESTMENT		**CONTACT INFORMATION**	
Regular	$3,000	*Vanguard U.S. Growth*	
IRA	$1,000	*Telephone: (800) 662-7447*	
		www.vanguard.com	

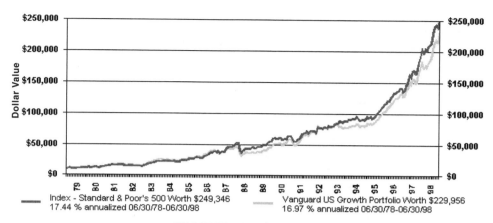

Index - Standard & Poor's 500 Worth $249,346
17.44 % annualized 06/30/78-06/30/98

Vanguard US Growth Portfolio Worth $229,956
16.97 % annualized 06/30/78-06/30/98

GROWTH OF $10,000

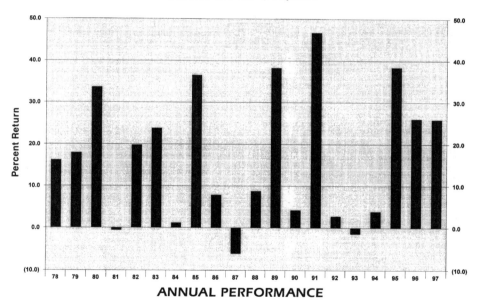

ANNUAL PERFORMANCE

TOP 10 HOLDINGS	
Pfizer	Procter & Gamble
Monsanto	Bristol-Myers Squibb
Intel	Merch & Co.
Coca-Cola	Cisco Systems
General Electric	Walt Disney

WARBURG PINCUS CAPITAL APPRECIATION

OBJECTIVE: *Large-Cap Growth*
MANAGER: *Susan Black and George Wyper*

13

FUND OVERVIEW:

Warburg Pincus Capital Appreciation invests across a broadly diversified portfolio of U.S. securities. Portfolio managers Susan Black and George Wyper first try to find sectors they expect will outperform the overall market for one reason or another. They then search for the most promising companies within those sectors. They may also look for positive themes or patterns within businesses (like a change in management, the generation of large free cash flow, or a company share buy-back program), which could make them even more compelling.

This is a pure growth fund, but Black and Wyper try to find companies they believe are selling at a reasonable price, considering their projected growth. To see whether the valuation makes sense, they analyze such factors as a company's growth rate, debt-to-equity ratio, and amount of inside ownership. They also try to identify whether today's growth is sustainable into the future. Some areas of recent interest include financial services, energy, and technology. In particular, they like financial services because of the sector's significant top-line growth and ongoing consolidation in the industry.

ANNUALIZED RETURNS		PORTFOLIO STATISTICS	
1-Year	33.17%	Beta	0.90%
3-Year	30.03%	Turnover	238.11%
5-Year	22.22%	12-Month Yield	0.31%
Overall Rank	1	12b-1 Fee	0.00%
Risk Rank	3	Expense Ratio	1.01%
MINIMUM INVESTMENT		**CONTACT INFORMATION**	
Regular	$2,500	*Warburg Pincus Capital Appreciation*	
IRA	$500	*Telephone: (800) 927-2874*	
		www.warburg.com	

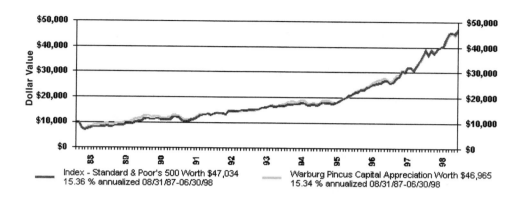

Index - Standard & Poor's 500 Worth $47,034
15.36 % annualized 08/31/87-06/30/98

Warburg Pincus Capital Appreciation Worth $46,965
15.34 % annualized 08/31/87-06/30/98

GROWTH OF $10,000

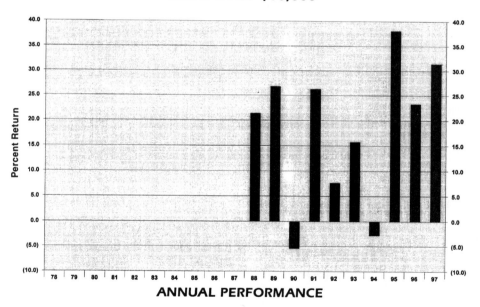

ANNUAL PERFORMANCE

TOP 10 HOLDINGS	
Loral Space & Comm.	La Quinta Inns
US West	BankAmerica
IBM	Noble Drilling
Credit Suisse	USG Corp.
Reliastar Finl. Corp.	BCE Inc.

WESTWOOD EQUITY

OBJECTIVE: *Large-Cap Growth*
MANAGER: *Susan Byrne*

14

FUND OVERVIEW:

Susan Byrne's number-one rule of investing is "Try not to ever lose money." It's a goal she doesn't always achieve, of course. But when she buys each stock for Westwood Equity's portfolio, she first attempts to figure out how much it could go down. In her search for individual companies, Byrne employs a top-down approach, beginning with an analysis of overall economic trends to identify sectors or industries poised for growth. Once that work has been done, she starts looking for individual securities that are most likely to benefit.

Byrne's analysis includes searching for a catalyst that can drive a stock higher. When she finds one, she checks out what other analysts are saying about the company. She'll only buy if she feels her peers are underestimating a company's potential. Specifically, Byrne wants to invest in businesses that she is almost certain will come through with positive earnings surprises, surpassing all Wall Street estimates. She sets a target for every stock in the portfolio, and revises it up or down based on the actual reported numbers. This sometimes means she gets out of high-fliers before they run out of steam. But she'd rather play it safe than risk being shocked by a disappointment.

ANNUALIZED RETURNS		PORTFOLIO STATISTICS	
1-Year	18.07%	Beta	0.77
3-Year	27.67%	Turnover	61.00%
5-Year	23.03%	12-Month Yield	0.64%
Overall Rank	2	12b-1 Fee	0.25%
Risk Rank	2	Expense Ratio	1.59%
MINIMUM INVESTMENT		**CONTACT INFORMATION**	
Regular	$1,000	*Westwood Equity Fund*	
IRA	$1,000	*Telephone: (800) 422-3554*	
		www.gabelli.com	

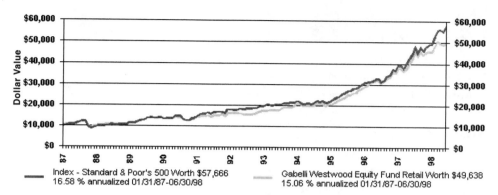

GROWTH OF $10,000

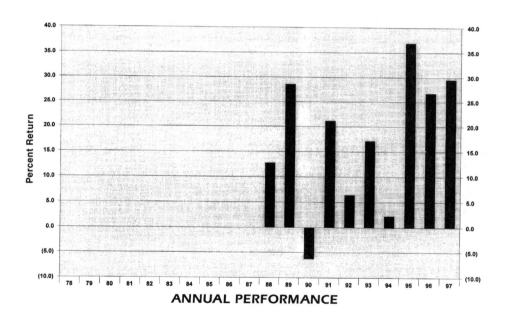

ANNUAL PERFORMANCE

TOP 10 HOLDINGS

CVS Corp.	Eaton Corp.
IBM	ALCOA
Lucent Technologies	Campbell Soup
Bell Atlantic	SBC Communications
Conseco	Mobil Corp.

WHITE OAK GROWTH

OBJECTIVE:	*Large-Cap Growth*	**15**
MANAGER:	*James D. Oelschlager*	

FUND OVERVIEW:

White Oak Growth has showered its investors with plenty of money in recent years. This concentrated fund contains around 25 stocks focused in three primary market sectors: financials, technology, and drugs. Manager James Oelschlager has been in these areas for the past decade, even before starting this fund. He believes in staying put and running with his winners, which makes the portfolio extremely tax-efficient. With such concentration comes volatility, of course, and this fund can give investors a bumpy ride. Over the long haul, however, it has been a big winner.

White Oak Growth focuses on established large-cap companies selling at attractive valuations based on expected future earnings. Stocks are monitored based on their five-year growth rates relative to their price-to-earnings multiple. Oelschlager doesn't try to time the market; he generally stays fully invested at all times. He continues to be excited about technology, his largest sector, believing that, going forward, it will be the strongest area for growth in the economy. Furthermore, he remains positive on the pipeline for new drugs and continuing consolidation in the financial services area.

ANNUALIZED RETURNS		PORTFOLIO STATISTICS	
1-Year	31.37%	Beta	1.34%
3-Year	34.92%	Turnover	7.90%
5-Year	28.45%	12-Month Yield	0.00%
Overall Rank	3	12b-1 Fee	0.00%
Risk Rank	4	Expense Ratio	0.97%

MINIMUM INVESTMENT		CONTACT INFORMATION	
Regular	$2,000	*White Oak Growth*	
IRA	$2,000	*Telephone: (888) 462-5386*	
		www.oakassociates.com	

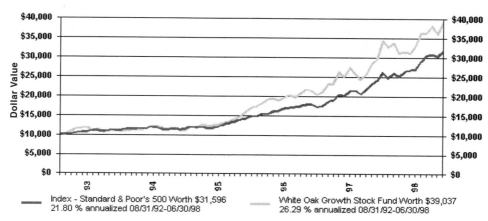

Index - Standard & Poor's 500 Worth $31,596
21.80 % annualized 08/31/92-06/30/98

White Oak Growth Stock Fund Worth $39,037
26.29 % annualized 08/31/92-06/30/98

GROWTH OF $10,000

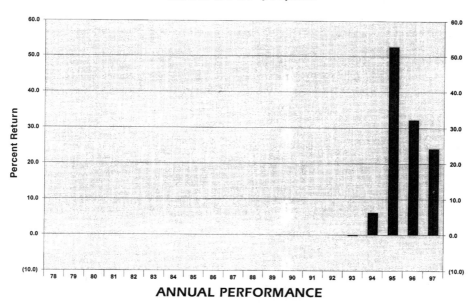

ANNUAL PERFORMANCE

TOP 10 HOLDINGS	
Cisco Systems	American Intl. Group
Pfizer	Medtronic
Oracle Corp.	Citicorp
NationsBank	Intel
Applied Materials	Parametric Tech.

WILSHIRE TARGET LARGE CO. GROWTH

OBJECTIVE:	*Large-Cap Growth*	**16**
MANAGER:	*Thomas Stevens*	

FUND OVERVIEW:

You might think of Wilshire Target Large Company Growth as a stylized index fund. The process of putting the portfolio together begins by culling through the 2,500 largest companies from the Wilshire 5000 index (a benchmark consisting of all publicly traded U.S. stocks). From here, manager Thomas Stevens picks out 200 or so of the biggest names with above-average earnings or sales growth. Stevens further favors established companies with solid market recognition, as opposed to up-and-coming turnaround situations. He remains fully invested, opting to switch among holdings as economic conditions change, instead of raising cash.

Stevens reports that five-year earnings growth on the companies in his portfolio remains well above that of the S&P 500, demonstrating the high quality and record of success exemplified by his chosen companies. The fund's sector weighting makeup is also much different from the S&P 500, with almost 30 percent of the portfolio in technology stocks. Its heavy exposure to this area has been beneficial so far, but it could hurt the fund more than its peers if techs take a tumble.

ANNUALIZED RETURNS		PORTFOLIO STATISTICS	
1-Year	32.09%	Beta	1.13
3-Year	31.94%	Turnover	13.00%
5-Year	24.18%	12-Month Yield	0.18%
Overall Rank	2	12b-1 Fee	0.25%
Risk Rank	3	Expense Ratio	0.60%
MINIMUM INVESTMENT		**CONTACT INFORMATION**	
Regular	$2,500	*Wilshire Target Large Co. Growth*	
IRA	$2,500	*Telephone: (888) 200-6796*	
		www.wilfunds.com	

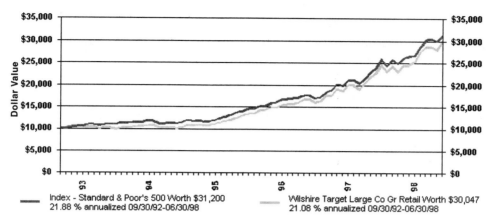

GROWTH OF $10,000

Index - Standard & Poor's 500 Worth $31,200
21.88 % annualized 09/30/92-06/30/98

Wilshire Target Large Co Gr Retail Worth $30,047
21.08 % annualized 09/30/92-06/30/98

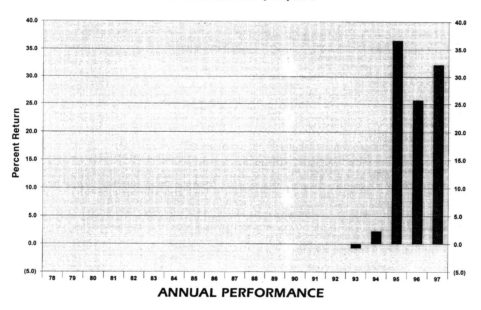

ANNUAL PERFORMANCE

TOP 10 HOLDINGS	
General Electric	Procter & Gamble
Microsoft	Wal-Mart
Intel	Johnson & Johnson
Coca-Cola	American Intl. Group
Merck & Co.	Hewlett-Packard

AMERICAN CENTURY EQUITY GROWTH

OBJECTIVE: *Large-Cap Value*
MANAGER: *William Martin and Jeff Tyler*

17

FUND OVERVIEW:

American Century Equity Growth managers William Martin and Jeff Tyler use a quantitative approach to running their fund. They begin by drawing ideas from the 2,500 largest companies traded in the United States, which means there are plenty of small caps represented as well. Using a portfolio optimization model, they make sure holdings in the portfolio match the risk characteristics of the S&P 500, while seeing to it that no more than 25 percent of all assets are invested in the same industry. "This gives the fund balance and stability, which are favorable characteristics during periods of increased market volatility," the managers note.

When it comes to picking individual stocks, the model takes many factors into consideration, including whether a company is underpriced based on earnings growth, business fundamentals, or intrinsic value. Martin and Tyler remain fully invested at all times and tend to focus on the largest names. However, they often include a number of small companies in an effort to enhance returns. They are also working to reduce turnover, which has grown with the increase in assets. This will make the portfolio more tax-efficient.

ANNUALIZED RETURNS		PORTFOLIO STATISTICS	
1-Year	37.74%	Beta	0.98
3-Year	32.03%	Turnover	75.00%
5-Year	23.62%	12-Month Yield	0.85%
Overall Rank	1	12b-1 Fee	0.00%
Risk Rank	3	Expense Ratio	1.00%

MINIMUM INVESTMENT		CONTACT INFORMATION
Regular	$2,500	*American Century Equity*
IRA	$1,000	*Growth Fund*
		Telephone: (800) 345-2021
		www.americancentury.com

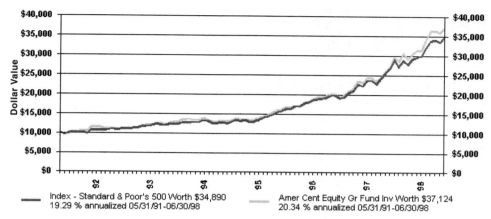

GROWTH OF $10,000

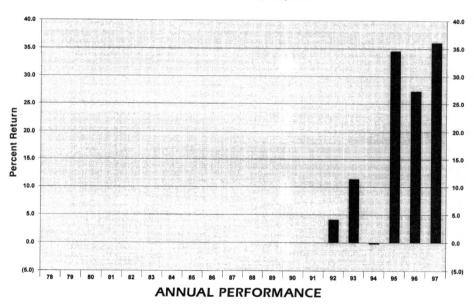

ANNUAL PERFORMANCE

TOP 10 HOLDINGS	
Ford Motor Co.	United Technologies
Unilever	Bell South
Morgan Stanley Dean Witter	Lucent Technologies
Chevron	Schlumberger
First Union Corp.	Caterpillar

BABSON VALUE

OBJECTIVE:	*Large-Cap Value*	
MANAGER:	*Nick Whitridge*	*18*

FUND OVERVIEW:

Nick Whitridge is always on the lookout for bargains, whether he's buying cars, suits, appliances, or stocks. When hunting for companies to add to the Babson Value portfolio, he hunts for names that are unloved by Wall Street, and therefore undervalued based on earnings, assets, or dividends. Such measures as price-to-book and price-to-earnings ratios are extremely important yardsticks to him. But before he'll buy a stock, he checks to be sure a company's balance sheet has enough money to give managers time to turn things around. He also wants to take on a relatively low degree of market risk.

This discipline fits well with Whitridge's natural contrarian instincts. He strives to spot companies that will outperform the market by exceeding investor expectations. Because he claims to like each holding equally, he keeps a constant 2.5 percent weighting of every stock, meaning there are about 40 names in the portfolio. To figure out when it's time to sell, Whitridge uses a relative-strength price test to uncover those securities that have become overvalued. The fund's overall price-to-earnings ratio is usually 20 percent lower than the S&P 500, reflecting the fund's value bent.

ANNUALIZED RETURNS		PORTFOLIO STATISTICS	
1-Year	25.07%	Beta	0.84
3-Year	25.12%	Turnover	17.00%
5-Year	22.32%	12-Month Yield	0.99%
Overall Rank	1	12b-1 Fee	0.00%
Risk Rank	3	Expense Ratio	0.96%
MINIMUM INVESTMENT		**CONTACT INFORMATION**	
Regular	$1,000	*Babson Value Fund*	
IRA	$250	*Telephone: (800) 422-2766*	
		www.jbfunds.com	

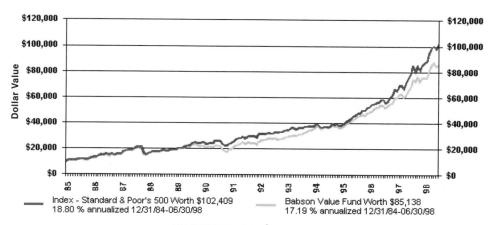

GROWTH OF $10,000

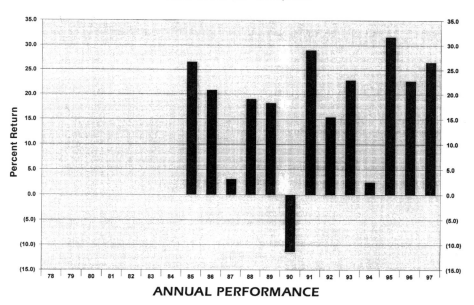

ANNUAL PERFORMANCE

TOP 10 HOLDINGS

Tenet Healthcare	Allstate
Illinova	Xerox
Harcourt General	Student Loan Corp.
Wells Fargo & Co.	Boeing
Travelers Group	Dana Corp.

CLIPPER FUND

OBJECTIVE:	*Large-Cap Value*	*19*
MANAGER:	*James Gipson*	

FUND OVERVIEW:

Clipper Fund skipper James Gipson runs a tight ship. He looks for a few select large-cap stocks that are priced right, and he will hold large amounts of cash when he can't find any. His portfolio may contain as few as 10 to 15 names, as it has recently, especially when he's gloomy about the outlook for the overall market. A cautious approach? You bet. Yet Gipson has managed to perform right in line with the S&P 500, a tough job for even the most aggressive fund.

Gipson is most concerned about preserving capital. He looks for industry leaders selling below intrinsic value. That number is determined by using a dividend and cash flow discounting model, or by looking at price-to-earnings ratios and comparing the sales transactions of like businesses. Balance sheet strength and the ability to generate earnings are other key factors in the appraisal process. Gipson attempts to keep turnover down, to reduce taxes. But he won't hesitate to trim a holding when he feels the time is right to do so. "Our first choice is to buy stock in a good company cheaply and then hold it forever," he says. "We will sell overvalued stocks, however, rather than expose (the) portfolio to potential loss."

ANNUALIZED RETURNS		PORTFOLIO STATISTICS	
1-Year	19.46%	Beta	0.68
3-Year	24.60%	Turnover	31.00
5-Year	20.62%	12-Month Yield	1.46%
Overall Rank	2	12b-1 Fee	0.00%
Risk Rank	2	Expense Ratio	1.08%
MINIMUM INVESTMENT		**CONTACT INFORMATION**	
Regular	$5,000	*lipper Fund*	
IRA	$2,000	*Telephone: (800) 776-5033*	
		www.clipperfund.com	

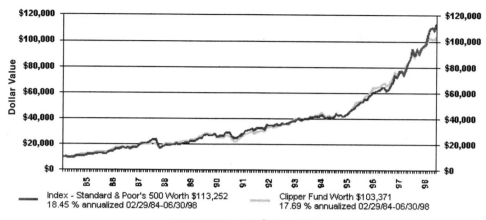

Index - Standard & Poor's 500 Worth $113,252
18.45 % annualized 02/29/84-06/30/98

Clipper Fund Worth $103,371
17.69 % annualized 02/29/84-06/30/98

GROWTH OF $10,000

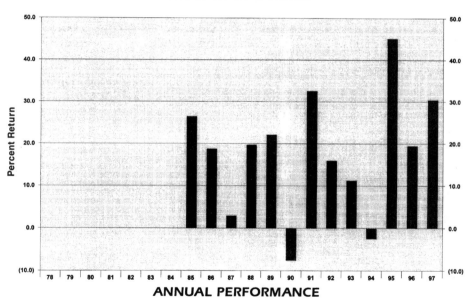

ANNUAL PERFORMANCE

TOP 10 HOLDINGS	
Philip Morris	Nike
Wal-Mart Stores	Johnson & Johnson
McDonald's	Toys R Us
Mattel	Old Republic
Golden West Financial	PepsiCo

DODGE & COX STOCK

| OBJECTIVE: | *Large-Cap Value* | *20* |
| MANAGER: | *Team Managed* | |

FUND OVERVIEW:

The Dodge & Cox Stock fund, founded in 1965, takes a price-disciplined approach to investing in large-cap companies. The management team won't buy or sell a stock unless it meets their projected price target. They use a bottom-up approach to company selection, emphasizing fundamental analysis. Still, several themes stand out. The fund has a high weighting in cyclically sensitive areas, such as chemicals, autos, paper/forest products, and transportation. It also maintains a lower exposure than the S&P 500 to the consumer products, health care, and telephone sectors, because valuations in these areas are too high, given the managers' assessment of future earnings potential. "We strive to invest in companies with strong business franchises, good prospects for improving profitability, and current valuations that we believe reflect relatively low investor expectations," notes fund president John A. Gunn.

Stocks in the portfolio generally have below-average price-to-earnings, price-to-book, and market cap-to-sales ratios. Because every investment is made with a three- to five-year time horizon, turnover is consistently low, which increases the overall tax efficiency of this time-tested performer.

ANNUALIZED RETURNS		PORTFOLIO STATISTICS	
1-Year	17.89%	Beta	0.81
3-Year	24.07%	Turnover	19.00%
5-Year	30.13%	12-Month Yield	1.51%
Overall Rank	2	12b-1 Fee	0.00%
Risk Rank	3	Expense Ratio	0.56%
MINIMUM INVESTMENT		**CONTACT INFORMATION**	
Regular	$2,500	*Dodge & Cox Stock Fund*	
IRA	$1,000	*Telephone: (800) 621-3979*	

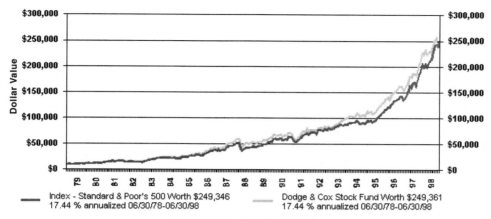

Index - Standard & Poor's 500 Worth $249,346
17.44 % annualized 06/30/78-06/30/98

Dodge & Cox Stock Fund Worth $249,361
17.44 % annualized 06/30/78-06/30/98

GROWTH OF $10,000

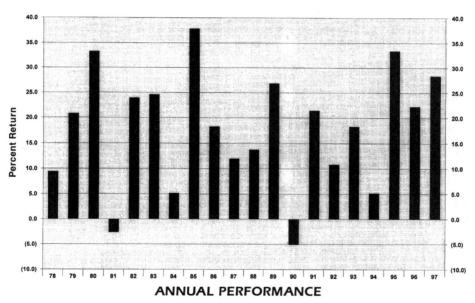

ANNUAL PERFORMANCE

TOP 10 HOLDINGS

General Motors	ALCOA
Union Pacific	Digital Equipment
Citicorp	Pharmacia & Upjohn
American Express	FDX Corp.
Dow Chemical	IBM

LEGG MASON VALUE TRUST

| OBJECTIVE: | *Large-Cap Value* | **21** |
| MANAGER: | *William H. Miller III* | |

FUND OVERVIEW:

Let's get the bad news out of the way first. Legg Mason Value Trust has a huge 12b-1 fee of .95 percent, which normally would be reason enough for me to stay away from it. It has also grown quite large in a short period of time. But there is a good reason for that. Manager Bill Miller has steered the fund to excellent returns, thanks to shrewd stock picking, low turnover, and a keen value bias. For that reason, I'm willing to overlook these negatives, assuming that Miller can continue to deliver despite the obstacles in his way.

Miller is quick to point out that he is an investor, not a speculator. He doesn't try to guess the direction of the market or which industries are most likely to outperform. He builds his portfolio one name at a time. "We do intensive research on our holdings and try to buy companies whose prices represent large discounts to our assessment of the intrinsic value of the business," he says. "We use an economic value approach to our analytical process, which involves going well beyond simple accounting-based measures of value." He runs a tightly focused portfolio of about 35 to 40 names, and isn't afraid to concentrate in specific sectors when he thinks it's wise to do so.

ANNUALIZED RETURNS		PORTFOLIO STATISTICS	
1-Year	37.90%	Beta	1.07
3-Year	39.24%	Turnover	13.60%
5-Year	29.25%	12-Month Yield	1.44%
Overall Rank	1	12b-1 Fee	0.94%
Risk Rank	4	Expense Ratio	1.73%
MINIMUM INVESTMENT		**CONTACT INFORMATION**	
Regular	$1,000	*Legg Mason Value Trust*	
IRA	$1,000	*Telephone: (800) 822-5544*	
		www.leggmason.com	

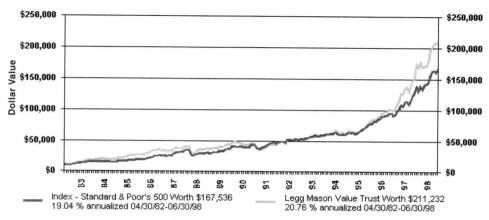

Index - Standard & Poor's 500 Worth $167,536
19.04 % annualized 04/30/82-06/30/98

Legg Mason Value Trust Worth $211,232
20.76 % annualized 04/30/82-06/30/98

GROWTH OF $10,000

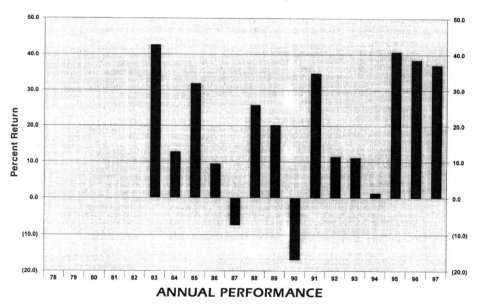

ANNUAL PERFORMANCE

TOP 10 HOLDINGS

Dell Computer	Compaq Computer
Federal Natl. Mtg. Assn.	America Online
IBM	Circus Circus
Chase Manhattan	MBNA Corp.
Western Digital	Lloyds TSB Group

OAK VALUE FUND

OBJECTIVE:	*Large-Cap Value*	***22***
MANAGER:	*David Carr and George Brumley III*	

FUND OVERVIEW:

David Carr and George Brumley didn't have a background in money management when they started their investment firm in 1986. But what they did have was a keen interest in the teachings of Warren Buffett. They studied Buffett's Berkshire Hathaway annual reports and used them to help form the foundation of the investment discipline they follow today. The results have been impressive. Their Oak Value Fund looks for companies selling at a discount to intrinsic value. Like Buffett, they refer to their approach as looking for "good businesses with good management at attractive prices." Carr and Brumley search for strong franchises and value stocks that can be had at a discount to the cash flow the business is expected to generate over the next several years. They personally visit more than 100 companies each year, looking for new ideas. The two say they strive to build a portfolio full of companies whose products or services they understand, with management they respect.

It's not surprising that Oak Value contains many of the same names found in Buffett's Berkshire Hathaway portfolio, including Coca-Cola, Walt Disney and *The Washington Post*. Berkshire Hathaway is also among the fund's top holdings.

ANNUALIZED RETURNS		PORTFOLIO STATISTICS	
1-Year	33.53%	Beta	0.68
3-Year	33.99%	Turnover	22.00%
5-Year	25.35%	12-Month Yield	0.00%
Overall Rank	1	12b-1 Fee	0.00%
Risk Rank	2	Expense Ratio	1.59%
MINIMUM INVESTMENT		**CONTACT INFORMATION**	
Regular	$2,500	*Oak Value Fund*	
IRA	$1,000	*Telephone: (800) 680-4199*	
		www.oakvalue.com	

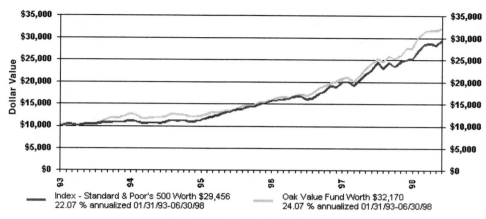

Index - Standard & Poor's 500 Worth $29,456
22.07 % annualized 01/31/93-06/30/98

Oak Value Fund Worth $32,170
24.07 % annualized 01/31/93-06/30/98

GROWTH OF $10,000

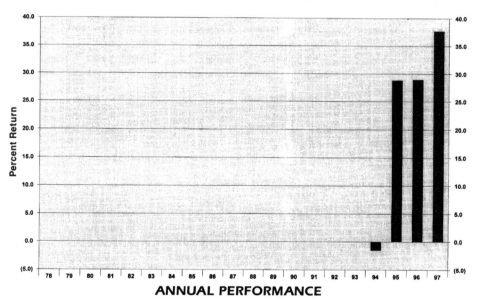

ANNUAL PERFORMANCE

TOP 10 HOLDINGS	
United Asset Management	Washington Post Cl B
Pulitzer Publishing	AFLAC
EW Scripps	RLI
RP Scherer	Dun & Bradstreet
Walt Disney	General Re

OAKMARK

OBJECTIVE:	*Large-Cap Value*	**23**
MANAGER:	*Robert Sanborn*	

FUND OVERVIEW:

As a kid growing up in Chicago, Robert Sanborn learned the importance of watching your wallet. His parents never had a lot of money and shopped mostly in discount department stores. He did the same thing, before becoming a success on Wall Street. So it is only natural that Sanborn chooses to stick with his penny-pinching ways when picking investments for his Oakmark Fund. He uses a disciplined long-term value approach to stock selection. Specifically, he looks for companies selling for at least 40 percent less than what a rational person would pay for the entire business, given its future prospects. He also wants to own companies in which management holds a substantial portion of the outstanding stock, to make sure their interests are aligned with his.

Sanborn is a cautious investor, but he doesn't believe in overdiversification. He typically devotes half of the fund's assets to his top 20 positions. He trades infrequently, although he'll get rid of a stock once it reaches 90 percent of its fair value, even if he still likes the fundamentals. You won't find any technology names in the Oakmark portfolio. Sanborn will only invest in businesses he understands and sees as likely to survive for decades to come.

ANNUALIZED RETURNS		PORTFOLIO STATISTICS	
1-Year	18.37%	Beta	0.77
3-Year	24.08%	Turnover	19.93%
5-Year	21.92%	12-Month Yield	0.88%
Overall Rank	2	12b-1 Fee	0.00%
Risk Rank	2	Expense Ratio	1.03%

MINIMUM INVESTMENT		CONTACT INFORMATION	
Regular	$1,000	*The Oakmark Fund*	
IRA	$500	*Telephone: (800) 625-6275*	
		www.oakmark.com	

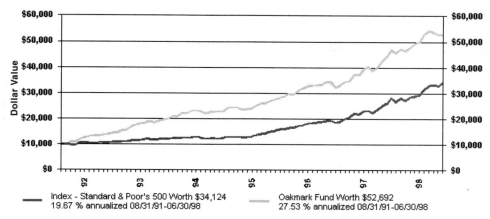

GROWTH OF $10,000

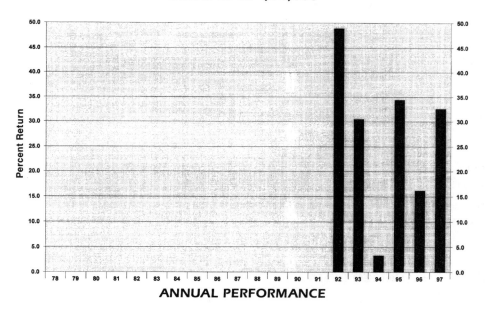

ANNUAL PERFORMANCE

TOP 10 HOLDINGS	
Philip Morris	Black & Decker
Banc One	US West
Lockheed Martin	Columbia/HCA
Tele-Communications Inc.	Nike
Mellon Bank	Anheuser Busch

SELECTED AMERICAN SHARES

		24
OBJECTIVE:	*Large-Cap Value*	
MANAGER:	*Christopher Davis*	

FUND OVERVIEW:

If you had to make a short list of the best mutual fund managers of all time, there's no question that Shelby Davis would show up near the top. His New York Venture Fund has been an outstanding performer since its inception in 1969. Perhaps he inherited much of his investment skill from his late father, who was a Wall Street legend in his own right. Unfortunately, New York Venture is a load fund, meaning you pay a commission to get in. In 1993, Shelby took over management of Selected American Shares, which is a nearly identical fund that is available on a no-load basis. Shelby relinquished day-to-day portfolio management duties to his son, Chris, in 1997, although he remains the firm's chief investment officer. Shelby still spends his days providing guidance on investment themes, strategies, and individual stock selection, while Chris pulls the trigger.

The Davis investment philosophy calls for finding overlooked, undervalued companies with promising long-term prospects. The Davises believe in doing rigorous research, visiting with management, and actively managing risk. They also favor proven businesses with long histories of earnings growth.

ANNUALIZED RETURNS		PORTFOLIO STATISTICS	
1-Year	27.39%	Beta	1.01
3-Year	31.35%	Turnover	26.00%
5-Year	22.70%	12-Month Yield	0.57%
Overall Rank	2	12b-1 Fee	0.25%
Risk Rank	3	Expense Ratio	0.95%
MINIMUM INVESTMENT		**CONTACT INFORMATION**	
Regular	$1,000	*Selected American Shares*	
IRA	$1,000	*Telephone: (800) 243-1575*	
		Website: www.selectedfunds.com	

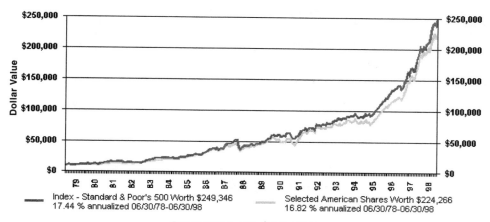

GROWTH OF $10,000

Index - Standard & Poor's 500 Worth $249,346
17.44 % annualized 06/30/78-06/30/98

Selected American Shares Worth $224,266
16.82 % annualized 06/30/78-06/30/98

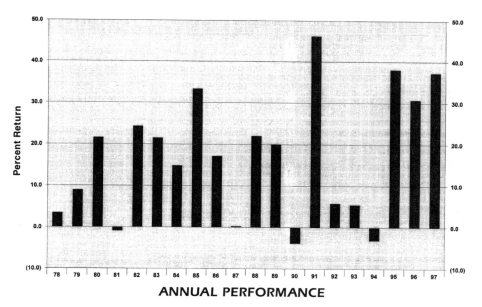

ANNUAL PERFORMANCE

TOP 10 HOLDINGS

American Express	IBM
Wells Fargo & Co.	General Re
Travelers Group	McDonald's
Morgan Stanley Dean Witter	Halliburton
Hewlett-Packard	BankAmerica

THE TORRAY FUND

| OBJECTIVE: | *Large-Cap Value* | **25** |
| MANAGER: | *Robert E. Torray* | |

FUND OVERVIEW:

Robert Torray is finally getting some much-deserved recognition. His Torray Fund went relatively unnoticed by investors for years, despite its standout performance compared to the S&P 500. Then people began to pay attention, and assets in the fund increased fourfold during 1997. Is all that new money impacting Torray's ability to keep posting strong numbers? No, he insists. And he has no plans to close the fund at this time. "So far, cash flow from shareholders has proven to be a tremendous advantage," he claims. "It has funded promising new investments and additions to existing holdings that otherwise could not have been made without selling stocks we prefer to maintain."

Torray says his investment style is simple. He'll buy stocks in the best companies at a fair price and keep them indefinitely. He'll consider small, medium, or large capitalization companies, although the latter have been getting most of his attention lately. His chosen companies have favorable economic characteristics, like rising sales and earnings, a strong competitive position, capable management, and a solid balance sheet. Torray runs a concentrated portfolio. More than half of all assets are placed in his top 20 holdings.

ANNUALIZED RETURNS		PORTFOLIO STATISTICS	
1-Year	37.15%	Beta	0.86
3-Year	35.40%	Turnover	11.72%
5-Year	26.44%	12-Month Yield	0.33%
Overall Rank	1	12b-1 Fee	0.00%
Risk Rank	3	Expense Ratio	1.12%
MINIMUM INVESTMENT		**CONTACT INFORMATION**	
Regular	$10,000	*The Torray Fund*	
IRA	$10,000	*Telephone: (800) 443-3036*	

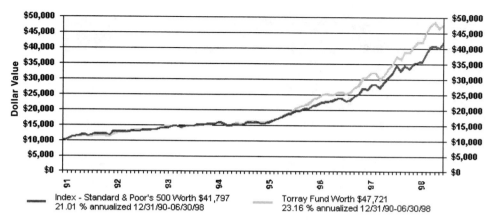

Index - Standard & Poor's 500 Worth $41,797
21.01 % annualized 12/31/90-06/30/98

Torray Fund Worth $47,721
23.16 % annualized 12/31/90-06/30/98

GROWTH OF $10,000

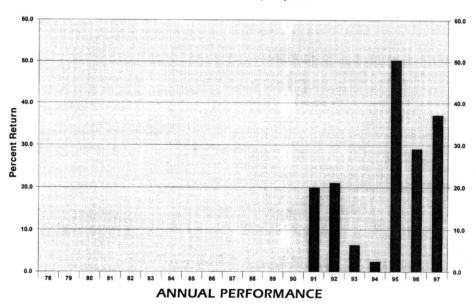

ANNUAL PERFORMANCE

TOP 10 HOLDINGS

AT&T	DuPont
Travelers Group	Archer Daniels Midland
Electronic Data Systems	US West
SLM Holding Corp.	Northrop Grumman
Loral Space & Communications	Banc One

VANGUARD WINDSOR II

| OBJECTIVE: | *Large-Cap Value* | **26** |
| MANAGER: | *Multiple Managers* | |

FUND OVERVIEW:

Vanguard Windsor II has one of the lowest expense ratios of any managed fund in the industry. It employs a time-tested, value-oriented approach to stock selection, looking for income-producing equities selling at low prices relative to earnings and assets, along with above-average dividend yields. Windsor II focuses on sizable, financially healthy companies that are deemed to be undervalued or out-of-favor with the rest of Wall Street. The theory is that patient investors who discover such securities early and hold on will eventually be handsomely rewarded.

Windsor II is managed by four separate advisory firms. Each relies on its own research and analysis, allowing the fund to benefit from differing points of view. However, all strictly follow the fund's value-oriented strategy. This should lower the risk that the fund will underperform because of decisions made by a single adviser. Windsor II buys only large and medium-size companies. It avoids any investment deemed to be speculative. This fund is appropriate for investors who want stock market exposure but prefer to subject themselves to only a modest amount of volatility.

ANNUALIZED RETURNS		PORTFOLIO STATISTICS	
1-Year	30.42%	Beta	0.84
3-Year	30.17%	Turnover	30.00%
5-Year	22.29%	12-Month Yield	1.89%
Overall Rank	1	12b-1 Fee	0.00%
Risk Rank	3	Expense Ratio	0.36%
MINIMUM INVESTMENT		**CONTACT INFORMATION**	
Regular	$3,000	*Vanguard Windsor II*	
IRA	$1,000	*Telephone: (800) 662-7447*	
		www.vanguard.com	

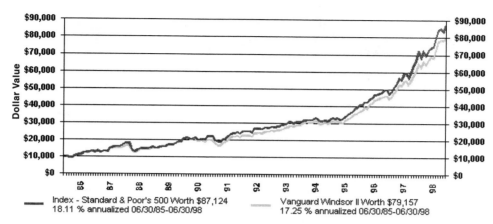

Index - Standard & Poor's 500 Worth $87,124
18.11 % annualized 06/30/85-06/30/98

Vanguard Windsor II Worth $79,157
17.25 % annualized 06/30/85-06/30/98

GROWTH OF $10,000

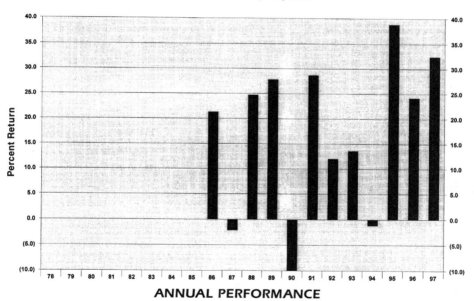

ANNUAL PERFORMANCE

TOP 10 HOLDINGS

Chase Manhattan	Waste Management
Ford Motor Co.	US West
GTE	BankAmerica
Sears Roebuck & Co.	SBC Communications
Anheuser Busch	Chrysler

VONTOBEL U.S. VALUE

OBJECTIVE:	*Large-Cap Value*	**27**
MANAGER:	*Edwin Walczak*	

FUND OVERVIEW:

If Warren Buffett ran a mutual fund, Ed Walczak thinks it would look a lot like Vontobel U.S. Value. Walczak is an admitted Buffett disciple who has refined his investment style over the years to resemble the "Oracle of Omaha's." Walczak screens through a universe of some 3,000 stocks looking for those that are statistically cheap. Each company is ranked, from highest to lowest, as measured by profitability and price-to-book value. He's looking for companies selling at a discount to the market. Once the screens are done, Walczak digs deeper to see how the fundamentals shape up. He pays close attention to the predictability of future earnings, the generation of free cash flow, whether the business is providing a competitive return, the level of debt, elements of a franchise, the current regulatory environment, and whether management is shareholder-friendly.

When Walczak can't find enough companies meeting his criteria for the fund, which has been the case recently, he'll raise cash, calling it "the residual of being unable to find sensible investment ideas." Because he wants to see proven track records, he only owns, seasoned businesses in his portfolio.

ANNUALIZED RETURNS		PORTFOLIO STATISTICS	
1-Year	30.41%	Beta	0.56
3-Year	28.35%	Turnover	26.55%
5-Year	21.23%	12-Month Yield	0.49%
Overall Rank	1	12b-1 Fee	0.00%
Risk Rank	1	Expense Ratio	1.56%
MINIMUM INVESTMENT		**CONTACT INFORMATION**	
Regular	$1,000	*Vontobel U.S. Value Fund*	
IRA	$1,000	*Telephone: (800) 527-9500*	
		www.vusa.com	

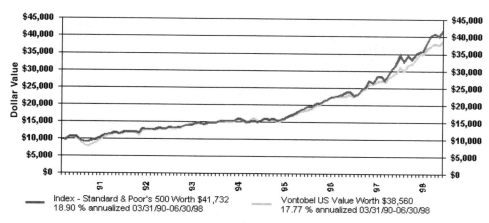

GROWTH OF $10,000

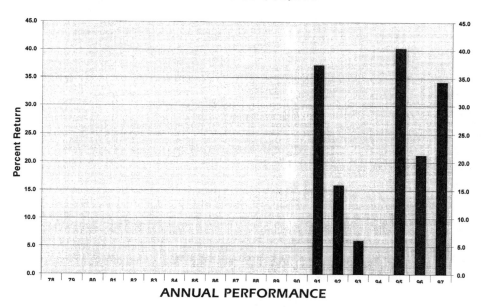

ANNUAL PERFORMANCE

TOP 10 HOLDINGS	
Federal Natl. Mtg. Assn.	McDonald's
American Intl. Group	Unum Corp.
Chubb	Gannett
Coca-Cola	Knight-Ridder
WM Wrigley	Wells Fargo & Co.

BRAMWELL GROWTH

OBJECTIVE:	*Mid-Cap Growth*	*28*
MANAGER:	*Elizabeth R. Bramwell*	

FUND OVERVIEW:

Elizabeth Bramwell uses a blended approach to find stocks for her Bramwell Growth Fund portfolio. She begins from a top-down perspective, looking at such macroeconomic variables as inflation and interest rates. This helps her determine which broad industries or themes are likely to benefit most from current conditions. From here, she does bottom-up analysis, focusing on company-specific variables like competitive industry dynamics, uniqueness of products and services, market leadership, and management expertise. On the financial side, Bramwell searches for stocks with high returns on sales and equity, favorable debt-to-equity ratios, and strong earnings and cash flow growth. She gets information from many sources, and she meets with management by attending the frequent analyst meetings held near her New York office.

Bramwell has been managing money for some three decades. Before launching her own fund in 1994, she built a great record at Gabelli Growth. Her present focus is on companies offering innovative new products and services that are beneficiaries of lower interest rates and effective users of technology. She also likes stocks that exploit the rising standard of living around the globe.

ANNUALIZED RETURNS		PORTFOLIO STATISTICS	
1-Year	39.46%	Beta	1.13
3-Year	26.57%	Turnover	26.00%
5-Year	N/A	12-Month Yield	0.00%
Overall Rank	3	12b-1 Fee	0.25%
Risk Rank	4	Expense Ratio	1.71%
MINIMUM INVESTMENT		**CONTACT INFORMATION**	
Regular	$1,000	*Bramwell Growth Fund*	
IRA	$500	*Telephone: (800) 272-6227*	

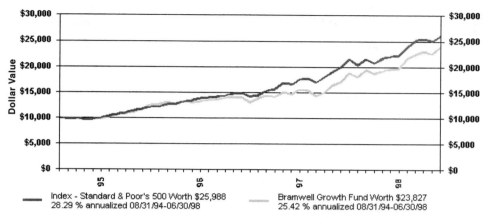

GROWTH OF $10,000

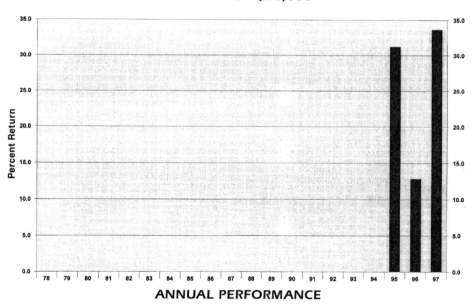

ANNUAL PERFORMANCE

TOP 10 HOLDINGS	
Computer Sciences	General Electric
Walgreen	Home Depot
Illinois Tool Works	Washington Mutual
Dell Computer	Allstate
Robert Half Intl.	Kohls Corp.

CGM FOCUS FUND

OBJECTIVE: *Mid-Cap Growth*
MANAGER: *Ken Heebner*

29

FUND OVERVIEW:

Ken Heebner has always been a man of convictions. He doesn't believe in owning too many companies, just 20 or 30 of his best ideas. That's one reason his CGM Capital Development Fund has whipped the competition for more than two decades, and further proof that good stock picking can lead to index-beating returns. Unfortunately, Capital Development has been closed to new investors since the 1980s. But now there's a way to tap into Heebner's expertise in an even more concentrated portfolio. CGM Focus will usually contain less than 20 of his favorite names. "At any given time, there are only so many stocks out there with superior risk–reward profiles," Heebner explains. "Those stocks are the ones I want to own and the only ones I want to own."

Heebner looks for sectors and companies likely to produce positive earnings surprises. He conducts extensive research on each stock and maintains regular contact with management. But he doesn't fall in love with any idea and is willing to pull the trigger at a moment's notice. This often leads to high turnover and frequent shifts among sectors. A risky approach, indeed, but one that has showered investors with excellent returns over time.

ANNUALIZED RETURNS		PORTFOLIO STATISTICS	
1-Year	N/A	Beta	N/A
3-Year	N/A	Turnover	N/A
5-Year	N/A	12-Month Yield	N/A
Overall Rank	N/A	12b-1 Fee	0.00%
Risk Rank	N/A	Expense Ratio	N/A

MINIMUM INVESTMENT		CONTACT INFORMATION
Regular	$2,500	*CGM Focus Fund*
IRA	$1,000	*Telephone: (800) 345-4048*
		www.cgmfunds.com

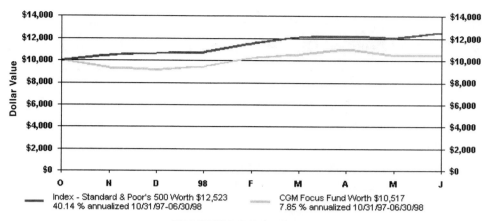

GROWTH OF $10,000

TOP 10 HOLDINGS	
USG	Chase Manhattan
Amerin	Continental Airlines
Delta Air Lines	Brylane
AMR	Airborne Freight
Compaq Computer	UAL

MAIRS & POWER GROWTH

OBJECTIVE:	*Mid-Cap Growth*	
MANAGER:	*George A. Mairs*	***30***

FUND OVERVIEW:

George Mairs likes to find investment ideas in his own backyard. That's why his Mairs & Power Growth fund has a large concentration of companies based in Minnesota. In fact, he focuses his research efforts on finding good businesses in the upper Midwest. His rationale is that he can add value to the research process that way because he understands these local firms better than Wall Street and can visit them in person. That doesn't mean he won't consider companies in other parts of the country. He will, but usually only when he can't find an equivalent idea in the same sector locally. This regional focus certainly hasn't hampered performance. Mairs & Power Growth continually seems to outshine the competition.

Mairs looks for high-quality companies with predictable earnings, above-average return on equity, market dominance, and financial strength. He stays fully invested at all times and favors a buy-and-hold strategy. Mairs will sell a holding once he believes it has become fully priced. He'll then use the proceeds to either establish a new position or add to an existing one. He likes mid caps because they offer comparable returns to small caps with less risk.

ANNUALIZED RETURNS		PORTFOLIO STATISTICS	
1-Year	16.16%	Beta	0.85
3-Year	28.26%	Turnover	5.07%
5-Year	24.52%	12-Month Yield	1.11%
Overall Rank	2	12b-1 Fee	0.00%
Risk Rank	3	Expense Ratio	0.83%
MINIMUM INVESTMENT		**CONTACT INFORMATION**	
Regular	$2,500	*Mairs & Power Growth Fund*	
IRA	$1,000	*Telephone: (800) 304-7404*	

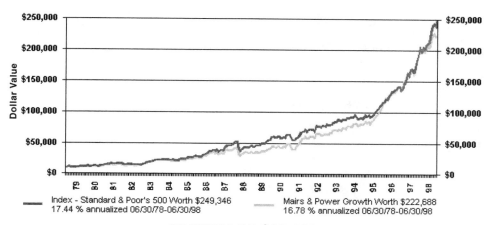

GROWTH OF $10,000

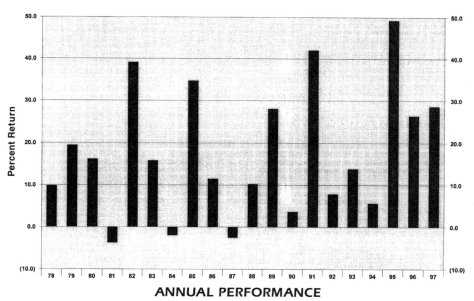

ANNUAL PERFORMANCE

TOP 10 HOLDINGS	
ADC Telecommunications	TCE Financial
Emerson Electric	Honeywell
Norwest Corp.	US Bancorp
Medtronic	Minnesota Mng. & Mfg.
Pfizer	Ecolab

NICHOLAS

OBJECTIVE:	*Mid-Cap Growth*	**31**
MANAGER:	*Albert O. Nicholas*	

FUND OVERVIEW:

When Albert Nicholas first started managing this fund in 1969, he concentrated mostly on big, blue-chip names. Over the years, however, you could say he has downsized somewhat, favoring more midsize companies. This has been especially true in recent years. As a value investor, Nicholas insists that many of the larger names are highly overpriced.

Patience is a virtue in the Nicholas investment strategy. He is a fundamentally oriented manager who looks for stocks with low price-to-earnings ratios and consistent, above-average earnings growth. He holds his positions, on average, three years or more. He doesn't try to forecast short-term market swings, but will preserve gains by selling what he deems to be overvalued securities. Even though Nicholas is now cautious about the direction of the economy, the fund remains fully invested in companies he considers to be fairly priced with rapid earnings growth. (Current earnings momentum is an important factor in his overall investment process.) Nicholas generally won't buy Initial Public Offerings or foreign stocks, because they are too risky. This fund has consistently outperformed its peers over time, with lower-than-average volatility.

ANNUALIZED RETURNS		PORTFOLIO STATISTICS	
1-Year	30.80%	Beta	0.92
3-Year	29.69%	Turnover	15.15%
5-Year	20.64%	12-Month Yield	0.40%
Overall Rank	1	12b-1 Fee	0.00%
Risk Rank	3	Expense Ratio	0.71%
MINIMUM INVESTMENT		**CONTACT INFORMATION**	
Regular	$500	*Nicholas Fund*	
IRA	$500	*Telephone: (800) 227-5987*	

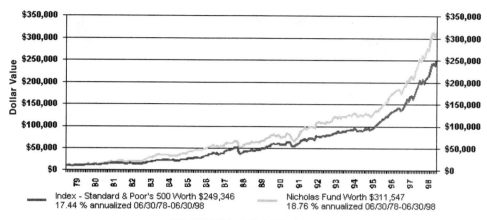

Index - Standard & Poor's 500 Worth $249,346
17.44 % annualized 06/30/78-06/30/98

Nicholas Fund Worth $311,547
18.76 % annualized 06/30/78-06/30/98

GROWTH OF $10,000

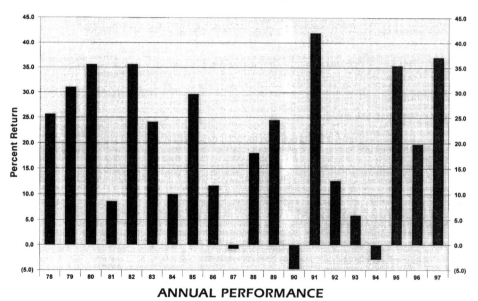

ANNUAL PERFORMANCE

TOP 10 HOLDINGS

Mercury General	SunAmerica
Federal Natl. Mtg. Assn.	Fifth Third Bancorp
Federal Home Ln. Mtg. Corp.	Wallace Computer Svcs.
Marshall & Ilsley	General Motors Cl. H
Travelers Group	Tyco Intl.

SAFECO GROWTH

OBJECTIVE:	*Mid-Cap Growth*	*32*
MANAGER:	*Tom Maguire*	

FUND OVERVIEW:

Although SAFECO Growth manager Tom Maguire can invest in any stocks he wants, he has been keeping most of his money in small caps these days. But that hasn't stopped him from buying a nice array of big blue chips as well, including Philip Morris and Avon Products. As a result, I've placed this fund in the mid-cap growth category. Ironically, even though small caps have slightly underperformed their larger brethren over the past few years, SAFECO Growth has shone, giving further testament to Maguire's stock-picking talents. He seeks capital appreciation by owning a portfolio of roughly 50 securities. He's more aggressive than his peers, favoring lesser-known companies. Maguire's also not afraid to place a lot of money in the businesses he likes the most.

As a fundamental manager, Maguire focuses on company product lines, growth rates, financial strength, and management. As his portfolio grows in size, he is increasingly paying more attention to liquidity and valuation when purchasing comparatively unseasoned stocks. This strategy has served him well thus far. But as new money continues to flow in, the challenge will be for Maguire to continue his winning ways with an inherently less nimble asset base.

ANNUALIZED RETURNS		PORTFOLIO STATISTICS	
1-Year	44.63%	Beta	0.83
3-Year	33.35%	Turnover	82.57%
5-Year	26.02%	12-Month Yield	0.00%
Overall Rank	2	12b-1 Fee	0.00%
Risk Rank	4	Expense Ratio	0.84%

MINIMUM INVESTMENT		CONTACT INFORMATION	
Regular	$1,000	*SAFECO Growth Fund*	
IRA	$250	*Telephone: (800) 624-5711*	
		www.safecofunds.com	

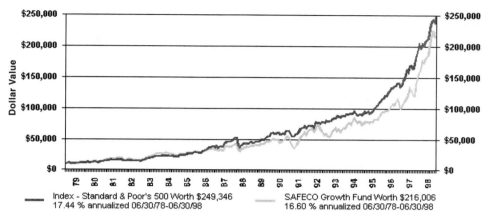

GROWTH OF $10,000

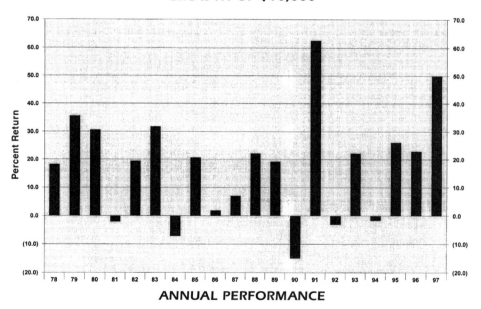

ANNUAL PERFORMANCE

TOP 10 HOLDINGS

Green Tree Financial	Avon Products
Chancellor Media	Philip Morris
Family Golf Centers	SFX Broadcasting
Micros Systems	Tetra Technologies
United Stationers	Danka Business Systems

STRONG GROWTH

OBJECTIVE: *Mid-Cap Growth*
MANAGER: *Ronald Ognar*

33

FUND OVERVIEW:

Strong Growth fund manager Ronald Ognar doesn't care what size a company is. He just wants to make sure it's growing and in an industry with solid fundamentals. There is a good and bad side to this investment approach. The good is that Ognar can exploit the best performing part of the market at any given time (assuming he's right). The downside is that Ognar is a style drifter, swithing around from small- and large-caps, so you don't always know what kind of fund you own. That's why when you look at the portfolio in total, you can only conclude that this is a true mid-cap offering.

Ognar favors companies with demonstrated earnings growth. He especially likes those businesses with good financial and accounting policies, a competitive edge, signs that capital is producing a high return, effective marketing and product development departments, prospects for above-average sales and profit growth, and stable management. Ognar also has a strict valuation discipline, and will only buy stocks trading at significant discounts to their projected growth rates. A holding gets booted out either when its valuation becomes excessive or he finds a better buy elsewhere.

ANNUALIZED RETURNS		PORTFOLIO STATISTICS	
1-Year	26.26%	Beta	1.17
3-Year	25.05%	Turnover	144.30%
5-Year	N/A	12-Month Yield	0.00%
Overall Rank	3	12b-1 Fee	0.00%
Risk Rank	4	Expense Ratio	1.30%
MINIMUM INVESTMENT		**CONTACT INFORMATION**	
Regular	$1,000	*Strong Growth Fund*	
IRA	$250	*Telephone: (800) 368-1030*	
		www.strongfunds.com	

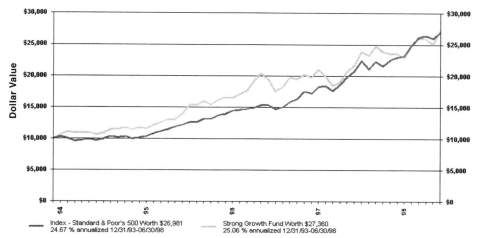

Index - Standard & Poor's 500 Worth $26,981
24.67 % annualized 12/31/93-06/30/98

Strong Growth Fund Worth $27,360
25.06 % annualized 12/31/93-06/30/98

GROWTH OF $10,000

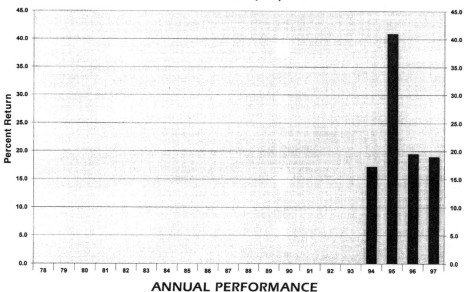

ANNUAL PERFORMANCE

TOP 10 HOLDINGS	
Cendant	Lowes Cos.
Kohls Corp.	Robert Half Intl.
Pfizer	HBO & Co.
Microsoft	Chancellor Media
Peoplesoft	Merck & Co.

T. ROWE PRICE MID-CAP GROWTH

| **OBJECTIVE:** | *Mid-Cap Growth* | |
| **MANAGER:** | *Brian W. H. Berghuis* | *34* |

FUND OVERVIEW:

Brian Berghuis is convinced his mid-cap stock universe is quite attractive going into 1999. He feels many of his companies are poised to do extremely well after being somewhat neglected in recent years. Berghuis looks for stocks with market values in the $300 million to $4 billion range and with earnings that are growing at a faster-than-average rate. He sticks mostly with domestic equities, although he'll buy other securities if he feels a purchase is appropriate.

Berghuis invests based on the belief that good research, not opinions on the overall economic environment, are what will lead him to superior long-term results. "We devote our time to carefully researching and evaluating company fundamentals," he says. "While we typically examine a multitude of factors before we invest, and virtually never invest before a face-to-face meeting with a company's management, several of the criteria we focus on include the growth in the company's industry sector, the growth rate we foresee for the company over the next several years, the strength of a company's business model, management we respect, strong financial characteristics, and reasonable valuations."

ANNUALIZED RETURNS		PORTFOLIO STATISTICS	
1-Year	29.89%	Beta	0.79
3-Year	26.98%	Turnover	42.60%
5-Year	22.82%	12-Month Yield	0.00%
Overall Rank	2	12b-1 Fee	0.00%
Risk Rank	3	Expense Ratio	0.94%

MINIMUM INVESTMENT		CONTACT INFORMATION
Regular	$2,500	*T. Rowe Price Mid-Cap Growth Fund*
IRA	$1,000	*Telephone: (800) 638-5660*
		www.troweprice.com

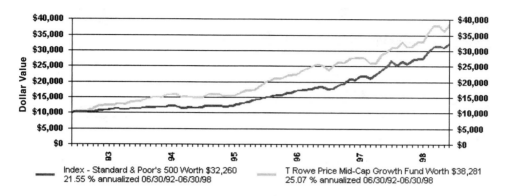

GROWTH OF $10,000

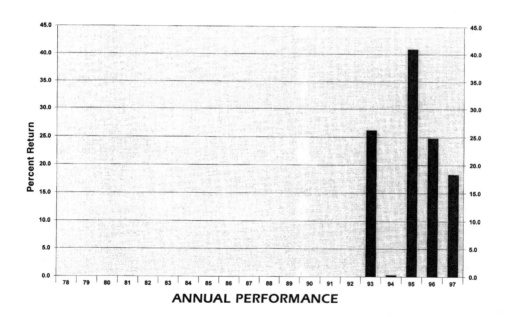

ANNUAL PERFORMANCE

TOP 10 HOLDINGS

Outdoor Systems
Warnaco Group
US Foodservice
Suiza Foods
Trimas Corp.

Affiliated Computer Svcs.
Danaher Corp.
Royal Caribbean Cruises
Culligan Water Tech.
Ace Ltd.

EXCELSIOR VALUE AND RESTRUCTURING

| OBJECTIVE: | *Mid-Cap Value* | **35** |
| MANAGER: | *David Williams* | |

FUND OVERVIEW:

For years, David Williams's Excelsior Value and Restructuring Fund was one of the best kept secrets in the mutual funds world. Then word of his great performance started to trickle into the media. Along with this sudden exposure came a huge inflow of new assets. So far, so good. Williams tells me he has been able to handle the fresh cash without a problem, at least for now.

This astute U.S. Trust manager looks for stocks that are predicted to benefit from either an expected restructuring or the redeployment of assets and operations. Such companies may include those involved in prospective mergers, consolidations, liquidations, spin-offs, or financial reorganizations. Because these stocks are troubled to begin with, Williams can usually pick them up on the cheap, often for less than 15 times earnings. But such a strategy is fraught with risk. After all, these businesses are often in bad shape to begin with. If the restructuring isn't successful, they might not survive. Williams increases his chances for success by first meeting with management. Then he makes sure the portfolio is diversified among close to 90 names. With that strategy, he surmises, there's a good chance something will always be working.

ANNUALIZED RETURNS		PORTFOLIO STATISTICS	
1-Year	26.55%	Beta	0.92
3-Year	30.16%	Turnover	37.00%
5-Year	26.65%	12-Month Yield	0.35%
Overall Rank	1	12b-1 Fee	0.00%
Risk Rank	3	Expense Ratio	0.85%
MINIMUM INVESTMENT		**CONTACT INFORMATION**	
Regular	$500	*Excelsior Value and Restructuring*	
IRA	$500	*Fund*	
		Telephone: (800) 446-1012	

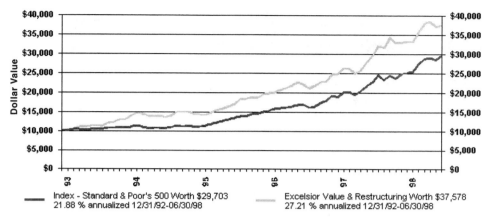

Index - Standard & Poor's 500 Worth $29,703
21.88 % annualized 12/31/92-06/30/98

Excelsior Value & Restructuring Worth $37,578
27.21 % annualized 12/31/92-06/30/98

GROWTH OF $10,000

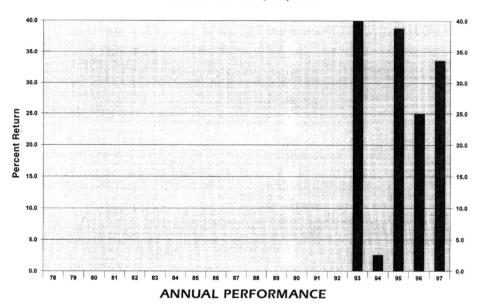

ANNUAL PERFORMANCE

TOP 10 HOLDINGS	
Union Pacific	Avon Products
Computer Associates	Eastman Kodak
IBM	Alcatel Alsthom
Texas Instruments	JP Morgan
Xerox	Frontier

FIRST EAGLE FUND OF AMERICA

OBJECTIVE:	*Mid-Cap Value*	**36**
MANAGER:	*Team Managed*	

FUND OVERVIEW:

The focus of the First Eagle Fund of America is to find quality companies undergoing significant change. Lead portfolio manager Harold Levy contends that positive change can have a tremendous impact on a business, although the market is slow to realize that fact. This creates inefficiencies in the market, which he hopes to capitalize on. Among the changes Levy looks for are: new management, acquisitions, share repurchases, divestitures, technological breakthroughs, or changes in strategy. Then, he figures out whether the stock is worth owning from a valuation perspective. "We look at a company as if we were buying the whole business, [which is] the way a rational businessman would price an acquisition," Levy says. He targets a return of 50 percent over a 12- to 18-month time frame for every idea under consideration. If he thinks a stock can achieve that ambitious goal, it will likely find its way into the portfolio.

You can never be certain that change will be good for a company. That's why Levy is constantly reevaluating his decisions. He hopes to limit his errors by doing extensive research and visiting his holdings on a regular basis to get a firsthand sense of how things are progressing.

ANNUALIZED RETURNS		PORTFOLIO STATISTICS	
1-Year	37.37%	Beta	0.83
3-Year	33.24%	Turnover	37.00%
5-Year	24.07%	12-Month Yield	0.00%
Overall Rank	1	12b-1 Fee	0.00%
Risk Rank	3	Expense Ratio	1.50%
MINIMUM INVESTMENT		**CONTACT INFORMATION**	
Regular	$2,000	*First Eagle Fund of America*	
IRA	$2,000	*Telephone: (800) 451-3623*	

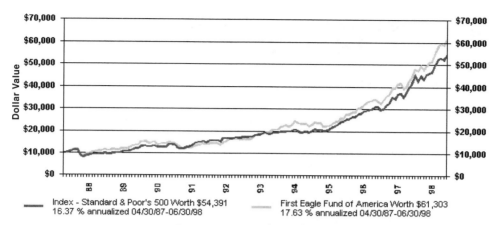

GROWTH OF $10,000

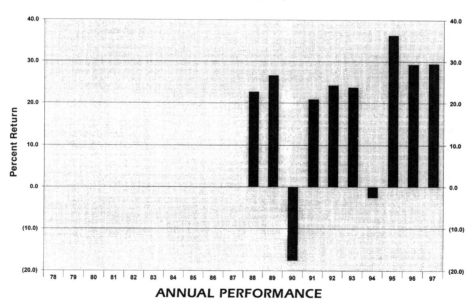

ANNUAL PERFORMANCE

TOP 10 HOLDINGS	
Finova Group	US Airways
Bank Boston	Allegiance
Storage Technology	Ceridian Corp.
Comcast Corp.	Gulfstream Aerospace
Biogen	Amgen

GABELLI ASSET

OBJECTIVE:	*Mid-Cap Value*	
MANAGER:	*Mario Gabelli*	*37*

FUND OVERVIEW:

Mario Gabelli doesn't mind that some people view his investment style as being boring. He focuses on a company's free cash flow, defined as earnings before interest, taxes, depreciation, and amortization, less the capital expenditures needed to grow the business. "Rising free cash flow often foreshadows net earnings improvement," he says. "Unlike Wall Street's ubiquitous earnings momentum players, we do not try to forecast earnings with accounting precision and then trade stocks based on quarterly expectations and realities." Instead, he positions himself in front of long-term earnings uptrends.

Gabelli also closely analyzes assets and liabilities, paying attention to inventories, receivables, and potential legal issues. His goal is to come up with a private market value estimate of what a company is worth. He then wants to buy the company's stock for less than that number. Often, Gabelli finds a catalyst that leads him to believe earnings will rise, thus increasing the private market value. At other times, he's attracted by a management change or spin-off. Once he has put his money on the line, Gabelli tends to be patient, though vocal, in seeing that his companies perform up to expectations.

ANNUALIZED RETURNS		PORTFOLIO STATISTICS	
1-Year	32.53%	Beta	0.78
3-Year	25.51%	Turnover	22.00%
5-Year	19.57%	12-Month Yield	0.17%
Overall Rank	2	12b-1 Fee	0.23%
Risk Rank	2	Expense Ratio	N/A
MINIMUM INVESTMENT		**CONTACT INFORMATION**	
Regular	$1,000	*Gabelli Asset Fund*	
IRA	$1,000	*Telephone: (800) 422-3554*	
		www.gabelli.com	

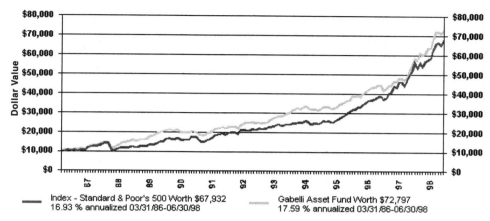

Index - Standard & Poor's 500 Worth $67,932
16.93 % annualized 03/31/86-06/30/98

Gabelli Asset Fund Worth $72,797
17.59 % annualized 03/31/86-06/30/98

GROWTH OF $10,000

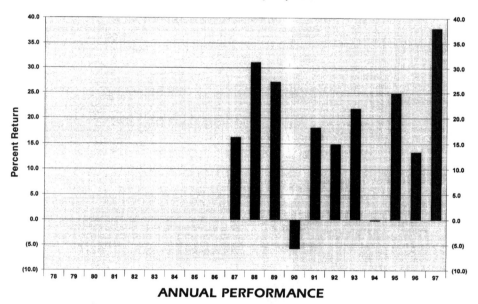

ANNUAL PERFORMANCE

TOP 10 HOLDINGS

Telesp...Pfd.	**Deere & Co.**
Time Warner	**Chris-Craft Inds.**
American Express	**Neiman Marcus**
Tele-Communications Inc.	**Quaker Oats**
United Television	**Century Tel. Ent.**

MUHLENKAMP FUND

| OBJECTIVE: | *Mid-Cap Value* | *38* |
| MANAGER: | *Ronald Muhlenkamp* | |

FUND OVERVIEW:

Ron Muhlenkamp will fill his portfolio with whatever he thinks will make the most money. That usually means a heavy weighting in stocks, although he'll emphasize bonds when interest rates exceed the return he expects to get from equities. Muhlenkamp doesn't believe in applying historical standards to today's market, because economic conditions are always changing. Instead, he constantly evaluates the current business cycle to see which industries appear to be most attractive.

Muhlenkamp is a value-oriented investor. He views a company's return on equity and price-to-book value ratio as important numbers for determining whether a stock is attractively priced. Instead of buying growth at a reasonable price, he wants *profitability* at a reasonable price. Muhlenkamp strives to generate a maximum total return for shareholders consistent with taking a reasonable amount of risk. He will only invest in securities that he expects to outpace the rate of inflation by at least 5 to 6 percent for stocks, and at least 3 percent for bonds. Another major advantage to this fund is its small minimum initial investment of just $200 for regular accounts, and $1 for IRAs.

ANNUALIZED RETURNS		PORTFOLIO STATISTICS	
1-Year	32.90%	Beta	0.83
3-Year	31.98%	Turnover	13.89%
5-Year	21.37%	12-Month Yield	0.30%
Overall Rank	1	12b-1 Fee	0.00%
Risk Rank	3	Expense Ratio	1.33%

MINIMUM INVESTMENT		CONTACT INFORMATION	
Regular	$200	*Muhlenkamp Fund*	
IRA	$1	*Telephone: (800) 860-3863*	
		www.muhlenkamp.com	

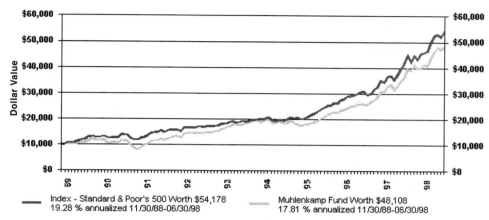

GROWTH OF $10,000

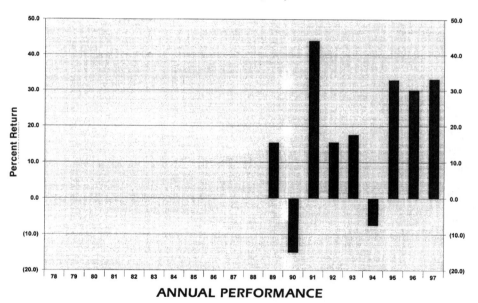

ANNUAL PERFORMANCE

TOP 10 HOLDINGS

Green Tree Financial	Ford Motor Co.
Federal Natl. Mtg. Assn.	Conseco
Mellon Bank	AMR Corp.
Philip Morris	SunAmerica
National RV Holdings	Aeroquip Vickers

NEUBERGER & BERMAN PARTNERS

OBJECTIVE:	*Mid-Cap Value*	**39**
MANAGER:	*Michael Kassen and Robert Gendelman*	

FUND OVERVIEW:

The number-one rule managers of the Neuberger & Berman Partners follow is: "Never forget the fundamentals when pursuing growth." "Whenever we analyze a stock, we ask ourselves, 'If we had all the money in the world, would we be interested in buying the company for the price represented by the stock?'" explains portfolio comanager Michael Kassen. "To decide, we look at the fundamentals: earnings, cash flow, plus the company's track record through all parts of the market cycle." You won't find many Fortune 100 stocks in this fund. Kassen and fellow manager Robert Gendelman feel it's too hard to gain an edge over other investors with these big companies. Instead, they focus primarily on mid caps, which are small enough to give them access to management. They also attend industry conferences and look for ideas. Before making an investment, they examine a company's balance sheet, contact suppliers, and talk with competitors about the business.

Kassen and Gendelman hope to buy stocks at a discount to their underlying value. They are especially fond of "fallen angels"—growth stocks that have tumbled to new lows but remain fundamentally strong.

ANNUALIZED RETURNS		PORTFOLIO STATISTICS	
1-Year	19.25%	Beta	0.89
3-Year	25.55%	Turnover	77.00%
5-Year	20.47%	12-Month Yield	0.55%
Overall Rank	3	12b-1 Fee	0.00%
Risk Rank	3	Expense Ratio	0.81%
MINIMUM INVESTMENT		**CONTACT INFORMATION**	
Regular	$1,000	*Neuberger & Berman Partners Fund*	
IRA	$1,000	*Telephone: (800) 877-9700*	
		www.nbfunds.com	

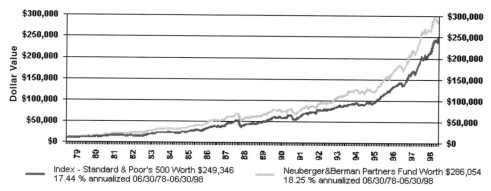

Index - Standard & Poor's 500 Worth $249,346
17.44 % annualized 06/30/78-06/30/98

Neuberger&Berman Partners Fund Worth $286,054
18.25 % annualized 06/30/78-06/30/98

GROWTH OF $10,000

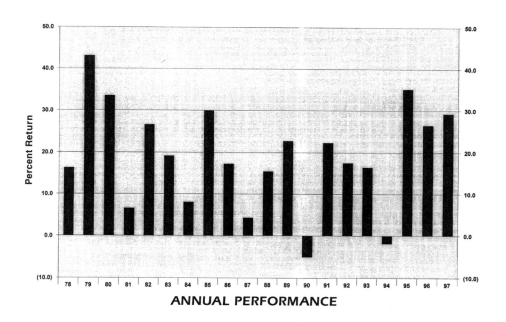

ANNUAL PERFORMANCE

TOP 10 HOLDINGS	
Allstate	Burlington Northern
Enron	Credit Suisse
Exel Ltd.	Travelers Group
Crown Cork & Seal	Comcast Corp.
DuPont	Praxair

SOUND SHORE

OBJECTIVE:	*Mid-Cap Value*	**40**
MANAGER:	*T. Gibbs Kane*	

FUND OVERVIEW:

Who would be interested in investing in companies that have pretty much lost their Wall Street sponsorship? T. Gibbs Kane, that's who. The Sound Shore fund manager looks for stocks that are in the doghouse with investors but still have earnings power. "Our investment style is described as being from the value school, meaning we are very sensitive to how a security is priced before we begin our research to ascertain if the valuation is a true reflection of the company's fundamentals," Kane says. "We begin with a universe of the largest companies listed on the U.S. exchanges— 1,250 companies with market capitalizations above $1 billion. From this start, we rank each company into deciles based on estimated PE (on earnings for the next four quarters) versus other stocks and the company's own 15-year 'normal' PE." Those names that wind up in the top two deciles get the most serious consideration.

Kane sets price targets for every stock in his rather concentrated portfolio. He'll sell a position once it reaches that number, even if the fundamentals are still intact. He also prides himself in visiting companies and talking with management, and will raise cash when he can't find anywhere to put it.

ANNUALIZED RETURNS		PORTFOLIO STATISTICS	
1-Year	20.53%	**Beta**	0.83
3-Year	28.23%	**Turnover**	35.28%
5-Year	21.48%	**12-Month Yield**	0.42%
Overall Rank	1	**12b-1 Fee**	0.00%
Risk Rank	3	**Expense Ratio**	1.10%
MINIMUM INVESTMENT		**CONTACT INFORMATION**	
Regular	$10,000	*Sound Shore Fund*	
IRA	$250	*Telephone: (800) 551-1980*	
		www.soundshorefund.com	

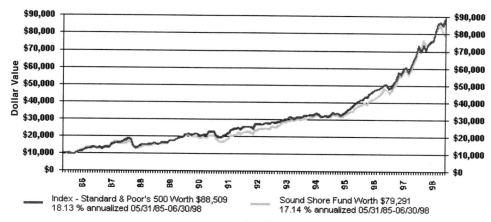

GROWTH OF $10,000

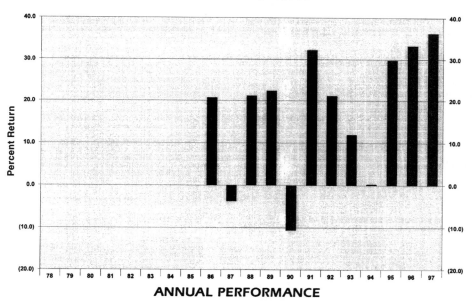

ANNUAL PERFORMANCE

TOP 10 HOLDINGS

Loews	Fannie Mae
Magna International	First Union
Banc One	Occidental Petroleum
Hasbro	IBM
Allstate	CalEnergy

T. ROWE PRICE VALUE

OBJECTIVE:	*Mid-Cap Value*	*41*
MANAGER:	*Brian Rogers*	

FUND OVERVIEW:

T. Rowe Price Value is one of two funds on my Powerhouse Performers list for 1999 that are managed by Brian Rogers. (The other is T. Rowe Price Equity Income, entry 64 in this chapter.) Although Value is only a few years old, it has managed to beat the return of the S&P 500 every year since inception, a feat only a handful of funds have achieved. Rogers also has a terrific record at Equity Income. (Value, a much smaller fund, allows him to focus on stock picking, without worrying about the dividend component required at Equity Income.).

"We emphasize investments in companies we determine to be undervalued in terms of price/earnings, price/cash flow, and price/asset ratios; replacement value calculations; or a range of other analytical frameworks," Rogers explains. "Many of our holdings are contrarian in nature, since we purchase shares of companies that have been out-of-favor and priced accordingly in the marketplace. We believe companies meeting our criteria prove an attractive combination of limited downside risk and reasonable upside potential." It's not surprising that many of Rogers's ideas are restructuring plays. He's also enamored of financial stocks.

ANNUALIZED RETURNS		PORTFOLIO STATISTICS	
1-Year	19.69%	Beta	0.65
3-Year	26.87%	Turnover	73.10%
5-Year	N/A	12-Month Yield	0.88%
Overall Rank	1	12b-1 Fee	0.00%
Risk Rank	2	Expense Ratio	1.10%
MINIMUM INVESTMENT		**CONTACT INFORMATION**	
Regular	$2,500	*T. Rowe Price Value Fund*	
IRA	$1,000	*Telephone: (800) 638-5660*	
		www.troweprice.com	

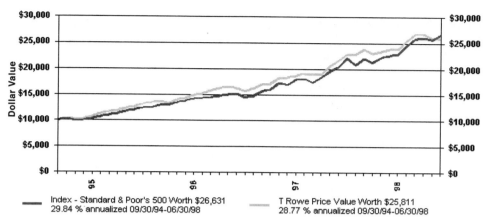

Index - Standard & Poor's 500 Worth $26,631
29.84 % annualized 09/30/94-06/30/98

T Rowe Price Value Worth $25,811
28.77 % annualized 09/30/94-06/30/98

GROWTH OF $10,000

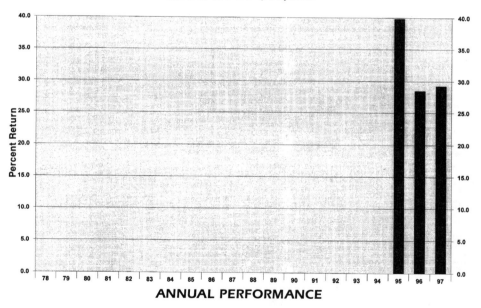

ANNUAL PERFORMANCE

TOP 10 HOLDINGS

Loews	Toys R Us
Alcatel Alsthom	General Signal
Great Lakes Chemical	Amerada Hess
Amoco	RJR Nabisco
Starwood Hotels & Resorts	Newmont Mining

TWEEDY, BROWNE AMERICAN VALUE

| OBJECTIVE: | *Mid-Cap Value* | *42* |
| MANAGER: | *Team Managed* | |

FUND OVERVIEW:

The managers of Tweedy, Browne American Value aren't shy about telling you they run their portfolio using the principles espoused in *Security Analysis,* the classic written by the late Columbia University Business School Professor Benjamin Graham. Graham talked about evaluating companies based on their "intrinsic value," which is the amount a rational businessperson would pay for the entire business. Graham claimed that investments made at a 40 to 50 percent discount to intrinsic value provided investors with a margin of safety. Once the market price rises toward intrinsic value, he recommended selling the stock and reinvesting the proceeds in other, more attractive ideas.

Therefore, Tweedy, Browne American Value holds stocks with one or more of the following characteristics: low stock price in relation to book value, low price-to-earnings ratio, low price-to-cash flow ratio, above-average dividend yield, and recent stock purchases by insiders. Managers Christopher Browne, John Spears, and William Browne own some 200 small, medium, and large stocks, including a few foreign companies. This conservative fund has consistently managed to keep up with the S&P 500 while incurring less risk.

ANNUALIZED RETURNS		PORTFOLIO STATISTICS	
1-Year	30.25%	Beta	0.75
3-Year	29.07%	Turnover	1.00%
5-Year	N/A	12-Month Yield	0.70%
Overall Rank	1	12b-1 Fee	0.00%
Risk Rank	2	Expense Ratio	1.38%
MINIMUM INVESTMENT		**CONTACT INFORMATION**	
Regular	$2,500	*Tweedy, Browne American*	
IRA	$500	*Value Fund*	
		Telephone: (800) 432-4789	

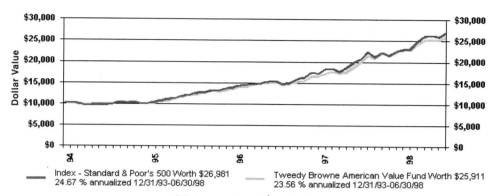

GROWTH OF $10,000

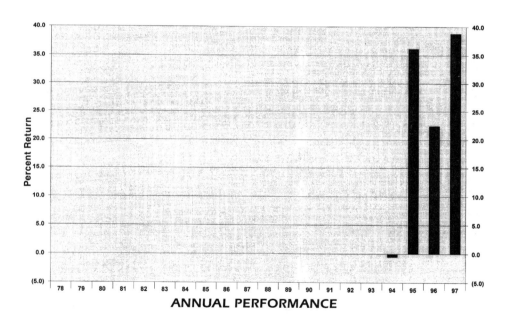

ANNUAL PERFORMANCE

TOP 10 HOLDINGS	
Chase Manhattan	Federal Home Ln. Mtg. Corp.
Philip Morris	UST Corp.
Popular Inc.	Transatlantic Holdings
Lehman Bros.	GATX Corp.
American Express	Household International

WEITZ HICKORY

OBJECTIVE:	*Mid-Cap Value*	*43*
MANAGER:	*Richard Lawson*	

FUND OVERVIEW:

Richard Lawson adheres to three simple principles when managing the Weitz Hickory Fund. He looks for growing businesses that are reasonably priced, he concentrates his portfolio in a limited number of names, and he invests with a time horizon of three to five years. "I attempt to identify good companies which I think are able to grow shareholder value at an attractive rate over many years, and buy them at a discount to what I think the company is worth today," Lawson explains. His strategy has produced index-beating returns throughout the fund's history, with one exception. In 1994, Hickory tumbled 17.2 percent a year when the S&P broke even. This shows the inherent risk you take in such a concentrated portfolio. When you have several losers, it definitely impacts performance. By the same token, holding a select group of winners has allowed the fund to be a real standout in recent years.

Lawson typically holds between 20 and 25 names in the portfolio. Of late, he has been focusing on the telecommunications, financial services, and real estate sectors. An added plus is that Lawson eats his own cooking, and says he has all of his own personal investment assets in Hickory.

ANNUALIZED RETURNS		PORTFOLIO STATISTICS	
1-Year	61.99%	Beta	0.68
3-Year	44.61%	Turnover	11.00%
5-Year	29.94%	12-Month Yield	1.45%
Overall Rank	1	12b-1 Fee	0.00%
Risk Rank	4	Expense Ratio	1.50%

MINIMUM INVESTMENT		CONTACT INFORMATION
Regular	$25,000 (less through some discount brokers)	*Weitz Hickory Fund*
IRA	$25,000 (less through some discount brokers)	*Telephone: (800) 232-4161*

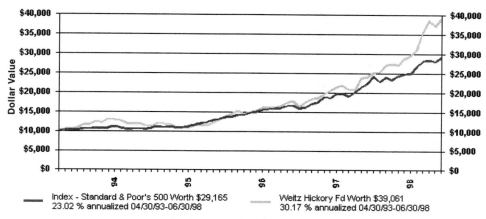

GROWTH OF $10,000

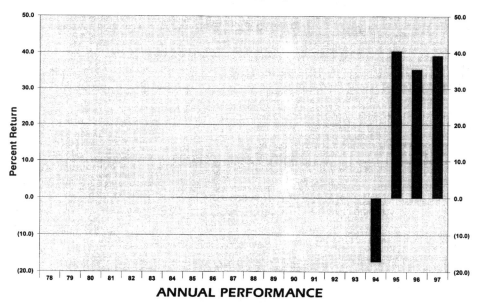

ANNUAL PERFORMANCE

TOP 10 HOLDINGS

Centennial Cellular

Redwood Trust

Century Communications

360 Communications

Novastar Financial

Valassis Communications

Capital One Financial

Resource Bancshares

Imperial Cr. Inds.

Core Comm.

WEITZ VALUE PORTFOLIO

OBJECTIVE:	*Mid-Cap Value*	**44**
MANAGER:	*Wallace Weitz*	

FUND OVERVIEW:

Weitz Value has an objective similar to Hickory's, along with many of the same investments. There are, however, a few differences. For one thing, this fund has a different manager. For another, the portfolio is much more diversified, which reduces some of the concentration risk. And its asset base is considerably larger. Manager Wallace Weitz tries to find companies he can buy for half of their intrinsic value, or what he thinks they are worth whole.

So which Weitz fund should you buy? Both Hickory and Value have excellent records and are highly recommended, but I expect Hickory to do better than Value over time because of its greater concentration. However, this also means you can expect it to deliver a higher degree of volatility. If you don't have a long time horizon, Value may be more appropriate. Both funds have a high minimum of $25,000, although you can get in for less through some of the discount brokers. But if you invest in both Value and Hickory, the companies let you get in for a combined minimum of $25,000. This means you can spread your $25,000 across both funds, maybe putting $12,500 in both Hickory and Value to begin with.

ANNUALIZED RETURNS		PORTFOLIO STATISTICS	
1-Year	47.51%	Beta	0.64
3-Year	33.03%	Turnover	16.00%
5-Year	23.02%	12-Month Yield	N/A
Overall Rank	1	12b-1 Fee	0.00%
Risk Rank	3	Expense Ratio	1.27%

MINIMUM INVESTMENT		CONTACT INFORMATION
Regular	$25,000 (less through some discount brokers)	*Weitz Hickory Fund* *Telephone: (800) 232-4161*
IRA	$25,000 (less through some discount brokers)	

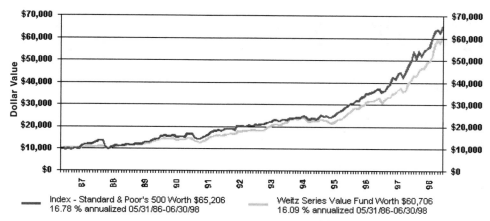

Index - Standard & Poor's 500 Worth $65,206
16.78 % annualized 05/31/86-06/30/98

Weitz Series Value Fund Worth $60,706
16.09 % annualized 05/31/86-06/30/98

GROWTH OF $10,000

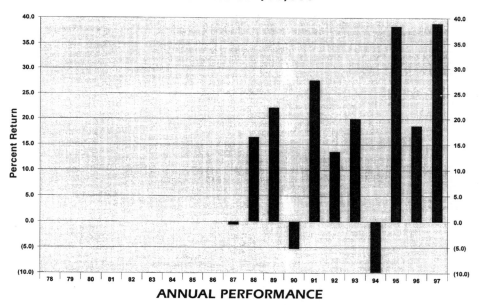

ANNUAL PERFORMANCE

TOP 10 HOLDINGS

Redwood Trust	Tele-Communications Inc.
360 Communications	Countrywide Credit
Centennial Cellular	Comcast Corp.
US West	Resource Bancshares
Century Communications	Valassis Communications

YACKTMAN FOCUSED

OBJECTIVE:	*Mid-Cap Value*	*45*
MANAGER:	*Donald Yacktman*	

FUND OVERVIEW:

Don Yacktman has never been shy about putting a lot of money in his favorite investments. Now he has a chance to take this idea of concentration to a new level. Yacktman Focused contains nothing but the 10 to 15 best ideas he and his analysts come across. When I visited Yacktman's office recently, he gushed about how this was the fund he and his analysts invest much of their own personal money in. That's a good sign. But understand that Yacktman tends to fall in love with out-of-favor companies and won't flinch at putting upward of 20 percent in a single name. If he's right, shareholders are rewarded. But if he's wrong, you'll definitely feel the pain.

Yacktman is a long-term investor who looks to buy traditional growth stocks after they have been whacked down in price. He wants businesses with high returns on tangible assets, shareholder-oriented management that spends cash wisely, and low valuations. Yacktman's goal is to provide the highest returns consistent with taking a minimal amount of risk. Remember, risk is relative in a concentrated fund like this. Don't expect the portfolio to move in line with the S&P 500. This fund is a big bet on a very talented stock picker.

ANNUALIZED RETURNS		PORTFOLIO STATISTICS	
1-Year	14.03%	Beta	N/A
3-Year	N/A	Turnover	N/A
5-Year	N/A	12-Month Yield	0.41%
Overall Rank	N/A	12b-1 Fee	0.00%
Risk Rank	N/A	Expense Ratio	1.25%
MINIMUM INVESTMENT		**CONTACT INFORMATION**	
Regular	$2,500	*Yacktman Focused Fund*	
IRA	$500	*Telephone: (800) 525-8258*	
		www.yacktman.com	

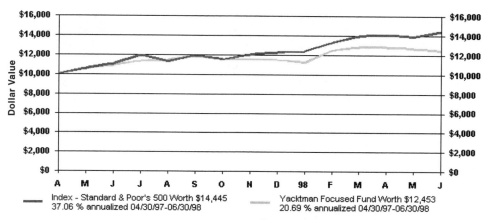

Index - Standard & Poor's 500 Worth $14,445
37.06 % annualized 04/30/97-06/30/98

Yacktman Focused Fund Worth $12,453
20.69 % annualized 04/30/97-06/30/98

GROWTH OF $10,000

TOP 10 HOLDINGS	
Department 56	Rollins
Philip Morris	United Asset Management
First Data	Fruit of the Loom
Franklin Covey	Reebok International
First Health Corp.	Intimate Brands

BARON SMALL CAP

OBJECTIVE:	*Small-Cap Growth*
MANAGER:	*Cliff Greenberg*

46

FUND OVERVIEW:

Even though Cliff Greenberg hasn't been managing a mutual fund for long, he has been making money in small-cap stocks for years. Before joining Baron in 1997, Greenberg spent 12 years running a prominent New York hedge fund. He tries to find companies with superior prospects that can be purchased at attractive prices. Greenberg won't buy a stock unless he thinks it can go up at least 50 percent over a two-year period, and he won't hesitate to overweight his favorite ideas in the portfolio.

Greenberg has an eclectic style. He says most of his investments fall into one of the following categories: growth stocks, fallen angels, or special situations. Growth companies either have new products or are involved in blossoming industries. They are also growing by at least 20 percent a year. Fallen angels are stocks that have tumbled dramatically in price. This often happens because Wall Street is concerned about current earnings prospects. Greenberg digs deeper to see whether the long-term fundamentals have materially changed. If not, he's interested. Finally, special situations encompass spin-offs, recapitalizations, equity stubs, and the like.

ANNUALIZED RETURNS		PORTFOLIO STATISTICS	
1-Year	N/A	Beta	N/A
3-Year	N/A	Turnover	N/A
5-Year	N/A	12-Month Yield	N/A
Overall Rank	N/A	12b-1 Fee	0.25%
Risk Rank	N/A	Expense Ratio	N/A

MINIMUM INVESTMENT		CONTACT INFORMATION
Regular	$2,000	*Baron Small Cap Fund*
IRA	$2,000	*Telephone: (800) 992-2766*
		www.baronfunds.com

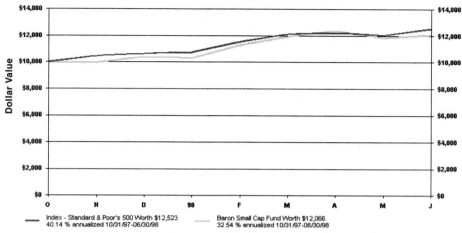

GROWTH OF $10,000

TOP 10 HOLDINGS

Culligan Water Technologies	Premier Parks
Counsel	Iron Mountain
AMF Bowling	Choicepoint
Universal Outdoor Holdings	Metro Networks
United Stationers	UNOVA

BJURMAN MICRO-CAP GROWTH

OBJECTIVE:	*Small-Cap Growth*	*47*
MANAGER:	*Team Managed*	

FUND OVERVIEW:

The Bjurman Micro-Cap Growth Fund looks for high-growth companies with market capitalizations between $30 million and $300 million at the time of initial investment. The management team, lead by O. Thomas Barry, seeks out undervalued stocks with superior earnings growth characteristics. They typically screen through a universe of 1,900 companies, using five different models. The models look at such attributes as earnings growth, earnings strength, earnings revisions, price-to-earnings, price-to-growth, and price-to-cash flow ratios. Then the managers take a top-down look at the economy to identify the 10 to 15 most promising industries to be invested in over the next 12 to 18 months. With the two lists in hand, Barry and his associates compile a list of up to 200 of the most attractive companies and begin doing additional fundamental and technical research.

To make sure the portfolio is well diversified, no more than 5 percent of assets are placed in any one stock, nor more than 15 percent in a single industry. This fund is fairly new, although its adviser, George D. Bjurman & Associates, has been managing money for more than 28 years.

ANNUALIZED RETURNS		PORTFOLIO STATISTICS	
1-Year	43.40%	Beta	N/A
3-Year	N/A	Turnover	22.00%
5-Year	N/A	12-Month Yield	N/A
Overall Rank	N/A	12b-1 Fee	0.25%
Risk Rank	N/A	Expense Ratio	1.80%

MINIMUM INVESTMENT		CONTACT INFORMATION
Regular	$5,000	*Bjurman Micro-Cap Growth Fund*
IRA	$2,000	*Telephone: (800) 227-7264*
		www.bjurmanfunds.com

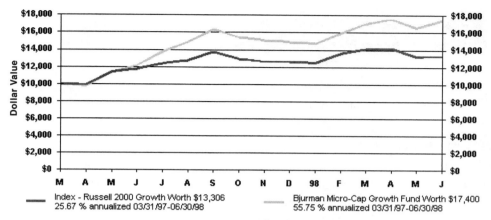

Index - Russell 2000 Growth Worth $13,306
25.67 % annualized 03/31/97-06/30/98

Bjurman Micro-Cap Growth Fund Worth $17,400
55.75 % annualized 03/31/97-06/30/98

GROWTH OF $10,000

TOP 10 HOLDINGS	
Bank of Commerce	**THO**
Analytical Surveys	**Dominion Homes**
PSC	**Harborside Healthcare**
AmeriLink	**Forensic Technologies**
Party City	**American Disposal Services**

FREMONT U.S. MICRO-CAP

| OBJECTIVE: | *Small-Cap Growth* | *48* |
| MANAGER: | *Robert Kern* | |

FUND OVERVIEW:

Bob Kern is a true pioneer of micro-cap investing. He first got interested in small companies in the late 1960s, when he realized they offered more access to management and had less Wall Street coverage. He focuses exclusively on the smallest 5 percent of all publicly traded companies—those with market capitalizations from $10 million to $400 million. That may sound limiting, but there are more than 4,700 qualifying companies for him to choose from. Kern says this is one of the least efficient sectors of the domestic equities market, which creates attractive opportunities for research-driven stock pickers like himself and for shareholders of the Fremont U.S. Micro-Cap Fund.

Kern places his emphasis on the business prospects for individual companies, not overall economic trends. Before committing any money, he scours through financial statements and meets with key decision makers to discuss their strategies for future growth. He's looking for businesses in their early stages of growth, where earnings can grow faster than inflation. The majority of the portfolio is normally invested in technology, health care, and consumer and services companies, where a high degree of innovation takes place.

ANNUALIZED RETURNS		PORTFOLIO STATISTICS	
1-Year	1.92%	Beta	0.81
3-Year	26.05%	Turnover	125.00%
5-Year	N/A	12-Month Yield	0.00%
Overall Rank	4	12b-1 Fee	0.00%
Risk Rank	4	Expense Ratio	1.87%
MINIMUM INVESTMENT		**CONTACT INFORMATION**	
Regular	$2,000	*Fremont U.S. Micro-Cap Fund*	
IRA	$1,000	*Telephone: (800) 548-4539*	
		www.fremontfunds.com	

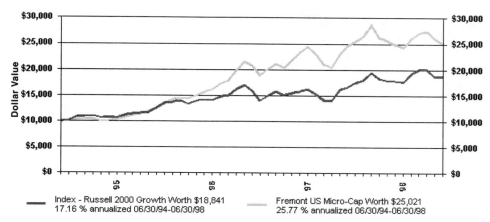

GROWTH OF $10,000

Index - Russell 2000 Growth Worth $18,841
17.16 % annualized 06/30/94-06/30/98

Fremont US Micro-Cap Worth $25,021
25.77 % annualized 06/30/94-06/30/98

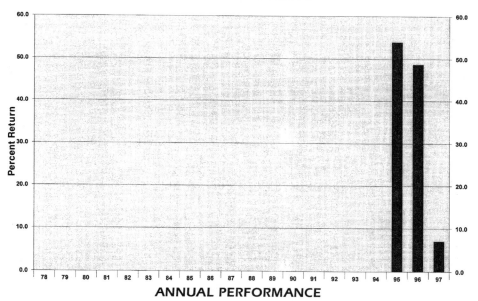

ANNUAL PERFORMANCE

TOP 10 HOLDINGS

Saga Communications	Warrantech Corp.
MDSI Mobile Data	Specialty Teleconstructors
Advance paradigm	AFC Cable Systems
Peerless	ISG Intl. Software
Richey Electronics	NuCo2 Inc.

HENLOPEN

OBJECTIVE:	*Small-Cap Growth*	*49*
MANAGER:	*Team Managed*	

Fund Overview:

Henlopen's three managers—Michael Hershey, Paul Larson, and Lorenzo Villalon—look for dominant small companies with rapid earnings growth. Their eclectic investment philosophy calls for purchasing stocks with strong momentum that they believe can carry the share price significantly higher over a one- or two-year period. But this isn't a pure momentum play, since they will also buy cyclical and out-of-favor companies if the price is right. The fund's average holding reported annual gains of 25 percent over the past three years, which is well ahead of companies in the S&P 500.

The experienced trio remain true to their convictions. They will overweight favorite names and quickly pull out of companies they no longer like. This "quick draw" approach means the fund is more volatile than many of its peers, but its performance has more than compensated for its inherently bumpy ride. Henlopen has landed among the top 15 percent of all small cap funds since inception in 1992 and has easily surpassed its direct benchmark, the Russell 2000. Henlopen also has a small asset base, which gives it an extra advantage as it navigates through this risk-laden area of the market.

ANNUALIZED RETURNS		PORTFOLIO STATISTICS	
1-Year	32.78%	Beta	0.93
3-Year	24.50%	Turnover	140.60%
5-Year	20.93%	12-Month Yield	4.92%
Overall Rank	3	12b-1 Fee	0.00%
Risk Rank	4	Expense Ratio	1.60%
MINIMUM INVESTMENT		**CONTACT INFORMATION**	
Regular	$10,000	*Henlopen Fund*	
IRA	$2,000	*Telephone: (800) 922-0224*	

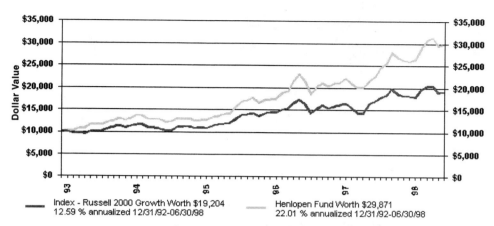

Index - Russell 2000 Growth Worth $19,204
12.59 % annualized 12/31/92-06/30/98

Henlopen Fund Worth $29,871
22.01 % annualized 12/31/92-06/30/98

GROWTH OF $10,000

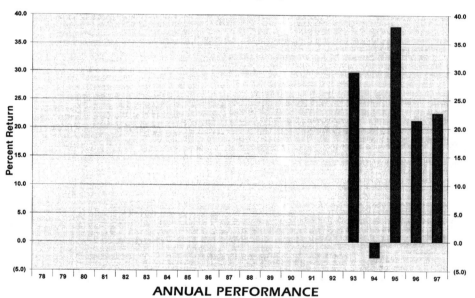

ANNUAL PERFORMANCE

TOP 10 HOLDINGS

Markel Corp.	Checkpoint Systems
Steiner Leisure	Unisys Corp.
Igen Intl.	Action Performance
Alydaar Software	Aim Safety
Integrated Circuit Systems	CCB Financial

JURIKA & VOYLES MINI-CAP

OBJECTIVE:	*Small-Cap Growth*	**50**
MANAGER:	*Team Managed*	

FUND OVERVIEW:

Jurika & Voyles Mini-Cap is in the midst of change. After several years of excellent performance, the fund's former manager left at the end of 1997. The portfolio is now in the hands of 11 of the firm's analysts. The new managers immediately began slicing the portfolio from 150 to a more manageable 60 to 90 stocks. They have also vowed to reduce annual turnover, which had run as high as 300 percent, to no more than half of that rate. This should make the fund more tax-efficient.

Jurika & Voyles Mini-Cap invests in stocks with market capitalizations from $150 million to $1.7 billion, in line with the Russell 2000. Each analyst is expected to contribute his or her best recommendations. One requirement is that a company's price-to-earnings ratio must be below the benchmark index. The team also seeks strong balance sheets and definable catalysts for growth. Firms with long-term debt-to-total capitalization ratios of more than 50 percent are automatically discarded, unless they generate enough cash to cover these liabilities. Lead manager Paul Meeks points out that the fund is unlikely to invest in companies with less than a 30 percent total return potential over a two-year period.

ANNUALIZED RETURNS		PORTFOLIO STATISTICS	
1-Year	10.28%	Beta	0.70
3-Year	23.18%	Turnover	304.88%
5-Year	N/A	12-Month Yield	0.00%
Overall Rank	3	12b-1 Fee	0.00%
Risk Rank	4	Expense Ratio	1.50%
MINIMUM INVESTMENT		**CONTACT INFORMATION**	
Regular	$10,000	*Jurika & Voyles Mini-Cap Fund*	
IRA	$10,000	*Telephone: (800) 584-6878*	
		Website: www.jurika.com	

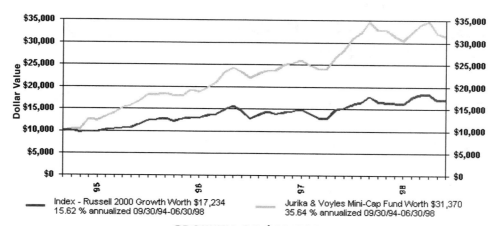

GROWTH OF $10,000

Index - Russell 2000 Growth Worth $17,234
15.62 % annualized 09/30/94-06/30/98

Jurika & Voyles Mini-Cap Fund Worth $31,370
35.64 % annualized 09/30/94-06/30/98

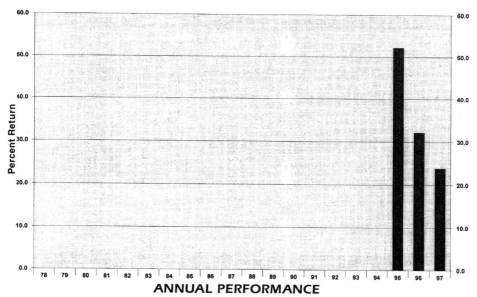

ANNUAL PERFORMANCE

TOP 10 HOLDINGS

Symantec Corp.	Amerin Corp.
Amerus Life Holdings	Penncorp Financial
Doncasters PLC	Kaufman & Broad
Genesee & WYO	Helen of Troy
MAF Bancorp	Pilgrims Pride

MANAGERS SPECIAL EQUITY

OBJECTIVE:	*Small-Cap Growth*	**51**
MANAGER:	*Team Managed*	

FUND OVERVIEW:

Managers Special Equity gives you access to four leading small-cap stock pickers in one portfolio. It farms out 26 percent of the portfolio to Timothy Ebright of Liberty Investment Management, 36 percent to Andrew Knuth of Westport Asset Management, 30 percent to Gary Pilgrim of Pilgrim Baxter & Associates (who also runs the popular PBHG Growth Fund), and 8 percent to Bob Kern of Kern Capital Management. Each person has a unique style and approach to small-cap investing. Ebright searches for companies that have predictable earnings and are selling at less than intrinsic value. Knuth will only buy stocks trading at or below the market's price-to-earnings multiple. Pilgrim focuses on companies with high earnings momentum. And Kern directs his efforts toward finding micro-cap stocks that are succeeding through new product innovation. Therefore, you get a blend of growth, earnings momentum, and value in one package.

Because of all the managers involved, Managers Special Equity's portfolio is quite large. No single holding accounts for more than 2 percent of total assets. This is a great fund for investors seeking to keep only one small-cap name in their portfolio.

ANNUALIZED RETURNS		PORTFOLIO STATISTICS	
1-Year	19.85%	Beta	0.78
3-Year	24.91%	Turnover	49.00%
5-Year	18.90%	12-Month Yield	0.10%
Overall Rank	3	12b-1 Fee	0.00%
Risk Rank	4	Expense Ratio	1.35%
MINIMUM INVESTMENT		**CONTACT INFORMATION**	
Regular	$2,000	*Managers Special Equity Fund*	
IRA	$500	*Telephone: (800) 835-3879*	
		www.managersfunds.com	

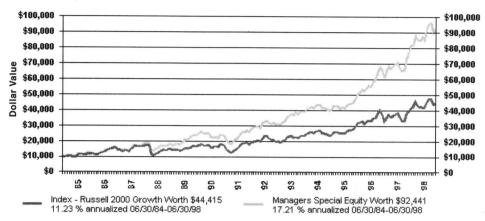

GROWTH OF $10,000

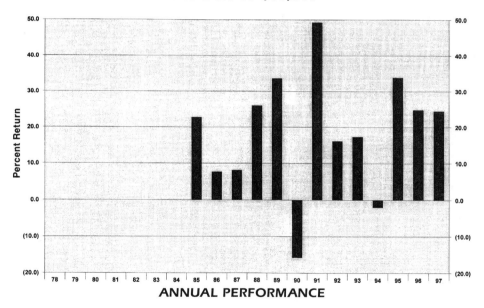

ANNUAL PERFORMANCE

TOP 10 HOLDINGS	
Xtra Corp.	Pittston Co. Brinks Grp.
Airborne Freight	Downey Financial
American Radio Systems	MacFrugals Bargains
Emmis Broadcasting	Policy Mgmt.
Allied Cap Corp.	C&D Technologies

NICHOLAS LIMITED EDITION

| OBJECTIVE: | *Small-Cap Growth* | **52** |
| MANAGER: | *David O. Nicholas* | |

FUND OVERVIEW:

David Nicholas describes his approach to investing as seeking growth at a reasonable price. He buys small and mid cap stocks in companies that appear to be attractively priced relative to their growth prospects. He's much more concerned about individual company selection than about the overall market. He also believes that reducing the downside is essential to achieving superior long-term results. Accordingly, he won't invest more than five percent of total assets in companies with track records shorter than three years. Nicholas hunts for stocks with price-to-earnings ratios that are low in relation to earnings growth. Alternatively, he likes stocks that are cheap compared to book value. Above-average secular earnings growth and strong current earnings momentum are other important factors he looks for.

The Nicholas Limited Edition portfolio is made up of around 60 stocks in such diversified industries as health care, financial services, media, and industrial products. Nicholas is convinced that large multinational company growth could be restrained at some point, which would further benefit the smaller companies he invests in.

ANNUALIZED RETURNS		PORTFOLIO STATISTICS	
1-Year	18.28%	Beta	0.67
3-Year	24.14%	Turnover	37.05%
5-Year	17.81%	12-Month Yield	0.01%
Overall Rank	3	12b-1 Fee	0.00%
Risk Rank	4	Expense Ratio	0.85%
MINIMUM INVESTMENT		**CONTACT INFORMATION**	
Regular	$2,000	*Nicholas Limited Edition*	
IRA	$2,000	*Telephone: (800) 227-5987*	

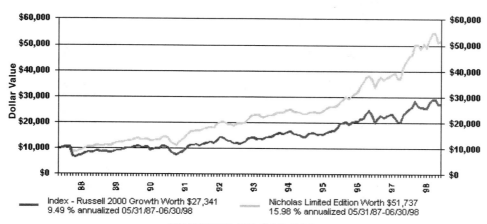

Index - Russell 2000 Growth Worth $27,341
9.49 % annualized 05/31/87-06/30/98

Nicholas Limited Edition Worth $51,737
15.98 % annualized 05/31/87-06/30/98

GROWTH OF $10,000

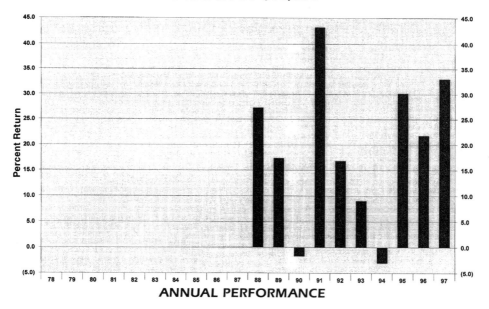

ANNUAL PERFORMANCE

TOP 10 HOLDINGS	
Heartland Express	ARM Financial Group
Intl. Speedway	Res-Care
Harborside Healthcare	Poe & Brown Inc.
Assisted Living Concepts	Sofamor/Danek Group
Dentsply Intl.	National Surgery Centers

SCHRODER U.S. SMALLER COMPANIES

OBJECTIVE: *Small-Cap Growth*
MANAGER: *Fariba Talebi*

53

FUND OVERVIEW:

The Schroder U.S. Smaller Companies Fund looks for emerging businesses able to grow earnings regardless of what's happening with the overall economy. Manager Fariba Talebi follows a bottom-up approach to individual stock selection, concentrating on underfollowed and misunderstood companies that can offer superior future growth. The fund pursues its capital appreciation objective by investing in U.S.-domiciled companies with market capitalizations of $1.5 billion or less at the time of initial purchase. This makes it a true small-cap portfolio. In addition to a positive earnings outlook, Talebi searches for companies with strong management that are selling at favorable prices in relation to book value and earnings. She is definitely conscious of how much she is being asked to pay for these companies. This is clearly a small-cap fund, but Talebi has the option of buying larger names when she feels it's appropriate. However, she currently believes that smaller companies are more attractive than their larger brethren, based on valuations.

This fund is sponsored by Schroder Capital Management, a prestigious London-based investment firm with some $150 billion in assets.

ANNUALIZED RETURNS		PORTFOLIO STATISTICS	
1-Year	15.10%	Beta	0.76
3-Year	26.83%	Turnover	34.45%
5-Year	N/A	12-Month Yield	0.00%
Overall Rank	3	12b-1 Fee	0.00%
Risk Rank	4	Expense Ratio	1.48%

MINIMUM INVESTMENT		CONTACT INFORMATION
Regular	$10,000	*Schroder U.S. Smaller Companies*
IRA	$2,000	*Fund*
		Telephone: (800) 290-9826

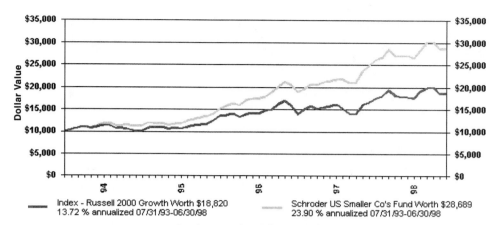

Index - Russell 2000 Growth Worth $18,820
13.72 % annualized 07/31/93-06/30/98

Schroder US Smaller Co's Fund Worth $28,689
23.90 % annualized 07/31/93-06/30/98

GROWTH OF $10,000

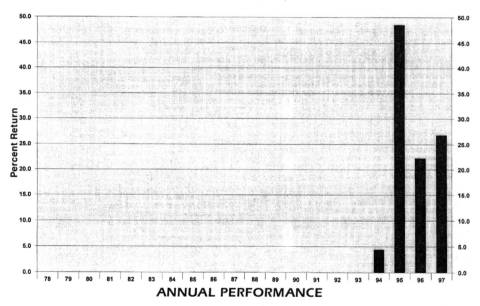

ANNUAL PERFORMANCE

TOP 10 HOLDINGS	
US Foodservice	Proffitt's
AO Smith	Sola International
Aliant Communications	New England Business Service
PartnerRe Holdings	Outback Steakhouse
Analogic	Electro Rent

T. ROWE PRICE SMALL-CAP STOCK

OBJECTIVE:	*Small-Cap Growth*	*54*
MANAGER:	*Greg A. McCrickard*	

FUND OVERVIEW:

I classify T. Rowe Price Small-Cap Stock as a growth fund, but manager Greg McCrickard actually invests in both growth- and value-oriented securities. He says this flexible approach gives him access to more opportunities, and the value component helps to temper overall volatility. The fund is also highly diversified; the average holding makes up less than 1.5 percent of the portfolio. This is both good and bad. It reduces risk, but it can prevent the fund from reaping the full rewards of its biggest winners. McCrickard is prone to take his gains sooner than most (although he's not a frequent trader), and he generally avoids concentrating too heavily in any one sector or industry.

McCrickard uses a variety of fundamental checkpoints to evaluate potential holdings. Among other things, he wants companies with sound financial structures, good management, attractive niches, pricing flexibility, and strong insider ownership. Because of his value component, McCrickard keeps a close eye on how much he's willing to pay for a stock, checking to see whether price-to-cash flow and price-to-earnings ratios are attractive relative to estimated earnings growth.

ANNUALIZED RETURNS		PORTFOLIO STATISTICS	
1-Year	20.89%	Beta	0.55
3-Year	23.92%	Turnover	22.90%
5-Year	19.51%	12-Month Yield	0.16%
Overall Rank	3	**12b-1 Fee**	0.00%
Risk Rank	3	**Expense Ratio**	1.02%
MINIMUM INVESTMENT		CONTACT INFORMATION	
Regular	$2,500	*T. Rowe Price Small-Cap Stock Fund*	
IRA	$1,000	*Telephone: (800) 638-5660*	
		www.troweprice.com	

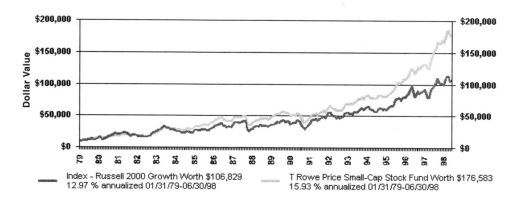

Index - Russell 2000 Growth Worth $106,829
12.97 % annualized 01/31/79-06/30/98

T Rowe Price Small-Cap Stock Fund Worth $176,583
15.93 % annualized 01/31/79-06/30/98

GROWTH OF $10,000

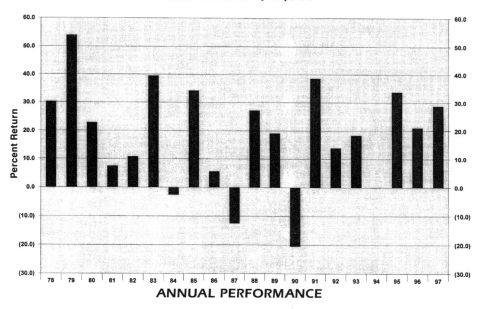

ANNUAL PERFORMANCE

TOP 10 HOLDINGS

JP Foodservice
Aliant Communications
Analogic Corp.
Summit Bancorp
Carson Pirie Scott & Co.

AO Smith Corp.
Coinmach Laundry
Harleysville Group
Richfood Holdings
Cowles Media

BABSON ENTERPRISE II

OBJECTIVE:	*Small-Cap Value*	
MANAGER:	*Lance James and Peter Schliemann*	

FUND OVERVIEW:

Babson Enterprise II managers Lance James and Peter Schliemann invest in profitable small companies that are dominant forces in their respective industries. But they want to buy these businesses when they are undervalued, allowing them to enjoy further price appreciation without all the risk normally associated with funds in this category. A company is considered to be selling at a fair price if it is reasonable relative to such measures as price-to-earnings, price-to-sales, and price-to-book value ratios.

James and Schliemann have been comanaging the fund since its inception in 1991. They work with a team of analysts to sift through thousands of ideas, in search of those with the best fundamentals. "We're looking for companies that are currently out of favor in the marketplace, but with the opportunity to improve their profitability," James explains. "This is how we buy good companies cheaply." Babson Enterprise II owns stocks with market capitalizations from $250 million to $1 billion at the time of initial purchase. The fund's turnover rate is low for an offering of this nature—another positive, because it helps to keep a lid on year-end tax liability.

ANNUALIZED RETURNS		PORTFOLIO STATISTICS	
1-Year	18.21%	Beta	0.65
3-Year	24.16%	Turnover	21.00%
5-Year	17.46%	12-Month Yield	0.17%
Overall Rank	3	12b-1 Fee	0.00%
Risk Rank	3	Expense Ratio	1.28%
MINIMUM INVESTMENT		**CONTACT INFORMATION**	
Regular	$1,000	*Babson Enterprise II*	
IRA	$250	*Telephone: (800) 422-2766*	
		www.jbfunds.com	

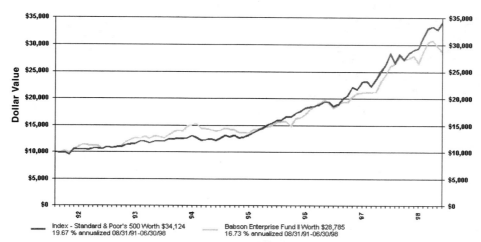

GROWTH OF $10,000

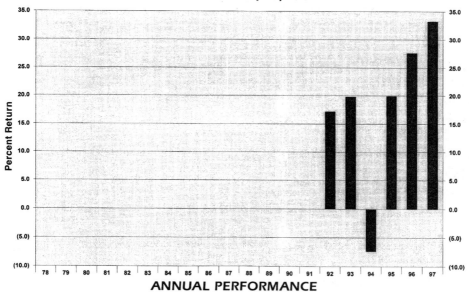

ANNUAL PERFORMANCE

TOP 10 HOLDINGS

Golden St. Bancorp
Carlisle Cos.
Herman Miller
BJ's Wholesale Club
Commerce Bancorp

Dun & Bradstreet
Nabors Inds.
Central Newspapers
Sea Containers
Interface

FASCIANO FUND

OBJECTIVE:	*Small-Cap Value*	**56**
MANAGER:	*Michael Fasciano*	

FUND OVERVIEW:

Michael Fasciano runs a fund that gives investors exposure to small cap stocks, while letting them sleep soundly at night. His low-risk approach to investing in this area of the market usually prevents the Fasciano Fund from having any blockbuster years. But it also tends to tame the potential downside. Fasciano looks for companies with solid financial conditions, strong cash flows, demonstrated profitability, heavy insider ownership, and conservative valuations. In addition, he wants steady growth, low- or soft-tech businesses. There are no high-flying Internet stocks in this portfolio.

"We are targeting a conservative balance between risk and reward," Fasciano explains. "This approach keeps your investment dollars working hard, but with some measure of safety." His process tries to screen out companies that are chronically troubled, unproven, or highly speculative. He looks for stocks with low price-to-earnings and price-to-growth rate ratios, high returns on assets, and strong cash flows. Fasciano's bottom-up approach calls for visiting companies and getting to know management. Even though the fund has been around for more than a decade, it still has a relatively small asset base, a major plus in the small-cap arena.

ANNUALIZED RETURNS		PORTFOLIO STATISTICS	
1-Year	33.20%	Beta	0.65
3-Year	25.53%	Turnover	16.90%
5-Year	20.45%	12-Month Yield	0.24%
Overall Rank	2	12b-1 Fee	0.00%
Risk Rank	3	Expense Ratio	1.30%
MINIMUM INVESTMENT		**CONTACT INFORMATION**	
Regular	$1,000	*Fasciano Fund*	
IRA	$1,000	*Telephone: (800) 848-6050*	
		www.fascianofunds.com	

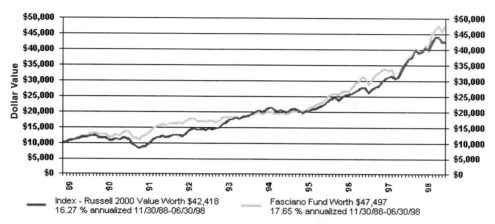

Index - Russell 2000 Value Worth $42,418
16.27 % annualized 11/30/88-06/30/98

Fasciano Fund Worth $47,497
17.65 % annualized 11/30/88-06/30/98

GROWTH OF $10,000

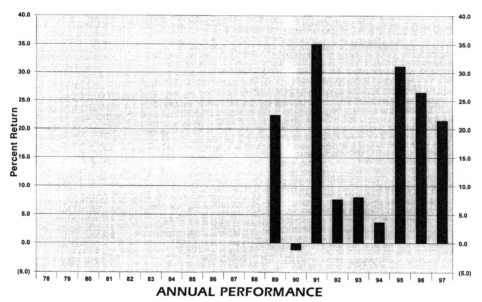

ANNUAL PERFORMANCE

TOP 10 HOLDINGS	
Pulitzer Publishing	Intl. Speedway
Central Parking Corp.	Concord EFS
Cardinal Health	Keane
Ocwen Financial	Resource Amer.
Emmis Broadcasting	CDW Computer Ctrs.

GREENSPRING

OBJECTIVE:	*Small-Cap Value*	*57*
MANAGER:	*Charles Carlson*	

FUND OVERVIEW:

Greenspring has been called the perfect fund for "chickens." Even though manager Charles Carlson is most interested in preserving principal during tough times for the market, he has managed to perform well even in the face of a bullish tide. Carlson seeks out hard-core value investments that should hold up well even when the market turns south. He will buy both stocks and bonds, although equities make up a majority of his portfolio. Carlson focuses on securities selling for low prices relative to the underlying company's free cash flow, earnings, and/or book value. He tries to find catalysts that could cause future earnings surprises and is most interested in underfollowed companies.

"At the core of the Greenspring Fund's investment philosophy is the belief that the preservation of capital during difficult market conditions, combined with strong gains during more favorable times, will lead to superior returns over an entire market cycle," Carlson notes. That makes Greenspring a perfect fund for investors seeking small-cap exposure and the ability to sleep comfortably at night. Just keep in mind that this fund won't perform as strongly as its peers if stock prices keep shooting to the moon.

ANNUALIZED RETURNS		PORTFOLIO STATISTICS	
1-Year	9.22%	Beta	0.36
3-Year	16.92%	Turnover	46.17%
5-Year	14.06%	12-Month Yield	3.34%
Overall Rank	3	12b-1 Fee	0.00%
Risk Rank	1	Expense Ratio	1.00%

MINIMUM INVESTMENT		CONTACT INFORMATION	
Regular	$2,000	*Greenspring Fund*	
IRA	$1,000	*Telephone: (800) 366-3863*	

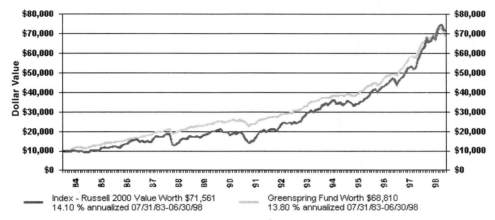

Index - Russell 2000 Value Worth $71,561
14.10 % annualized 07/31/83-06/30/98

Greenspring Fund Worth $68,810
13.80 % annualized 07/31/83-06/30/98

GROWTH OF $10,000

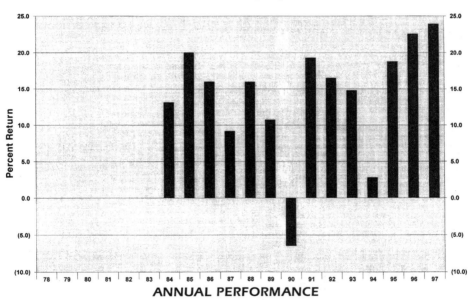

ANNUAL PERFORMANCE

TOP 10 HOLDINGS

ATC Group Services	Castle Energy Corp.
Crestar Financial	Prime Retail
Barringer Technologies	Reliastar Financial
US Industries	Criimi Mae
Ocwen Asset Invt. Corp.	Griffin Corp.

HOTCHKIS & WILEY SMALL CAP

OBJECTIVE:	*Small-Cap Value*	
MANAGER:	*James Miles and David Green*	**58**

FUND OVERVIEW:

The perfect stock for James Miles and David Green is one that everyone else is trying to sell because of an analyst's downgrade, a lawsuit, or an earnings disappointment. They figure Wall Street gets too excited when stocks are going up, and overly pessimistic when they're on the way down. Besides, even when everyone else is negative on a particular industry, there are always individual companies with attractive growth rates, growing earnings, and sound fundamentals. Those are the stocks Miles and Green hope to unearth during any quake in the market, which is when such stocks go on sale.

They find their ideas by screening through a database of some 3,000 companies, paying close attention to those with favorable valuation characteristics, such as low price-to-earnings ratios. From here, they do their own fundamental research, which includes conversations with company management. They sell when a stock's price-to-earnings multiple is 1.5 times greater than the market, or when its long-term business prospects deteriorate. Miles and Green are relatively new to fund management, but so far they're doing a terrific job with a fund that was nothing to write home about before they came on board.

ANNUALIZED RETURNS		PORTFOLIO STATISTICS	
1-Year	22.23%	Beta	0.64
3-Year	21.94%	Turnover	88.00%
5-Year	16.62%	12-Month Yield	0.18%
Overall Rank	3	12b-1 Fee	0.00%
Risk Rank	4	Expense Ratio	1.00%
MINIMUM INVESTMENT		**CONTACT INFORMATION**	
Regular	$10,000	*Hotchkis & Wiley Small Cap Fund*	
IRA	$10,000	*Telephone: (800) 236-4479*	

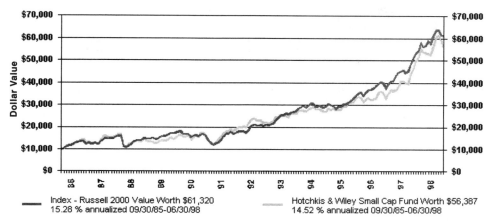

Index - Russell 2000 Value Worth $61,320
15.28 % annualized 09/30/85-06/30/98

Hotchkis & Wiley Small Cap Fund Worth $56,387
14.52 % annualized 09/30/85-06/30/98

GROWTH OF $10,000

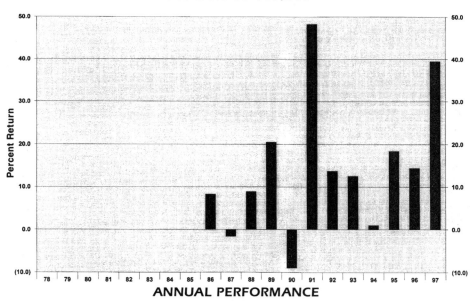

ANNUAL PERFORMANCE

TOP 10 HOLDINGS

American Coin Merchandising	Avteam
Dominicks Supermarkets	Redwood Tr. Inc.
Friedmans	Denison Intl. PLC
Micros Systems	ESG Re. Ltd.
Stoneridge	Groupe AB SA ADR

SCUDDER SMALL COMPANY VALUE

OBJECTIVE:	*Small-Cap Value*	**59**
MANAGER:	*Team Managed*	

FUND OVERVIEW:

Scudder Small Company Value targets tiny companies with big potential. This team-managed fund uses proprietary computer models to find small U.S. companies selling at prices that don't reflect their long-term potential. Stocks are valued based on such measures as price-to-earnings, price-to-book value, and price-to-cash flow ratios. Managers look for favorable trends that could lead to strong earnings growth and therefore stock price momentum.

In line with this style, many of the fund's holdings are often out-of-favor with the rest of Wall Street. "We seek to exploit inefficiencies in the small-cap segment of the U.S. stock market and add value through quantitative equity analysis, portfolio construction, and efficient trading," explain lead managers James Eysenbach and Philip Fortuna. "We do not attempt to add value through market timing, either by moving between stocks and cash or among various segments of the equity markets."

This fund is more quantitative than others in the small-cap value category. It has historically been less volatile than both the Russell 2000 and S&P 500 indexes, which is what you would expect from an offering of this nature.

ANNUALIZED RETURNS		PORTFOLIO STATISTICS	
1-Year	23.14%	Beta	N/A
3-Year	N/A	Turnover	43.64%
5-Year	N/A	12-Month Yield	0.31%
Overall Rank	N/A	12b-1 Fee	0.00%
Risk Rank	N/A	Expense Ratio	1.50%
MINIMUM INVESTMENT		**CONTACT INFORMATION**	
Regular	$2,500	*Scudder Small Company Value Fund*	
IRA	$1,000	*Telephone: (800) 343-2890*	
		funds.scudder.com	

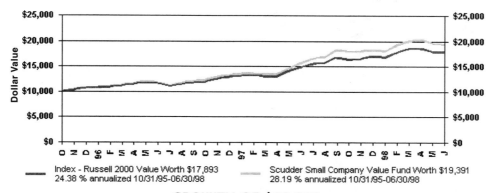

Index - Russell 2000 Value Worth $17,893
24.38 % annualized 10/31/95-06/30/98

Scudder Small Company Value Fund Worth $19,391
28.19 % annualized 10/31/95-06/30/98

GROWTH OF $10,000

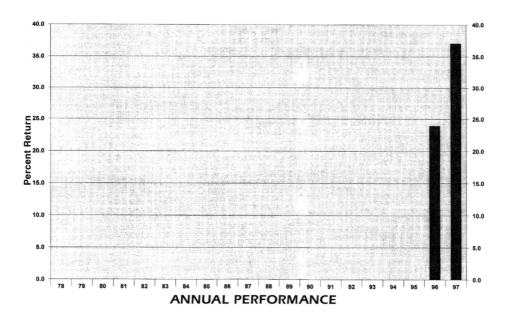

ANNUAL PERFORMANCE

TOP 10 HOLDINGS

LS Starrett	NACCO Industries
US Home	Energen
NCH	Puerto Rican Cement
Guilford Mills	Ameron Intl.
Harleysville Group	Banknorth Group

SKYLINE SMALL CAP VALUE PLUS

OBJECTIVE:	*Small-Cap Value*	*60*
MANAGER:	*Kenneth Kailin*	

FUND OVERVIEW:

Skyline Small Cap Value Plus manager Kenneth Kailin looks for above-average companies selling at below-average prices. As a value investor, he wants stocks with price-to-earnings ratios that are at least 20 percent below the overall market. He prefers to see earnings per share grow by at least 15 percent annually, or faster than the average publicly traded company. Special emphasis is placed on factors that may lead to this growth, such as the closing of inefficient plants, recent acquisitions, or new store openings.

Kailin's universe is equities with market capitalizations between $400 million and $2 billion. His portfolio of 35 to 55 holdings contains many companies that he calls "neglected," meaning they enjoy little or no coverage by Wall Street analysts. He likes this because such stocks can experience strong price appreciation once other investors catch on. Kailin screens for stocks using his previously mentioned guidelines. Those that pass this first stage are researched further by Skyline analysts. All ideas go through an investment committee, but Kailin has the final say on whether a recommended stock gets added to the portfolio.

ANNUALIZED RETURNS		PORTFOLIO STATISTICS	
1-Year	17.50%	Beta	0.73
3-Year	24.28%	Turnover	104.00%
5-Year	17.22%	12-Month Yield	0.00%
Overall Rank	3	12b-1 Fee	0.00%
Risk Rank	3	Expense Ratio	1.51%
MINIMUM INVESTMENT		CONTACT INFORMATION	
Regular	$1,000	*Skyline Small Cap Value Plus Fund*	
IRA	$1,000	*Telephone: (800) 458-5222*	

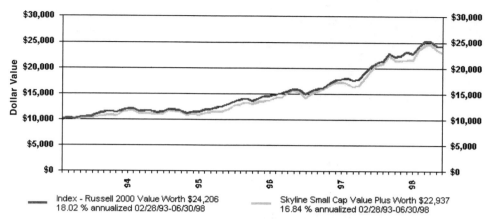

Index - Russell 2000 Value Worth $24,206
18.02 % annualized 02/28/93-06/30/98

Skyline Small Cap Value Plus Worth $22,937
16.84 % annualized 02/28/93-06/30/98

GROWTH OF $10,000

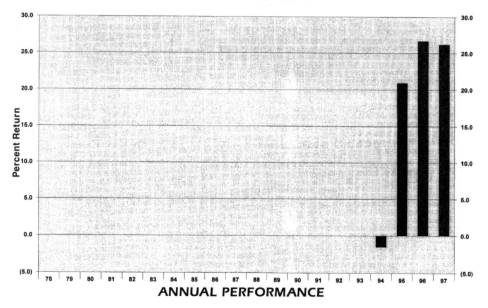

ANNUAL PERFORMANCE

TOP 10 HOLDINGS

Brylane
United Stationers
Integrated Health
CDI com.
CMAC Investment Corp.

Trigon Healthcare
Hughes Supply
Furniture Brands Intl.
World Color Press
Pentair

STRATTON SMALL-CAP YIELD

OBJECTIVE: *Small-Cap Value*
MANAGER: *Frank Reichel*

61

FUND OVERVIEW:

Small-cap stocks are not normally considered a good source of dividends, but Frank Reichel begs to differ. His Stratton Small-Cap Yield fund seeks to generate both capital appreciation and current income by investing in the common and convertible stock of companies with market capitalizations from $50 million to $500 million. He also tries to keep risk under control by buying only companies that have been around for more than three years and pay an established dividend. Reichel reasons that the dividend requirement helps to reduce price volatility.

The portfolio is invested using both a top-down and a bottom-up approach. Reichel looks for equities with yields greater than the small-cap benchmark Russell 2000 index. Once he has his list narrowed down, he screens for companies with low price-to-earnings and price-to-cash flow multiples. He further favors stocks with demonstrated earnings growth and positive earnings revisions. By charter, Reichel is prohibited from investing in IPOs or tobacco-related stocks. It's also interesting to note that the management fee is based on performance. It goes up if Reichel beats the index, down if he trails it.

ANNUALIZED RETURNS		PORTFOLIO STATISTICS	
1-Year	21.48%	Beta	0.63
3-Year	22.48%	Turnover	26.27%
5-Year	15.76%	12-Month Yield	0.88%
Overall Rank	3	12b-1 Fee	0.00%
Risk Rank	3	Expense Ratio	1.62%
MINIMUM INVESTMENT		**CONTACT INFORMATION**	
Regular	$2,000	*Stratton Small-Cap Yield Fund*	
IRA	None	*Telephone: (800) 472-4226*	
		www.strattonmgt.com	

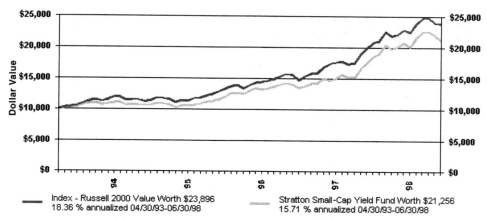

GROWTH OF $10,000

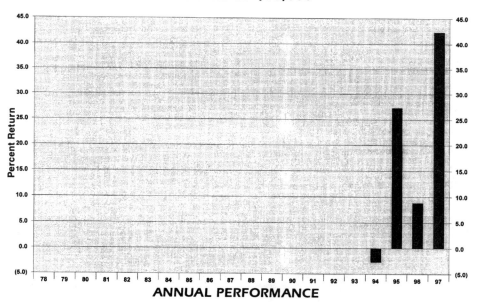

ANNUAL PERFORMANCE

TOP 10 HOLDINGS

Interra Finl.
Eaton Vance Corp.
Primex Technologies
Kuhlman Corp.
TB Woods Corp.

Commercial Intertech
Standard Motor Prods.
Technitrol
Greenbrier Cos.
AO Smith Corp.

THIRD AVENUE SMALL-CAP VALUE

| **OBJECTIVE:** | *Small-Cap Value* | |
| **MANAGER:** | *Martin J. Whitman/Curtis Jensen* | |

FUND OVERVIEW:

Marty Whitman isn't offended when people refer to him as a vulture. After all, that's what he calls himself. Whitman is a dedicated value investor, but not in the traditional sense. He looks for special situations where he can get in cheap, often because investors worry about the businesses' ability to continue as a going concern. His ideal company has an exceptionally strong financial position, as measured by a lack of debt and the presence of high-quality assets. To Whitman and co-manager Curtis Jensen (Whitman's former student), a perfect stock also has a "reasonable" management team, understandable business, and can be had for no more than 50 cents on the $1 for what it would be worth if taken over by another entity. "There are trade-offs involved in following our approach," Whitman admits. "In almost all cases, when we acquire a security, the near-term earnings outlook is terrible." But that, he believes, also reduces his downside; the stock is presumably trading at a low level because this bleak prognosis has already been factored in.

When Whitman can't find enough equities, he'll buy distressed bonds or even hold cash. He's a buy-and-hold investor and an exceptional stock picker.

ANNUALIZED RETURNS		PORTFOLIO STATISTICS	
1-Year	5.83%	Beta	N/A
3-Year	N/A	Turnover	38.00%
5-Year	N/A	12-Month Yield	0.50%
Overall Rank	N/A	12b-1 Fee	0.00%
Risk Rank	N/A	Expense Ratio	1.65%

MINIMUM INVESTMENT		CONTACT INFORMATION	
Regular	$1,000	*Third Avenue Small-Cap Value Fund*	
IRA	$500	*Telephone: (800) 443-1021*	
		www.mjwhitman.com	

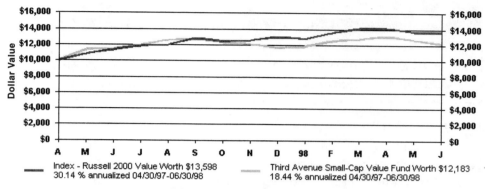

Index - Russell 2000 Value Worth $13,598
30.14 % annualized 04/30/97-06/30/98

Third Avenue Small-Cap Value Fund Worth $12,183
18.44 % annualized 04/30/97-06/30/98

GROWTH OF $10,000

TOP 10 HOLDINGS

Nissan Fire & Marine	Planar Systems
MBIA	Alico
Skyline	Xircom
Alexander & Baldwin	FSI International
Tejon Ranch	Deltic Timber

HEARTLAND VALUE PLUS

OBJECTIVE:	*Equity Income*	**63**
MANAGER:	*William Nasgovitz and Patrick Retzer*	

FUND OVERVIEW:

Heartland Value Plus seeks both capital appreciation and current income by investing in micro-cap stocks. These are the tiniest publicly traded companies; their market capitalizations are usually below $750 million. Managers Bill Nasgovitz and Patrick Retzer use value criteria to select their stocks, and they look primarily for income-producing securities. These aren't always easy to find in the small-cap universe because many emerging companies don't pay dividends. In addition to common stocks, the fund will hold preferreds, convertibles, and real estate investment trusts (REITs). They also buy corporate bonds, to enhance the fund's yield.

Nasgovitz is a Ben Graham disciple who evaluates securities based on such variables as price-to-earnings ratios, undervalued assets, the potential for favorable developments, and the amount of insider ownership. Retzger specializes in fixed-income securities and plays a more integral role in that part of the portfolio. The fund's yield should be higher than the S&P 500's, but this really isn't a good income vehicle. It should be viewed more as a conservative way to gain micro-cap exposure, with a bond component to cushion volatility.

ANNUALIZED RETURNS		PORTFOLIO STATISTICS	
1-Year	17.32%	Beta	0.26
3-Year	22.35%	Turnover	27.00%
5-Year	N/A	12-Month Yield	3.44%
Overall Rank	3	12b-1 Fee	0.25%
Risk Rank	2	Expense Ratio	1.23%
MINIMUM INVESTMENT		**CONTACT INFORMATION**	
Regular	$1,000	*Heartland Value Plus Fund*	
IRA	$1,000	*Telephone: (800) 432-7856*	

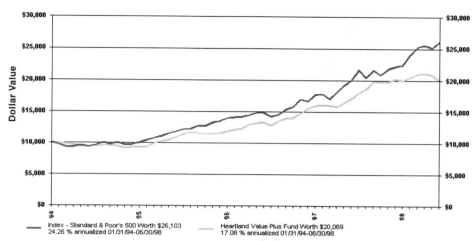

GROWTH OF $10,000

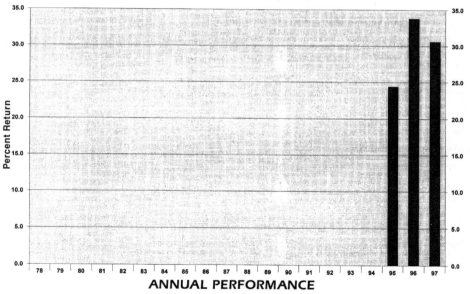

ANNUAL PERFORMANCE

TOP 10 HOLDINGS	
Fleming Cos.	Unisource Energy
WPL Holdings	London Pac Group
Central & South West	Southwestern Energy
USX-Delhi Group	Rochester Gas & Elec.
Dames & Moore	Akita Drilling

T. ROWE PRICE EQUITY INCOME

OBJECTIVE:	*Equity Income*	
MANAGER:	*Brian Rogers*	**64**

FUND OVERVIEW:

T. Rowe Price Equity Income takes a conservative approach to generating both consistent income and long-term capital growth. It is managed by Brian Rogers, whose value-oriented strategy has made this fund a real standout. (You may be familiar with Rogers from his regular appearances as a panelist on the PBS program *Wall $treet Week.*) Rogers looks for dividend-paying stocks that appear to be temporarily undervalued for one reason or another. The yield component offers some downside protection against both overall market declines and potential future disappointments from these sometimes troubled companies.

Research is the cornerstone of Rogers's investment approach. He and his analysts screen through hundreds of stocks looking for promising candidates. They then do a bottom-up evaluation of each business to see whether the story really checks out. To make the cut, a company must have an established operating history, a high dividend and low price-to-earnings ratio relative to the S&P, and a sound balance sheet. The portfolio contains mostly large blue-chip names and is extremely diversified, making it an attractive conservative equity investment.

ANNUALIZED RETURNS		PORTFOLIO STATISTICS	
1-Year	19.39%	Beta	0.64
3-Year	23.96%	Turnover	23.90%
5-Year	19.59%	12-Month Yield	2.22%
Overall Rank	2	12b-1 Fee	0.00%
Risk Rank	2	Expense Ratio	0.79%

MINIMUM INVESTMENT		CONTACT INFORMATION	
Regular	$2,500	*T. Rowe Price Equity Income*	
IRA	$1,000	*Telephone: (800) 638-5660*	
		www.troweprice.com	

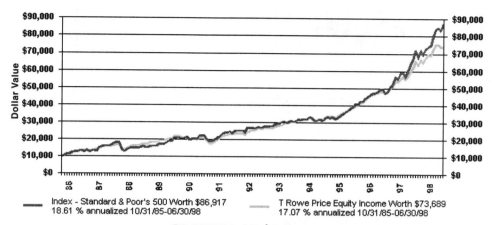

Index - Standard & Poor's 500 Worth $86,917
18.61 % annualized 10/31/85-06/30/98

T Rowe Price Equity Income Worth $73,689
17.07 % annualized 10/31/85-06/30/98

GROWTH OF $10,000

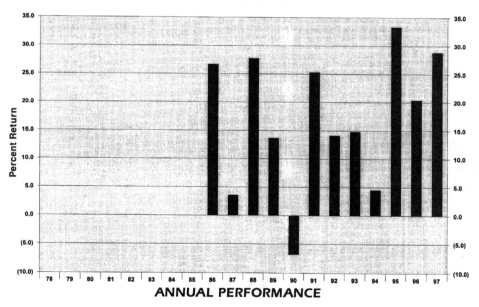

ANNUAL PERFORMANCE

TOP 10 HOLDINGS

AT&T Corp.	American Home Prods.
Mellon Bank	Union Pac Corp.
Dow Chemical	Exxon Corp.
Atlantic Richfield	Philip Morris
Alltel Corp.	SBC Communications

AMERICAN CENTURY INCOME & GROWTH

OBJECTIVE:	*Growth and Income*	
MANAGER:	*John Schniedwind and Kurt Borgwardt*	

FUND OVERVIEW:

Armed with a computer database of 2,500 stocks, John Schniedwind and Kurt Borgwardt search for attractive ideas to put in their American Century Income & Growth Portfolio. Every company is ranked according to earnings momentum and valuation characteristics, to make sure the fund pays a fair price for its holdings. The model also verifies that no more than 25 percent of the portfolio is put in any one industry. The overall goal of this quantitatively driven strategy is to beat the S&P 500 index while generating a yield that's at least 30 percent higher. This is a stiff challenge, but the fund has been able to meet it since inception.

Like most of the other funds in this category, this one doesn't have much of an income component. The portfolio does hold some high-yielding utility and energy stocks, but there are almost no bonds. In the past, the fund experienced a high degree of turnover stemming from strong new asset growth; fresh cash causes the model to reallocate holdings to keep everything in balance. However, Schniedwind and Borgwardt have vowed to make an effort to reduce this frequent trading.

ANNUALIZED RETURNS		PORTFOLIO STATISTICS	
1-Year	34.75%	**Beta**	0.96
3-Year	31.30%	**Turnover**	102.00%
5-Year	22.68%	**12-Month Yield**	1.32%
Overall Rank	1	**12b-1 Fee**	0.00%
Risk Rank	3	**Expense Ratio**	0.65%

MINIMUM INVESTMENT		CONTACT INFORMATION
Regular	$2,500	*American Century Income &*
IRA	$1,000	*Growth Fund*
		Telephone: (800) 345-2021
		www.americancentury.com

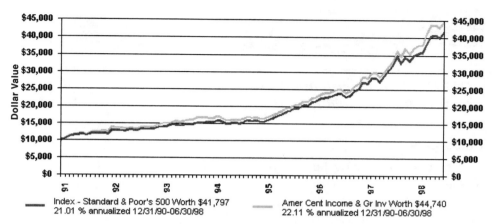

Index - Standard & Poor's 500 Worth $41,797
21.01 % annualized 12/31/90-06/30/98

Amer Cent Income & Gr Inv Worth $44,740
22.11 % annualized 12/31/90-06/30/98

GROWTH OF $10,000

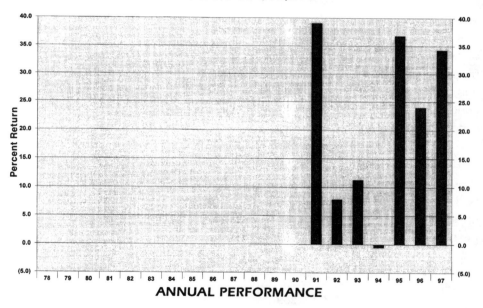

ANNUAL PERFORMANCE

TOP 10 HOLDINGS

Ford Motor Co.	Atlantic Richfield
United Technologies	Morgan Stanley Dean Witter
Microsoft	First Union Corp.
Merck & Co.	Chevron
Ameritech Corp.	Exxon

BARON GROWTH & INCOME

OBJECTIVE:	*Growth and Income*	
MANAGER:	*Ronald Baron*	**66**

FUND OVERVIEW:

Instead of buying large-cap dividend-paying stocks, like most fund managers in this category, Ron Baron fills his Baron Growth & Income with small and midsize companies. He follows a bottom-up, fundamentally driven approach of looking for undervalued stocks that he believes could go up at least 50 percent over a two-year period. Many of Baron's holdings are obscure and underfollowed at the time of his initial purchase, which is why they are selling for attractive prices. Before committing capital, Baron does extensive research on a company's financial structure, product demand, profitability, barriers to entry, and quality of management. He maintains a diversified portfolio of 50 to 80 stocks, but he prefers to concentrate on his best ideas. Normally, one-third of net assets are kept in the fund's top ten holdings.

To produce the "income" component, Baron invests about 20 percent of the portfolio in high-yielding real estate investments trusts (REITs), although many of his other stocks pay some amount of dividend as well. He will also buy convertible bonds and other income-producing assets, but equities are the primary focus. His ambitious goal is to achieve a 15 to 25 percent annual return.

ANNUALIZED RETURNS		PORTFOLIO STATISTICS	
1-Year	19.83%	Beta	0.83
3-Year	26.62%	Turnover	25.20%
5-Year	N/A	12-Month Yield	0.06%
Overall Rank	2	12b-1 Fee	0.25%
Risk Rank	4	Expense Ratio	1.39%

MINIMUM INVESTMENT		CONTACT INFORMATION	
Regular	$2,000	*Baron Growth & Income Fund*	
IRA	$2,000	*Telephone: (800) 992-2766*	
		www.baronfunds.com	

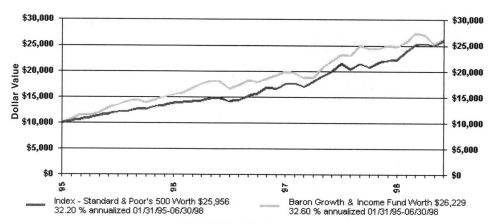

Index - Standard & Poor's 500 Worth $25,956
32.20 % annualized 01/31/95-06/30/98

Baron Growth & Income Fund Worth $26,229
32.60 % annualized 01/31/95-06/30/98

GROWTH OF $10,000

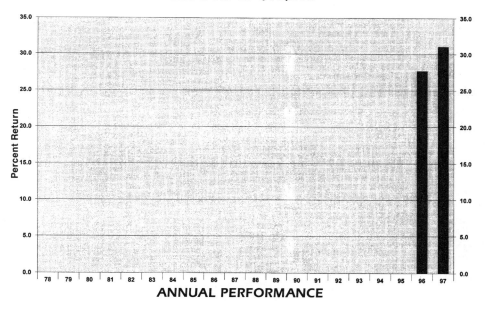

ANNUAL PERFORMANCE

TOP 10 HOLDINGS	
Charles Schwab	Starwood Hotels & Resorts
Manor Care	Corrections Corp. Amer.
Heftel Broadcasting	CCA Prison Relaty
Sunburst Hospitality	Spieker Properties
American Radio Systems	Smart & Final

CHICAGO TRUST GROWTH & INCOME

OBJECTIVE:	*Growth and Income*	**67**
MANAGER:	*Jerold L. Stodden*	

FUND OVERVIEW:

What you get with the Chicago Trust Growth & Income fund is a portfolio of mostly blue-chip companies, many of which pay a dividend. Manager Jerold Stodden invests mostly in common stocks, but he also buys preferreds, convertible securities, and fixed-income instruments. In fact, by prospectus he is able to put most or all of his assets in cash equivalents for defensive purposes, although the chance of that happening is quite remote. Additionally, he can keep up to 20 percent of the portfolio in foreign securities.

Stodden remains optimistic not only about the positions in his fund, but also about the market overall. "The absence of a recession, continued subdued inflation, and slower growth can provide a solid longer-term foundation for the stock market—especially consistent, top-quality growth situations (like the ones in Chicago Trust Growth & Income)," he says. "We recognize that volatility may occur in our portfolio during periods when the stock market is dominated by themes which are contrary to our investment approach. Our longer-term stock selection process will continue to focus on fundamentally strong companies which are able to demonstrate traits of consistent top- and bottom-line growth."

ANNUALIZED RETURNS		PORTFOLIO STATISTICS	
1-Year	28.82%	Beta	0.97
3-Year	30.32%	Turnover	25.00%
5-Year	N/A	12-Month Yield	0.09%
Overall Rank	1	12b-1 Fee	0.25%
Risk Rank	3	Expense Ratio	1.00%

MINIMUM INVESTMENT		CONTACT INFORMATION
Regular	$2,500	*Chicago Trust Growth & Income*
IRA	$500	*Telephone: (800) 992-8151*
		www.alleghanyfunds.chicago-trust
		.com

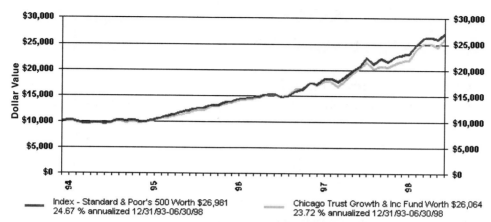

GROWTH OF $10,000

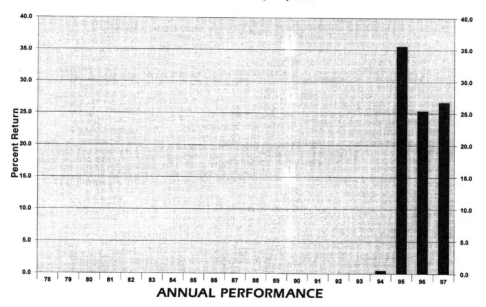

ANNUAL PERFORMANCE

TOP 10 HOLDINGS	
Illinois Tools Works	Pfizer
Norwest corp.	Cardinal Health
Federal Home Ln. Mtg. Corp.	Sysco Corp.
American Intl. Group	Newell Co.
Royal Dutch Petroleum	Walgreen

LEXINGTON CORPORATE LEADERS

OBJECTIVE:	*Growth and Income*	
MANAGER:	*Lawrence Kantor*	**68**

FUND OVERVIEW:

Lexington Corporate Leaders was set up as a unit trust in 1935. Its objective was to generate long-term capital growth and income by buying an equal number of shares from a fixed list of 30 American blue-chip companies. Today, that number has been reduced to 25. Because of this unusual policy, if a stock splits, the extra shares are promptly sold and the proceeds are reinvested among other positions. In addition, the fund is prohibited from adding new positions, except in the case of a spin-off. As a result, Lexington Corporate Leaders doesn't own companies in industries that have evolved since its founding, such as computer technology and airlines. Still, most companies in the fund are highly diversified, giving investors some exposure to virtually every segment of the economy, both in the United States and abroad. A stock is removed from the portfolio only if it fails to pay a dividend or is delisted from the exchange.

Fund manager Lawrence Kantor clearly has little flexibility when it comes to adding or deleting names from the fund's list of holdings. That hasn't hurt, though. The fund has consistently been a strong performer since inception, giving the S&P 500 a good run for its money.

ANNUALIZED RETURNS		PORTFOLIO STATISTICS	
1-Year	17.64%	Beta	0.84
3-Year	25.26%	Turnover	N/A
5-Year	19.41%	12-Month Yield	N/A
Overall Rank	2	12b-1 Fee	0.00%
Risk Rank	3	Expense Ratio	0.61%

MINIMUM INVESTMENT		CONTACT INFORMATION	
Regular	$1,000	*Lexington Corporate Leaders Trust*	
IRA	$1,000	*Fund*	
		Telephone: (800) 526-0056	

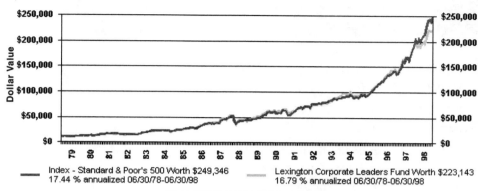

Index - Standard & Poor's 500 Worth $249,346
17.44 % annualized 06/30/78-06/30/98

Lexington Corporate Leaders Fund Worth $223,143
16.79 % annualized 06/30/78-06/30/98

GROWTH OF $10,000

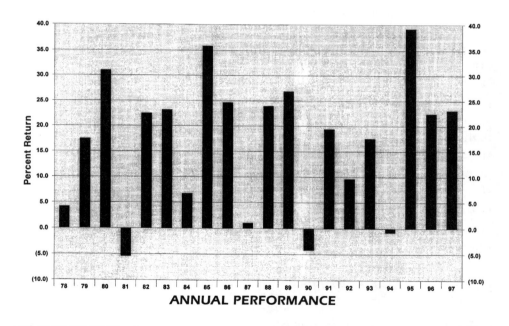

ANNUAL PERFORMANCE

TOP 10 HOLDINGS	
General Electric	Burlington Northern
Procter & Gamble	DuPont
Chevron	Lucent Technologies
Columbia Energy Group	Exxon
Mobil	AT&T

MARSICO GROWTH & INCOME

OBJECTIVE:	*Growth and Income*	**69**
MANAGER:	*Tom Marsico*	

FUND OVERVIEW:

One of the best all-around growth and income funds over the past decade has been Janus Growth & Income. For much of that time, the man responsible was Tom Marsico. Marsico managed Janus Growth & Income from May 31, 1991, to August 7, 1997, steering it to a 21.19 percent annualized gain, compared to 18.59 percent for the S&P 500. Now, Marsico has a new fund with the same mandate. Marsico Growth & Income was launched at the beginning of 1998. Because it looks and feels just like the portfolio he ran at Janus, it's reasonable to expect Marsico's winning ways at his own shop will continue. Plus, his new fund is much smaller, which is always a major advantage.

Marsico Growth & Income tries to identify quality companies with high growth potential before they are fully recognized by Wall Street. Marsico buys mostly blue chips, especially those experiencing a positive element of change. He further looks for globally diverse companies with strong franchises and brand names. The investment objective of this fund is long-term capital growth, with minimal emphasis on income. Marsico can also own bonds and other fixed-income securities, but you should think of this fund as a pure stock offering.

ANNUALIZED RETURNS		PORTFOLIO STATISTICS	
1-Year	N/A	Beta	N/A
3-Year	N/A	Turnover	N/A
5-Year	N/A	12-Month Yield	N/A
Overall Rank	N/A	12b-1 Fee	0.25%
Risk Rank	N/A	Expense Ratio	N/A
MINIMUM INVESTMENT		**CONTACT INFORMATION**	
Regular	$2,500	*Marsico Growth & Income Fund*	
IRA	$1,000	*Telephone: (888) 860-8686*	
		www.marsicofunds.com	

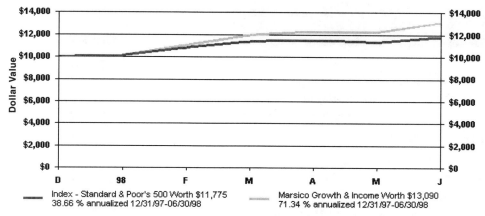

Index - Standard & Poor's 500 Worth $11,775
38.66 % annualized 12/31/97-06/30/98

Marsico Growth & Income Worth $13,090
71.34 % annualized 12/31/97-06/30/98

GROWTH OF $10,000

TOP 10 HOLDINGS	
Premier Parks	Lucent Technologies
Dell Computer	Merrill Lynch
Ford Motor	Citicorp
Volkswagen	Warner-Lambert
Pfizer	Delta & Pine Land

SMITH BREEDEN EQUITY MARKET PLUS

OBJECTIVE:	*Growth and Income*	*70*
MANAGER:	*John Sprow*	

FUND OVERVIEW:

The Smith Breeden Equity Market Plus Fund's objective is to provide a greater return than the S&P 500 without taking on any additional risk. Manager John Sprow divides the portfolio into two segments: one for the S&P 500 index and the other for fixed-income investments. Sprow doesn't generally buy individual stocks for the S&P 500 segment. Instead, he gets his equity exposure through S&P 500 futures and swaps. This generates indexlike returns without requiring any up-front money to enter into these contracts. Therefore, most of the portfolio's cash gets put to work in the fixed-income segment, namely in U.S. government, mortgage-backed, and corporate debt securities. These investments generate income and have the potential to achieve capital appreciation. The income component allows the fund to outperform the S&P 500 when properly constructed. In other words, you get the market's return (from the S&P 500 derivatives), any dividends, plus the yield and appreciation from the fixed-income instruments.

If this seems like an exotic strategy, it is. But Sprow has consistently achieved his objective with less volatility than the S&P.

ANNUALIZED RETURNS		PORTFOLIO STATISTICS	
1-Year	28.08%	Beta	0.96
3-Year	30.51%	Turnover	182.00%
5-Year	23.23%	12-Month Yield	2.89%
Overall Rank	1	12b-1 Fee	0.00%
Risk Rank	3	Expense Ratio	0.88%

MINIMUM INVESTMENT		CONTACT INFORMATION
Regular	$1,000	*Smith Breeden Equity Market Plus*
IRA	$250	*Fund*
		Telephone: (800) 221-3137
		www.smithbreeden.com

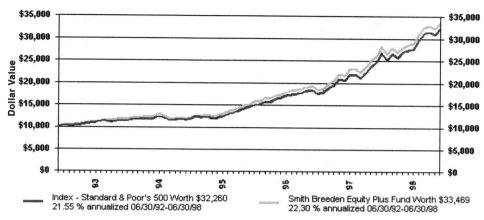

Index - Standard & Poor's 500 Worth $32,260
21.55 % annualized 06/30/92-06/30/98

Smith Breeden Equity Plus Fund Worth $33,469
22.30 % annualized 06/30/92-06/30/98

GROWTH OF $10,000

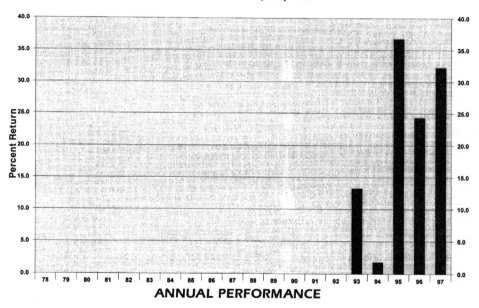

TOP 10 HOLDINGS

GNMA ARM	GNMA 7%
FHLMC TBA 6.5%	GNMA 7.5%
FNMA ARM	GNMA ARM
FHLMC 6.5%	FHLMC TBA 6%
GNMA 5%	GNMA ARM

SSgA GROWTH & INCOME

OBJECTIVE:	*Growth and Income*	**71**
MANAGER:	*L. Emerson Tuttle*	

FUND OVERVIEW:

Like many other funds in this category, SSgA Growth & Income is purely a stock portfolio. It contains a combination of small- and mid-cap companies, many of which pay only a very small dividend. Nevertheless, the fund's investment objective is to achieve both long-term capital growth and current income. Manager L. Emerson Tuttle's goal is to provide greater long-term returns than the overall U.S. equity market, without incurring more risk. His portfolio strategy combines market economics with fundamental research. He begins by assessing current economic conditions and forecasting his expectations for the coming months. Then he examines each sector in the S&P 500 index to see how it is performing relative to the overall market. Tuttle gives greater weight in the portfolio to those sectors he expects will outperform the index. In that pursuit, he selects those stocks in each sector that appear to be most attractive.

SSgA is part of State Street Global Advisors, an international investment firm with more than $280 billion in assets. The company stresses performance and expects its managers to stay ahead of the pack. Tuttle joined State Street in 1981 and is assisted by four other portfolio managers in running this fund.

ANNUALIZED RETURNS		PORTFOLIO STATISTICS	
1-Year	34.34%	Beta	0.98
3-Year	29.17%	Turnover	38.31%
5-Year	N/A	12-Month Yield	0.48%
Overall Rank	2	12b-1 Fee	0.08%
Risk Rank	3	Expense Ratio	0.94%
MINIMUM INVESTMENT		**CONTACT INFORMATION**	
Regular	$1,000	*SSgA Growth and Income Fund*	
IRA	$250	*Telephone: (800) 647-7327*	
		www.ssgafunds.com	

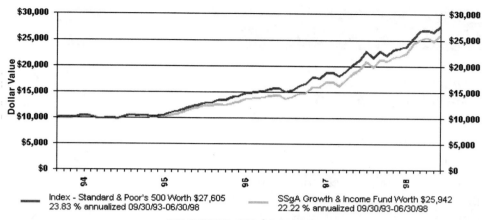

Index - Standard & Poor's 500 Worth $27,605
23.83 % annualized 09/30/93-06/30/98

SSgA Growth & Income Fund Worth $25,942
22.22 % annualized 09/30/93-06/30/98

GROWTH OF $10,000

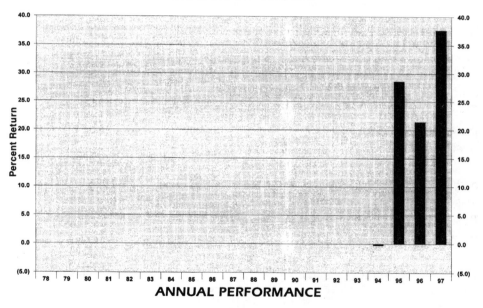

ANNUAL PERFORMANCE

TOP 10 HOLDINGS	
Northern Trust	**Linear Technology**
Alltel Corp.	**Franklin Resources**
Mobil	**Merck & Co.**
Time Warner	**Walt Disney**
Lucent Technologies	**Cisco Systems**

WARBURG PINCUS GROWTH & INCOME

OBJECTIVE:	*Growth and Income*	*72*
MANAGER:	*Brian Posner*	

FUND OVERVIEW:

Before Brian Posner took the reins of Warburg Pincus Growth & Income at the end of 1996, the fund was on a downward spiral. Assets had plummeted from $1.2 billion to $450 million as a result of lackluster performance. When Posner arrived from Fidelity Investments, he completely revamped the portfolio and made this fund a formidable challenger in the growth and income category.

Posner takes a total return approach to investing; he focuses on equities he deems to have the best risk-adjusted return prospects. He especially likes to find stocks that are temporarily depressed for cyclical or other clearly identifiable reasons. He gets positive on such companies when he also sees a management change or restructuring take place. New products and services that could add to earnings and cash flow are also desirable.

The fund's industry weightings generally approximate those of the S&P 500. Because of Posner's emphasis on risk control, this fund should be less volatile than the overall market. Incidentally, you can read more about Posner, his background, and his investment process in Chapter 2, where I take you inside the mind of one of the industry's leading fund managers.

ANNUALIZED RETURNS		PORTFOLIO STATISTICS	
1-Year	26.28%	Beta	0.89
3-Year	16.14%	Turnover	114.00%
5-Year	14.37%	12-Month Yield	0.70%
Overall Rank	3	12b-1 Fee	0.00%
Risk Rank	3	Expense Ratio	1.17%
MINIMUM INVESTMENT		**CONTACT INFORMATION**	
Regular	$2,500	*Warburg Pincus Growth & Income*	
IRA	$500	*Telephone: (800) 927-2874*	
		www.warburg.com	

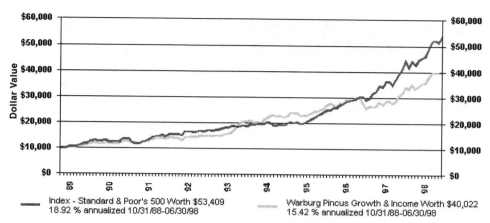

Index - Standard & Poor's 500 Worth $53,409
18.92 % annualized 10/31/88-06/30/98

Warburg Pincus Growth & Income Worth $40,022
15.42 % annualized 10/31/88-06/30/98

GROWTH OF $10,000

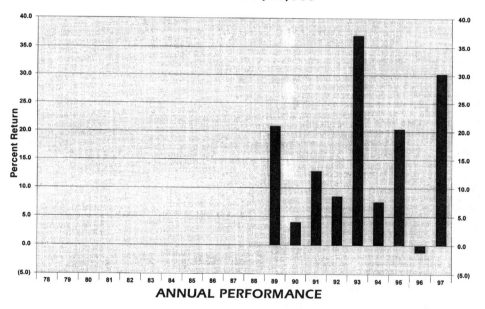

ANNUAL PERFORMANCE

TOP 10 HOLDINGS	
British Petroleum	Philip Morris
Chrysler	Citicorp
IBM	Seagate Technology
Allstate	USG Corp.
Exxon	Bell Atlantic

ASM INDEX 30

OBJECTIVE:	*Index*	**73**
MANAGER:	*Steven Adler*	

FUND OVERVIEW:

The Dow Jones Industrial Average is the benchmark most commonly used to report on the health of the overall stock market. It's also the oldest. But there are only two funds tracking this venerable index. (A majority of the rest focus on the S&P 500.) ASM Index 30, begun in 1991, has been around the longest. (The fund doesn't call itself the Dow 30 because, until recently, Dow Jones refused to license the name.)

As we discussed earlier, the Dow Jones Industrial Average consists of 30 broadly diversified blue chips companies, including JP Morgan, Merck, Walt Disney, IBM, and American Express. While the Dow has slightly underperformed the S&P 500 in recent years, over long stretches of time it has done a bit better. For those looking for a quality core holding you can hold on to for years to come, ASM Index 30 is definitely worth considering.

The fund's expense ratio has fallen considerably in recent years and now stands at 0.41 percent. Granted, that's more than most S&P 500 funds charge. But it's still far less than you would pay for a comparable actively managed large-cap offering.

ANNUALIZED RETURNS		PORTFOLIO STATISTICS	
1-Year	18.25%	Beta	1.00
3-Year	25.17%	Turnover	265.00%
5-Year	19.57%	12-Month Yield	1.50%
Overall Rank	2	12b-1 Fee	0.00%
Risk Rank	3	Expense Ratio	0.41%
MINIMUM INVESTMENT		**CONTACT INFORMATION**	
Regular	$1,000	*ASM Index 30 Fund*	
IRA	$500	*Telephone: (800) 445-2763*	

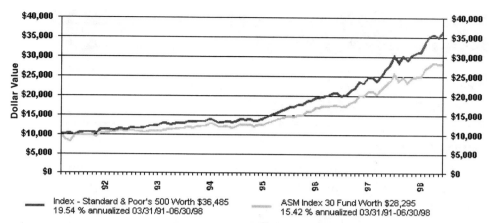

Index - Standard & Poor's 500 Worth $36,485
19.54 % annualized 03/31/91-06/30/98

ASM Index 30 Fund Worth $28,295
15.42 % annualized 03/31/91-06/30/98

GROWTH OF $10,000

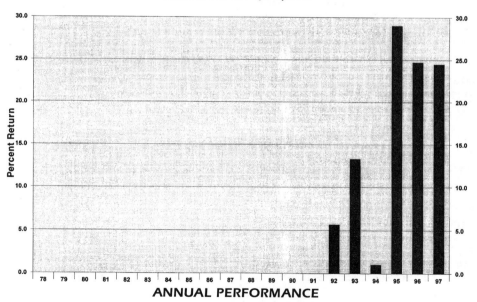

ANNUAL PERFORMANCE

TOP 10 HOLDINGS

JP Morgan	Walt Disney
IBM	American Express
Minnesota Mng. & Mfg.	ALCOA
Merch & Co.	Travelers Group
Chevron	United Technologies

BRIDGEWAY ULTRA-LARGE 35 INDEX

OBJECTIVE:	*Index*	**74**
MANAGER:	*John Montgomery*	

FUND OVERVIEW:

Bridgeway Ultra-Large 35 Index calls itself a hybrid between the Dow and S&P 500. This unique offering, which has the lowest expense ratio of any fund in this book, consists of equal percentages of the 35 largest U.S. companies, excluding tobacco stocks and allowing for industry diversification. Holdings include General Motors, GTE, Intel, AT&T, Merck, Coca-Cola, Fannie Mae, and DuPont. What's great about this fund, besides its bare-bones costs, is that manager John Montgomery runs it with an eye on keeping taxes to an absolute minimum. In fact, his goal is to never have a capital gains distribution. (The fund is fairly new, having been launched in July 1997, so it's too soon to tell how successful he is at reaching this objective.)

Bridgeway Ultra-Large 35 Index has everything you could want in a fund: Low expenses, tax efficiency, and quality management. By the way, you won't find the past performance of the index Montgomery follows anywhere. He made it up. This fund has done better than the S&P 500 since inception, an accomplishment few funds can boast about. And if the recent large-cap stock dominance continues in 1999, this fund should continue to shine.

ANNUALIZED RETURNS		PORTFOLIO STATISTICS	
1-Year	N/A	Beta	N/A
3-Year	N/A	Turnover	N/A
5-Year	N/A	12-Month Yield	N/A
Overall Rank	N/A	12b-1 Fee	0.00%
Risk Rank	N/A	Expense Ratio	N/A

MINIMUM INVESTMENT		CONTACT INFORMATION	
Regular	$2,000	*Bridgeway Ultra Large 35 Index*	
IRA	$500	*(800) 661-3550*	

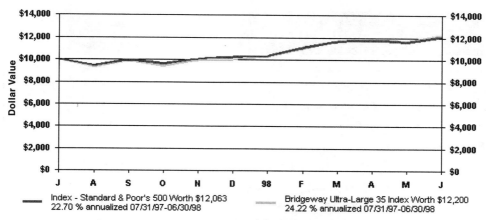

GROWTH OF $10,000

TOP 10 HOLDINGS	
General Motors	Walt Disney
GTE	Merck & Co.
DuPont	Coca-Cola
Intel	Fannie Mae
AT&T	SBC Communications

VANGUARD INDEX 500

| OBJECTIVE: | *Index* | ***75*** |
| MANAGER: | *George Sauter* | |

FUND OVERVIEW:

Vanguard Index 500 is the granddaddy of all index funds. It is the largest and best performing of the portfolios that try to replicate the price and yield performance of the S&P 500. It does so by following a computer model that guides the fund to invest in all 500 stocks in the index in approximately the exact same proportions. (The S&P 500, as you probably know by now, is dominated by large blue-chip stocks and represents approximately 70 percent of the total capitalization of all U.S. equities.) By nature, the fund will be close to fully invested at all times, holding only a tiny level of cash to meet redemptions. The fund's returns since inception have been virtually identical to the S&P 500, less Vanguard's bare-bones expense ratio.

Assuming no mass redemption requests come in, this fund should be highly tax-efficient because turnover is low. It would make a nice large-cap core holding in almost any portfolio, although I tend to prefer the Vanguard Total Stock Market Portfolio (which we will discuss next) even more, for those who want to own just one index fund. For more on the role indexing should play in your overall portfolio, you might want to reread my comments in Chapter 3.

ANNUALIZED RETURNS		PORTFOLIO STATISTICS	
1-Year	30.07%	Beta	1.00
3-Year	30.12%	Turnover	5.00%
5-Year	22.94%	12-Month Yield	1.24%
Overall Rank	1	12b-1 Fee	0.00%
Risk Rank	3	Expense Ratio	0.19%

MINIMUM INVESTMENT		CONTACT INFORMATION
Regular	$3,000	*Vanguard Index Trust 500 Portfolio*
IRA	$1,000	*Telephone: (800) 662-7447*
		www.vanguard.com

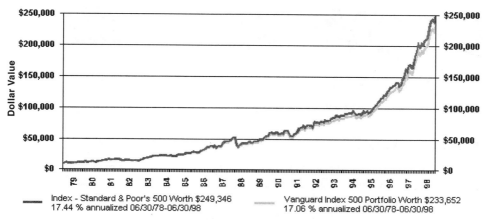

Index - Standard & Poor's 500 Worth $249,346
17.44 % annualized 06/30/78-06/30/98

Vanguard Index 500 Portfolio Worth $233,652
17.06 % annualized 06/30/78-06/30/98

GROWTH OF $10,000

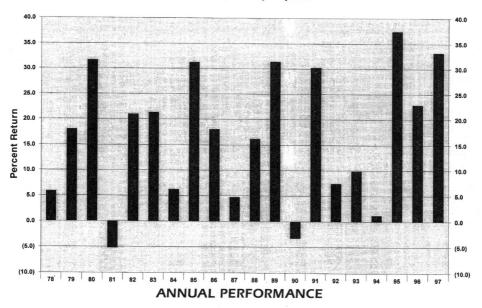

ANNUAL PERFORMANCE

TOP 10 HOLDINGS	
General Electric	Royal Dutch Pete.
Coca-Cola	Intel
Microsoft	Philip Morris
Exxon	Procter & Gamble
Merck & Co.	IBM

VANGUARD TOTAL STOCK MARKET

OBJECTIVE:	*Index*	*76*
MANAGER:	*George Sauter*	

FUND OVERVIEW:

Unlike the Vanguard Index 500 fund, which only gives you exposure to blue-chip America, Vanguard Total Stock Market allows you to invest in equities of all sizes—large and small. Although 70 percent of the portfolio looks just like the S&P 500, 20 percent is in mid-cap stocks and the remaining 10 percent is in small caps. This gives you access to the entire U.S. equity market. The fund is designed to parallel the performance of the Wilshire 5000 Index, which consists of all regularly traded U.S. stocks on the three major exchanges. However, it normally will hold only a representative sample of some 2,000 positions because the cost of owning all 5,000 would be quite high.

If you are looking for the simplest approach to gaining exposure to the entire stock market without having to do any work, this fund is a great choice. It is so diversified, it could technically be the only fund you own for your U.S. market exposure. I'm not recommending that approach, but as far as index funds are concerned, this one is my favorite. The actual manager isn't that important; the fund is run by a computer, so this can truly be a buy-and-hold investment.

ANNUALIZED RETURNS		PORTFOLIO STATISTICS	
1-Year	28.53%	**Beta**	0.95
3-Year	27.69%	**Turnover**	2.00%
5-Year	21.21%	**12-Month Yield**	1.22%
Overall Rank	1	**12b-1 Fee**	0.00%
Risk Rank	3	**Expense Ratio**	0.20%

MINIMUM INVESTMENT		CONTACT INFORMATION
Regular	$3,000	*Vanguard Total Stock Market*
IRA	$1,000	*Portfolio*
		Telephone: (800) 662-7447
		www.vanguard.com

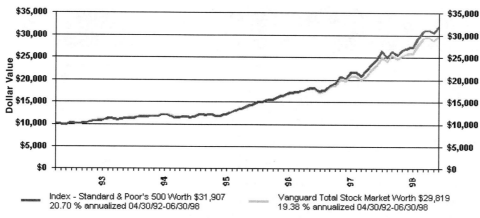

Index - Standard & Poor's 500 Worth $31,907
20.70 % annualized 04/30/92-06/30/98

Vanguard Total Stock Market Worth $29,819
19.38 % annualized 04/30/92-06/30/98

GROWTH OF $10,000

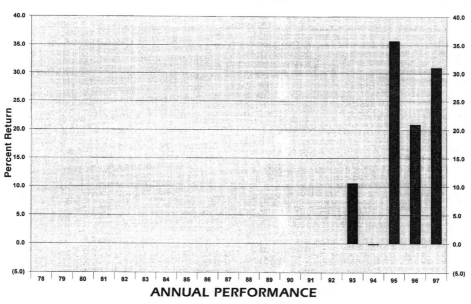

ANNUAL PERFORMANCE

TOP 10 HOLDINGS	
General Electric	**Pfizer**
Microsoft	**Intel**
Coca-Cola	**Wal-Mart Stores**
Exxon	**Procter & Gamble**
Merck & Co.	**AT&T**

DODGE & COX BALANCED

OBJECTIVE:	*Balanced*	**77**
MANAGER:	*Team Managed*	

FUND OVERVIEW:

Dodge & Cox Balanced seeks to provide regular income, protection of principal, and the opportunity for long-term appreciation in one value-oriented fund. The investment team running the portfolio changes the proportion of assets in stocks, bonds, and cash to align with expectations for future business and investment prospects. Under normal conditions, no more than 75 percent of the portfolio will be kept in stocks; the rest is mostly in bonds and other investment-grade securities. The fund's prospectus points out that "a substantial position will be maintained in common stocks which, in the view of Dodge & Cox, have a favorable outlook for long-term growth of principal and income." Prospective earnings and a dividend component are the major considerations managers use when making equity selections. Individual companies are evaluated on financial strength and the overall economic stability of the industry.

To temper volatility, investments in any one stock or bond will rarely make up more than 2 percent of total assets. Managers tend to hold on for the long haul, meaning annual turnover is low. There are some 80 stocks and 120 bonds in the portfolio, representing mostly blue-chip names and government securities.

ANNUALIZED RETURNS		PORTFOLIO STATISTICS	
1-Year	15.35%	Beta	0.56
3-Year	17.73%	Turnover	32.00%
5-Year	15.16%	12-Month Yield	3.12%
Overall Rank	3	12b-1 Fee	0.00%
Risk Rank	1	Expense Ratio	0.55%
MINIMUM INVESTMENT		**CONTACT INFORMATION**	
Regular	$2,500	*Dodge & Cox Balanced Fund*	
IRA	$1,000	*Telephone: (800) 621-3979*	

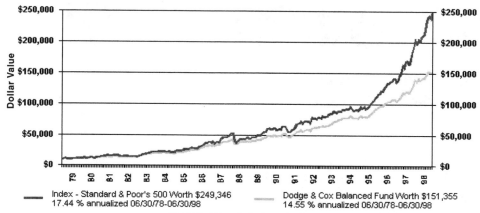

Index - Standard & Poor's 500 Worth $249,346   Dodge & Cox Balanced Fund Worth $151,355
17.44 % annualized 06/30/78-06/30/98   14.55 % annualized 06/30/78-06/30/98

GROWTH OF $10,000

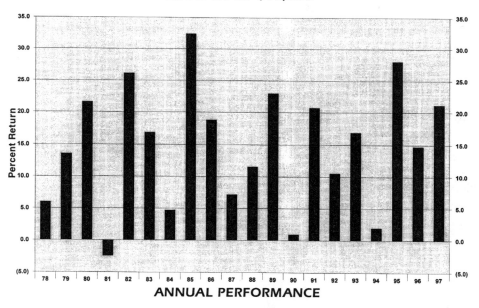

ANNUAL PERFORMANCE

TOP 10 HOLDINGS	
General Motors	K-Mart
Citicorp	Pharmacia & Upjohn
Motorola	FDX Corp.
Dow Chemical	ALCOA
American Express	Union Pacific

MONTAG & CALDWELL BALANCED

OBJECTIVE:	*Balanced*	**78**
MANAGER:	*Ronald E. Canakaris*	

FUND OVERVIEW:

Montag & Caldwell Balanced takes a total return approach to investing by spreading the fund across blue-chip companies, corporate and U.S. government bonds, and a slight reserve of cash. Instead of worrying about which asset classes to put the money to work in, manager Ronald Canakaris focuses on finding the best investments for each area of the portfolio. The fund's strategic target allocation calls for stocks to make up 50 to 70 percent of total assets, with the bulk of the rest in senior fixed-income securities. However, if Canakaris believes one asset class is exceedingly more attractive than another, he can navigate outside of these parameters.

Canakaris is positive on the outlook for stocks, assuming the economy and corporate profits continue to grow. He also believes bonds still provide attractive yields and appreciation potential. "With economic growth likely to slow and inflation well-controlled, we think there is the potential for positive bond market returns in the period ahead," he predicts. In addition to gradually lengthening maturities, he will continue to seek high-yielding corporate and agency issues. Meantime, the fund's cash component is at under 5 percent.

ANNUALIZED RETURNS		PORTFOLIO STATISTICS	
1-Year	23.85%	Beta	0.71
3-Year	22.78%	Turnover	28.13%
5-Year	N/A	12-Month Yield	1.43%
Overall Rank	2	12b-1 Fee	0.25%
Risk Rank	2	Expense Ratio	1.25%

MINIMUM INVESTMENT		CONTACT INFORMATION
Regular	$2,500	*Montag & Caldwell Balanced Fund*
IRA	$50	*Telephone: (800) 992-8151*
		www.alleghanyfunds
		.chicago-trust.com

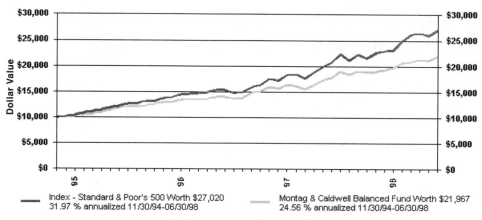

GROWTH OF $10,000

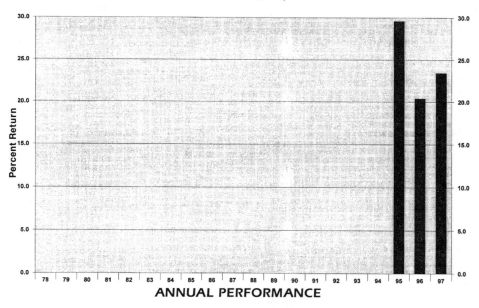

ANNUAL PERFORMANCE

TOP 10 HOLDINGS	
Cisco Systems	Coca-Cola
Gillette	Bristol-Myers Squibb
Procter & Gamble	Home Depot
Johnson & Johnson	Medtronic
Pfizer	Oracle Corp.

RAINIER BALANCED PORTFOLIO

OBJECTIVE: *Balanced*
MANAGER: *Team Managed*

79

FUND OVERVIEW:

Rainier Balanced is designed to provide long-term capital appreciation and regular income, with less return and risk than the S&P 500. The portfolio is allocated among equities, fixed-income instruments, and short-term cash equivalents. Stocks will normally make up 35 to 65 percent of the portfolio, and bonds will constitute from 30 to 55 percent. The remainder will be in cash. The management team uses a strategic asset allocation approach, putting money where it is expected to do best, given short-term trends in the economy. Shifts from one asset to another are gradual, though, and aggressive market timing is avoided.

The equity portion of the portfolio is invested by Jim Margard, who also runs another Powerhouse Performer, Rainier Core Equity (see entry 8). This fund is appropriate for conservative investors who prefer to have their stock and bond exposure in one place. Note that the fund has a minimum initial investment requirement of $25,000. I realize that's steep for most people. However, if you buy it through a no-load, no-transaction-fee program at one of the discount brokers, you can get in for as little as $2,500.

ANNUALIZED RETURNS		PORTFOLIO STATISTICS	
1-Year	21.57%	Beta	0.60
3-Year	20.67%	Turnover	133.00%
5-Year	N/A	12-Month Yield	1.72%
Overall Rank	2	12b-1 Fee	0.25%
Risk Rank	1	Expense Ratio	1.18%
MINIMUM INVESTMENT		**CONTACT INFORMATION**	
Regular	$25,000	*Rainier Balanced Portfolio*	
IRA	$25,000	*Telephone: (800) 248-6314*	

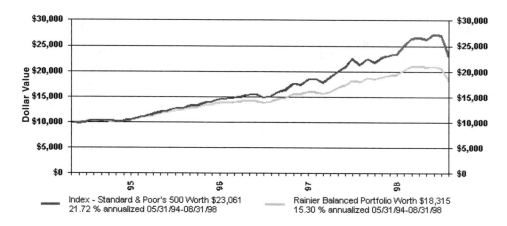

Index - Standard & Poor's 500 Worth $23,061
21.72 % annualized 05/31/94-08/31/98

Rainier Balanced Portfolio Worth $18,315
15.30 % annualized 05/31/94-08/31/98

GROWTH OF $10,000

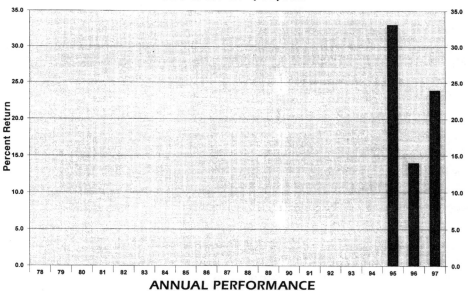

ANNUAL PERFORMANCE

TOP 10 HOLDINGS	
US Treasury Note 6.5%	Bell Atlantic
US Treasury Note 6.375%	US Treasury Note 6.5%
Microsoft	Marsh & McLennan
US Treasury Note 7.25%	US Treasury Note 7.75%
Household International	US Treasury Note 6.75%

VALUE LINE ASSET ALLOCATION

OBJECTIVE:	*Balanced*	**80**
MANAGER:	*Team Managed*	

FUND OVERVIEW:

Unlike a traditional balanced fund, which maintains a pretty steady weighting of stocks, bonds, and cash, Value Line Asset Allocation's managers shift exposure to these asset classes, depending on what their computer model tells them. What's amazing is that even though the fund has averaged less than a 50 percent exposure to equities since inception, it has managed to keep up with the S&P 500 all-stock index. And it has done so in spite of owning a highly diversified list of some 200 mostly small- and mid-cap companies across a wide variety of industries. "Our highly disciplined strategy is to invest exclusively in stocks with strong earnings and strong price momentum, quickly selling issues that fail to make the grade," fund chairman Jean Bernhard Buttner notes.

Because Value Line's proprietary stock model is currently somewhat cautious, the fund's equity exposure is slightly below its neutral benchmark of 55 percent. Another 30 percent is in U.S. Treasuries, and the remainder is resting in cash. Value Line Asset Allocation is great for investors looking for both stock and bond diversification in one fund. But if you already have elements of both in your portfolio, this fund might be redundant.

ANNUALIZED RETURNS		PORTFOLIO STATISTICS	
1-Year	28.26%	Beta	0.47
3-Year	27.55%	Turnover	58.00%
5-Year		12-Month Yield	1.37%
Overall Rank	1	12b-1 Fee	0.25%
Risk Rank	2	Expense Ratio	1.15%

MINIMUM INVESTMENT		CONTACT INFORMATION
Regular	$1,000	*Value Line Asset Allocation Fund*
IRA	$1,000	*Telephone: (800) 223-0818*
		www.valueline.com

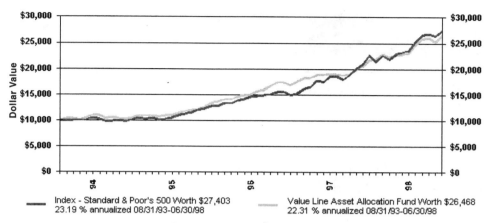

Index - Standard & Poor's 500 Worth $27,403
23.19 % annualized 08/31/93-06/30/98

Value Line Asset Allocation Fund Worth $26,468
22.31 % annualized 08/31/93-06/30/98

GROWTH OF $10,000

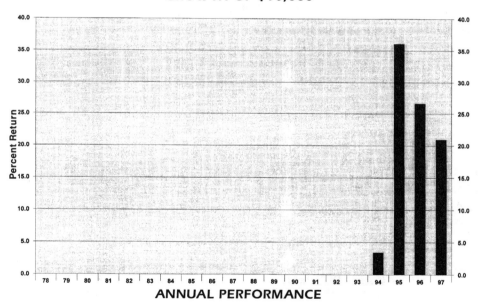

ANNUAL PERFORMANCE

TOP 10 HOLDINGS	
Russell 2000 Index (Fut.)	US Treasury Bond 7.25%
US Treasury Note 6.5%	US Treasury Note 5.875%
US Treasury Note 6.375%	S&P 400 Midcap Index (Fut.)
US Treasury Note 6.75%	FNMA Debenture 6.5%
FHLMC Debenture 7.1%	US Treasury Note 7.75%

WESTWOOD BALANCED

| **OBJECTIVE:** | *Balanced* | **81** |
| **MANAGER:** | *Susan Byrne* | |

FUND OVERVIEW:

Westwood Balanced manager Susan Byrne takes a top-down approach to investing. She begins by looking at the overall economic environment, starting with inflation. If conditions seem right for equities, she'll place up to 70 percent of the portfolio in stocks, with the remainder in fixed-income instruments and cash. Byrne also buys preferreds, real estate investment trusts (REITs), and high-grade convertible securities.

Westwood Balanced seeks to provide shareholders with both capital appreciation and current income. No less than 25 percent of the portfolio will be invested in bonds and other fixed-income instruments at all times. If Byrne believes the outlook for equities is bleak, she can temporarily put the entire portfolio in U.S. government securities, certificates of deposit, or other cash-equivalent investments to preserve capital.

A few years ago, Byrne entered into an agreement with prominent fund manager Mario Gabelli for the marketing of her Westwood family of funds. When you call for information, you'll be connected to Gabelli's office, even though he has nothing to do with the fund's management.

ANNUALIZED RETURNS		PORTFOLIO STATISTICS	
1-Year	15.33%	Beta	0.54
3-Year	20.69%	Turnover	110.00%
5-Year	17.44%	12-Month Yield	2.21%
Overall Rank	2	12b-1 Fee	0.25%
Risk Rank	1	Expense Ratio	1.36%

MINIMUM INVESTMENT		CONTACT INFORMATION	
Regular	$1,000	*Westwood Balanced*	
IRA	$1,000	*Telephone: (800) 422-3554*	
		www.gabelli.com	

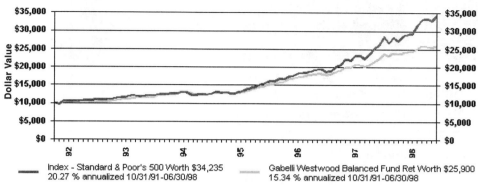

Index - Standard & Poor's 500 Worth $34,235
20.27 % annualized 10/31/91-06/30/98

Gabelli Westwood Balanced Fund Ret Worth $25,900
15.34 % annualized 10/31/91-06/30/98

GROWTH OF $10,000

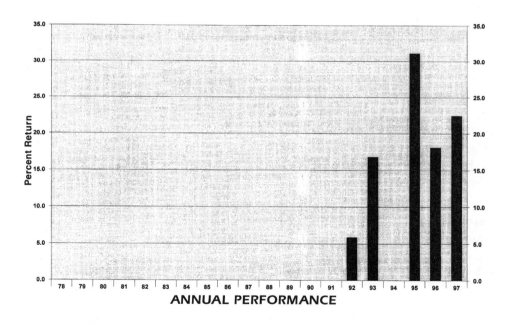

ANNUAL PERFORMANCE

TOP 10 HOLDINGS	
SBC Communications	Pennzoil
Lucent Technologies	Bell Atlantic
IBM	Tenet Healthcare
Conseco	Eaton Corp.
CVS Corp.	Campbell Soup

AMERICAN AADVANTAGE INTERNATIONAL EQUITY

OBJECTIVE:	*International*	*82*
MANAGER:	*Team Managed*	

FUND OVERVIEW:

It's not every day that you come across a fund run by an airline. AMR Investments is a multibillion-dollar asset management firm that has long run pension funds for employees of American Airlines. Several years ago, the company decided to offer its investment products to the general public by forming a series of mutual funds. International Equity is a real standout. AMR has hired the managers of three other top-notch international funds to run American AAdvantage International. The team includes Sarah Ketterer of Hotchkis & Wiley International, Dominic Caldecott of Morgan Stanley International Equity, and Gary Motyl of Franklin Capital Accumulator. Each manages one-third of the portfolio, and they all follow a value approach to selecting companies around the globe. Together, they have put together a highly diversified, mostly large-cap portfolio with some 300 names.

The managers are limited by prospectus to investing only in the more developed markets of Europe and Asia, which means you won't get much exposure to emerging countries. Note that you are best investing in the fund's "Plan Ahead" shares, which have a lower expense ratio.

ANNUALIZED RETURNS		PORTFOLIO STATISTICS	
1-Year	11.66%	Beta	0.53
3-Year	16.03%	Turnover	21.00%
5-Year	3	12-Month Yield	1.65%
Overall Rank	2	12b-1 Fee	0.00%
Risk Rank	2	Expense Ratio	1.15%

MINIMUM INVESTMENT		CONTACT INFORMATION
Regular	$2,500	*American AAdvantage International*
IRA	$2,500	*Equity Fund*
		Telephone: (800) 388-3344
		www.aafunds.com

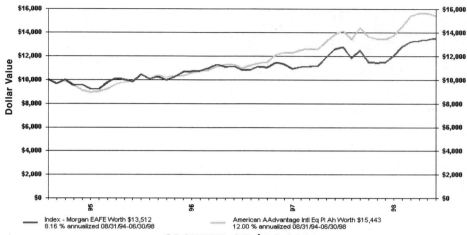

Index - Morgan EAFE Worth $13,512
8.16 % annualized 08/31/94-06/30/98

American AAdvantage Intl Eq Pl Ah Worth $15,443
12.00 % annualized 08/31/94-06/30/98

GROWTH OF $10,000

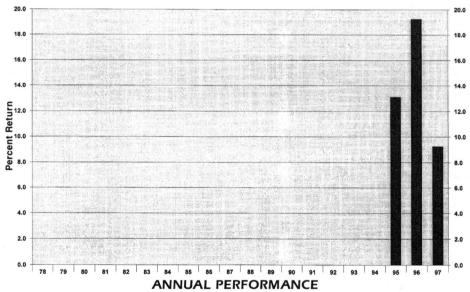

ANNUAL PERFORMANCE

TOP 10 HOLDINGS

Nestle	Sony
Akzo Nobel NV	Fuji Photo Film
Elf Aquitaine SA	Electrolux
Philips Electronics NV	Telefonica de Espana
Internationale Nederl Groep	Nycomed

AMERICAN/20TH CENTURY INTERNATIONAL DISCOVERY

OBJECTIVE:	*International*	*83*
MANAGER:	*Team Managed*	

FUND OVERVIEW:

The team that manages American/20th Century International Discovery Fund invests in foreign companies with market capitalizations of less than $1 billion. This is clearly one of the riskiest international funds you can buy; it takes overseas volatility to a new level by concentrating on unseasoned, emerging growth businesses. However, the most significant gains in foreign markets over time have come from small-cap stocks. In fact, the difference in performance between small- and large-cap equities is much more pronounced overseas than in the United States. To enhance the fund's liquidity, at least half of the portfolio's assets will be invested in developed foreign countries at all times. The rest can be dispersed among the emerging markets.

Because of the nature of this fund, and to address possible liquidity issues, American/20th Century has a hefty $10,000 minimum initial investment. It also assesses a 2 percent redemption fee on shares redeemed within 180 days, to discourage short-term trading. Therefore, this is not an investment to consider unless you have a long time horizon and a portfolio of at least $100,000 (to make sure this fund doesn't compose more than 10 percent of the total).

ANNUALIZED RETURNS		PORTFOLIO STATISTICS	
1-Year	28.94%	**Beta**	0.48
3-Year	28.87%	**Turnover**	65.00%
5-Year	N/A	**12-Month Yield**	0.18%
Overall Rank	3	**12b-1 Fee**	0.00%
Risk Rank	3	**Expense Ratio**	1.75%

MINIMUM INVESTMENT		CONTACT INFORMATION
Regular	$10,000	*American / 20th Century*
IRA	$10,000	*International Discovery Fund*
		Telephone: (800) 345-2021
		www.americancentury.com

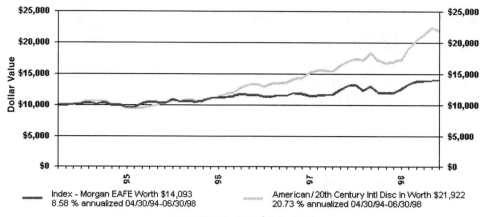

GROWTH OF $10,000

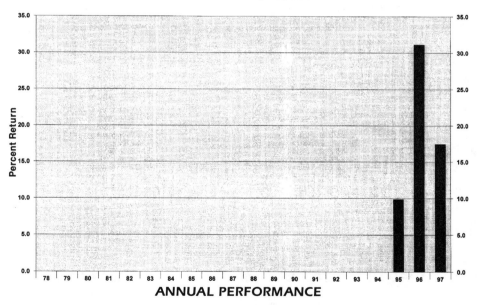

ANNUAL PERFORMANCE

TOP 10 HOLDINGS	
Marschollek Lautenschlager	Internatio-Mueller
Newcort Credit Group	Porsche
TT Tieto	Georg Fischer
Kempen & Co.	Havas Advertising
Esselte Cl B	Richemont

ARTISAN INTERNATIONAL

OBJECTIVE:	*International*
MANAGER:	*Mark Yockey*

84

FUND OVERVIEW:

Mark Yockey begins the process of investing his Artisan International Fund by looking around the world and figuring out where he would most like to put his money to work. He favors those countries with improving economic conditions, and avoids those that appear to be overvalued. He pays attention to such measures as gross domestic product growth, corporate profitability, current accounting and currency issues, and changes in interest rates. Having made those decisions, he looks for those companies best positioned to profit. He concentrates on stocks with above-average financials and accelerating earnings per share. He also keeps an eye on price, avoiding businesses trading at unsustainable or unusually high valuations.

Yockey is presently most enthusiastic about Europe, where he has invested the biggest bulk of his assets. "To our mind, Europe offers the greatest investment potential in a generation," he insists. "The reasons include privatization, deregulation, increasing competition, merger activity, and a burgeoning commitment to enhancing shareholder value." In Asia, he's most positive on Hong Kong, which he's convinced has favorable long-term prospects.

ANNUALIZED RETURNS		PORTFOLIO STATISTICS	
1-Year	13.99%	Beta	N/A
3-Year	N/A	Turnover	39.96%
5-Year	N/A	12-Month Yield	1.21%
Overall Rank	N/A	12b-1 Fee	0.00%
Risk Rank	N/A	Expense Ratio	1.41%
MINIMUM INVESTMENT		**CONTACT INFORMATION**	
Regular	$1,000	*Artisan International Fund*	
IRA	$1,000	*Telephone: (800) 344-1770*	

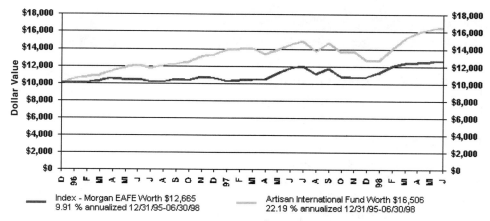

Index - Morgan EAFE Worth $12,665
9.91 % annualized 12/31/95-06/30/98

Artisan International Fund Worth $16,506
22.19 % annualized 12/31/95-06/30/98

GROWTH OF $10,000

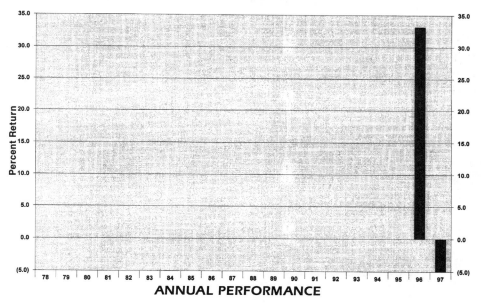

ANNUAL PERFORMANCE

TOP 10 HOLDINGS	
COLT Telecom Group	Riograndense Telecom Pfd.
Metronet Communications	Novartis
Union Bank Switzerland	Credit Suisse
Nokia Cl B	Cap Gemini
Vest-Wood	Energis

BT INTERNATIONAL EQUITY

OBJECTIVE:	*International*	**85**
MANAGER:	*Team Managed*	

FUND OVERVIEW:

There are three managers at the helm of BT International Equity: Michael Levy, Robert Reiner, and Julie Wang. They search the world for attractive investment ideas, and are currently most keen on Europe. "In our opinion, continental European markets continue to offer the best prospects, especially in France and in the periphery," the managers say. "European unification should reward companies that have taken the crucial steps required to be successful in the increasingly competitive marketplace." As a result, a large majority of the portfolio has been placed in Europe, with only small allotments to Asia. The managers view Japan as a trading market that will remain extremely volatile until serious measures are taken to restructure the economy. They also feel Southeast Asia is a risky place for investors, and thus maintain only a token weighting there.

This fund, which has one of the best records in the international growth category, invests in both large and small securities around the world. The primary emphasis, however, is on established companies in developed countries.

ANNUALIZED RETURNS		PORTFOLIO STATISTICS	
1-Year	21.00%	Beta	0.72
3-Year	23.28%	Turnover	55.00%
5-Year	20.39%	12-Month Yield	0.05
Overall Rank	3	12b-1 Fee	0.00%
Risk Rank	3	Expense Ratio	1.50%
MINIMUM INVESTMENT		**CONTACT INFORMATION**	
Regular	$2,500	*BT International Equity Fund*	
IRA	$500	*Telephone: (800) 730-1313*	

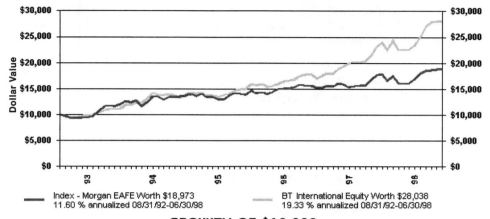

Index - Morgan EAFE Worth $18,973
11.60 % annualized 08/31/92-06/30/98

BT International Equity Worth $28,038
19.33 % annualized 08/31/92-06/30/98

GROWTH OF $10,000

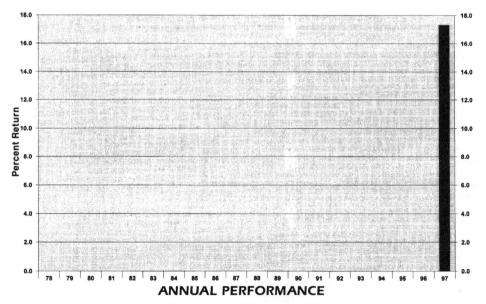

ANNUAL PERFORMANCE

TOP 10 HOLDINGS

Credito Italiano	Hagemeyer
Telecen-Communicaco Pessoais	Telecom Italia
Generale díEnterprises	Renault
Newcourt Credit Group	AXA-UAP
Banque Nationale de Paris	ING Groep

MANAGERS INTERNATIONAL EQUITY

OBJECTIVE:	*International*	**86**
MANAGER:	*Team Managed*	

FUND OVERVIEW:

Managers International Equity gives one half of the portfolio to each of two different managers: William Holzer of Scudder Kemper Investments and John Reinsberg of Lazard Asset Management. The concept is similar to the one described for American AAdvantage International Equity. Two approaches to selecting overseas investments are offered in one fund. Holzer is a top-down thematic investor who views the world as a single global economy. He first develops themes that target the fastest growing or most profitable segments. He then works with Scudder's analysts to identify companies that could benefit from the effects of these themes. Reinsberg uses a bottom-up value approach. He focuses on individual stocks that are believed to be financially strong and inexpensively priced.

The end result is a broad portfolio of names from around the world. Because part of the diversification benefit of international investing is the result of currency fluctuations, the portfolio managers don't hedge their exposure back to U.S. dollars. Both Holzer and Reinsberg are fairly conservative, take a long-term view on investing, and are normally diversified across at least three countries.

ANNUALIZED RETURNS		PORTFOLIO STATISTICS	
1-Year	15.33%	Beta	0.53
3-Year	16.53%	Turnover	37.00%
5-Year	16.18%	12-Month Yield	1.16%
Overall Rank	3	12b-1 Fee	0.00%
Risk Rank	2	Expense Ratio	1.44%

MINIMUM INVESTMENT		CONTACT INFORMATION
Regular	$2,000	*Managers International Equity*
IRA	$500	*Telephone: (800) 835-3879*
		www.managersfunds.com

Index - Morgan EAFE Worth $45,451
12.87 % annualized 12/31/85-06/30/98

Managers International Equity Fund Worth $58,987
15.25 % annualized 12/31/85-06/30/98

GROWTH OF $10,000

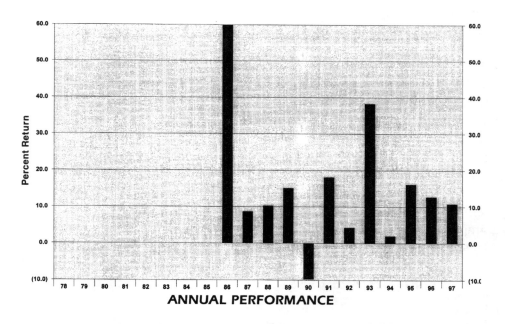

ANNUAL PERFORMANCE

TOP 10 HOLDINGS	
AXA SA	BAT Industries
Unilever	Sny
Viag AG	Nordbanken
British Aerospace	Philips Elec. Com.
Hoechst AG	Matsushita El. Ind.

OAKMARK INTERNATIONAL

| OBJECTIVE: | *International* | **87** |
| MANAGER: | *David Herro and Michael Welsh* | |

FUND OVERVIEW:

Oakmark International's David Herro and Michael Welsh are very dedicated to their value-oriented investment style. They have strict guidelines for determining whether a stock is worth buying or selling. They choose companies from around the world, that trade at a discount to current or potential free cash flow, where management will use that money to enhance shareholder value. A stock must also sell at no less than a 15 percent discount from what Herro and Welsh consider to be its fair market value. Once a holding approaches fair value, they get rid of it. Herro and Welsh feel currency is a separate issue, and will only hedge when they think the portfolio will suffer if they don't.

When evaluating an individual business, Herro and Welsh consider the relative political and economic stability in the issuer's home country, the applicable accounting practices, and the company's ownership structure. The fund invests in both mature markets (Japan, Canada, and the United Kingdom), as well as less developed areas (Mexico and Thailand), and selected emerging markets. There are no limits on the fund's geographic distribution, though Herro and Walsh are normally spread over at least five countries outside the United States.

ANNUALIZED RETURNS		PORTFOLIO STATISTICS	
1-Year	-10.77%	Beta	0.60
3-Year	11.15%	Turnover	61.28%
5-Year	10.48%	12-Month Yield	3.64%
Overall Rank	3	12b-1 Fee	0.00%
Risk Rank	3	Expense Ratio	1.26%

MINIMUM INVESTMENT		CONTACT INFORMATION	
Regular	$1,000	*Oakmark International*	
IRA	$500	*Telephone: (800) 625-6275*	
		www.oakmark.com	

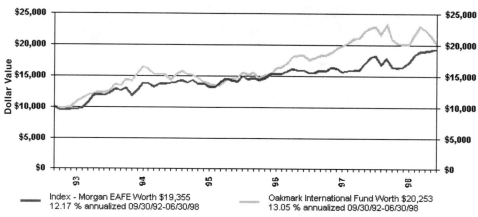

Index - Morgan EAFE Worth $19,355
12.17 % annualized 09/30/92-06/30/98

Oakmark International Fund Worth $20,253
13.05 % annualized 09/30/92-06/30/98

GROWTH OF $10,000

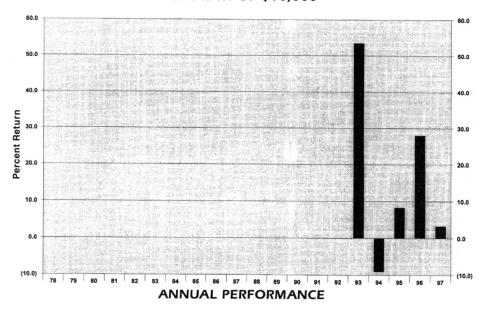

ANNUAL PERFORMANCE

TOP 10 HOLDINGS	
Saatchi & Saatchi	Guinness PLC
Sedgwick Group	Lion Nathan
Tomkins PLC	Fila Holdings
Tate & Lyle	Telecom Italia SPA
Volvo Aktiebolaget	Pernod-Ricard

FOUNDERS WORLDWIDE GROWTH

OBJECTIVE:	*Global*	**88**
MANAGER:	*Michael Gerding*	

FUND OVERVIEW:

Michael Gerding and his analysts travel the world, looking for the most attractive growth companies. He'll buy anything, anywhere, as long as it meets his criteria. To sift through the enormous international opportunities at his disposal, Gerding looks for companies with strong fundamentals, and he often meets face-to-face with managers to get to know their businesses even better. Unlike other fund managers in this category, Gerding doesn't have any target allocations to particular countries. He just looks for the most promising stocks, wherever they might be. He's allowed to invest anywhere in the world, including the United States. By charter, the fund will always diversify its assets across three or more countries, and it won't keep more than 50 percent in any one place.

Even though Gerding is a bottom-up investor, he does factor in local political, economic, and social factors when considering a potential investment. "As we look around the globe, we are finding many of the best investment opportunities in Europe," Gerding says. "As was the case in the United States, corporate restructuring in Europe will likely have a very broad impact on both countries and companies (that) will last for many years to come."

ANNUALIZED RETURNS		PORTFOLIO STATISTICS	
1-Year	14.96%	Beta	0.56
3-Year	16.08%	Turnover	82.00%
5-Year	16.55%	12-Month Yield	0.12%
Overall Rank	3	12b-1 Fee	0.25%
Risk Rank	2	Expense Ratio	1.44%

MINIMUM INVESTMENT		CONTACT INFORMATION	
Regular	$1,000	*Founders Worldwide Growth Fund*	
IRA	$500	*Telephone: (800) 232-4161*	
		www.founders.com	

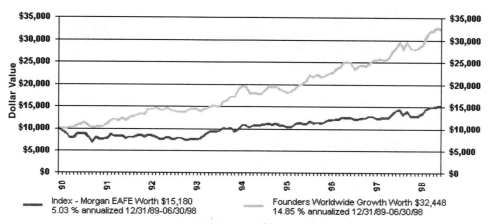

Index - Morgan EAFE Worth $15,180
5.03 % annualized 12/31/89-06/30/98

Founders Worldwide Growth Worth $32,448
14.85 % annualized 12/31/89-06/30/98

GROWTH OF $10,000

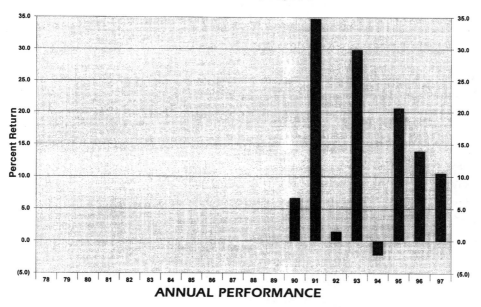

ANNUAL PERFORMANCE

TOP 10 HOLDINGS	
Ladbroke Group PLC	YPF Sociedad Anonima ADR
Credito Italiano	Baan Co NV
Sony	Total SA ADR
Marschollek Lauten	Unitas Bank
Ver Ned Uitgeversbedr	Next PLC

JANUS WORLDWIDE

| OBJECTIVE: | *Global* | **89** |
| MANAGER: | *Helen Young Hayes* | |

FUND OVERVIEW:

Janus Worldwide has been a real standout in the global fund category, and this performance has not gone unnoticed. Money is pouring in to manager Helen Young Hayes at such a rapid pace, she was forced to close Worldwide's sister fund, Janus Overseas, when assets approached $5 billion. Her reasoning was that Overseas concentrates on smaller companies outside the United States, and liquidity was starting to become an issue. But Worldwide's portfolio is some three times bigger. Is she going to close this fund too? No, says Hayes. Her rationale is that because she loads Worldwide's portfolio with larger stocks and can also include the United States in the mix, she can invest a larger asset base with ease. So far, that has been true.

Hayes doesn't base investment decisions solely on country or industry cycles, but macroeconomic trends do play a role in the selection process. She searches for companies with growing earnings and an increasing demand for their products. Hayes likes to buy stocks at a discount to their project growth rates, and she favors companies that are pumping up profits by reducing debt or restructuring. She'll unload a holding once it reaches her predetermined target.

ANNUALIZED RETURNS		PORTFOLIO STATISTICS	
1-Year	26.32%	**Beta**	0.68
3-Year	28.85%	**Turnover**	79.00%
5-Year	23.51%	**12-Month Yield**	0.39%
Overall Rank	2	**12b-1 Fee**	0.00%
Risk Rank	3	**Expense Ratio**	0.94%

MINIMUM INVESTMENT		CONTACT INFORMATION
Regular	$2,500	*Janus Worldwide Fund*
IRA	$500	*Telephone: (800) 525-3713*
		www.janus.com

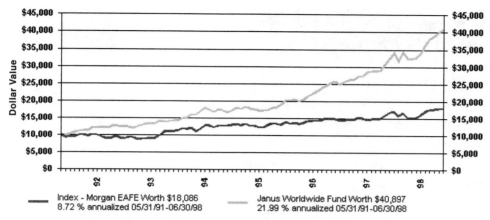

Index - Morgan EAFE Worth $18,086
8.72 % annualized 05/31/91-06/30/98

Janus Worldwide Fund Worth $40,897
21.99 % annualized 05/31/91-06/30/98

GROWTH OF $10,000

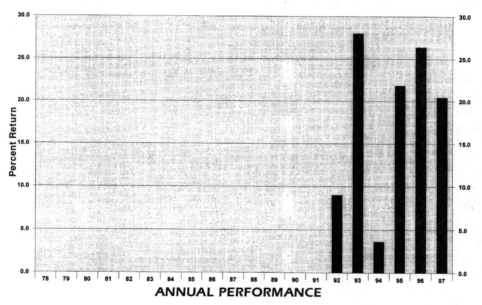

ANNUAL PERFORMANCE

TOP 10 HOLDINGS	
Philips Electronics	Nationale Elf.
Rentokil Initial ORD	Lyonnaise Des Eaux
Philips Elec. Com.	Volkswagen
Akzo NV	Monsanto
Siebe PLC	Cap Gemini Sogeti ORD

MONTGOMERY SELECT 50

OBJECTIVE:	*Global*	*90*
MANAGER:	*Team Managed*	

FUND OVERVIEW:

Montgomery Select 50 gives you access to the best ideas from Montgomery Asset Management's top portfolio managers. Each of the firm's five investment teams picks the best ideas from their individual areas of expertise, which include growth, micro-cap, equity income, international, and emerging markets. This means you get a portfolio with companies of all sizes and industries, located around the globe.

"Because of this built-in diversification, these seasoned Montgomery managers can be less concerned about how their stock picks will ultimately fit within the context of the fund's other holdings," says Kevin Hamilton, chair of Select 50's oversight committee. "Instead, they are free to choose those securities that they believe truly offer the greatest potential for growth."

I have found that most managers only have a small handful of truly great ideas at any one time, so this concept makes a great deal of sense. And Montgomery's managers are all very experienced. Therefore, rather than buying any individual fund from the family, I prefer this aggressive offering, which gives investors access to the firm's most promising ideas.

ANNUALIZED RETURNS		PORTFOLIO STATISTICS	
1-Year	15.43%	Beta	N/A
3-Year	N/A	Turnover	157.93%
5-Year	N/A	12-Month Yield	N/A
Overall Rank	N/A	12b-1 Fee	0.00%
Risk Rank	N/A	Expense Ratio	1.82%
MINIMUM INVESTMENT		**CONTACT INFORMATION**	
Regular	$1,000	*Montgomery Select 50 Fund*	
IRA	$1,000	*Telephone: (800) 572-3863*	
		www.montgomeryfunds.com	

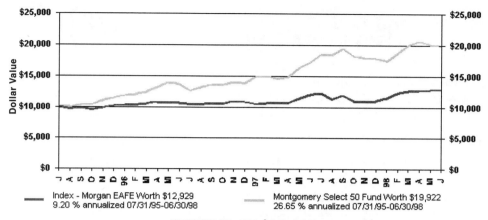

GROWTH OF $10,000

Index - Morgan EAFE Worth $12,929
9.20 % annualized 07/31/95-06/30/98

Montgomery Select 50 Fund Worth $19,922
26.65 % annualized 07/31/95-06/30/98

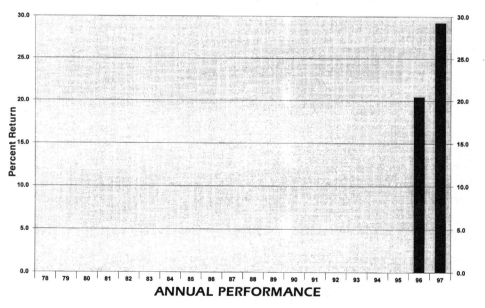

ANNUAL PERFORMANCE

TOP 10 HOLDINGS	
Mannesmann	ING Groep
Akbank Turk Anonim Sirketi	Cooper
Bank Leumi Le-Israel	Transporta Gas Sur B
Brisa Auto-Estradas	Telecom Italia
Philips Electronics	HA-LO Industries

TWEEDY, BROWNE GLOBAL VALUE

| OBJECTIVE: | *Global* | *91* |
| MANAGER: | *Team Managed* | |

FUND OVERVIEW:

Tweedy, Browne Global Value's three managers apply the time-tested value approach of the late Benjamin Graham to international investing. Graham, a former Columbia University Business School professor, wrote the 1934 classic *Security Analysis*. He suggested buying companies that could be had for a minimum 40 percent discount from their true intrinsic value. He also advised paying attention to price-to-earnings ratios, book value, and similar benchmarks. This is the same discipline these managers follow at their other Powerhouse Performer fund, American Value (see entry 42). The difference is that this portfolio is made up mostly of foreign securities, although you will find a few U.S. companies inside as well.

You could argue that this is one of the less risky international offerings available, because all overseas investments are hedged back to the U.S. dollar. This eliminates currency risk, which can be either good or bad, depending on the direction of the dollar. When the dollar is declining, you're better off in an unhedged fund because the return from currency fluctuations alone will be impressive. Conservative investors wanting international exposure should feel very comfortable entrusting their money to Tweedy, Browne.

ANNUALIZED RETURNS		PORTFOLIO STATISTICS	
1-Year	21.32%	Beta	0.53
3-Year	22.94%	Turnover	8.00%
5-Year	18.07%	12-Month Yield	4.45%
Overall Rank	2	12b-1 Fee	0.00%
Risk Rank	2	Expense Ratio	1.42%
MINIMUM INVESTMENT		**CONTACT INFORMATION**	
Regular	$2,500	*Tweedy, Browne Global Value Fund*	
IRA	$500	*Telephone: (800) 432-4789*	

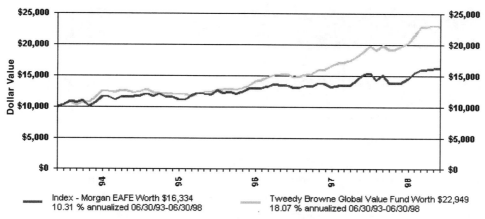

GROWTH OF $10,000

Index - Morgan EAFE Worth $16,334
10.31 % annualized 06/30/93-06/30/98

Tweedy Browne Global Value Fund Worth $22,949
18.07 % annualized 06/30/93-06/30/98

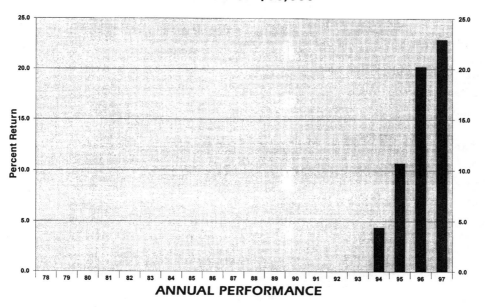

ANNUAL PERFORMANCE

TOP 10 HOLDINGS	
Nestle	Akzo NV
Pharmacia & Upjohn	Chase Manhattan
Unilever NV	BTR PLC
Matsushita Elec. Indl. Ltd.	Lehman Brothers
Kone Corp.	Fuji Photo Film

LOOMIS SAYLES BOND

OBJECTIVE:	*Corporate Bond (Intermediate)*	*92*
MANAGER:	*Daniel J. Fuss*	

FUND OVERVIEW:

Loomis Sayles Bond manager Daniel J. Fuss is one of the best fixed-income investors around. He strives to generate a high total return through a combination of current income and capital appreciation. He invests most of his fund's assets in bonds, although up to 20 percent of the portfolio can be placed in preferred stocks. The fixed-income side can include corporate and U.S. government obligations, plus commercial paper, zero coupon bonds, and mortgage-backed securities. In addition, the prospectus allows Fuss to invest up to 20 percent of the portfolio overseas, and up to 35 percent in junk bonds. Fuss isn't shy about exploiting this flexibility when he think conditions warrant it. In early 1998, for example, he was busy looking for battered bargains in Southeast Asia and Latin America.

Loomis Sayles Bond should be viewed as a long-term investment because the securities tend to have extended maturities, and thus a heightened degree of volatility. You'll notice the fund's minimum investment is $250,000. However, that can be reduced to just $2,500 by going through one of the many brokerage firm no-load, no-transaction-fee programs.

ANNUALIZED RETURNS		PORTFOLIO STATISTICS	
1-Year	10.93%	Beta	N/A
3-Year	N/A	Turnover	N/A
5-Year	N/A	12-Month Yield	6.05%
Overall Rank	N/A	12b-1 Fee	0.25%
Risk Rank	N/A	Expense Ratio	N/A

MINIMUM INVESTMENT		CONTACT INFORMATION	
Regular	$250,000	*Loomis Sayles Bond Fund*	
IRA	$250,000	*Telephone: (800) 633-3330*	
		www.loomissayles.com	

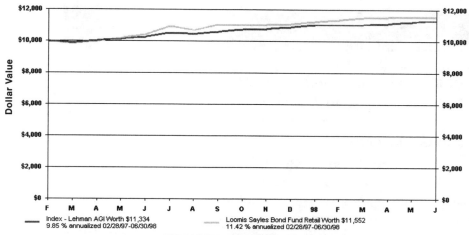

Index - Lehman AGI Worth $11,334
9.85 % annualized 02/28/97-06/30/98

Loomis Sayles Bond Fund Retail Worth $11,552
11.42 % annualized 02/28/97-06/30/98

GROWTH OF $10,000

TOP 10 HOLDINGS	
Canadian Govt. 0%	Republic Brazil 10.125%
FNMA 0%	TCI Comm. Inc. 7.875%
Philip Morris Cos. 7.75%	Time Warner 7.57%
Province Manitoba 6.5%	US Treasury 6%
Province Manitoba 7.75%	US Treasury 6.25%

STRONG CORPORATE BOND

| **OBJECTIVE:** | *Corporate Bond (Intermediate)* | *93* |
| **MANAGER:** | *Jeffrey Koch and John Bender* | |

FUND OVERVIEW:

The Strong Corporate Bond Fund is designed for investors seeking a high level of current income with a moderate degree of share price fluctuation. This is not a short-term parking place for your money. Instead, it is designed to be part of the fixed-income mix of a long-term portfolio. The fund doesn't come with any specific maturity restrictions, but the fund's average maturity will normally be in the 7- to 12-year range. At least 65 percent of the portfolio's total assets will usually be invested in the bonds of corporate issuers. The rest can be in any type of fixed-income security, such as U.S. government and mortgage-backed issues. A majority of the fund is placed in investment-grade debt obligations—those rated BBB or higher by Standard & Poor's. Up to 25 percent can be invested in lower-grade junk bonds and preferred stocks.

Managers Jeffrey Koch and John Bender believe careful research is paramount to their success. They use intense analysis to uncover securities that are ignored, dismissed, or underappreciated by other investors. Koch and Bender feel they can add the most value by attempting to be positioned in the right industries and sectors of the market at the right time.

ANNUALIZED RETURNS		PORTFOLIO STATISTICS	
1-Year	12.58%	Beta	1.18
3-Year	10.61%	Turnover	542.40%
5-Year	10.26%	12-Month Yield	6.43%
Overall Rank	1	12b-1 Fee	0.00%
Risk Rank	5	Expense Ratio	1.00%
MINIMUM INVESTMENT		**CONTACT INFORMATION**	
Regular	$2,500	*Strong Corporate Bond Fund*	
IRA	$250	*Telephone: (800) 368-1683*	
		www.strong-funds.com	

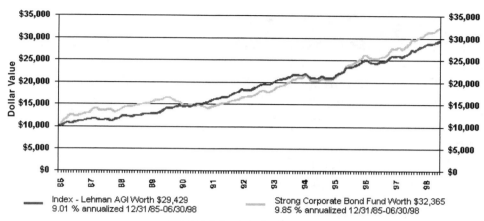

Index - Lehman AGI Worth $29,429
9.01 % annualized 12/31/85-06/30/98

Strong Corporate Bond Fund Worth $32,365
9.85 % annualized 12/31/85-06/30/98

GROWTH OF $10,000

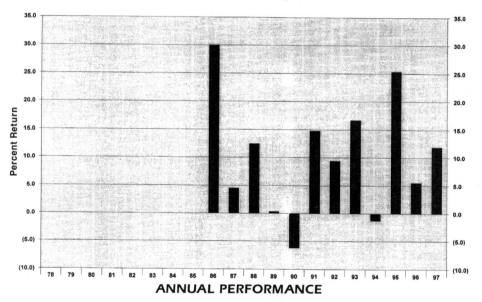

ANNUAL PERFORMANCE

TOP 10 HOLDINGS	
ARA Svcs. Inc. 10.625%	Socgen Real Estate 7.64%
Banco Sud Amer. 7.6%	Time Warner Ent. 8.375%
Cablevision Sys. 8.125%	US Treasury 6.5%
Gruma SA de CV 7.625%	US Treasury 6.625%
Mohegan Tribal Gm 13.5%	Worldcom Inc. 8.88%

LEXINGTON GNMA

OBJECTIVE:	*Mortgage-Backed Securities (Intermediate)*	**94**
MANAGER:	*Denis Jamison*	

FUND OVERVIEW:

If you're looking for high current yield, credit safety, and liquidity, few investments compare to mortgage-backed Government National Mortgage Association (GNMA) certificates, or Ginnie Maes. The GNMA is a U.S. government agency that pools mortgages together and sells them in the form of certificates. Each certificate represents an undivided part-ownership in one of these pools. Every mortgage in the pool is guaranteed by a certain government agency, meaning they are very safe. In fact, Ginnie Maes and the other securities in the Lexington GNMA portfolio are guaranteed as to the timely payment of principal and interest by Uncle Sam.

Still, the price and yield of shares in the fund will fluctuate with interest rates. GNMAs are also subject to early prepayments from homeowners wishing to refinance their loans at lower rates. High prepayments will have a negative impact on the fund's relative performance. And because prepayments tend to get reinvested at lower yields, the dividend-per-share payouts will be reduced. You shouldn't expect to see much overall volatility, in this fund and you will enjoy a generous yield that currently comes in at around 7 percent.

ANNUALIZED RETURNS		PORTFOLIO STATISTICS	
1-Year	10.13%	Beta	0.65
3-Year	8.27%	Turnover	134.28%
5-Year	6.92%	12-Month Yield	5.87%
Overall Rank	1	12b-1 Fee	0.00%
Risk Rank	2	Expense Ratio	1.01%
MINIMUM INVESTMENT		**CONTACT INFORMATION**	
Regular	$1,000	*Lexington GNMA Income Fund*	
IRA	$1,000	*Telephone: (800) 526-0056*	

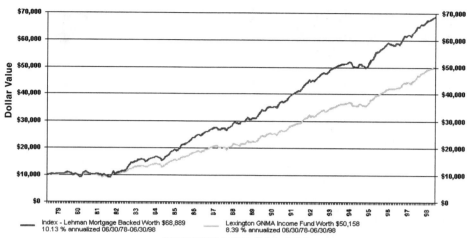

Index - Lehman Mortgage Backed Worth $68,889
10.13 % annualized 06/30/78-06/30/98

Lexington GNMA Income Fund Worth $50,158
8.39 % annualized 06/30/78-06/30/98

GROWTH OF $10,000

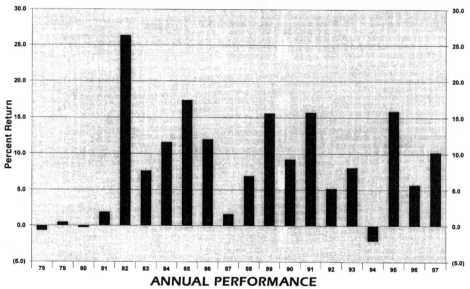

ANNUAL PERFORMANCE

TOP 10 HOLDINGS	
GNMA 7%	GNMA 7%
GNMA 6.5%	GNMA Project Loan 8.2%
GNMA Project Loan 8.15%	GNMA 9.25%
US Treasury Note 5.75%	GNMA 7.875%
GNMA 8.125%	GNMA 8.125%

VANGUARD GNMA

OBJECTIVE:	*Mortgage-Backed Securities (Intermediate)*	
MANAGER:	*Paul D. Kaplan*	

FUND OVERVIEW:

Here's another vehicle for capturing monthly income, liquidity, and relative safety through investing in a portfolio of mortgage-backed Government National Mortgage Association (GNMA) certificates, or Ginnie Maes. You'll remember from the previous profile that the GNMA is a U.S. government agency that pools mortgages together and sells them in the form of certificates. These pools are guaranteed by the government. What's the difference between the Vanguard and Lexington funds? Not much. Both are excellent choices. In fact, even though Lexington's expense ratio is slightly higher, the performance of the two funds has been almost identical. The one advantage to the Lexington fund is its availability through many of the no-load, no-transaction-fee programs. You have to pay a commission to purchase the Vanguard GNMA through a discount broker.

The other difference of note is that Vanguard GNMA's manager, Paul Kaplan, considers himself to be a bargain hunter. He buys issues that he feels offer the best relative value. He also runs the portfolio with an eye toward reducing its exposure to interest-rate risk.

ANNUALIZED RETURNS		PORTFOLIO STATISTICS	
1-Year	8.91%	Beta	0.80
3-Year	8.00%	Turnover	3.00%
5-Year	6.96%	12-Month Yield	6.80%
Overall Rank	1	12b-1 Fee	0.00%
Risk Rank	3	Expense Ratio	0.30%

MINIMUM INVESTMENT		CONTACT INFORMATION
Regular	$3,000	*Vanguard GNMA Portfolio*
IRA	$3,000	*Telephone: (800) 662-7447*
		www.vanguard.com

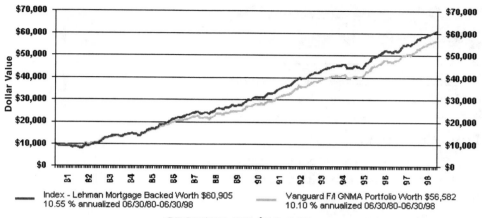

GROWTH OF $10,000

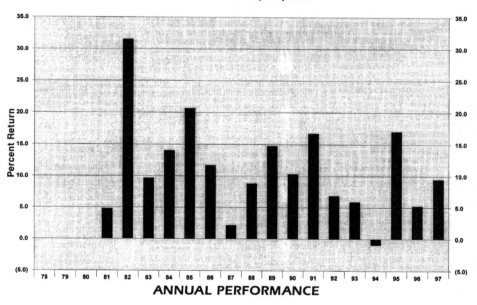

ANNUAL PERFORMANCE

TOP 10 HOLDINGS	
GNMA 6%	GNMA 8%
GNMA 6.5%	GNMA 8.25%
GNMA 7%	GNMA 8.5%
GNMA 7.5%	GNMA 9%
GNMA 7.75%	GNMA 9.5%

STRONG GOVERNMENT SECURITIES

		96
OBJECTIVE:	*General Government Bond*	
MANAGER:	*Bradley Tank and John Bender*	

FUND OVERVIEW:

The Strong Government Securities Fund works to produce a high level of current income with a moderate degree of share price fluctuation. It is appropriate for investors who need a greater level of monthly income than shorter-term funds can provide, but wish to enjoy the low credit risk associated with securities backed by the U.S. government.

Managers Bradley Tank and John Bender will normally keep at least 90 percent of the fund's assets in U.S. government securities at all times, with the remainder in other investment-grade debt obligations. There are no maturity restrictions on the portfolio, although the average maturity is usually between 5 and 10 years. "Our fixed-income management process includes a top-down analysis of the economy, interest rates, and the supply of and demand for credit," Tank explains. "We then conduct a rigorous security analysis of any issue we're considering."

One advantage to this fund is that, by law, interest income earned from U.S. Treasury securities is exempt from state and local taxes, which is good for investors in high-tax states.

ANNUALIZED RETURNS		PORTFOLIO STATISTICS	
1-Year	10.13%	Beta	0.97
3-Year	7.54%	Turnover	474.90%
5-Year	6.94%	12-Month Yield	5.64%
Overall Rank	2	12b-1 Fee	0.00%
Risk Rank	3	Expense Ratio	0.80%
MINIMUM INVESTMENT		**CONTACT INFORMATION**	
Regular	$2,500	*Strong Corporate Bond Fund*	
IRA	$250	*Telephone: (800) 368-1683*	
		www.strong-funds.com	

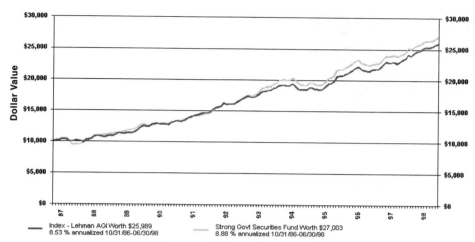

Index - Lehman AGI Worth $25,989
8.53 % annualized 10/31/86-06/30/98

Strong Govt Securities Fund Worth $27,003
8.88 % annualized 10/31/86-06/30/98

GROWTH OF $10,000

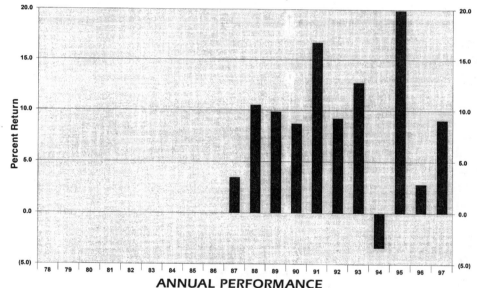

ANNUAL PERFORMANCE

TOP 10 HOLDINGS

FHA Project Loan 7.4%
FNMA 6.103%
FNMA 7.778%
GNMA 6%
GNMA 9%

Socgen Real Est. 7.64%
US Treasury 6.25%
US Treasury 6.5%
US Treasury 6.625%

STRONG HIGH-YIELD MUNICIPAL BOND

OBJECTIVE:	*Federal Municipal Bond*	*97*
MANAGER:	*Mary-Kay H. Bourbulas*	

FUND OVERVIEW:

Investors seeking income that is federally tax-exempt should consider the Strong High-Yield Municipal Bond Fund. This portfolio invests primarily in long-term, medium- and lower-quality municipal obligations. There are no maturity restrictions; the fund's average portfolio maturity is between 15 and 25 years, which means its share price will fluctuate significantly as interest rates change.

"Our goal is to deliver steady performance by diversifying our investments with respect to position size, sectors, and state concentration," explains portfolio manager Mary-Kay Bourbulas. "Another element of our strategy is keeping a comfortable portion of the portfolio in liquid, rated municipal issues." Bourbulas likes to invest along themes that she believes offer solid growth potential. The most prominent one is the aging of America, which got her interested in hospitals, retirement facilities, and assisted-living centers. "Before we purchase any unrated bond, we conduct thorough research," she adds. "The research process is essential to identifying issues that are attractive on their own merits, regardless of changes in interest rates or in the economy's growth."

ANNUALIZED RETURNS		PORTFOLIO STATISTICS	
1-Year	12.05%	Beta	1.01
3-Year	9.55%	Turnover	42.20%
5-Year	N/A	12-Month Yield	5.63%
Overall Rank	1	12b-1 Fee	0.00%
Risk Rank	3	Expense Ratio	0.69%

MINIMUM INVESTMENT		CONTACT INFORMATION
Regular	$2,500	*Strong High-Yield Municipal*
IRA	$250	*Bond Fund*
		Telephone: (800) 368-1683
		www.strong-funds.com

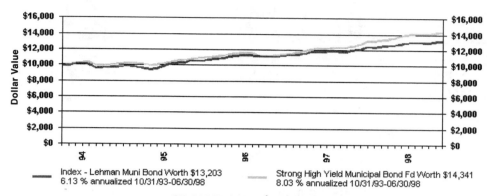

Index - Lehman Muni Bond Worth $13,203
6.13 % annualized 10/31/93-06/30/98

Strong High Yield Municipal Bond Fd Worth $14,341
8.03 % annualized 10/31/93-06/30/98

GROWTH OF $10,000

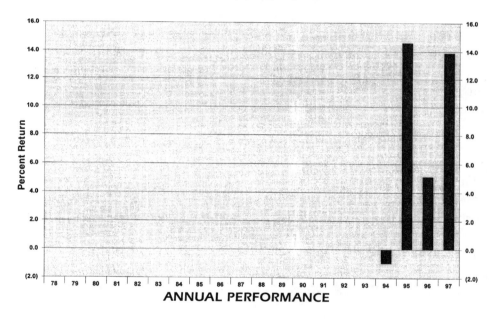

ANNUAL PERFORMANCE

TOP 10 HOLDINGS

AL Public Park Auth. 8%	ND Hlth Facl. Rev. 8.875%
IA Mort Elder Care 8.75%	PA Auth Hlth. Rev. 9%
IL Exposition Auth. 7%	PA IDA CDA Hlth 8.375%
IN EDR MFHR Apts. 8.75%	PA IDA Revenue 8%
NC HFC Revenue 8.5%	WI Hlth. & Edu. Facl. 8%

NORTHEAST INVESTORS TRUST

OBJECTIVE:	*High-Yield Corporate*	*98*
MANAGER:	*Ernest Monrad and Bruce Monrad*	

FUND OVERVIEW:

The father-and-son team of Ernest and Bruce Monrad tries to generate income for shareholders through investing in both corporate bonds and stocks. But, unlike other managers of funds of this nature, the Monrads also try to achieve as much capital appreciation as possible. The proportions of stocks and bonds vary based on market conditions. Since 1970, about 80 percent of all assets have been held in fixed-income securities, preferred stocks, and cash. Only a small portion has been put in common stocks, usually for liquidity purposes and to increase the potential for capital gains. The Monrads also avoid keeping more than 25 percent of the portfolio exposed to any one industry.

A combination of in-house and Wall Street research is used for selecting and evaluating securities for the fund. The Monrads place heavy emphasis on value. When they find an attractive bond, they'll also consider adding shares of the company's stock if the price is right. As an added booster, the Monrads can use leverage, borrowing up to 25 percent of the portfolio's net assets. This enhances the fund's buying power when they are bullish, and gives them adequate cash to meet redemptions without having to liquidate any holdings.

ANNUALIZED RETURNS		PORTFOLIO STATISTICS	
1-Year	12.63%	Beta	0.07
3-Year	15.24%	Turnover	33.44%
5-Year	13.55%	12-Month Yield	8.08%
Overall Rank	1	12b-1 Fee	0.00%
Risk Rank	3	Expense Ratio	0.64%
MINIMUM INVESTMENT		**CONTACT INFORMATION**	
Regular	$1,000	*Northeast Investors Trust*	
IRA	$1,000	*Telephone: (800) 225-6704*	

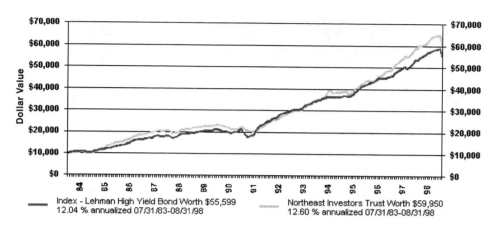

Index - Lehman High Yield Bond Worth $55,599
12.04 % annualized 07/31/83-08/31/98

Northeast Investors Trust Worth $59,950
12.60 % annualized 07/31/83-08/31/98

GROWTH OF $10,000

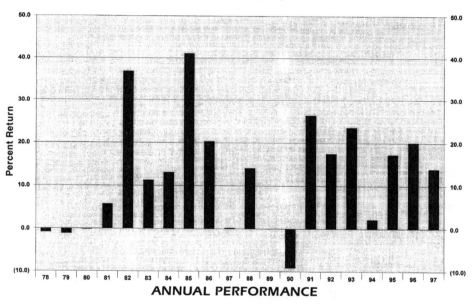

ANNUAL PERFORMANCE

TOP 10 HOLDINGS

American Standard 10.5%	Republic of Brazil 6.77%
Americold Corp B 11.5%	Rockefeller Center 0%
Argentina 9.75%	Specialty Foods 10.25%
Boyd Gaming 9.5%	Stone Container 12.58%
Gaylord Container 12.75%	Trump Atlantic City 11.25%

STRONG HIGH-YIELD BOND

OBJECTIVE:	*High-Yield Corporate*	**99**
MANAGER:	*Jeffrey Koch*	

FUND OVERVIEW:

Strong High-Yield Bond Fund manager Jeffrey Koch follows a straight-forward discipline. "Our approach to investing in the high-yield market begins with a top-down review of macroeconomic factors likely to influence both the real economy and financial asset prices," he says. "Among others, these factors include worldwide economic growth, inflation, interest rates, monetary policy, fiscal policy, and governmental regulation." Once Koch formulates an opinion on these factors, he positions the portfolio accordingly. "Because the success of an investment in a high-yield bond is ultimately a result of the issuer's creditworthiness, our research analysts rigorously examine the fundamentals of all of the securities in which we invest," he adds.

Strong High-Yield Bond primarily owns medium- and lower-quality corporate debt obligations, or junk bonds, in the pursuit of current income and capital growth. It offers both a higher yield and a greater degree of risk than other bond funds. In addition, keep in mind that high-yield bonds tend to be impacted more by the economy than interest rates, which makes them especially unattractive in times of recession.

ANNUALIZED RETURNS		PORTFOLIO STATISTICS	
1-Year	15.02%	Beta	N/A
3-Year	N/A	Turnover	390.80%
5-Year	N/A	12-Month Yield	8.45%
Overall Rank	N/A	12b-1 Fee	0.00%
Risk Rank	N/A	Expense Ratio	0.60%

MINIMUM INVESTMENT		CONTACT INFORMATION
Regular	$2,500	*Strong High-Yield Bond Fund*
IRA	$250	*Telephone: (800) 368-1683*
		www.strong-funds.com

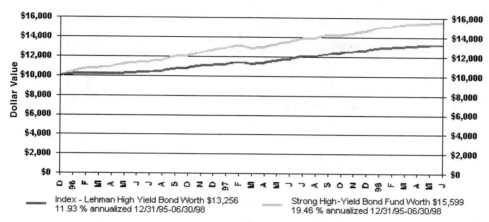

Index - Lehman High Yield Bond Worth $13,256
11.93 % annualized 12/31/95-06/30/98

Strong High-Yield Bond Fund Worth $15,599
19.46 % annualized 12/31/95-06/30/98

GROWTH OF $10,000

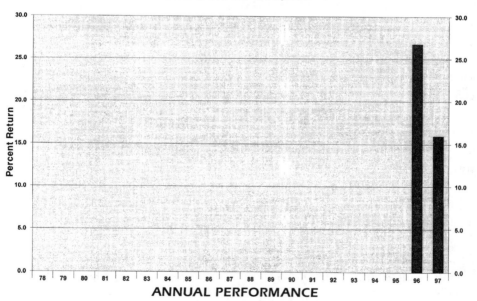

ANNUAL PERFORMANCE

TOP 10 HOLDINGS

Bay View Capital 9.125%
Food 4 Less Hldgs. 13.625%
Nextel Comm Step 0%
Chancellor Media 144A Pfd. 12%
Verio 144A (Unit) 13.5%

Nextlink Comm. 12.5%
Time Warner Cl K Pfd. 10.25%
USAir 9.625%
Atlas Air 10.75%
Jordan Telecom 144A Step 0%

VALUE LINE AGGRESSIVE INCOME TRUST

OBJECTIVE:	*High-Yield Corporate*	**100**
MANAGER:	*Team Managed*	

FUND OVERVIEW:

Value Line Aggressive Income invests primarily in lower-rated, fixed-income securities issued by smaller and unseasoned companies. These securities are otherwise known as "junk bonds." You take more risk that your money will be returned, and therefore are compensated by a higher yield. The fund's objective is to maximize current income. Capital appreciation, although a secondary consideration, can come from the improved credit rating of a company in the portfolio or from lower interest rates in general. At least 80 percent of the bonds in this fund are rated B++ or lower by the *Value Line Investment Survey.* The rest of the mix may include U.S. government securities, convertible bonds, and warrants. Value Line follows about 3,500 companies, which are rated from A++ to C. Companies with the best financial strength are given an A++, followed by A+, and so on. Those rated C usually have serious financial troubles. The bonds in this fund are right on the border.

You face many risks when investing in junk bonds, including limited liquidity. That's why it's important to own a number of different issues in a fund like this, to quell volatility.

ANNUALIZED RETURNS		PORTFOLIO STATISTICS	
1-Year	12.52%	Beta	0.40
3-Year	16.35%	Turnover	276.00%
5-Year	11.85%	12-Month Yield	8.69%
Overall Rank	1	12b-1 Fee	0.00%
Risk Rank	4	Expense Ratio	1.10%
MINIMUM INVESTMENT		**CONTACT INFORMATION**	
Regular	$1,000	*Value Line Aggressive Income Trust*	
IRA	$1,000	*Telephone: (800) 223-0818*	
		www.valueline.com	

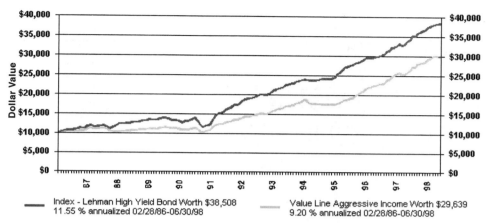

Index - Lehman High Yield Bond Worth $38,508
11.55 % annualized 02/28/86-06/30/98

Value Line Aggressive Income Worth $29,639
9.20 % annualized 02/28/86-06/30/98

GROWTH OF $10,000

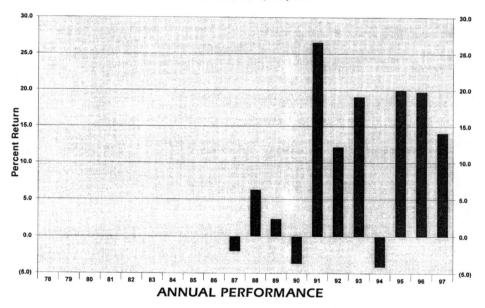

ANNUAL PERFORMANCE

TOP 10 HOLDINGS

Primus Telecomm 11.75%   National Energy 10.75%
IXC Communications 12.5%   Sprint Spectrum Step 0%
Cort Furniture Rental 12%   Spanish Brdcst. 144A 14.25%
Colt Telecom (Unit) Step 0%   Ocwen Financial 11.875%
National Energy 10.75%   Rogers Cablesystems 10%

7

PUTTING YOUR
PORTFOLIO TOGETHER

Now that you know what mutual funds are, how they work, what to look for when choosing them, and which ones appear to be most promising for the year ahead, it's time to put together your own personal investment plan. In a moment, I'll give you an asset allocation test, to help you determine which types of funds might be most appropriate for you, given your stage in life and your comfort level. Then I will reveal my specific portfolio recommendations (complete with the precise percentage allocations to selected funds from the Powerhouse Performers list) that correspond to your score on the test.

WHAT IS ASSET ALLOCATION?

═══ You may have heard the term *asset allocation* before. But what exactly does it mean? In a nutshell, asset allocation is the process of figuring out how much of your investment capital should be placed in each of the three main asset classes: stocks, bonds, and cash. (I'm leaving out precious metals, artworks, limited partnerships, commodities, options, futures, and various other possibilities. For most people, these asset classes aren't practical.)

"Investment capital," for purposes of our continuing discussion in this chapter, includes only money you have set aside for the long term. It is an amount above and beyond the money you need to live on. It *does not* include a home that you own, cash in a savings account that you plan to spend soon (say, on a car or vacation), insurance policies, or any emergency funds you may have set aside to get you through rough financial periods. It *does* include your 401(k)s, 403(b)s, and IRAs, although you will probably have to assemble separate fund portfolios for these accounts, because most company retirement plans give you a select list to choose from. (Nevertheless, the principles and allocation guidelines we are about to discuss apply to them as well.)

RISK VERSUS REWARD

≡ You've no doubt heard the cliché "No pain, no gain." It certainly applies to investing. Every investment comes with some degree of risk. With stocks, you risk that the overall market will fall or that your underlying companies will suffer financially—or even go out of business. The same is true for corporate bonds. Even bank savings accounts carry the risk that your financial institution will fail, and your balance may be above the amount covered by federal depository insurance. The only no-risk investments out there are Treasury bills, notes, and bonds, which are ansaction-fee supermarkets, which is my preferred way of buying them.

FIGURE 7.1   THE $150,000 LUNCH?

You may have more money to invest than you think. Simply cutting back on some of life's indulgences can pump up your portfolio by almost $400,000 over time. Here are just a few examples:

Cut Back On	Savings per Month	Savings per Year	30-Year Growth
Eating lunch out	$ 65	$ 780	$148,702
Coffee	22	260	49,567
Impulse Purchases	43	520	99,135
Clothes	40	480	91,173
Total savings	$170	$2,040	$388,577

These hypothetical figures assume a 10 percent annual rate of return compounded at the same rate as contributions over a 30-year period in a tax-deferred account. All numbers are in today's dollars. The tabulation is for illustrative purposes only. Actual investment returns will vary.

---

will fluctuate in value as interest rates change (assuming you don't hold on through maturity).

As you might have guessed, the level of return you can expect to receive from an investment corresponds directly with the degree of risk you take. Small-company and foreign stocks, the most volatile of all, have historically showered investors with the highest returns. Equities in general have done much better than fixed-income investments. Corporate bonds pay higher rates than risk-free Treasuries. And insured bank savings accounts normally pay the least.

But there is another risk that most people don't think about: "opportunity risk." If you aren't willing to endure the volatility associated with stocks, at least for a portion of your portfolio, you risk suffering low returns that might not even keep up with the rate of inflation. (See Figure 7.2.) Consider these statistics. Stocks have provided a rate of return far superior to that of any other asset class over time. From 1979 to 1998, according to data provided by Smith Barney, the S&P 500 rose at an annualized rate of 17.22 percent, including reinvested dividends. That compares to 7.17 percent for 90-day Treasury bills and 11.07 percent for long-term government bonds. The returns during the most recent 10-year bull market have been even higher for stocks: 18.07 percent annually for the S&P, while 90-day bills provided a paltry 5.35 percent, and long-term government bonds returned 11.12 percent. If this trend continues in the future, and I have every reason to believe it will, you will build more wealth from stocks than from any other asset class. (Interestingly, although small and foreign stocks have done better than the S&P 500 over extended periods of time, both have lagged the index considerably over the past decade.)

It is generally assumed that the younger you are, the more your portfolio should be allocated to stocks. This makes sense for two reasons. First, equities generally don't provide much income, a disadvantage that becomes increasingly important in retirement. Second, stocks can be extremely

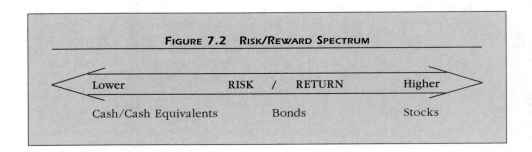

FIGURE 7.2   RISK/REWARD SPECTRUM

Lower   RISK / RETURN   Higher

Cash/Cash Equivalents   Bonds   Stocks

volatile over the short term, so the longer your time horizon, the less you will be impacted by such fluctuations. Nevertheless, some of the most astute elderly investors I know keep anywhere from 80 to 100 percent of their portfolios in equities at all times, even as they near the age of eligibility to receive a televised happy birthday greeting from Willard Scott.

DOLLAR COST AVERAGING

Investors of all ages can profit from volatility by using a technique known as "dollar cost averaging." Simply put, this means investing a fixed amount in your favorite funds on a regular basis, regardless of what's going on with the market. In that way, you buy more shares when the market is down, and fewer shares when it is up. This is precisely what you do when you contribute to your 401(k), SEP-IRA, or 403(b) plan at work. Your company (or you, if you're self-employed) takes regular contributions out of your paycheck and sends them in to your selected funds each month or quarter. Dollar cost averaging doesn't necessarily increase your overall returns, especially during strong bull markets. But it certainly lessens your volatility, and it's often the only way people can afford to invest. (See Figure 7.3.)

FIGURE 7.3   DOLLAR COST AVERAGING AT WORK

Regular Investment	Per-Share Price	Shares Acquired
$ 200	$10	20
200	8	25
200	5	40
200	8	25
200	10	20
Total $1,000	$41	130

Average Cost Per Share = $7.69 ($1,000 ÷ 130 shares)

Average Price Per Share = $8.20 ($41 ÷ 5)

By regularly investing the same dollar amount in your account, you take advantage of market fluctuations by buying more fund shares when prices are low, fewer as prices rise. This strategy, however, does not guarantee profit or protection against loss in declining markets. This is only a hypothetical illustration. It does not project the future performance of any particular investment.

By the way, don't think you can't get a monthly income check from your non-dividend-paying stock funds. You can. Simply sign up for what's called "systematic withdrawal." This program allows you to have a certain amount redeemed automatically from your funds each month. You might think of it as dollar cost averaging in reverse.

INVESTOR PROFILE

≡ Now back to that test I told you about. My friends at discount broker Charles Schwab & Co. created an investor profile quiz to help people determine which asset allocation plan is most appropriate for them. The quiz takes into consideration such things as age, personality, and tolerance for risk. In the end, you get an overall score, which can be matched up with the model portfolios that follow. (The portfolios are mine, not Schwab's.) Keep in mind that the test assumes we're talking about *investment capital,* or money being set aside for at least five years.

Take a few moments to circle the most appropriate answer for each question below. Better yet, make a copy of the test first, so that your spouse (or significant other) can take it too. Then total your score and match it up with the corresponding model portfolio.

Calculate your total and match it up with the appropriate model portfolio. Is this where you want your investment level to be? Read all five portfolio descriptions before you decide.

1. AGGRESSIVE ALL-STOCK PORTFOLIO: 86 TO 100 POINTS (FIGURE 7.4)

≡ This portfolio is most appropriate for those under age 40. They have a 20- to 30-year time horizon before they'll need the money. It assumes you are looking for high growth and are willing to endure substantial year-to-year volatility in that pursuit. The suggested subasset class breakdown for this portfolio is as follows:

40% Large-Cap Funds

20% Mid-Cap Funds

20% Small-Cap Funds

20% International Funds

INVESTOR PROFILE TEST*

Points

1. My current age is:
   a) under 31 8
   b) 31 to 40 6
   c) 41 to 50 4
   d) 51 to 60 2
   e) over 60 0

2. Over the next few years, I expect my income to:
   a) decline 0
   b) stay about the same 1
   c) increase 2
   d) fluctuate 0

3. My investment experience is best described as follows:
   a) I've never invested in stocks, either directly or through stock
      mutual funds 2
   b) I've invested a small amount of money in stocks or stock funds 6
   c) I've occasionally invested a fair amount in stocks or stock funds . . . 10
   d) I've invested in commodities, options, international stocks, or
      limited partnerships 14
   e) I have money in a company retirement plan (i.e., a 401(k) or
      SEP-IRA), but am not sure whether I'm invested in stock funds
      or other types of investments 0

4. I plan to start withdrawing money from my investments in:
   a) less than 5 years 0
   b) 5 to 10 years 10
   c) 11 to 15 years 20
   d) more than 15 years 30

5. When I begin withdrawing the money I've accumulated, I plan to
   spend it in:
   a) less than a year 0
   b) less than 5 years 2
   c) less than 10 years 8
   d) at least 10 years 10

(Continued)

6. How might you respond to fluctuations in your investment?

    a) I'm very concerned any time my investments lose value and will sell quickly if they start to lose money. 0

    b) Day-to-day market moves make me uncomfortable. If an investment loses 5 percent or more over a full quarter, I am likely to sell it and look for a better alternative. 4

    c) I realize there are lots of random day-to-day movements in the market. I usually wait until I have watched the performance of an investment for at least a year before making changes. 10

    d) Even if poor market conditions result in losses of up to 20 percent in a given year, I try to follow a consistent, long-term investment plan. 14

7. Consider the range of high and low returns that might result from a $10,000 investment in four different areas over a 10-year period. Keep in mind that investments offering higher returns often involve greater risks. Which range of possible outcomes would be most acceptable to you?

Value of $10,000 after 10 years:

Investment A

Best case $45,412

Worst case   6,979 . . . . 10 pts.

Investment B

Best case $82,425

Worst case   4,186 . . . . 15 pts.

Investment C

Best case $27,000

Worst case   9,622 . . . . 5 pts.

Investment D

Best case $12,689

Worst case   10,118 . . . . 2 pts.

8. When I buy car insurance, I:

    a) choose the lowest deductible amount to ensure maximum coverage even though my policy costs more. 0

    b) choose a moderate deductible level in order to reduce the premium. . 2

    c) choose a high deductible in order to pay a low premium, even though many losses may not be covered. 5

    d) choose to carry no insurance. 7

Your Total Points . . . . _____

* Reprinted with the permission of Charles Schwab & Co.

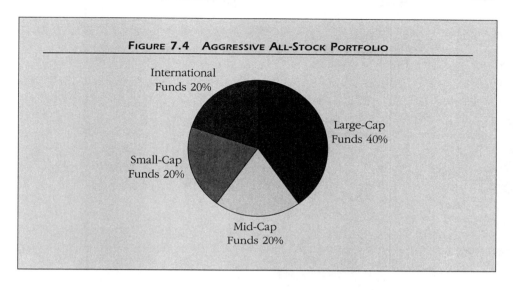

Figure 7.4 Aggressive All-Stock Portfolio

International Funds 20%

Large-Cap Funds 40%

Small-Cap Funds 20%

Mid-Cap Funds 20%

Specific Recommended Funds and Weightings for a $20,000 Portfolio:

$4,000 U.S. Global Leaders Growth (20%)

$4,000 Oak Value (20%)

$4,000 Muhlenkamp Fund (20%)

$2,000 Baron Small Cap (10%)

$2,000 Berger Small Cap Value (10%)

$2,000 Artisan International (10%)

$2,000 Managers International Equity (10%)

2. MODERATE ALL-STOCK PORTFOLIO: 71 TO 85 POINTS (FIGURE 7.5)

This portfolio is most appropriate for those ages 40 to 50 who have a 10- to 20-year time horizon, or for younger investors seeking a lower-risk approach to equity investing. It is fully invested, primarily in the stocks of more seasoned and value-oriented companies, yet it assumes you are willing

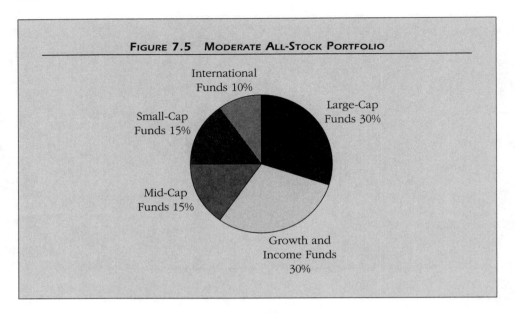

FIGURE 7.5   MODERATE ALL-STOCK PORTFOLIO

to endure substantial year-to-year volatility in the pursuit of high growth. The suggested subasset class breakdown for this portfolio is as follows:

30% Large-Cap Funds

30% Growth and Income Funds

15% Mid-Cap Funds

15% Small-Cap Funds

10% International Funds

Specific Recommended Funds and Weightings for a $20,000 Portfolio:

$3,000 U.S. Global Leaders Growth (15%)

$3,000 Oak Value (15%)

$3,000 Baron Growth & Income (15%)

$3,000 Warburg Pincus Growth & Income (15%)

$3,000 Muhlenkamp Fund (15%)

$3,000 Berger Small Cap Value (15%)

$2,000 Artisan International (10%)

3. MODERATE STOCK AND BOND PORTFOLIO: 56 TO 70 POINTS (FIGURE 7.6)

This portfolio is designed for those ages 50 to 70 who are looking to maintain a majority weighting in stocks, but with a solid fixed-income component to temper volatility. It assumes you are willing to enjoy slightly lower returns in exchange for less risk. The suggested subasset class fund breakdown for this portfolio is:

20% Large-Cap Funds

20% Growth and Income Funds

10% Mid-Cap Funds

5% Small-Cap Funds

5% International Funds

20% Corporate Bond Funds

10% Mortgage-Backed Securities Funds

10% High-Yield Corporate Funds

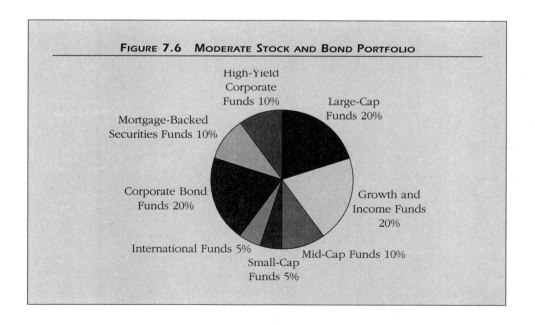

FIGURE 7.6 MODERATE STOCK AND BOND PORTFOLIO

High-Yield Corporate Funds 10%

Large-Cap Funds 20%

Mortgage-Backed Securities Funds 10%

Corporate Bond Funds 20%

Growth and Income Funds 20%

International Funds 5%

Small-Cap Funds 5%

Mid-Cap Funds 10%

Specific Recommended Funds and Weightings for a $20,000 Portfolio:

$4,000 U.S. Global Leaders Growth (20%)

$4,000 Warburg Pincus Growth & Income (20%)

$2,000 Muhlenkamp Fund (10%)

$1,000 Babson Enterprise II (5%)

$1,000 Artisan International (5%)

$4,000 Strong Corporate Bond (20%)

$2,000 Lexington GNMA (10%)

$2,000 Northeast Investors Trust (10%)

4. BALANCED STOCK AND BOND PORTFOLIO: 41 TO 55 POINTS (FIGURE 7.7)

This portfolio is most appropriate for those over age 50 seeking a balanced portfolio with 50 percent stocks and 50 percent bonds. While it will provide a moderate degree of income, its primary goal is to grow capital

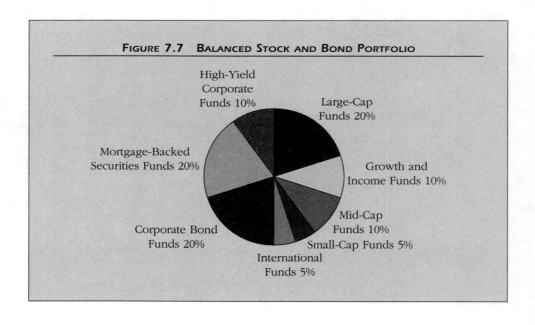

FIGURE 7.7   BALANCED STOCK AND BOND PORTFOLIO

High-Yield Corporate Funds 10%

Large-Cap Funds 20%

Mortgage-Backed Securities Funds 20%

Growth and Income Funds 10%

Corporate Bond Funds 20%

Mid-Cap Funds 10%

Small-Cap Funds 5%

International Funds 5%

without subjecting investors to a high degree of risk. The suggested subasset class breakdown for this portfolio is as follows:

20% Large-Cap Funds

10% Growth and Income Funds

10% Mid-Cap Funds

5% Small-Cap Funds

5% International Funds

20% Corporate Bond Funds

20% Mortgage-Backed Securities Funds

10% High-Yield Corporate Funds

Specific Recommended Funds and Weightings for a $20,000 Portfolio:

$4,000 U.S. Global Leaders Growth (20%)

$2,000 Warburg Pincus Growth & Income (10%)

$2,000 Muhlenkamp Fund (10%)

$1,000 Babson Enterprise II (5%)

$1,000 Managers International Equity (5%)

$4,000 Strong Corporate Bond (20%)

$4,000 Lexington GNMA (20%)

$2,000 Northeast Investors Trust (10%)

5. CONSERVATIVE INCOME PRODUCER: 0 TO 40 POINTS (FIGURE 7.8)

This portfolio maintains a small exposure to dividend-paying stocks for growth, but concentrates on bond investments to provide a steady stream of monthly income. It is most appropriate for people in retirement who are looking to live off their investments while enduring only a minimal amount of volatility. The suggested subasset class breakdown for this portfolio is:

30% Growth and Income Funds

30% Corporate Bond Funds

20% Mortgage-Backed Securities Funds

20% High-Yield Corporate Funds

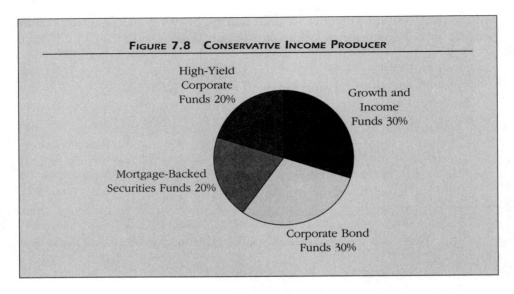

FIGURE 7.8   CONSERVATIVE INCOME PRODUCER

High-Yield Corporate Funds 20%

Growth and Income Funds 30%

Mortgage-Backed Securities Funds 20%

Corporate Bond Funds 30%

Specific Recommended Funds and Weightings for a $20,000 Portfolio:

$3,000 Warburg Pincus Growth & Income (15%)

$3,000 Baron Growth & Income (15%)

$6,000 Strong Corporate Bond (30%)

$4,000 Lexington GNMA (20%)

$4,000 Northeast Investors Trust (20%)

HOW THE PORTFOLIOS WERE PUT TOGETHER

The five model portfolios assume you have at least $20,000 to invest. If you have less, that's perfectly fine. Make the necessary adjustments, keeping in mind that each fund has a minimum initial investment requirement. This means you may not be able to buy as many funds as suggested, at least in the beginning. For example, let's say your score leads you to the Aggressive All-Stock Portfolio. This 100 percent globally diversified equity plan calls for putting 40 percent in large caps, 20 percent in mid caps, 20 percent in small caps, and 20 percent in international funds. If you have only $10,000 to invest, you won't be able to meet the minimums for both U.S. Global Leaders Growth and Oak Value, so consider putting the entire

40 percent in just one of those funds instead. If you have only $5,000, you might start with one large-cap fund and one mid-cap fund, with the goal of adding a small-cap fund and an international offering when you can afford them. The secret is to get started as early as possible.

You don't have to buy the exact funds I recommend. These just happen to be among my favorite Powerhouse Performers in each category that have the lowest minimum investment requirements. Almost all of them are available through the various no-load, no-transaction-fee supermarkets, which is my preferred way of buying them. Feel free to mix, match, and substitute as you feel is appropriate. If you would rather buy Papp America Abroad or Marsico Focus instead of U.S. Global Leaders Growth, for instance, go ahead. All are large-cap growth funds from my Powerhouse Performers list. If you have a bigger portfolio and can meet the minimum requirements of funds like First Eagle Fund of America or Weitz Valve, these are excellent choices as well. Likewise, if you're in a high tax bracket, you might consider replacing a corporate or high-yield bond fund with a tax-free municipal fund instead. (By the way, I will be updating these portfolios, recommended funds, and the entire "Powerhouse Performers" roster in each annual edition of this book. So be sure to look for the *New York Institute of Finance Guide To Mutual Funds 2000,* which will be available in bookstores by next January.)

Keep one final thing in mind. I purposely made sure that every model portfolio held a blend of both growth and value funds. If you're going to make substitutions, I suggest you maintain this balance. After all, growth and value aren't always in vogue at the same time. Therefore, part of your diversification plan should call for holding funds that adhere to both disciplines. I also believe that a maximum 20 percent international weighting is appropriate for aggressive investors. Some advisers recommend putting even more money overseas. But given that most U.S. companies are global anyway, and considering the political and economic turmoil in many foreign countries right now, I'm perfectly comfortable capping this weighting at 20 percent. Again, this is something you can modify to your own personal preferences.

TIMING THE MARKET

After you have set your asset allocation plan, it makes sense to review it as you grow older and/or as your needs change. But once you have decided on the right program for *you,* stick with it religiously and avoid trying

Every investor who qualifies should consider putting the maximum $2,000 a year into an IRA account. Even if you can't deduct the contribution, this money will compound tax-free until you withdraw it. Keep in mind that IRA stands for Individual *Retirement* Account, which means this money should not be touched until you need it in your golden years. If you try to tap into an IRA before you turn 59½, the government slaps you with a 10 percent penalty in addition to any income taxes due, unless you have a qualified reason.

There are now two types of IRAs: Traditional and Roth. What follows is a brief rundown of the benefits and requirements for both:

Eligibility

Traditional IRA: Individuals under age 70½ (and their spouses) who have earned income, regardless of the amount.

Roth IRA: Individuals of any age (and their spouses) with earned income and with adjusted gross income below $110,000 (for single filers) or $160,000 (for those filing a joint return).

Deductibility of Contribution

Traditional IRA: Contribution is fully deductible if the investor is not covered by an employer-sponsored retirement plan. If the investor is covered by an employer-sponsored retirement plan, a partial deduction may be permitted for those falling within these income guidelines: $30,000 to $40,000 for single filers; $50,000 to $60,000 for those filing jointly. Above these amounts, you can still contribute to a traditional IRA, but will not receive a tax deduction.

Roth IRA: No deduction permitted.

Annual Contribution Limits

Traditional IRA: Individuals (and their spouses) may contribute up to $2,000 per year (or 100 percent of compensation, whichever is less).

Roth IRA: Individuals (and their spouses) may contribute up to $2,000 (or 100 percent of compensation, whichever is less) with the following limits: The ability to contribute phases out at income levels between $95,000 and $110,000 for individuals and between $150,000 and $160,000 for those filing joint returns.

Tax Treatment of Distributions

Traditional IRA: Total deductible contributions and interest taxed as ordinary income in the year of withdrawal. Nondeductible contributions are not taxed, although the interest earned from them is. Distributions made before age 59½ may be subject to a 10 percent penalty. Early penalty-free withdrawals can be made prior to age 59½ upon death, disability, the purchase of a first-time home (up to $10,000 lifetime maximum), to fund higher education expenses, to pay for medical expenses in excess of 7.5 percent of adjusted gross income, or for health insurance premiums if unemployed more than 12 weeks.

Roth IRA: Distributions made after age 59½ are tax-free if the Roth IRA has been held for more than five years. Distributions made before age 59½ may be subject to a 10 percent penalty. Early penalty-free withdrawals can be made prior to age 59½ upon death, disability, the purchase of a first home (up to $10,000 lifetime maximum), to fund higher education expenses, to pay for medical expenses in excess of 7.5 percent of adjusted gross income, or for health insurance premiums if unemployed more than 12 weeks. You can also withdraw your contributed principal from a Roth IRA without tax or penalty at any time.

Minimum Distribution Requirements

Traditional IRA: Distributions must start by age 70½.

Roth IRA: No requirements.

to time the market. If you have made a decision to be 100 percent invested in a globally diversified equity portfolio, don't get creative by switching back and forth from stocks to bonds, based on whether you're bullish or bearish at the moment. The reason? No one has proven that you can successfully time the market over the long haul. It simply can't be done.

The only thing we know for sure is that the market has an upward bias. I can't tell you where it will be tomorrow, next week, or even next year, but I have faith that it will be higher 10 years from now than it is today. It would be great to be able to avoid every bear market. The problem is, the nasty bears creep up without warning. And study after study has shown that investors who simply stay put and ride out the inevitable market swings always come out far ahead of traders who try to guess what will happen next by switching back and forth, which is an exercise in futility.

I continually reinforce the idea that investment capital is money you are willing to put away for long periods of time. In this way, you can afford to ride out the sometimes grueling short-term volatility that I guarantee you will be forced to endure. One of the questions on the test you just took asked how you would feel if your $10,000 investment fell to a mere $4,186 over a 10-year period. If that kind of possibility scares you to death, lighten up on or entirely avoid stocks. But as the question also implies, that $10,000 could grow significantly. Again, the more risk you take, the greater your potential reward, but the more fluctuations you will be forced to endure.

THE 25 BEST
INTERNET SITES FOR
MUTUAL FUND INVESTORS

If you have a computer with access to the Internet, you can now tap into more information about mutual funds than you ever dreamed possible, by visiting the plethora of financial sites that pop up daily on the World Wide Web. These locations allow you to do research, download performance charts, track your portfolio online, and even chat in real time with other investors. The bad news is that most of these sites aren't worth your time. A majority of the so-called investment sites out there are mere advertisements for certain products or services. They contain little, if any, objective investment information. Others with more substance charge a subscription fee, which can get pretty steep.

In this chapter, I uncover 25 of the best sites I have run across for mutual fund investors. The sites can be accessed absolutely free. A few have premium content you have to pay for, but I recommend you just stick with the stuff that's available at no cost.

I offer a few caveats before you proceed. Anyone can set up and contribute to an Internet site, so always be suspicious of advice you receive online; much of it is self-serving. Occasionally, you'll find companies touting their own stock under the auspices of a seemingly legitimate financial column. Another thing: think twice before giving your e-mail address to anyone, unless you're open to being deluged with junk announcements. In some cases, you must reveal this information to gain access to a site. Otherwise, keep all personal data to yourself.

Finally, beyond what you can access through the Internet, a number of helpful computer software programs are available to help monitor and improve the results of your portfolio. Quicken and Microsoft Money, for example, will keep track of your cost basis for every fund. These programs are complete personal finance solutions, and they allow for such other features as check writing and budgeting. For fund analysis, you should consider the Value Line No-Load Analyzer for Windows program, which is available on CD-ROM. This service contains a database of more than 3,000 no-load and low-load funds, and features sophisticated sorting, screening, filtering, portfolio analysis, and graphics capabilities. A special trial offer to receive this service can be found at the back of this book. I admit to being somewhat biased; Value Line provided much of the data used in this Guide. However, this powerful and comprehensive tool is easy to use and is accessible without logging on to the Internet.

Now that the formalities are out of the way, here (in no particular order) are my picks for the year's 25 best Websites for mutual fund investors. Be sure to look for an updated list of new sites in each annual edition of this book.

1. **The Mutual Fund Channel**   www.mutualfundchannel.com

   The Mutual Fund Channel allows you to get customized fund performance data, profiles, portfolio valuations, and other investment information delivered right to your desktop by using the latest Internet broadcast technology. After you download the site's free BackWeb software (which can take up to 30 minutes to download with slower modems), you can track up to 20 different funds. The closing prices and percentage changes are automatically delivered to your computer every afternoon, along with any related news, and then flashed across your screen like a ticker tape.

2. **Morningstar.Net**   www.morningstar.net

   Morningstar, a fund-rating service, has put together a rather impressive site full of fund manager interviews, portfolio tracking software, late-breaking financial news, chat rooms, market analysis, and snapshot fund profiles containing the company's trademark star ratings. The site allows you to monitor the progress of your fund portfolio online, and an X-ray feature shows how broadly diversified your overall holdings are, across various asset classes and investment styles. Of greatest value are the archive of reports and insightful articles on the personalities and trends within the fund industry.

3. **Quicken.com** www.quicken.com

   While not strictly a site for fund investors, Quicken.com contains an array of useful areas covering everything from tracking your investments to running your small business more effectively. The mutual fund page contains not only fund profiles and manager interviews, but also broad-based articles on subjects like the wisdom of small-cap investing. Quicken's Mutual Fund Finder lets you search for funds using your own specific criteria, like low minimum investment requirements. It also has direct links to other helpful sites for investors, and analyses of various fund investment strategies.

4. **Dr. Ed Yardeni's Economics Network** www.yardeni.com

   Ed Yardeni is the well-respected chief economist of Deutsche Morgan Grenfell in New York. He says he hopes his site will be the number-one source of economic and financial information for investors. There's reason to believe it will. Yardeni has filled it with more economic data and analysis than you could ever hope for, including the portfolio strategy reports presented to Deutsche Morgan Grenfell's clients. Yardeni also includes his past speeches, commentaries on such topics as the Year 2000 problem, plus his latest forecasts for interest rates and economic growth around the world.

5. **Invest-O-Rama** www.investorama.com

   Invest-O-Rama, run by a freelance financial journalist, is more of a directory to other interesting Internet sites than anything else. The home page gives you access to market commentaries from various contributors (mostly newsletter writers), stock and fund quotes, and charting capabilities. But the real attraction is Invest-O-Rama's ability to connect you with company and fund research material from other online sources. It contains direct links to virtually every major fund family's Internet site, along with articles on topics such as "The Advantage of No-Load Mutual Funds" and "How Many Funds Should I Own?"

6. **Investor Words** www.investorwords.com

   I think the glossary in the back of this book is pretty comprehensive, but it's nothing compared to what you'll find at the Investor Words Internet site. Billed as "the biggest, best investing glossary on the Web," it contains definitions for some 4,000 investment-related words, from *alpha* to *zero-coupon bond.* Within most definitions, you will find links to other related words, to further your understanding of every concept. Given the financial industry's knack for throwing around confusing gobbledygook, this site is bound to be a frequent stop for every serious investor.

7. **Microsoft Investor**   www.investor.msn.com

   Microsoft Investor is a site that's full of potential. Unfortunately, it's pretty stingy about giving away free information. For the most valuable services, you will have to fork over a subscription fee of $9.95. Nevertheless, the complimentary news articles on various personal finance subjects are worth your perusal. The site is clearly targeted more toward stock investors, although the "Money Insider" column contains a lot of general advice on topics like controlling taxable gains. There are also occasional freebie fund-manager interviews and continuous news updates from MSNBC.

8. **Yahoo Finance**   www.quote.yahoo.com

   It's not that pretty to look at, but Yahoo Finance is a great source of comprehensive, up-to-the-minute investment information. On the stock side, it reports on the day's major corporate developments. It also has a page devoted exclusively to news relating to mutual funds, such as new fund launches, cash flow trends, and manager changes. Additionally, it includes free links to fund-related stories written by reporters from TheStreet.com, a subscriber-based Internet service. What's more, Yahoo Finance has a fund message board and can provide a quick printout of top performers across various time periods.

9. **Wall Street Research Net**   www.wsrn.com

   Wall Street Research Net contains thousands of links to help you conduct fundamental research on both actively traded companies and mutual funds. It can also assist you in locating important economic data that could impact the market. In addition to mutual fund news, collected from various sources on the Web, the site provides a daily list of the fund world's biggest gainers and losers. Furthermore, you will find a glossary of commonly used mutual fund terms here, profiles of Morningstar's managers of the year, and insightful commentary on other important business topics of interest to investors.

10. **Daily Rocket**   www.dailyrocket.com

When you call up the Daily Rocket site on your computer, you'll be greeted with a recap of the day on Wall Street, followed by several somewhat dated features primarily of interest to stock investors. What's of more value to fund lovers can be found by clicking on the "articles" icon at the top of the home page and selecting "mutual funds." There you will find a small archive of stories of special appeal to beginning investors. Subjects include "Navigating Through a Mutual Fund Prospectus," "Deciphering the Mutual Fund Rating System," and "Open-End Funds vs. Closed-End Funds."

11. **FinanCenter.com**   www.financenter.com

How much will you need to save to enjoy the retirement of your dreams? What is the total return you have actually earned from your least favorite mutual fund? Do you make enough to buy that brand new home you've been eyeing on the other side of town? For the answers to these questions and more, log in to FinanCenter.com. You'll find dozens of calculators here that work through various "what if" scenarios with you. You supply the raw data and the calculators give numerical responses to everything from estimated living expenses 30 years in the future to the amount you must save to become a millionaire.

12. **ICI Mutual Fund Connection**   www.ici.org

The Investment Company Institute is the trade association for the fund industry. Its Website is packed with statistical fund information, along with the association's most recent press releases and research reports. You can also listen to ICI's weekly 60-second "Informed Investor" radio reports, which cover topics of interest to fund shareholders. This site will give you a better understanding of the various issues affecting the fund industry. In addition, the "About Mutual Fund Shareholders" section contains some fascinating information on the demographic characteristics of the average fund investor.

13. **U.S. Securities and Exchange Commission**   www.sec.gov

By tapping in to the SEC Website, you'll be able to access the huge database of legal documents that mutual funds are required to file with the government. You can pull down prospectuses and other detailed papers filed by every fund company. This is an effective and quick way to do research on funds you own or are considering. It can also lead you to brand new funds that have registered with the SEC but are not yet available to the public. Incidentally, you can use this same database to search for 10-Ks, 10-Qs, and other material that must be filed with the SEC by public companies as well.

14. **Vanguard Online**   www.vanguard.com

Almost every major fund company now has its own Internet site, but this one from the Vanguard Group stands out. It is more than just a commercial message for the company's various funds. Instead, it contains a wealth of educational material. Vanguard Online has an area called "The University," which features a series of ten courses answering such questions as "What is a mutual fund?" "How do you build a portfolio?" and "What are the best ways to rebalance your portfolio?" You'll also find help tools for retirement planning and a library of in-depth fund material.

15. **Find a Fund**   www.findafund.com

Find a Fund is one of the newest Internet sites built especially for mutual fund investors. It contains a spotlight article, which examines recent trends and changes in a new market sector each week. The site also includes a library of mutual fund basics and performance profiles for almost every fund. Find a Fund allows you to compare the holdings and sector weightings of two different funds, to see if owning both really offers diversification. In addition, you will find average performance numbers for various fund categories here, which is useful for evaluating how your funds compare to their peers.

16. **Mutual Fund Investor's Center**   www.mfea.com

This site, sponsored by the Mutual Fund Education Alliance, contains in-depth profiles of select fund managers, thoughts from leaders in the field, and a news center with recent developments in the industry. The education center teaches users about the basics of fund investing, goes over the various types of funds available, discusses the tax ramifications of fund ownership, and has a special feature on investing for women. Finally, the site's planning center lets you go through various scenarios to make informed decisions about investing for college, retirement, and your child's (children's) future.

17. **Fund Alarm**   www.fundalarm.com

Almost every fund site gives you some kind of advice on buying funds. Fund Alarm is the only one specializing in telling you when to sell. It is updated at the beginning of each month and follows more than 1,900 funds. A fund is likely to earn a "three alarm" sell signal if it undergoes a bad change in management or its performance lags behind its benchmark over a consistent time period. Fund Alarm is run by Roy Weitz, who is not even in the investment business. His offbeat thoughts about key personalities and changes in the industry are enlightening, even if I don't always agree with him.

18. **Bloomberg Website**   www.bloomberg.com

Michael Bloomberg's investment information empire is into just about every medium imaginable now (radio, TV, print, computer terminals), so it was only a matter of time before he put up his own Internet address as well. The site is flush with news straight from the Bloomberg wires, including a section packed with mutual fund-related stories. If you're looking for the latest developments on fund companies and the industry in general, this is about the most comprehensive source around. The site also updates the equity indexes throughout the day and lets you tap into Bloomberg Radio and TV live.

19. **Fund $pot**   www.fundspot.com

Fund $pot is a site that will connect you to other areas on the Internet that are of interest to fund investors. You'll find links to mutual fund news, portfolio manager interviews, and fund family Websites. "Interactive Spot" will take you to worksheets and financial calculators useful for college, retirement, and general financial planning. If you feel like chatting about your newest fund discovery, the site can direct you to an investor forum where you can talk to your heart's content. To round things out, Fund $pot will lead you to sites with portfolio tracking capabilities, research, and current quotes.

20. **Mutual Funds Interactive**   www.fundsinteractive.com

Mutual Funds Interactive is awash with useful information and articles written by its founder, Marla Brill, and by a team of contributing fund experts. This isn't the prettiest site around, but there are discussion groups where you can chat about everything from retirement planning to which Websites you like the most. You'll also find Value Line screening tools, the results of various fund-related surveys, manager profiles, and links to fund family home pages. The "Mutual Fund Features" section is especially interesting. It contains dozens of articles culled from numerous columnists and publications.

21. **Mutual Fund Café**   www.mfcafe.com

This cleverly named site invites you to pull up a modem, grab some hot java, and catch up on the freshest fund industry information. Written primarily for fund professionals, the Mutual Fund Café is loaded with behind-the-scenes news that will be of interest to any serious investor. Categorized into such cleverly named sections as "Top Bananas," "Market Share Pie," "Burgers 'n' Acquisitions," "Legal Stew," and "Bean Counters," the site won't teach you the basics of fund investing (there are plenty of previously mentioned online locations that do that). But it will show you how the fund business *really* works.

22. **The Young Investor Website**   www.younginvestor.com

It may take a little coaxing to persuade your children to log on to a site where they can learn about how to handle money, but once they get here, I think they'll thank you for the advice. The Young Investor Website is run by Liberty Financial, sponsor of the Stein Roe Young Investor Fund. It is, of course, somewhat self-serving; the company would love to have users invest in the fund as well. Still, this colorful and creative site educates kids about financial matters and investing through a series of games, including "Currency Crossword" and the brain-teaser "Money-Tration," without much advertising hype.

23. **Young Investor's Guide to Accumulating Wealth**

This site is also written with young people in mind, but is appropriate for adults as well. It is run by 22-year-old college business student and Web entrepreneur Gregg Fidan. Fidan tells me he got interested in stocks after the crash of 1987 and developed this site to help young and inexperienced investors alike learn how to invest and accumulate wealth. Fidan and his guest contributors (investment professionals) explain such things as how funds work, the best way to start saving, and why people should invest in the first place. He also has a forum where readers can submit questions.

24. **IBC Financial Data**   www.ibcdata.com

   You'll notice that there are no money market funds among my list of "100 Powerhouse Performers." That's because money market yields change so often, it's hard to keep track of who is offering the best deals. One way you can stay ahead of the curve is by visiting the IBC Financial Data site. IBC is in the business of tracking money funds and yields. You can't access all of its services without paying a fee, but the freebies are all you need. A click of the mouse gives you a rundown of the highest yielding funds. Another section goes over the finer points of selecting and evaluating these cash-equivalent investments.

25. **Index Funds Online**   www.indexfundsonline.com

   If you opt to keep part of your portfolio in index funds, or just want to learn more about how these investments work, you'll find the content of Index Funds Online to be of interest. The site, run by diehard indexers, has excerpts from books on indexing and reprints of related articles from various publications. The "Index Information" center contains short descriptions for each of the major global indexes (i.e., number of stocks included and market capitalizations), along with a listing of funds available to track these indexes. The site also updates how well the various indexes have performed on a weekly basis.

VALUE LINE
PERFORMANCE DATA FOR
SOME 8,000 FUNDS

What follows are comprehensive performance results and rankings for some 8,000 stock and bond mutual funds from the *Value Line Mutual Fund Survey*. I believe this is the most exhaustive collection of fund data you will find in any book on the market today. The directory starts out with a listing of stock funds, and then gives a roster of bond offerings. The following information (where available) is provided for each entry:

Fund Name. Funds are listed in alphabetical order, with stock funds up front, and bond funds in the back. Almost every fund you own or are considering can probably be found somewhere on these pages.

Objective. This is a brief description of the fund's investment objective (i.e., growth, foreign, corporate bond, and so on).

Annualized Return for 1, 3, and 5 Years. Here you will find every fund's average annual return over the past one-, three- and five-year periods, where applicable, as compiled by Value Line. (All performance data is as of June 30, 1998, unless otherwise noted.)

Overall Rank. This number, compiled exclusively by Value Line, shows how a given fund stacks up next to its peers. Ratings are on a scale of 1 through 5. Funds with a 1 ranking have performed best, and those rated 5 have done the poorest.

Risk Rank. Another proprietary Value Line statistic, the risk rank number tells you how much volatility a fund has subjected its investors to. It is also based on a scale of 1 through 5, with 1 being least risky, and 5 being riskiest.

Maximum Sales Load. If a fund has a front-end sales load, it will be noted here. (Remember: If you're making fund selections on your own, you should favor no-load funds.) Also, many load funds have several share classes which come with back-ended redemption fees, instead of up-front sales commissions. In other words, you pay on the way "out" rather than on the way "in." Therefore, although some load funds in this directory may have several other share classes with "0" listed as the maximum sales load, be aware that you can almost always count on being hit with steep exit fees on these funds.

Expense Ratio. Every fund has an expense ratio. This number represents the percentage that gets deducted from the fund's net asset value each year, to cover all charges related to managing your money.

Toll-Free Telephone. This is the toll-free telephone number you can call to request a prospectus and more information on the listed fund.

Many thanks to the good folks at Value Line who helped to put this performance directory together. They truly did a first-rate job.

Stock Fund Name	Objective	Annualized Return for			Rank		Max Load	Expense Ratio	Toll-Free Telephone
		1 Year	3 Years	5 Years	Overall	Risk			

STOCK FUNDS

Stock Fund Name	Objective	1 Year	3 Years	5 Years	Overall	Risk	Max Load	Expense Ratio	Toll-Free Telephone
AAL Capital Growth Fund A	Growth	33.71	29.25	20.62	2	3	4.75	0.98	800 553-6319
AAL Capital Growth Fund B	Growth	32.44					0	1.89	800 553-6319
AAL Equity Income Fund A	Utilities	23.65	17.67		3	2	4	1.15	800 553-6319
AAL Equity Income Fund B	Utilities	22.42					0	1.99	800 553-6319
AAL International Fund A	Foreign	−0.68					4	2.10	800 553-6319
AAL International Fund B	Foreign	−1.68					0	2.94	800 553-6319
AAL Mid Cap Stock Fund A	Small Co	15.30	18.63	15.14	4	4	4	1.35	800 553-6319
AAL Mid Cap Stock Fund B	Small Co	14.14					0	2.29	800 553-6319
AAL Small Cap Stock Fund A	Small Co	11.10					4	2.06	800 553-6319
AAL Small Cap Stock Fund B	Small Co	10.05					0	3.00	800 553-6319
AARP Balanced Stock & Bond Fund	Balanced	17.06	17.95		3	1	0	0.91	800 253-2277
AARP Capital Growth Fund	Growth	26.75	28.03	19.64	2	3	0	0.88	800 253-2277
AARP Diversified Growth Fund	Growth	16.79					0	0.00	800 253-2277
AARP Diversified Income with Growth	Income	8.85					0	0.00	800 253-2277
AARP Global Growth Fund	Global	16.19					0	1.75	800 253-2277
AARP Growth & Income Fund	Growth/Inc	21.78	26.20	20.74	1	2	0	0.71	800 253-2277
AARP International Stock Fund	Foreign	23.39					0	1.75	800 253-2277
AARP Small Company Stock	Small Co	17.76					0	1.75	800 253-2277
AARP US Stock Index Fund	Growth	29.22					0	0.50	800 253-2277
ABN AMRO Asian Tiger Fund Comn Shs	Pacific	−53.16	−17.20		5	5	4.5	1.59	800 443-4725
ABN AMRO Asian Tiger Fund Inv Shs	Pacific	−53.55	−17.81		5	5	4.5	1.84	800 443-4725
ABN AMRO Balanced Fund Comn Shs	Balanced	18.42	18.79		3	1	0	0.92	800 443-4725
ABN AMRO Balanced Fund Inv Shs	Balanced	18.04	18.47	13.27	3	1	4.5	1.17	800 443-4725
ABN AMRO Growth Fund Comn Shs	Growth	28.34	25.66		2	3	0	1.01	800 443-4725
ABN AMRO Growth Fund Inv Shs	Growth	28.03	25.34	18.36	2	3	4.5	1.26	800 443-4725
ABN AMRO Intl Equity Comn Shs	Foreign	8.39	13.37		4	3	0	1.33	800 443-4725
ABN AMRO Intl Equity Inv Shs	Foreign	7.99	12.91	12.75	4	4	4.5	1.58	800 443-4725
ABN AMRO Latin American Fd Comn Shs	Foreign	−22.14					0	1.47	800 443-4725
ABN AMRO Small Cap Fund Comn Shs	Small Co	11.91	19.21	13.98	4	4	0	1.03	800 443-4725
ABN AMRO Small Cap Fund Inv Shs	Small Co	11.50	18.88	13.65	4	4	0	1.03	800 443-4725
ABN AMRO Value Fund Comn Shs	Growth	22.80	25.81	18.47	2	3	0	1.01	800 443-4725
ABN AMRO Value Fund Inv Shs	Growth	22.77	25.53	18.79	1	3	0	1.26	800 443-4725
Academy Value Fund	Growth/Inc	−3.57	6.26		5	3		2.00	
Accessor Growth Fund	Growth	34.27	29.65	24.64	2	3	0	0.93	800 759-3504
Accessor International Equity Fund	Foreign	13.99	17.96		4	3	0	1.52	800 759-3504
Accessor Small to Midcap Portfolio	Small Co	38.09	31.13		2	3	0	1.15	800 759-3504
Accessor Value & Income	Income	27.08	27.67	20.14	1	3	0	1.05	800 759-3504
Achievement Balanced Fund Instl	Balanced	15.59	16.20		3	2	4.5	0.90	800 472-0577
Achievement Balanced Fund Retail	Balanced	15.38	15.92		3	2	4.5	1.15	800 472-0577
Achievement Equity Fund Instl	Growth	20.20	22.93		3	3	4.5	0.90	800 472-0577
Achievement Equity Fund Retail	Growth	19.95	20.35		2	3	4.5	1.15	800 472-0577
Acorn Fund	Small Co	26.87	22.86	16.69	3	3	0	0.56	800 922-6769
Acorn International Fund	Foreign	11.59	15.66	13.50	3	2	0	1.19	800 922-6769
Acorn USA	Small Co	31.57					0	1.41	800 922-6769
Addison Capital Shares	Growth	19.34	25.71	18.54	2	2	0	1.81	800 526-6397
Adrian Day Global Opportunity Fund	Global	−24.08					0	2.50	800 426-6635
Advantus Cornerstone Fund A	Growth	6.76	22.80		3	3	5	1.09	800 665-6005
Advantus Cornerstone Fund B	Growth	5.78	21.86		2	3	0	1.98	800 665-6005
Advantus Cornerstone Fund C	Growth	5.65	21.72		3	3	0	1.98	800 665-6005
Advantus Enterprise Fund A	Small Co	11.89	11.36		4	4	5	1.28	800 665-6005
Advantus Enterprise Fund B	Small Co	10.91	11.79		5	4	0	2.18	800 665-6005
Advantus Enterprise Fund C	Small Co	10.92	11.76		5	4	0	2.18	800 665-6005
Advantus Horizon Fund A	Growth/Inc	31.58	25.86	19.38	3	4	5	1.43	800 665-6005
Advantus Horizon Fund B	Growth/Inc	30.55	24.98		2	4	0	2.18	800 665-6005
Advantus Horizon Fund C	Growth/Inc	31.39	25.17		2	4	0	2.18	800 665-6005
Advantus Index 500 Fund A	Growth/Inc	28.91					5	0.70	800 665-6005
Advantus Index 500 Fund B	Growth/Inc	27.80					0	1.60	800 665-6005

Stock Fund Name	Objective	Annualized Return for			Rank		Max Load	Expense Ratio	Toll-Free Telephone
		1 Year	3 Years	5 Years	Overall	Risk			
Advantus Index 500 Fund C	Growth/Inc	27.73					0	1.60	800 665-6005
Advantus Intl Balanced Fd Inc A	Balanced	4.49	11.28		3	2	5	1.51	800 665-6005
Advantus Intl Balanced Fd Inc C	Balanced	3.60	10.44		4	2	0	2.37	800 665-6005
Advantus Spectrum Fund A	AssetAlloc	21.01	17.41	12.96	3	2	5	1.26	800 665-6005
Advantus Spectrum Fund B	AssetAlloc	20.30	16.74		3	2	0	1.90	800 665-6005
Advantus Spectrum Fund C	AssetAlloc	20.14	16.61		3	2	0	1.90	800 665-6005
Advantus Venture Fund A	Growth	21.45					5	1.35	800 665-6005
Advantus Venture Fund B	Growth	20.10					0	2.25	800 665-6005
Advantus Venture Fund C	Growth	20.45					0	2.25	800 665-6005
Aetna Ascent Fund A	AssetAlloc	16.40					0	2.36	800 238-6263
Aetna Ascent Fund I	AssetAlloc	17.00	21.56		2	2	0	1.61	800 238-6263
Aetna Balanced Fund A	Flexible	21.50	18.95	14.13	3	2	0	2.02	800 238-6263
Aetna Balanced Fund I	Flexible	22.06	19.70	15.08	3	2	0	1.24	800 238-6263
Aetna Crossroads Fund A	AssetAlloc	14.99					0	2.44	800 238-6263
Aetna Crossroads Fund I	AssetAlloc	15.41	19.64		3	1	0	1.68	800 238-6263
Aetna Growth & Income A	Growth/Inc	24.90	28.14	20.39	1	3	0	1.78	800 238-6263
Aetna Growth & Income I	Growth/Inc	25.51	28.99	21.02	1	3	0	1.00	800 238-6263
Aetna Growth Fund A	Growth	32.00	26.88		3	4	0	1.96	800 238-6263
Aetna Growth Fund I	Growth	32.63	27.70		1	3	0	1.17	800 238-6263
Aetna International Fund A	Foreign	20.47	22.78		3	3	0	2.64	800 238-6263
Aetna International Fund I	Foreign	21.20	23.62	16.73	3	3	0	1.72	800 238-6263
Aetna Legacy Fund A	AssetAlloc	12.10					0	2.47	800 238-6263
Aetna Legacy Fund I	AssetAlloc	12.48	14.48		3	1	0	1.72	800 238-6263
Aetna Small Company Fund A	Small Co	22.62	23.85		2	4	0	2.33	800 238-6263
Aetna Small Company Fund I	Small Co	23.23	24.62		2	4	0	1.61	800 238-6263
AHA Diversified Equity	Growth	24.99	28.55	21.96	1	3	0	0.17	800 332-2111
AHA Investment Balanced	Balanced	17.56	20.30	15.30	2	2	0	0.23	800 332-2111
AIM Advisor Flex Fund C	AssetAlloc	18.87	18.77	15.59	2	1	0	2.20	800 347-4246
AIM Advisor International Value C	Foreign	12.72	19.40		3	3	0	0.85	800 347-4246
AIM Advisor Large Cap Value Fund C	Growth/Inc	21.36	23.45	19.08	2	3	0	2.20	800 347-4246
AIM Advisor Real Estate Fund C	Real Est	5.85	17.30		3	3	0	1.17	800 347-4246
AIM Aggressive Growth Fund	Agg Growth	16.67	16.63	22.51	4	5	5.5	1.06	800 347-4246
AIM America Value A	Growth	18.60					4.75	2.00	800 347-4246
AIM America Value B	Growth	17.88						2.17	800 347-4246
AIM Balanced A	Balanced	21.69	22.77	17.01	1	2	4.75	0.98	800 347-4246
AIM Balanced B	Balanced	20.80	21.81		2	2	0	1.83	800 347-4246
AIM Blue Chip Fund A	Growth/Inc	30.85	28.97	22.48	1	3	5.5	1.31	800 347-4246
AIM Blue Chip Fund B	Growth/Inc	29.92					0	2.10	800 347-4246
AIM Capital Development Fund A	Growth	25.96					5.5	1.34	800 347-4246
AIM Capital Development Fund B	Growth	25.04					0	2.04	800 347-4246
AIM Charter Fund A	Growth/Inc	22.25	23.95	18.06	3	3	5.5	1.09	800 347-4246
AIM Charter Fund B	Growth/Inc	21.43	23.05		3	3		1.09	800 347-4246
AIM Constellation Fund A	Agg Growth	17.99	17.56	17.56	4	4	5.5	1.09	800 347-4246
AIM Emerging Markets A	Foreign	−39.69	−12.29	−3.03	5	5	4.75	2.17	800 347-4246
AIM Emerging Markets B	Foreign	−40.03	−12.73	−3.54	5	5		2.62	800 347-4246
AIM Europe Growth A	European	29.37	21.47	15.11	3	3	4.75	1.75	800 347-4246
AIM Europe Growth B	European	28.45	20.67	14.36	3	3	0	2.40	800 347-4246
AIM Global Aggressive Growth A	Global	5.11	16.61		4	4	4.75	1.74	800 347-4246
AIM Global Aggressive Growth B	Global	4.51	15.96		4	4	0	2.28	800 347-4246
AIM Global Cons Products & Svcs A	Growth	40.18	33.85		2	4	4.75	1.75	800 347-4246
AIM Global Cons Products & Svcs B	Growth	37.06	32.37		2	4		2.37	800 347-4246
AIM Global Financial Services A	Financial	25.14	26.10		3	3	4.75	2.36	800 347-4246
AIM Global Financial Services B	Financial	24.49	25.50		3	3	0	2.86	800 347-4246
AIM Global Growth & Income A	Global	25.91	20.64	15.40	2	1	4.75	1.64	800 347-4246
AIM Global Growth & Income B	Global	25.19	19.84	14.64	2	1	0	2.21	800 347-4246
AIM Global Growth A	Global	19.13	21.51		3	3	4.75	1.81	800 347-4246
AIM Global Growth B	Global	18.49	20.86		3	3	0	2.35	800 347-4246
AIM Global Health Care A	Health	14.83	23.34	17.84	4	4	4.75	2.27	800 347-4246

289

Stock Fund Name	Objective	Annualized Return for 1 Year	3 Years	5 Years	Rank Overall	Risk	Max Load	Expense Ratio	Toll-Free Telephone
AIM Global Health Care B	Health	14.20	22.72	17.19	4	4	0	2.29	800 347-4246
AIM Global Infrastructure A	Other	2.86	11.31		4	3	0	2.03	800 347-4246
AIM Global Infrastructure B	Other	2.39	10.71		5	3	4.75	2.53	800 347-4246
AIM Global Resources A	Energy/Res	−10.73	8.53		4	5	4.75	2.10	800 347-4246
AIM Global Resources B	Energy/Res	−11.12	7.62		5	5	0	2.60	800 347-4246
AIM Global Telecommunications A	Technology	22.20	15.26	13.51	4	5	4.75	2.34	800 347-4246
AIM Global Telecommunications B	Technology	21.63	14.66	12.60	4	5	0	2.34	800 347-4246
AIM Global Utilities A	Utilities	23.41	20.54	11.77	3	2	5.5	1.12	800 347-4246
AIM Global Utilities B	Utilities	22.51	19.66		3	2	0	1.89	800 347-4246
AIM International Equity A	Foreign	12.67	17.30	16.33	4	3	5.5	1.47	800 347-4246
AIM International Equity B	Foreign	11.79	16.40		4	3	0	2.27	800 347-4246
AIM International Growth A	Foreign	9.60	13.46	8.83	4	3	4.75	1.82	800 347-4246
AIM International Growth B	Foreign	8.97	12.75	8.13	4	3	0	2.47	800 347-4246
AIM Japan Growth A	Pacific	−16.27	−0.37	−0.15	5	3	4.75	2.08	800 347-4246
AIM Japan Growth B	Pacific	−16.77	−0.98	−0.80	5	3		2.73	800 347-4246
AIM Latin American Growth A	Foreign	−29.83	0.23	1.30	5	5	4.75	2.06	800 347-4246
AIM Latin American Growth B	Foreign	−30.16	−0.23	0.89	5	5	0	2.60	800 347-4246
AIM Mid Cap Growth A	Growth	30.14	13.63	18.27	3	4	4.75	1.43	800 347-4246
AIM Mid Cap Growth B	Growth	29.36	12.88	19.31	4	5	0	1.43	800 347-4246
AIM New Pacific Growth A	Pacific	−54.39	−19.07	−9.39	5	5	4.75	1.65	800 347-4246
AIM New Pacific Growth B	Pacific	−52.55	−18.39	−9.99	5	5	0	2.30	800 347-4246
AIM Select Growth Fund A	Growth	22.06	21.00	16.89	3	4	5.5	1.13	800 347-4246
AIM Select Growth Fund B	Growth	20.98	19.96		4	4	0	2.04	800 347-4246
AIM Small Cap Equity A	Small Co	35.80					4.75	1.95	800 347-4246
AIM Small Cap Equity B	Small Co	34.84						2.60	800 347-4246
AIM Summit Fund	Growth	28.84	24.37	19.48	3	4	8.5	0.67	800 347-4246
AIM Value Fund A	Growth	26.59	22.70	20.45	2	3	5.5	1.04	800 347-4246
AIM Value Fund B	Growth	25.58	21.70		2	3	0	1.86	800 347-4246
AIM Weingarten Fund A	Growth	29.78	24.63	19.81	2	3	5.5	1.05	800 347-4246
AIM Weingarten Fund B	Growth	28.76	23.63		3	3		1.87	800 347-4246
AIM Worldwide Growth A	Global	13.90	14.25	10.15	4	3	4.75	1.78	800 347-4246
AIM Worldwide Growth B	Global	13.08	13.49	9.38	4	3	0	2.43	800 347-4246
Alger Balanced Fund A	Balanced	26.83					4.75	2.16	800 992-3863
Alger Balanced Fund B	Balanced	25.91	18.04	14.33	3	2	0	2.89	800 992-3863
Alger Capital Appreciation Fund A	Growth	29.58					4.75	1.47	800 992-3863
Alger Capital Appreciation Fund B	Growth	28.56	27.03		4	4	0	2.21	800 992-3863
Alger Growth Fund A	Growth	35.15					4.75	1.34	800 992-3863
Alger Growth Fund B	Growth	34.13	24.08	22.28	3	4	0	2.01	800 992-3863
Alger Midcap Growth Fund A	Growth	29.34					4.75	1.52	800 992-3863
Alger Midcap Growth Fund B	Growth	28.29	20.57	23.33	3	4	0	2.13	800 992-3863
Alger Retirement Cap Appreciation	Agg Growth	37.94	24.41		3	5	0	1.46	800 992-3863
Alger Retirement Growth Fund	Growth	36.02	25.27		3	4	0	0.97	800 992-3863
Alger Retirement Midcap Growth Fund	Growth	34.92	25.46		3	4	0	1.27	800 992-3863
Alger Retirement Small Cap Fund	Small Co	28.25	21.12		4	5	0	1.05	800 992-3863
Alger Small Cap Fund A	Small Co	20.05					4.75	1.40	800 992-3863
Alger Small Cap Fund B	Small Co	19.15	12.33	15.51	4	5	0	2.14	800 992-3863
Alliance All-Asia Fund Adv	Pacific	−42.10					0	3.21	800 221-5672
Alliance All-Asia Fund Class A	Pacific	−42.37	−15.47		5	4	4.25	3.45	800 221-5672
Alliance All-Asia Fund Class B	Pacific	−42.80	−16.06		5	4	0	4.15	800 221-5672
Alliance All-Asia Fund Class C	Pacific	−42.61	−16.00		5	4	0	4.15	800 221-5672
Alliance Balanced Shares A	Balanced	24.99	18.46	13.51	3	2	4.25	1.40	800 221-5672
Alliance Balanced Shares Adv	Balanced	25.27					0	1.22	800 221-5672
Alliance Balanced Shares B	Balanced	24.03	17.24	12.62	3	2	0	2.17	800 221-5672
Alliance Balanced Shares C	Balanced	23.98	17.24	12.99	3	2	0	2.15	800 221-5672
Alliance Conservative Inv A	Balanced	14.57	11.50	8.37	3	1	4.25	1.41	800 221-5672
Alliance Conservative Inv B	Balanced	13.82	10.74	7.64	3	1	0	2.11	800 221-5672
Alliance Conservative Inv C	Balanced	13.72	10.70		3	1	0	2.10	800 221-5672
Alliance Fund A	Growth	21.80	22.39	18.61	3	4	4.25	1.03	800 221-5672

Stock Fund Name	Objective	Annualized Return for			Rank		Max Load	Expense Ratio	Toll-Free Telephone
		1 Year	3 Years	5 Years	Overall	Risk			
Alliance Fund Adv	Growth	22.13					0	0.83	800 221-5672
Alliance Fund B	Growth	20.84	21.35	17.58	3	4	0	1.85	800 221-5672
Alliance Fund C	Growth	20.98	21.40	17.63	3	4	0	1.83	800 221-5672
Alliance Global Environment Fund A	Global	18.36	24.34	16.42	3	4	4.25	2.39	800 221-5672
Alliance Global Small Cap A	Global	12.51	20.06	14.77	3	3	4.25	2.12	800 221-5672
Alliance Global Small Cap Adv	Global	12.86					0	1.82	800 221-5672
Alliance Global Small Cap B	Global	11.70	19.21	13.81	4	3	0	2.82	800 221-5672
Alliance Global Small Cap C	Global	11.67	19.25	13.97	4	3	0	2.80	800 221-5672
Alliance Growth & Income A	Growth/Inc	28.51	27.83	20.45	1	3	4.25	0.92	800 221-5672
Alliance Growth & Income Adv	Growth/Inc	29.34					0	0.71	800 221-5672
Alliance Growth & Income B	Growth/Inc	27.60	26.73	19.53	2	3	0	0.92	800 221-5672
Alliance Growth & Income C	Growth/Inc	27.60	26.72	17.74	3	4	0	1.71	800 221-5672
Alliance Growth Fund A	Growth	34.25	27.23	21.76	2	3	4.25	1.26	800 221-5672
Alliance Growth Fund Adv	Growth	34.64					0	0.98	800 221-5672
Alliance Growth Fund B	Growth	33.31	26.35	21.03	2	3	0	1.88	800 221-5672
Alliance Growth Fund C	Growth	33.33	26.35		2	3	0	1.97	800 221-5672
Alliance Growth Investors A	Growth/Inc	19.88	17.43	12.88	3	2	4.25	1.72	800 221-5672
Alliance Growth Investors B	Growth/Inc	19.10	16.64	12.12	3	2	0	2.42	800 221-5672
Alliance Growth Investors C	Growth/Inc	18.92	16.60		3	2	0	2.42	800 221-5672
Alliance Income Builder Fund A	Balanced	16.43	17.98		3	1	4.25	2.09	800 221-5672
Alliance Income Builder Fund Adv	Balanced	16.66					0	1.68	800 221-5672
Alliance Income Builder Fund B	Balanced	15.58	17.12		3	1	0	2.80	800 221-5672
Alliance Income Builder Fund C	Balanced	15.63	17.14	11.87	3	1	0	2.80	800 221-5672
Alliance International Fund A	Foreign	6.79	10.58	10.05	4	3	4.25	1.77	800 221-5672
Alliance International Fund Adv	Foreign	6.98					0	1.64	800 221-5672
Alliance International Fund B	Foreign	5.91	9.65	9.13	4	3	0	2.63	800 221-5672
Alliance International Fund C	Foreign	5.85	9.64	9.13	4	3	0	2.61	800 221-5672
Alliance New Europe Fund A	European	36.48	24.70	22.23	2	3	4.25	1.89	800 221-5672
Alliance New Europe Fund Adv	European	36.63					0	1.57	800 221-5672
Alliance New Europe Fund B	European	35.39	23.79	21.36	2	3	0	2.59	800 221-5672
Alliance New Europe Fund C	European	35.44	23.81	21.38	2	3	0	2.59	800 221-5672
Alliance Premier Growth Fund A	Growth	43.14	34.05	25.87	3	4	4.25	1.57	800 221-5672
Alliance Premier Growth Fund Adv	Growth	43.70					0	1.25	800 221-5672
Alliance Premier Growth Fund B	Growth	42.30	33.13	25.11	3	4	0	2.25	800 221-5672
Alliance Premier Growth Fund C	Growth	42.23	33.14	25.13	3	4	0	2.24	800 221-5672
Alliance Quasar Fund A	Small Co	21.12	30.86	21.84	3	4	4.25	1.67	800 221-5672
Alliance Quasar Fund Adv	Small Co	21.36					0	1.58	800 221-5672
Alliance Quasar Fund B	Small Co	20.18	29.85	20.88	3	4	0	2.51	800 221-5672
Alliance Quasar Fund C	Small Co	20.21	29.84	20.91	3	4	0	2.50	800 221-5672
Alliance Real Estate Investment A	Real Est	7.27					4.25	2.73	800 221-5672
Alliance Real Estate Investment Adv	Real Est	7.45					0	1.45	800 221-5672
Alliance Real Estate Investment B	Real Est	7.19					0	2.44	800 221-5672
Alliance Real Estate Investment C	Real Est	6.48					0	2.43	800 221-5672
Alliance Strategic Balanced Fd Adv	Balanced	16.18					0	1.10	800 221-5672
Alliance Strategic Balanced Fund A	Balanced	16.46	14.64	10.89	3	1	4.25	1.40	800 221-5672
Alliance Strategic Balanced Fund B	Balanced	15.58	13.87	10.13	3	1	0	2.10	800 221-5672
Alliance Strategic Balanced Fund C	Balanced	15.58	13.84		3	1	0	2.10	800 221-5672
Alliance Technology A	Technology	29.00	19.69	27.11	4	5	4.25	1.67	800 221-5672
Alliance Technology Adv	Technology	29.36					0	1.39	800 221-5672
Alliance Technology B	Technology	28.10	18.87	19.68	4	5	0	2.39	800 221-5672
Alliance Technology C	Technology	28.10	18.87	19.68	4	5	0	2.38	800 221-5672
Alliance Utility Income Fund A	Utilities	37.78	19.41		3	3	4.25	1.50	800 221-5672
Alliance Utility Income Fund Adv	Utilities	38.11					0	1.20	800 221-5672
Alliance Utility Income Fund B	Utilities	36.85	18.60		3	3	0	2.20	800 221-5672
Alliance Utility Income Fund C	Utilities	36.78	18.61		3	3	0	2.20	800 221-5672
Alliance Worldwide Privatization A	Global	9.18	17.64		4	3	4.25	1.71	800 221-5672
Alliance Worldwide Privatization Ad	Global	9.82					0	1.43	800 221-5672
Alliance Worldwide Privatization B	Global	8.16	16.78		4	3	0	2.43	800 221-5672

Stock Fund Name	Objective	Annualized Return for			Rank		Max Load	Expense Ratio	Toll-Free Telephone
		1 Year	3 Years	5 Years	Overall	Risk			
Alliance Worldwide Privatization C	Global	8.16	16.78		4	3	0	2.41	800 221-5672
Alliance/Regent Sector Opp Fund A	Growth	35.23					4.25	3.00	800 221-5672
Alliance/Regent Sector Opp Fund Adv	Growth	35.72					0	2.70	800 221-5672
Alliance/Regent Sector Opp Fund B	Growth	34.45					0	3.70	800 221-5672
Alliance/Regent Sector Opp Fund C	Growth	34.36					0	3.70	800 221-5672
Alpine Intl Real Estate Equity B	Real Est	13.64	5.66		4	3	0	2.86	888 785-5578
Alpine Intl Real Estate Equity C	Real Est	13.55	5.66		4	3	0	2.90	888 785-5578
Alpine Intl Real Estate Equity Y	Real Est	14.66	6.60	5.40	4	4	0	1.82	888 785-5578
Alpine US Real Estate Equity A	Real Est	28.92	30.30		2	4	4.75	1.77	800 343-2898
Alpine US Real Estate Equity B	Real Est	27.96	29.40		2	4	0	2.52	800 343-2898
Alpine US Real Estate Equity C	Real Est	27.98					0	2.52	800 343-2898
Alpine US Real Estate Equity Y	Real Est	29.18	27.50		3	4	0	1.50	800 343-2898
Amana Income Fund	Income	21.78	17.66	12.26	3	2	0	1.69	800 728-8762
AMCAP Fund	Growth	34.61	24.33	19.38	2	3	5.75	0.68	800 421-0180
Amer Cent Balanced Fund Adv	Balanced	21.79					0	1.25	800 345-2021
Amer Cent Balanced Fund Inv	Balanced	22.08	17.37	13.54	3	2	0	1.00	800 345-2021
Amer Cent Equity Gr Fund Inv	Growth	37.74	32.04	23.62	1	3	0	1.00	800 345-2021
Amer Cent Equity Inc Fd Adv	Growth/Inc	17.19					0	1.25	800 345-2021
Amer Cent Equity Inc Fd Inv	Growth/Inc	18.56	22.56		2	2	0	1.00	800 345-2021
Amer Cent Global Gold Fd Inv	Gold	–31.72	–19.56	–12.01	5	5	0	0.75	800 345-2021
Amer Cent Global Nat Res Inv	Energy/Res	–4.23	8.60		5	3	0	0.75	800 345-2021
Amer Cent Income & Gr Inv	Growth/Inc	34.76	31.31	22.69	1	3	0	0.65	800 345-2021
Amer Cent Real Estate Fd Inv	Real Est	8.37					0		800 345-2021
Amer Cent Strat All Aggr Adv	AssetAlloc	20.86					0	1.45	800 345-2021
Amer Cent Strat All Aggr Inv	AssetAlloc	21.15					0	1.20	800 345-2021
Amer Cent Strat All Cons Adv	AssetAlloc	14.26					0	1.25	800 345-2021
Amer Cent Strat All Cons Inv	AssetAlloc	14.47					0	1.00	800 345-2021
Amer Cent Strat All Mod Adv	AssetAlloc	18.58					0	1.35	800 345-2021
Amer Cent Strat All Mod Inv	AssetAlloc	18.85					0	1.10	800 345-2021
Amer Cent Utilities Fund Inv	Utilities	36.28	23.09	13.77	3	3	0	0.74	800 345-2021
Amer Cent Value Fund Adv	Growth	17.49					0	1.25	800 345-2021
Amer Cent Value Fund Inv	Growth	17.94	22.84		1	3	0	1.00	800 345-2021
Amer Cent-20th Century Giftrust Inv	Small Co	4.66	4.74	15.61	5	5	0	1.00	800 345-2021
Amer Cent-20th Century Growth Adv	Growth	35.24					0		800 345-2021
Amer Cent-20th Century Growth Inv	Growth	35.57	22.95	18.20	3	4	0	1.00	800 345-2021
Amer Cent-20th Century Heritage Inv	Growth	13.11	16.88	14.15	4	4	0	1.00	800 345-2021
Amer Cent-20th Century Intl Disc In	Foreign	28.95	28.88		3	3	0	1.75	800 345-2021
Amer Cent-20th Century Intl Gr Adv	Foreign	25.45					0	1.66	800 345-2021
Amer Cent-20th Century Intl Gr Inv	Foreign	25.75	23.56	18.29	3	3	0	1.38	800 345-2021
Amer Cent-20th Century New Opps Inv	Small Co	16.77					0	1.50	800 345-2021
Amer Cent-20th Century Select Inv	Growth	30.65	25.96	17.49	3	3	0	1.00	800 345-2021
Amer Cent-20th Century Ultra Adv	Agg Growth	30.82					0	0.80	800 345-2021
Amer Cent-20th Century Ultra Inv	Agg Growth	31.15	25.70	19.79	3	4	0	1.00	800 345-2021
Amer Cent-20th Century Vista Adv	Agg Growth	1.83					0	1.25	800 345-2021
Amer Cent-20th Century Vista Inv	Agg Growth	2.06	6.06	10.26	5	5	0	1.00	800 345-2021
America's Utility Fund	Utilities	23.51	16.92	9.56	3	2	0	1.21	800 487-3863
American AAdvantage Balanced Instl	Balanced	18.17	18.20	14.55	3	1	0	0.60	800 231-4252
American AAdvantage Balanced Mlge	Balanced	17.85	17.77		3	1	0	0.35	800 231-4252
American AAdvantage Balanced Pl Ah	Balanced	17.70	17.85		3	1	0	0.92	800 231-4252
American AAdvantage Gr & Inc Instl	Growth/Inc	21.77	24.53	19.38	1	2	0	0.61	800 231-4252
American AAdvantage Gr & Inc Mlge	Growth/Inc	21.59	24.07		1	2	0	0.35	800 231-4252
American AAdvantage Gr & Inc Pl Ah	Growth/Inc	21.39	24.09		1	2	0	0.95	800 231-4252
American AAdvantage Intl Eq Instl	Foreign	11.86	17.77	17.11	3	2	0	0.83	800 231-4252
American AAdvantage Intl Eq Mileage	Foreign	11.28	16.92		3	2	0	0.59	800 231-4252
American AAdvantage Intl Eq Pl Ah	Foreign	11.67	16.04		3	2	0	1.16	800 231-4252
American Balanced Fund	Balanced	13.97	17.58	14.13	3	1	5.75	0.65	800 421-0180
American Growth Fund A	Growth	7.37					5.75	1.61	800 525-2406
American Growth Fund B	Growth	6.58					0	2.24	800 525-2406

292

Stock Fund Name	Objective	Annualized Return for			Rank		Max Load	Expense Ratio	Toll-Free Telephone
		1 Year	3 Years	5 Years	Overall	Risk			
American Growth Fund C	Growth	6.69					0	2.31	800 525-2406
American Growth Fund D	Growth	7.67	12.28	11.52	4	3	5.75	1.76	800 525-2406
American Heritage Fund	Agg Growth	−24.00	5.35	−8.87	5	5	0	5.31	800 828-5050
American Mutual Fund	Growth/Inc	20.02	22.01	16.93	2	2	5.75	0.58	800 421-0180
American National Growth	Growth	19.79	20.34	17.80	3	3	5.75	0.96	800 231-4639
American National Income	Income	22.32	20.93	16.91	2	2	5.75	1.05	800 231-4639
American Pension Capital Income	Income	15.03	26.77	19.44	3	2	0	1.77	800 544-6060
American Pension Growth Fund	Global	4.39	11.51	11.50	4	3	0	2.24	800 544-6060
American Pension Yorktown Classic V	Growth	−0.91	11.06	11.38	4	4	0	2.65	800 544-6060
American Performance Aggress Growth	Small Co	−0.43	6.84	8.61	5	5	5	1.08	800 762-7085
American Performance Equity	Growth	24.61	28.63	21.34	1	3	5.26	1.05	800 762-7085
Amerindo Technology Fund	Technology	36.65					0	2.78	888 TECHFUND
Ameristar Capital Growth Fund A	Growth	28.55					4.75	1.18	800-852-0045
Ameristar Core Income Fund A	Income	10.54					3	1.12	800-852-0045
Ameristar Dividend Growth Fund A	Growth/Inc	26.18					4.75	1.30	800-852-0045
Ameristock Mutual Fund	Growth/Inc	31.85					0	0.56	800 394-5064
AmSouth Balanced Fund	Balanced	18.02	15.66	13.06	3	1	4.5	1.08	800 451-8382
AmSouth Equity Fund	Growth	24.75	23.74	18.76	2	3	4.5	1.06	800 451-8382
AmSouth Regional Equity	Growth	14.96	21.01	15.71	3	3	4.5	1.06	800 451-8382
Amway Mutual Fund	Growth	18.39	24.01		3	3	3	0.50	800 346-2670
Analytic Defensive Equity Fund	Growth/Inc	26.20	20.74	15.70	2	1	0	1.32	800 374-2633
Anchor Capital Accumulation Trust	Growth	14.04	16.80	11.07	3	2	0	1.12	
Aon Asset Allocation Fund	AssetAlloc	21.44	22.20		3	2	0	0.56	800 266-3637
Aon International Equity Fund	Foreign	5.34					0	1.38	800 266-3637
Aon REIT Index Fund	Real Est	7.11					0	0.87	800 266-3637
Aon S&P 500 Index Fund	Growth	29.97					0	0.53	800 266-3637
APEX MidCap Growth	Agg Growth	12.05	−6.86	−3.24	5	4	5.75	5.25	
Aquila Cascadia Equity Fund A	Growth	10.21						1.18	800 228-4227
Aquila Cascadia Equity Fund C	Growth	9.27					0	1.22	800 228-4227
Aquila Cascadia Equity Fund Y	Growth	10.40					0	1.22	800 228-4227
Aquila Rocky Mountain Equity Fund A	Growth	14.47	15.32		3	2	4.25	1.49	800 228-4227
Aquila Rocky Mountain Equity Fund C	Growth	13.55					0	2.27	800 228-4227
Aquila Rocky Mountain Equity Fund Y	Growth	14.37					0	1.24	800 228-4227
Aquinas Balanced Fund	Balanced	18.25	17.07		3	1	0	1.46	800 423-6369
Aquinas Equity Growth Fund	Growth	32.65	27.50		2	3	0	1.49	800 423-6369
Aquinas Equity Income Fund	Income	18.19	22.33		2	2	0	1.38	800 423-6369
Arch Balanced Portfolio B	Balanced	15.10	15.42	12.06	3	1	0	1.97	800 452-2724
Arch Balanced Portfolio Instl	Balanced	15.95	16.25	12.50	3	1	0	1.37	800 452-2724
Arch Balanced Portfolio Invest	Balanced	15.68	16.14		3	1	4.5	1.27	800 452-2724
Arch Balanced Portfolio Trust	Balanced	16.24	16.59	12.88	3	1	0	0.97	800 452-2724
Arch Growth & Income Eq Inv A	Growth	20.75	23.97	18.50	2	3	4.5	1.04	800 452-2724
Arch Growth & Income Eq Inv B	Growth	19.89	23.19		2	3	0	1.74	800 452-2724
Arch Growth & Income Eq Trust	Growth	21.08	24.38	18.77	2	3	0	0.74	800 452-2724
Arch International Equity Fd A	Foreign	11.34	13.21		4	3	0	1.50	800 452-2724
Arch International Equity Fd B	Foreign	10.82	12.51		4	3	0	2.20	800 452-2724
Arch International Equity Fd Instl	Foreign	11.36	13.17		4	3	0	1.76	800 452-2724
Arch International Equity Trust	Foreign	11.58	14.06		4	3	0	1.20	800 452-2724
Arch Small Cap Equity B	Small Co	10.77	11.44	13.72	4	4	0	2.05	800 452-2724
Arch Small Cap Equity Instl	Small Co	11.49	12.20		4	4	0	1.25	800 452-2724
Arch Small Cap Equity Inv	Small Co	11.61	12.19	14.22	4	4	4.5	1.25	800 452-2724
Arch Small Cap Equity Trust	Small Co	11.96	12.67	13.98	4	4	4.5	1.05	800 452-2724
Ariel Appreciation Fund	Small Co	34.42	29.22	19.51	2	2	0	1.33	800 292-7435
Ariel Growth Fund	Small Co	29.68	26.33	18.39	2	2	0	0.46	800 292-7435
Ark Balanced Fund Instl	Balanced	24.03	18.36		3	2	0	0.74	888 427-5386
Ark Balanced Fund Retail	Balanced	23.77	18.05		3	2	4.75	0.96	888 427-5386
Ark Blue Chip Equity Institutional	Growth	28.37						0.70	888 427-5386
Ark Blue Chip Equity Retail	Growth	28.07					3	1.04	888 427-5386
Ark Capital Growth Instl	Growth	32.54	24.91		3	4	0	0.39	888 427-5386

293

Stock Fund Name	Objective	Annualized Return for			Rank		Max Load	Expense Ratio	Toll-Free Telephone
		1 Year	3 Years	5 Years	Overall	Risk			
Ark Capital Growth Retail	Growth	32.34	24.71		3	4	4.75	0.56	888 427-5386
Ark Equity Income Instl	Income	19.63					0	0.83	888 427-5386
Ark Equity Income Retail	Income	19.31					4.75		888 427-5386
Ark International Equity Retail	Foreign	8.85					0	0.16	888 427-5386
Ark Mid-Cap Equity Instl	Growth	29.06					0	0.65	888 427-5386
Ark Small Cap Equity Instl	Small Co	25.25						0.95	888 427-5386
Ark Small Cap Equity Retail	Small Co	24.96					0	1.11	888 427-5386
Armada Equity Growth Fund Instl	Growth/Inc	29.81	28.55	19.70	2	3	0	0.98	800 622-3863
Armada Equity Growth Fund Retail	Growth/Inc	29.48	28.39	20.05	2	3	3.75	1.22	800 622-3863
Armada Equity Income Fund Instl	Income	19.99	23.12		2	2	0	1.01	800 622-3863
Armada Equity Income Fund Retail	Income	19.85	22.84		2	2	3.75	1.26	800 622-3863
Armada Small Cap Value Instl	Growth/Inc	9.20	19.38		3	3	0	0.97	800 622-3863
Armada Small Cap Value Retail	Growth/Inc	8.77	19.04		3	3	3.75	1.22	800 622-3863
Armstrong Associates Fund	Growth	13.31	14.18	13.89	3	2	0	1.40	
Artisan International Fund	Foreign	13.99					0	1.42	800 454-1770
ASM Index 30 Fund	Growth/Inc	18.25	25.18	19.57	2	3	0	0.42	800 445-2763
Atlas Balanced Fund A	Balanced	21.19	18.98		3	1	3	1.23	800 933-2852
Atlas Balanced Fund B	Balanced	20.52	18.34		3	1	0	1.73	800 933-2852
Atlas Emerging Growth Fund A	Foreign	13.42					3		800 933-2852
Atlas Emerging Growth Fund B	Foreign	12.64					0		800 933-2852
Atlas Global Growth Fund A	Global	21.03					3	1.68	800 933-2852
Atlas Global Growth Fund B	Global	20.40					0	2.23	800 933-2852
Atlas Growth & Income Fund A	Growth/Inc	29.57	26.07	19.19	2	3	3	1.13	800 933-2852
Atlas Growth & Income Fund B	Growth/Inc	29.62	25.67		1	3	0	1.13	800 933-2852
Atlas Strategic Growth Fund A	Growth	23.96	23.10		3	3	3	1.25	800 933-2852
Atlas Strategic Growth Fund B	Growth	23.12	19.98		3	3	0	1.75	800 933-2852
Austin Global Equity Fund	Global	28.75	18.86		3	3	0	2.50	800 551-1980
Avondale Total Return Fund	Growth/Inc	17.65	16.29	13.50	3	2	0	1.83	800 998-3190
Babson Enterprise Fund	Small Co	16.90	20.82	16.75	3	3	0	1.08	800 422-2766
Babson Enterprise Fund II	Growth	18.22	24.16	17.47	3	3	0	1.28	800 422-2766
Babson Growth Fund	Growth	28.17	26.59	20.41	2	3	0	0.83	800 422-2766
Babson Shadow Stock Fund	Small Co	21.98	20.87	16.43	3	2	0	1.13	800 422-2766
Babson Value Fund	Growth/Inc	25.07	25.12	22.33	1	3	0	0.97	800 422-2766
Babson-Stewart Ivory International	Foreign	6.48	11.55	11.66	4	2	0	1.19	800 422-2766
Baron Asset Fund	Small Co	25.06	26.64	23.22	2	4	0	1.40	800 992-2766
Baron Growth and Income Fund	Growth/Inc	19.84	26.62		2	4	0	1.40	800 992-2766
Barr Rosenberg Ser Tr Intl Sm Cap I	Foreign	−5.10					0	1.50	800 555-5737
Barr Rosenberg Ser Tr Intl Sm Cap S	Foreign	−5.47					0	1.50	800 555-5737
Barr Rosenberg Ser Tr Japan Instl	Pacific	−39.52	−17.31	−10.91	5	5	0	1.42	800 555-5737
Barr Rosenberg Ser Tr Japan Select	Pacific	−39.66					0	1.50	800 555-5737
Barr Rosenberg Ser Tr US Sm Cap I	Small Co	19.68	26.34	23.59	3	3	0	1.07	800 555-5737
Barr Rosenberg Ser Tr US Sm Cap Sel	Small Co	18.98					0	1.15	800 555-5737
Bartlett Basic Value A	Growth	23.30	22.23	18.19	2	2	4.75	1.13	800 822-5544
Bartlett Value International A	Foreign	−6.35	9.80	10.71	5	3	0	1.81	800 822-5544
BB&K Diversa Fund	AssetAlloc	14.05	14.07	10.54	3	1	0	1.84	800 882-8383
BB&K International Equity Fund	Foreign	13.04	14.14	11.35	3	3	0	1.45	800 882-8383
BB&T Balanced A	Balanced	17.17	16.31		3	1	4.5	1.19	800 228-1872
BB&T Balanced Trust	Balanced	17.48	16.59		3	1	0	0.95	800 228-1872
BB&T Growth & Income Stock A	Growth/Inc	19.56	24.29	18.76	2	2	4.5	1.09	800 228-1872
BB&T Growth & Income Stock Trust	Growth/Inc	19.84	24.60	19.00	2	2	0	0.84	800 228-1872
BEA Emerging Markets	Foreign	−30.00	−5.19	−0.53	5	4	0	1.49	800 401-2230
BEA Emerging Markets Adv	Foreign	−33.86					0		800 401-2230
BEA Global Telecom Adv	Technology	46.93					0	1.65	800 401-2230
BEA International Equity	Foreign	26.12	18.62	13.11	3	3	0	1.16	800 401-2230
BEA International Equity Adv	Foreign	25.66					0	1.41	800 401-2230
BEA US Core Equity Portfolio	Growth	25.82	27.85		1	3	0	1.00	800 401-2230
Bear Stearns Insiders Select Fund A	Growth	25.91	25.93		2	3	4.75	1.65	800 766-4111
Bear Stearns Insiders Select Fund C	Growth	25.22	25.26		2	3	0	2.15	800 766-4111

294

Stock Fund Name	Objective	Annualized Return for			Rank		Max Load	Expense Ratio	Toll-Free Telephone
		1 Year	3 Years	5 Years	Overall	Risk			
Bear Stearns Insiders Select Fund Y	Growth	26.43	26.31		2	3	0	1.15	800 766-4111
Bear Stearns Large Cap Value A	Growth/Inc	24.25	25.82		2	3	4.75	1.50	800 766-4111
Bear Stearns Large Cap Value C	Growth/Inc	23.70	25.22		3	3	0	2.00	800 766-4111
Bear Stearns Large Cap Value Y	Growth/Inc	24.84					0	1.00	800 766-4111
Bear Stearns S&P STARS A	Growth/Inc	30.94	26.69		3	4	4.75	1.50	800 766-4111
Bear Stearns S&P STARS C	Growth/Inc	30.21	26.02		3	4	0	2.00	800 766-4111
Bear Stearns S&P STARS Y	Growth/Inc	31.51					0	1.00	800 766-4111
Bear Stearns Small Cap Value A	Small Co	28.29	25.27		3	4	5.5	1.50	800 766-4111
Bear Stearns Small Cap Value C	Small Co	27.66	24.61		3	4	0	2.00	800 766-4111
Bear Stearns Small Cap Value Y	Small Co	28.97	25.84		3	4	0	1.00	800 766-4111
Benchmark Balanced A	Balanced	21.24	18.18		3	2	0	0.61	800 637-1380
Benchmark Balanced C	Balanced	20.92					0	0.85	800 637-1380
Benchmark Balanced D	Balanced	20.78					0	1.00	800 637-1380
Benchmark Diversified Growth A	Growth	30.66	27.47	17.53	3	3	0	0.67	800 637-1380
Benchmark Diversified Growth D	Growth	30.24	27.02		2	3	0	1.06	800 637-1380
Benchmark Equity Index A	Growth/Inc	29.61	29.82	22.18	1	3	0	0.22	800 637-1380
Benchmark Equity Index C	Growth/Inc	29.34					0	0.46	800 637-1380
Benchmark Equity Index D	Growth/Inc	29.14	29.47		1	3	0	0.61	800 637-1380
Benchmark Focused Growth A	Growth	31.49	26.02		3	4	0	0.92	800 637-1380
Benchmark Focused Growth C	Growth	31.15					0	1.15	800 637-1380
Benchmark Focused Growth D	Growth	31.00	25.63		3	4	0	1.30	800 637-1380
Benchmark International Growth A	Foreign	15.14	12.35		4	2	0	1.06	800 637-1380
Benchmark International Growth D	Foreign	14.66	11.89		4	2	0	1.45	800 637-1380
Benchmark Intl Equity Index A	Foreign	5.44					0		800 637-1380
Benchmark Small Company Index A	Small Co	16.02	18.41	14.03	4	4	0	0.31	800 637-1380
Benchmark Small Company Index D	Small Co	21.96	20.23		3	4	0	0.71	800 637-1380
Berger 100 Fund	Growth	18.16	16.45	12.59	3	4	0	1.39	800 333-1001
Berger Growth and Income Fund	Growth/Inc	21.73	20.13	14.86	3	2	0	1.50	800 333-1001
Berger New Generation Fund	Growth	36.86					0	1.66	800 333-1001
Berger Small Company Growth Fund	Small Co	27.13	24.17		3	5	0	1.66	800 333-1001
Bernstein International Value	Foreign	17.82	19.67	13.81	3	2	0	1.27	
Berwyn Fund	Small Co	13.33	14.77	14.77	4	3	0	1.20	800 992-6757
Berwyn Income Fund	Flexible	8.88	12.21	10.92	3	1	0	0.65	800 992-6757
Bishop Equity Fund Instl	Growth	27.53					0	1.23	800 262-9565
Bjurman Micro-Cap Growth Fund	Small Co	43.41					0	1.80	800 227-7264
BlackRock Balanced Fund Instl	Balanced	22.36	21.66	16.13	2	2	0	0.84	800 388-8734
BlackRock Balanced Fund Inv A	Balanced	21.80	21.15	15.67	2	2	4.5	1.24	800 388-8734
BlackRock Balanced Fund Inv B	Balanced	20.82	20.23		2	2	0	2.05	800 388-8734
BlackRock Balanced Fund Inv C	Balanced	20.82					0	2.03	800 388-8734
BlackRock Balanced Fund Service	Balanced	22.01	21.29		2	2	0	1.14	800 388-8734
BlackRock Emerging Markets A	Foreign	−42.94	−10.93		5	5	5	2.25	800 388-8734
BlackRock Emerging Markets B	Foreign	−43.35					0	2.98	800 388-8734
BlackRock Emerging Markets C	Foreign	−43.33					0	2.58	800 388-8734
BlackRock Emerging Markets Instl	Foreign	−42.61	−10.46		5	5	0	1.78	800 388-8734
BlackRock Emerging Markets Svc	Foreign	−42.72	−10.71		5	5	0	2.08	800 388-8734
BlackRock Index Equity Instl	Growth/Inc	29.85	27.54	21.35	1	3	0	0.18	800 388-8734
BlackRock Index Equity Invest A	Growth/Inc	29.39	27.05	20.91	1	3	3	0.65	800 388-8734
BlackRock Index Equity Invest B	Growth/Inc	28.23					0	1.38	800 388-8734
BlackRock Index Equity Invest C	Growth/Inc	28.22					0	1.38	800 388-8734
BlackRock Index Equity Service	Growth/Inc	29.60	27.27		1	3	0	0.48	800 388-8734
BlackRock Intl Equity Instl	Foreign	10.12	12.03	10.92	4	3	0	1.06	800 388-8734
BlackRock Intl Equity Inv A	Foreign	9.45	11.52	9.71	4	3	5	1.53	800 388-8734
BlackRock Intl Equity Inv B	Foreign	8.74	10.71		4	3	0	2.27	800 388-8734
BlackRock Intl Equity Inv C	Foreign	8.75					0	2.28	800 388-8734
BlackRock Intl Equity Service	Foreign	9.69	11.65		4	3	0	1.36	800 388-8734
BlackRock Large Cap Grth Eq Instl	Growth	34.91	29.48	20.20	2	3	0	0.87	800 388-8734
BlackRock Large Cap Grth Eq Inv B	Growth	33.28					0	2.01	800 388-8734
BlackRock Large Cap Grth Eq Inv C	Growth	33.28					0	2.02	800 388-8734

Stock Fund Name	Objective	Annualized Return for			Rank		Max Load	Expense Ratio	Toll-Free Telephone
		1 Year	3 Years	5 Years	Overall	Risk			
BlackRock Large Cap Grth Eq Svc	Growth	34.61	29.16		2	3	0	1.10	800 388-8734
BlackRock Large Cap Val Eq Instl	Growth	23.36	26.80	21.13	1	2	0	0.84	800 388-8734
BlackRock Large Cap Val Eq Inv A	Growth	24.78	26.92	21.05	1	2	4.5	1.26	800 388-8734
BlackRock Large Cap Val Eq Inv B	Growth	21.89					0	2.00	800 388-8734
BlackRock Large Cap Val Eq Inv C	Growth	22.01					0	2.01	800 388-8734
BlackRock Large Cap Val Eq Svc	Growth	23.08	26.33		2	4	0	1.09	800 388-8734
BlackRock Midcap Growth Eq Instl	Growth	24.38					0	1.13	800 388-8734
BlackRock Midcap Growth Eq Inv A	Growth	23.67					0	1.59	800 388-8734
BlackRock Midcap Growth Eq Inv B	Growth	22.64					0	2.32	800 388-8734
BlackRock Midcap Growth Eq Inv C	Growth	22.76					0	2.35	800 388-8734
BlackRock Midcap Growth Eq Svc	Growth	23.93					0	1.44	800 388-8734
BlackRock Midcap Value Eq Instl	Growth/Inc	17.96					0	1.15	800 388-8734
BlackRock Midcap Value Eq Inv A	Growth/Inc	17.79					0	1.61	800 388-8734
BlackRock Midcap Value Eq Inv B	Growth/Inc	17.13					0	2.32	800 388-8734
BlackRock Midcap Value Eq Inv C	Growth/Inc	17.13					0	2.33	800 388-8734
BlackRock Midcap Value Eq Svc	Growth/Inc	17.98					0	1.44	800 388-8734
BlackRock Select Equity Instl	Growth/Inc	26.84	28.93		1	3	0	0.79	800 388-8734
BlackRock Select Equity Invest A	Growth/Inc	26.33	28.45		1	3	4.5	1.27	800 388-8734
BlackRock Select Equity Invest B	Growth/Inc	25.32					0	2.01	800 388-8734
BlackRock Select Equity Invest C	Growth/Inc	25.32					0	2.01	800 388-8734
BlackRock Select Equity Service	Growth/Inc	24.76	28.57		1	3	0	1.09	800 388-8734
BlackRock Sm Cap Gr Eq Inv A	Small Co	10.85	20.03		4	5	4.5	1.34	800 388-8734
BlackRock Sm Cap Gr Eq Inv B	Small Co	16.03					0	2.07	800 388-8734
BlackRock Sm Cap Gr Eq Inv C	Small Co	16.03					0	2.07	800 388-8734
BlackRock Sm Cap Val Eq Instl	Small Co	17.88	23.20	18.09	3	3	0	0.87	800 388-8734
BlackRock Sm Cap Val Eq Invest A	Small Co	17.32	22.70	17.70	3	3	3	1.34	800 388-8734
BlackRock Sm Cap Val Eq Invest B	Small Co	16.47	21.54		3	3	0	2.07	800 388-8734
BlackRock Sm Cap Val Eq Invest C	Small Co	16.47					0	2.04	800 388-8734
BlackRock Sm Cap Val Eq Service	Small Co	17.49	22.83		3	3	0	1.17	800 388-8734
BNY Hamilton Equity Income Instl	Income	21.81					0	0.86	800 426-9363
BNY Hamilton Equity Income Inv	Income	21.51	22.88	16.31	2	2	0	0.99	800 426-9363
BNY Hamilton Intl Equity Instl	Foreign	9.97					0	1.22	800 426-9363
BNY Hamilton Intl Equity Investor	Foreign	9.73					0	1.46	800 426-9363
BNY Hamilton Large Cap Instl	Growth	28.11					0	0.81	800 426-9363
BNY Hamilton Large Cap Investor	Growth	27.95					0	1.07	800 426-9363
BNY Hamilton Small Cap Instl	Small Co	12.73					0	0.96	800 426-9363
BNY Hamilton Small Cap Investor	Small Co	12.64					0	1.19	800 426-9363
Boston 1784 Asset Allocation Fund	AssetAlloc	19.30	18.08		3	1	0	0.97	800 252-1784
Boston 1784 Growth & Income Fund	Growth/Inc	29.36	24.36	20.41	2	3	0	0.88	800 252-1784
Boston 1784 Growth Fund	Growth	11.63					0	0.88	800 252-1784
Boston 1784 International Equity A	Foreign	2.32	11.99		4	3	0	1.23	800 252-1784
Boston Balanced Fund	Balanced	27.47						1.02	800-449-8782
Bramwell Growth Fund	Growth	39.46	26.58		3	4	0	1.72	800 272-6227
Brandes International Equity Instl	Foreign	15.17					0	2.46	800 237-7119
Brandywine Blue Fund	Growth	10.02	17.07	18.64	4	4	0	1.08	800 338-1579
Brandywine Fund	Growth	6.06	15.86	17.55	4	4	0	1.04	800 338-1579
Brazos Real Estate Fund	Real Est	4.18					0	1.25	800 336-9970
Brazos Small Cap Fund	Small Co	35.96					0	1.35	800 336-9970
Bremer Growth Stock Fund	Growth	26.58					0	1.05	800-595-5552
Bridges Investment Fund	Growth	22.84	22.94	17.84	1	2	0	0.81	800-595-5552
Bridgeway Aggressive Growth	Agg Growth	18.09	26.60		3	4	0	1.96	800 661-3550
Bridgeway Social Responsibility	Growth	35.31	26.06		2	3	0	1.50	800 661-3550
Bridgeway Ultra-Small Company Port	Small Co	17.70	31.35		3	5	0	1.58	800 661-3550
Brinson Global Equity Fund	Global	8.99	18.37		3	2	0	1.00	800 448-2430
Brinson Global Fund	AssetAlloc	8.28	14.39	10.97	3	1	0	0.99	800 448-2430
Brinson Non US Equity Fund	Foreign	4.86	15.94		4	2	0	1.00	800 448-2430
Brinson US Balanced Fund	Balanced	12.19	13.73		3	1	0	0.88	800 448-2430
Brinson US Equity Fund	Growth/Inc	21.48	27.89		1	3	0	0.80	800 448-2430

Stock Fund Name	Objective	Annualized Return for			Rank		Max Load	Expense Ratio	Toll-Free Telephone
		1 Year	3 Years	5 Years	Overall	Risk			
Brown Capital Management Balanced	Balanced	25.52	20.17	16.66	2	2	0	1.20	800 525-3863
Brown Capital Management Equity	Growth	30.92	24.48	19.75	2	3	0	1.20	800 525-3863
Brown Capital Management Small Co	Small Co	24.29	21.36	18.78	3	4	0	1.50	800 525-3863
Bruce Fund	Flexible	29.78	18.50	13.79	4	4	0	1.69	
Brundage Story & Rose Equity Fund	Growth/Inc	21.68	23.78	17.95	3	3	0	1.28	800 320-2212
BT Investment Capital Appreciation	Growth	29.71	18.43	17.63	4	4	0	1.25	800 730-1313
BT Investment Equity 500 Index	Growth/Inc	29.32	29.38	22.41	1	3	0	0.25	800 730-1313
BT Investment Equity Appreciation	Growth	30.30	19.31		3	4	0	1.00	800 730-1313
BT Investment Instl Asset Mgt	AssetAlloc	24.01	21.19		2	2	0	0.60	800 730-1313
BT Investment International Equity	Foreign	21.00	23.29	20.40	3	3	0	1.50	800 730-1313
BT Investment Latin American Eq	Foreign	−13.75	14.19		4	5	0	2.00	800 730-1313
BT Investment Lifecycle Long Range	AssetAlloc	23.57	20.71		2	2	0	1.00	800 730-1313
BT Investment Lifecycle Mid Range	AssetAlloc	19.42	16.30		3	1	0	1.00	800 730-1313
BT Investment Lifecycle Short Range	AssetAlloc	13.74	10.62		3	1	0	1.00	800 730-1313
BT Investment Pacific Basin Equity	Pacific	−55.26	−19.53		5	5	0	1.75	800 730-1313
BT Investment Small Cap Fund	Small Co	23.25	17.47		4	5	0	1.25	800 730-1313
Buffalo Balanced Fund	Balanced	15.09	15.73		3	1	0	1.05	800 492-8332
Buffalo Equity Fund	Growth	19.10	24.02		3	3	0	1.09	800 492-8332
Buffalo USA Global Fund	Global	8.13	22.14		3	3	0	1.13	800 492-8332
Bull & Bear Gold Investors	Gold	−43.45	−24.78	−18.28	5	5	0	2.77	800 847-4200
Bull & Bear Special Equities Fund	Agg Growth	20.45	12.09	8.30	4	5	0	1.19	800 847-4200
Bull & Bear US and Overseas Fund	Global	15.07	10.06	9.04	5	4	0	3.00	800 847-4200
Burnham Fund A	Growth/Inc	25.86	23.53	16.65	2	2	5	1.10	800 874-3863
Burnham Fund B	Growth/Inc	24.77	22.76		2	3	0	2.10	800 874-3863
Burnham Fund C	Growth/Inc	24.85	22.34		2	2	0	2.10	800 874-3863
Calamos Convertible Fund A	Converts	20.17	20.71	15.46	2	2	4.75	1.40	800 823-7386
Calamos Convertible Fund C	Converts	19.61					0	2.00	800 823-7386
Calamos Convertible Fund I	Converts	20.66					0		800 823-7386
Calamos Global Growth and Income A	Global	19.36					4.75	2.00	800 823-7386
Calamos Global Growth and Income C	Global	20.46					0	2.50	800 823-7386
Calamos Growth and Income Fund A	Converts	24.56	24.62	16.68	2	2	4.75	2.00	800 823-7386
Calamos Growth and Income Fund C	Converts	23.93					0	2.50	800 823-7386
Calamos Growth Fund A	Growth	30.12	27.15	18.30	3	4	4.75	2.00	800 823-7386
Calamos Growth Fund C	Growth	29.49					0	2.50	800 823-7386
Calamos Strategic Income Fund	Converts	13.34	11.10	7.99	3	1	4.75	2.10	800 823-7386
Caldwell & Orkin Market Opportunity	AssetAlloc	34.15	29.78	19.23	2	1	0	1.29	800 237-7073
California Invest Tr S&P 500 Index	Growth/Inc	30.07	29.95	22.32	1	3	0	0.20	800 225-8778
California Invest Tr S&P MidCap	Agg Growth	26.96	21.67	16.67	3	3	0	0.40	800 225-8778
Calvert New Africa Fund	Foreign	24.54	10.72		4	4	2.5	3.00	800 368-2745
Calvert Social Equity Portfolio A	Growth	11.54	18.51	11.25	4	3	4.75	1.17	800 368-2745
Calvert Social Managed Growth A	Balanced	21.61	16.77	12.43	3	2	4.75	1.14	800 368-2745
Calvert Social Managed Growth C	Balanced	20.31	15.46		3	1	0	1.42	800 368-2745
Calvert World Values Intl Equity A	Foreign	20.36	17.47	14.29	3	3	4.75	1.76	800 368-2745
Canandaigua National Equity	Growth	12.15	19.75	16.03	3	4	0	0.54	303 572-5401
Capital Exchange Fund	Growth/Inc	29.38	29.13	24.15	1	3	0	0.69	800 225-6265
Capital Income Builder	Income	21.27	21.34	15.99	2	1	5.75	0.65	800 421-0180
Capital Management Mid Cap Instl	Growth	18.53	21.11		3	3	2.5	1.50	800 525-3863
Capital Management Mid Cap Inv	Growth	17.34	20.52		3	3	3	1.25	800 525-3863
Capital Value Fund	AssetAlloc	22.12	15.86	13.59	3	2	3.5	2.38	800 525-3863
Capital World Growth & Income	Global	15.35	20.99	18.73	2	2	5.75	0.82	800 421-0180
Cappiello-Rushmore Emerging Growth	Small Co	−0.14	3.77	8.11	5	5	0	1.50	800 343-3355
Cappiello-Rushmore Growth Fund	Growth	20.72	17.50	17.47	4	4	0	1.50	800 343-3355
Cappiello-Rushmore Utility Income	Utilities	25.42	16.07	8.33	3	2	0	1.05	800 343-3355
Capstone Growth Fund	Growth	21.23	24.42	16.25	3	3	0	1.20	800 262-6631
Capstone New Zealand Fund	Foreign	−41.11	−7.02	−2.37	4	4	0	2.67	800 262-6631
Capstone Nikko Japan Fund	Pacific	−31.00	−10.41	−8.57	5	4	0	2.57	800 262-6631
Cardinal Aggressive Growth Fund	Agg Growth	8.46	10.26	9.15	5	4	4.5	2.00	800 848-7734
Cardinal Balanced Fund	Balanced	22.42	19.05	14.23	3	2	4.5	1.64	800 848-7734

Stock Fund Name	Objective	Annualized Return for			Rank		Max Load	Expense Ratio	Toll-Free Telephone
		1 Year	3 Years	5 Years	Overall	Risk			
Cardinal Fund	Growth/Inc	25.69	26.37	18.51	2	3	4.5	1.06	800 848-7734
Carillon Inv Tr Capital Fund	AssetAlloc	0.78	7.76	8.46	3	1	5	1.03	800 999-1840
Carl Domino Equity Income Fund	Growth/Inc	15.79					0	1.51	800 506-9922
Carolinas Fund Institutional Class	Growth	24.20	17.63		2	3	0	1.73	800 543-8721
Carolinas Fund Investors Class	Growth	23.61	16.81		3	3	3.5	2.22	800 543-8721
Centurion TAA Fund	AssetAlloc	−3.20	0.51	−6.82	4	1	4.75	2.65	800 400-6432
Century Shares Trust	Financial	34.54	32.67	19.88	2	3	0	0.82	800 321-1928
CGCM Balanced Fund	Balanced	13.83	18.31	14.30	3	1	0	1.00	800-544-7835
CGCM Emerging Markets Equity	Foreign	−35.65	−5.90		5	4	0	1.60	800-544-7835
CGCM International Equity	Foreign	8.69	12.34		4	3	0	0.97	800-544-7835
CGCM Large Cap Growth	Growth	30.77	27.13		3	4	0	0.62	800-544-7835
CGCM Large Cap Value Equity	Growth/Inc	25.33	26.26		2	3	0	0.78	800-544-7835
CGCM Small Cap Growth	Small Co	15.53	18.85	19.99	4	5	0	0.90	800-544-7835
CGCM Small Cap Value Equity	Small Co	19.22	24.10		2	3	0	0.90	800-544-7835
CGM Capital Development Fund	Growth	11.81	26.70	16.76	4	4	0	1.07	800 345-4048
CGM Mutual Fund	Balanced	4.01	14.84	10.93	4	3	0	0.98	800 345-4048
CGM Realty Fund	Real Est	6.09	23.49		3	3	0	1.00	800 345-4048
Chase Balanced Fund	Balanced	23.15	19.24	14.11	3	2	0	1.00	800 34-VISTA
Chase Core Equity Fund	Growth	30.79	29.09	20.11	2	3	0	1.20	800 34-VISTA
Chase Equity Growth Fund	Growth	35.16	29.95	20.88	3	3	0	1.11	800 34-VISTA
Chase Equity Income Fund	Growth/Inc	25.84	26.94	19.06	3	3	0	1.00	800 34-VISTA
Chase Small Cap Fund	Small Co	14.53	25.03	17.48	3	4	0	1.00	800 34-VISTA
Chase Vista Balanced Fund A	Balanced	20.06	18.90	14.44	3	1	4.5	1.25	800 34-VISTA
Chase Vista Balanced Fund B	Balanced	19.18	18.09		3	1	0	2.00	800 34-VISTA
Chase Vista Capital Growth Fund A	Growth	25.95	22.85	17.85	3	3	5.75	1.29	800 34-VISTA
Chase Vista Capital Growth Fund B	Growth	25.32	22.24		3	3	0	1.80	800 34-VISTA
Chase Vista Capital Growth Fund I	Growth	26.44					0	0.92	800 34-VISTA
Chase Vista Equity Income Fund A	Income	20.91	27.63		2	2	4.75	1.50	800 34-VISTA
Chase Vista Equity Income Fund B	Income	20.54					0	2.25	800 34-VISTA
Chase Vista European Fund A	European	43.28					4.75	1.75	800 34-VISTA
Chase Vista European Fund B	European	42.90					0	2.53	800 34-VISTA
Chase Vista Growth & Income Fund A	Growth/Inc	24.47	23.62	17.00	2	3	4.75	1.27	800 34-VISTA
Chase Vista Growth & Income Fund B	Growth/Inc	24.00	23.06		2	3	0	1.76	800 34-VISTA
Chase Vista Growth & Income Fund I	Growth/Inc	24.91					0	0.86	800 34-VISTA
Chase Vista Intl Equity Fund A	Foreign	8.07	9.42	7.60	4	3	4.75	2.00	800 34-VISTA
Chase Vista Intl Equity Fund B	Foreign	7.46	8.88		4	3	0	2.50	800 34-VISTA
Chase Vista Japan Fund A	Pacific	−20.92					4.75	1.75	800 34-VISTA
Chase Vista Japan Fund B	Pacific	−21.46					0	2.50	800 34-VISTA
Chase Vista Large Cap Equity Fund A	Growth	28.01					4.75	1.27	800 34-VISTA
Chase Vista Large Cap Equity Fund B	Growth	27.50					0	1.71	800 34-VISTA
Chase Vista Large Cap Equity Fund I	Growth	28.81	27.96	21.11	1	3	0	0.50	800 34-VISTA
Chase Vista Select Balanced	Balanced	18.83					0		800 34-VISTA
Chase Vista Select Equity Income	Income	19.22					0		800 34-VISTA
Chase Vista Select Intl Equity	Foreign	12.41					0		800 34-VISTA
Chase Vista Select Large Cap Equity	Growth	29.74					0		800 34-VISTA
Chase Vista Select Large Cap Growth	Growth	37.35					0		800 34-VISTA
Chase Vista Select New Growth Opp	Growth	26.86					0		800 34-VISTA
Chase Vista Select Small Cap Value	Small Co	12.21					0		800 34-VISTA
Chase Vista Sm Cap Opportunities A	Small Co	30.96					4.75		800 34-VISTA
Chase Vista Sm Cap Opportunities B	Small Co	30.12					0		800 34-VISTA
Chase Vista Small Cap Equity A	Small Co	20.27	26.79		3	4	4.75	1.46	800 34-VISTA
Chase Vista Small Cap Equity B	Small Co	19.41	25.44		2	4	0	2.17	800 34-VISTA
Chase Vista Small Cap Equity I	Small Co	20.65					0	1.10	800 34-VISTA
Chase Vista Southeast Asian Fund A	Pacific	−53.14					4.75	1.75	800 34-VISTA
Chase Vista Southeast Asian Fund B	Pacific	−53.56					0	2.52	800 34-VISTA
Chesapeake Aggressive Growth Fund	Agg Growth	11.20	12.56	18.51	4	5	3	1.42	800 525-3863
Chesapeake Growth Fund A	Growth	14.88	15.87		4	4	3	1.55	800 525-3863
Chesapeake Growth Fund C	Growth	12.83	14.53		4	4	0	2.73	800 525-3863

Stock Fund Name	Objective	Annualized Return for			Rank		Max Load	Expense Ratio	Toll-Free Telephone
		1 Year	3 Years	5 Years	Overall	Risk			
Chesapeake Growth Fund D	Growth	14.11	15.27		4	4	1.5	2.08	800 525-3863
Chesapeake Growth Fund Instl	Growth	15.27	16.17		4	4	0	1.21	800 525-3863
Chicago Trust Balanced Fund	Balanced	22.25					0	1.00	800 992-8151
Chicago Trust Growth & Inc Fund	Growth/Inc	28.82	30.33		1	3	0	1.00	800 992-8151
Chicago Trust Talon Fund	Growth	7.90	20.41		4	4	0	1.30	800 992-8151
Citicorp Select 200	AssetAlloc	8.00					0	1.50	800 721-1899
Citicorp Select 300	AssetAlloc	9.34					0	1.50	800 721-1899
Citicorp Select 400	AssetAlloc	9.28					0	1.75	800 721-1899
Citicorp Select 500	AssetAlloc	10.32					0	1.75	800 721-1899
CitiFunds Balanced Portfolio	Balanced	16.85	15.06	11.86	3	2	4.75	0.55	800 721-1899
CitiFunds International Equity	Foreign	10.52	9.66	9.05	4	3	4.75	1.00	800 721-1899
CitiFunds Large Cap Growth Port	Growth	33.75	26.93	19.73	2	3	4.75	1.05	800 721-1899
Citizens Emerging Growth	Foreign	33.13						2.12	800 223-7010
Citizens Global Equity	Global	21.82	18.61		3	3		2.18	800 223-7010
Clipper Fund	Growth	19.46	24.60	20.62	2	2	0	1.08	800 776-5033
Cohen & Steers Realty Shares	Real Est	6.57	19.72	14.19	3	3	0	1.06	800 437-9912
Cohen & Steers Special Equity Fund	Real Est	17.47					0		800 437-9912
Colonial Fund A	Balanced	20.53	20.97	16.63	2	2	5.75	1.14	800 345-6611
Colonial Fund B	Balanced	19.67	20.05	15.27	3	2	0	1.90	800 345-6611
Colonial Global Equity A	Global	17.95	19.20	17.25	3	3	5.75	1.55	800 345-6611
Colonial Global Equity B	Global	17.14	18.26	16.26	3	3	0	2.30	800 345-6611
Colonial Global Utilities A	Utilities	20.84	18.28	11.73	3	2	5.75	1.53	800 345-6611
Colonial Global Utilities B	Utilities	19.86	17.35		3	2	0	2.28	800 345-6611
Colonial Global Utilities C	Utilities	19.93	17.37		3	2	0	2.28	800 345-6611
Colonial International Horizons A	Foreign	10.09	15.15	11.77	4	3	5.75	1.62	800 345-6611
Colonial International Horizons B	Foreign	9.38	14.33	11.03	4	3	0	2.37	800 345-6611
Colonial Intl Fund for Growth A	Foreign	−4.99	7.65		5	3	5.75	1.75	800 345-6611
Colonial Intl Fund for Growth B	Foreign	−5.63	6.79		5	3	0	2.50	800 345-6611
Colonial Intl Fund for Growth C	Foreign	−5.68	6.77		5	3	0	2.50	800 345-6611
Colonial Select Value Fund A	Growth	34.37	27.21	21.14	2	3	5.75	1.30	800 345-6611
Colonial Select Value Fund B	Growth	33.32	26.25	20.24	2	3	0	1.77	800 345-6611
Colonial Small Cap Value Fund A	Small Co	18.91	21.20	20.13	3	4	5.75	1.36	800 345-6611
Colonial Small Cap Value Fund B	Small Co	18.05	20.32	19.25	3	4	0	2.07	800 345-6611
Colonial Small Cap Value Fund C	Small Co	18.13					0	2.07	800 345-6611
Colonial Strategic Balanced Fund A	Balanced	17.67					4.75	1.65	800 345-6611
Colonial Strategic Balanced Fund B	Balanced	17.18					0	2.10	800 345-6611
Colonial Strategic Balanced Fund C	Balanced	17.16					0	2.10	800 345-6611
Colonial US Stock Fund A	Growth/Inc	28.66	26.42	19.62	2	3	5.75	1.45	800 345-6611
Colonial US Stock Fund B	Growth/Inc	27.67	25.47	18.89	2	3	0	2.20	800 345-6611
Colonial US Stock Fund C	Growth/Inc	27.73	25.47		2	3	0	2.18	800 345-6611
Colonial Utilities Fund A	Utilities	28.44	20.06	11.79	3	2	4.75	1.22	800 345-6611
Colonial Utilities Fund B	Utilities	27.51	19.21	11.00	3	2	0	1.97	800 345-6611
Columbia Balanced Fund	Balanced	19.76	18.03	14.24	3	1	0	0.68	800 547-1707
Columbia Common Stock Fund	Growth/Inc	24.61	26.35	20.10	1	2	0	0.76	800 547-1707
Columbia Growth Fund	Growth	33.70	28.15	21.53	2	3	0	0.71	800 547-1707
Columbia International Stock Fund	Foreign	7.10	17.70	13.26	4	3	0	1.58	800 547-1707
Columbia Real Estate Equity Fund	Real Est	10.15	22.94		3	3	0	1.01	800 547-1707
Columbia Small Cap Fund	Small Co	28.34					0	1.49	800 547-1707
Columbia Special Fund	Small Co	13.88	16.46	15.48	4	4	0	0.98	800 547-1707
Commerce Balanced Fund I	Balanced	21.62	18.69		3	2	3.5	1.38	800 305-2140
Commerce Growth Fund I	Growth	32.16	27.72		2	3	3.5	1.09	800 305-2140
Commerce International Equity I	Foreign	4.25	11.79		4	3	3.5	1.72	800 305-2140
Commerce MidCap Fund I	Agg Growth	29.25	20.77		3	4	3.5	1.16	800 305-2140
Comstock Partners Capital Value A	AssetAlloc	−27.67	−15.91	−10.89	5	2	4.5	1.28	800 645-6561
Comstock Partners Capital Value B	AssetAlloc	−28.13	−16.55	−11.58	5	2	0	2.03	800 645-6561
Comstock Partners Capital Value C	AssetAlloc	−28.30					0	2.07	800 645-6561
Comstock Partners Capital Value R	AssetAlloc	−27.46					0	1.19	800 645-6561
Concert Invmt Series Growth & Inc 1	Growth/Inc	21.96	24.05	18.27	2	3	8.5	0.89	800 221-3627

299

Stock Fund Name	Objective	Annualized Return for			Rank		Max Load	Expense Ratio	Toll-Free Telephone
		1 Year	3 Years	5 Years	Overall	Risk			
Concert Invmt Series Growth & Inc A	Growth/Inc	21.75	23.40		2	3	5.5	1.14	800 221-3627
Concert Invmt Series Growth & Inc B	Growth/Inc	20.91	22.54		2	3	0	1.89	800 221-3627
Concert Invmt Series Growth Fund 1	Growth	29.79	26.03	19.43	2	3	8.5	0.94	800 221-3627
Concert Invmt Series Growth Fund A	Growth	29.46	25.06		2	3	5.5	1.18	800 221-3627
Concert Invmt Series Growth Fund B	Growth	28.44	24.21		1	3	0	1.93	800 221-3627
Concorde Income Fund	Income	5.75					0	2.00	
Concorde Value Fund	Growth	20.12	22.45	15.98	3	3	0	0.68	
Conseco Asset Allocation A	AssetAlloc	23.87					5.75	1.50	800 986-3384
Conseco Asset Allocation Y	AssetAlloc	24.51					0	1.00	800 986-3384
Conseco Equity Fund A	Growth	29.89					5	1.50	800 986-3384
Conseco Equity Fund Y	Growth	29.92					0	1.00	800 986-3384
Copley Fund	Growth/Inc	23.48	16.60	9.65	3	2	0	1.00	800 424-8570
CoreFund Balanced A	Balanced	23.63	19.25	13.94	3	2	5.5	1.03	800 355-2673
CoreFund Balanced Y	Balanced	23.83	19.52	14.31	3	2	0	0.78	800 355-2673
CoreFund Core Equity A	Growth	21.59	27.13	20.36	2	3	5.5	1.24	800 355-2673
CoreFund Core Equity Y	Growth	21.90	27.55		2	3		0.99	800 355-2673
CoreFund Equity Index A	Growth	29.17					5.5	0.37	800 355-2673
CoreFund Equity Index Y	Growth	28.76	29.58	22.02	1	3	0	0.37	800 355-2673
CoreFund Growth Equity A	Growth/Inc	39.19	30.28	20.19	2	3	5.5	1.21	800 355-2673
CoreFund Growth Equity Y	Growth/Inc	39.69	30.69	20.50	2	3	0	0.96	800 355-2673
CoreFund International Growth A	Foreign	7.35	12.92	10.72	4	3	5.5	1.45	800 355-2673
CoreFund International Growth Y	Foreign	7.58	13.17	10.97	4	3	0	1.20	800 355-2673
CoreFund Special Equity A	Growth	13.78	22.15		4	4	5.5	1.32	800 355-2673
CoreFund Special Equity Y	Growth	14.74	16.20		4	4		1.07	800 355-2673
Cornercap Balanced Fund	Balanced	16.22					0	1.50	800 728-0670
Cornercap Growth	Growth	22.05	23.53	17.07	3	3	0	1.56	800 728-0670
Countrywide Aggressive Growth	Agg Growth	11.38					4.5	1.95	800 543-8721
Countrywide Equity Fund A	Growth	26.09	24.57	16.77	2	2	4	1.25	800 543-8721
Countrywide Equity Fund C	Growth	25.04	23.56		2	2	0	2.00	800 543-8721
Countrywide Growth/Value Fund	Growth	18.47					4.5	1.95	800 543-8721
Countrywide Utility A	Utilities	24.77	17.74	11.38	3	3	4	1.20	800 543-8721
Countrywide Utility C	Utilities	23.71	16.83		3	3	0	2.00	800 543-8721
Cowen Income + Growth Fund A	Income	16.36	18.59	13.27	3	2	4.75	1.21	800 221-5616
Cowen Opportunity Fund A	Small Co	2.14	12.70	13.03	3	4	4.75	1.38	800 221-5616
CRA Realty Shares Instl	Real Est	10.23					0	1.00	800 932-7781
Crabbe Huson Asset Allocation	AssetAlloc	11.31	11.88	11.06	3	2	0	1.55	800 541-9732
Crabbe Huson Equity Fund	Growth	9.81	15.40	15.03	3	3	0	1.36	800 541-9732
Crabbe Huson Real Estate Inv	Real Est	9.92					0	1.50	800 541-9732
Crabbe Huson Small Cap Instl	Small Co	−1.01					0	1.00	800 541-9732
Crabbe Huson Small Cap Retail	Small Co	−1.37					0	1.50	800 541-9732
Crabbe Huson Special Fund	Growth	−16.29	1.52	8.39	5	3	0	1.50	800 541-9732
CrestFunds Capital Apprec Inv Class	Agg Growth	29.50	23.37	18.19	3	3	4.5	1.03	800 451-5435
CrestFunds Capital Apprec Tr Class	Agg Growth	29.55	23.40	18.69	2	3	0	1.05	800 451-5435
Crestfunds Life Vision Balanced	Balanced	15.23					0		800 451-5435
Crestfunds Life Vision Growth & Inc	Growth/Inc	15.92					0		800 451-5435
Crestfunds Life Vision Max Growth	Growth	19.78					0		800 451-5435
CrestFunds Special Equity Inv	Small Co	12.00	16.78	12.90	4	4	4.5	1.03	800 451-5435
CrestFunds Special Equity Inv B	Small Co	10.96	15.66		4	4	0	1.88	800 451-5435
CrestFunds Special Equity Trust	Small Co	12.00	16.81	12.92	4	4	0	1.02	800 451-5435
CrestFunds Value Inv A	Growth/Inc	23.24	24.67	18.30	2	3	4.5	1.03	800 451-5435
CrestFunds Value Inv B	Growth/Inc	22.34	20.21		3	3	0	1.68	800 451-5435
CrestFunds Value Trust	Growth/Inc	23.25	24.66	18.28	1	3	0	1.02	800 451-5435
CRM Small Cap Value Fund Inv	Small Co	16.00					0	1.46	800 551-1980
Croft-Leominster Income Fund	Income	12.71	11.26		4	2	0	1.10	800 551-0990
Croft-Leominster Value Fund	Growth	17.30	24.35		3	3	0	1.50	800 551-0990
Cruelty Free Value Fund	Growth	17.46					0		
Cutler Approved List Equity Fund	Income	24.95	26.34	19.44	2	3	0	1.25	800 228-8537
Cutler Equity Income Fund	Income	21.53	27.17	19.20	2	3	0	1.20	800 228-8537

300

Stock Fund Name	Objective	Annualized Return for			Rank		Max Load	Expense Ratio	Toll-Free Telephone
		1 Year	3 Years	5 Years	Overall	Risk			
Davis Convertible Securities Fund A	Converts	15.04	22.38	15.88	3	2	4.75	1.08	800 279-0279
Davis Convertible Securities Fund B	Converts	13.90	20.78		3	2	0	2.01	800 279-0279
Davis Financial Fund A	Financial	33.93	37.46	26.81	1	3	4.75	1.07	800 279-0279
Davis Financial Fund B	Financial	32.72	36.22		1	3	0	2.02	800 279-0279
Davis Growth Opportunity Fund A	Growth	16.19	19.94		4	5	4.75	1.46	800 279-0279
Davis Growth Opportunity Fund B	Growth	15.22	19.05	19.31	4	5	0	2.08	800 279-0279
Davis Intl Total Return Fund A	Foreign	−6.43	3.41		5	4	4.75	1.70	800 279-0279
Davis Intl Total Return Fund B	Foreign	−7.41	2.65		5	4	0	2.51	800 279-0279
Davis New York Venture Fund A	Growth	24.13	28.36	22.43	2	3	4.75	0.91	800 279-0279
Davis New York Venture Fund B	Growth	23.06	27.14		2	3	0	1.79	800 279-0279
Davis New York Venture Fund C	Growth	23.13	27.17		2	3	0	1.73	800 279-0279
Davis Real Estate Fund A	Real Est	11.37	23.75		3	3	4.75	1.29	800 279-0279
Davis Real Estate Fund B	Real Est	10.45	22.62		3	3	0	2.23	800 279-0279
Dean Balanced Fund A	Balanced	15.24					5.25		888 899-8343
Dean Large Cap Value Fund A	Growth	17.99					5.25		888 899-8343
Dean Small Cap Value Fund A	Small Co	26.34					5.25		888 899-8343
Dean Witter Global Asset Alloc B	AssetAlloc	2.98	10.58		4	2		2.53	800 869-6397
Delafield Fund	Growth	8.76	20.02		3	2	0	1.29	800 221-3079
Delaware Grp Aggressive Growth B	Agg Growth	56.79					0	2.44	800 523-4640
Delaware Grp Blue Chip A	Growth/Inc	25.28					4.75		800 523-4640
Delaware Grp Blue Chip B	Growth/Inc	24.38					0		800 523-4640
Delaware Grp Blue Chip C	Growth/Inc	24.35					0		800 523-4640
Delaware Grp Decatur Income Fund A	Income	20.88	24.47	18.89	2	2	4.75	0.88	800 523-4640
Delaware Grp Decatur Income Fund B	Income	19.99	23.47		2	2	0	1.69	800 523-4640
Delaware Grp Decatur Income Fund C	Income	20.01					0	1.69	800 523-4640
Delaware Grp Decatur Income Instl	Income	20.85	24.61	19.00	2	2	0	0.69	800 523-4640
Delaware Grp Decatur Tot Ret A	Income	21.30	25.61	19.81	2	3	4.75	1.13	800 523-4640
Delaware Grp Decatur Tot Ret B	Income	20.16	24.60		2	2	0	1.81	800 523-4640
Delaware Grp Decatur Tot Ret C	Income	20.38					0	1.81	800 523-4640
Delaware Grp Decatur Tot Ret Instl	Income	21.63	25.95	20.14	2	3	0	0.81	800 523-4640
Delaware Grp Delaware Fund A	Balanced	20.66	19.84	14.73	3	2	4.75	0.97	800 523-4640
Delaware Grp Delaware Fund B	Balanced	19.71	18.87		3	2	0	1.74	800 523-4640
Delaware Grp Delaware Fund C	Balanced	19.87					0	1.74	800 523-4640
Delaware Grp Delaware Fund Instl	Balanced	20.89	20.02		3	2	0	0.74	800 523-4640
Delaware Grp DelCap A	Growth	21.26	18.22	14.93	3	4	4.75	1.36	800 523-4640
Delaware Grp DelCap B	Growth	20.40	17.41		4	4	0	2.04	800 523-4640
Delaware Grp DelCap C	Growth	20.43					0	2.04	800 523-4640
Delaware Grp DelCap Instl	Growth	21.65	18.59		3	4	0	1.04	800 523-4640
Delaware Grp Devon Fund A	Growth/Inc	29.59	29.16		1	3	4.75	1.25	800 523-4640
Delaware Grp Devon Fund B	Growth/Inc	28.54	28.22		1	3	0	1.94	800 523-4640
Delaware Grp Devon Fund C	Growth/Inc	28.67					0	1.94	800 523-4640
Delaware Grp Devon Fund Instl	Growth/Inc	29.99	29.13		1	3	0	0.94	800 523-4640
Delaware Grp Emerging Markets A	Foreign	−36.91					4.75	2.00	800 523-4640
Delaware Grp Emerging Markets B	Foreign	−37.41					0	2.70	800 523-4640
Delaware Grp Emerging Markets C	Foreign	−37.36					0	2.70	800 523-4640
Delaware Grp Emerging Markets I	Foreign	−36.72					0	1.70	800 523-4640
Delaware Grp Global Assets Fund A	AssetAlloc	9.23	14.98		3	1	4.75	1.25	800 523-4640
Delaware Grp Global Assets Fund B	AssetAlloc	8.44	14.19		3	1	0	1.95	800 523-4640
Delaware Grp Global Assets Fund C	AssetAlloc	8.48					0	1.95	800 523-4640
Delaware Grp Global Assets Instl	AssetAlloc	9.54	15.30		3	1	0	0.95	800 523-4640
Delaware Grp Intl Equity A	Foreign	3.64	14.52	12.80	3	3	4.75	1.85	800 523-4640
Delaware Grp Intl Equity B	Foreign	2.94	13.78		4	3	0	2.55	800 523-4640
Delaware Grp Intl Equity C	Foreign	2.94					0	2.55	800 523-4640
Delaware Grp Intl Equity Instl	Foreign	3.80	14.81		4	3	0	1.55	800 523-4640
Delaware Grp Small-Cap Value A	Small Co	14.06	22.56	15.59	3	3	4.75	1.39	800 523-4640
Delaware Grp Small-Cap Value B	Small Co	13.30	21.71		2	3	0	2.13	800 523-4640
Delaware Grp Small-Cap Value C	Small Co	13.32					0	2.13	800 523-4640
Delaware Grp Small-Cap Value Instl	Small Co	14.44	22.94	15.93	3	3	0	1.13	800 523-4640

Stock Fund Name	Objective	Annualized Return for			Rank		Max Load	Expense Ratio	Toll-Free Telephone
		1 Year	3 Years	5 Years	Overall	Risk			
Delaware Grp Social Awareness A	Growth	34.00					4.75		800 523-4640
Delaware Grp Social Awareness B	Growth	32.96					0		800 523-4640
Delaware Grp Social Awareness C	Growth	32.96					0		800 523-4640
Delaware Grp Trend Fund A	Agg Growth	24.11	19.61	16.45	4	4	4.75	1.08	800 523-4640
Delaware Grp Trend Fund B	Agg Growth	23.09	18.69		4	4	0	2.09	800 523-4640
Delaware Grp Trend Fund C	Agg Growth	23.10					0	2.09	800 523-4640
Delaware Grp Trend Fund Instl	Agg Growth	23.65	19.65	16.59	4	4	0	1.08	800 523-4640
Delaware-Voyageur Growth Stock Fund	Growth	17.16	21.70	17.22	3	3	4.75	1.75	800 523-4640
Depositors Fund of Boston	Growth/Inc	29.46	30.90	22.96	1	3	0	0.71	800 225-6265
DFA Continental Small Company	European	22.41	12.94	14.96	3	3	0	0.72	888-326-5327
DFA Emerging Markets	Foreign	−35.29	−7.60		5	5	0	1.15	888-326-5327
DFA International Small Cap Value	Foreign	−14.90					0	0.99	888-326-5327
DFA International Value	Foreign	5.85	10.28		4	3	0	0.65	888-326-5327
DFA Japanese Small Company	Pacific	−45.56	−22.43	−17.38	5	5	0	0.74	888-326-5327
DFA Large Cap International	Foreign	7.80	12.12	10.45	4	3	0	0.51	888-326-5327
DFA Pacific Rim Small Company	Pacific	−59.01	−20.44	−9.30	5	5	0	0.83	888-326-5327
DFA Real Estate Securities	Real Est	8.33	18.15	11.24	4	2	0	0.80	888-326-5327
DFA United Kingdom Small Company	European	17.89	15.87	13.93	3	2	0	0.69	888-326-5327
DFA US 6-10 Small Company	Small Co	15.94	19.10	16.42	4	4	0	0.46	888-326-5327
DFA US 9-10 Small Company	Small Co	18.14	15.90	17.06	4	4	0	0.61	888-326-5327
DFA US Large Cap Value	Growth/Inc	34.63	28.41	20.96	2	3	0	0.36	888-326-5327
DFA US Large Company	Growth/Inc	30.00	29.94	22.79	1	3	0	0.15	888-326-5327
DFA US Small Cap Value	Small Co	20.12	23.35	20.72	3	3	0	0.61	888-326-5327
DG Equity Fund	Growth/Inc	31.55	29.01	22.43	2	3	3.5	0.96	800 530-7377
DG Opportunity Fund	Small Co	12.73	18.37		4	5	3.5	1.14	800 530-7377
Diversification Fund	Growth/Inc	29.45	27.71	21.48	1	3	4	0.78	800 225-6265
Dodge & Cox Balanced Fund	Balanced	15.36	17.74	15.16	3	1	0	0.55	800 621-3979
Dodge & Cox Stock Fund	Growth/Inc	17.90	24.07	20.14	2	3	0	0.57	800 621-3979
Domini Social Equity Fund	Growth	32.96	30.33	22.55	2	3	0	1.23	800 762-6814
Dreyfus Aggressive Growth	Agg Growth	−30.15					0	0.60	800 645-6561
Dreyfus Aggressive Value	Small Co	9.27					0	1.24	800 645-6561
Dreyfus Appreciation Fund	Growth	28.34	31.06	24.15	1	3	0	0.88	800 645-6561
Dreyfus Asset Allocation Tot Ret	AssetAlloc	17.46	17.00		3	2	0	0.66	800 645-6561
Dreyfus Balanced Fund	Balanced	12.69	14.95	14.08	3	1	0	0.96	800 645-6561
Dreyfus Basic S&P 500 Stock Index	Growth/Inc	29.76	29.87		1	3	0	0.20	800 645-6561
Dreyfus Disciplined Stock Fund R	Growth/Inc	31.45	30.64	22.57	1	3	0	1.15	800 645-6561
Dreyfus Emerging Leaders Fund	Growth	25.19					0	1.39	800 645-6561
Dreyfus Emerging Markets Fund	Foreign	−29.59					0	0.98	800 645-6561
Dreyfus Equity Dividend Fund	Growth/Inc	15.63					0	1.27	800 645-6561
Dreyfus Fund	Growth/Inc	13.31	14.84	12.55	4	3	0	0.71	800 645-6561
Dreyfus Global Growth LP	Global	9.44	13.43	10.58	4	3	3	0.67	800 645-6561
Dreyfus Growth and Income	Growth/Inc	12.62	16.10	13.71	4	3	0	1.01	800 645-6561
Dreyfus Growth Opportunity	Growth	9.02	18.16	14.36	4	3	0	0.52	800 645-6561
Dreyfus International Growth Fund	Foreign	1.84	8.86		5	3	0	0.96	800 645-6561
Dreyfus International Stock Index	Foreign	4.10					0		800 645-6561
Dreyfus International Value Fund	Foreign	8.76					0	1.49	800 645-6561
Dreyfus Large Company Value	Growth	12.93	26.02		3	3	0	1.22	800 645-6561
Dreyfus MidCap Index	Growth	26.48	23.44	17.87	3	3	0	0.50	800 645-6561
Dreyfus Midcap Value Fund	Growth	14.48					0	1.25	800 645-6561
Dreyfus New Leaders Fund	Small Co	17.89	19.99	17.00	3	3	0	1.12	800 645-6561
Dreyfus Premier Aggressive Growth A	Agg Growth	−27.67	−10.07	−3.85	5	5	5.75	1.20	800 334-6899
Dreyfus Premier Aggressive Growth B	Agg Growth	−28.25					0	1.95	800 334-6899
Dreyfus Premier Aggressive Growth C	Agg Growth	−28.95					0	1.99	800 334-6899
Dreyfus Premier Aggressive Growth R	Agg Growth	−27.76					0	0.76	800 334-6899
Dreyfus Premier Balanced A	Balanced	18.23	21.43		2	2	5.75	1.25	800 334-6899
Dreyfus Premier Balanced B	Balanced	17.23	20.46		3	2	0	2.00	800 334-6899
Dreyfus Premier Balanced C	Balanced	17.34	20.33		3	2	0	2.00	800 334-6899
Dreyfus Premier Balanced R	Balanced	18.54	21.74		2	2	0	1.00	800 334-6899

Stock Fund Name	Objective	Annualized Return for			Rank		Max Load	Expense Ratio	Toll-Free Telephone
		1 Year	3 Years	5 Years	Overall	Risk			
Dreyfus Premier Core Value A	Growth	15.41	23.58	19.42	2	3	0	1.12	800 334-6899
Dreyfus Premier Core Value Instl	Growth	15.49	23.69	19.54	1	3	0	0.51	800 334-6899
Dreyfus Premier Core Value R	Growth	15.38	23.84		2	3	0	0.44	800 334-6899
Dreyfus Premier Growth and Income A	Growth/Inc	13.85					5.75	1.24	800 334-6899
Dreyfus Premier Growth and Income B	Growth/Inc	13.14					0	2.00	800 334-6899
Dreyfus Premier Growth and Income C	Growth/Inc	13.03					0	2.00	800 334-6899
Dreyfus Premier Growth and Income R	Growth/Inc	14.01					0	0.99	800 334-6899
Dreyfus Premier International Gr A	Foreign	9.68	13.69	11.46	4	3	5.75	1.30	800 334-6899
Dreyfus Premier International Gr B	Foreign	8.83	12.82	9.70	4	3	0	2.05	800 334-6899
Dreyfus Premier International Gr C	Foreign	8.78					0	2.10	800 334-6899
Dreyfus Premier International Gr R	Foreign	9.76					0	1.09	800 334-6899
Dreyfus Premier Large Co Stock A	Income	31.62	30.28		1	3	5.75	0.57	800 334-6899
Dreyfus Premier Large Co Stock R	Income	31.97	30.59		1	3	0	0.45	800 334-6899
Dreyfus Premier Mid Cap Stk A	Growth	25.25	29.20		1	3	0	0.67	800 334-6899
Dreyfus Premier Mid Cap Stk R	Growth	25.63	29.57		1	3	0	1.10	800 334-6899
Dreyfus Premier Small Company Stk A	Small Co	15.34	20.56		3	4	5.75	0.74	800 334-6899
Dreyfus Premier Small Company Stk B	Small Co	14.37	19.60		4	4	0	1.12	800 334-6899
Dreyfus Premier Small Company Stk C	Small Co	14.37	19.60		4	4	0	1.12	800 334-6899
Dreyfus Premier Small Company Stk R	Small Co	15.53	20.80		3	4	0	0.62	800 334-6899
Dreyfus Premier Value Fund A	Small Co	11.00	18.54	12.63	3	3	5.75	1.18	800 334-6899
Dreyfus Premier Value Fund B	Small Co	10.11	17.65	11.76	4	3	0	1.93	800 334-6899
Dreyfus Premier Value Fund C	Small Co	10.04					0	2.00	800 334-6899
Dreyfus Premier Value Fund R	Small Co	10.73					0	0.94	800 334-6899
Dreyfus Premier Worldwide Growth A	Global	28.29	27.37		1	3	5.75	1.19	800 334-6899
Dreyfus Premier Worldwide Growth B	Global	27.31	26.40		1	3	0	2.00	800 334-6899
Dreyfus Premier Worldwide Growth C	Global	27.30	26.35		1	3	0	1.99	800 334-6899
Dreyfus Premier Worldwide Growth R	Global	28.57					0	0.95	800 334-6899
Dreyfus S&P 500 Index Fund	Growth/Inc	29.51	29.51	22.38	1	3	0	0.25	800 645-6561
Dreyfus Small Cap Stock Index	Small Co	19.29					0	0.17	800 645-6561
Dreyfus Small Company Value Fund	Small Co	11.67	27.61		2	3	0	1.23	800 645-6561
Dreyfus Third Century Fund	Growth	30.15	29.62	20.28	2	3	0	0.49	800 645-6561
Driehaus International Growth Fund	Foreign	31.56					0		800 560-6111
Eagle Growth Shares	Growth	9.70	14.20	7.48	5	3	8.5	2.75	800 749-9933
Eastcliff Growth Fund	Growth	33.86					0	1.30	
Eastcliff Regional Small Cap Value	Small Co	11.06					0	1.30	
Eastcliff Total Return Fund	Growth/Inc	29.36	27.30	18.52	2	3	0	1.30	800 338-1579
Eaton Vance Balanced A	Balanced	19.24	19.46	15.59	2	2	4.5	0.97	800 225-6265
Eaton Vance Balanced B	Balanced	18.16	18.32		3	2	0	1.93	800 225-6265
Eaton Vance Greater China Growth A	Pacific	−53.89	−13.38	−3.98	5	5	5.75	2.14	800 225-6265
Eaton Vance Greater China Growth B	Pacific	−54.24	−13.87	−4.69	5	5	0	2.14	800 225-6265
Eaton Vance Greater India Fund A	Foreign	−27.20	−12.39		5	5	0	2.93	800 225-6265
Eaton Vance Greater India Fund B	Foreign	−27.18	−13.09		5	5	0	2.97	800 225-6265
Eaton Vance Growth Fund A	Growth	23.27	25.00	17.61	2	3	5.75	2.04	800 225-6265
Eaton Vance Growth Fund B	Growth	22.48	23.61		2	3	0	2.04	800 225-6265
Eaton Vance Marathon Prime Rate Res	Flexible	7.07	7.00	6.83	3	1	0	1.35	800 225-6265
Eaton Vance Special Equities Fund A	Growth	21.87	21.49	13.63	3	4	4.75	1.25	800 225-6265
Eaton Vance Special Equities Fund B	Growth	19.55	18.52		3	4	0	3.20	800 225-6265
Eaton Vance Stock Fund A	Growth/Inc	26.69	26.72	19.13	2	3	5.75	1.18	800 225-6265
Eaton Vance Stock Fund B	Growth/Inc	25.56	25.18		2	2	0	2.09	800 225-6265
Eaton Vance Utilities Fund A	Utilities	26.75	18.66	9.30	3	2	4.75	1.13	800 225-6265
Eaton Vance Utilities Fund B	Utilities	25.58	17.65		3	2	0	2.04	800 225-6265
Eaton Vance Worldwide Dev Res B	Energy/Res	−39.22	−8.14	−1.27	5	5	0	2.40	800 225-6265
Eaton Vance Worldwide Health Sci A	Health	−1.14	20.06	17.85	4	4	5.75	2.00	800 225-6265
Eclipse Balanced Fund	Balanced	21.93	18.30	14.27	3	1	0	0.84	800 872-2710
Eclipse Equity Fund	Small Co	28.20	28.15	19.48	2	3	0	1.14	800 872-2710
Eclipse Growth and Income Fund	Growth/Inc	34.11	28.39		1	2	0	0.94	800 872-2710
Ehrenkrantz Growth	Growth	8.29	7.69	7.23	3	1	0	1.90	800 424-8570
Elfun Diversified Fund	Flexible	18.52	18.49	14.97	2	1	0	3.41	800 242-0134

303

Stock Fund Name	Objective	Annualized Return for			Rank		Max Load	Expense Ratio	Toll-Free Telephone
		1 Year	3 Years	5 Years	Overall	Risk			
Elfun Global Fund	Global	13.81	15.60	15.69	3	3	0	0.13	800 242-0134
Elfun Trusts	Growth	26.90	28.61	22.49	1	3	0	0.13	800 242-0134
Endowments Fund	Growth/Inc	19.67	22.03	16.79	2	2	0	0.74	800 421-0180
Enterprise Capital Appreciation	Agg Growth	30.20	20.96	16.59	3	4	4.75	1.65	800 432-4320
Enterprise Equity Income A	Income	16.84	23.94	17.87	2	2	4.75	1.50	800 432-4320
Enterprise Growth Portfolio	Growth	31.05	32.95	27.26	2	4	4.75	1.42	800 432-4320
Enterprise International Growth A	Foreign	4.94	13.33	11.55	4	2	4.75	1.71	800 432-4320
ESC Strategic Appreciation A	Growth	19.58	21.84		3	3	4.5	1.82	800 261-3863
ESC Strategic Appreciation D	Growth	19.27	22.41		3	4	4.5	2.34	800 261-3863
ESC Strategic Global Equity A	Global	4.95	11.03		5	3	4.5	2.25	800 261-3863
ESC Strategic Global Equity D	Global	4.64	10.72		5	3	1.5	2.78	800 261-3863
ESC Strategic Growth Fund A	Growth	9.63					4.5	2.00	800 261-3863
ESC Strategic Growth Fund D	Growth	9.13					1.5	2.50	800 261-3863
ESC Strategic Income Fund A	Income	6.04	5.29		3	1	4.5	1.65	800 261-3863
ESC Strategic Income Fund D	Income	5.51	4.76		3	1	1.5	2.15	800 261-3863
ESC Strategic Small Cap Fund A	Small Co	10.36	26.24		4	4	4.5	1.66	800 261-3863
ESC Strategic Small Cap Fund D	Small Co	10.02	25.89		4	4	1.5	2.50	800 261-3863
ESC Strategic Value A	Growth/Inc	6.19					4.5		800 261-3863
ESC Strategic Value D	Growth/Inc	5.68					1.5		800 261-3863
EuroPacific Growth Fund	Foreign	7.65	16.19	15.55	4	3	5.75	0.88	800 421-0180
Evergreen Aggressive Growth Fund A	Agg Growth	22.63	18.63	14.65	4	5	4.75	1.01	800 343-2898
Evergreen Aggressive Growth Fund B	Agg Growth	22.01					0	2.05	800 343-2898
Evergreen Aggressive Growth Fund C	Agg Growth	22.21					0	2.05	800 343-2898
Evergreen Aggressive Growth Fund Y	Agg Growth	22.74					0	1.03	800 343-2898
Evergreen American Retirement A	Flexible	14.46	16.29		3	1	0.0475	1.37	800 343-2898
Evergreen American Retirement B	Flexible	13.62	15.42		3	1	0	2.11	800 343-2898
Evergreen American Retirement C	Flexible	13.59	15.44		3	1	0	2.12	800 343-2898
Evergreen American Retirement Y	Flexible	14.74	16.51	12.56	3	1	0	1.09	800 343-2898
Evergreen Balanced Fund B	Balanced	16.09	18.44	13.40	3	1	0	1.34	800 343-2898
Evergreen Blue Chip Fund B	Growth/Inc	25.73	26.27	17.97	3	3	0	1.58	800 343-2898
Evergreen Emerging Markets Growth A	Foreign	−11.11	7.10		5	4	4.75	1.75	800 343-2898
Evergreen Emerging Markets Growth B	Foreign	−11.97	6.32		5	4	0	2.51	800 343-2898
Evergreen Emerging Markets Growth C	Foreign	−11.99	6.32		5	4	0	2.54	800 343-2898
Evergreen Emerging Markets Growth Y	Foreign	−10.81	7.39		5	4	0	1.49	800 343-2898
Evergreen Fd for Tot Ret A	Income	21.73	25.76	17.67	2	2	5.75	1.24	800 343-2898
Evergreen Fd for Tot Ret B	Income	20.79	24.75	16.86	2	2	0	2.00	800 343-2898
Evergreen Fd for Tot Ret C	Income	20.83	24.79	16.84	2	2	0	1.66	800 343-2898
Evergreen Foundation Fund A	Balanced	21.36	18.67		3	2	4.75	1.25	800 343-2898
Evergreen Foundation Fund B	Balanced	20.44	17.78		3	2	0	2.00	800 343-2898
Evergreen Foundation Fund C	Balanced	20.51	17.63		3	2	0	2.00	800 343-2898
Evergreen Foundation Fund Y	Balanced	21.59	18.77	15.56	3	2	0	0.99	800 343-2898
Evergreen Fund A	Agg Growth	23.87	23.40		2	2	4.75	1.43	800 343-2898
Evergreen Fund B	Agg Growth	22.94	22.53		1	2	0	2.17	800 343-2898
Evergreen Fund C	Agg Growth	22.92	22.52		1	2	0	2.18	800 343-2898
Evergreen Fund Y	Agg Growth	24.20	23.78	19.60	2	2	0	1.18	800 343-2898
Evergreen Global Leaders Fund A	Global	16.94					4.75	1.76	800 343-2898
Evergreen Global Leaders Fund B	Global	16.14					0	2.50	800 343-2898
Evergreen Global Leaders Fund C	Global	16.01					0	2.51	800 343-2898
Evergreen Global Leaders Fund Y	Global	17.19					0	1.50	800 343-2898
Evergreen Global Opp A	Global	12.60	9.59	11.82	4	3	4.75	1.87	800 343-2898
Evergreen Global Opp B	Global	11.77	8.75		4	3	0	2.51	800 343-2898
Evergreen Global Opp C	Global	11.79	8.72		4	3	0	2.53	800 343-2898
Evergreen Growth & Income A	Growth/Inc	22.27					4.75	1.47	800 343-2898
Evergreen Growth & Income B	Growth/Inc	21.44	24.02		1	2	0	2.25	800 343-2898
Evergreen Growth & Income C	Growth/Inc	21.44	23.93		1	2	0	2.25	800 343-2898
Evergreen Growth & Income Y	Growth/Inc	22.63	25.14	20.46	2	2	0	1.21	800 343-2898
Evergreen Income and Growth A	Income	15.57	16.38		3	2	4.75	1.45	800 343-2898
Evergreen Income and Growth B	Income	14.65	15.51		3	2	0	2.20	800 343-2898

Stock Fund Name	Objective	Annualized Return for			Rank		Max Load	Expense Ratio	Toll-Free Telephone
		1 Year	3 Years	5 Years	Overall	Risk			
Evergreen Income and Growth C	Income	14.63	15.61		3	2	0	2.20	800 343-2898
Evergreen Income and Growth Y	Income	15.74	16.63	11.77	3	2	0	1.20	800 343-2898
Evergreen Intl Equity A	Foreign	−4.02	7.33		5	3	4.75	1.24	800 343-2898
Evergreen Intl Equity B	Foreign	−4.63	6.61		5	3	0	1.99	800 343-2898
Evergreen Intl Equity C	Foreign	−4.59	6.67		5	3	0	1.99	800 343-2898
Evergreen Intl Equity Y	Foreign	−3.69	7.64		5	3	0	0.99	800 343-2898
Evergreen Intl Growth Fund B	Foreign	18.42	19.12	14.18	3	2	0	2.38	800 343-2898
Evergreen Latin America Fund A	Foreign	−22.18	9.50		5	5	5.75	1.86	800 343-2898
Evergreen Latin America Fund B	Foreign	−22.73	8.68		5	5	0	2.61	800 343-2898
Evergreen Latin America Fund C	Foreign	−22.94	8.60		5	5		2.61	800 343-2898
Evergreen Micro Cap Fund A	Small Co	24.87	17.80		4	4	4.75	1.78	800 343-2898
Evergreen Micro Cap Fund B	Small Co	27.45	18.04		4	3	0	2.67	800 343-2898
Evergreen Micro Cap Fund C	Small Co	27.43	18.02		4	3	0	2.68	800 343-2898
Evergreen Micro Cap Fund Y	Small Co	28.69	19.17	12.50	4	3	0	1.36	800 343-2898
Evergreen Natural Resources A	Energy/Res	−22.39	2.18		5	4	4.75	2.01	800 343-2898
Evergreen Natural Resources B	Energy/Res	−22.99	1.40		5	4	0	2.78	800 343-2898
Evergreen Natural Resources C	Energy/Res	−23.06	1.37		5	4		2.79	800 343-2898
Evergreen Omega Fund A	Agg Growth	31.02	22.97	17.52	3	4	4.75	1.31	800 343-2898
Evergreen Omega Fund B	Agg Growth	29.91	21.89		3	4	0	2.16	800 343-2898
Evergreen Omega Fund C	Agg Growth	29.96	21.90		3	4	0	2.17	800 343-2898
Evergreen Precious Metals Fund B	Gold	−34.14	−16.41	−9.97	5	5	0	2.48	800 343-2898
Evergreen Small Cap Equity Inc A	Small Co	13.53	22.88		3	2	4.75	1.71	800 343-2898
Evergreen Small Cap Equity Inc B	Small Co	12.60	21.98		3	2	0	2.46	800 343-2898
Evergreen Small Cap Equity Inc C	Small Co	12.61	21.95		3	2	0	2.44	800 343-2898
Evergreen Small Cap Equity Inc Y	Small Co	13.80	23.26		3	2	0	1.38	800 343-2898
Evergreen Small Company Gr A	Small Co	5.59					5.75	1.92	800 343-2898
Evergreen Small Company Gr B	Small Co	8.91	8.76	12.58	4	4	0	1.77	800 343-2898
Evergreen Small Company Gr C	Small Co	4.80					0	2.68	800 343-2898
Evergreen Strategic Growth Fund B	Growth	27.71	24.08	18.17	3	3	0	1.19	800 343-2898
Evergreen Tax Strat Foundation A	Balanced	15.07	15.62		3	1	4.75	1.38	800 343-2898
Evergreen Tax Strat Foundation B	Balanced	14.28	17.93		3	1	0	2.14	800 343-2898
Evergreen Tax Strat Foundation C	Balanced	14.23	16.52		3	1	0	2.14	800 343-2898
Evergreen Utility A	Utilities	22.68	17.75		3	3	4.75	0.99	800 343-2898
Evergreen Utility B	Utilities	21.69	16.82		3	3	0	1.75	800 343-2898
Evergreen Utility C	Utilities	21.44	16.84		3	3	0	1.75	800 343-2898
Evergreen Utility Y	Utilities	22.62	16.34		3	2	0	0.94	800 343-2898
Evergreen Value Fund A	Growth/Inc	20.62	21.97	17.95	3	3	4.75	0.92	800 343-2898
Evergreen Value Fund B	Growth/Inc	19.58	21.04	16.46	3	3	0	1.67	800 343-2898
Evergreen Value Fund C	Growth/Inc	19.45	21.02		3	3	0	1.66	800 343-2898
Evergreen Value Fund Y	Growth/Inc	20.79	22.23	18.51	3	3	0	0.67	800 343-2898
Excelsior Blended Equity Fund	Growth	35.82	27.46	21.56	1	3	0	0.99	800 446-1012
Excelsior Energy and Natural Res	Energy/Res	9.17	21.88	12.94	4	4	0	0.98	800 446-1012
Excelsior Income & Growth Fund	Income	13.35	18.01	14.94	3	2	0	1.02	800 446-1012
Excelsior Instl Balanced Fund	Balanced	13.18	14.79		3	1		0.70	800 446-1012
Excelsior Instl Equity Fund	Growth	33.21	27.22		2	3	0	0.70	800 446-1012
Excelsior Instl Income Fund	Income	10.45	7.00		3	1		0.50	800 446-1012
Excelsior Instl International Eq	Foreign	0.72	8.42		4	3		1.43	800 446-1012
Excelsior Instl Optimum Growth Fund	Agg Growth	45.70					0	0.70	800 446-1012
Excelsior Instl Value Equity Fund	Growth	25.12					0	0.70	800 446-1012
Excelsior International Fund	Foreign	2.08	10.18	9.68	4	3	0	1.43	800 446-1012
Excelsior Latin America Fund	Foreign	−28.13	6.69	5.38	5	5	0	1.50	800 446-1012
Excelsior Pacific/Asia Fund	Pacific	−45.87	−14.48	−5.24	5	4	0	1.52	800 446-1012
Excelsior Pan European	European	30.96	24.27	19.46	2	3	0	1.42	800 446-1012
Excelsior Small Cap Fund	Small Co	4.80	4.29	8.90	5	5	0	0.94	800 446-1012
Excelsior Value & Restructuring	Growth	26.56	30.16	26.66	1	3	0	0.86	800 446-1012
Exchange Fund of Boston	Growth/Inc	29.43	28.41	21.48	1	3	0	0.77	800 225-6265
Executive Investors Blue Chip Fund	Income	22.71	25.07	16.46	3	3	4.75	0.75	800 423-4026
Fairmont Fund	Small Co	7.94	14.34	15.46	4	4	0	1.63	

Stock Fund Name	Objective	Annualized Return for			Rank		Max Load	Expense Ratio	Toll-Free Telephone
		1 Year	3 Years	5 Years	Overall	Risk			
Fairport Growth & Income Fund	Growth/Inc	14.55	21.66		3	3	0	1.77	800 332-6459
Fairport Midwest Growth Fund	Growth	16.08	19.20		3	3	0	1.50	800 332-6459
FAM Equity Income	Income	18.54					0	1.50	800 932-3271
FAM Value Fund	Small Co	33.92	23.01	17.18	3	3	0	1.24	800 932-3271
Fasciano Fund	Small Co	33.20	25.53	20.46	2	3	0	1.30	800 338-1579
FBL Blue Chip Portfolio	Growth	20.42	24.92	19.92	2	3	0	1.51	800 247-4170
FBL Managed Portfolio	Flexible	1.52	11.56	8.85	3	1	0	1.84	800 247-4170
FBL Value Growth Portfolio	Growth/Inc	−3.99	11.67	9.19	3	2	0	1.61	800 247-4170
FBP Contrarian Balanced Fund	Balanced	17.90	19.24	15.79	2	2	0	1.04	800 543-8721
FBP Contrarian Equity Fund	Growth	21.48	24.47		2	3	0	1.15	800 543-8721
FBR Financial Services Fund	Financial	39.17					0	1.65	888 888-0025
FBR Small Cap Financial Fund	Financial	32.20					0	1.65	888 888-0025
FBR Small Cap Growth/Value Fund	Small Co	28.83					0	1.65	888 888-0025
Federated Aggressive Growth A	Agg Growth	32.09					5.5	1.71	800 245-5051
Federated Aggressive Growth B	Agg Growth	31.32					0	2.55	800 245-5051
Federated Aggressive Growth C	Agg Growth	31.16					0	2.59	800 245-5051
Federated American Leaders A	Growth/Inc	28.30	27.66	20.69	1	3	5.5	1.14	800 245-5051
Federated American Leaders B	Growth/Inc	27.23	26.68		1	3	0	1.95	800 245-5051
Federated American Leaders C	Growth/Inc	27.23	26.70	18.90	1	3	0	1.95	800 245-5051
Federated American Leaders F	Growth/Inc	28.12	27.60		1	3	1	1.19	800 245-5051
Federated Asia Pacific Growth A	Pacific	−48.49					5.5	1.79	800 245-5051
Federated Asia Pacific Growth B	Pacific	−48.70					0	2.53	800 245-5051
Federated Asia Pacific Growth C	Pacific	−48.66					0	2.54	800 245-5051
Federated Cap Appreciation Fund A	Growth/Inc	27.97	26.87	19.79	2	3	5.5	1.25	800 245-5051
Federated Cap Appreciation Fund B	Growth/Inc	27.13					0	2.01	800 245-5051
Federated Cap Appreciation Fund C	Growth/Inc	26.95					0	2.01	800 245-5051
Federated Emerging Markets A	Foreign	−24.66					5.5	1.97	800 245-5051
Federated Emerging Markets B	Foreign	−25.22					0	2.73	800 245-5051
Federated Emerging Markets C	Foreign	−25.26					0	2.72	800 245-5051
Federated Equity Income A	Income	16.13	24.35	18.19	2	2	5.5	1.06	800 245-5051
Federated Equity Income B	Income	15.33					0	1.87	800 245-5051
Federated Equity Income C	Income	15.33	23.43	17.29	3	2	0	1.87	800 245-5051
Federated Equity Income F	Income	15.90	24.03		2	2	1	1.36	800 245-5051
Federated European Growth A	European	29.42					5.5	1.75	800 245-5051
Federated European Growth B	European	28.40					0	2.50	800 245-5051
Federated European Growth C	European	28.45					0	2.50	800 245-5051
Federated Growth Strategies A	Growth	26.95	28.01	18.58	3	4	0	1.04	800 245-5051
Federated Growth Strategies B	Growth	26.07					0	2.03	800 245-5051
Federated Growth Strategies C	Growth	26.33					0	1.90	800 245-5051
Federated Intl Equity Fund A	Foreign	27.83	15.62	13.53	3	3	5.5	1.70	800 245-5051
Federated Intl Equity Fund B	Foreign	26.82					0	2.58	800 245-5051
Federated Intl Equity Fund C	Foreign	26.86	10.46		4	3	0	2.58	800 245-5051
Federated Intl Small Company A	Foreign	30.71					5.5	1.97	800 245-5051
Federated Intl Small Company B	Foreign	29.73					0	2.72	800 245-5051
Federated Intl Small Company C	Foreign	29.75					0	2.72	800 245-5051
Federated Latin American Growth A	Foreign	−31.23					5.5	1.97	800 245-5051
Federated Latin American Growth B	Foreign	−31.83					0	2.73	800 245-5051
Federated Latin American Growth C	Foreign	−31.79					0	2.73	800 245-5051
Federated Managed Aggr Gr (IS)	Agg Growth	18.09	16.27		3	2	0	1.05	800 245-5051
Federated Managed Aggr Gr (Select)	Agg Growth	17.37	15.55		3	2	0	1.75	800 245-5051
Federated Managed Gr & Inc (IS)	Balanced	15.23	11.47		3	1	0	1.05	800 245-5051
Federated Managed Gr & Inc (Select)	Balanced	14.43	10.76		3	1	0	1.75	800 245-5051
Federated Managed Growth (IS)	AssetAlloc	15.62	14.47		3	1	0	1.05	800 245-5051
Federated Managed Growth (Select)	AssetAlloc	14.66	13.67		3	1	0	1.75	800 245-5051
Federated Max Cap (IS)	Growth/Inc	29.56	29.73		1	3	0	0.31	800 245-5051
Federated Max Cap (ISS)	Growth/Inc	29.00	29.34		1	3	0	0.62	800 245-5051
Federated Mid Cap	Agg Growth	26.10	22.76	17.20	3	3	0	0.60	800 245-5051
Federated Mini Cap	Small Co	14.88	17.13	13.00	4	4	0	0.76	800 245-5051

Stock Fund Name	Objective	Annualized Return for			Rank		Max Load	Expense Ratio	Toll-Free Telephone
		1 Year	3 Years	5 Years	Overall	Risk			
Federated Small Cap Strategies A	Small Co	15.06					5.5	1.39	800 245-5051
Federated Small Cap Strategies B	Small Co	14.22					0	2.14	800 245-5051
Federated Small Cap Strategies C	Small Co	14.23					0	2.14	800 245-5051
Federated Stock & Bond A	Balanced	19.14	19.14	14.27	3	1	5.5	1.21	800 245-5051
Federated Stock & Bond B	Balanced	18.31					0	1.98	800 245-5051
Federated Stock & Bond C	Balanced	18.21					0	1.94	800 245-5051
Federated Stock Trust	Growth/Inc	27.69	28.28	20.97	1	2	0	1.00	800 245-5051
Federated Utility Fund A	Utilities	21.55	19.00	12.33	3	2	5.5	1.15	800 245-5051
Federated Utility Fund B	Utilities	20.72					0	1.90	800 245-5051
Federated Utility Fund C	Utilities	20.65	18.11	11.53	4	3	0	1.90	800 245-5051
Federated Utility Fund F	Utilities	21.60					0	1.12	800 245-5051
Federated World Utility A	Utilities	20.65	21.61		2	2	5.5	1.32	800 245-5051
Federated World Utility B	Utilities	19.66					0	2.08	800 245-5051
Federated World Utility C	Utilities	19.72					0	2.07	800 245-5051
Federated World Utility F	Utilities	20.57	21.19		2	2	0	1.32	800 245-5051
Fidelity Adv Balanced Fund A	Balanced	19.18					5.25	1.50	800 522-7297
Fidelity Adv Balanced Fund B	Balanced	18.47					0		800 522-7297
Fidelity Adv Balanced Fund Instl	Balanced	19.89					0		800 522-7297
Fidelity Adv Balanced Fund T	Balanced	19.21	16.07	11.18	3	2	3.5	1.17	800 522-7297
Fidelity Adv Consumer Industries A	Growth	36.62					5.75	1.75	800 522-7297
Fidelity Adv Consumer Industries B	Growth	35.40					0	2.50	800 522-7297
Fidelity Adv Consumer Industries I	Growth	36.83					0	1.48	800 522-7297
Fidelity Adv Consumer Industries T	Growth	36.06					3.5	1.97	800 522-7297
Fidelity Adv Cyclical Industries A	Growth	19.15					5.25	1.75	800 522-7297
Fidelity Adv Cyclical Industries B	Growth	18.20					0	2.50	800 522-7297
Fidelity Adv Cyclical Industries I	Growth	19.46					0	1.48	800 522-7297
Fidelity Adv Cyclical Industries T	Growth	18.94					3.5	2.00	800 522-7297
Fidelity Adv Equity Growth A	Growth	28.65					5.25	1.32	800 522-7297
Fidelity Adv Equity Growth B	Growth	27.76					0	1.93	800 522-7297
Fidelity Adv Equity Growth Instl	Growth	29.24	25.02	21.08	2	3	0	0.77	800 522-7297
Fidelity Adv Equity Growth T	Growth	28.53	24.30	20.27	2	3	3.5	1.31	800 522-7297
Fidelity Adv Equity Income A	Income	22.44					5.25	1.46	800 522-7297
Fidelity Adv Equity Income B	Income	21.71	22.20		2	2	0	1.81	800 522-7297
Fidelity Adv Equity Income Instl	Income	22.99	23.55		1	2	0	0.80	800 522-7297
Fidelity Adv Equity Income T	Income	22.33	22.81	19.44	2	2	3.5	0.67	800 522-7297
Fidelity Adv Financial Services A	Financial	39.98					5.75	1.75	800 522-7297
Fidelity Adv Financial Services B	Financial	38.76					0	2.50	800 522-7297
Fidelity Adv Financial Services I	Financial	40.12					0	1.47	800 522-7297
Fidelity Adv Financial Services T	Financial	39.76					3.5	1.97	800 522-7297
Fidelity Adv Growth and Income A	Growth/Inc	32.16					5.25	1.50	800 522-7297
Fidelity Adv Growth and Income B	Growth/Inc	33.09					0	2.25	800 522-7297
Fidelity Adv Growth and Income I	Growth/Inc	32.68					0	1.07	800 522-7297
Fidelity Adv Growth and Income T	Growth/Inc	32.00					3.5	1.50	800 522-7297
Fidelity Adv Growth Opportunities A	Growth	24.69					5.25	1.48	800 522-7297
Fidelity Adv Growth Opportunities B	Growth	23.83					0		800 522-7297
Fidelity Adv Growth Opportunities I	Growth	25.15					0		800 522-7297
Fidelity Adv Growth Opportunities T	Growth	24.52	23.69	20.55	2	2	3.5	1.18	800 522-7297
Fidelity Adv Health Care A	Health	30.18					5.25	1.75	800 522-7297
Fidelity Adv Health Care B	Health	29.06					0	2.50	800 522-7297
Fidelity Adv Health Care I	Health	30.40					0	1.49	800 522-7297
Fidelity Adv Health Care T	Health	29.96					3.5	1.75	800 522-7297
Fidelity Adv Large Cap Fund A	Growth	30.26					5.25	1.75	800 522-7297
Fidelity Adv Large Cap Fund B	Growth	29.85					0	2.50	800 522-7297
Fidelity Adv Large Cap Fund Instl	Growth	31.10					0	1.50	800 522-7297
Fidelity Adv Large Cap Fund T	Growth	30.54					3.5	2.00	800 522-7297
Fidelity Adv Mid Cap Fund A	Growth	26.44					5.25	1.56	800 522-7297
Fidelity Adv Mid Cap Fund B	Growth	25.74					0	2.38	800 522-7297
Fidelity Adv Mid Cap Fund Instl	Growth	27.14					0	1.50	800 522-7297

Stock Fund Name	Objective	Annualized Return for			Rank		Max Load	Expense Ratio	Toll-Free Telephone
		1 Year	3 Years	5 Years	Overall	Risk			
Fidelity Adv Mid Cap Fund T	Growth	26.41					3.5	1.60	800 522-7297
Fidelity Adv Natural Resources A	Energy/Res	−1.64					5.25	1.66	800 522-7297
Fidelity Adv Natural Resources B	Energy/Res	−2.21					0	2.28	800 522-7297
Fidelity Adv Natural Resources I	Energy/Res	−1.29					0	1.06	800 522-7297
Fidelity Adv Natural Resources T	Energy/Res	−1.71	12.64	11.93	4	4	3.5	1.46	800 522-7297
Fidelity Adv Overseas Fund A	Foreign	10.62					5.25	1.16	800 522-7297
Fidelity Adv Overseas Fund B	Foreign	9.84					0	2.37	800 522-7297
Fidelity Adv Overseas Fund I	Foreign	11.02					0	1.43	800 522-7297
Fidelity Adv Overseas Fund T	Foreign	10.50	14.68	13.12	4	3	3.5	2.12	800 522-7297
Fidelity Adv Strat Opportunities A	Agg Growth	16.05					5.25	0.97	800 522-7297
Fidelity Adv Strat Opportunities B	Agg Growth	15.66	14.96		4	4	0	1.80	800 522-7297
Fidelity Adv Strat Opportunities I	Agg Growth	16.50	15.52	13.78	4	4	0	1.57	800 522-7297
Fidelity Adv Strat Opportunities T	Agg Growth	16.26	15.58	13.52	4	4	3.5	1.24	800 522-7297
Fidelity Adv Technology Fund A	Technology	16.43					5.25	1.75	800 522-7297
Fidelity Adv Technology Fund B	Technology	15.38					0	2.50	800 522-7297
Fidelity Adv Technology Fund I	Technology	16.66					0	1.44	800 522-7297
Fidelity Adv Technology Fund T	Technology	17.88					3.5	2.00	800 522-7297
Fidelity Adv Technoquant Growth A	Growth	14.83					5.25	1.75	800 522-7297
Fidelity Adv Technoquant Growth B	Growth	14.07					0	2.50	800 522-7297
Fidelity Adv Technoquant Growth I	Growth	15.15					0	1.50	800 522-7297
Fidelity Adv Technoquant Growth T	Growth	14.55					3.5	2.00	800 522-7297
Fidelity Adv Utilities Growth A	Utilities	35.07					5.75	1.75	800 522-7297
Fidelity Adv Utilities Growth B	Utilities	34.04					0	2.50	800 522-7297
Fidelity Adv Utilities Growth I	Utilities	35.45					0	1.50	800 522-7297
Fidelity Adv Utilities Growth T	Utilities	34.79					3.5	2.00	800 522-7297
Fidelity Asset Manager	AssetAlloc	18.82	17.55	12.96	3	1	0	0.78	800 544-8888
Fidelity Asset Manager: Growth	AssetAlloc	23.00	21.99	15.84	3	2	0	0.86	800 544-8888
Fidelity Asset Manager: Income	AssetAlloc	12.19	11.25	9.25	3	1	0	0.76	800 544-8888
Fidelity Balanced Fund	Balanced	22.19	16.95	11.44	3	1	0	0.71	800 544-8888
Fidelity Blue Chip Growth Fund	Growth	29.27	23.92	22.10	2	3	3	0.72	800 544-8888
Fidelity Canada Fund	Foreign	4.26	11.28	6.72	5	3	3	0.92	800 544-8888
Fidelity Capital Appreciation	Agg Growth	20.82	20.19	17.07	3	3	0	0.70	800 544-8888
Fidelity Congress Street Fund	Growth	15.70	24.61	20.00	2	3	0	0.62	800 544-8888
Fidelity Contrafund	Growth	29.71	25.69	20.37	2	3	3	0.68	800 544-8888
Fidelity Convertible Securities	Converts	23.35	18.02	13.98	3	2	0	0.74	800 544-8888
Fidelity Destiny I	Growth	26.57	25.46	22.66	1	2	8.24	0.34	800 544-8888
Fidelity Destiny II	Growth	28.90	25.62	22.81	2	2	8.24	0.50	800 544-8888
Fidelity Disciplined Equity Fund	Growth	32.36	25.16	20.50	2	3	0	0.64	800 544-8888
Fidelity Diversified International	Foreign	14.88	20.43	16.39	3	2	0	1.23	800 544-8888
Fidelity Dividend Growth Fund	Growth/Inc	34.59	30.78	26.88	1	3	0	0.90	800 544-8888
Fidelity Emerging Growth Fund	Agg Growth	35.77	22.48	20.19	3	4	3	1.09	800 544-8888
Fidelity Emerging Markets Fund	Foreign	−49.11	−18.45	−7.54	5	5	3	1.35	800 544-8888
Fidelity Equity-Income Fund	Income	23.20	25.82	20.16	1	2	0	0.68	800 544-8888
Fidelity Equity-Income II	Income	26.99	24.92	19.47	2	3	0	0.70	800 544-8888
Fidelity Europe Cap Appreciation	European	36.53	27.46		2	3	3	1.17	800 544-8888
Fidelity Europe Fund	European	34.75	27.27	23.25	1	2	3	1.19	800 544-8888
Fidelity Exchange Fund	Growth	25.38	28.57	20.64	1	3	0	0.63	800 544-8888
Fidelity Export Fund	Global	26.89	27.45		3	4	3	0.98	800 544-8888
Fidelity Fifty Fund	Agg Growth	20.06	21.06		3	4	3	0.82	800 544-8888
Fidelity France Fund	European	40.94					3	2.00	800 544-8888
Fidelity Freedom 2000	AssetAlloc	15.96					0	0.08	800 544-8888
Fidelity Freedom 2010	AssetAlloc	19.79					0	0.08	800 544-8888
Fidelity Freedom 2020	AssetAlloc	21.74					0	0.08	800 544-8888
Fidelity Freedom 2030	AssetAlloc	22.04					0	0.08	800 544-8888
Fidelity Fund	Growth/Inc	33.54	29.47	22.60	1	3	0	0.58	800 544-8888
Fidelity Germany Fund	European	44.22					3	2.00	800 544-8888
Fidelity Global Balanced Fund	Balanced	13.30	13.80	9.27	3	2	0	1.49	800 544-8888
Fidelity Growth & Income Fund	Growth/Inc	27.96	28.52	21.88	1	2	0	0.73	800 544-8888

Stock Fund Name	Objective	Annualized Return for			Rank		Max Load	Expense Ratio	Toll-Free Telephone
		1 Year	3 Years	5 Years	Overall	Risk			
Fidelity Growth Company Fund	Growth	21.04	21.38	18.48	2	3	3	0.71	800 544-8888
Fidelity Hong Kong & China Fund	Pacific	−40.85					3	1.31	800 544-8888
Fidelity International Growth & Inc	Foreign	11.14	14.33	11.35	4	2	0	1.15	800 544-8888
Fidelity International Value Fund	Foreign	8.74	15.12		4	3	0	1.33	800 544-8888
Fidelity Japan Fund	Pacific	−22.92	−4.54	−3.67	5	4	3	1.43	800 544-8888
Fidelity Japan Small Companies Fund	Pacific	−29.36					3	1.43	800 544-8888
Fidelity Large Cap Stock	Growth	31.08	26.61		2	3	0	1.01	800 544-8888
Fidelity Latin America Fund	Foreign	−22.29	13.30	6.56	5	5	3	1.29	800 544-8888
Fidelity Low-Priced Stock Fund	Small Co	21.92	24.14	20.76	1	2	3	0.97	800 544-8888
Fidelity Magellan Fund	Growth	28.97	22.08	19.32	2	3	3	0.60	800 544-8888
Fidelity Mid-Cap Stock Fund	Growth	36.74	26.37		3	3	0	1.00	800 544-8888
Fidelity New Millennium Fund	Agg Growth	22.98	28.72	24.30	3	4	3	0.99	800 544-8888
Fidelity Nordic Fund	European	32.92					3	1.46	800 544-8888
Fidelity OTC Portfolio	Small Co	22.61	21.20	18.69	2	4	3	0.77	800 544-8888
Fidelity Overseas Fund	Foreign	10.70	15.18	13.42	4	3	0	1.23	800 544-8888
Fidelity Pacific Basin	Pacific	−26.59	−6.80	−1.07	5	4	3	1.32	800 544-8888
Fidelity Puritan Fund	Balanced	18.96	19.70	15.63	3	2	0	0.65	800 544-8888
Fidelity Real Estate Invest Port	Real Est	6.82	19.22	12.13	3	3	0	0.84	800 544-8888
Fidelity Retirement Growth Fund	Growth	29.29	20.92	17.36	3	3	0	0.64	800 544-8888
Fidelity Select Air Transportation	Other	46.31	21.00	18.92	3	5	3	1.94	800 544-6666
Fidelity Select Automotive	Other	16.32	17.58	11.20	3	3	3	1.58	800 544-6666
Fidelity Select Biotechnology	Health	13.24	16.30	11.59	4	4	3	1.53	800 544-6666
Fidelity Select Brokerage & Invest	Financial	57.73	42.26	27.81	2	4	3	1.43	800 544-6666
Fidelity Select Chemicals	Other	1.47	14.20	16.21	4	3	3	1.66	800 544-6666
Fidelity Select Computers	Technology	25.15	21.85	30.56	4	5	3	1.35	800 544-6666
Fidelity Select Construct & Housing	Other	32.21	25.06	18.15	3	3	3	2.45	800 544-6666
Fidelity Select Consumer Industries	Other	41.65	29.85	20.33	2	3	3	2.21	800 544-6666
Fidelity Select Cyclical Industries	Other	16.88					3	2.50	800 544-6666
Fidelity Select Defense & Aerospace	Technology	24.87	25.69	23.85	3	4	3	1.70	800 544-6666
Fidelity Select Devel Commun	Technology	22.77	12.33	17.59	4	5	3	1.57	800 544-6666
Fidelity Select Electronics	Technology	−0.57	19.97	30.14	4	5	3	1.13	800 544-6666
Fidelity Select Energy Portfolio	Energy/Res	8.54	18.04	11.81	4	4	3	1.50	800 544-6666
Fidelity Select Energy Service	Energy/Res	9.56	32.63	20.14	4	5	3	1.31	800 544-6666
Fidelity Select Environmental Svcs	Other	5.93	12.05	9.38	5	4	3	2.33	800 544-6666
Fidelity Select Financial Services	Financial	42.29	38.01	26.72	1	4	3	1.32	800 544-6666
Fidelity Select Food & Agriculture	Other	21.25	22.67	20.07	3	3	3	1.51	800 544-6666
Fidelity Select Gold Portfolio	Gold	−36.73	−14.10	−7.79	5	5	3	1.42	800 544-6666
Fidelity Select Health Care	Health	32.32	32.22	30.58	1	3	3	1.20	800 544-6666
Fidelity Select Home Finance	Financial	26.71	37.09	31.60	2	4	3	1.23	800 544-6666
Fidelity Select Indl Materials	Other	2.78	7.03	10.83	5	4	3	1.93	800 544-6666
Fidelity Select Industrial Equip	Other	15.23	21.38	21.10	2	4	3	1.58	800 544-6666
Fidelity Select Insurance	Financial	35.61	34.02	22.76	2	3	3	1.48	800 544-6666
Fidelity Select Leisure	Other	51.60	29.05	23.09	3	3	3	1.44	800 544-6666
Fidelity Select Medical Delivery	Health	19.21	22.60	24.36	3	4	3	1.56	800 544-6666
Fidelity Select Multimedia	Other	42.69	21.60	21.97	3	4	3	1.76	800 544-6666
Fidelity Select Natural Gas	Energy/Res	6.36	12.97	6.97	4	4	3	1.70	800 544-6666
Fidelity Select Natural Resources	Energy/Res	−1.35					3	2.50	800 544-6666
Fidelity Select Paper & Forest	Other	0.83	6.30	13.00	4	4	3	2.10	800 544-6666
Fidelity Select Precious Metal	Gold	−38.87	−19.84	−9.76	5	5	3	1.73	800 544-6666
Fidelity Select Regional Banks	Financial	35.98	38.39	26.68	1	3	3	1.27	800 544-6666
Fidelity Select Retailing	Other	52.39	32.20	20.87	3	4	3	1.82	800 544-6666
Fidelity Select Software & Comp Svs	Technology	37.20	25.94	22.94	3	5	3	1.43	800 544-6666
Fidelity Select Technology	Technology	17.23	19.60	21.93	4	5	3	1.32	800 544-6666
Fidelity Select Telecommunications	Technology	38.71	23.98	20.01	3	4	3	1.55	800 544-6666
Fidelity Select Transportation	Other	17.75	18.93	15.14	4	3	3	1.62	800 544-6666
Fidelity Select Utilities Growth	Utilities	30.84	25.28	14.64	3	3	3	1.34	800 544-6666
Fidelity Small Cap Selector	Small Co	22.31	18.47		3	4	3	0.91	800 544-8888
Fidelity Southeast Asia Fund	Pacific	−52.73	−18.99	−5.58	5	5	3	1.32	800 544-8888

| Stock Fund Name | Objective | Annualized Return for | | | Rank | | Max Load | Expense Ratio | Toll-Free Telephone |
		1 Year	3 Years	5 Years	Overall	Risk			
Fidelity Spartan Market Index Fund	Growth/Inc	29.90	29.86	22.68	1	3	0	0.19	800 544-6666
Fidelity Stock Selector	Growth	26.70	24.73	20.08	2	3	0	0.69	800 544-8888
Fidelity Technoquant Growth	Growth	16.52					3	1.37	800 544-8888
Fidelity Trend Fund	Growth	14.95	17.28	12.69	4	4	0	0.65	800 544-8888
Fidelity United Kingdom Fund	European	27.04					3	1.96	800 544-8888
Fidelity US Equity Index	Growth/Inc	29.84	29.93	22.79	1	3	0	0.28	800 544-8888
Fidelity Utilities Fund	Utilities	34.83	24.29	15.57	2	2	0	0.84	800 544-8888
Fidelity Value Fund	Growth	13.99	21.03	18.51	3	3	0	0.64	800 544-8888
Fidelity Worldwide Fund	Global	14.23	16.08	14.82	3	3	0	1.18	800 544-8888
Fiduciary Capital Growth	Growth	11.38	18.24	15.00	3	3	0	1.20	800 338-1579
Fiduciary Exchange Fund	Growth/Inc	29.43	27.29	20.64	1	3	0	0.75	800 225-6265
59 Wall St European Equity	European	32.28	22.50	19.16	3	3	0	1.36	800 625-5759
59 Wall St Pacific Basin Equity	Pacific	−25.94	−5.58	−0.68	5	4	0	1.26	800 625-5759
59 Wall St Small Co	Small Co	18.30	18.93	12.15	4	4	0	1.10	800 625-5759
First American Balanced A	Balanced	13.79	17.49	14.55	3	1	4.5	1.13	800 637-2548
First American Balanced B	Balanced	13.04	18.92	14.52	3	2	0	1.80	800 637-2548
First American Balanced Instl	Balanced	14.31	17.88		3	1	0	0.80	800 637-2548
First American Equity Income A	Income	25.38	23.78	17.57	2	2	4.5	1.00	800 637-2548
First American Equity Income B	Income	24.43	22.92		2	2	0	1.75	800 637-2548
First American Equity Income I	Income	25.75	24.15		2	2	0	0.75	800 637-2548
First American Equity Index A	Growth/Inc	29.26	29.44	22.41	1	3	4.5	0.60	800 637-2548
First American Equity Index B	Growth/Inc	28.30	28.50		1	3	0	1.35	800 637-2548
First American Equity Index Instl	Growth/Inc	29.59	29.77		1	3	0	0.35	800 637-2548
First American Health Sciences A	Health	8.11					4.5	1.15	800 637-2548
First American Health Sciences B	Health	7.27					0	1.90	800 637-2548
First American Health Sciences I	Health	8.42					0	0.90	800 637-2548
First American Intl A	Foreign	23.80	19.20		4	4	4.5	1.92	800 637-2548
First American Intl B	Foreign	25.58	19.12		3	3	0	2.67	800 637-2548
First American Intl I	Foreign	26.94	20.30		3	3	0	1.72	800 637-2548
First American Intl Index A	Foreign	3.80					4.5	0.92	800 637-2548
First American Large Cap Growth A	Growth	28.31	25.13	19.35	2	3	4.5	1.05	800 637-2548
First American Large Cap Growth B	Growth	27.13	24.13		1	3	0	1.80	800 637-2548
First American Large Cap Growth I	Growth	28.47	25.39		2	3	0	0.80	800 637-2548
First American Large Cap Val A	Growth/Inc	15.45	24.68	20.33	2	3	4.5	1.05	800 637-2548
First American Large Cap Val B	Growth/Inc	14.56	23.74		3	3	0	1.80	800 637-2548
First American Large Cap Val Instl	Growth/Inc	15.86	25.05		2	3	0	0.80	800 637-2548
First American Mid Cap Value A	Agg Growth	9.33	23.88	19.68	3	3	4.5	1.14	800 637-2548
First American Mid Cap Value B	Agg Growth	8.49	22.94		2	4	0	1.90	800 637-2548
First American Mid Cap Value Instl	Agg Growth	9.60	24.21		3	3	0	0.89	800 637-2548
First American Real Estate Secs A	Real Est	8.45					4.5	0.80	800 637-2548
First American Real Estate Secs B	Real Est	7.58					0	1.80	800 637-2548
First American Real Estate Secs I	Real Est	8.71	18.46		3	2	0	0.80	800 637-2548
First American Regional Equity A	Small Co	14.49	18.92	18.99	4	4	4.5	1.15	800 637-2548
First American Regional Equity B	Small Co	13.62	18.01		4	4	0	1.90	800 637-2548
First American Regional Equity Inst	Small Co	14.79	19.20		4	4	0	0.90	800 637-2548
First American Small Cap Growth A	Small Co	12.54	13.79		4	4	4.5	1.15	800 637-2548
First American Small Cap Growth B	Small Co	11.51	12.99		4	4	0	1.90	800 637-2548
First American Small Cap Growth I	Small Co	12.70	14.09		4	4	0	0.90	800 637-2548
First American Small Cap Value A	Small Co	14.19					4.5	1.37	800 637-2548
First American Small Cap Value I	Small Co	14.43						1.06	800 637-2548
First American Strategy Agg Growth	Agg Growth	16.80					0	0.60	800 637-2548
First American Strategy Gr & Inc	Growth/Inc	13.98					0	0.60	800 637-2548
First American Strategy Growth Fund	Growth	15.48					0	0.60	800 637-2548
First American Strategy Income Fund	Income	13.32					0	0.60	800 637-2548
First American Technology A	Technology	20.59	17.66		4	5	4.5	1.15	800 637-2548
First American Technology B	Technology	19.97	16.79		4	5	0	1.90	800 637-2548
First American Technology I	Technology	21.11	17.91		4	5	0	0.90	800 637-2548
First Eagle Fund of America	Agg Growth	37.34	33.24	24.08	1	3	0	1.50	800 451-3623

Stock Fund Name	Objective	Annualized Return for			Rank		Max Load	Expense Ratio	Toll-Free Telephone
		1 Year	3 Years	5 Years	Overall	Risk			
First Eagle International Fund	Foreign	22.36					0	2.70	800 451-3623
First Funds Growth and Income I	Growth/Inc	32.55	28.25		1	3	0	0.83	800 442-1941
First Funds Growth and Income II	Growth/Inc	32.21					5.75	1.14	800 442-1941
First Funds Growth and Income III	Growth/Inc	31.16	26.85		1	3	0	1.94	800 442-1941
First Investors Blue Chip	Growth/Inc	22.38	24.98	18.32	2	3	6.25	1.64	800 423-4026
First Investors Global Fund	Global	13.11	16.56	13.94	4	3	6.25	1.83	800 423-4026
First Investors Mid Cap Opportunity	Growth	16.94	16.03	12.55	4	4	6.25	1.50	800 423-4026
First Investors Special Sit A	Small Co	12.49	13.68	13.09	4	4	6.25	2.23	800 423-4026
First Investors Total Return A	Flexible	16.12	16.84	13.09	3	2	6.25	1.49	800 423-4026
First Omaha Balanced Fund	Balanced	12.01					0	1.16	800 662-4203
First Omaha Equity	Growth	13.03	18.78		3	2	0	1.04	800 662-4203
First Omaha Small Cap Value Fund	Small Co	7.08					0	1.34	800 662-4203
First Source Mono Income Div Equity	Growth/Inc	27.85					5	1.62	800 554-3862
First Source Mono Income Equity	Income	18.12					5	1.37	800 554-3862
First Source Mono Income Special Eq	Small Co	1.87					5	1.39	800 554-3862
Firstar Balanced Growth Instl	Balanced	19.12	17.20	13.74	3	2	0	0.75	800 982-8909
Firstar Balanced Growth Retail	Balanced	18.81	16.90	13.53	3	2	4	1.00	800 982-8909
Firstar Equity Index Instl	Growth/Inc	29.67	29.73	22.59	1	3	0	0.65	800 982-8909
Firstar Equity Index Retail	Growth/Inc	29.35	29.07	22.18	1	3	4	0.63	800 982-8909
Firstar Growth & Income Instl	Growth/Inc	31.41	30.50	21.74	1	2	0	0.88	800 982-8909
Firstar Growth & Income Retail	Growth/Inc	31.09	30.18	21.53	1	2	4	1.12	800 982-8909
Firstar Growth Instl	Growth	28.71	24.04	18.85	2	3	0	0.90	800 982-8909
Firstar Growth Retail	Growth	28.37	23.75	18.65	2	3	4	1.14	800 982-8909
Firstar International Equity Instl	Foreign	−16.74	0.63		5	3	0	1.50	800 982-8909
Firstar International Equity Retail	Foreign	−16.91	0.36		5	3	4	1.75	800 982-8909
Firstar MicroCap Instl	Small Co	31.32					0	1.97	800 982-8909
Firstar MicroCap Retail	Small Co	31.05					4	1.95	800 982-8909
Firstar Special Growth Fund Instl	Agg Growth	15.58	20.74	17.33	3	4	0	1.12	800 982-8909
Firstar Special Growth Fund Retail	Agg Growth	15.31	20.40	17.13	3	4	4	1.13	800 982-8909
Firsthand Technology Value Fund	Technology	−2.36	34.89		4	5	0	1.93	888 884-2675
Flag Investors Communications Fd A	Utilities	50.81	32.78	21.11	3	4	4.5	1.11	800 767-3524
Flag Investors Communications Fd B	Utilities	49.44	31.64		3	4	0	1.86	800 767-3524
Flag Investors Communications Fd D	Utilities	50.18	32.21	21.21	3	4	1.5	1.50	800 767-3524
Flag Investors Emerging Growth A	Small Co	10.71	18.91	16.92	4	5	4.5	1.44	800 767-3524
Flag Investors Emerging Growth B	Small Co	9.95					0	2.19	800 767-3524
Flag Investors Emerging Growth I	Small Co	10.81					0	1.19	800 767-3524
Flag Investors Equity Partners Fd A	Growth	25.52	26.95	14.37	2	3	4.5	1.35	800 767-3524
Flag Investors Equity Partners Fd B	Growth	24.61	26.12		2	3	0	2.10	800 767-3524
Flag Investors Equity Partners Fd I	Growth	25.82					0	1.10	800 767-3524
Flag Investors International Fund	Foreign	10.88	14.47	12.53	4	3	4.5	1.50	800 767-3524
Flag Investors RE Securities Instl	Real Est	7.71					0	1.25	800 767-3524
Flag Investors Real Estate Sec A	Real Est	7.22	18.44		2	3	4.5	1.25	800 767-3524
Flag Investors Real Estate Sec B	Real Est	6.42	17.57		2	3	0	2.00	800 767-3524
Flag Investors Value Builder A	Balanced	22.38	24.39	18.64	1	2	4.5	1.15	800 767-3524
Flag Investors Value Builder B	Balanced	21.47	23.43		1	2	0	2.02	800 767-3524
Flag Investors Value Builder D	Balanced	21.93	22.68	17.30	2	2	0	1.50	800 767-3524
Flag Investors Value Builder Instl	Balanced	22.68					0	1.02	800 767-3524
Flagship Golden Rainbow	Flexible	9.43	11.18	9.55	3	1	4.2	1.07	800 227-4648
Flagship Utility Inc A	Utilities	19.41	14.64		3	2	4.2	1.50	800 227-4648
Flagship Utility Inc C	Utilities	18.73	13.98		3	2	0		800 227-4648
Flex Funds Muirfield Fund	AssetAlloc	11.21	14.28	12.89	4	3	0	1.29	800 325-3539
Flex Funds Total Return Utilities	Utilities	30.42	21.93		3	2	0	1.67	800 325-3539
FMC Select Fund	Growth	25.44	26.56		1	2	0	1.10	800 932-7781
Focus Trust	Growth	39.80	27.16		2	3	0	2.00	800 665-2550
Fortis Asset Allocation A	AssetAlloc	21.40	16.70	14.01	3	2	4.75	2.00	800 800-2638
Fortis Asset Allocation B	AssetAlloc	20.72					0	2.02	800 800-2638
Fortis Asset Allocation C	AssetAlloc	20.74					0	2.02	800 800-2638
Fortis Asset Allocation H	AssetAlloc	20.74	16.06		3	2	0	2.02	800 800-2638

311

Stock Fund Name	Objective	Annualized Return for			Rank		Max Load	Expense Ratio	Toll-Free Telephone
		1 Year	3 Years	5 Years	Overall	Risk			
Fortis Cap Appreciation A	Small Co	23.96	12.84	11.71	3	5	4.5	2.10	800 800-2638
Fortis Cap Appreciation B	Small Co	23.30	12.26		3	5	0	2.06	800 800-2638
Fortis Cap Appreciation C	Small Co	23.28	12.27		3	5	0	2.06	800 800-2638
Fortis Cap Appreciation H	Small Co	23.28	12.25		3	5	0	2.06	800 800-2638
Fortis Capital Fund A	Growth	29.72	21.63	18.26	3	3	4.75	1.18	800 800-2638
Fortis Capital Fund B	Growth	28.77	20.71		3	3	0	1.92	800 800-2638
Fortis Capital Fund C	Growth	28.72	20.72		3	3	0	1.92	800 800-2638
Fortis Capital Fund H	Growth	28.75	20.74		3	3	0	2.46	800 800-2638
Fortis Fiduciary Fund A	Growth	30.52	22.05	18.77	3	3	4.75	1.41	800 800-2638
Fortis Fiduciary Fund B	Growth	29.52	21.18		3	3	0	2.16	800 800-2638
Fortis Fiduciary Fund C	Growth	29.54	21.14		3	3	0	2.16	800 800-2638
Fortis Fiduciary Fund H	Growth	29.52	21.48		3	3	0	2.16	800 800-2638
Fortis Global Growth Portfolio A	Global	15.11	17.94	15.42	4	3	4.75	1.44	800 800-2638
Fortis Global Growth Portfolio B	Global	14.27	17.09		4	3	0	2.18	800 800-2638
Fortis Global Growth Portfolio C	Global	14.26	17.09		4	3	0	2.18	800 800-2638
Fortis Global Growth Portfolio H	Global	14.27	17.08		4	3	0	2.18	800 800-2638
Fortis Growth Fund A	Agg Growth	23.03	18.01	13.75	4	4	4.75	1.07	800 800-2638
Fortis Growth Fund B	Agg Growth	22.14	17.17		4	4	0	1.81	800 800-2638
Fortis Growth Fund C	Agg Growth	22.18	17.19		4	4	0	1.81	800 800-2638
Fortis Growth Fund H	Agg Growth	22.13	17.20		4	4	0	1.81	800 800-2638
Founders Balanced Fund	Balanced	15.26	20.17	16.40	2	1	0	0.99	800 525-2440
Founders Blue Chip Fund	Growth/Inc	19.92	23.55	19.05	1	2	0	1.09	800 525-2440
Founders Discovery Fund	Small Co	20.76	17.93	14.47	4	5	0	1.52	800 525-2440
Founders Frontier Fund	Small Co	11.52	15.02	14.32	4	4	0	1.54	800 525-2440
Founders Growth Fund	Growth	27.90	28.08	22.04	2	3	0	1.10	800 525-2440
Founders International Equity	Foreign	22.09					0	1.85	800 525-2440
Founders Passport Fund	Foreign	15.77	18.49		3	2	0	1.53	800 525-2440
Founders Special Fund	Agg Growth	20.04	16.82	15.15	4	4	0	1.30	800 525-2440
Founders Worldwide Growth	Global	14.96	16.09	16.56	3	2	0	1.45	800 525-2440
Fountain Square Balanced Fund A	Balanced	16.82	18.22		3	2	4.5	1.00	888 799-5353
Fountain Square Balanced Fund C	Balanced	16.16					0	1.75	888 799-5353
Fountain Square Equity Income A	Income	29.18					4.5	1.00	888 799-5353
Fountain Square Equity Income C	Income	28.18					0	1.75	888 799-5353
Fountain Square Intl Equity C	Foreign	12.99					0	2.19	888 799-5353
Fountain Square MidCap Fund A	Growth/Inc	19.08	19.11		3	4	4.5	1.00	888 799-5353
Fountain Square Midcap Fund C	Growth/Inc	18.19					0	1.75	888 799-5353
Fountain Square Qual Growth Fund A	Growth	23.24	27.08	19.90	2	3	4.5	1.00	888 799-5353
Fountain Square Qual Growth Fund C	Growth	22.54					0	1.75	888 799-5353
FPA Capital Fund	Small Co	22.56	25.03	25.13	2	3	6.5	0.84	800 982-4372
FPA Paramount Fund	Growth/Inc	−1.21	10.99	11.75	4	3	6.5	0.86	800 982-4372
FPA Perennial Fund	Growth/Inc	19.94	19.96	14.69	3	2	6.5	1.16	800 982-4372
Franklin Asset Allocation Fund	AssetAlloc	11.77	16.27	13.70	3	1	4.5	1.12	800 342-5236
Franklin Balance Sheet	Small Co	19.04	20.94	19.34	2	2	1.5	1.08	800 342-5236
Franklin CA Growth Fund I	Growth	19.18	23.75	26.04	3	4	4.5	1.00	800 342-5236
Franklin Convertible Securities I	Converts	7.32	14.49	12.88	3	2	4.5	1.01	800 342-5236
Franklin Convertible Securities II	Converts	6.55					1	1.74	800 342-5236
Franklin Corporate Qual Dividend	Income	4.94	5.24	4.28	3	1	1.5	1.03	800 342-5236
Franklin DynaTech Fund I	Technology	16.59	19.40	17.79	3	4	4.5	1.04	800 342-5236
Franklin Equity Fund Adv	Growth	22.53					0	0.70	800 342-5236
Franklin Equity Fund I	Growth	22.43	24.73	19.70	2	3	4.5	0.89	800 342-5236
Franklin Equity Fund II	Growth	21.70	23.80		1	3	1	1.70	800 342-5236
Franklin Equity Income I	Income	19.39	19.40	15.06	3	2	4.5	0.97	800 342-5236
Franklin Equity Income II	Income	18.50					1	1.72	800 342-5236
Franklin Global Health Care I	Health	−2.66	20.12	18.49	4	5	4.5	1.14	800 342-5236
Franklin Global Utilities Fund I	Utilities	21.85	21.59	16.66	3	3	4.5	1.05	800 342-5236
Franklin Global Utilities Fund II	Utilities	20.91	20.77		2	3	1	1.82	800 342-5236
Franklin Gold Fund Adv	Gold	−30.87					0	0.98	800 342-5236
Franklin Gold Fund I	Gold	−30.79	−14.96	−8.14	5	5	4.5	1.18	800 342-5236

Stock Fund Name	Objective	Annualized Return for			Rank		Max Load	Expense Ratio	Toll-Free Telephone
		1 Year	3 Years	5 Years	Overall	Risk			
Franklin Gold Fund II	Gold	−31.05	−15.55		5	5	1	1.98	800 342-5236
Franklin Growth Fund Adv	Growth	16.71					0	0.66	800 342-5236
Franklin Growth Fund I	Growth	16.44	20.63	18.31	2	2	4.5	0.89	800 342-5236
Franklin Growth Fund II	Growth	15.56	19.74		3	2	1	1.66	800 342-5236
Franklin Income Fund Adv	Income	11.58					0	0.57	800 342-5236
Franklin Income Fund I	Flexible	11.46	12.35	9.75	3	1	4.25	0.72	800 342-5236
Franklin Income Fund II	Flexible	10.90	11.94		3	1	1	1.22	800 342-5236
Franklin Mutual Beacon Fund I	Growth/Inc	20.32					4.5	1.09	800 342-5236
Franklin Mutual Beacon Fund II	Growth/Inc	19.53					0	1.74	800 342-5236
Franklin Mutual Discovery Fund I	Global	20.42					4.5	1.33	800 342-5236
Franklin Mutual Discovery Fund II	Global	19.73					0	1.98	800 342-5236
Franklin Mutual European Fund I	European	29.16					4.5	1.37	800 342-5236
Franklin Mutual European Fund II	European	28.60					0	2.02	800 342-5236
Franklin Mutual Qualified Fund I	Growth/Inc	18.59					4.5	1.10	800 342-5236
Franklin Mutual Qualified Fund II	Growth/Inc	17.83					0	1.75	800 342-5236
Franklin Mutual Shares Fund I	Growth/Inc	18.17					4.5	1.07	800 342-5236
Franklin Mutual Shares Fund II	Growth/Inc	17.37					0	1.72	800 342-5236
Franklin Natural Resources Fund Adv	Energy/Res	−8.00					0	0.64	800 342-5236
Franklin Natural Resources Fund I	Energy/Res	−7.61	13.84		4	4	4.5	0.96	800 342-5236
Franklin Real Estate Securities I	Real Est	6.90	19.64		3	2	4.5	1.00	800 342-5236
Franklin Real Estate Securities II	Real Est	6.10	18.70		3	2	1	1.75	800 342-5236
Franklin Rising Dividends Fund I	Growth/Inc	19.16	24.92	16.44	3	3	4.5	1.41	800 342-5236
Franklin Small Cap Growth Adv	Small Co	14.25					0	0.67	800 342-5236
Franklin Small Cap Growth I	Small Co	13.85	20.53	23.10	3	4	4.5	0.88	800 342-5236
Franklin Small Cap Growth II	Small Co	13.03					1	1.67	800 342-5236
Franklin Utilities Fund Adv	Utilities	21.45					0	0.62	800 342-5236
Franklin Utilities Fund I	Utilities	21.27	14.34	8.43	3	3	4.25	0.75	800 342-5236
Franklin/Temp Conservative Trgt I	Growth/Inc	9.54					4.5	0.79	800 342-5236
Franklin/Temp Conservative Trgt II	Growth/Inc	8.65					1	1.51	800 342-5236
Franklin/Temp Growth Trgt Fund I	Growth	9.94					4.5	0.76	800 342-5236
Franklin/Temp Growth Trgt Fund II	Growth	9.79					1	1.51	800 342-5236
Franklin/Temp Moderate Trgt Fund I	Growth	9.14					4.5	0.82	800 342-5236
Franklin/Temp Moderate Trgt Fund II	Growth	7.86					1	1.50	800 342-5236
Fremont Emerging Markets	Foreign	−28.50					0	0.00	800 548-4539
Fremont Global Fund	Global	7.88	13.71	11.79	3	2	0	0.85	800 548-4539
Fremont Growth Fund	Growth	22.59	26.10	20.07	2	3	0	0.85	800 548-4539
Fremont International Growth Fund	Foreign	−5.05	5.44		4	3	0	1.50	800 548-4539
Fremont International Small Cap	Foreign	−24.96	−3.22		5	4	0	1.50	800 548-4539
Fremont US Micro-Cap	Small Co	1.93	26.05		4	4	0	1.88	800 548-4539
Fundamental Investors Fund	Growth/Inc	22.42	24.63	20.40	1	2	5.75	0.63	800 421-0180
FundManager Growth With Income Adv	Growth/Inc	19.18	21.82	17.32	2	2	4.5	1.67	800 344-9033
FundManager Managed Tot Ret Adv	Growth/Inc	14.08	12.45	11.42	3	1	4.5	2.19	800 344-9033
FundManager Portfolios Agg Gr Adv	Agg Growth	20.66	16.93	15.18	3	3	4.5	1.71	800 344-9033
FundManager Portfolios Growth Adv	Growth	21.53	23.07	18.49	2	2	4.5	1.70	800 344-9033
Gabelli ABC Fund	Growth	10.79	10.00	9.75	3	1	0	0.87	800 422-3554
Gabelli Asset Fund	Growth	32.53	25.51	19.58	2	2	0	0.22	800 422-3554
Gabelli Equity Income Fund	Income	23.87	23.62	17.97	1	2	0	1.78	800 422-3554
Gabelli Global Convertible Secs Fd	Converts	5.11	7.91		4	2	0	2.48	800 422-3554
Gabelli Global Couch Potato	Other	47.79	27.64		3	3	4.5	1.78	800 422-3554
Gabelli Global Telecommunications	Technology	37.49	24.33		3	3	4.5	1.78	800 422-3554
Gabelli Gold Fund	Gold	−41.41	−21.72		5	5	0	3.24	800 422-3554
Gabelli Growth Fund	Growth	37.16	31.13	22.85	2	3	0	1.43	800 422-3554
Gabelli International Growth	Foreign	19.84	20.69		3	3	0	2.46	800 422-3554
Gabelli Small Cap Growth Fund	Small Co	24.35	22.81	18.08	3	3	0	1.73	800 422-3554
Gabelli Value Fund	Agg Growth	43.37	27.80	22.60	3	4	5.5	1.42	800 422-3554
Gabelli Westwood Balanced Fund Ret	Balanced	15.33	20.69	17.45	2	1	0	1.36	800 937-8966
Gabelli Westwood Balanced Fund Svc	Balanced	15.01	20.43	17.05	2	1	0	2.37	800 937-8966
Gabelli Westwood Equity Fund Retail	Growth/Inc	18.08	27.67	23.03	2	2	0	1.59	800 937-8966

313

Stock Fund Name	Objective	Annualized Return for			Rank		Max Load	Expense Ratio	Toll-Free Telephone
		1 Year	3 Years	5 Years	Overall	Risk			
Gabelli Westwood Equity Fund Svc	Growth/Inc	17.83	27.30		2	2	0	0.85	800 937-8966
Gabelli Westwood Small Cap Fund	Small Co	19.77					0	1.89	800 937-8966
Galaxy Asset Allocation Instl	AssetAlloc	18.55	18.96	14.78	2	1	0	1.22	800 628-0414
Galaxy Asset Allocation Retail A	AssetAlloc	18.36	18.76	14.60	2	1	0	1.37	800 628-0414
Galaxy Asset Allocation Retail B	AssetAlloc	17.53					0	2.20	800 628-0414
Galaxy Equity Growth Instl	Growth	29.58	27.00	20.77	1	3	0	0.96	800 628-0414
Galaxy Equity Growth Retail A	Growth	29.06	26.45	20.44	1	3	3.75	1.32	800 628-0414
Galaxy Equity Growth Retail B	Growth	28.25					0	2.37	800 628-0414
Galaxy Equity Income Instl	Growth/Inc	22.51	23.76	18.29	1	2	0	0.98	800 628-0414
Galaxy Equity Income Retail A	Growth/Inc	21.92	23.20	17.88	1	2	3.75	1.44	800 628-0414
Galaxy Equity Value Fund Instl	Growth/Inc	27.88	25.56	20.44	1	3	0	1.05	800 628-0414
Galaxy Equity Value Fund Retail A	Growth/Inc	27.40	25.05	20.05	2	3	3.75	1.38	800 628-0414
Galaxy Equity Value Fund Retail B	Growth/Inc	26.58					0	2.41	800 628-0414
Galaxy Growth and Income Fund Ret B	Growth/Inc	22.01					0	2.32	800 628-0414
Galaxy Growth and Income Fund Trust	Growth/Inc	23.29	24.31	20.02	1	2	0	1.03	800 628-0414
Galaxy Intnl Equity Fund Instl	Foreign	17.51	18.65	15.18	3	3	0	1.39	800 628-0414
Galaxy Intnl Equity Fund Retail A	Foreign	16.81	17.93		4	3	3.75	1.92	800 628-0414
Galaxy Large Company Index Retail A	Growth/Inc	29.55	29.76	22.59	1	3	0	0.40	800 628-0414
Galaxy Small Cap Value Retail A	Small Co	13.50	23.11	19.14	2	3	3.75	1.56	800 628-0414
Galaxy Small Cap Value Trust	Small Co	18.36	25.11	20.38	3	3	0	1.04	800 628-0414
Galaxy Small Company Eq Instl	Small Co	8.85	17.49	17.28	4	5	0	1.18	800 628-0414
Galaxy Small Company Eq Retail A	Small Co	8.38	16.91	16.84	4	5	0	1.46	800 628-0414
Galaxy Small Company Eq Retail B	Small Co	7.77					0	2.66	800 628-0414
Galaxy Small Company Index Retail A	Small Co	18.81	21.27	17.00	3	3	0	0.40	800 628-0414
Galaxy Utility Index Retail A	Utilities	29.86	19.98	11.95	3	3	0	0.40	800 628-0414
GAM Asian Capital	Pacific	−55.24	−23.24		5	5	5	4.66	800 356-5740
GAM Europe Fund	European	29.75	25.22	19.64	3	3	5	1.96	800 356-5740
GAM Global Fund Class A	Global	32.18	24.98	25.55	3	4	5	1.83	800 356-5740
GAM Global Fund Class D	Global	31.93					3.5	2.25	800 356-5740
GAM International Fund Class A	Foreign	26.51	21.37	23.88	3	4	5	1.68	800 356-5740
GAM International Fund Class D	Foreign	26.35					3.5	1.84	800 356-5740
GAM Japan Fund	Pacific	−18.10	5.61		5	3	5	2.20	800 356-5740
GAM North America Fund	Global	29.77	30.83	22.20	1	3	5	2.24	800 356-5740
GAM Pacific Basin Fund Class A	Pacific	−46.78	−13.93	−3.78	5	5	5	1.98	800 356-5740
GAM Pacific Basin Fund Class D	Pacific	−45.08					3.5	2.14	800 356-5740
GAMerica Capital	Growth	51.91	27.86		3	4	5	4.79	800 356-5740
Gateway Cincinnati Fund	Growth	26.12	24.49		2	2	0	1.98	800 354-6339
Gateway Fund	Growth/Inc	14.43	11.75	10.20	3	1	0	1.07	800 354-6339
Gateway Small Cap Index Fund	Small Co	16.44	17.61	12.12	4	3	0	1.50	800 354-6339
GE Global Equity Fund A	Global	12.03	14.50	13.96	4	3	5.75	1.60	800 242-0134
GE Global Equity Fund B	Global	11.50	16.05		4	3	0	2.10	800 242-0134
GE Global Equity Fund C	Global	12.25	16.67		4	3	0	1.35	800 242-0134
GE Global Equity Fund D	Global	12.62	17.11		4	3	0	1.10	800 242-0134
GE International Equity A	Foreign	12.64	14.71		4	3	5.75	1.60	800 242-0134
GE International Equity B	Foreign	12.14	14.20		4	3	0	2.10	800 242-0134
GE International Equity C	Foreign	12.91	14.91		4	3	0	1.35	800 242-0134
GE International Equity D	Foreign	13.43	15.29		4	3	0	1.03	800 242-0134
GE Mid-Cap Fund A	Growth	16.76	20.28		4	4	5.75	1.31	800 242-0134
GE Mid-Cap Fund B	Growth	16.17	19.52		4	4	0	2.06	800 242-0134
GE Premier Growth Fund A	Growth	34.38					5.75	1.40	800 242-0134
GE Premier Growth Fund B	Growth	33.73					0	1.90	800 242-0134
GE Premier Growth Fund C	Growth	34.50					0	1.15	800 242-0134
GE Premier Growth Fund D	Growth	34.73					0	0.90	800 242-0134
GE S&S Program	Growth/Inc	28.47	28.85	21.59	1	3	0	0.12	800 242-0134
GE Strategic Investment A	Flexible	17.35	17.71	14.03	3	1	5.75	1.15	800 242-0134
GE Strategic Investment B	Flexible	16.57	16.06		3	1	0	1.65	800 242-0134
GE Strategic Investment C	Flexible	17.68	16.92	13.09	3	1	0	0.90	800 242-0134
GE Strategic Investment D	Flexible	17.95	17.15		3	1	0	0.65	800 242-0134

314

Stock Fund Name	Objective	Annualized Return for			Rank		Max Load	Expense Ratio	Toll-Free Telephone
		1 Year	3 Years	5 Years	Overall	Risk			
GE US Equity A	Growth	27.12	28.30	20.46	1	3	4.75	1.00	800 242-0134
GE US Equity B	Growth	26.50	25.83		1	3	0	1.50	800 242-0134
GE US Equity C	Growth	27.44	26.69	19.59	2	3	0	0.75	800 242-0134
GE US Equity D	Growth	27.75	26.93		1	3	0	0.50	800 242-0134
GE Value Equity Fund A	Growth/Inc	24.42	28.32		2	3	5.75	1.30	800 242-0134
GE Value Equity Fund B	Growth/Inc	23.63	27.60		2	3	0	2.05	800 242-0134
General Securities Fund	Flexible	2.98	14.54	14.45	4	3	0	1.44	800 577-9217
George Putnam Fund of Boston A	Balanced	16.77	19.54	15.44	2	1	5.75	0.52	800 225-1581
George Putnam Fund of Boston B	Balanced	15.82	18.63		3	1	0	1.81	800 225-1581
George Putnam Fund of Boston M	Balanced	16.17	18.91		3	1	3.5	1.56	800 225-1581
Gintel Fund	Growth	20.19	24.73	14.26	3	3	0	1.70	800 243-5808
Glenmede Emerging Markets	Foreign	−42.61	−12.86		5	5	0	1.76	800 442-8299
Glenmede Equity Portfolio	Income	26.05	27.88	20.87	2	3	0	0.15	800 442-8299
Glenmede Instl International	Foreign	9.69	14.71	14.13	4	3	0	0.99	800 442-8299
Glenmede International Portfolio	Foreign	10.21	15.67	15.28	3	3	0	0.14	800 442-8299
Glenmede Large Cap Value	Growth	24.78	23.96	18.95	3	3	0	0.15	800 442-8299
Glenmede Small Cap	Small Co	11.45	22.08	18.19	3	3	0	0.12	800 442-8299
GMO Tr Pelican III	Growth	7.51	17.00	15.38	2	3	0	2.01	
Golden Oak Growth Portfolio A	Agg Growth	40.92	24.90	18.22	3	4	5.75	1.35	800 545-6331
Golden Oak Growth Portfolio I	Agg Growth	41.05	25.15	18.53	3	4	0	1.07	800 545-6331
Goldman Sachs Asian Growth A	Pacific	−56.72	−22.05		5	5	5.5	1.67	800 292-4726
Goldman Sachs Asian Growth B	Pacific	−56.92					0	2.21	800 292-4726
Goldman Sachs Balanced Fund B	Balanced	11.19					0	1.75	800 292-4726
Goldman Sachs Capital Growth A	Growth	35.86	28.37	21.96	2	3	5.5	1.63	800 292-4726
Goldman Sachs Capital Growth B	Growth	34.62					0	2.15	800 292-4726
Goldman Sachs CORE US Equity Fund A	Growth/Inc	29.30	28.15	22.64	1	3	5.5	1.28	800 292-4726
Goldman Sachs CORE US Equity Fund B	Growth/Inc	28.65					0	1.83	800 292-4726
Goldman Sachs Growth & Income A	Growth/Inc	14.40	23.68	20.82	3	3	5.5	1.21	800 292-4726
Goldman Sachs Growth & Income B	Growth/Inc	13.62					0	1.93	800 292-4726
Goldman Sachs Intl Equity Fund A	Foreign	10.61	18.32	14.41	3	3	5.5	1.69	800 292-4726
Goldman Sachs Intl Equity Fund B	Foreign	10.01					0	2.23	800 292-4726
Goldman Sachs Small Cap Value A	Small Co	19.32	21.80		3	4	5.5	1.60	800 292-4726
Goldman Sachs Small Cap Value B	Small Co	18.49					0	2.35	800 292-4726
Government Street Equity Fund	Growth	21.43	24.84	17.70	2	3	0	0.88	800 543-8721
Govett Asia Fund A	Pacific	−55.81	−18.85		5	5	4.95	2.50	800 225-2222
Govett Emerging Markets Equity A	Foreign	−37.64	−7.69	−0.69	5	5	4.95	2.50	800 225-2222
Govett International Equity Fund A	Foreign	3.72	10.74	10.17	4	4	4.95	2.50	800 225-2222
Govett Latin America Fund A	Foreign	−31.37	5.38		5	5	4.95	2.50	800 225-2222
Govett Smaller Companies Fund A	Small Co	1.56	0.78	16.61	5	5	4.95	1.95	800 225-2222
Gradison Established Value Fund	Growth	14.05	19.30	16.19	3	2	0	1.11	800 869-5999
Gradison Opportunity Value Fund	Small Co	19.60	21.84	16.26	3	3	0	1.33	800 869-5999
GrandView Realty Growth Fund	Real Est	17.17	23.75		3	3	4.5	1.99	800 525-3863
GrandView S&P REIT Index Fund	Real Est	4.58	14.53		3	3	3	1.05	800 525-3863
Granum Value Fund	Growth	18.26					0		888-547-2686
Green Century Balanced Fund	Balanced	13.13	16.71	11.95	3	4	0	2.50	800 934-7336
Green Century Equity Fund	Growth	32.66	30.05	22.39	2	3	0	1.50	800 934-7336
Greenspring Fund	Growth	9.22	16.62	14.07	3	1	0	1.00	800 366-3863
Griffin Growth & Income A	Growth/Inc	15.74	24.07		2	3	4.5	0.60	800 676-4450
Griffin Growth & Income B	Growth/Inc	15.30	23.60		2	3	0	0.93	800 676-4450
Growth Fund of America	Growth	29.10	20.84	19.00	3	3	5.75	0.72	800 421-0180
Growth Fund of Washington	Growth	31.68	27.78	18.83	2	3	4.75	1.25	800 348-4782
Guardian Asset Allocation Fund A	AssetAlloc	18.83	20.63	15.63	3	2	4.5	0.95	800 221-3253
Guardian Baillie Gifford Emrg Mkt A	Foreign	−32.88					4.5	2.31	800 221-3253
Guardian Baillie Gifford Emrg Mkt B	Foreign	−34.26					0	4.24	800 221-3253
Guardian Baillie Gifford Intl Fd A	Foreign	15.93	18.53	14.66	3	3	4.5	1.62	800 221-3253
Guardian Park Avenue Fund A	Growth	29.47	29.27	22.13	2	3	4.5	0.79	800 221-3253
Guardian Park Avenue Small Cap A	Small Co	26.28					4.5	1.36	800 221-3253
Guardian Park Avenue Small Cap B	Small Co	25.12					0	2.26	800 221-3253

Stock Fund Name	Objective	Annualized Return for			Rank		Max Load	Expense Ratio	Toll-Free Telephone
		1 Year	3 Years	5 Years	Overall	Risk			
Guinness Flight Asia Blue Chip	Pacific	−52.45					0	1.98	800 915-6565
Guinness Flight Asia Small Cap	Pacific	−62.67					0	1.84	800 915-6565
Guinness Flight China & Hong Kong	Pacific	−49.31	−4.82		5	5	0	1.69	800 915-6565
Harbor Capital Appreciation	Growth	34.90	27.27	24.68	2	4	0	0.70	800 422-1050
Harbor Growth Fund	Growth	15.86	16.85	12.96	4	4	0	1.12	800 422-1050
Harbor International Fund	Foreign	8.54	19.21	18.79	3	3	0	0.97	800 422-1050
Harbor International Growth Fund	Foreign	19.08	21.98		3	3	0	1.02	800 422-1050
Harbor International II Fund	Foreign	−1.48					0	1.17	800 422-1050
Harbor Value Fund	Growth/Inc	20.90	24.79	19.07	2	2	0	0.83	800 422-1050
Harris Insight Balanced Fund A	Balanced	19.24					4.5	1.13	800 982-8782
Harris Insight Balanced Fund C	Balanced	19.64					0	1.13	800 982-8782
Harris Insight Equity A	Growth/Inc	30.63	29.00	21.21	2	3	4.5	1.13	800 982-8782
Harris Insight Equity C	Growth/Inc	31.06					0	0.88	800 982-8782
Harris Insight Equity Income A	Income	29.15					4.5	1.18	800 982-8782
Harris Insight Equity Income C	Income	29.50					0	0.93	800 982-8782
Harris Insight Growth Fund A	Growth	28.04					4.5	1.35	800 982-8782
Harris Insight Growth Fund C	Growth	28.39					0	1.10	800 982-8782
Harris Insight Index Fund A	Growth/Inc	29.39					4.5	0.70	800 982-8782
Harris Insight Index Fund C	Growth/Inc	29.74					0	0.45	800 982-8782
Harris Insight Intl Equity A	Foreign	−10.83					4.5	1.65	800 982-8782
Harris Insight Intl Equity C	Foreign	−10.52					0	1.40	800 982-8782
Harris Insight Small Cap Opp A	Small Co	22.69					4.5	1.45	800 982-8782
Harris Insight Small Cap Opp C	Small Co	23.12					0	1.20	800 982-8782
Harris Insight Small Cap Value A	Small Co	23.30					0	0.99	800 982-8782
Harris Insight Small Cap Value C	Small Co	23.62					0	0.99	800 982-8782
Hartford Advisors Fund A	Growth	23.09					5.5	1.87	888 843-5517
Hartford Advisors Fund B	Growth	22.27					0	3.04	888 843-5517
Hartford Capital Appreciation A	Agg Growth	20.61					5.5	1.45	888 843-5517
Hartford Capital Appreciation B	Agg Growth	19.70					0	3.20	888 843-5517
Hartford Dividend & Growth A	Growth/Inc	21.43					5.5	2.06	888 843-5517
Hartford Dividend & Growth B	Growth/Inc	20.69					0	3.64	888 843-5517
Hartford Intl Opportunity A	Foreign	7.08					5.5	2.93	888 843-5517
Hartford Intl Opportunity B	Foreign	6.43					0	6.60	888 843-5517
Hartford Small Company A	Small Co	18.22					5.5	2.24	888 843-5517
Hartford Small Company B	Small Co	16.37					0	5.49	888 843-5517
Hartford Stock Fund A	Growth	31.89					5.5	4.12	888 843-5517
Hartford Stock Fund B	Growth	30.94					0	3.33	888 843-5517
Haven Fund	Growth	17.39	22.10	17.29	1	3	0	1.33	800 844-4836
Heartland Large Cap Value Fund	Growth/Inc	12.44					0	2.12	800 432-7856
Heartland Mid Cap Value Fund	Foreign	17.95					0	1.46	800 432-7856
Heartland Small Cap Contrarian	Small Co	1.40	11.29		4	3	0	1.34	800 432-7856
Heartland Value Fund	Small Co	12.21	18.99	18.06	3	3	0	1.12	800 432-7856
Heartland Value Plus Fund	Income	17.32	22.35		3	2	0	1.24	800 432-7856
Heitman Real Estate Fund Advisor	Real Est	6.35	18.27		3	2	4.75	1.59	800 435-1405
Heitman Real Estate Fund Instl	Real Est	6.94	20.68	13.12	3	3	0	1.59	800 435-1405
Henlopen Fund	Growth	32.79	24.50	20.93	3	4	0	1.60	800-922-0224
Heritage Capital Appreciation Tr A	Agg Growth	46.67	30.99	22.14	2	3	4.75	1.27	800 421-4184
Heritage Capital Appreciation Tr C	Agg Growth	45.77	30.45		1	3	0	2.07	800 421-4184
Heritage Income Growth Trust A	Growth/Inc	18.72	23.16	17.25	2	2	4.75	1.34	800 421-4184
Heritage Income Growth Trust C	Growth/Inc	17.72	22.25		1	2	0	2.10	800 421-4184
Heritage Series Tr Eagle Intl Eq A	Foreign	10.06					4.75	1.97	800 421-4184
Heritage Series Tr Eagle Intl Eq C	Foreign	9.26					0	2.72	800 421-4184
Heritage Series Tr Eagle Intl Eq E	Foreign	9.38	13.66		4	3	0	2.60	800 421-4184
Heritage Series Trust Growth Eq A	Growth	40.92					4.75	1.63	800 421-4184
Heritage Series Trust Growth Eq C	Growth	39.90					0	2.38	800 421-4184
Heritage Small Cap Stock Fund A	Small Co	13.67	27.12	21.19	3	4	4.75	1.25	800 421-4184
Heritage Small Cap Stock Fund C	Small Co	12.82	26.27		3	4	0	2.04	800 421-4184
Heritage Value Equity Fd A	Growth/Inc	6.65	17.83		2	3	4.75	1.63	800 421-4184

316

Stock Fund Name	Objective	Annualized Return for			Rank		Max Load	Expense Ratio	Toll-Free Telephone
		1 Year	3 Years	5 Years	Overall	Risk			
Heritage Value Equity Fd C	Growth/Inc	5.85	16.92		3	3	0	2.38	800 421-4184
Highlands Growth Fund	Growth	28.96	21.75	16.22	3	3	0	1.71	800 325-3539
HighMark Balanced Instl	Balanced	15.77	17.64	14.33	3	1	0	1.09	800 433-6884
HighMark Balanced Retail	Balanced	15.49	17.38	14.02	3	1	4.5	1.07	800 433-6884
HighMark Blue Chip Growth Instl	Growth	24.68	23.98		2	3	0	0.95	800 433-6884
HighMark Convertible Secs Instl	Converts	9.73	12.60		4	2	0	0.85	800 433-6884
HighMark Emerg Growth Instl	Small Co	20.41	18.85		4	4	0	0.26	800 433-6884
HighMark Growth Fund Instl	Growth	35.72	29.48		1	3	0	1.24	800 433-6884
HighMark Growth Fund Retail	Growth	35.43	29.46		1	3	4.5	1.04	800 433-6884
HighMark Income Equity Instl	Income	20.33	23.88	18.27	2	2	0	1.21	800 433-6884
HighMark Income Equity Retail	Income	19.94	23.72	18.24	2	2	4.5	1.06	800 433-6884
HighMark Value Momentum Instl	Growth/Inc	21.38	26.47	20.69	2	3	0	0.94	800 433-6884
HighMark Value Momentum Retail	Growth/Inc	21.32	26.27	20.43	2	3	4.5	1.03	800 433-6884
Hilliard Lyons Growth Fund	Growth	21.92	25.60	19.32	2	4	4.75	1.30	800 444-1854
Hodges Fund	Growth	26.53	26.40	18.79	3	4	2.5	1.91	800 388-8512
HomeState PA Growth Fund	Growth	25.04	24.22	22.99	3	4	4.75	1.57	800 232-0224
HomeState Select Opportunities	Small Co	18.37					4.75		800 232-0224
Homestead Value Fund	Growth/Inc	18.57	22.92	19.15	2	2	0	0.79	800 258-3030
Horace Mann Growth Fund	Growth	15.12	23.29		3	3	0	0.63	800 999-1030
Hotchkis & Wiley Balanced Fund	Balanced	13.29	14.71	12.72	3	1	0	0.94	800 796-5606
Hotchkis & Wiley Equity Income	Growth/Inc	22.60	22.89	18.25	3	3	0	0.87	800 796-5606
Hotchkis & Wiley Global Eq Fund	Global	7.60					0	1.00	800 796-5606
Hotchkis & Wiley International Fund	Foreign	7.77	15.83	15.03	4	2	0	0.94	800 796-5606
Hotchkis & Wiley Mid Cap Fund	Growth	14.99					0	1.00	800 796-5606
Hotchkis & Wiley Small Cap Fund	Small Co	22.24	21.95	16.63	3	4	0	1.00	800 796-5606
HSBC Growth & Income Fund	Growth/Inc	25.46	25.63	19.16	2	3	5	0.83	800 634-2536
Hudson Capital Appreciation A	Growth	18.09	29.82	19.79	3	4	4.5	2.03	800 722-2458
Hudson Capital Appreciation B	Growth	17.56					0	2.56	800 722-2458
Hudson Capital Appreciation N	Growth	18.01					0	1.81	800 722-2458
IAA Asset Allocation Fund	AssetAlloc	8.10	14.16	11.74	3	1	0	1.46	800 245-2100
IAA Trust Growth Fund	Growth	10.97	20.12	16.56	2	3	0	1.16	800 245-2100
IAI Balanced Fund	Balanced	24.57	22.26	15.40	3	2	0	1.25	800 945-3863
IAI Capital Appreciation Fund	Growth	15.58					0	1.25	800 945-3863
IAI Developing Countries Fund	Foreign	−36.33	−9.22		5	5	0	2.00	800 945-3863
IAI Emerging Growth Fund	Small Co	8.96	12.74	13.02	4	5	0	1.23	800 945-3863
IAI Growth & Income Fund	Growth/Inc	19.78	22.76	16.89	2	3	0	1.24	800 945-3863
IAI Growth Fund	Growth	25.38	19.73		3	3	0	1.25	800 945-3863
IAI International Fund	Foreign	−7.10	5.90	8.10	5	3	0	1.67	800 945-3863
IAI MidCap Growth Fund	Growth	14.66	14.78	16.76	4	3	0	1.25	800 945-3863
IAI Regional Fund	Growth	11.27	19.07	15.69	3	3	0	1.21	800 945-3863
IAI Value Fund	Growth	44.80	26.11	19.41	4	4	0	1.25	800 945-3863
ICAP Discretionary Equity Port	Growth	22.72	27.16		1	3	0	0.80	888 221-4227
ICAP Equity Portfolio	Growth	22.94	28.42		1	3	0	0.80	888 221-4227
ICON Asia Region	Pacific	−34.98	−9.59	−5.87	5	3	0	1.66	888 389-ICON
ICON Basic Materials	Other	−22.04					0	1.45	888 389-ICON
ICON Healthcare	Health	24.67					0	1.45	888 389-ICON
ICON Leisure	Other	18.26					0	1.48	888 389-ICON
ICON North Europe Region	European	28.23					0	1.66	888 389-ICON
ICON South Europe Region	European	45.85					0	1.69	888 389-ICON
ICON Technology	Technology	2.19					0	1.47	888 389-ICON
ICON Tranportation	Other	9.55					0	1.61	888 389-ICON
IDEX Aggressive Growth Portfolio A	Agg Growth	37.00	21.82		3	4	5.5	1.85	800 851-9777
IDEX Aggressive Growth Portfolio B	Agg Growth	36.73					0	2.50	800 851-9777
IDEX Aggressive Growth Portfolio C	Agg Growth	36.72	21.59		3	4	0	2.37	800 851-9777
IDEX Balanced Portfolio A	Balanced	24.93	22.54		2	1	5	1.85	800 851-9777
IDEX Balanced Portfolio B	Balanced	24.15					0	2.50	800 851-9777
IDEX Balanced Portfolio C	Balanced	24.28	21.89		2	1	0	2.40	800 851-9777
IDEX C.A.S.E. Portfolio A	Growth	5.18					5.5	1.85	800 851-9777

Stock Fund Name	Objective	Annualized Return for			Rank		Max Load	Expense Ratio	Toll-Free Telephone
		1 Year	3 Years	5 Years	Overall	Risk			
IDEX C.A.S.E. Portfolio B	Growth	4.59					0	2.50	800 851-9777
IDEX C.A.S.E. Portfolio C	Growth	4.67					0	2.40	800 851-9777
IDEX Capital Appreciation A	Growth	26.91					5.5	1.85	800 851-9777
IDEX Capital Appreciation B	Growth	26.53					0	2.50	800 851-9777
IDEX Capital Appreciation C	Growth	26.51	20.48		3	4	0	2.40	800 851-9777
IDEX Global Portfolio A	Global	27.60	28.24	23.74	2	3	5.5	1.91	800 851-9777
IDEX Global Portfolio B	Global	27.34					0	2.73	800 851-9777
IDEX Global Portfolio C	Global	27.50	28.19		2	3	0	2.63	800 851-9777
IDEX Growth Portfolio A	Growth	43.60	30.67	21.14	3	4	5.5	1.55	800 851-9777
IDEX Growth Portfolio B	Growth	43.43					0	2.32	800 851-9777
IDEX Growth Portfolio C	Growth	43.48	30.40		3	4	0	1.55	800 851-9777
IDEX International Equity Fund A	Foreign	9.07					5.5	1.70	800 851-9777
IDEX International Equity Fund B	Foreign	8.38					0	2.35	800 851-9777
IDEX International Equity Fund C	Foreign	8.52					0	2.25	800 851-9777
IDEX Strategic Total Return A	AssetAlloc	14.74	19.15		3	2	5.5	1.85	800 851-9777
IDEX Strategic Total Return B	AssetAlloc	13.95					0	2.50	800 851-9777
IDEX Strategic Total Return C	AssetAlloc	14.06	19.64		3	2	0	2.40	800 851-9777
IDEX Tactical Asset Allocation A	AssetAlloc	14.61					5.5	1.85	800 851-9777
IDEX Tactical Asset Allocation B	AssetAlloc	13.80					0	2.50	800 851-9777
IDEX Tactical Asset Allocation C	AssetAlloc	13.91					0	2.40	800 851-9777
IDEX Value Equity Fund A	Growth/Inc	25.77					5.5	1.50	800 851-9777
IDEX Value Equity Fund B	Growth/Inc	13.77					0	1.50	800 851-9777
IDEX Value Equity Fund C	Growth/Inc	13.82					0	2.05	800 851-9777
IDS Blue Chip Advantage Fund	Growth/Inc	21.30	26.94	20.85	2	3	5	0.78	800 328-8300
IDS Discovery Fund	Small Co	14.70	18.24	13.36	4	4	5	1.13	800 328-8300
IDS Diversified Equity Income	Income	17.01	20.42	15.44	3	2	5	0.88	800 328-8300
IDS Equity Select	Growth/Inc	25.97	26.72	17.82	3	3	5	0.83	800 328-8300
IDS Equity Value B	Growth/Inc	13.87	21.24	16.14	3	2	0	1.61	800 328-8300
IDS Global Growth Fund	Global	23.95	15.93	13.42	3	3	5	1.27	800 328-8300
IDS Growth Fund	Growth	20.78	26.64	22.40	3	4	5	0.89	800 328-8300
IDS International Fund	Foreign	13.04	13.85	11.62	4	3	5	1.18	800 328-8300
IDS Managed Allocation Fund	Flexible	12.17	14.35	12.07	4	2	5	0.84	800 328-8300
IDS Mutual	Balanced	14.42	16.37	13.08	3	1	5	0.83	800 328-8300
IDS New Dimensions Fund	Growth	28.04	27.20	20.86	2	3	5	0.91	800 328-8300
IDS Precious Metals Fund	Gold	−37.61	−11.98	−4.63	5	5	5	1.51	800 328-8300
IDS Progressive Fund	Small Co	18.23	19.48	16.09	3	2	5	1.10	800 328-8300
IDS Research Opportunities A	Growth	21.07					5	1.52	800 328-8300
IDS Research Opportunities B	Growth	20.22					0	2.25	800 328-8300
IDS Research Opportunities Y	Growth	21.21					0	1.45	800 328-8300
IDS Small Company Index A	Small Co	17.83					5	1.00	800 328-8300
IDS Small Company Index B	Small Co	16.91					0	1.76	800 328-8300
IDS Small Company Index Y	Small Co	17.80					0	0.82	800 328-8300
IDS Stock Fund	Growth/Inc	23.47	22.99	17.83	2	2	5	0.78	800 328-8300
IDS Strategist Balanced Fund	Balanced	15.25						0.62	800 328-8300
IDS Strategist Emerging Markets Fd	Foreign	−32.04						2.20	800 328-8300
IDS Strategist Equity Fund	Growth/Inc	22.84						0.58	800 328-8300
IDS Strategist Equity Income Fund	Income	17.32						1.07	800 328-8300
IDS Strategist Growth Fund	Growth	20.77						0.99	800 328-8300
IDS Strategist Growth Trends Fund	Growth	17.15						0.92	800 328-8300
IDS Strategist Quality Income Fund	Corp-Inv	9.62						1.03	800 328-8300
IDS Strategist Special Growth Fund	Agg Growth	21.18						1.39	800 328-8300
IDS Strategist Total Return Fund	Growth/Inc	12.28						1.26	800 328-8300
IDS Strategist World Growth Fund	Foreign	24.05						1.65	800 328-8300
IDS Strategy Aggressive B	Agg Growth	34.78	23.62	17.39	3	4	0	1.77	800 328-8300
IDS Utilities Income Fund	Utilities	28.47	22.17	14.23	3	2	5	0.87	800 328-8300
Income Fund of America	Income	18.12	18.96	14.55	2	1	5.75	0.61	800 421-0180
Independence One Equity Plus Fd	Growth	29.57					0	0.40	800 245-0242
Intrust Intl Stock Fund Instl	Foreign	9.08					0		888 266-8787

Stock Fund Name	Objective	Annualized Return for			Rank		Max Load	Expense Ratio	Toll-Free Telephone
		1 Year	3 Years	5 Years	Overall	Risk			
Intrust Stock Fund Instl	Growth	11.98					0		888 266-8787
INVESCO Asian Growth Fund	Pacific	−60.08					0	2.05	800 525-8085
INVESCO Balanced Fund	Balanced	20.67	22.71		2	1	0	1.29	800 525-8085
INVESCO Dynamics Fund	Agg Growth	37.36	25.15	20.86	2	4	0	1.08	800 525-8085
INVESCO European Small Company	European	20.43	23.93		3	3	0	1.62	800 525-8085
INVESCO Growth Fund	Growth/Inc	29.60	27.70	18.90	3	3	0	1.07	800 525-8085
INVESCO Industrial Income	Income	19.89	21.17	16.09	3	2	0	0.92	800 525-8085
INVESCO International European	European	44.22	30.19	22.95	2	3	0	1.25	800 525-8085
INVESCO International Growth	Foreign	2.99	11.61	9.50	4	3	0	1.71	800 525-8085
INVESCO International Pacific Basin	Pacific	−46.42	−14.72	−6.41	5	4	0	1.24	800 525-8085
INVESCO Latin American Growth Fund	Foreign	−30.77	4.85		4	5	0	1.76	800 525-8085
INVESCO Multi-Asset Allocation	AssetAlloc	16.12	18.51		3	1	0	1.55	800 525-8085
INVESCO Small Company Growth Fund	Small Co	20.55	19.66	16.60	4	5	0	0.74	800 525-8085
INVESCO Small Company Value Fund	Small Co	14.03	18.10		2	3	0	1.25	800 525-8085
INVESCO Strategic Energy	Energy/Res	5.71	20.86	9.40	4	4	0	1.35	800 525-8085
INVESCO Strategic Environmental	Other	16.62	17.35	13.49	4	4	0	1.72	800 525-8085
INVESCO Strategic Financial Serv	Financial	38.25	37.84	24.97	2	4	0	0.99	800 525-8085
INVESCO Strategic Gold	Gold	−52.24	−20.22	−14.65	5	5	0	1.07	800 525-8085
INVESCO Strategic Health Sciences	Health	29.43	30.03	23.91	3	4	0	1.08	800 525-8085
INVESCO Strategic Leisure	Other	35.03	19.42	17.26	3	3	0	1.41	800 525-8085
INVESCO Strategic Technology	Technology	15.84	21.14	21.27	4	4	0	1.05	800 525-8085
INVESCO Strategic Utilities	Utilities	29.54	21.29	12.74	3	2	0	1.22	800 525-8085
INVESCO Total Return Fund	AssetAlloc	18.96	19.35	16.62	2	1	0	0.86	800 525-8085
INVESCO Value Equity Fund	Growth/Inc	20.68	23.73	19.78	2	3	0	1.04	800 525-8085
INVESCO Worldwide Capital Goods	Global	12.29	19.00		4	3	0	2.11	800 525-8085
INVESCO Worldwide Communications	Technology	44.84	29.63		2	4	0	1.66	800 525-8085
Investment Company of America	Growth/Inc	24.37	25.35	19.58	1	2	5.75	0.56	800 421-0180
Investors Research Fund	Agg Growth	8.82	15.43	10.95	3	2	5.75	1.77	800 732-1733
Ivy Asia Pacific Fund A	Pacific	−58.20					5.75		800 456-5111
Ivy Asia Pacific Fund B	Pacific	−58.54					0		800 456-5111
Ivy Asia Pacific Fund C	Pacific	−58.52					0		800 456-5111
Ivy Canada Fund A	Foreign	−31.50	−7.80	−5.65	4	5	5.75	2.80	800 456-5111
Ivy Canada Fund B	Foreign	−31.75	−8.29		5	5	0	3.00	800 456-5111
Ivy Canada Fund C	Foreign	−31.61					0	3.00	800 456-5111
Ivy China Region Fd A	Pacific	−51.59	−12.91		5	5	5.75	2.37	800 456-5111
Ivy China Region Fd B	Pacific	−51.94	−13.62		5	5	0	3.00	800 456-5111
Ivy China Region Fd C	Pacific	−51.86					0	2.93	800 456-5111
Ivy Developing Nations Fund A	Foreign	−46.89	−10.91		5	5	5.75	2.33	800 456-5111
Ivy Developing Nations Fund B	Foreign	−47.43	−11.54		5	5	0	3.00	800 456-5111
Ivy Developing Nations Fund C	Foreign	−47.41					0	3.00	800 456-5111
Ivy Global Fund A	Global	−10.69	7.31	9.04	5	4	5.75	2.05	800 456-5111
Ivy Global Fund B	Global	−11.46	6.61		5	4	0	2.80	800 456-5111
Ivy Global Fund C	Global	−11.53					0	2.76	800 456-5111
Ivy Global Natural Resources A	Energy/Res	−21.85					5.75		800 456-5111
Ivy Global Natural Resources B	Energy/Res	−22.46					0		800 456-5111
Ivy Global Natural Resources C	Energy/Res	−22.71					0		800 456-5111
Ivy Global Science and Technology A	Technology	18.57					5.75	2.21	800 456-5111
Ivy Global Science and Technology B	Technology	17.58					0	2.90	800 456-5111
Ivy Global Science and Technology C	Technology	17.74					0	2.95	800 456-5111
Ivy Global Science and Technology I	Technology	18.57					0	2.95	800 456-5111
Ivy Growth Fund A	Growth	15.51	18.19	14.83	4	3	5.75	0.00	800 456-5111
Ivy Growth Fund B	Growth	14.47	16.66		4	3	0	2.31	800 456-5111
Ivy Growth Fund C	Growth	14.19					0	2.26	800 456-5111
Ivy Growth with Income A	Growth	19.49	20.42		3	3	5.75	1.66	800 456-5111
Ivy Growth with Income B	Growth	18.55	20.34		3	2	0	2.38	800 456-5111
Ivy Growth with Income C	Growth	18.63	21.94		3	2	0	2.39	800 456-5111
Ivy International Fund A	Foreign	4.44	15.51	16.04	4	3	5.75	1.59	800 456-5111
Ivy International Fund B	Foreign	3.57	14.55		3	3	0	2.43	800 456-5111

| Stock Fund Name | Objective | Annualized Return for | | | Rank | | Max Load | Expense Ratio | Toll-Free Telephone |
		1 Year	3 Years	5 Years	Overall	Risk			
Ivy International Fund C	Foreign	3.59					0	2.41	800 456-5111
Ivy International Fund II Cl A	Foreign	−1.95					5.75		800 456-5111
Ivy International Fund II Cl B	Foreign	−2.73					0		800 456-5111
Ivy International Fund II Cl C	Foreign	−2.73							800 456-5111
Ivy International Fund II Cl I	Foreign	−1.95					0		800 456-5111
Ivy Intl Small Companies Fund A	Foreign	−6.97					5.75		800 456-5111
Ivy Intl Small Companies Fund B	Foreign	−7.78					0		800 456-5111
Ivy Intl Small Companies Fund C	Foreign	−7.73					0		800 456-5111
Ivy Intl Small Companies Fund I	Foreign	−7.90					0		800 456-5111
Ivy Pan Europe Fund A	European	22.97					5.75		800 456-5111
Ivy Pan Europe Fund B	European	26.87					0		800 456-5111
Ivy Pan Europe Fund C	European	26.89					0		800 456-5111
Ivy South America Fund A	Foreign	−26.85	6.36		5	5	5.75	2.48	800 456-5111
Ivy South America Fund B	Foreign	−27.39	5.80		5	5	0	3.00	800 456-5111
Ivy South America Fund C	Foreign	−27.41					0	3.00	800 456-5111
Ivy US Emerging Growth Fd A	Small Co	16.94	17.52	19.40	4	5	5.75	0.00	800 456-5111
Ivy US Emerging Growth Fd B	Small Co	16.03	13.86		4	5	0	2.48	800 456-5111
Ivy US Emerging Growth Fd C	Small Co	16.09					0	2.45	800 456-5111
Jamestown International Equity Fund	Foreign	16.59					0	1.60	800 525-3863
Janus Balanced Fund	Balanced	25.46	22.29	16.62	2	1	0	1.10	800 525-3713
Janus Enterprise Fund	Growth	28.01	20.05	17.74	3	4	0	1.04	800 525-3713
Janus Equity Income Fund	Income	35.61						1.66	800 525-3713
Janus Fund	Growth	31.58	25.47	19.14	1	3	0	0.86	800 525-3713
Janus Growth & Income Fund	Growth/Inc	37.45	33.66	22.64	2	4	0	0.96	800 525-3713
Janus Mercury Fund	Agg Growth	37.16	24.34	24.17	3	4	0	0.92	800 525-3713
Janus Olympus Fund	Growth	39.23					0	1.45	800 525-3713
Janus Overseas Fund	Foreign	21.88	28.47		2	3	0	1.07	800 525-3713
Janus Special Situations Fund	Growth	42.60					0	1.34	800 525-3713
Janus Twenty Fund	Growth	47.21	35.93	23.59	2	4	0	0.91	800 525-3713
Janus Venture Fund	Small Co	30.39	15.87	14.15	3	4	0	0.92	800 525-3713
Janus Worldwide Fund	Global	26.32	28.85	23.52	2	3	0	0.95	800 525-3713
Japan Fund	Pacific	−22.09	−3.10	−5.01	5	4	0	1.21	800 525-2470
Jensen Portfolio	Growth/Inc	17.24	22.20	16.75	3	3	0	1.32	800 221-4384
John Hancock Emerging Growth A	Small Co	17.60	17.73	17.69	4	4	5	1.29	800 225-5291
John Hancock Emerging Growth B	Small Co	16.65	16.82	16.80	4	4	0	2.02	800 225-5291
John Hancock Global A	Global	11.49	14.82	13.64	4	4	5	1.81	800 225-5291
John Hancock Global B	Global	10.78	14.04	12.91	4	4	0	2.49	800 225-5291
John Hancock Global Rx A	Health	23.64	25.55	22.37	3	4	5	1.68	800 225-5291
John Hancock Global Rx B	Health	22.80	24.66		3	4	0	2.46	800 225-5291
John Hancock Global Tech A	Technology	25.90	14.97	21.26	4	5	5	1.01	800 225-5291
John Hancock Global Tech B	Technology	24.99	19.28		4	5	0	2.24	800 225-5291
John Hancock Growth & Income A	Growth/Inc	27.47	29.56	20.00	2	3	5	1.12	800 225-5291
John Hancock Growth & Income B	Growth/Inc	26.49	28.97	19.29	2	3	0	2.19	800 225-5291
John Hancock Growth A	Growth	21.98	20.14	15.58	3	4	5	1.44	800 225-5291
John Hancock Growth B	Growth	21.20	19.29		3	4	0	1.44	800 225-5291
John Hancock Independence Equity A	Growth	32.34	29.04	21.99	1	3	5	1.44	800 225-5291
John Hancock Independence Equity B	Growth	31.37						2.14	800 225-5291
John Hancock International A	Foreign	−2.28	7.16		4	4	5	0.18	800 225-5291
John Hancock International B	Foreign	−2.94	6.40		5	4	0	0.44	800 225-5291
John Hancock Pacific Basin A	Pacific	−46.88	−13.91	−4.94	5	4	5	3.00	800 225-5291
John Hancock Pacific Basin B	Pacific	−47.30	−14.53		5	5		2.76	800 225-5291
John Hancock Regional Bank A	Financial	35.66	35.76		1	3	5	1.41	800 225-5291
John Hancock Regional Bank B	Financial	34.74	34.83	26.50	1	3	0	2.00	800 225-5291
John Hancock Sovereign Balanced A	Balanced	17.53	16.92	12.90	3	1	5	1.25	800 225-5291
John Hancock Sovereign Balanced B	Balanced	16.74	14.75	11.33	3	2	0	1.95	800 225-5291
John Hancock Sovereign Investors A	Growth/Inc	20.34	22.75	16.94	2	2	5	1.10	800 225-5291
John Hancock Sovereign Investors B	Growth/Inc	19.41	21.81		2	2		1.86	800 225-5291
John Hancock Sovereign Investors Y	Growth/Inc	9.13	18.97	14.31	2	3	0	0.88	800 225-5291

Stock Fund Name	Objective	Annualized Return for			Rank		Max Load	Expense Ratio	Toll-Free Telephone
		1 Year	3 Years	5 Years	Overall	Risk			
John Hancock Special Equities A	Small Co	10.61	12.43	13.71	4	5	5	1.43	800 225-5291
John Hancock Special Equities B	Small Co	9.76	11.60		4	5	0	2.34	800 225-5291
John Hancock Special Equities C	Small Co	11.12	12.92	14.23	4	5	0	1.45	800 225-5291
John Hancock Special Opport A	Growth	21.55	19.77		3	4	5	1.50	800 225-5291
John Hancock Special Opport B	Growth	20.75	18.86		3	4	0	2.29	800 225-5291
John Hancock Special Value A	Growth	11.02	16.01		4	3	5	1.67	800 225-5291
John Hancock Special Value B	Growth	10.17	15.16		4	3	0	0.00	800 225-5291
JP Morgan Emerging Markets Equity	Foreign	−39.30	−9.05		5	4	0	1.65	800 766-7722
JP Morgan European Equity Fund	European	33.91					0	1.42	800 766-7722
JP Morgan Instl Disciplined Equity	Growth	30.57					0	0.45	800 766-7722
JP Morgan Instl Diversified Fund	Balanced	18.00	18.52		3	1	0	0.65	800 766-7722
JP Morgan Instl Emerging Markets Eq	Foreign	−39.38	−8.89		5	4	0	1.37	800 766-7722
JP Morgan Instl European Equity	European	34.97					0	1.00	800 766-7722
JP Morgan Instl Gl Strategic Inc	Global	8.07					0	0.65	800 766-7722
JP Morgan Instl International Eq	Foreign	6.13	11.77		4	3	0	0.93	800 766-7722
JP Morgan Instl Intl Opportunities	Foreign	−0.28					0	0.99	800 766-7722
JP Morgan Instl Japan Equity Fund	Pacific	−35.88					0	1.00	800 766-7722
JP Morgan Instl Tax Aware Discip Eq	Growth	31.57					0	0.55	800 766-7722
JP Morgan Instl US Equity Fund	Growth	26.50	26.32		1	3	0	0.60	800 766-7722
JP Morgan Instl US Small Company	Small Co	17.25	19.92		3	3	0	0.80	800 766-7722
JP Morgan International Equity	Foreign	5.96	11.55	7.51	4	2	0	1.12	800 766-7722
JP Morgan Intl Opportunities	Foreign	−0.44					0	1.20	800 766-7722
JP Morgan Japan Equity Fund	Pacific	−37.40					0	1.42	800 766-7722
JP Morgan Small Co Opportunities	Small Co	23.35					0	1.20	800 766-7722
JP Morgan Tax Aware Eq Select Shs	Growth	29.67					0	0.85	800 766-7722
JP Morgan US Equity Fund	Growth	26.16	26.05	20.47	1	3	0	0.79	800 766-7722
JP Morgan US Small Company Fund	Small Co	17.00	19.97		3	3	0	0.92	800 766-7722
Jundt Growth Fund A	Growth	26.62					5.25	2.18	800 370-0612
Jundt Growth Fund B	Growth	25.66					0	2.92	800 370-0612
Jundt Growth Fund C	Growth	26.03					0	2.92	800 370-0612
Jundt Growth Fund I	Growth	26.93					5.25	1.92	800 370-0612
Jundt Opportunity Fund A	Small Co	46.22					5.25	2.14	800 370-0612
Jundt Opportunity Fund B	Small Co	45.18					0	2.89	800 370-0612
Jundt Opportunity Fund C	Small Co	45.06					0	2.89	800 370-0612
Jundt Opportunity Fund I	Small Co	46.66					5.25	1.89	800 370-0612
Jundt US Emerging Growth Fund A	Small Co	34.32					5.25	1.80	800 370-0612
Jundt US Emerging Growth Fund B	Small Co	31.55					0	2.55	800 370-0612
Jundt US Emerging Growth Fund C	Small Co	31.60					0	2.55	800 370-0612
Jundt US Emerging Growth Fund I	Small Co	31.01					5.25	1.55	800 370-0612
Jurika & Voyles Balanced Fund	Balanced	8.96	14.72	13.78	3	2	0	1.07	800 584-6878
Jurika & Voyles Mini-Cap Fund	Small Co	10.29	23.20		3	4	0	1.50	800 584-6878
Jurika & Voyles Value + Growth Fd	Growth	11.61	18.29		4	4	0	1.26	800 584-6878
Kalmar Growth With Value Small Cap	Small Co	23.68					0		800 282-2319
Kaufmann Fund	Small Co	13.45	19.14	19.80	4	4	0	1.89	800 261-0555
Keeley Small Cap Value Fund	Small Co	36.46	30.21		2	4	4.5	2.45	800 533-5344
Kemper Blue Chip Fund A	Growth/Inc	20.68	26.01	17.58	2	3	5.75	1.19	800 621-1048
Kemper Blue Chip Fund B	Growth/Inc	19.56	24.94		2	3	0	2.08	800 621-1048
Kemper Blue Chip Fund C	Growth/Inc	19.62	24.99		2	3	0	2.01	800 621-1048
Kemper Contrarian Fund A	Growth/Inc	22.35	25.33	19.96	1	3	5.75	1.35	800 621-1048
Kemper Contrarian Fund B	Growth/Inc	21.27					0	2.26	800 621-1048
Kemper Contrarian Fund C	Growth/Inc	21.17					0	2.47	800 621-1048
Kemper Europe Fund A	European	27.70					5.75	1.42	800 621-1048
Kemper Europe Fund B	European	26.36					0	2.31	800 621-1048
Kemper Europe Fund C	European	26.68					0	2.28	800 621-1048
Kemper Growth Fund A	Growth	24.55	21.02	14.75	3	3	5	1.06	800 621-1048
Kemper Growth Fund B	Growth	23.23	19.78		3	3	0	2.12	800 621-1048
Kemper Growth Fund C	Growth	23.68	19.98		3	3	0	2.01	800 621-1048
Kemper Horizon 10+ Portfolio A	Growth/Inc	17.24					5.75	1.51	800 621-1048

| Stock Fund Name | Objective | Annualized Return for | | | Rank | | Max Load | Expense Ratio | Toll-Free Telephone |
		1 Year	3 Years	5 Years	Overall	Risk			
Kemper Horizon 10+ Portfolio B	Growth/Inc	16.28						2.36	800 621-1048
Kemper Horizon 10+ Portfolio C	Growth/Inc	16.32					0	2.61	800 621-1048
Kemper Horizon 20+ Portfolio A	Growth	19.06					5.75	1.69	800 621-1048
Kemper Horizon 20+ Portfolio B	Growth	17.81					0	2.47	800 621-1048
Kemper Horizon 20+ Portfolio C	Growth	17.97					0	2.48	800 621-1048
Kemper Horizon 5 Portfolio A	Income	13.11					5.75	1.51	800 621-1048
Kemper Horizon 5 Portfolio B	Income	12.51						2.15	800 621-1048
Kemper Horizon 5 Portfolio C	Income	12.43					0	2.16	800 621-1048
Kemper International Fund A	Foreign	12.04	16.94	14.20	4	3	5.75	2.49	800 621-1048
Kemper International Fund B	Foreign	11.07	14.87		4	3	0	2.58	800 621-1048
Kemper International Fund C	Foreign	11.15	15.03		4	3	0	2.47	800 621-1048
Kemper Retirement Fund I	Flexible	14.41	15.57	11.69	3	1	5	0.84	800 621-1048
Kemper Retirement Fund II	Flexible	12.98	13.14	10.11	3	1	5	0.90	800 621-1048
Kemper Retirement Fund III	Flexible	14.15	14.10	11.59	3	1	5	0.95	800 621-1048
Kemper Retirement Fund IV	Flexible	14.68	13.61	10.65	3	1	5	0.96	800 621-1048
Kemper Retirement Fund V	Flexible	16.31	14.77		3	1	5	0.94	800 621-1048
Kemper Small Cap Equity Fund A	Small Co	9.24	16.91	14.98	4	4	5.75	0.90	800 621-1048
Kemper Small Cap Equity Fund B	Small Co	7.94	15.61		4	4	0	2.04	800 621-1048
Kemper Small Cap Equity Fund C	Small Co	8.78	15.93		4	4	0	1.95	800 621-1048
Kemper Small Cap Value A	Small Co	9.27	20.78	18.98	3	3	5.75	1.32	800 621-1048
Kemper Small Cap Value B	Small Co	8.29					0	2.34	800 621-1048
Kemper Small Cap Value C	Small Co	8.37					0	2.24	800 621-1048
Kemper Small Cap Value I	Small Co	12.18					0	0.89	800 621-1048
Kemper Technology Fund A	Technology	22.47	18.97	21.25	4	5	5.75	0.89	800 621-1048
Kemper Technology Fund B	Technology	21.31	17.79		4	5	0	1.85	800 621-1048
Kemper Technology Fund C	Technology	21.63	5.05		5	5	0	1.76	800 621-1048
Kemper Total Return Fund A	Balanced	17.65	18.76	13.07	3	2	5.75	1.01	800 621-1048
Kemper Total Return Fund B	Balanced	16.56	17.69		3	2	0	1.95	800 621-1048
Kemper Total Return Fund C	Balanced	16.64	17.77		3	2	0	1.90	800 621-1048
Kemper Value and Growth Fund A	Growth	23.51					5.75	1.56	800 621-1048
Kemper Value and Growth Fund C	Growth	22.26					0	2.35	800 621-1048
Kemper Worldwide 2004 Fund	Growth	14.59	11.89		3	1	0	1.16	800 621-1048
Kemper-Dreman High Return Fund A	Growth/Inc	20.50	30.23	22.29	2	2	5.75	1.22	800 621-1048
Kemper-Dreman High Return Fund B	Growth/Inc	19.48					0	2.12	800 621-1048
Kemper-Dreman High Return Fund C	Growth/Inc	8.81					0	2.10	800 621-1048
Kemper-Dreman High Return Fund I	Growth/Inc	10.16					0	0.83	800 621-1048
Kent Growth & Income Instl	Growth/Inc	26.20	25.39	18.69	1	2	0	0.92	800 633-5368
Kent Growth & Income Invest	Growth/Inc	25.83	25.06	18.97	1	2		1.17	800 633-5368
Kent Index Equity Instl	Growth	29.49	29.41		1	3	0	0.43	800 633-5368
Kent Index Equity Invest	Growth	29.18	28.82	21.80	1	3	4	0.68	800 633-5368
Kent Intl Growth Fund Instl	Foreign	5.43	12.98		4	3	0	1.05	800 633-5368
Kent Intl Growth Fund Invest	Foreign	5.19	12.68	10.23	4	3	4	1.30	800 633-5368
Kent Small Company Growth Instl	Small Co	15.32	20.80		3	3	0	0.93	800 633-5368
Kent Small Company Growth Invest	Small Co	15.00	20.48	16.20	3	3	4	1.18	800 633-5368
KeyPremier Aggressive Growth Fund	Agg Growth	11.44					4.5	0.66	800 766-3960
KeyPremier Established Growth Fund	Growth	26.99					4.5	0.44	800 766-3960
Kiewit Equity Portfolio	Growth	29.08	24.59		1	3	0	0.80	800 254-3948
Kobren Insight Conserv Alloc Fund	AssetAlloc	13.12					0	1.00	800 895-9936
Kobren Insight Growth Fund	Growth	13.93					0	1.00	800 895-9936
Kobren Insight Moderate Growth Fund	Growth/Inc	16.77					0	1.00	800 895-9936
Lazard Emerging Markets	Foreign	−34.51	0.49		5	4	0	1.28	800 823-6300
Lazard Equity Portfolio	Growth	21.51	24.63	21.53	2	3	0	0.87	800 823-6300
Lazard International Equity Port	Foreign	18.22	18.71	16.09	3	3	0	0.89	800 823-6300
Lazard International Small Cap Port	Foreign	16.31	13.78		4	3	0	1.09	800 823-6300
Lazard Small Cap Portfolio	Small Co	10.96	18.64	17.74	3	3	0	0.82	800 823-6300
Legg Mason Special Invest Trust	Small Co	22.29	23.56	16.60	3	4	0	1.84	800 822-5544
Legg Mason Total Return Trust	Growth/Inc	23.31	28.06	19.67	2	2	0	1.89	800 822-5544
Legg Mason Value Trust	Growth	37.91	39.24	29.26	1	4	0	1.74	800 822-5544

Stock Fund Name	Objective	Annualized Return for			Rank		Max Load	Expense Ratio	Toll-Free Telephone
		1 Year	3 Years	5 Years	Overall	Risk			
Lepercq-Istel Fund	Growth/Inc	25.15	18.82	14.53	4	4	0	1.64	800 655-7766
Lexington Convertible Securities	Converts	13.81	12.16	10.64	4	3	0	2.50	800 526-0056
Lexington Corporate Leaders Fund	Growth/Inc	17.65	25.27	19.42	2	3	0	0.62	800 526-0056
Lexington Crosby Sm Cap Asia Growth	Pacific	−64.74					0	2.28	800 526-0056
Lexington Global Fund	Global	8.10	15.36	13.39	4	3	0	1.75	800 526-0056
Lexington Goldfund	Gold	−32.81	−15.52	−9.68	5	5	0	1.58	800 526-0056
Lexington Growth and Income Fund	Growth/Inc	25.92	27.86	18.64	2	3	0	1.17	800 526-0056
Lexington International Fund	Foreign	2.42	12.14		4	3	0	1.75	800 526-0056
Lexington Smallcap Value Fund	Small Co	4.71					0	2.74	800 526-0056
Lexington Strategic Invt Fund	Gold	−38.40	−23.43	−12.85	5	5	5.75	2.50	800 526-0056
Lexington Strategic Silver Fund	Gold	−17.32	−6.15	−1.25	5	5	5.75	1.96	800 526-0056
Lexington Troika Dialog Russia Fund	Foreign	−62.38					0	2.07	800 526-0056
Lexington Worldwide Emerging Mkts	Foreign	−34.45	−8.04	−0.64	5	4	0	1.82	800 526-0056
LifeUSA Aggressive Growth Fund	Agg Growth	20.12					5.75	0.50	800 864-4725
LifeUSA Balanced Fund	Balanced	10.46					5.75	0.50	800 864-4725
LifeUSA Global Fund	Global	−1.10					5.75	0.50	800 864-4725
LifeUSA Growth Fund	Growth	19.66					5.75	0.50	800 864-4725
Lighthouse Contrarian Fund	Growth	−1.26					0	2.24	800 282-2340
Lindner Bulwark Fund	Flexible	−10.08	−3.26		5	4	0	0.62	
Lindner Dividend Fund	Income	14.75	13.17	10.46	3	1	0	0.31	
Lindner Growth Fund	Growth	0.31	11.23	10.64	4	3	0	0.44	
Lindner International Fund	Foreign	−20.31	−0.45		5	4	0	1.07	
Lindner Utilities Fund	Utilities	15.54	21.37		3	4	0	0.48	
Lindner/Ryback Small-Cap Fund	Small Co	15.24	21.87		3	4	0	0.96	
LMH Fund Ltd	Growth/Inc	13.03	17.83	13.97	3	2	0	2.63	800 366-6223
LongLeaf Partners Fund	Growth	31.94	25.83	23.29	1	2	0	0.94	800 445-9469
LongLeaf Partners Realty Fund	Real Est	7.28					0	1.24	800 445-9469
LongLeaf Partners Small Cap	Small Co	25.08	28.64	20.59	1	1	0	1.09	800 445-9469
Loomis Sayles Core Value Instl	Growth/Inc	19.18	24.05	19.56	2	3	0	0.85	800 626-9390
Loomis Sayles Core Value Retail	Growth/Inc	19.14					0		800 626-9390
Loomis Sayles Growth Fund Instl	Growth	25.70	21.78	17.22	3	4	0	0.85	800 626-9390
Loomis Sayles Growth Fund Retail	Growth	25.42					0		800 626-9390
Loomis Sayles Intl Equity Instl	Foreign	−1.62	7.94	11.06	4	3	0	1.00	800 626-9390
Loomis Sayles Intl Equity Retail	Foreign	−2.01					0		800 626-9390
Loomis Sayles Mid Cap Growth Instl	Growth	24.77					0		800 626-9390
Loomis Sayles Mid Cap Growth Retail	Growth	24.36					0		800 626-9390
Loomis Sayles Mid Cap Value Instl	Growth/Inc	19.87					0		800 626-9390
Loomis Sayles Mid Cap Value Retail	Growth/Inc	19.77					0		800 626-9390
Loomis Sayles Sm Cap Growth Instl	Small Co	29.08					0		800 626-9390
Loomis Sayles Sm Cap Growth Retail	Small Co	23.02					0		800 626-9390
Loomis Sayles Small Cap Val Instl	Small Co	14.78	25.84	18.64	3	3	0	1.00	800 626-9390
Loomis Sayles Small Cap Val Retail	Small Co	14.45					0		800 626-9390
Loomis Sayles Strat Value Instl	Growth	11.95					0		800 626-9390
Loomis Sayles Strat Value Retail	Growth	13.69					0		800 626-9390
Loomis Sayles Worldwide Instl	Global	−1.59					0		800 626-9390
Loomis Sayles Worldwide Retail	Global	−1.98					0		800 626-9390
Lord Abbett Affiliated Fund A	Growth/Inc	18.32	23.47	19.26	2	3	5.75	0.65	800 426-1130
Lord Abbett Affiliated Fund B	Growth/Inc	17.45					6.1	0.71	800 426-1130
Lord Abbett Affiliated Fund C	Growth/Inc	17.53					0	0.71	800 426-1130
Lord Abbett Balanced Fund A	Balanced	13.07					4.75	0.78	800 426-1130
Lord Abbett Balanced Fund C	Balanced	12.02					0	1.26	800 426-1130
Lord Abbett Developing Growth A	Small Co	23.82	25.90	24.58	3	4	5.75	0.56	800 426-1130
Lord Abbett Developing Growth B	Small Co	22.92					0	0.92	800 426-1130
Lord Abbett Developing Growth C	Small Co	22.98					0	0.89	800 426-1130
Lord Abbett Equity 1990	Flexible	14.38	23.30	18.40	3	3	5.5	0.74	800 426-1130
Lord Abbett Global Equity Series A	Global	9.60	12.53	9.85	4	2	5.75	1.51	800 426-1130
Lord Abbett Global Equity Series B	Global	8.82					0	1.11	800 426-1130
Lord Abbett Global Equity Series C	Global	8.72					0	0.97	800 426-1130

323

| Stock Fund Name | Objective | Annualized Return for | | | Rank | | Max Load | Expense Ratio | Toll-Free Telephone |
		1 Year	3 Years	5 Years	Overall	Risk			
Lord Abbett Growth & Income A	Growth/Inc	20.01					5.75	0.61	800 426-1130
Lord Abbett Growth & Income C	Growth/Inc	19.17	23.00		2	2	0	2.05	800 426-1130
Lord Abbett International Series A	Foreign	39.07					5.75	0.51	800 426-1130
Lord Abbett International Series B	Foreign	38.13					0	0.87	800 426-1130
Lord Abbett International Series C	Foreign	38.13					0	0.87	800 426-1130
Lord Abbett Mid-Cap Value Fund A	Growth	23.53	23.71	17.41	2	2	5.75	1.25	800 426-1130
Lord Abbett Mid-Cap Value Fund B	Growth	23.13					0	1.29	800 426-1130
Lord Abbett Mid-Cap Value Fund C	Growth	23.14					0	1.28	800 426-1130
Lord Abbett Research Large Cap A	Growth/Inc	18.48	23.96	21.43	2	3	5.75	1.52	800 426-1130
Lord Abbett Research Large Cap B	Growth/Inc	17.92					0	1.07	800 426-1130
Lord Abbett Research Large Cap C	Growth/Inc	17.91					0	1.54	800 426-1130
Lord Abbett Research Small Cap A	Small Co	13.56					5.75	0.61	800 426-1130
Lord Abbett Research Small Cap B	Small Co	12.60					0	0.93	800 426-1130
Lord Abbett Research Small Cap C	Small Co	12.65					0	1.25	800 426-1130
Lutheran Brotherhood Fund	Growth/Inc	25.83	25.13	17.88	2	3	5	0.88	800 328-4552
Lutheran Brotherhood Mid Cap Growth	Growth	18.87					5		800 328-4552
Lutheran Brotherhood Opp Growth	Agg Growth	3.47	8.97	12.57	4	5	5	1.29	800 328-4552
Lutheran Brotherhood World Growth	Foreign	4.55					5	1.91	800 328-4552
MainStay Capital Appreciation A	Agg Growth	30.86	26.08		3	4	5.5	1.10	800 624-6782
MainStay Capital Appreciation B	Agg Growth	29.97	25.38	20.10	3	4	0	1.09	800 624-6782
MainStay Convertible Fund A	Converts	12.20	12.89		3	1	5.5	1.46	800 624-6782
MainStay Convertible Fund B	Converts	10.49	11.89	11.95	3	1	0	2.08	800 624-6782
MainStay Equity Index Fund	Growth/Inc	31.92	30.05	23.80	1	3	5.5	0.80	800 624-6782
MainStay Institutional EAFE Index	Foreign	4.41	9.75	9.00	4	3	0	0.94	800 695-2126
MainStay Institutional Growth Eq	Growth	31.46	27.58	21.47	3	4	0	0.93	800 695-2126
MainStay Institutional Indexed Eq	Growth/Inc	29.67	29.76	22.53	1	3	0	0.30	800 695-2126
MainStay Institutional Multi-Asset	AssetAlloc	23.43	23.42	16.85	2	2	0	0.76	800 695-2126
MainStay Institutional Value Equity	Growth/Inc	14.64	20.36	16.70	3	2	0	0.93	800 695-2126
MainStay Instl Intl Equity Instl	Foreign	7.78	14.74		4	3		1.00	800 695-2126
MainStay Instl Intl Equity Service	Foreign	7.16	14.24		4	3		1.25	800 695-2126
MainStay International Equity A	Foreign	9.50	14.26		4	3	5.5	1.99	800 624-6782
MainStay Total Return Fund A	Flexible	21.97	18.80		3	2	5.5	1.15	800 624-6782
MainStay Total Return Fund B	Flexible	21.21	18.17	14.56	3	2	0	1.65	800 624-6782
MainStay Value Fund A	Growth/Inc	14.27	19.86		2	2	5.5	1.13	800 624-6782
MainStay Value Fund B	Growth/Inc	13.55	19.17	15.55	3	2	0	1.11	800 624-6782
Mairs & Power Balanced Fund	Balanced	20.39	22.05	16.54	2	2	0	0.92	800 304-7404
Mairs & Power Growth	Growth	16.16	28.26	24.52	2	3	0	0.84	800 304-7404
Managers Capital Appreciation Fund	Growth	43.11	24.20	20.02	3	4	0	1.32	800 835-3879
Managers Income Equity	Income	22.69	24.03	18.87	1	2	0	1.32	800 835-3879
Managers International Equity Fund	Foreign	15.33	16.54	16.18	3	2	0	1.45	800 835-3879
Managers Special Equity	Small Co	19.85	24.91	18.90	3	4	0	1.35	800 835-3879
Map-Equity Fund	Growth	23.26	28.26	20.60	1	2	4.75	0.82	800 559-5535
Markman Aggressive Growth	Flexible	19.23	15.23		3	3	0	0.95	800 707-2771
Markman Conservative	Flexible	11.44	11.70		3	1	0	0.95	800 707-2771
Markman Moderate	Flexible	17.26	14.84		3	2	0	0.95	800 707-2771
Marquis Balanced Class A	Balanced	17.03	15.68		3	1	3.5	0.90	800-480-4111
Marquis Balanced Class B	Balanced	16.12	15.12		3	1	0	1.65	800-480-4111
Marquis Growth Equity A	Growth	25.18					3.5	1.00	800-480-4111
Marquis Growth Equity B	Growth	24.34					0	1.75	800-480-4111
Marquis Value Equity A	Growth	25.62	25.06		1	3	3.5	1.00	800-480-4111
Marquis Value Equity B	Growth	24.96	24.32		2	3	0	1.75	800-480-4111
Marshall Equity Income Fund	Income	20.36	23.61		2	2	0	1.20	800 236-8560
Marshall International Stock Fund	Foreign	6.93	14.72		4	3	0	1.61	800 236-8560
Marshall Large-Cap Growth & Income	Growth/Inc	22.28	23.44		3	3	0	1.23	800 236-8560
Marshall Mid-Cap Growth Fund	Growth	31.69	24.57		3	4	0	1.20	800 236-8560
Marshall Mid-Cap Value Fund	Growth	19.02	17.94		3	2	0	1.23	800 236-8560
MAS Funds Balanced	Balanced	17.55	18.99	14.69	3	1	0	0.58	800 354-8185
MAS Funds Emerging Markets Port	Foreign	−33.60	−4.47		5	5	0	0.91	800 354-8185

Stock Fund Name	Objective	Annualized Return for			Rank		Max Load	Expense Ratio	Toll-Free Telephone
		1 Year	3 Years	5 Years	Overall	Risk			
MAS Funds Equity Portfolio	Growth	23.36	25.27	19.85	2	3	0	0.61	800 354-8185
MAS Funds International Equity	Foreign	9.65	13.69	11.05	4	3	0	0.66	800 354-8185
MAS Funds MidCap Growth	Small Co	52.03	33.10	24.41	3	4	0	0.63	800 354-8185
MAS Funds MidCap Value Portfolio	Small Co	30.20	33.06		1	4	0	0.91	800 354-8185
MAS Funds Multi-Asset-Class	AssetAlloc	15.29	17.99		3	2	0	0.70	800 354-8185
MAS Funds Small Cap Value	Small Co	18.28	27.20	21.10	3	4	0	0.86	800 354-8185
MAS Funds Value Portfolio	Growth/Inc	11.72	23.07	20.75	3	2	0	0.59	800 354-8185
Mason Street Aggressive Growth A	Agg Growth	22.71					4.75	1.30	888 627-6678
Mason Street Aggressive Growth B	Agg Growth	21.93					0	1.95	888 627-6678
Mason Street Asset Allocation A	AssetAlloc	16.66					4.75	1.35	888 627-6678
Mason Street Asset Allocation B	AssetAlloc	15.94					0	2.00	888 627-6678
Mason Street Growth & Income A	Growth/Inc	24.44					4.75	2.76	888 627-6678
Mason Street Growth & Income B	Growth/Inc	23.58					0	1.85	888 627-6678
Mason Street Growth A	Growth	31.74					4.75	1.30	888 627-6678
Mason Street Growth B	Growth	30.85					0	1.95	888 627-6678
Mason Street Index 500 A	Growth	28.98					4.75	0.85	888 627-6678
Mason Street Index 500 B	Growth	28.14					0	1.50	888 627-6678
Mason Street International Equity A	Foreign	−1.74					4.75	1.65	888 627-6678
Mason Street International Equity B	Foreign	−2.41					0	2.30	888 627-6678
Mass Investors Growth Stock A	Growth	45.60	35.35	24.57	2	4	5.75	0.71	800 343-2829
Mass Investors Growth Stock B	Growth	44.53	34.22		2	4	0	1.53	800 343-2829
Mass Investors Trust A	Growth/Inc	28.89	31.28	22.92	1	3	5.75	0.74	800 343-2829
MassMutual Instl Balanced S	Balanced	14.78	15.82		3	1	0	0.53	
MassMutual Instl Intl Equity S	Foreign	17.16	18.25		3	3	0	1.02	
MassMutual Instl Small Cap Value S	Small Co	20.07	23.94		3	3	0	0.63	
MassMutual Instl Value Equity S	Growth/Inc	20.41	24.13		2	2	0	0.53	
Masters' Select Equity Fund	Growth	27.77					0	1.47	800 960-0188
MasterWorks Asset Allocation	AssetAlloc	28.30	19.92		3	2	0	0.75	800 776-0179
MasterWorks Growth Stock Fund	Growth	20.07	9.48		4	5	0	0.81	800 776-0179
MasterWorks Lifepath 2000 Instl	AssetAlloc	10.87	9.61		2	1	0	0.95	800 776-0179
MasterWorks Lifepath 2010 Instl	AssetAlloc	15.70	15.21		3	1	0	0.95	800 776-0179
MasterWorks Lifepath 2020 Instl	AssetAlloc	20.27	19.23		2	2	0	0.95	800 776-0179
MasterWorks Lifepath 2030 Instl	AssetAlloc	23.69	22.32		2	3	0	0.95	800 776-0179
MasterWorks Lifepath 2040 Instl	AssetAlloc	25.48	25.24		1	3	0	0.95	800 776-0179
MasterWorks S&P 500 Stock Fund	Growth	29.85	29.90		1	3	0	0.22	800 776-0179
Mathers Fund	Growth	0.48	0.20	0.48	4	1	0	1.03	800 962-3863
Matrix Growth Fund	Growth	32.28	26.24	17.44	3	3	0	1.75	800 354-6339
Matterhorn Growth Fund	Growth	11.38	11.53	11.62	4	3	0	4.00	800 543-2875
Matthews Asian Convert Secs Fund	Pacific	−34.81	−6.87		5	4	0	1.90	800 789-2742
Matthews Korea Fund	Pacific	−69.33	−39.45		5	5	0	2.50	800 789-2742
Matthews Pacific Tiger Fund	Pacific	−60.51	−19.21		5	5	0	1.90	800 789-2742
Maxus Equity Fund	Growth/Inc	13.01	18.69	16.42	3	2	0	1.87	800 446-2987
Maxus Income Fund	Flexible	8.26	9.35	7.20	3	1	0	1.91	800 446-2987
Maxus Laureate Fund	Growth/Inc	16.98	17.92		4	3	0	3.00	800 446-2987
McM Balanced Fund	Balanced	21.05	20.52		2	2	0	0.60	800 788-9485
McM Equity Investment Fund	Growth	29.76	25.88		2	4	0	0.75	800 788-9485
Megatrends Fund	Flexible	11.22	16.60	11.87	4	3	0	1.81	800 426-6635
Mentor Capital Growth A	Growth	36.09	26.84	18.59	2	3	5.75	1.41	800 382-0016
Mentor Capital Growth B	Growth	35.09	25.88	17.70	2	3	0	2.16	800 382-0016
Mentor Growth Portfolio B	Growth	17.74	22.14	17.98	4	4	5.75	2.03	800 382-0016
Mentor Income & Growth A	Growth/Inc	12.35	17.75	15.10	3	1	5.75	1.36	800 382-0016
Mentor Income & Growth B	Growth/Inc	11.39	16.86	14.25	3	1	0	2.12	800 382-0016
Mentor Perpetual Global Port A	Global	14.35	19.67		3	3	5.75	1.89	800 382-0016
Mentor Perpetual Global Port B	Global	13.51	18.73		3	3	0	2.76	800 382-0016
Mentor Strategy Portfolio A	Agg Growth	16.91	16.12		4	2	5.75	1.40	800 382-0016
Mentor Strategy Portfolio B	Agg Growth	16.55	15.45		4	2	0	2.21	800 382-0016
Merger Fund	Growth	11.18	11.57	11.37	3	1	0	1.36	800 343-8959
Meridian Fund	Small Co	16.78	17.31	14.23	3	3	0	0.95	800 446-6662

| Stock Fund Name | Objective | Annualized Return for | | | Rank | | Max Load | Expense Ratio | Toll-Free Telephone |
		1 Year	3 Years	5 Years	Overall	Risk			
Meridian Value Fund	Growth	25.81	31.28		3	4	0	2.51	800 446-6662
Merrill Lynch Basic Value A	Growth/Inc	23.23	24.30	19.81	1	2	5.25	0.54	800 637-3863
Merrill Lynch Basic Value B	Growth/Inc	21.97	23.03	18.59	1	2	0	1.57	800 637-3863
Merrill Lynch Capital Fund A	Flexible	17.34	18.75	16.27	2	1	5.25	0.55	800 637-3863
Merrill Lynch Capital Fund B	Flexible	16.17	17.55	15.08	3	1	0	1.56	800 637-3863
Merrill Lynch Consults Intl Port	Foreign	2.02	11.69	8.78	4	3	0		800 637-3863
Merrill Lynch Dev Cap Markets A	Foreign	−36.19	−4.87	1.77	5	4	5.25	1.53	800 637-3863
Merrill Lynch Dragon B	Pacific	−58.17	−21.61	−8.19	5	5	0	2.37	800 637-3863
Merrill Lynch Dragon D	Pacific	−57.84	−20.99	−7.48	5	5	6.5	1.61	800 637-3863
Merrill Lynch Eurofund A	European	37.00	26.08	22.80	2	2	5.25	1.04	800 637-3863
Merrill Lynch Eurofund B	European	35.58	24.77	21.53	2	2	0	2.06	800 637-3863
Merrill Lynch Eurofund C	European	35.23	24.61		2	2	0	2.10	800 637-3863
Merrill Lynch Eurofund D	European	36.66	25.75		2	2	5.25	1.30	800 637-3863
Merrill Lynch Fund for Tomorrow A	Growth	15.61	18.78	15.54	4	4	5.25	0.89	800 637-3863
Merrill Lynch Fund for Tomorrow B	Growth	14.45	17.53	14.39	4	4	0	1.94	800 637-3863
Merrill Lynch Fundamental Growth B	Growth	30.70	28.74	20.66	2	3	0	2.02	800 637-3863
Merrill Lynch Global Alloc B	AssetAlloc	6.60	13.84	11.23	3	1	0	1.85	800 637-3863
Merrill Lynch Global Alloc D	AssetAlloc	7.42	14.71	12.23	3	1	6.5	0.95	800 637-3863
Merrill Lynch Global Holdings A	Global	7.44	13.69	11.79	4	3	5.25	1.39	800 637-3863
Merrill Lynch Global Holdings B	Global	6.35	12.63	10.64	4	3	0	2.37	800 637-3863
Merrill Lynch Global Resources Tr A	Energy/Res	−17.90	0.43	3.58	5	4	5.25	1.01	800 637-3863
Merrill Lynch Global Resources Tr B	Energy/Res	−18.75	−0.43	2.56	5	4	0	2.13	800 637-3863
Merrill Lynch Global Util Fund A	Utilities	25.42	20.86	14.05	3	3	6.5	0.87	800 637-3863
Merrill Lynch Global Util Fund B	Utilities	24.41	19.94	13.18	3	3	0	1.59	800 637-3863
Merrill Lynch Global Value A	Global	30.09					5.25	0.99	800 637-3863
Merrill Lynch Global Value B	Global	28.76					0	2.02	800 637-3863
Merrill Lynch Global Value C	Global	28.76					0	2.02	800 637-3863
Merrill Lynch Global Value D	Global	29.68					5.25	1.25	800 637-3863
Merrill Lynch Growth A	Growth	−0.19	16.14	17.18	4	4	5.25	0.76	800 637-3863
Merrill Lynch Growth B	Growth	−1.22	14.94	15.97	4	4	0	1.83	800 637-3863
Merrill Lynch Growth C	Growth	−1.21	14.94		4	4	0	1.79	800 637-3863
Merrill Lynch Growth D	Growth	−0.46	18.30		4	4	5.25	1.01	800 637-3863
Merrill Lynch Healthcare A	Health	24.36	27.91	20.27	2	3	5.25	1.38	800 637-3863
Merrill Lynch Healthcare B	Health	23.02	26.62	19.08	3	3	0	2.44	800 637-3863
Merrill Lynch Latin America A	Foreign	−26.75	7.45		5	5	5.25	1.49	800 637-3863
Merrill Lynch Latin America B	Foreign	−27.53	6.35	3.43	5	5	0	2.50	800 637-3863
Merrill Lynch Latin America C	Foreign	−27.52	6.32		5	5	0	2.54	800 637-3863
Merrill Lynch Latin America D	Foreign	−26.91	7.28	4.30	5	5	4	1.74	800 637-3863
Merrill Lynch Pacific A	Pacific	−21.36	2.94	3.76	5	4	5.25	0.87	800 637-3863
Merrill Lynch Pacific B	Pacific	−22.20	1.88	2.67	5	4	0	1.97	800 637-3863
Merrill Lynch Phoenix A	Growth	28.79	19.00	14.64	3	4	5.25	1.26	800 637-3863
Merrill Lynch Phoenix B	Growth	27.54	17.81	13.49	3	4	0	2.26	800 637-3863
Merrill Lynch Special Value A	Small Co	16.28	23.17	18.88	3	4	5.25	1.02	800 637-3863
Merrill Lynch Special Value B	Small Co	15.09	21.90	19.47	3	4	0	2.05	800 637-3863
Merrill Lynch Strategic Dividend A	Income	23.25	24.77	16.24	2	2	5.25	0.90	800 637-3863
Merrill Lynch Strategic Dividend B	Income	22.09	23.51	16.36	2	2	0	1.94	800 637-3863
Merrill Lynch Technology A	Technology	−15.38	2.15	8.57	5	5	5.25	1.30	800 637-3863
Merrill Lynch Technology B	Technology	−16.19	1.08	7.45	5	5	0	2.34	800 637-3863
Merriman Asset Allocation Fund	AssetAlloc	5.42	8.98	7.69	4	2	0	1.78	800 423-4893
Merriman Capital Appreciation Fund	Growth	10.51	12.62	9.80	4	3	0	1.79	800 423-4893
Merriman Growth and Income Fund	Growth/Inc	14.39	17.34	12.48	3	2	0	1.71	800 423-4893
Merriman Leveraged Growth Fund	Growth	12.10	15.16	11.92	4	4	0	4.13	800 423-4893
Meyers Pride Value Fund	Growth	17.00					0	2.09	800 410-3337
MFR Emerging Markets Total Return A	AssetAlloc	0.54					4.75	2.00	888 743-6432
MFR Emerging Markets Total Return B	AssetAlloc	−0.23					0	2.75	888 743-6432
MFR Global Asset Allocation A	AssetAlloc	18.37					4.75	2.00	888 743-6432
MFR Global Asset Allocation B	AssetAlloc	16.93					0	2.75	888 743-6432
MFS Capital Opportunities Fund A	Agg Growth	34.86	28.58	22.10	1	3	5.75	1.29	800 343-2829

Stock Fund Name	Objective	Annualized Return for			Rank		Max Load	Expense Ratio	Toll-Free Telephone
		1 Year	3 Years	5 Years	Overall	Risk			
MFS Capital Opportunities Fund B	Agg Growth	33.92	23.83		3	3	0	2.09	800 343-2829
MFS Capital Opportunities Fund C	Agg Growth	33.90					0	2.08	800 343-2829
MFS Emerging Growth Fund A	Agg Growth	26.31	25.50	17.59	3	4	5.75	1.23	800 343-2829
MFS Emerging Growth Fund B	Agg Growth	25.38	24.53	21.59	3	4	0	1.97	800 343-2829
MFS Emerging Growth Fund C	Agg Growth	25.36					0	1.35	800 343-2829
MFS For & Col Emerging Markets Eq A	Foreign	−25.76					4.75	2.51	800 343-2829
MFS For & Col Emerging Markets Eq B	Foreign	−26.12					0	3.04	800 343-2829
MFS For & Col Emerging Markets Eq C	Foreign	−26.14					0	3.00	800 343-2829
MFS For & Col International Gr A	Foreign	−0.62					4.75	1.99	800 343-2829
MFS For & Col International Gr B	Foreign	−1.11					0	2.53	800 343-2829
MFS For & Col International Gr C	Foreign	−1.05					0	2.50	800 343-2829
MFS For & Col Intl Growth & Inc A	Foreign	18.15					4.75	2.39	800 343-2829
MFS For & Col Intl Growth & Inc B	Foreign	17.59					0	2.94	800 343-2829
MFS For & Col Intl Growth & Inc C	Foreign	17.49					0	2.64	800 343-2829
MFS Growth Opportunities Fund A	Growth	28.67	26.58	19.88	3	4	5.75	0.84	800 343-2829
MFS Growth Opportunities Fund B	Growth	27.54	25.46		3	4	0	0.80	800 343-2829
MFS Large Cap Growth Fund A	Agg Growth	32.88	27.91		1	3	5.75	1.30	800 343-2829
MFS Large Cap Growth Fund B	Agg Growth	31.88	26.92	20.03	2	3	0	2.05	800 343-2829
MFS Managed Sectors A	Agg Growth	22.99	21.04		3	4	5.75	2.21	800 343-2829
MFS Managed Sectors B	Agg Growth	22.23	20.21	16.80	3	4	0	1.31	800 343-2829
MFS Midcap Growth Fund A	Small Co	25.72	19.81		3	4	5.75	1.49	800 343-2829
MFS Midcap Growth Fund B	Small Co	24.75	18.84		3	4	0	2.30	800 343-2829
MFS Midcap Growth Fund C	Small Co	24.79	18.86		3	4	0	2.24	800 343-2829
MFS Research Fund A	Growth/Inc	26.39	28.07	22.47	2	3	5.75	0.95	800 343-2829
MFS Research Fund B	Growth/Inc	25.16	27.02		2	3	0	1.74	800 343-2829
MFS Research Fund C	Growth/Inc	25.56	26.38		2	3	0	1.71	800 343-2829
MFS Strategic Growth Fund A	Growth	47.60					5.25		800 343-2829
MFS Strategic Growth Fund B	Growth	45.02					0		800 343-2829
MFS Strategic Growth Fund C	Growth	46.64					0		800 343-2829
MFS Strategic Growth Fund I	Growth	46.43					0		800 343-2829
MFS Total Return A	Balanced	18.12	18.63	14.11	3	1	4.75	0.92	800 343-2829
MFS Total Return B	Balanced	17.60	17.88		3	1	0	2.15	800 343-2829
MFS Total Return C	Balanced	17.55	17.88		3	1	0	1.61	800 343-2829
MFS Utilities A	Utilities	30.21	27.61		1	2	4.75	1.10	800 343-2829
MFS Utilities B	Utilities	29.28	22.04		3	2	0	1.89	800 343-2829
MFS Utilities C	Utilities	29.35	26.67		1	2	0	1.86	800 343-2829
MFS World Asset Allocation A	AssetAlloc	11.50	15.34		3	1	4.75	1.39	800 343-2829
MFS World Asset Allocation B	AssetAlloc	10.93	14.68		3	1	0	1.99	800 343-2829
MFS World Asset Allocation C	AssetAlloc	10.96	14.73		3	1	0	1.96	800 343-2829
MFS World Equity B	Global	15.09	19.32	15.98	3	3	0	2.43	800 343-2829
MFS World Equity C	Global	15.03	19.35		3	3	0	2.41	800 343-2829
MFS World Growth A	Global	11.68	16.82		4	3	5.75	1.54	800 343-2829
MFS World Growth B	Global	10.93	15.95		4	3	0	2.31	800 343-2829
MFS World Growth C	Global	10.90	15.99		4	3	0	2.26	800 343-2829
MFS World Total Return A	Balanced	16.37	16.41	13.96	3	1	4.75	1.59	800 343-2829
MFS World Total Return B	Balanced	15.54	15.59		3	1	0	2.27	800 343-2829
MFS World Total Return C	Balanced	15.57	15.63		3	1	0	2.25	800 343-2829
Midas Fund	Gold	−53.57	−26.30	−11.98	5	5	0	1.90	800 400-6432
Mississippi Opportunity Fund A	Growth	19.44	15.43		4	4	3.5	2.11	800 543-8721
MMA Praxis Growth Fund	Growth	13.94	20.31		3	2	0	1.72	800 977-2947
MMA Praxis International Fund	Foreign	14.64					0	2.00	800 977-2947
Monetta Balanced Fund	Balanced	15.54					0	1.09	800 666-3882
Monetta Fund	Small Co	14.03	12.26	10.69	4	4	0	1.48	800 666-3882
Monetta Large-Cap Equity	Growth	15.24					0	1.52	800 666-3882
Monetta Mid-Cap Equity	Growth	20.91	21.08	19.83	3	3	0	1.26	800 666-3882
Monetta Small-Cap Equity	Small Co	29.62					0	1.84	800 666-3882
Monitor Growth Investment Shares	Growth	28.54	26.38	19.98	2	3	4	1.06	800 253-0412
Monitor Growth Trust Shares	Growth	28.85	26.68		1	3	0	0.81	800 253-0412

327

Stock Fund Name	Objective	Annualized Return for			Rank		Max Load	Expense Ratio	Toll-Free Telephone
		1 Year	3 Years	5 Years	Overall	Risk			
Monitor Income Equity Invmt Shares	Income	24.18					5.5		800 253-0412
Monitor Income Equity Trust Shares	Income	24.99	23.73	17.26	2	1	0	1.08	800 253-0412
Montag & Caldwell Balanced Fund	Balanced	23.86	22.79		2	2	0	1.25	800 992-8151
Montag & Caldwell Growth Fund	Growth	32.56	33.43		2	4	0	1.23	800 992-8151
Monterey Murphy New World Biotech	Health	−3.87	−1.89		5	4	0	2.64	800 628-9403
Monterey Murphy New World Tech Conv	Growth	−4.73	9.51	7.25	4	2	0	2.44	800 628-9403
Monterey Murphy New World Tech Fund	Technology	−7.58	3.37		4	5	0	2.44	800 628-9403
Monterey OCM Gold Fund	Gold	−28.01	−4.70	−17.15	5	5	4.5	2.44	800 628-9403
Monterey PIA Equity Fund	Growth	18.40	24.06	13.14	3	4	4.5	2.44	800 628-9403
Montgomery Emerging Asia	Pacific	−63.45					0	2.20	800 572-3863
Montgomery Emerging Markets Fund	Foreign	−39.20	−7.90	−0.01	5	5	0	1.59	800 572-3863
Montgomery Equity Income Fund	Income	15.83	22.03		2	2	0	1.46	800 572-3863
Montgomery Global Communications Fd	Technology	45.45	24.79	19.27	3	4	0	1.91	800 572-3863
Montgomery Global Opport Fund	Global	27.12	24.70		3	3	0	1.90	800 572-3863
Montgomery Growth Fund	Growth	17.37	20.84		3	3	0	1.25	800 572-3863
Montgomery Instl Emerging Markets	Foreign	−38.05	−6.39		5	5	0	1.92	800 572-3863
Montgomery Intl Growth Fund	Foreign	23.35					0	1.66	800 572-3863
Montgomery Intl Small Cap Fund P	Foreign	4.13					0	2.15	800 572-3863
Montgomery Intl Small Cap Fund R	Foreign	4.46	15.05		4	3	0	1.90	800 572-3863
Montgomery Latin America	Foreign	−25.42					0		800 572-3863
Montgomery Select 50 Fund	Growth/Inc	15.44					0	1.82	800 572-3863
Montgomery Small Cap Fund	Small Co	23.23	22.29	16.73	3	4	0	1.24	800 572-3863
Montgomery Small Cap Opportunities	Small Co	11.86					0	1.50	800 572-3863
Montgomery US Asset Allocation	AssetAlloc	14.73	17.66		3	2	0	1.43	800 572-3863
Montgomery US Emerging Growth Fund	Small Co	21.76	22.32		2	4	0	1.70	800 572-3863
Morg Stan Dean Witter Amer Val B	Growth	39.61	27.28	19.81	2	4	0	1.46	800 869-6397
Morg Stan Dean Witter Bal Growth C	Balanced	18.18	19.26		3	1	0	1.92	800 869-6397
Morg Stan Dean Witter Bal Income C	Balanced	12.85	12.97		3	1	0	1.88	800 869-6397
Morg Stan Dean Witter Cap Apprec B	Growth	8.25					0	2.00	800 869-6397
Morg Stan Dean Witter Cap Growth B	Growth	25.01	22.18	16.30	3	4	0	1.84	800 869-6397
Morg Stan Dean Witter Conv Sec B	Converts	10.95	15.16	12.31	3	1	0	1.84	800 869-6397
Morg Stan Dean Witter Develop Gr B	Small Co	20.45	17.75	17.00	4	5	0	1.68	800 869-6397
Morg Stan Dean Witter Dividend Gr B	Growth/Inc	22.35	24.69	18.49	2	2	0	1.16	800 869-6397
Morg Stan Dean Witter European Gr B	European	30.09	25.95	24.58	1	2	0	2.42	800 869-6397
Morg Stan Dean Witter Finan Svc B	Financial	44.60					0		800 869-6397
Morg Stan Dean Witter Gl Div Gr B	Global	7.34	15.81		4	2	0	2.01	800 869-6397
Morg Stan Dean Witter Gl Util B	Utilities	31.43	21.03		3	3	0	1.79	800 869-6397
Morg Stan Dean Witter Hlth Sci Tr B	Health	17.86	17.94	15.87	4	5	0	2.25	800 869-6397
Morg Stan Dean Witter Inc Builder B	Growth/Inc	17.36						1.85	800 869-6397
Morg Stan Dean Witter Information B	Technology	36.15					0	2.01	800 869-6397
Morg Stan Dean Witter Intl Sm Cap B	Foreign	−6.50	1.21		5	3	0	2.92	800 869-6397
Morg Stan Dean Witter Japan Fund B	Pacific	−27.10						2.43	800 869-6397
Morg Stan Dean Witter Mid Cap Gr B	Growth	25.87	25.39		3	4	0	1.99	800 869-6397
Morg Stan Dean Witter Mkt Leader B	Growth	19.00					0		800 869-6397
Morg Stan Dean Witter Nat Res Dev B	Energy/Res	1.41	15.91	12.14	4	3	0	1.77	800 869-6397
Morg Stan Dean Witter Pacific Gr B	Pacific	−53.73	−20.84	−8.38	5	5	0	2.44	800 869-6397
Morg Stan Dean Witter Pr Met&Min B	Gold	−37.07	−18.85	−11.98	5	5	0	2.28	800 869-6397
Morg Stan Dean Witter Strategist B	AssetAlloc	21.69	19.12	14.48	3	2	0	1.57	800 869-6397
Morg Stan Dean Witter Utilities B	Utilities	29.36	17.95	11.03	3	2	0	1.67	800 869-6397
Morg Stan Dean Witter Value-Added B	Growth/Inc	21.84	21.92	17.61	2	3	0	1.45	800 869-6397
Morgan Grenfell Emrg Markets Eq	Foreign	−35.53	−7.02		5	4	0	1.25	800 550-6426
Morgan Grenfell European Equity	European	30.50					0	0.90	800 550-6426
Morgan Grenfell European Sm Cap Eq	European	22.50	12.87		3	3	0	1.25	800 550-6426
Morgan Grenfell International Eq	Foreign	7.87	14.70		4	3	0	0.90	800 550-6426
Morgan Grenfell Intnl Small Cap	Foreign	−0.52	4.31		5	3	0	1.25	800 550-6426
Morgan Grenfell Smaller Co Instl	Small Co	18.88	20.35		4	4	0	1.25	800 550-6426
Morgan Keegan Southern Capital	Growth	25.32	26.63	18.34	3	3	3	2.00	800 564-2113
Morgan Stanley Active Ctry Instl A	Foreign	13.61	18.26	12.85	4	3	0	0.80	800 548-7786

Stock Fund Name	Objective	Annualized Return for			Rank		Max Load	Expense Ratio	Toll-Free Telephone
		1 Year	3 Years	5 Years	Overall	Risk			
Morgan Stanley Active Ctry Instl B	Foreign	13.26					0	1.05	800 548-7786
Morgan Stanley Aggress Eq Instl A	Agg Growth	32.63	36.44		1	3	0	1.00	800 548-7786
Morgan Stanley Aggress Eq Instl B	Agg Growth	32.35					0	1.25	800 548-7786
Morgan Stanley Aggress Eq Ret A	Agg Growth	30.93					4.75	1.57	800 548-7786
Morgan Stanley Aggress Eq Ret B	Agg Growth	29.94					0	2.25	800 548-7786
Morgan Stanley Aggress Eq Ret C	Agg Growth	29.90					0	2.32	800 548-7786
Morgan Stanley American Value A	Small Co	28.26	25.32		3	3	4.75	1.50	800 548-7786
Morgan Stanley American Value B	Small Co	27.30					0	2.25	800 548-7786
Morgan Stanley American Value C	Small Co	27.40	24.39		3	3	0	2.25	800 548-7786
Morgan Stanley Asian Equity Inst A	Pacific	−61.78	−26.08	−9.30	5	5	0	0.50	800 548-7786
Morgan Stanley Asian Equity Inst B	Pacific	−61.76					0	0.50	800 548-7786
Morgan Stanley Asian Growth A	Pacific	−60.57	−25.86		5	5	4.75	1.84	800 548-7786
Morgan Stanley Asian Growth B	Pacific	−60.89	−26.38		5	5	0	2.59	800 548-7786
Morgan Stanley Asian Growth C	Pacific	−60.88	−26.42	−11.09	5	5	0	2.59	800 548-7786
Morgan Stanley Balanced Port A	Balanced	16.28	14.64	11.92	3	1	0	0.71	800 548-7786
Morgan Stanley Balanced Port B	Balanced	14.90					0	0.95	800 548-7786
Morgan Stanley Dean Witter Growth B	Growth	21.98	19.91	15.12	3	3	0	1.63	800 869-6397
Morgan Stanley Emerging Markets A	Foreign	−34.31	−5.22		5	5	4.75	2.21	800 548-7786
Morgan Stanley Emerging Markets B	Foreign	−34.76	−5.86		5	5	0	2.96	800 548-7786
Morgan Stanley Emerging Markets C	Foreign	−34.73	−6.33		5	5	0	2.96	800 548-7786
Morgan Stanley Emrg Growth Instl A	Small Co	31.57	17.44	15.19	3	4	0	1.25	800 548-7786
Morgan Stanley Emrg Growth Instl B	Small Co	30.24					0	1.25	800 548-7786
Morgan Stanley Emrg Mkts Instl A	Foreign	−32.72	−3.63	4.38	5	5	0	1.69	800 548-7786
Morgan Stanley Emrg Mkts Instl B	Foreign	−32.89					0	1.94	800 548-7786
Morgan Stanley Eq Gr Port Instl A	Growth	33.45	32.79	26.06	1	3	0	0.80	800 548-7786
Morgan Stanley Eq Gr Port Instl B	Growth	33.30					0	1.05	800 548-7786
Morgan Stanley European Eq Instl A	European	27.73	21.78	22.61	2	2	0	1.00	800 548-7786
Morgan Stanley European Eq Instl B	European	27.53					0	1.25	800 548-7786
Morgan Stanley Global Eq Alloc A	Global	16.17	20.41	15.22	3	2	4.75	1.70	800 548-7786
Morgan Stanley Global Eq Alloc B	Global	15.33	19.51		3	2	0	2.45	800 548-7786
Morgan Stanley Global Eq Alloc C	Global	15.37					0	2.45	800 548-7786
Morgan Stanley Global Eq Instl A	Global	20.76	22.41	21.60	2	2	0	1.00	800 548-7786
Morgan Stanley Global Eq Instl B	Global	20.12					0	1.25	800 548-7786
Morgan Stanley Inter Magnum Inst A	Foreign	8.41					0	1.00	800 548-7786
Morgan Stanley Inter Magnum Inst B	Foreign	8.07					0	1.25	800 548-7786
Morgan Stanley Intl Eq Port Instl A	Foreign	16.42	19.73	19.15	3	2	0	1.00	800 548-7786
Morgan Stanley Intl Eq Port Instl B	Foreign	16.15					0	1.25	800 548-7786
Morgan Stanley Intl Magnum A	Foreign	21.81					4.75	1.65	800 548-7786
Morgan Stanley Intl Magnum B	Foreign	7.55					0	2.40	800 548-7786
Morgan Stanley Intl Magnum C	Foreign	7.55					0	2.40	800 548-7786
Morgan Stanley Intl Small Cap	Foreign	8.28	11.21		4	2	0	1.15	800 548-7786
Morgan Stanley Japanese Equity A	Pacific	−22.72	2.79		5	4	0	1.00	800 548-7786
Morgan Stanley Japanese Equity B	Pacific	−23.08					0	1.25	800 548-7786
Morgan Stanley Latin Am Eq Instl A	Foreign	−17.00	22.70		4	5	0	1.70	800 548-7786
Morgan Stanley Latin Am Eq Instl B	Foreign	−17.39					0	1.95	800 548-7786
Morgan Stanley Latin Amer Equity A	Foreign	−17.37	21.90		4	5	4.75	2.24	800 548-7786
Morgan Stanley Latin Amer Equity B	Foreign	−17.82					0	2.99	800 548-7786
Morgan Stanley Latin Amer Equity C	Foreign	−17.86	21.04		4	5	0	2.99	800 548-7786
Morgan Stanley Sm Cap Val Instl A	Small Co	27.75	25.55	18.90	3	3	0	1.00	800 548-7786
Morgan Stanley Sm Cap Val Instl B	Small Co	27.57					0	1.25	800 548-7786
Morgan Stanley Technology Inst A	Technology	30.66					0	1.25	800 548-7786
Morgan Stanley Technology Inst B	Technology	30.43					0	1.50	800 548-7786
Morgan Stanley US Real Estate A	Real Est	8.04					4.75	1.55	800 548-7786
Morgan Stanley US Real Estate B	Real Est	7.23					0	2.30	800 548-7786
Morgan Stanley US Real Estate C	Real Est	7.20					0	2.30	800 548-7786
Morgan Stanley US Real Estate Ins B	Real Est	5.38					0	1.25	800 548-7786
Morgan Stanley Val Eq Port Instl A	Growth/Inc	26.12	24.26	19.51	1	3	0	0.70	800 548-7786
Morgan Stanley Val Eq Port Instl B	Growth/Inc	25.98					0	0.95	800 548-7786

Stock Fund Name	Objective	Annualized Return for			Rank		Max Load	Expense Ratio	Toll-Free Telephone
		1 Year	3 Years	5 Years	Overall	Risk			
Mosaic Balanced Fund	Balanced	19.49	21.55	14.78	3	2	0	0.73	888 670-3600
Mosaic Foresight Fund	Foreign	−12.01	5.16	4.49	5	4	0	2.50	888 670-3600
Mosaic Investors Fund	Growth	25.58	23.11	16.42	3	3	0	0.56	888 670-3600
Mosaic Mid-Cap Growth Fund	Small Co	14.47	12.58	10.87	4	3	0	0.31	888 670-3600
MSB Fund	Growth	28.93	26.02	19.19	2	3	0	1.43	800 661-3938
Muhlenkamp Fund	Growth/Inc	32.91	31.98	21.38	1	3	0	1.33	800 860-3863
Munder Accelerating Growth Fund A	Growth	12.80	13.00	11.61	4	4	5.5	1.20	800 438-5789
Munder Accelerating Growth Fund B	Growth	11.51	11.80		4	4	0	1.95	800 438-5789
Munder Accelerating Growth Fund C	Growth	11.77					0	1.95	800 438-5789
Munder Accelerating Growth Fund K	Growth	12.22	12.81	12.09	4	4	0	1.20	800 438-5789
Munder Accelerating Growth Fund Y	Growth	12.51	13.08	11.74	4	4	0	0.95	800 438-5789
Munder All Season Moderate A	Growth/Inc	8.62					5.5	0.85	800 438-5789
Munder All Season Moderate Y	Growth/Inc	8.68					0	0.55	800 438-5789
Munder All-Season Aggressive Y	Growth	15.02					0	0.55	800 438-5789
Munder Balanced Fund A	Balanced	15.87	15.50	11.42	3	2	5.5	1.22	800 438-5789
Munder Balanced Fund B	Balanced	15.06	14.64		3	2	0	1.97	800 438-5789
Munder Balanced Fund C	Balanced	14.82					0	1.97	800 438-5789
Munder Balanced Fund K	Balanced	15.80	15.50	11.43	3	2	0	1.22	800 438-5789
Munder Balanced Fund Y	Balanced	16.19	15.77	11.74	3	2	0	0.97	800 438-5789
Munder Framlington Emerg Markets A	Foreign	−28.34					5.5	1.79	800 438-5789
Munder Framlington Emerg Markets B	Foreign	−30.18					0	2.54	800 438-5789
Munder Framlington Emerg Markets C	Foreign	−28.87					0	2.54	800 438-5789
Munder Framlington Emerg Markets K	Foreign	−28.34					0	1.79	800 438-5789
Munder Framlington Emerg Markets Y	Foreign	−28.12					0	1.54	800 438-5789
Munder Framlington Healthcare A	Health	8.74					5.5	1.55	800 438-5789
Munder Framlington Healthcare B	Health	7.94					0	2.30	800 438-5789
Munder Framlington Healthcare C	Health	7.94					0	2.30	800 438-5789
Munder Framlington Healthcare Y	Health	8.82					0	1.30	800 438-5789
Munder Framlington Intl Growth A	Foreign	5.59					5.5	1.55	800 438-5789
Munder Framlington Intl Growth C	Foreign	5.05					0	2.30	800 438-5789
Munder Framlington Intl Growth K	Foreign	5.59					0	1.55	800 438-5789
Munder Framlington Intl Growth Y	Foreign	5.86					0	1.30	800 438-5789
Munder Growth & Income Fund A	Growth/Inc	23.19	24.02		2	2	0	1.20	800 438-5789
Munder Growth & Income Fund B	Growth/Inc	3.69	16.48		4	3	0	1.95	800 438-5789
Munder Growth & Income Fund C	Growth/Inc	22.04					0	1.95	800 438-5789
Munder Growth & Income Fund K	Growth/Inc	23.17	24.04		2	2	0	1.20	800 438-5789
Munder Growth & Income Fund Y	Growth/Inc	23.49	24.35		2	2	0	0.96	800 438-5789
Munder Index 500 Fund A	Growth/Inc	29.73	29.69	22.52	1	3	2.5	0.39	800 438-5789
Munder Index 500 Fund B	Growth/Inc	29.28					0	0.74	800 438-5789
Munder Index 500 Fund K	Growth/Inc	29.53	29.51	22.42	1	3	0	0.54	800 438-5789
Munder Index 500 Fund Y	Growth/Inc	29.87	29.83	22.71	1	3	0	0.25	800 438-5789
Munder International Equity A	Foreign	4.29	11.75	10.71	4	3	5.5	1.26	800 438-5789
Munder International Equity B	Foreign	3.51	10.83		4	3	0	2.01	800 438-5789
Munder International Equity C	Foreign	3.36					0	2.01	800 438-5789
Munder International Equity K	Foreign	4.21	11.73	10.72	4	3	0	1.26	800 438-5789
Munder International Equity Y	Foreign	4.46	12.04	10.97	4	3	0	1.01	800 438-5789
Munder Micro-Cap Equity Fund A	Small Co	37.79					5.5	1.50	800 438-5789
Munder Micro-Cap Equity Fund B	Small Co	36.66					0	1.50	800 438-5789
Munder Micro-Cap Equity Fund C	Small Co	36.74					0	1.25	800 438-5789
Munder Micro-Cap Equity Fund K	Small Co	37.69					0	1.50	800 438-5789
Munder Micro-Cap Equity Fund Y	Small Co	37.97					0	1.25	800 438-5789
Munder Mid Cap Growth Fund B	Growth	4.08					0	1.99	800 438-5789
Munder Mid Cap Growth Fund C	Growth	4.09					0	1.99	800 438-5789
Munder Mid Cap Growth Fund K	Growth	4.81					0	1.24	800 438-5789
Munder Mid Cap Growth Fund Y	Growth	5.18					0	0.99	800 438-5789
Munder Multi-Season Growth Fund A	Growth	25.01	26.65		2	3	5.5	1.25	800 438-5789
Munder Multi-Season Growth Fund B	Growth	24.10	25.79		2	3	0	2.00	800 438-5789
Munder Multi-Season Growth Fund C	Growth	24.08	25.73		2	3	0	2.00	800 438-5789

Stock Fund Name	Objective	Annualized Return for			Rank		Max Load	Expense Ratio	Toll-Free Telephone
		1 Year	3 Years	5 Years	Overall	Risk			
Munder Multi-Season Growth Fund K	Growth	25.04	26.68		2	3	0	1.25	800 438-5789
Munder Multi-Season Growth Fund Y	Growth	25.27	27.00		2	3	0	1.00	800 438-5789
Munder Netnet Fund	Technology	86.69					0	1.48	800 438-5789
Munder Real Estate Equity Invst A	Real Est	8.88	18.99		3	3	5.5	1.35	800 438-5789
Munder Real Estate Equity Invst B	Real Est	8.07	18.09		3	3	0	2.10	800 438-5789
Munder Real Estate Equity Invst C	Real Est	8.12					0	2.10	800 438-5789
Munder Real Estate Equity Invst Y	Real Est	9.19	19.24		2	3	0	1.10	800 438-5789
Munder Small Cap Value Fund A	Small Co	24.36					5.5	1.38	800 438-5789
Munder Small Cap Value Fund B	Small Co	23.40					0	2.13	800 438-5789
Munder Small Cap Value Fund C	Small Co	23.42					0	2.13	800 438-5789
Munder Small Cap Value Fund K	Small Co	24.53					0	1.39	800 438-5789
Munder Small Cap Value Fund Y	Small Co	24.82					0	1.13	800 438-5789
Munder Small Co Gwth Fund A	Small Co	12.00	25.45	18.78	4	4	5.5	1.22	800 438-5789
Munder Small Co Gwth Fund B	Small Co	11.09	24.25		4	4	0	1.97	800 438-5789
Munder Small Co Gwth Fund C	Small Co	10.14					0	1.97	800 438-5789
Munder Small Co Gwth Fund K	Small Co	11.95	25.45	18.77	4	4	0	1.22	800 438-5789
Munder Small Co Gwth Fund Y	Small Co	12.17	25.71	19.00	4	4	0	0.97	800 438-5789
Munder Value Fund A	Growth	25.53					5.5	1.27	800 438-5789
Munder Value Fund B	Growth	24.93					0	2.02	800 438-5789
Munder Value Fund C	Growth	24.78					0	2.02	800 438-5789
Munder Value Fund K	Growth	25.84					0	1.27	800 438-5789
Munder Value Fund Y	Growth	26.13					0	0.95	800 438-5789
Mutual Beacon Fund Z	Growth/Inc	20.77	22.23	19.26	1	2	0	0.74	800 342-5236
Mutual Discovery Fund Z	Global	20.84	24.16	22.10	1	2	0	1.35	800 342-5236
Mutual European Fund Z	European	29.83					4.5	1.03	800 342-5236
Mutual Qualified Fund Z	Growth/Inc	19.04	22.25	19.73	2	2	0	0.75	800 342-5236
Mutual Shares Fund Z	Growth/Inc	18.58	22.46	19.47	2	2	0	0.72	800 342-5236
Nations Balanced Assets Invest A	Balanced	16.35	17.86	13.23	3	1	0	1.25	800 321-7854
Nations Balanced Assets Invest B	Balanced	15.47	17.16	12.59	3	1	0	1.75	800 321-7854
Nations Balanced Assets Invest C	Balanced	15.40	17.17	12.48	3	1	0	1.50	800 321-7854
Nations Balanced Assets Pr A	Balanced	16.46	18.06	13.45	3	1	0	1.01	800 321-7854
Nations Capital Growth Invest A	Growth	34.19	26.05	19.91	2	3	0	1.21	800 321-7854
Nations Capital Growth Invest B	Growth	33.07	25.10	19.00	2	3	0	1.96	800 321-7854
Nations Capital Growth Invest C	Growth	33.43	25.49	19.20	2	3	0	1.46	800 321-7854
Nations Capital Growth Pr A	Growth	34.42	26.34	20.18	2	3	0	0.97	800 321-7854
Nations Disciplined Equity Inv A	Agg Growth	32.35	27.27		2	3	0	1.29	800 321-7854
Nations Disciplined Equity Inv B	Agg Growth	31.40	26.47		1	3	0	1.78	800 321-7854
Nations Disciplined Equity Inv C	Agg Growth	31.42	26.72		1	3	0	1.54	800 321-7854
Nations Disciplined Equity Pr A	Agg Growth	32.68	27.60	20.44	2	3	0	1.04	800 321-7854
Nations Emerging Gr Inv A	Agg Growth	18.24	19.73	17.32	4	4	0	1.22	800 321-7854
Nations Emerging Gr Inv B	Agg Growth	17.32	18.80	16.43	4	4	0	1.48	800 321-7854
Nations Emerging Gr Inv C	Agg Growth	17.42	19.12	16.62	4	4	0	1.48	800 321-7854
Nations Emerging Gr Pr A	Agg Growth	18.42	19.93		3	4	0	0.98	800 321-7854
Nations Emerging Markets Inv A	Foreign	−31.32	−4.66		5	4	0	1.99	800 321-7854
Nations Emerging Markets Inv B	Foreign	−31.72	−5.31		5	4	0	2.74	800 321-7854
Nations Emerging Markets Inv C	Foreign	−31.77	−5.14		5	4	0	2.24	800 321-7854
Nations Emerging Markets Pr A	Foreign	−31.06	−4.40		5	4	0	1.74	800 321-7854
Nations Equity Income Inv A	Income	16.93	20.87	16.32	2	2	0	1.11	800 321-7854
Nations Equity Income Inv B	Income	16.07	20.21		3	2	0	1.66	800 321-7854
Nations Equity Income Inv C	Income	16.35	20.37	15.63	3	2	0	1.41	800 321-7854
Nations Equity Income Pr A	Income	17.14	21.18		2	2	0	0.91	800 321-7854
Nations Equity Index Tr A	Growth	29.59	29.99		1	3	0	0.35	800 321-7854
Nations Intl Growth Inv C	Foreign	4.48					0		800 321-7854
Nations Intl Growth Pr B	Foreign	6.00					0		800 321-7854
Nations Intnl Equity Invest A	Foreign	5.51	11.61	10.07	4	3	0	1.38	800 321-7854
Nations Intnl Equity Invest B	Foreign	4.67	10.86	9.31	4	3	0	2.16	800 321-7854
Nations Intnl Equity Invest C	Foreign	4.79	11.06	9.38	4	3	0	1.66	800 321-7854
Nations Intnl Equity Pr A	Foreign	5.79	11.91		4	3	0	1.16	800 321-7854

331

Stock Fund Name	Objective	Annualized Return for			Rank		Max Load	Expense Ratio	Toll-Free Telephone
		1 Year	3 Years	5 Years	Overall	Risk			
Nations Lifegoal Balanced Invest A	Balanced	14.24					0	0.50	800 321-7854
Nations Lifegoal Balanced Invest C	Balanced	13.98					0	0.91	800 321-7854
Nations Lifegoal Balanced Primary A	Balanced	14.27					0	0.25	800 321-7854
Nations Lifegoal Balanced Primary B	Balanced	14.08					0	0.75	800 321-7854
Nations Lifegoal Growth Investor A	Growth	11.86					0	0.50	800 321-7854
Nations Lifegoal Growth Investor C	Growth	11.03					0	0.91	800 321-7854
Nations Lifegoal Growth Primary A	Growth	11.90					0	0.25	800 321-7854
Nations Lifegoal Growth Primary B	Growth	11.64					0	0.75	800 321-7854
Nations Lifegoal Inc & Gr Invest A	Growth/Inc	9.29					0	0.50	800 321-7854
Nations Lifegoal Inc & Gr Invest C	Growth/Inc	8.54					0	0.91	800 321-7854
Nations Lifegoal Inc & Gr Primary A	Growth/Inc	9.45						0.25	800 321-7854
Nations Lifegoal Inc & Gr Primary B	Growth/Inc	9.45					0	0.25	800 321-7854
Nations Managed Index Investor A	Growth	29.70					0	0.75	800 321-7854
Nations Managed Index Investor C	Growth	29.37					0	1.00	800 321-7854
Nations Managed Index Primary A	Growth	30.00					0	0.50	800 321-7854
Nations Managed Sm Cap Index Inv A	Small Co	21.13					0	0.75	800 321-7854
Nations Managed Sm Cap Index Inv C	Small Co	20.81					0	1.00	800 321-7854
Nations Managed Sm Cap Index Pr A	Small Co	21.30					0	0.50	800 321-7854
Nations Managed Sm Cap Index Pr B	Small Co	20.70					0	1.00	800 321-7854
Nations Pacific Growth Inv A	Pacific	−49.54	−16.76		5	5	0	2.55	800 321-7854
Nations Pacific Growth Inv B	Pacific	−49.93	−17.24		5	5	0	2.42	800 321-7854
Nations Pacific Growth Inv C	Pacific	−49.26	−16.81		5	5	0	1.92	800 321-7854
Nations Pacific Growth Pr A	Pacific	−49.40	−16.49		5	5	0	1.42	800 321-7854
Nations Small Company Growth Inv C	Small Co	16.40					0		800 321-7854
Nations Value Fund Invest A	Growth/Inc	22.65	24.48	19.47	2	3		1.19	800 321-7854
Nations Value Fund Invest B	Growth/Inc	21.85	23.78		2	3	0	1.72	800 321-7854
Nations Value Fund Invest C	Growth/Inc	22.01	24.74	18.78	2	3	0	1.47	800 321-7854
Nations Value Fund Pr A	Growth/Inc	22.98	24.79	19.63	1	3	0	0.97	800 321-7854
Nationwide Fund D	Growth/Inc	37.89	35.00	24.23	1	2	4.5	0.60	800 848-0920
Nationwide Growth Fund D	Growth	26.69	23.86	19.49	2	3	4.5	0.64	800 848-0920
Nationwide Mid Cap Growth Fund D	Growth	25.18	19.33	17.22	3	3	0	0.94	800 848-0920
Navellier Aggressive Growth Port	Agg Growth	17.40					0	2.00	800 887-8671
Navellier Aggressive Micro Cap Port	Small Co	23.19					0	1.55	800 887-8671
Navellier Mid Cap Growth Port	Growth	26.52					0	0.86	800 887-8671
Navellier Series Aggressive Sm Cap	Small Co	13.69	15.94		4	5	0	1.55	800 887-8671
Neuberger&Berman Adv Mgmt Tr Bal	Balanced	18.74	14.62	10.87	4	2	0	1.03	800 877-9700
Neuberger&Berman AMT Growth Port	Growth	27.33	20.84	16.69	3	4	0	0.91	800 877-9700
Neuberger&Berman Focus Assets	Growth	21.85					0	1.50	800 877-9700
Neuberger&Berman Focus Fund	Growth	22.43	22.74	20.42	3	4	0	0.86	800 877-9700
Neuberger&Berman Focus Trust	Growth	22.33	22.68		3	4	0	0.53	800 877-9700
Neuberger&Berman Genesis Assets	Small Co	14.17					0		800 877-9700
Neuberger&Berman Genesis Fund	Small Co	14.49	25.09	18.75	3	3	0	1.17	800 877-9700
Neuberger&Berman Genesis Trust	Small Co	14.41	25.05	18.86	3	3	0	0.80	800 877-9700
Neuberger&Berman Guardian Assets	Growth/Inc	16.58					0	1.50	800 877-9700
Neuberger&Berman Guardian Fund	Growth/Inc	17.41	19.15	17.66	3	3	0	0.80	800 877-9700
Neuberger&Berman Guardian Trust	Growth/Inc	17.30	19.05		3	3	0	0.46	800 877-9700
Neuberger&Berman International	Foreign	15.56	19.61		3	3	0	1.22	800 877-9700
Neuberger&Berman Manhattan Assets	Agg Growth	26.87					0	1.50	800 877-9700
Neuberger&Berman Manhattan Fund	Agg Growth	27.38	20.91	17.41	3	4	0	0.99	800 877-9700
Neuberger&Berman Manhattan Trust	Agg Growth	27.21	20.86	17.41	3	4	0	0.59	800 877-9700
Neuberger&Berman NYCDC Soc Resp Tr	Growth	22.39	25.63		2	3	0	0.63	800 877-9700
Neuberger&Berman Partners Assets	Growth	18.45					0	1.50	800 877-9700
Neuberger&Berman Partners Fund	Growth	19.25	25.56	20.48	3	3	0	0.81	800 877-9700
Neuberger&Berman Partners Trust	Growth	19.12	25.52		1	3	0	0.49	800 877-9700
Neuberger&Berman Soc Resp Trust	Growth	27.44					0		800 877-9700
New Alternatives Fund	Other	6.70	10.97	8.76	4	3	4.75	1.15	800 423-8383
New Century Capital	Growth	23.93	22.41	18.11	2	3	0	1.47	888-639-0102
New Century I Portfolio	Income	17.88	16.74	13.29	3	1	0	1.61	888-639-0102

Stock Fund Name	Objective	Annualized Return for			Rank		Max Load	Expense Ratio	Toll-Free Telephone
		1 Year	3 Years	5 Years	Overall	Risk			
New Economy Fund	Growth	34.43	23.93	17.89	3	3	5.75	0.81	800 421-0180
New England Balanced Fund A	Balanced	13.97	16.65	14.04	3	1	5.75	1.29	800 225-5478
New England Balanced Fund B	Balanced	12.70	15.66		3	1	0	2.08	800 225-5478
New England Balanced Fund C	Balanced	12.68	14.19		3	1	0	2.08	800 225-5478
New England Balanced Fund Y	Balanced	14.34	17.15		3	1	0		800 225-5478
New England Capital Growth Fund A	Growth	24.26	20.51	16.79	3	3	5.75	1.51	800 225-5478
New England Capital Growth Fund B	Growth	23.16	19.51		3	3	0	2.26	800 225-5478
New England Capital Growth Fund C	Growth	23.16	19.53		3	3	0	2.26	800 225-5478
New England Equity Income A	Income	16.22					5.75		800 225-5478
New England Growth Fund A	Growth	31.63	27.01	21.02	3	4	6.5	1.15	800 225-5478
New England Growth Opportunities A	Growth/Inc	32.62	28.37	21.33	1	3	5.75	1.21	800 225-5478
New England Growth Opportunities B	Growth/Inc	31.59					0	2.05	800 225-5478
New England Growth Opportunities C	Growth/Inc	31.51	27.30		2	3	0	2.05	800 225-5478
New England International Equity A	Foreign	-2.43	2.92	5.39	5	3	5.75	1.75	800 225-5478
New England International Equity B	Foreign	-3.00	2.24		5	3	0	2.50	800 225-5478
New England International Equity C	Foreign	-3.05	2.26		5	4	0	2.50	800 225-5478
New England International Equity Y	Foreign	-1.75	3.77		5	3	0	1.15	800 225-5478
New England Star Advisers Fund Tr A	Agg Growth	24.07	23.88		3	3	5.75	1.66	800 225-5478
New England Star Advisers Fund Tr B	Agg Growth	23.16	22.98		2	3	0	2.43	800 225-5478
New England Star Advisers Fund Tr C	Agg Growth	23.13	22.99		2	3	0	1.43	800 225-5478
New England Star Advisers Fund Tr Y	Agg Growth	24.36	24.32		2	3	0	1.43	800 225-5478
New England Star Small Cap A	Small Co	20.77					5.75	2.46	800 225-5478
New England Star Small Cap B	Small Co	19.80					0	3.21	800 225-5478
New England Star Small Cap C	Small Co	19.80					0	3.21	800 225-5478
New England Star Worldwide Fund A	Global	3.08					5.75	2.15	800 225-5478
New England Star Worldwide Fund B	Global	2.31					0	2.90	800 225-5478
New England Star Worldwide Fund C	Global	2.37					0	2.90	800 225-5478
New England Value Fund A	Growth/Inc	15.14	22.20	18.66	3	3	5.75	1.25	800 225-5478
New England Value Fund B	Growth/Inc	14.13	21.29		3	3	0	2.04	800 225-5478
New England Value Fund C	Growth/Inc	14.33	21.37		3	3	0	2.04	800 225-5478
New England Value Fund Y	Growth/Inc	15.39	22.53		3	3	0	1.04	800 225-5478
New Perspective Fund	Global	18.37	19.21	18.79	3	2	5.75	0.79	800 421-0180
Newport Greater China B	Pacific	-52.59					0	2.90	800 345-6611
Newport Greater China C	Pacific	-52.54					0	2.90	800 345-6611
Newport Japan Opportunities Fund A	Pacific	-20.53					5.75	2.00	800 345-6611
Newport Japan Opportunities Fund B	Pacific	-21.16					0	2.75	800 345-6611
Newport Japan Opportunities Fund C	Pacific	-21.09					0	2.75	800 345-6611
Newport Tiger Cub Fund A	Pacific	-50.41					5.75	2.25	800 345-6611
Newport Tiger Cub Fund B	Pacific	-50.87					0	3.00	800 345-6611
Newport Tiger Cub Fund C	Pacific	-50.87					0	3.00	800 345-6611
Newport Tiger Fund A	Pacific	-55.95	-19.06	-5.13	5	5	5.75	1.69	800 345-6611
Newport Tiger Fund B	Pacific	-56.26	-19.66		5	5	0	2.48	800 345-6611
Newport Tiger Fund C	Pacific	-56.25	-19.66		5	5	1	2.48	800 345-6611
Newport Tiger Fund T	Pacific	-55.80	-18.85	-4.98	5	5	5.75	1.48	800 345-6611
Nicholas Equity Income Fund	Growth/Inc	17.99	17.52		3	2	0	1.18	800 227-5987
Nicholas Fund	Growth	30.80	29.69	20.65	1	3	0	0.72	800 227-5987
Nicholas II Fund	Small Co	32.20	27.85	20.34	2	3	0	0.61	800 227-5987
Nicholas Limited Edition	Small Co	18.29	24.14	17.82	3	4	0	0.86	800 227-5987
Nicholas-Applegate Bal Gr A	Balanced	26.67	18.80	13.32	3	3	5.25	1.61	800 551-8045
Nicholas-Applegate Bal Gr B	Balanced	26.05	18.20	12.76	3	3	0	2.25	800 551-8045
Nicholas-Applegate Bal Gr C	Balanced	25.68	18.01	12.65	3	3	0	2.25	800 551-8045
Nicholas-Applegate Bal Gr I	Balanced	27.49	19.63	14.52	3	3	0	1.00	800 551-8045
Nicholas-Applegate Bal Gr Q	Balanced	26.52	19.35	13.81	3	3	0	1.26	800 551-8045
Nicholas-Applegate Core Gr A	Growth	24.23	19.85	13.94	4	4	5.25	1.59	800 551-8045
Nicholas-Applegate Core Gr B	Growth	23.40	19.12	13.21	4	4	0	2.25	800 551-8045
Nicholas-Applegate Core Gr C	Growth	23.53	19.21	13.29	4	4	0	2.14	800 551-8045
Nicholas-Applegate Core Gr I	Growth	24.93	20.54	14.57	3	4	0	1.00	800 551-8045
Nicholas-Applegate Core Gr Q	Growth	24.52	20.15	14.23	3	4	0	1.25	800 551-8045

Stock Fund Name	Objective	Annualized Return for			Rank		Max Load	Expense Ratio	Toll-Free Telephone
		1 Year	3 Years	5 Years	Overall	Risk			
Nicholas-Applegate Emerging Gr A	Small Co	14.25	17.37	14.94	4	5	5.25	1.72	800 551-8045
Nicholas-Applegate Emerging Gr B	Small Co	13.31	16.46	14.51	4	5	0	2.61	800 551-8045
Nicholas-Applegate Emerging Gr C	Small Co	13.49	16.64	14.24	4	5	0	2.35	800 551-8045
Nicholas-Applegate Emerging Gr I	Small Co	15.04	18.12	16.04	4	5	0	1.17	800 551-8045
Nicholas-Applegate Emerging Gr Q	Small Co	14.65	17.99	15.94	4	5	0	1.51	800 551-8045
Nicholas-Applegate Emrg Countries A	Foreign	−19.62	8.77		4	4	5.25	2.26	800 551-8045
Nicholas-Applegate Emrg Countries B	Foreign	−19.52	8.34		4	4	0	2.90	800 551-8045
Nicholas-Applegate Emrg Countries C	Foreign	−19.53	8.34		4	4	0	2.90	800 551-8045
Nicholas-Applegate Emrg Countries I	Foreign	−18.55	9.63		4	4	0	1.65	800 551-8045
Nicholas-Applegate Emrg Countries Q	Foreign	−18.74	9.44		4	4	0	1.91	800 551-8045
Nicholas-Applegate Gl Gr & Income I	Global	32.76					0		800 551-8045
Nicholas-Applegate Growth Equity A	Growth	24.04	19.44	13.89	4	4	5.25	1.39	800 551-8045
Nicholas-Applegate Growth Equity B	Growth	23.09	18.45	12.97	4	4	0	2.21	800 551-8045
Nicholas-Applegate Growth Equity C	Growth	23.09	18.45		3	4	0	2.21	800 551-8045
Nicholas-Applegate Income & Gr A	Growth/Inc	21.71	21.64	15.44	3	2	5.25	1.60	800 551-8045
Nicholas-Applegate Income & Gr B	Growth/Inc	21.19	21.04	14.83	3	2	0	2.25	800 551-8045
Nicholas-Applegate Income & Gr C	Growth/Inc	20.96	20.87	14.78	3	2	0	2.25	800 551-8045
Nicholas-Applegate Income & Gr I	Growth/Inc	22.43	22.37	14.34	3	2	0	1.00	800 551-8045
Nicholas-Applegate Income & Gr Q	Growth/Inc	22.23	22.09	15.88	3	2	0	1.25	800 551-8045
Nicholas-Applegate Intl Core Gr A	Foreign	24.01					5.25	1.95	800 551-8045
Nicholas-Applegate Intl Core Gr B	Foreign	24.24					0	2.59	800 551-8045
Nicholas-Applegate Intl Core Gr C	Foreign	23.23					0	2.41	800 551-8045
Nicholas-Applegate Intl Core Gr I	Foreign	24.63					0	1.40	800 551-8045
Nicholas-Applegate Intl Core Gr Q	Foreign	25.30					0	2.67	800 551-8045
Nicholas-Applegate Intl Sm Cap Gr A	Foreign	30.22	24.34	15.82	3	3	5.25	1.95	800 551-8045
Nicholas-Applegate Intl Sm Cap Gr B	Foreign	29.55	23.64	14.97	3	3	0	2.60	800 551-8045
Nicholas-Applegate Intl Sm Cap Gr C	Foreign	29.57	23.65	14.99	3	3	0	2.60	800 551-8045
Nicholas-Applegate Intl Sm Cap Gr I	Foreign	30.93	25.02	16.29	3	3	0	1.40	800 551-8045
Nicholas-Applegate Intl Sm Cap Gr Q	Foreign	30.75	24.73	16.02	3	3	0	1.66	800 551-8045
Nicholas-Applegate Large Cap Gr A	Growth	46.18					5.25		800 551-8045
Nicholas-Applegate Large Cap Gr B	Growth	45.23					0		800 551-8045
Nicholas-Applegate Large Cap Gr C	Growth	45.42					0		800 551-8045
Nicholas-Applegate Large Cap Gr I	Growth	47.11					0	1.00	800 551-8045
Nicholas-Applegate Large Cap Gr Q	Growth	46.49					0		800 551-8045
Nicholas-Applegate Mini Cap Growth	Small Co	32.56					0	1.57	800 551-8045
Nicholas-Applegate Value Fund I	Growth/Inc	38.45					0	1.00	800 551-8045
Nicholas-Applegate Worldwide Gr A	Global	25.13	22.35	16.84	3	3	5.25	1.86	800 551-8045
Nicholas-Applegate Worldwide Gr B	Global	24.48	21.67	16.15	3	3	0	2.50	800 551-8045
Nicholas-Applegate Worldwide Gr C	Global	24.34	21.59	16.12	3	3	0	2.50	800 551-8045
Nicholas-Applegate Worldwide Gr I	Global	25.61	22.97	17.37	3	3	0	1.35	800 551-8045
Nicholas-Applegate Worldwide Gr Q	Global	25.64	22.75	17.19	3	3	0	1.61	800 551-8045
Nomura Pacific Basin Fund	Pacific	−39.30	−9.59	−2.92	5	4	0	1.39	800 833-0018
North American Balanced Fund A	Balanced	15.83	15.82		3	1	4.75	1.34	800 872-8037
North American Balanced Fund B	Balanced	15.04	15.05		3	1	0	1.99	800 872-8037
North American Balanced Fund C	Balanced	15.07	15.06	12.15	3	1	0	1.34	800 872-8037
North American Equity-Income A	Income	18.97	19.89		3	2	4.75	1.34	800 872-8037
North American Equity-Income B	Income	18.18	19.10		3	2	0	1.99	800 872-8037
North American Equity-Income C	Income	18.16	19.11	15.94	3	2	0	1.99	800 872-8037
North American Global Equity A	Global	17.16	17.14		3	3	4.75	1.75	800 872-8037
North American Global Equity B	Global	17.00	16.61		3	3	0	2.40	800 872-8037
North American Global Equity C	Global	16.93	16.61	12.15	3	3	0	2.40	800 872-8037
North American Growth and Income A	Growth/Inc	27.31	27.59		2	3	4.75	1.34	800 872-8037
North American Growth and Income B	Growth/Inc	26.43	26.78		2	3	0	1.99	800 872-8037
North American Growth and Income C	Growth/Inc	26.42	26.74	19.84	2	3	0	1.99	800 872-8037
North American Growth Equity Fund A	Growth	27.96					4.75	1.65	800 872-8037
North American Growth Equity Fund B	Growth	27.20					0	2.30	800 872-8037
North American Growth Equity Fund C	Growth	27.15					0	2.30	800 872-8037
North American Intl Growth & Inc A	Foreign	4.73	10.77		4	2	4.75	1.75	800 872-8037

Stock Fund Name	Objective	Annualized Return for			Rank		Max Load	Expense Ratio	Toll-Free Telephone
		1 Year	3 Years	5 Years	Overall	Risk			
North American Intl Growth & Inc B	Foreign	3.77	10.03		4	2	0	2.40	800 872-8037
North American Intl Growth & Inc C	Foreign	4.12	13.10		4	3	0	2.40	800 872-8037
North American Intl Small Cap A	Foreign	14.52					4.75	1.90	800 872-8037
North American Intl Small Cap B	Foreign	13.75					0	2.55	800 872-8037
North American Intl Small Cap C	Foreign	13.90					0	2.55	800 872-8037
North American Small/Mid Cap Fund A	Small Co	30.65					4.75	1.68	800 872-8037
North American Small/Mid Cap Fund B	Small Co	29.70					0	2.33	800 872-8037
North American Small/Mid Cap Fund C	Small Co	29.73					0	2.33	800 872-8037
Northeast Investors Growth Fund	Growth	37.38	32.86	24.08	1	3	0	1.12	800 225-6704
Northern Growth Equity Fund	Growth	32.22	27.26		2	3	0	1.33	800 595-9111
Northern Income Equity Fund	Income	18.29	18.90		3	1	0	1.00	800 595-9111
Northern Intl Growth Equity Fund	Foreign	14.57	12.26		4	2	0	1.63	800 595-9111
Northern Intl Select Equity Fund	Foreign	13.32	10.03		4	3	0	1.66	800 595-9111
Northern Select Equity Fund	Agg Growth	31.07	28.64		2	3	0	1.00	800 595-9111
Northern Small Cap Fund	Small Co	19.06	20.61		3	3	0	1.00	800 595-9111
Northern Stock Index Fund	Growth	29.04					0	2.23	800 595-9111
Northern Technology Fund	Technology	36.63					0	2.02	800 595-9111
Northstar Balance Sheet Opp Fund A	Flexible	21.62			3	2	4.75	1.41	800 595-7827
Northstar Balance Sheet Opp Fund B	Flexible	19.24	13.76		3	2	0	2.10	800 595-7827
Northstar Balance Sheet Opp Fund C	Flexible	19.99					0	2.10	800 595-7827
Northstar Balance Sheet Opp Fund T	Flexible	20.35	18.10	12.56	3	2	0	1.83	800 595-7827
Northstar Growth & Value Fund A	Growth	15.80					4.75	1.85	800 595-7827
Northstar Growth & Value Fund B	Growth	14.92					0	0.11	800 595-7827
Northstar Growth & Value Fund C	Growth	14.82					0	0.11	800 595-7827
Northstar Growth Fund A	Growth	20.27	10.60		4	4	4.75	1.32	800 595-7827
Northstar Growth Fund B	Growth	19.56	20.52		3	3	0	2.12	800 595-7827
Northstar Growth Fund C	Growth	19.47	20.43		3	3	0	2.10	800 595-7827
Northstar Growth Fund T	Growth	19.59	20.57	15.11	3	3	0	2.03	800 595-7827
Northstar Income & Growth A	Growth/Inc	10.00	14.61		3	1	4.75	1.08	800 595-7827
Northstar Income & Growth B	Growth/Inc	9.21	13.80		3	1	0	1.83	800 595-7827
Northstar Income & Growth C	Growth/Inc	9.27	13.63		3	1	0	1.12	800 595-7827
Northstar Special Fund A	Small Co	16.93	15.98		4	5	4.75	0.01	800 595-7827
Northstar Special Fund B	Small Co	16.09	13.47		4	4	0	2.11	800 595-7827
Northstar Special Fund C	Small Co	16.06					0	2.16	800 595-7827
Northstar Special Fund T	Small Co	16.21	15.27	12.41	4	4	0	1.99	800 595-7827
Norwest Contrarian Stock I	Growth	2.85	8.30		5	3	0	1.72	800 338-1348
Norwest Diversified Eq Fd A	Growth	24.30	25.05	20.28	2	4	4.5	1.02	800 338-1348
Norwest Diversified Eq Fd B	Growth	23.38					0	2.41	800 338-1348
Norwest Diversified Eq Fd I	Growth	24.33	25.05	20.28	1	3	0	1.31	800 338-1348
Norwest Growth Balanced Fund I	Balanced	20.19	18.13		3	2	0	1.16	800 338-1348
Norwest Growth Equity Fund A	Growth	19.83			2	3	4.5	1.95	800 338-1348
Norwest Growth Equity Fund B	Growth	18.94					0	3.02	800 338-1348
Norwest Growth Equity Fund I	Growth	19.83	20.20		3	3	0	1.84	800 338-1348
Norwest Income Bond Fund A	Flexible	12.18	7.40	5.03	3	1	3.75	1.17	800 338-1348
Norwest Income Bond Fund B	Flexible	11.23	6.63		3	1	0	2.25	800 338-1348
Norwest Income Bond Fund I	Flexible	12.18	7.43		3	1	0	1.02	800 338-1348
Norwest Income Equity Fund A	Income	24.95	26.58	20.93	1	2	4.5	0.85	800 338-1348
Norwest Income Equity Fund B	Income	24.24					0	1.96	800 338-1348
Norwest Income Equity Fund I	Income	24.95	26.69		1	2	0	1.30	800 338-1348
Norwest Index Fund I	Growth/Inc	29.70	29.19		2	3	0	0.25	800 338-1348
Norwest International Fund A	Foreign	5.62	11.96		4	3	4.5	1.72	800 338-1348
Norwest International Fund B	Foreign	4.87	11.10		4	3	0	2.76	800 338-1348
Norwest International Fund I	Foreign	5.67	11.95		4	3	0	1.44	800 338-1348
Norwest Large Co Growth Fd I	Growth	37.12	29.17	22.66	2	4	0	1.00	800 338-1348
Norwest Moderate Bal Fund I	Balanced	16.48	13.58		3	1	0	1.04	800 338-1348
Norwest Small Co Growth Fund I	Small Co	11.88	20.04	18.27	4	4	0	1.25	800 338-1348
Norwest Small Co Stock Fund A	Small Co	7.05	12.96		5	5	4.5	1.67	800 338-1348
Norwest Small Co Stock Fund B	Small Co	6.25	12.05		5	5	0	2.73	800 338-1348

Stock Fund Name	Objective	Annualized Return for			Rank		Max Load	Expense Ratio	Toll-Free Telephone
		1 Year	3 Years	5 Years	Overall	Risk			
Norwest Small Co Stock Fund I	Small Co	7.10	12.96		5	5	0	1.56	800 338-1348
Norwest ValuGrowth Stock A	Growth	19.66	21.72	15.93	3	3	4.5	1.01	800 338-1348
Norwest ValuGrowth Stock B	Growth	18.92	20.74		3	3	0	2.48	800 338-1348
Norwest ValuGrowth Stock I	Growth	19.64	21.23	15.34	3	3	0	1.33	800 338-1348
Numeric Investors Growth & Value	Growth	33.85					0	1.00	800 686-3742
Numeric Investors Growth Fund	Small Co	14.88					0	1.00	800 686-3742
Numeric Investors Micro Cap Fund	Small Co	24.82					0	1.00	800 686-3742
O'Shaughnessy Aggressive Growth	Agg Growth	20.95					0	2.00	800 797-0773
O'Shaughnessy Cornerstone Growth4	Growth	30.50					0	1.56	800 797-0773
O'Shaughnessy Cornerstone Value	Growth/Inc	14.20					0	2.00	800 797-0773
O'Shaughnessy Dogs of the Market	Growth/Inc	19.36					0	2.00	800 797-0773
Oak Hall Small Cap Contrarian Fund	Small Co	29.87	22.07	9.42	3	4	0	2.93	800 228-8537
Oak Value Fund	Growth	33.53	33.99	25.36	1	2	0	1.59	800 680-4199
Oakmark Equity Income Fund	Balanced	21.51					0	1.50	800 625-6275
Oakmark Fund	Growth	18.38	24.10	21.92	2	2	0	1.03	800 625-6275
Oakmark International Fund	Foreign	–10.78	11.15	10.49	3	3	0	1.26	800 625-6275
Oakmark International Small Cap	Foreign	–24.95					0	1.96	800 625-6275
Oakmark Select Fund	Growth	44.30					0	1.13	800 625-6275
Oakmark Small Cap Fund	Small Co	15.91					0	1.45	800 625-6275
Oberweis Emerging Growth Port	Small Co	–6.07	8.52	11.50	4	5	0	1.44	800 245-7311
Oberweis Micro-Cap	Small Co	5.57					0	1.83	800 245-7311
Oberweis Mid Cap Portfolio	Small Co	20.73					0	1.83	800 245-7311
Old Dominion	Growth/Inc	6.03	16.78	14.17	3	3	4	1.16	800 441-6580
Olstein Financial Alert Fund	Agg Growth	26.47					0	2.27	800-799-2113
One Group Disciplined Value Fid	Growth	28.10	22.74	17.39	3	3	0	0.98	800 480-4111
One Group Equity Index Inv A	Growth/Inc	29.54	32.58	24.12	1	3	4.5	0.55	800 480-4111
One Group Growth Opportunities Fid	Small Co	30.78	26.01	18.99	3	4	0	0.99	800 480-4111
One Group Income Equity Fid	Income	23.19	26.15	20.20	2	2	4.5	1.02	800 480-4111
One Group International Eq Index	Foreign	9.36	11.71	10.87	4	3	4.5	1.11	800 480-4111
One Group Large Company Value Fid	Growth	21.37	20.26	16.87	3	3	0	0.97	800 480-4111
One Group Small Cap Fund A	Growth	9.87	13.85	11.56	5	4	4.5	1.27	800 480-4111
One Group Value Growth Fund	Growth/Inc	32.10	28.09	19.50	2	3	4.5	1.24	800 480-4111
Oppenheimer Capital Appreciation A	Agg Growth	30.10	27.99	21.85	2	3	5.75	1.02	800 525-7048
Oppenheimer Capital Appreciation B	Agg Growth	29.08					0	1.92	800 525-7048
Oppenheimer Capital Appreciation C	Agg Growth	29.05	27.02		2	3	0	1.88	800 525-7048
Oppenheimer Convertible Sec A	Converts	13.83	14.71		3	1	5.75	0.97	800 525-7048
Oppenheimer Convertible Sec B	Converts	12.92	13.86		3	1	0	1.72	800 525-7048
Oppenheimer Convertible Sec C	Converts	12.97					0	1.70	800 525-7048
Oppenheimer Convertible Sec M	Converts	13.40	14.20	13.71	3	1	3.25	1.46	800 525-7048
Oppenheimer Developing Markets A	Foreign	–19.25					5.75	1.94	800 525-7048
Oppenheimer Developing Markets B	Foreign	–19.96					0	2.78	800 525-7048
Oppenheimer Developing Markets C	Foreign	–19.90					0	2.77	800 525-7048
Oppenheimer Disciplined Alloc A	AssetAlloc	14.44	14.48	11.95	3	1	5.75	1.11	800 525-7048
Oppenheimer Disciplined Alloc B	AssetAlloc	13.54					0	1.85	800 525-7048
Oppenheimer Disciplined Alloc C	AssetAlloc	13.55					0	1.93	800 525-7048
Oppenheimer Disciplined Value A	Growth	18.26	22.55	18.48	2	3	5.75	1.05	800 525-7048
Oppenheimer Disciplined Value B	Growth	17.39					0	1.88	800 525-7048
Oppenheimer Disciplined Value C	Growth	17.42					0	1.87	800 525-7048
Oppenheimer Disciplined Value Y	Growth	18.68					0		800 525-7048
Oppenheimer Discovery Fund A	Small Co	13.58	17.48	13.47	4	4	5.75	1.22	800 525-7048
Oppenheimer Discovery Fund B	Small Co	12.71	16.58		4	4	0	1.96	800 525-7048
Oppenheimer Discovery Fund C	Small Co	12.79					0	1.97	800 525-7048
Oppenheimer Enterprise Fund A	Growth	33.20					5.75	1.50	800 525-7048
Oppenheimer Enterprise Fund B	Growth	32.17					0	2.27	800 525-7048
Oppenheimer Enterprise Fund C	Growth	32.39					0	2.27	800 525-7048
Oppenheimer Equity Income A	Income	24.95	23.69	17.11	2	2	5.75	0.88	800 525-7048
Oppenheimer Equity Income B	Income	24.00	22.69		2	2	0	1.70	800 525-7048
Oppenheimer Equity Income C	Income	24.00					0	1.75	800 525-7048

336

Stock Fund Name	Objective	Annualized Return for			Rank		Max Load	Expense Ratio	Toll-Free Telephone
		1 Year	3 Years	5 Years	Overall	Risk			
Oppenheimer Global Fund A	Global	17.91	20.01	18.99	3	3	5.75	1.13	800 525-7048
Oppenheimer Global Fund B	Global	17.00	19.05		3	3	0	1.96	800 525-7048
Oppenheimer Global Fund C	Global	16.98					0	1.97	800 525-7048
Oppenheimer Global Gwth & Inc A	Global	25.30	22.18	18.45	3	3	5.75	1.43	800 525-7048
Oppenheimer Global Gwth & Inc B	Global	24.37					0	1.19	800 525-7048
Oppenheimer Global Gwth & Inc C	Global	24.34	21.26		3	3	0	2.20	800 525-7048
Oppenheimer Gold & Special Min A	Gold	−30.23	−12.91	−6.11	5	5	5.75	1.34	800 525-7048
Oppenheimer Gold & Special Min B	Gold	−30.73					0	2.16	800 525-7048
Oppenheimer Gold & Special Min C	Gold	−30.74					0	2.18	800 525-7048
Oppenheimer Growth Fund A	Growth	14.77	20.97	18.10	3	2	5.75	1.01	800 525-7048
Oppenheimer Growth Fund B	Growth	13.81	19.90		3	2	0	1.85	800 525-7048
Oppenheimer Growth Fund C	Growth	13.83					0	1.87	800 525-7048
Oppenheimer Growth Fund Y	Growth	15.05	21.08		3	2	0	1.91	800 525-7048
Oppenheimer International Growth A	Foreign	22.30					5.75	0.94	800 525-7048
Oppenheimer International Growth B	Foreign	21.42					0	0.26	800 525-7048
Oppenheimer International Growth C	Foreign	21.39					0	0.15	800 525-7048
Oppenheimer Main Street Inc & Gr A	Growth/Inc	27.34	24.03	21.34	2	3	5.75	0.94	800 525-7048
Oppenheimer Main Street Inc & Gr B	Growth/Inc	26.36	23.09		2	3	0	1.71	800 525-7048
Oppenheimer Main Street Inc & Gr C	Growth/Inc	26.34	23.09		2	3	0	1.71	800 525-7048
Oppenheimer Main Street Inc & Gr Y	Growth/Inc	27.62					0	0.60	800 525-7048
Oppenheimer Multiple Strategies A	AssetAlloc	13.45	16.44	13.77	3	1	5.75	3.30	800 525-7048
Oppenheimer Multiple Strategies C	AssetAlloc	12.98	15.28		3	1	0	1.98	800 525-7048
Oppenheimer Quest Balanced Value A	Growth/Inc	28.65	21.98	17.57	3	2	5.75	1.70	800 525-7048
Oppenheimer Quest Balanced Value B	Growth/Inc	28.07	21.45		3	2	0	2.30	800 525-7048
Oppenheimer Quest Balanced Value C	Growth/Inc	28.11	21.39		3	2	0	2.29	800 525-7048
Oppenheimer Quest Capital Value A	Growth	26.30					5.75	1.07	800 525-7048
Oppenheimer Quest Capital Value B	Growth	25.51					0	1.93	800 525-7048
Oppenheimer Quest Capital Value C	Growth	25.49					0	1.89	800 525-7048
Oppenheimer Quest Global Value A	Global	14.35	18.07	15.85	3	2	5.75	0.17	800 525-7048
Oppenheimer Quest Global Value B	Global	13.82	17.48		3	2	0	0.37	800 525-7048
Oppenheimer Quest Global Value C	Global	13.78	17.22		3	2	0	2.29	800 525-7048
Oppenheimer Quest Opp Value Fund A	Flexible	17.59	21.44	19.89	2	2	5.75	1.54	800 525-7048
Oppenheimer Quest Opp Value Fund B	Flexible	17.02	20.84		2	2	0	2.03	800 525-7048
Oppenheimer Quest Opp Value Fund C	Flexible	17.02	20.81		2	2	0	2.03	800 525-7048
Oppenheimer Quest Opp Value Fund Y	Flexible	18.30					0	1.42	800 525-7048
Oppenheimer Quest Small Cap Value A	Small Co	5.96	16.45	12.19	4	3	5.5	1.88	800 525-7048
Oppenheimer Quest Small Cap Value B	Small Co	5.47	15.86		4	3	0	2.37	800 525-7048
Oppenheimer Quest Small Cap Value C	Small Co	5.47	15.87		4	3	0	2.37	800 525-7048
Oppenheimer Quest Value Fund A	Growth	23.48	25.73	20.26	1	2	5.75	1.60	800 525-7048
Oppenheimer Quest Value Fund B	Growth	22.90	25.09		1	2	0	2.17	800 525-7048
Oppenheimer Quest Value Fund C	Growth	22.83	25.06		1	2	0	2.18	800 525-7048
Oppenheimer Quest Value Fund Y	Growth	23.88					0	1.23	800 525-7048
Oppenheimer Real Asset Fund A	AssetAlloc	−24.75					5.75	1.74	800 525-7048
Oppenheimer Real Asset Fund B	AssetAlloc	−25.29					0	2.56	800 525-7048
Oppenheimer Real Asset Fund C	AssetAlloc	−25.25					0	2.56	800 525-7048
Oppenheimer Real Asset Fund Y	AssetAlloc	−24.68					0	1.57	800 525-7048
Oppenheimer Total Return A	Flexible	29.18	25.69	18.10	2	2	5.75	0.89	800 525-7048
Oppenheimer Total Return B	Flexible	28.13	24.80	15.46	2	2	0	1.70	800 525-7048
ORI Growth Fund A	Growth	18.29	23.06		3	4	4.25	2.00	800 407-7298
OVB Capital Appreciation A	Growth	38.49	26.07		3	4	0	1.27	800 545-6331
OVB Capital Appreciation B	Growth	38.22	25.80		3	4	0	1.52	800 545-6331
OVB Emerging Growth A	Small Co	23.81	12.25		4	5	0	1.34	800 545-6331
OVB Emerging Growth B	Small Co	23.39	11.91		4	5	0	1.59	800 545-6331
Pacific Advisors Balanced	Balanced	13.85	14.73	9.06	3	1	5.75	3.28	800 282-6693
Pacific Advisors Income & Equity	Growth/Inc	13.44	8.13	6.51	3	1	4.75	1.85	800 282-6693
Pacific Advisors Small Cap	Small Co	8.11	11.95	14.64	4	4	5.75	3.18	800 282-6693
Pacific Horizon Agg Growth Fund	Small Co	17.65	18.81	13.60	4	5	4.5	1.50	800 332-3863
Pacific Horizon Blue Chip SRF Cl	Growth	29.39	30.15	23.40	1	3	0	0.96	800 332-3863

Stock Fund Name	Objective	Annualized Return for			Rank		Max Load	Expense Ratio	Toll-Free Telephone
		1 Year	3 Years	5 Years	Overall	Risk			
Pacific Horizon Capital Income	Converts	10.85	18.85	14.32	3	2	4.5	1.12	800 332-3863
PaineWebber Asia Pacific Growth A	Pacific	−53.00					4.5	2.33	800 647-1568
PaineWebber Asia Pacific Growth B	Pacific	−53.37					0	3.12	800 647-1568
PaineWebber Asia Pacific Growth C	Pacific	−53.37					0	3.10	800 647-1568
PaineWebber Balanced A	Balanced	24.15	19.82	14.38	3	2	4.5	1.46	800 647-1568
PaineWebber Balanced B	Balanced	23.12	18.93	13.50	3	2	0	2.22	800 647-1568
PaineWebber Balanced C	Balanced	23.18	17.10	12.42	3	2	0	2.21	800 647-1568
PaineWebber Emerging Mkts A	Foreign	−36.54	−8.52		5	4	4.5	2.44	800 647-1568
PaineWebber Emerging Mkts B	Foreign	−36.93	−9.11		5	4	0	3.19	800 647-1568
PaineWebber Emerging Mkts C	Foreign	−37.04	−9.45		5	4	0	3.19	800 647-1568
PaineWebber Financial Svc Growth A	Financial	30.64	34.62	24.62	1	3	4.5	1.22	800 647-1568
PaineWebber Financial Svc Growth B	Financial	29.68	33.76	23.77	2	3	0	1.97	800 647-1568
PaineWebber Financial Svc Growth C	Financial	29.66	33.61	23.79	2	3	0	1.97	800 647-1568
PaineWebber Global Equity A	Global	10.35	13.42	13.59	4	3	4.5	1.44	800 647-1568
PaineWebber Global Equity B	Global	9.38					0	2.26	800 647-1568
PaineWebber Global Equity C	Global	4.33	11.64		4	3	0	2.20	800 647-1568
PaineWebber Growth & Income Fd A	Growth/Inc	26.65	28.12	19.09	1	3	4.5	1.15	800 647-1568
PaineWebber Growth & Income Fd B	Growth/Inc	25.74	27.14	16.65	2	3	0	1.93	800 647-1568
PaineWebber Growth & Income Fd C	Growth/Inc	25.66	27.02	16.58	2	3	0	1.92	800 647-1568
PaineWebber Growth & Income Fd Y	Growth/Inc	26.96	25.87	15.48	3	3	0	0.88	800 647-1568
PaineWebber Growth A	Growth	32.81	23.52	16.33	3	4	4.5	1.27	800 647-1568
PaineWebber Growth B	Growth	31.75	22.54	15.42	3	4	0	2.06	800 647-1568
PaineWebber Growth C	Growth	31.69	22.50	15.39	3	4	0	2.07	800 647-1568
PaineWebber Growth Y	Growth	33.35	23.68	16.52	3	4	0	1.00	800 647-1568
PaineWebber Mid Cap Fund A	Growth	12.12	17.52	15.82	4	4	4.5	1.57	800 647-1568
PaineWebber Mid Cap Fund B	Growth	11.19	16.60	14.91	4	4	0	2.32	800 647-1568
PaineWebber Mid Cap Fund C	Growth	11.30	16.38	14.79	4	4	0	2.35	800 647-1568
PaineWebber PACE Intnl Emerging Mkt	Foreign	−34.52					0	1.50	800 647-1568
PaineWebber PACE Intnl Equity	Foreign	9.95					0	1.21	800 647-1568
PaineWebber PACE Large Co Growth Eq	Growth	37.04					0	1.00	800 647-1568
PaineWebber PACE Large Co Value Eq	Growth/Inc	21.28					0	0.98	800 647-1568
PaineWebber PACE Sm/Med Co Grwth Eq	Growth	25.60					0	1.00	800 647-1568
PaineWebber PACE Sm/Med Co Value Eq	Small Co	21.40					0	1.00	800 647-1568
PaineWebber Small Cap Value A	Small Co	23.81	19.39	14.13	4	4	4.5	2.00	800 647-1568
PaineWebber Small Cap Value B	Small Co	22.92	18.45	13.42	4	4	0	2.75	800 647-1568
PaineWebber Small Cap Value C	Small Co	22.85	18.39	13.37	4	4	0	2.77	800 647-1568
PaineWebber Tactical Alloc A	AssetAlloc	29.20	28.92	21.24	1	3	4.5	0.99	800 647-1568
PaineWebber Tactical Alloc B	AssetAlloc	27.71	28.13	20.52	2	3	0	1.74	800 647-1568
PaineWebber Tactical Alloc C	AssetAlloc	28.22	28.07	20.52	2	3	0	1.75	800 647-1568
PaineWebber Utility Income A	Utilities	25.56	17.59		3	2	4.5	2.03	800 647-1568
PaineWebber Utility Income B	Utilities	24.53	16.60		3	2	0	2.78	800 647-1568
PaineWebber Utility Income C	Utilities	24.58	16.64		3	2	0	2.79	800 647-1568
Papp America Abroad Fund	Growth	14.08	27.63	24.44	3	3	0	1.22	800 421-4004
Papp America Pacific Rim	Pacific	13.29					0		800 421-4004
Papp Stock Fund	Growth	22.61	27.53	20.49	2	3	0	1.18	800 421-4004
Parkstone Aggressive Alloc Instl	Agg Growth	15.69					0	0.64	800 451-8377
Parkstone Balanced Allocation Instl	Balanced	15.30	15.01	12.32	3	1	0	0.55	800 451-8377
Parkstone Balanced Allocation Inv A	Balanced	15.00	14.61	12.00	3	1	4.5	0.67	800 451-8377
Parkstone Balanced Allocation Inv B	Balanced	14.08	13.81		3	1	0	1.05	800 451-8377
Parkstone Balanced Allocation Inv C	Balanced	14.10	13.86	11.37	3	1	0	1.05	800 451-8377
Parkstone Conservative Alloc Instl	Growth	12.83					0	0.60	800 451-8377
Parkstone Equity Income Fund Instl	Income	18.80	22.68	15.42	3	2	0	0.68	800 451-8377
Parkstone Equity Income Fund Inv A	Income	18.54	22.51		3	2	4.5	0.80	800 451-8377
Parkstone Equity Income Fund Inv B	Income	17.67	21.62		3	2	0	1.18	800 451-8377
Parkstone Equity Income Fund Inv C	Income	17.67	21.83	14.33	3	2	0	1.18	800 451-8377
Parkstone Intl Discovery Instl	Foreign	3.67	11.44	9.32	4	3	0	0.79	800 451-8377
Parkstone Intl Discovery Inv A	Foreign	3.52	11.24	9.14	4	3	4.5	0.92	800 451-8377
Parkstone Intl Discovery Inv B	Foreign	2.71	10.24		5	3	0	1.30	800 451-8377

338

Stock Fund Name	Objective	Annualized Return for			Rank		Max Load	Expense Ratio	Toll-Free Telephone
		1 Year	3 Years	5 Years	Overall	Risk			
Parkstone Intl Discovery Inv C	Foreign	2.77	10.37	8.88	4	3	0	1.30	800 451-8377
Parkstone Large Cap Fund Instl	Growth/Inc	36.03					0	0.56	800 451-8377
Parkstone Large Cap Fund Inv A	Growth/Inc	35.76					4.5	0.69	800 451-8377
Parkstone Large Cap Fund Inv B	Growth/Inc	34.69					0	1.06	800 451-8377
Parkstone Large Cap Fund Inv C	Growth/Inc	35.75					0	1.06	800 451-8377
Parkstone Mid Capitalization Instl	Growth	23.17	19.07	15.53	3	4	0	0.66	800 451-8377
Parkstone Mid Capitalization Inv A	Growth	23.00	19.02	15.40	3	4	4.5	0.78	800 451-8377
Parkstone Mid Capitalization Inv B	Growth	22.33	18.18		3	4	0	1.16	800 451-8377
Parkstone Mid Capitalization Inv C	Growth	22.52	18.36	15.74	3	4	0	1.16	800 451-8377
Parkstone Small Cap Instl	Small Co	3.19	13.97	16.00	4	5	0	0.67	800 451-8377
Parkstone Small Cap Inv A	Small Co	2.86	13.77	16.21	4	5	4.5	0.80	800 451-8377
Parkstone Small Cap Inv B	Small Co	2.20	13.01		5	5	0	1.18	800 451-8377
Parkstone Small Cap Inv C	Small Co	2.23	12.91	15.72	4	5	0	1.18	800 451-8377
Parnassus Equity Income Fund	Balanced	15.77	14.00	11.01	3	1	0	1.02	800 999-3505
Parnassus Fund	Growth	−2.12	5.66	10.90	5	5	3.5	1.11	800 999-3505
Pathfinder Fund	Small Co	13.93	16.57	12.47	4	5	0	1.28	800 444-4778
Pax World Fund	Balanced	23.81	21.01	15.28	2	1	0	0.91	800 767-1729
Payden & Rygel Global Balanced R	Balanced	13.96					0	0.69	800 572-9336
Payden & Rygel Growth & Income R	Growth/Inc	21.12					0	0.53	800 572-9336
Payden & Rygel International Eq R	Foreign	4.59					0	0.89	800 572-9336
Payden & Rygel Market Return Fund R	Flexible	29.28					0	0.45	800 572-9336
Payson Balanced Fund	Balanced	10.64	15.82	12.28	3	2	4	1.15	800 879-8900
Payson Value Fund	Growth/Inc	25.20	24.70	18.77	3	3		1.45	800 879-8900
PBHG Core Growth	Growth	10.88					0	1.36	800 433-0051
PBHG Emerging Growth	Small Co	5.12	13.60	23.23	4	5	0	1.27	800 433-0051
PBHG Growth Fund	Small Co	9.69	13.71	17.24	4	5	0	1.25	800 433-0051
PBHG Growth II Ins	Growth	13.30					0	1.20	800 433-0051
PBHG International Fund	Foreign	2.04	11.06		4	3	0	1.99	800 433-0051
PBHG Large Cap 20	Growth	52.65					0	1.49	800 433-0051
PBHG Large Cap Growth	Growth	36.62	31.55		3	4	0	1.22	800 433-0051
PBHG Large Cap Growth Ins	Growth	30.89					0		800 433-0051
PBHG Large Cap Value	Growth	24.04					0	1.27	800 433-0051
PBHG Limited Fund	Small Co	22.73					0	1.40	800 433-0051
PBHG Mid Cap Value Fund	Growth	39.32					0	1.50	800 433-0051
PBHG Select Equity	Growth	32.47	30.42		3	5	0	1.35	800 433-0051
PBHG Small Cap Value	Small Co	27.95					0	1.50	800 433-0051
PBHG Strategic Small Company	Small Co	17.46					0	1.45	800 433-0051
PBHG Technology & Communication	Technology	9.08					0	1.30	800 433-0051
Pegasus Equity Income A	Income	8.26	17.94		3	2	5	0.95	800 688-3350
Pegasus Equity Income B	Income	7.57	17.09		3	2	0	1.70	800 688-3350
Pegasus Equity Income I	Income	8.56	20.10		3	2	0	0.70	800 688-3350
Pegasus Equity Index Fund A	Growth	29.46	29.66	22.40	1	3	3	0.57	800 688-3350
Pegasus Equity Index Fund B	Growth	27.35					0	1.30	800 688-3350
Pegasus Equity Index Fund I	Growth	29.80	29.42	22.26	1	3	0	0.30	800 688-3350
Pegasus Growth and Value Fund A	Growth	18.57	23.06	17.89	3	3	5	1.09	800 688-3350
Pegasus Growth and Value Fund B	Growth	17.77					0	1.82	800 688-3350
Pegasus Growth and Value Fund I	Growth	18.81	23.25	18.00	3	3	0	0.82	800 688-3350
Pegasus Growth Fund A	Growth	31.39	28.02		1	3	5	1.04	800 688-3350
Pegasus Growth Fund B	Growth	30.32	27.10		1	3	0	1.79	800 688-3350
Pegasus Growth Fund I	Growth	31.56	25.61		2	3	0	0.79	800 688-3350
Pegasus International Equity A	Foreign	7.06	9.84		4	3	5	1.37	800 688-3350
Pegasus International Equity B	Foreign	6.54					0	1.60	800 688-3350
Pegasus International Equity I	Foreign	7.35	10.92		4	3	0	0.60	800 688-3350
Pegasus Intrinsic Value Fund A	Growth	15.16	20.81	16.53	2	1	5	1.06	800 688-3350
Pegasus Intrinsic Value Fund B	Growth	14.31					0	1.81	800 688-3350
Pegasus Intrinsic Value Fund I	Growth	15.46	20.83	16.55	2	1	0	0.81	800 688-3350
Pegasus Managed Assets Bal A	Growth/Inc	12.72	14.68		3	1	5	1.22	800 688-3350
Pegasus Managed Assets Bal B	Growth/Inc	11.95					0	0.97	800 688-3350

Stock Fund Name	Objective	Annualized Return for			Rank		Max Load	Expense Ratio	Toll-Free Telephone
		1 Year	3 Years	5 Years	Overall	Risk			
Pegasus Managed Assets Bal I	Growth/Inc	12.89	18.02		3	2	0	0.97	800 688-3350
Pegasus Managed Assets Conserv A	Flexible	11.50	13.56	11.27	3	1	5	1.24	800 688-3350
Pegasus Managed Assets Conserv B	Flexible	10.44	12.56		3	1	0	1.97	800 688-3350
Pegasus Managed Assets Conserv I	Flexible	11.69	13.66		3	1	0	0.97	800 688-3350
Pegasus Managed Assets Growth A	AssetAlloc	13.56					5	1.21	800 688-3350
Pegasus Managed Assets Growth B	AssetAlloc	12.78					0	1.96	800 688-3350
Pegasus Managed Assets Growth I	AssetAlloc	13.91					0	0.96	800 688-3350
Pegasus Mid-Cap Opportunity Fund A	Agg Growth	20.01	21.95	17.44	3	3	5	1.09	800 688-3350
Pegasus Mid-Cap Opportunity Fund B	Agg Growth	19.78					0	1.82	800 688-3350
Pegasus Mid-Cap Opportunity Fund I	Agg Growth	20.31	22.18	17.57	3	3	0	0.82	800 688-3350
Pegasus Small Cap Opportunity A	Small Co	19.25	26.07		2	3	5	1.19	800 688-3350
Pegasus Small Cap Opportunity B	Small Co	18.43	25.38		3	3	0	1.94	800 688-3350
Pegasus Small Cap Opportunity I	Small Co	19.69	26.74		3	3	0	0.94	800 688-3350
Pennsylvania Mutual Fund	Small Co	20.25	18.03	14.11	3	2	0	1.05	800 221-4268
Performance Large Cap Eq Consumer	Growth	31.81	30.93	21.57	1	3	4.7	1.06	800 737-3676
Performance Large Cap Eq Instl	Growth	32.16	31.30	21.89	1	3	0	0.86	800 737-3676
Performance Mid Cap Growth Consumer	Growth	21.53	24.79		1	3	4.5	1.19	800 737-3676
Performance Mid Cap Growth Instl	Growth	21.83	25.11		1	3	0	0.92	800 737-3676
Perkins Opportunity Fund	Small Co	−3.71	−0.77	15.01	4	5	4.75	1.99	800 998-3190
Permanent Aggressive Growth Port	Agg Growth	25.04	20.21	19.45	3	4	0	1.46	800 531-5142
Permanent Portfolio	AssetAlloc	8.54	4.73	5.31	4	1	0	1.91	800 531-5142
Perritt MicroCap Opportunities	Small Co	9.24	17.22	14.04	4	4	0	1.52	800 331-8936
Philadelphia Fund	Growth/Inc	29.62	23.60	16.63	3	3	0	1.53	800 749-9933
Phoenix Aberdeen Global Small Cap A	Global	7.98					4.75		800 243-4361
Phoenix Aberdeen Global Small Cap B	Global	7.25					0		800 243-4361
Phoenix Aberdeen New Asia A	Pacific	−43.60					4.75		800 243-4361
Phoenix Aberdeen New Asia B	Pacific	−44.04					0		800 243-4361
Phoenix Aggressive Growth Fund A	Agg Growth	29.70	23.47	18.67	3	4	4.75	1.20	800 243-4361
Phoenix Aggressive Growth Fund B	Agg Growth	28.89	22.61		3	4	0	1.97	800 243-4361
Phoenix Balanced Fund A	Balanced	18.36	16.50	11.50	3	2	4.75	0.98	800 243-4361
Phoenix Balanced Fund B	Balanced	17.44	15.63		3	2	0	1.76	800 243-4361
Phoenix Convertible Fund A	Converts	9.12	12.44	9.76	4	1	4.75	1.12	800 243-4361
Phoenix Convertible Fund B	Converts	8.37	11.60		4	1	0	1.90	800 243-4361
Phoenix Equity Opportunities A	Growth	34.31	17.60	13.76	3	4	4.75	1.22	800 243-4361
Phoenix Equity Opportunities B	Growth	33.09	16.73		3	4	0		800 243-4361
Phoenix Growth Fund A	Growth	26.61	23.00	17.69	2	3	4.75	1.10	800 243-4361
Phoenix Growth Fund B	Growth	25.66	22.10		2	3	0	1.88	800 243-4361
Phoenix Income & Growth A	Flexible	15.41	15.71	11.54	3	1	4.75	1.18	800 243-4361
Phoenix Income & Growth B	Flexible	14.54	14.84	10.73	3	1	0	1.18	800 243-4361
Phoenix Instl Balanced Port X	Balanced	18.96	17.66	12.45	3	2	0		800 243-4361
Phoenix Instl Balanced Port Y	Balanced	18.64	17.35	12.16	3	2	0		800 243-4361
Phoenix Instl Growth Stock Port X	Growth	28.68	23.88	18.29	2	3	0		800 243-4361
Phoenix Instl Growth Stock Port Y	Growth	28.35	23.57	18.00	3	3	0		800 243-4361
Phoenix Instl Real Estate Port X	Real Est	8.41					0		800 243-4361
Phoenix Instl Real Estate Port Y	Real Est	8.33					0		800 243-4361
Phoenix International A	Foreign	28.38	21.31	18.05	3	3	4.75	1.56	800 243-4361
Phoenix International B	Foreign	27.39	20.36		3	3	0		800 243-4361
Phoenix Mid Cap A	Growth	20.72	15.69	13.33	4	4	4.75	1.33	800 243-4361
Phoenix Mid Cap B	Growth	19.77	14.84		4	4	0	1.37	800 243-4361
Phoenix Real Estate Securities A	Real Est	5.68	18.80		2	3	4.75		800 243-4361
Phoenix Real Estate Securities B	Real Est	4.96	17.93		2	3	0		800 243-4361
Phoenix Small Cap A	Small Co	32.15					4.75	1.33	800 243-4361
Phoenix Small Cap B	Small Co	31.23					0		800 243-4361
Phoenix Strategic Allocation Fund A	AssetAlloc	20.61	15.43	11.91	3	2	4.75	1.17	800 243-4361
Phoenix Strategic Allocation Fund B	AssetAlloc	19.72	14.48		3	2	0		800 243-4361
Phoenix Strategic Theme A	Growth	25.78					4.75		800 243-4361
Phoenix Strategic Theme B	Growth	24.95					0		800 243-4361
Phoenix Worldwide Opportunities A	Global	31.45	21.86	19.70	3	3	4.75	1.52	800 243-4361

Stock Fund Name	Objective	Annualized Return for			Rank		Max Load	Expense Ratio	Toll-Free Telephone
		1 Year	3 Years	5 Years	Overall	Risk			
Phoenix Worldwide Opportunities B	Global	30.61	20.96		3	3	0		800 243-4361
Phoenix-Engemann Balanced Return A	Balanced	20.30	19.75	14.95	3	2	5.5	1.70	800 243-4361
Phoenix-Engemann Balanced Return B	Balanced	19.36	18.81		3	2	0	2.00	800 243-4361
Phoenix-Engemann Balanced Return C	Balanced	19.33	18.79		3	2	0	2.70	800 243-4361
Phoenix-Engemann Global Growth A	Global	13.04	18.93		3	4	5.5	0.80	800 243-4361
Phoenix-Engemann Growth Fund A	Growth	26.17	22.26	16.85	3	4	5.5	1.60	800 243-4361
Phoenix-Engemann Growth Fund B	Growth	25.37	21.32		2	4	0	2.30	800 243-4361
Phoenix-Engemann Growth Fund C	Growth	25.37	21.32		2	4	0	2.30	800 243-4361
Phoenix-Engemann Nifty Fifty A	Growth	22.06	24.49	19.16	2	4	5.5	1.60	800 243-4361
Phoenix-Engemann Nifty Fifty B	Growth	21.19	23.57		3	4	0	2.50	800 243-4361
Phoenix-Engemann Nifty Fifty C	Growth	21.19	23.57		3	4	0	2.50	800 243-4361
Phoenix-Engemann Sm & Mid-Cap Gr A	Agg Growth	21.34	32.72		2	5	4.75	1.80	800 243-4361
Phoenix-Engemann Value 25 A	Growth/Inc	11.61					5.5		800 243-4361
Phoenix-Engemann Value 25 B	Growth/Inc	10.73					0		800 243-4361
Phoenix-Engemann Value 25 C	Growth/Inc	10.67					0		800 243-4361
Pilgrim Amer Masters Asia-Pac Eq A	Pacific	−59.65					5.75	2.00	800 334-3444
Pilgrim Amer Masters Asia-Pac Eq B	Pacific	−60.11					0	2.75	800 334-3444
Pilgrim Amer Masters Asia-Pac Eq M	Pacific	−59.85					3.5	2.50	800 334-3444
Pilgrim Amer Masters LargeCap Val A	Growth/Inc	17.71					5.75	1.75	800 334-3444
Pilgrim Amer Masters LargeCap Val B	Growth/Inc	16.91						2.50	800 334-3444
Pilgrim Amer Masters LargeCap Val M	Growth/Inc	17.20					3.5	2.25	800 334-3444
Pilgrim Amer Masters MidCap Value A	Agg Growth	18.40					5.75	1.75	800 334-3444
Pilgrim Amer Masters MidCap Value B	Agg Growth	17.40						2.50	800 334-3444
Pilgrim Amer Masters MidCap Value M	Agg Growth	17.75					3.5	2.25	800 334-3444
Pilgrim America MagnaCap A	Growth	20.52	24.12	20.27	2	2	5.75	1.38	800 334-3444
Pilgrim America MagnaCap B	Growth	19.76					0	2.16	800 334-3444
Pilgrim America MagnaCap M	Growth	20.00					3.25	1.83	800 334-3444
Pillar Balanced Growth A	Balanced	19.11	18.50	13.54	3	1	5.5	1.05	800 932-7782
Pillar Balanced Growth B	Balanced	7.35					0	1.80	800 932-7782
Pillar Balanced Growth I	Balanced	19.61	18.84	13.85	3	1	0	0.80	800 932-7782
Pillar Equity Growth A	Growth	26.31					5.5	1.05	800 932-7782
Pillar Equity Growth B	Growth	25.29					0	1.80	800 932-7782
Pillar Equity Growth I	Growth	27.20					0	0.80	800 932-7782
Pillar Equity Income A	Income	18.75	24.31	17.09	2	2	0	1.05	800 932-7782
Pillar Equity Income B	Income	17.32					0	1.80	800 932-7782
Pillar Equity Income I	Income	19.86	27.39	19.03	2	2	0	0.80	800 932-7782
Pillar Equity Value A	Growth/Inc	23.60	25.98	19.16	2	3	0	1.05	800 932-7782
Pillar Equity Value B	Growth/Inc	22.86					0	1.80	800 932-7782
Pillar Equity Value I	Growth/Inc	24.43	26.51		1	3	5.5	0.80	800 932-7782
Pillar International Growth A	Foreign	3.80	10.96		4	3	5.5	1.75	800 932-7782
Pillar International Growth B	Foreign	1.34					0	2.50	800 932-7782
Pillar International Growth I	Foreign	3.50	11.03		4	3	0	1.50	800 932-7782
Pillar Mid Cap Value Class A	Small Co	19.88	15.78	11.69	4	3	5.5	1.05	800 932-7782
Pillar Mid Cap Value Class I	Small Co	22.53	16.84	12.41	3	3	0	0.80	800 932-7782
PIMCO Balanced Fund A	Balanced	19.40					5.5	1.15	800 426-0107
PIMCO Balanced Fund B	Balanced	18.59					0	1.90	800 426-0107
PIMCO Balanced Fund C	Balanced	18.59					0	1.90	800 426-0107
PIMCO Balanced Fund Instl	Balanced	20.02	18.44	13.86	3	1	0	0.70	800 426-0107
PIMCO Capital Appreciation A	Growth	32.39					5.5	1.11	800 426-0107
PIMCO Capital Appreciation Admin	Growth	32.55					0	0.70	800 426-0107
PIMCO Capital Appreciation B	Growth	31.39					0	1.85	800 426-0107
PIMCO Capital Appreciation C	Growth	31.40					0	1.86	800 426-0107
PIMCO Capital Appreciation Instl	Growth	32.97	29.67	22.07	2	3	0	0.71	800 426-0107
PIMCO Core Equity Fund Admin	Growth	41.55	26.43		3	4	0	1.07	800 426-0107
PIMCO Core Equity Fund Instl	Growth	41.83	26.73		2	3	0	0.82	800 426-0107
PIMCO Emerging Markets A	Foreign	−27.40					5.5	1.89	800 426-0107
PIMCO Emerging Markets B	Foreign	−27.86					0	2.62	800 426-0107
PIMCO Emerging Markets C	Foreign	−27.86					0	2.63	800 426-0107

341

Stock Fund Name	Objective	Annualized Return for			Rank		Max Load	Expense Ratio	Toll-Free Telephone
		1 Year	3 Years	5 Years	Overall	Risk			
PIMCO Emerging Markets Fund Admin	Foreign	−27.31	−4.78		5	4	0	1.61	800 426-0107
PIMCO Emerging Markets Fund Instl	Foreign	−27.08	−4.52	2.12	5	4	0	1.35	800 426-0107
PIMCO Enhanced Equity Fund Instl	Growth	32.33	28.76	20.92	1	3	0	0.74	800 426-0107
PIMCO Equity Income A	Income	21.36					5.5	1.13	800 426-0107
PIMCO Equity Income Admin	Income	21.58	23.04		2	2	0	0.95	800 426-0107
PIMCO Equity Income B	Income	20.47					0	1.87	800 426-0107
PIMCO Equity Income C	Income	20.51					0	1.87	800 426-0107
PIMCO Equity Income Instl	Income	21.84	24.77	18.12	2	2	0	0.71	800 426-0107
PIMCO Growth Fund A	Growth	41.03	26.51		2	3	5.5	1.11	800 426-0107
PIMCO Growth Fund B	Growth	39.97	25.57		3	3	0	1.86	800 426-0107
PIMCO Growth Fund C	Growth	39.98	25.55	19.37	2	3	0	1.86	800 426-0107
PIMCO Innovation Fund A	Technology	48.11	27.70		3	5	5.5	1.28	800 426-0107
PIMCO Innovation Fund B	Technology	46.95	26.74		3	5	0	2.03	800 426-0107
PIMCO Innovation Fund C	Technology	46.97	26.72		3	5	0	2.03	800 426-0107
PIMCO International Fund A	Foreign	9.95	11.69	8.59	4	3	5.5	1.90	800 426-0107
PIMCO International Fund B	Foreign	9.18	10.88		4	3	0	2.26	800 426-0107
PIMCO International Fund C	Foreign	9.18	10.89	7.78	4	3	0	2.25	800 426-0107
PIMCO Intl Developed Fund A	Foreign	15.65					5.5	1.54	800 426-0107
PIMCO Intl Developed Fund Admin	Foreign	15.33	14.36		4	3	0	1.38	800 426-0107
PIMCO Intl Developed Fund B	Foreign	14.13					0	2.28	800 426-0107
PIMCO Intl Developed Fund C	Foreign	14.38					0	2.28	800 426-0107
PIMCO Intl Developed Fund Instl	Foreign	15.69	14.69	13.04	4	3	0	1.13	800 426-0107
PIMCO Micro Cap Growth Admin	Small Co	33.70					0	0.96	800 426-0107
PIMCO Micro Cap Growth Instl	Small Co	33.95	29.86	24.91	3	4	0	0.71	800 426-0107
PIMCO Mid Cap Equity Fund Instl	Growth	30.40	22.63		3	4	0	0.88	800 426-0107
PIMCO Mid Cap Growth A	Growth	25.72					5.5	1.11	800 426-0107
PIMCO Mid Cap Growth Administrative	Growth	25.76	25.69		2	3	0	0.96	800 426-0107
PIMCO Mid Cap Growth B	Growth	24.76					0	1.85	800 426-0107
PIMCO Mid Cap Growth C	Growth	24.70					0	1.86	800 426-0107
PIMCO Mid Cap Growth Institutional	Growth	26.16	26.05	20.23	2	3	0	1.15	800 426-0107
PIMCO Opportunity Fund A	Agg Growth	13.87	11.14	9.83	4	5	5.5	1.25	800 426-0107
PIMCO Opportunity Fund C	Agg Growth	13.01	10.31	12.42	3	5	0	2.06	800 426-0107
PIMCO Precious Metals Fund A	Gold	−39.64	−22.40		5	5	5.5	1.90	800 426-0107
PIMCO Precious Metals Fund B	Gold	−40.50	−23.12		5	5	0	2.13	800 426-0107
PIMCO Precious Metals Fund C	Gold	−40.69	−23.15	−14.71	5	5	0	2.60	800 426-0107
PIMCO Renaissance Fund A	Growth/Inc	30.98	30.87	21.28	1	3	5.5	1.23	800 426-0107
PIMCO Renaissance Fund B	Growth/Inc	29.99	29.90		1	3	0	1.97	800 426-0107
PIMCO Renaissance Fund C	Growth/Inc	29.98	29.90	20.75	1	3	0	1.97	800 426-0107
PIMCO Small Cap Growth Admin	Small Co	18.90					0	1.50	800 426-0107
PIMCO Small Cap Growth Instl	Small Co	19.33	19.80	15.69	4	4	0	1.25	800 426-0107
PIMCO Small Cap Value A	Small Co	17.33					5.5	1.30	800 426-0107
PIMCO Small Cap Value Admin	Small Co	17.41					0	1.16	800 426-0107
PIMCO Small Cap Value B	Small Co	16.40					0	2.04	800 426-0107
PIMCO Small Cap Value C	Small Co	16.43					0	2.05	800 426-0107
PIMCO Small Cap Value Instl	Small Co	17.77	23.77	17.41	3	3	0	1.16	800 426-0107
PIMCO Stocksplus Fund A	Growth/Inc	28.98					0	1.10	800 426-0107
PIMCO Stocksplus Fund Admin	Growth/Inc	29.00					0	0.95	800 426-0107
PIMCO Stocksplus Fund B	Growth/Inc	27.97					0	1.88	800 426-0107
PIMCO Stocksplus Fund C	Growth/Inc	28.40					0	1.65	800 426-0107
PIMCO StocksPlus Instl	Growth/Inc	29.49	30.28	23.92	1	3	0	0.65	800 426-0107
PIMCO Strategic Balanced Instl	Balanced	22.10					0	0.90	800 426-0107
PIMCO Target Fund A	Growth	27.48	21.72	19.38	3	4	5.5	1.20	800 426-0107
PIMCO Target Fund B	Growth	26.45	20.79		4	4	0	1.94	800 426-0107
PIMCO Target Fund C	Growth	26.53	20.79	18.46	3	4	0	1.94	800 426-0107
PIMCO Value Fund A	Growth/Inc	18.86					5.5	1.11	800 426-0107
PIMCO Value Fund B	Growth/Inc	17.98					0	1.86	800 426-0107
PIMCO Value Fund C	Growth/Inc	17.98					0	1.86	800 426-0107
PIMCO Value Fund I	Growth/Inc	19.35	24.08	18.83	2	2	0	0.71	800 426-0107

Stock Fund Name	Objective	Annualized Return for			Rank		Max Load	Expense Ratio	Toll-Free Telephone
		1 Year	3 Years	5 Years	Overall	Risk			
Pin Oak Aggressive Stock Fund	Small Co	24.33	16.51	15.33	4	5	0	1.29	888 462-5386
Pioneer Balanced Fund A	Balanced	12.55	13.04	9.67	4	1	4.5	1.17	800 225-6292
Pioneer Balanced Fund B	Balanced	11.53	12.58		3	1	0	2.02	800 225-6292
Pioneer Balanced Fund C	Balanced	11.74					0	1.94	800 225-6292
Pioneer Capital Growth A	Growth	14.29	16.11	18.19	3	3	5.75	1.00	800 225-6292
Pioneer Capital Growth B	Growth	13.45	15.20		4	3	0	1.77	800 225-6292
Pioneer Capital Growth C	Growth	13.43					0	1.76	800 225-6292
Pioneer Emerging Markets Fund A	Foreign	−27.13	3.51		5	5	5.75	2.26	800 225-6292
Pioneer Emerging Markets Fund B	Foreign	−27.67	2.79		5	5	0	2.97	800 225-6292
Pioneer Emerging Markets Fund C	Foreign	−27.62					0	2.93	800 225-6292
Pioneer Equity Income Fund A	Income	27.63	24.95	17.70	2	2	5.75	1.11	800 225-6292
Pioneer Equity Income Fund B	Income	26.68	24.00		2	2	0	1.90	800 225-6292
Pioneer Equity Income Fund C	Income	26.61					0	1.93	800 225-6292
Pioneer Europe Fund A	European	38.23	27.60	24.44	1	3	5.75	1.78	800 225-6292
Pioneer Europe Fund B	European	37.11	26.59		1	3	0	2.68	800 225-6292
Pioneer Europe Fund C	European	37.34					0	2.62	800 225-6292
Pioneer Fund A	Growth/Inc	31.87	28.19	20.77	2	3	5.75	1.02	800 225-6292
Pioneer Fund B	Growth/Inc	30.68					0	1.84	800 225-6292
Pioneer Fund C	Growth/Inc	30.70					0	1.77	800 225-6292
Pioneer Gold Shares Fund A	Gold	−32.55	−16.62	−10.31	5	5	5.75	1.74	800 225-6292
Pioneer Gold Shares Fund B	Gold	−32.96	−16.64		5	5	0	2.51	800 225-6292
Pioneer Gold Shares Fund C	Gold	−33.07					0	2.38	800 225-6292
Pioneer Growth Shares A	Growth	40.93	36.15	24.90	3	4	5.75	1.05	800 225-6292
Pioneer Growth Shares B	Growth	39.76	35.15		3	4	0	1.80	800 225-6292
Pioneer Growth Shares C	Growth	39.95					0	1.78	800 225-6292
Pioneer II A	Growth/Inc	9.55	19.54	16.45	3	3	5.75	0.96	800 225-6292
Pioneer II B	Growth/Inc	8.36					0	1.87	800 225-6292
Pioneer II C	Growth/Inc	8.44					0	2.01	800 225-6292
Pioneer India Fund A	Foreign	−29.65	−15.95		5	5	5.75	2.28	800 225-6292
Pioneer India Fund B	Foreign	−30.21	−16.63		5	5	0	2.93	800 225-6292
Pioneer India Fund C	Foreign	−30.45					0	2.88	800 225-6292
Pioneer International Growth A	Foreign	−7.49	8.32	11.44	5	4	5.75	1.69	800 225-6292
Pioneer International Growth B	Foreign	−8.24	7.43		5	4	0	2.54	800 225-6292
Pioneer International Growth C	Foreign	−8.02					0	2.51	800 225-6292
Pioneer Mid-Cap Fund A	Small Co	25.63	15.00	12.08	4	4	5.75	0.87	800 225-6292
Pioneer Mid-Cap Fund B	Small Co	24.19					0	1.83	800 225-6292
Pioneer Mid-Cap Fund C	Small Co	24.40					0	1.92	800 225-6292
Pioneer Real Estate Shares A	Real Est	6.33	18.19		4	3	5.75	1.67	800 225-6292
Pioneer Real Estate Shares B	Real Est	5.60					0	2.42	800 225-6292
Pioneer Real Estate Shares C	Real Est	5.61					0	2.37	800 225-6292
Pioneer Small Company Fund A	Small Co	14.22					5.75	1.49	800 225-6292
Pioneer Small Company Fund B	Small Co	13.36					0	2.21	800 225-6292
Pioneer Small Company Fund C	Small Co	13.35					0	2.20	800 225-6292
Piper Balanced A	Balanced	18.80	15.66	12.99	3	1	4	1.73	800 866-7778
Piper Emerging Growth A	Small Co	23.24	21.21	17.42	3	4	4	1.23	800 866-7778
Piper Emerging Growth Y	Small Co	10.02					0	1.18	800 866-7778
Piper Growth & Income Fund A	Growth/Inc	24.49	25.08	19.76	2	3	4	1.34	800 866-7778
Piper Growth & Income Fund Y	Growth/Inc	10.67					0	1.32	800 866-7778
Piper Growth Fund A	Growth	26.84	22.73	16.65	3	3	4	1.26	800 866-7778
Piper Pacific European Growth A	Foreign	−0.12	6.63	8.07	5	3	4	1.72	800 866-7778
Piper Pacific European Growth Y	Foreign	−4.72					0	1.64	800 866-7778
Piper Small Company Growth Fund A	Small Co	26.48	21.06	14.25	4	4	4	1.34	800 866-7778
Polynous Growth Fund	Growth	13.43					4.5	2.73	800 924-3863
Preferred Asset Allocation Fund	AssetAlloc	21.84	20.33	15.92	2	1	0	0.99	800 662-4769
Preferred Growth Fund	Growth	34.14	25.57	21.67	2	4	0	0.84	800 662-4769
Preferred International Fund	Foreign	7.20	14.32	15.09	4	3	0	0.88	800 662-4769
Preferred Small Cap Fund	Small Co	16.99					0	0.90	800 662-4769
Preferred Value Fund	Growth/Inc	26.51	27.82	21.45	1	2	0	0.83	800 662-4769

343

Stock Fund Name	Objective	Annualized Return for			Rank		Max Load	Expense Ratio	Toll-Free Telephone
		1 Year	3 Years	5 Years	Overall	Risk			
Primary Income Fund	Growth/Inc	14.72	17.80	13.16	3	1	0	0.86	800 443-6544
Primary Trend Fund	Flexible	13.06	17.47	13.33	3	3	0	1.21	800 443-6544
Principal Balanced Fund A	Balanced	14.92	16.06	11.96	3	1	4.75	1.33	800 247-4123
Principal Balanced Fund B	Balanced	14.14	15.19		3	1	0	2.14	800 247-4123
Principal Blue Chip Fund A	Growth/Inc	19.56	24.23	18.54	2	3	4.75	1.33	800 247-4123
Principal Blue Chip Fund B	Growth/Inc	18.72	23.21		2	3	0	2.06	800 247-4123
Principal Blue Chip Fund R	Growth/Inc	18.91					0	1.89	800 247-4123
Principal Capital Value Fund A	Growth	25.94	27.09	19.47	1	2	4.75	0.70	800 247-4123
Principal Capital Value Fund B	Growth	24.79	25.92		2	2		1.50	800 247-4123
Principal Growth Fund A	Growth	30.57	24.38	20.77	2	3	4.75	1.03	800 247-4123
Principal Growth Fund B	Growth	30.05	23.65		3	3	0	1.48	800 247-4123
Principal Growth Fund R	Growth	29.75					0	1.69	800 247-4123
Principal International Fund A	Foreign	11.74	18.86	16.18	3	3	4.75	1.39	800 247-4123
Principal International Fund B	Foreign	10.95	17.94		3	3		2.10	800 247-4123
Principal MidCap Fund A	Small Co	18.11	21.41	19.09	3	3	4.75	1.26	800 247-4123
Principal MidCap Fund B	Small Co	17.59	20.68		3	3	0	1.69	800 247-4123
Principal Pres Div Achievers	Growth/Inc	21.46	26.17	18.31	2	3	4.5	1.20	800 826-4600
Principal Pres PSE Tech 100 Index	Technology	21.78					4.5	0.00	800 826-4600
Principal Pres S&P 100 Plus	Growth/Inc	29.38	28.58	21.91	2	3	4.5	0.90	800 826-4600
Principal Pres Select Value	Small Co	17.66	25.16		3	5	4.5	1.00	800 826-4600
Principal Utilities Fund A	Utilities	28.37	19.41	10.35	3	3	4.75	1.00	800 247-4123
Principal Utilities Fund B	Utilities	27.50	18.53		3	3	0	1.90	800 247-4123
Principal Utilities Fund R	Utilities	27.72					0	1.65	800 247-4123
Provident Inv Counsel Growth Fund	Growth	32.61	25.51	18.78	3	4	0	1.25	
Provident Inv Counsel Pinnacle Bal	Balanced	26.29	22.99	16.30	3	3	0	1.05	
Provident Inv Counsel Sm Cap Gr Fd	Small Co	13.50	19.57		4	5	0	0.98	
Prudent Bear Fund	Growth	−19.90					0	2.59	888 778-2327
Prudential Balanced Fund A	Balanced	14.00	14.39	11.38	4	2	5	1.29	800 225-1852
Prudential Balanced Fund B	Balanced	13.28	13.55	10.55	4	2	0	1.94	800 225-1852
Prudential Balanced Fund Z	Balanced	14.42	14.35		3	1	0		800 225-1852
Prudential Emerging Growth A	Small Co	26.36					5	1.21	800 225-1852
Prudential Emerging Growth B	Small Co	25.35					0	1.21	800 225-1852
Prudential Emerging Growth C	Small Co	25.35					0	1.21	800 225-1852
Prudential Emerging Growth Z	Small Co	26.82					0	1.21	800 225-1852
Prudential Equity Fund A	Growth	22.96	22.60	17.79	2	2	5	0.89	800 225-1852
Prudential Equity Fund B	Growth	22.11	21.69	18.11	2	2	0	1.64	800 225-1852
Prudential Equity Fund C	Growth	22.11	21.65		2	2	0	1.64	800 225-1852
Prudential Equity Income A	Income	27.56	24.70	18.42	3	3	5	1.11	800 225-1852
Prudential Equity Income B	Income	26.58	23.79	17.55	3	3	0	1.69	800 225-1852
Prudential Equity Income C	Income	26.59	23.79		3	3	0		800 225-1852
Prudential Europe Growth A	European	39.59	24.53		3	3	5		800 225-1852
Prudential Europe Growth B	European	38.13	23.48		3	3	0		800 225-1852
Prudential Global Genesis A	Global	1.99	8.57	11.49	5	3	5	1.53	800 225-1852
Prudential Global Genesis B	Global	1.24	7.72	10.63	5	3	0	2.48	800 225-1852
Prudential Global Genesis C	Global	1.24	7.73		5	3	0	1.53	800 225-1852
Prudential Global Utility Fund A	Utilities	22.92	19.34	13.76	3	2	5	1.21	800 225-1852
Prudential Global Utility Fund B	Utilities	22.00	18.45	12.77	3	2	0	1.99	800 225-1852
Prudential Instl-Active Balanced	Balanced	15.55	11.73		3	1	0		800 225-1852
Prudential Multi Sector A	Growth	16.80	17.03	15.36	4	3	5	1.29	800 225-1852
Prudential Multi Sector B	Growth	16.13	16.24	12.72	4	3	0	0.94	800 225-1852
Prudential Multi Sector C	Growth	16.13	16.27		4	3	0		800 225-1852
Prudential Natural Resources A	Energy/Res	−16.84	4.70	5.51	5	4	5	2.59	800 225-1852
Prudential Natural Resources B	Energy/Res	−17.48	3.70	4.58	5	4	0	1.48	800 225-1852
Prudential Pacific Growth A	Pacific	−39.48	−11.35	−4.12	5	4	5	1.48	800 225-1852
Prudential Pacific Growth B	Pacific	−39.96	−11.96	−5.08	5	4	0	2.23	800 225-1852
Prudential Pacific Growth C	Pacific	−39.96	−11.96		5	4	0	2.12	800 225-1852
Prudential Small Company Value A	Small Co	22.36	23.79	18.76	3	3	5	1.33	800 225-1852
Prudential Small Company Value B	Small Co	21.41	22.90	17.88	3	3	0	1.96	800 225-1852

344

Stock Fund Name	Objective	Annualized Return for			Rank		Max Load	Expense Ratio	Toll-Free Telephone
		1 Year	3 Years	5 Years	Overall	Risk			
Prudential Small Company Value C	Small Co	21.49	22.93		3	3	0		800 225-1852
Prudential Stock Index Z	Growth	29.43	29.08		1	3	0	0.52	800 225-1852
Prudential Utility Fund A	Utilities	27.40	24.08	14.81	3	2	5	0.58	800 225-1852
Prudential Utility Fund B	Utilities	26.43	23.13	13.98	3	2	0	1.57	800 225-1852
Prudential Utility Fund C	Utilities	26.28	23.07		2	2	0	0.58	800 225-1852
Prudential World Global Fund A	Global	11.91	15.94	16.28	4	3	5	1.71	800 225-1852
Prudential World Global Fund B	Global	11.16	15.17	15.49	4	3	0	2.07	800 225-1852
Prudential World Global Fund C	Global	11.04	15.13		4	3	0	2.09	800 225-1852
Prudential World Intl Stock Series	Foreign	7.96	14.35		4	3	0		800 225-1852
Purisima Total Return Fund	AssetAlloc	22.12					0	1.50	800 841-2858
Putnam Asia Pacific Growth A	Pacific	−31.07	−6.63	1.12	5	4	5.75	0.81	800 225-1581
Putnam Asia Pacific Growth B	Pacific	−31.55	−7.32	0.43	5	4	0	1.18	800 225-1581
Putnam Asia Pacific Growth M	Pacific	−31.40	−7.06		5	4	5	1.06	800 225-1581
Putnam Asset Alloc:Balanced A	Balanced	14.34	18.43		3	2	5.75	0.63	800 225-1581
Putnam Asset Alloc:Balanced B	Balanced	13.59	17.60		3	2	0	1.01	800 225-1581
Putnam Asset Alloc:Balanced C	Balanced	13.48	16.37		3	2	0	1.01	800 225-1581
Putnam Asset Alloc:Balanced M	Balanced	13.80	14.92		4	2	3.5	0.88	800 225-1581
Putnam Asset Alloc:Balanced Y	Balanced	14.29	17.60		3	2	0	1.22	800 225-1581
Putnam Asset Alloc:Conservative A	AssetAlloc	10.96	12.95		3	1	5.75	0.69	800 225-1581
Putnam Asset Alloc:Conservative B	AssetAlloc	9.85	12.04		3	1	0	1.06	800 225-1581
Putnam Asset Alloc:Conservative C	AssetAlloc	10.13	12.12		3	1	0	1.06	800 225-1581
Putnam Asset Alloc:Conservative M	AssetAlloc	10.37	11.17		3	1	3.5	0.94	800 225-1581
Putnam Asset Alloc:Conservative Y	AssetAlloc	10.44	11.14		3	1	0	1.22	800 225-1581
Putnam Asset Alloc:Growth A	AssetAlloc	16.56	20.46		2	2	5.75	0.70	800 225-1581
Putnam Asset Alloc:Growth B	AssetAlloc	15.74	19.65		3	2	0	1.08	800 225-1581
Putnam Asset Alloc:Growth C	AssetAlloc	15.70	19.59		3	2	0	1.08	800 225-1581
Putnam Asset Alloc:Growth M	AssetAlloc	16.06	19.91		3	2	3.5	0.95	800 225-1581
Putnam Asset Alloc:Growth Y	AssetAlloc	16.94	20.91		2	2	0	1.21	800 225-1581
Putnam Balanced Retirement A	Balanced	15.23	16.99	13.57	3	1	5.75	1.15	800 225-1581
Putnam Balanced Retirement B	Balanced	14.53	16.11		3	1	0	0.97	800 225-1581
Putnam Balanced Retirement M	Balanced	14.67	16.45		3	1	3.5	0.84	800 225-1581
Putnam Capital Appreciation A	Growth	22.96	28.64		2	2	5.75	0.53	800 225-1581
Putnam Capital Appreciation B	Growth	22.04	27.99		2	2	0	1.95	800 225-1581
Putnam Capital Appreciation M	Growth	22.40					3.5	1.70	800 225-1581
Putnam Conv Income-Growth Trust A	Converts	14.86	18.07	14.38	3	1	5.75	1.03	800 225-1581
Putnam Conv Income-Growth Trust B	Converts	14.00	17.15		3	1	0	0.89	800 225-1581
Putnam Conv Income-Growth Trust M	Converts	14.27	17.43		3	1	3.5	0.77	800 225-1581
Putnam Diversified Equity Tr A	Global	23.44	23.40		2	3	5.75	1.43	800 225-1581
Putnam Diversified Equity Tr B	Global	22.71	22.70		1	3	0	2.02	800 225-1581
Putnam Diversified Equity Tr M	Global	22.99					3.5	1.23	800 225-1581
Putnam Emerging Markets A	Foreign	−32.58					5.25	1.25	800 225-1581
Putnam Emerging Markets B	Foreign	−33.13					0	1.12	800 225-1581
Putnam Emerging Markets M	Foreign	−33.69					3.5	1.87	800 225-1581
Putnam Equity Income A	Income	19.86	24.33	19.45	1	2	5.75	1.06	800 225-1581
Putnam Equity Income B	Income	18.99	23.40		2	2	0	1.45	800 225-1581
Putnam Equity Income M	Income	19.30	23.74		2	2	3.5	1.45	800 225-1581
Putnam Europe Growth Fund A	European	35.22	27.00	24.19	2	3	5.75	1.45	800 225-1581
Putnam Europe Growth Fund B	European	34.26	26.04		2	3	0	2.20	800 225-1581
Putnam Europe Growth Fund M	European	34.56	26.38		2	3	3.5	2.02	800 225-1581
Putnam Fund for Growth & Income M	Growth/Inc	17.13	19.01		3	3	3.5	0.68	800 225-1581
Putnam Gl Natural Resources Fund A	Energy/Res	2.23	14.91	8.68	4	3	5.75	1.23	800 225-1581
Putnam Gl Natural Resources Fund B	Energy/Res	0.57	11.42		4	3	0	0.99	800 225-1581
Putnam Gl Natural Resources Fund M	Energy/Res	1.68					3.5	1.73	800 225-1581
Putnam Global Growth A	Global	18.26	20.50	16.38	3	3	5.75	1.24	800 225-1581
Putnam Global Growth B	Global	17.35	19.57	15.50	3	3	0	1.01	800 225-1581
Putnam Global Growth M	Global	17.65	19.87		3	3	3.5	0.88	800 225-1581
Putnam Growth & Income A	Growth/Inc	17.75	24.09	19.09	2	2	5.75	0.86	800 225-1581
Putnam Growth & Income B	Growth/Inc	16.83	23.15	18.34	2	2	0	0.81	800 225-1581

Stock Fund Name	Objective	Annualized Return for			Rank		Max Load	Expense Ratio	Toll-Free Telephone
		1 Year	3 Years	5 Years	Overall	Risk			
Putnam Growth & Income II A	Growth/Inc	16.18	23.34		2	2	5.75	0.52	800 225-1581
Putnam Growth & Income II B	Growth/Inc	15.30	22.42		3	2	0	0.89	800 225-1581
Putnam Growth & Income II M	Growth/Inc	15.52	22.73		3	2	3.5	0.77	800 225-1581
Putnam Growth Opportunities A	Growth	38.01					5.75	1.05	800 225-1581
Putnam Health Sciences Trust A	Health	26.89	30.84	25.69	2	3	5.75	1.08	800 225-1581
Putnam Health Sciences Trust B	Health	25.93	28.62	24.03	2	3	0	1.83	800 225-1581
Putnam International Growth Fund A	Foreign	20.80	22.04	18.56	3	3	5.75	1.42	800 225-1581
Putnam International Growth Fund B	Foreign	19.99	21.19		3	3	0	2.34	800 225-1581
Putnam International Growth Fund M	Foreign	20.18	21.11		3	3	3.5	2.09	800 225-1581
Putnam International Growth Fund Y	Foreign	21.08					0	1.74	800 225-1581
Putnam International Voyager A	Foreign	21.13					5.75	1.03	800 225-1581
Putnam International Voyager B	Foreign	20.12					0	0.96	800 225-1581
Putnam International Voyager M	Foreign	20.55					3.5	0.87	800 225-1581
Putnam Intl New Opportunities A	Foreign	3.11	13.69		4	4	5.75	0.89	800 225-1581
Putnam Intl New Opportunities B	Foreign	2.30					0	1.26	800 225-1581
Putnam Intl New Opportunities M	Foreign	2.60					3.5	1.14	800 225-1581
Putnam Investors Fund A	Growth	38.87	31.63	23.44	2	3	5.75	1.00	800 225-1581
Putnam Investors Fund B	Growth	37.83	30.64	22.45	2	3	0	1.75	800 225-1581
Putnam Investors Fund M	Growth	38.24	30.96		1	3	3.5	1.50	800 225-1581
Putnam New Opportunities A	Agg Growth	32.75	26.22	24.03	3	4	5.75	1.02	800 225-1581
Putnam New Opportunities B	Agg Growth	31.75	25.29	23.10	3	4	0	1.81	800 225-1581
Putnam New Opportunities M	Agg Growth	32.09	25.60		3	4	3.5	1.56	800 225-1581
Putnam New Value Fund A	Growth	9.43	20.85		2	3	5.75	1.22	800 225-1581
Putnam New Value Fund B	Growth	8.46					0	1.97	800 225-1581
Putnam New Value Fund M	Growth	8.70					3.5	1.72	800 225-1581
Putnam OTC & Emerging Growth A	Small Co	25.48	21.56	20.78	3	5	5.75	1.16	800 225-1581
Putnam OTC & Emerging Growth B	Small Co	24.62	20.73	19.42	3	5	0	1.91	800 225-1581
Putnam OTC & Emerging Growth M	Small Co	24.78	20.92		4	5	3.5	1.66	800 225-1581
Putnam Preferred Income	Income	10.79	9.95	7.87	3	1	3.25	0.85	800 225-1581
Putnam Utilities Growth & Income A	Utilities	23.56	20.58	13.80	3	2	5.75	1.05	800 225-1581
Putnam Utilities Growth & Income B	Utilities	22.60	17.10	11.45	3	2	0	0.92	800 225-1581
Putnam Utilities Growth & Income M	Utilities	29.59	16.79		3	2	3.5	0.78	800 225-1581
Putnam Vista Fund A	Growth	30.38	27.36	20.93	3	4	5.75	1.04	800 225-1581
Putnam Vista Fund B	Growth	29.43	26.41	20.02	3	4	0	0.90	800 225-1581
Putnam Vista Fund M	Growth	29.70	26.84		3	4	3.5	0.77	800 225-1581
Putnam Voyager Fund A	Agg Growth	32.14	25.71	21.79	2	4	5.75	0.50	800 225-1581
Putnam Voyager Fund B	Agg Growth	31.15	24.78	20.87	3	4	0	1.77	800 225-1581
Putnam Voyager Fund II A	Agg Growth	32.22	24.32	22.48	3	4	5.75	1.97	800 225-1581
Putnam Voyager Fund II B	Agg Growth	31.20					0	0.99	800 225-1581
Putnam Voyager Fund II M	Agg Growth	31.57					3.5	0.87	800 225-1581
Putnam Voyager Fund M	Agg Growth	31.48	25.07		3	4	3.5	1.52	800 225-1581
Putnam Voyager Fund Y	Agg Growth	32.48	26.03		2	4	0	0.77	800 225-1581
Quadra Value Equity	Growth	17.49					0	1.00	800-595-9291
Quaker Aggressive Growth Fund	Agg Growth	17.01					0	1.35	800 355-3553
Quaker Core Equity Fund	Growth	24.20					0	1.35	800 355-3553
Quaker Enhanced Stock Market Fund	Growth	25.42					0	1.00	800 355-3553
Quaker Small Cap Value Fund	Small Co	20.97					0	1.31	800 355-3553
Quantitative Fgn Frontier Fd Instl	Foreign	−32.16					0	2.01	800 331-1244
Quantitative Fgn Frontier Fd Ord	Foreign	−32.42	−5.72		4	4	0	2.68	800 331-1244
Quantitative Gr & Inc Instl	Growth/Inc	31.30	28.31	21.14	2	4	0	1.24	800 331-1244
Quantitative Gr & Inc Ord Shs	Growth/Inc	29.55	27.33	20.43	2	3	0	1.71	800 331-1244
Quantitative Intl Equity Instl	Foreign	1.57					0	1.69	800 331-1244
Quantitative Intl Equity Ord	Foreign	1.09	6.61	8.41	5	3	0	2.20	800 331-1244
Quantitative Numeric II Instl	Agg Growth	27.54	23.34		3	4	0	1.44	800 331-1244
Quantitative Numeric II Ord	Agg Growth	27.34					0	1.19	800 331-1244
Quantitative Small Cap Fund Ord	Agg Growth	10.57	17.59	17.04	4	4	0	1.90	800 331-1244
Quantitative Small Cap Fund Shs	Agg Growth	11.07	18.31	17.71	4	4	0	1.47	800 331-1244
Rainbow Fund	Growth/Inc	−2.84	12.43	8.91	4	3	0	0.96	

346

Stock Fund Name	Objective	Annualized Return for			Rank		Max Load	Expense Ratio	Toll-Free Telephone
		1 Year	3 Years	5 Years	Overall	Risk			
Rainier Balanced Portfolio	Balanced	21.58	20.67		2	1	0	1.19	800 248-6314
Rainier Core Equity	Growth	28.70	30.12		1	3	0	1.15	800 248-6314
Rainier Small/Mid Cap Equity	Small Co	24.14	27.11		1	3	0	1.15	800 248-6314
Rea-Graham Balanced Fund	Balanced	8.84	8.31	5.53	3	1	4.75	2.89	800 433-1998
Regional Opportunity Fund B	Growth	29.98					0	2.66	800 543-8721
Regions Growth Fund A	Growth/Inc	30.18	28.20		2	3	4.75	1.03	800 433-2829
Reich & Tang Equity Fund	Growth	7.29	15.11	14.20	4	3	0	1.21	800 221-3079
Republic Bank Equity Retail A	Growth	28.92					0		800 782-8183
Republic Bank Opportunity Retail A	Agg Growth	22.09					0	1.55	800 782-8183
Republic Bank Overseas Eq Retail A	Foreign	3.85					0		800 782-8183
Reserve Blue Chip Growth Fund A	Growth	23.02	17.29		3	3	4.5	1.75	800 637-1700
Reserve Convertible Securities A	Converts	−1.66					4.5	0.52	800 637-1700
Reserve Informed Investors Growth A	Growth	27.54	8.78		5	5	4.5	1.75	800 637-1700
Reserve International Equity Fund A	Foreign	2.30					4.5	2.00	800 637-1700
Reserve Large-Cap Value Fund A	Growth	27.60					4.5	1.75	800 637-1700
Reserve Mid-Cap Growth Fund A	Growth	5.32	8.69		5	4	4.5	1.75	800 637-1700
Reserve Small Cap Growth A	Small Co	13.07	11.83		5	5	4.5	2.00	800 637-1700
Reynolds Blue Chip Growth Fund	Growth	35.19	32.45	23.76	2	4	0	1.40	800 773-9665
Reynolds Opportunity Fund	Agg Growth	29.88	23.54	19.70	3	4	0	1.60	800 773-9665
Rightime Blue Chip Fund	Growth/Inc	19.18	14.48	12.54	3	2	4.75	2.09	800 242-1421
Rightime Fund	Flexible	14.29	9.39	9.62	3	2	0	2.45	800 242-1421
Rightime Mid Cap Fund	Growth	21.19	12.94	10.86	3	2	4.75	2.15	800 242-1421
Rightime Social Awareness Fund	Growth/Inc	22.60	17.35	12.34	3	2	4.75	2.35	800 242-1421
RIMCO Monument Small Cap Equity	Small Co	32.05	27.22		3	4	5.75	1.07	800 934-3883
RIMCO Monument Stock Fund	Growth/Inc	23.60	26.30		1	3	5.75	0.89	800 934-3883
Riverfront Balanced Fund A	Balanced	21.10	14.75		3	1	4.5	1.70	800 424-2295
Riverfront Balanced Fund B	Balanced	20.12	14.17		3	1	0	2.54	800 424-2295
Riverfront Income Equity A	Income	16.24	21.92	18.71	1	2	4.5	1.72	800 424-2295
Riverfront Income Equity B	Income	15.34	21.34		2	2	0	2.48	800 424-2295
Riverfront Stock Appreciation A	Growth	20.80	17.19	10.80	4	4	4.5	2.11	800 424-2295
Riverfront Stock Appreciation B	Growth	19.68	15.59	9.75	4	4	0	2.64	800 424-2295
Robertson Stephens Contrarian Fund	Global	−32.99	−5.23	1.45	5	4	0	2.48	800 766-3863
Robertson Stephens Dev Countries	Foreign	−37.32	−11.24		5	4	0	1.84	800 766-3863
Robertson Stephens Diversified Gr	Growth	29.11					0	2.28	800 766-3863
Robertson Stephens Emerging Growth	Small Co	35.41	26.24	22.64	3	5	0	1.50	800 766-3863
Robertson Stephens Gl Low Price	Global	−21.76					0	1.94	800 766-3863
Robertson Stephens Global Nat Res	Energy/Res	−19.03					0	1.94	800 766-3863
Robertson Stephens Global Value	Global	14.31					0		800 766-3863
Robertson Stephens Growth and Inc	Growth/Inc	20.91					0	1.71	800 766-3863
Robertson Stephens Info Age Fund	Technology	22.63					0	2.03	800 766-3863
Robertson Stephens Micro Cap Growth	Small Co	22.58					0	3.08	800 766-3863
Robertson Stephens Partners Fund	Growth	6.00					0	1.93	800 766-3863
Robertson Stephens Value + Growth	Growth	18.32	16.03	24.74	4	5	0	1.49	800 766-3863
Rockwood Growth Fund	Growth	−9.85	13.09	9.22	4	5	0	2.81	800 847-4200
Rodney Square Large Cap Gr Equity	Growth	23.17	25.45	20.42	3	4	4	1.40	800 336-9970
Royce Giftshares	Small Co	27.14					0	1.50	800 221-4268
Royce Global Services	Global	12.95	13.37		4	2	0	1.69	800 221-4268
Royce Low Priced Stock	Small Co	28.32	20.79		3	3	0	2.44	800 221-4268
Royce Micro Cap	Small Co	20.51	17.88	16.32	3	3	0	1.49	800 221-4268
Royce PMF2 Fund	Small Co	17.71					0	1.75	800 221-4268
Royce Premier Fund	Small Co	12.11	16.49	15.12	3	2	0	1.25	800 221-4268
Royce REvest Growth and Income	Growth/Inc	14.26	17.29		4	3	0	1.30	800 221-4268
Royce Total Return Fund	Growth/Inc	17.77	22.75		2	1	0	1.86	800 221-4268
RSI Retirement Emerg Growth Equity	Small Co	9.43	19.37	19.96	4	5	0	1.85	800 368-3527
RSI Retirement International Equity	Foreign	3.17	13.25	10.73	4	3	0	1.00	800 368-3527
RSI Retirement Value Equity	Growth	25.18	28.79	20.42	1	3	0	1.26	800 368-3527
Rushmore American Gas Index Fund	Other	22.92	20.81	12.05	3	2	0	0.85	800 343-3355
RYDEX Nova Fund	Agg Growth	37.70	38.18		2	4	0	1.11	800 820-0888

Stock Fund Name	Objective	Annualized Return for			Rank		Max Load	Expense Ratio	Toll-Free Telephone
		1 Year	3 Years	5 Years	Overall	Risk			
RYDEX OTC Fund	Agg Growth	40.89	36.79		3	5	0	1.13	800 820-0888
RYDEX Series Precious Metals Tr	Gold	−28.00	−16.73		5	5	0	1.45	800 820-0888
RYDEX Ursa Fund	Growth	−18.75	−17.62		5	3	0	1.34	800 820-0888
SAFECO Advisor Balanced Fund A	Balanced	12.74					0.75	1.52	800 426-6730
SAFECO Advisor Balanced Fund B	Balanced	11.84					0	2.28	800 426-6730
SAFECO Advisor Equity Fund A	Growth/Inc	21.46					4.5	1.24	800 426-6730
SAFECO Advisor Equity Fund B	Growth/Inc	20.17					0	1.81	800 426-6730
SAFECO Advisor Growth Fund A	Growth	44.68					4.5	1.06	800 426-6730
SAFECO Advisor Growth Fund B	Growth	43.49					0	1.88	800 426-6730
SAFECO Advisor Income Fund A	Income	24.36					4.5	1.11	800 426-6730
SAFECO Advisor Income Fund B	Income	24.06					0	1.87	800 426-6730
SAFECO Advisor Intl Stock Fund A	Foreign	11.14					4.5	1.87	800 426-6730
SAFECO Advisor Intl Stock Fund B	Foreign	10.15					0	2.64	800 426-6730
SAFECO Advisor Northwest Fund A	Growth	16.71					4.5	1.40	800 426-6730
SAFECO Advisor Northwest Fund B	Growth	16.14					0	2.18	800 426-6730
SAFECO Advisor Small Company A	Small Co	30.92					0.85	1.52	800 426-6730
SAFECO Advisor US Value Fund A	Growth/Inc	9.02					0.75	1.48	800 426-6730
SAFECO Advisor US Value Fund B	Growth/Inc	8.12					0	2.29	800 426-6730
SAFECO Balanced Fund	Balanced	12.31					0	1.23	800 426-6730
SAFECO Equity Fund	Growth/Inc	21.49	25.35	22.47	2	3	0	0.73	800 426-6730
SAFECO Growth Fund	Growth	44.63	33.35	26.03	2	4	0	0.85	800 426-6730
SAFECO Income Fund	Income	24.67	25.46	18.66	1	2	0	0.85	800 426-6730
SAFECO International Stock Fund	Foreign	8.99					0	1.63	800 426-6730
SAFECO Northwest Fund	Growth	17.30	18.94	15.00	3	3	0	1.09	800 426-6730
SAFECO Small Company Stock Fund	Small Co	31.30					0	1.33	800 426-6730
SAFECO US Value Fund	Growth/Inc	13.80					0	1.19	800 426-6730
Salomon Brothers Asia Growth Fund A	Pacific	−52.19					4.75	1.24	800 725-6666
Salomon Brothers Asia Growth Fund B	Pacific	−52.57					0	1.99	800 725-6666
Salomon Brothers Asia Growth Fund C	Pacific	−51.30					0	1.99	800 725-6666
Salomon Brothers Asia Growth Fund O	Pacific	−50.73					0	0.99	800 725-6666
Salomon Brothers Capital Fund A	Agg Growth	28.59					4.75	1.46	800 725-6666
Salomon Brothers Capital Fund B	Agg Growth	28.51					0	2.20	800 725-6666
Salomon Brothers Capital Fund C	Agg Growth	28.54					0	2.21	800 725-6666
Salomon Brothers Capital Fund O	Agg Growth	27.80	30.87	20.10	1	3	0	0.62	800 725-6666
Salomon Brothers Investor Fund A	Growth/Inc	23.06	28.51		1	4	4.75	0.95	800 725-6666
Salomon Brothers Investor Fund B	Growth/Inc	22.22	26.38		1	3	0	1.70	800 725-6666
Salomon Brothers Investor Fund C	Growth/Inc	22.21	23.88		1	3	0	1.70	800 725-6666
Salomon Brothers Investor Fund O	Growth/Inc	18.57	29.09	21.34	1	3	0	0.69	800 725-6666
Salomon Brothers Opportunity	Growth	21.72	25.21	19.58	2	3	0	1.16	800 725-6666
Salomon Brothers Total Return A	Income	15.24					4.75	0.77	800 725-6666
Salomon Brothers Total Return B	Income	14.31					0	1.52	800 725-6666
Salomon Brothers Total Return C	Income	14.46					0	1.52	800 725-6666
Salomon Brothers Total Return O	Income	15.45					0	0.52	800 725-6666
Sandhill Portfolio Manager Fund	AssetAlloc	14.01	16.37		3	2	0	1.85	800 527-9500
Santa Barbara Bender Growth Fund C	Growth	34.58					0	3.50	
Santa Barbara Bender Growth Fund Y	Growth	35.57					0	2.75	
Schroder Emerging Markets	Foreign	−35.94	−6.27		5	4	0	1.79	800 344-8332
Schroder International Fund	Foreign	5.06	12.42	13.32	4	3	0	0.99	800 344-8332
Schroder International Smaller Cos	Foreign	9.48					0	1.90	800 344-8332
Schroder Large Cap Equity	Growth	28.51	25.88		3	3	0	1.23	800 344-8332
Schroder Small Cap Value Inv	Small Co	30.69	29.22		4	4	0		800 344-8332
Schroder US Equity Fund	Growth	23.69	24.25	17.93	3	3	0	1.50	800 344-8332
Schroder US Smaller Co's Fund	Small Co	15.11	26.84		3	4	0	1.49	800 344-8332
Schwab 1000 Fund	Growth/Inc	30.14	28.98	21.80	1	3	0	0.49	800 266-5623
Schwab Analytics Fund	Growth	31.45					0	0.75	800 266-5623
Schwab Asset Dir Balanced Growth	AssetAlloc	16.51					0	0.89	800 266-5623
Schwab Asset Dir Conservative Gr	AssetAlloc	13.44					0	0.89	800 266-5623
Schwab Asset Dir High Growth	AssetAlloc	19.11					0	0.89	800 266-5623

Stock Fund Name	Objective	Annualized Return for			Rank		Max Load	Expense Ratio	Toll-Free Telephone
		1 Year	3 Years	5 Years	Overall	Risk			
Schwab International Index Fund	Foreign	8.53	13.14		4	3	0	1.15	800 266-5623
Schwab OneSource-Balanced Alloc	Balanced	15.66					0	0.50	800 266-5623
Schwab OneSource-Growth Alloc	Growth	17.66					0	0.50	800 266-5623
Schwab OneSource-Intl Alloc	Foreign	11.46					0	0.50	800 266-5623
Schwab S & P 500 Fund	Growth/Inc	29.64					0	0.49	800 266-5623
Schwab Small Cap Index Fund	Small Co	17.58	19.14		4	4	0	0.55	800 266-5623
Schwartz Value	Growth	12.77	16.16	12.86	4	2	0	1.86	800 543-8721
Scout Regional Fund	Flexible	14.42	15.10		3	2	0	0.86	800 422-2766
Scout Stock Fund	Growth/Inc	15.41	14.40	13.09	3	2	0	0.86	800 422-2766
Scout Worldwide Fund	Foreign	20.24	20.36		3	2	0	0.85	800 422-2766
Scudder 21st Century Growth Fund	Growth	17.44					0	1.75	800 225-2470
Scudder Balanced Fund	Balanced	21.62	19.16	14.93	3	2	0	1.02	800 225-2470
Scudder Classic Growth Fund	Growth	23.99					0	1.25	800 225-2470
Scudder Development Fund	Small Co	17.86	14.87	13.92	4	5	0	1.40	800 225-2470
Scudder Emerging Mkts Growth	Foreign	−20.93					0	2.00	800 225-2470
Scudder Global Discovery	Global	18.73	19.41	13.18	3	3	0	1.63	800 225-2470
Scudder Global Fund	Global	14.93	18.75	15.61	3	2	0	1.33	800 225-2470
Scudder Gold Fund	Gold	−35.45	−10.07	−3.64	5	5	0	1.60	800 225-2470
Scudder Greater Europe Growth Fd	European	51.16	33.46		1	3		1.81	800 225-2470
Scudder Growth & Income Fund	Growth/Inc	20.66	25.78	20.53	1	2	0	0.76	800 225-2470
Scudder International Fund	Foreign	14.56	16.68	14.31	4	3	0	1.17	800 225-2470
Scudder Intl Growth & Income	Growth/Inc	15.49					0	2.01	800 225-2470
Scudder Large Company Growth Fund	Growth	30.90	28.03	21.14	2	4	0	1.21	800 225-2470
Scudder Large Company Value	Growth	22.77	25.85	18.43	2	3	0	0.93	800 225-2470
Scudder Latin America Fund	Foreign	−17.54	13.92	11.53	4	5	0	1.89	800 225-2470
Scudder Micro Cap Fund	Small Co	22.75					0	1.75	800 225-2470
Scudder Pacific Opportunities Fund	Pacific	−51.72	−18.96	−8.45	5	5	0	1.94	800 225-2470
Scudder Pathway Series:Balanced	Balanced	11.52					0	0.00	800 225-2470
Scudder Pathway Series:Conservative	Income	11.07					0	0.00	800 225-2470
Scudder Pathway Series:Growth Port	Growth	12.86					0	0.00	800 225-2470
Scudder Pathway Series:Intl Port	Foreign	6.55					0	0.00	800 225-2470
Scudder Small Company Value Fund	Small Co	23.14					0	1.50	800 225-2470
Scudder Value Fund	Growth	26.76	27.24	20.55	1	3	0	1.24	800 225-2470
Second Fiduciary Exchange Fund	Growth/Inc	29.44	28.93	21.22	1	3	0	0.72	800 225-6265
Security Capital Real Estate Fund I	Real Est	11.80					0	0.94	888 732-8748
Security Capital Real Estate Fund R	Real Est	11.78					0	0.95	888 732-8748
Security Equity Fund A	Growth	29.65	29.05	22.42	1	3	5.75	1.03	800 888-2461
Security Equity Fund B	Growth	28.42	28.02		1	3		2.04	800 888-2461
Security Equity Global A	Global	6.98	15.60		4	3	5.75	2.00	800 888-2461
Security Equity Global B	Global	5.83	14.39		4	3	0	3.00	800 888-2461
Security Growth & Income A	Growth/Inc	20.93	21.79	14.59	3	3	5.75	2.26	800 888-2461
Security Growth & Income B	Growth/Inc	19.91	19.27		3	3	0	2.26	800 888-2461
Security Social Awareness A	Growth	27.83					5.75	1.42	800 888-2461
Security Social Awareness B	Growth	26.36					0	2.17	800 888-2461
Security Ultra A	Agg Growth	21.20	17.59	12.90	4	4	5.75	1.23	800 888-2461
Security Ultra B	Agg Growth	19.96	16.38		4	4		2.80	800 888-2461
Security Value Fund A	Growth	33.98					5.75		800 888-2461
Security Value Fund B	Growth	32.69					0		800 888-2461
Sefton Equity Value Fund	Growth	9.83	22.95		3	2	0	1.56	800-524-2776
SEI Emerging Markets Equity	Foreign	−36.68	−7.94		5	4	0	2.55	800 342-5734
SEI Instl Equity Income	Income	20.94	24.60	18.77	2	2	0	0.90	800 342-5734
SEI Instl Large Cap Value A	Growth/Inc	27.71	28.64	19.62	1	3	0	0.85	800 342-5734
SEI Instl Mgd Balanced	Balanced	20.55	19.18	12.82	3	1	0	0.75	800 342-5734
SEI Instl Mgd Capital Appreciation	Growth	28.99	28.41	19.12	2	3	0	0.84	800 342-5734
SEI Instl Mgd Small Cap A	Small Co	14.91	19.07	17.51	4	5	0	1.11	800 342-5734
SEI Instl Mgd Small Cap D	Small Co	14.52	18.65		4	5	5	0.86	800 342-5734
SEI Instl Mgd Tr Large Cap Growth A	Growth	36.13	31.75		2	4	0	0.27	800 342-5734
SEI Instl Mid-Cap Portfolio A	Agg Growth	27.10	25.34		3	3	0	1.00	800 342-5734

349

Stock Fund Name	Objective	Annualized Return for			Rank		Max Load	Expense Ratio	Toll-Free Telephone
		1 Year	3 Years	5 Years	Overall	Risk			
SEI International Equity Fund A	Foreign	6.07	11.90	8.67	4	3	0	1.25	800 342-5734
SEI International Equity Fund D	Foreign	3.52	10.68		4	3	5	1.65	800 342-5734
SEI S&P 500 Index A	Growth/Inc	29.56					0	1.84	800 342-5734
SEI S&P 500 Index E	Growth/Inc	29.78	29.94	22.76	1	3	0	0.54	800 342-5734
SEI Small Cap Value A	Small Co	20.84	24.43		2	3	0	0.45	800 342-5734
Selected American Shares	Growth/Inc	27.40	31.36	22.71	2	3	0	0.96	800 279-0279
Selected Special Shares	Small Co	36.32	23.83	18.95	3	4	0	1.28	800 279-0279
Seligman Capital Fund A	Agg Growth	27.35	24.72	16.86	3	4	4.75	1.05	800 221-2783
Seligman Capital Fund B	Agg Growth	26.26					0	1.82	800 221-2783
Seligman Capital Fund D	Agg Growth	26.33	23.77	15.66	3	4	0	1.82	800 221-2783
Seligman Comm & Info A	Technology	19.13	13.83	28.47	4	5	4.75	1.53	800 221-2783
Seligman Comm & Info B	Technology	18.11					0	2.30	800 221-2783
Seligman Comm & Info D	Technology	18.13	12.94	27.32	4	5	0	2.30	800 221-2783
Seligman Common Stock Fund A	Growth/Inc	17.29	20.44	16.37	3	2	4.75	1.13	800 221-2783
Seligman Common Stock Fund B	Growth/Inc	16.39					0	1.90	800 221-2783
Seligman Common Stock Fund D	Growth/Inc	16.46	19.52	15.30	3	2	0	1.90	800 221-2783
Seligman Frontier Fund A	Small Co	15.58	16.93	19.08	4	4	4.75	1.52	800 221-2783
Seligman Frontier Fund B	Small Co	14.67					0	2.33	800 221-2783
Seligman Frontier Fund D	Small Co	14.66	16.04	17.94	4	4	0	2.33	800 221-2783
Seligman Growth Fund A	Growth	26.23	25.44	18.59	3	3	4.75	1.18	800 221-2783
Seligman Growth Fund B	Growth	25.44					0	1.94	800 221-2783
Seligman Growth Fund D	Growth	25.44	24.32	17.03	3	4	0	1.94	800 221-2783
Seligman Henderson Emrg Mkts Gr A	Foreign	−30.37					4.75	2.22	800 221-2783
Seligman Henderson Emrg Mkts Gr B	Foreign	−30.94					0	3.80	800 221-2783
Seligman Henderson Emrg Mkts Gr D	Foreign	−30.94					0	3.80	800 221-2783
Seligman Henderson Gl Gr Opp A	Global	17.15					4.25	1.91	800 221-2783
Seligman Henderson Gl Gr Opp B	Global	16.28					0	2.53	800 221-2783
Seligman Henderson Gl Gr Opp D	Global	15.75					0	2.67	800 221-2783
Seligman Henderson Gl Smaller Cos A	Global	10.49	17.71	18.32	3	3	4.75	1.67	800 221-2783
Seligman Henderson Gl Smaller Cos B	Global	9.62					0	2.54	800 221-2783
Seligman Henderson Gl Smaller Cos D	Global	9.68	16.53	17.40	3	3	0	2.51	800 221-2783
Seligman Henderson Gl Technology A	Technology	14.48	16.21		4	5	4.75	1.67	800 221-2783
Seligman Henderson Gl Technology B	Technology	13.55					0	2.51	800 221-2783
Seligman Henderson Gl Technology D	Technology	13.39	15.04		4	5	0	2.52	800 221-2783
Seligman Henderson Intl Fund A	Foreign	10.73	14.58	12.69	4	3	4.75	1.78	800 221-2783
Seligman Henderson Intl Fund B	Foreign	9.71					0	0.00	800 221-2783
Seligman Henderson Intl Fund D	Foreign	9.71	13.69		4	3	0	0.00	800 221-2783
Seligman Income A	Flexible	13.37	11.76	9.66	3	1	4.75	1.14	800 221-2783
Seligman Income B	Flexible	12.56					0	1.90	800 221-2783
Seligman Income D	Flexible	12.49	10.89	8.79	3	1	0	1.90	800 221-2783
Seligman Large Cap Value A	Growth	29.47					4.75		800 221-2783
Seligman Large Cap Value B	Growth	28.42					0		800 221-2783
Seligman Large Cap Value D	Growth	28.54					0		800 221-2783
Seligman Small Cap Value A	Small Co	7.30					4.75		800 221-2783
Seligman Small Cap Value B	Small Co	6.48					0		800 221-2783
Seligman Small Cap Value D	Small Co	6.48					0		800 221-2783
Seneca Growth Fund	Growth	31.75					0	2.25	800 990-9331
Seneca Growth Fund Instl	Objective	32.75					0	1.30	800 990-9331
Seneca Mid-Cap EDGE Fund	Small Co	36.12					0	2.05	800 990-9331
Seneca Mid-Cap EDGE Instl	Small Co	36.97					0	1.34	800 990-9331
Seneca Real Estate Securities Fund	Real Est	1.95					0	2.54	800 990-9331
Seneca Real Estate Securities Instl	Real Est	3.12					0	1.79	800 990-9331
Sentinel Balanced Fund A	Balanced	17.19	17.28	12.80	3	1	5	1.16	800 282-3863
Sentinel Balanced Fund B	Balanced	16.26					4	0.99	800 282-3863
Sentinel Common Stock Fund A	Growth/Inc	21.05	25.28	18.88	2	2	5	1.04	800 282-3863
Sentinel Common Stock Fund B	Growth/Inc	20.11					4	2.35	800 282-3863
Sentinel Growth Fund A	Growth	21.32	22.66	15.38	3	3	5	0.67	800 282-3863
Sentinel Small Company A	Small Co	16.21	18.51	14.18	3	3	5	1.34	800 282-3863

350

Stock Fund Name	Objective	Annualized Return for			Rank		Max Load	Expense Ratio	Toll-Free Telephone
		1 Year	3 Years	5 Years	Overall	Risk			
Sentinel Small Company B	Small Co	15.19					4	2.53	800 282-3863
Sentinel World Fund A	Foreign	9.38	14.99	13.91	4	3	5	1.29	800 282-3863
Sentinel World Fund B	Foreign	11.33					4	2.16	800 282-3863
Sentry Fund	Growth	20.14	22.06	16.76	3	3	0	0.83	800 533-7827
Sequoia	Growth	48.23	39.55	27.11	1	3	0	1.00	800 686-6884
Sextant Growth Fund	Growth	5.67	12.73	9.62	5	4	0	0.34	800 728-8762
Shelby Fund	Growth	−8.87	6.20		4	5	0	1.13	800 774-3529
SIFE Trust Fund	Financial	32.49	32.89	24.36	2	3	5	1.25	800 231-0356
SIFE Trust Fund II A	Financial	31.94					5	1.50	800 231-0356
SIFE Trust Fund II B	Financial	24.89					0	2.22	800 231-0356
SIFE Trust Fund II C	Financial	25.10					0	2.25	800 231-0356
Sit Balanced	Balanced	18.35	19.07		3	2		1.00	800 332-5580
Sit Dev Markets Growth Fund	Foreign	−30.52	−1.21		5	4	0	2.00	800 332-5580
Sit International Growth Fund	Foreign	7.50	11.51	13.37	4	3	0	1.50	800 332-5580
Sit Large Cap Growth	Growth/Inc	35.35	30.64	22.86	2	3	0	1.00	800 332-5580
Sit Mid Cap Growth	Growth	22.19	23.97	18.46	3	4	0	0.92	800 332-5580
Sit Small Cap Growth Fund	Small Co	11.70	18.14		4	5		1.50	800 332-5580
Skyline Small Cap Value Plus	Small Co	17.50	24.28	17.23	3	3	0	1.51	800 458-5222
Skyline Special Equities	Small Co	16.62	25.78	18.71	2	3	0	1.49	800 458-5222
SMALLCAP World Fund	Global	9.24	16.35	15.42	4	3	5.75	1.07	800 421-0180
Smith Barney Aggr Grth A	Agg Growth	23.00	18.75	19.11	4	4	5	1.21	800 544-7835
Smith Barney Aggr Grth B	Agg Growth	22.04	17.75	18.19	4	4	0	2.02	800 544-7835
Smith Barney Aggr Grth L	Agg Growth	22.10	17.85	18.24	4	4	0	1.97	800 544-7835
Smith Barney Appreciation A	Growth	20.35	22.69	17.77	2	2	5	0.95	800 544-7835
Smith Barney Appreciation B	Growth	19.45	21.80	16.89	2	2	0	1.74	800 544-7835
Smith Barney Appreciation L	Growth	19.45	21.51	16.76	2	2		1.73	800 544-7835
Smith Barney Balanced A	Balanced	22.69	13.90	9.28	3	2	5	1.06	800 544-7835
Smith Barney Balanced B	Balanced	22.14	13.41	8.65	3	2	0	1.51	800 544-7835
Smith Barney Balanced O	Balanced	22.19	13.41	8.76	3	2	0	1.47	800 544-7835
Smith Barney Con Social Awareness A	Flexible	27.03	19.93	15.72	2	1	5	1.22	800 544-7835
Smith Barney Con Social Awareness B	Flexible	25.70	18.92	14.88	3	1	0	1.95	800 544-7835
Smith Barney Con Social Awareness L	Flexible	30.01	20.03	15.24	2	2	0	1.96	800 544-7835
Smith Barney Concert Peachtree Gr A	Growth	19.54	16.73		3	3	5	1.69	800 544-7835
Smith Barney Concert Peachtree Gr B	Growth	19.51	16.43		3	3	0	2.44	800 544-7835
Smith Barney Concert Peachtree Gr L	Growth	18.60	14.29		3	3	0	2.44	800 544-7835
Smith Barney Contrarian Fund A	Growth	5.25	10.73		4	3	5	1.52	800 544-7835
Smith Barney Contrarian Fund B	Growth	4.44	10.14		4	3	0	2.06	800 544-7835
Smith Barney Contrarian Fund L	Growth	4.37	10.14		4	3	0	2.04	800 544-7835
Smith Barney Conv A	Converts	9.05	13.25	10.36	4	1	5	1.23	800 544-7835
Smith Barney Conv B	Converts	8.57	12.84	9.66	4	1	0	1.73	800 544-7835
Smith Barney Conv O	Converts	8.66	12.71		3	1		1.74	800 544-7835
Smith Barney Emrg Markets Port A	Foreign	−41.53	−8.37		5	5	5	2.10	800 544-7835
Smith Barney Emrg Markets Port B	Foreign	−42.01	−9.09		5	5	0	2.88	800 544-7835
Smith Barney Emrg Markets Port L	Foreign	−42.01	−9.07		5	5	0	2.86	800 544-7835
Smith Barney European Portfolio A	European	30.68	20.61		3	3	5	1.78	800 451-2010
Smith Barney European Portfolio B	European	30.07	19.67		3	3	0	2.49	800 451-2010
Smith Barney European Portfolio L	European	29.45	19.61		3	3	0	2.47	800 451-2010
Smith Barney Fundamental Val A	Growth	13.39	17.78	15.55	2	2	5	1.14	800 544-7835
Smith Barney Fundamental Val B	Growth	12.48	16.88	14.56	4	2	0	1.90	800 544-7835
Smith Barney Fundamental Val L	Growth	7.11	14.97		4	3	0	1.89	800 544-7835
Smith Barney Intl Balanced Port A	Balanced	−0.80	6.11		5	2	5	1.26	800 451-2010
Smith Barney Intl Balanced Port B	Balanced	−6.36	3.65		5	3	0	1.73	800 451-2010
Smith Barney Intl Balanced Port L	Balanced	−6.10	3.64		5	3	0	2.52	800 451-2010
Smith Barney Intl Equity A	Foreign	10.48	11.21	11.74	4	3	5	1.29	800 451-2010
Smith Barney Intl Equity B	Foreign	9.63	11.41		4	3	0	2.06	800 451-2010
Smith Barney Intl Equity L	Foreign	9.63	10.70	11.10	4	3	0	2.07	800 451-2010
Smith Barney Intl Equity Y	Foreign	10.58	11.75		4	4	0	0.94	800 451-2010
Smith Barney Large Cap Blend A	Growth/Inc	19.31	22.41	16.54	2	2	5	1.12	800 544-7835

| Stock Fund Name | Objective | Annualized Return for | | | Rank | | Max Load | Expense Ratio | Toll-Free Telephone |
		1 Year	3 Years	5 Years	Overall	Risk			
Smith Barney Large Cap Blend B	Growth/Inc	18.60	21.95	16.03	3	2	0	1.59	800 544-7835
Smith Barney Large Cap Blend O	Growth/Inc	18.60	21.76		2	2		1.61	800 544-7835
Smith Barney Large Cap Value A	Income	21.73	24.46	17.65	2	2	5	0.92	800 451-2010
Smith Barney Large Cap Value B	Income	20.75	23.49		2	2		1.71	800 451-2010
Smith Barney Large Cap Value L	Income	20.77	23.48	16.41	2	2	0	1.69	800 451-2010
Smith Barney Natural Resources A	Energy/Res	−19.78	−0.24	−0.63	5	5	5	1.56	800 544-7835
Smith Barney Natural Resources B	Energy/Res	−20.29	−0.90		5	5	0	2.19	800 544-7835
Smith Barney Natural Resources L	Energy/Res	−20.18	−1.08		5	5	0	2.13	800 544-7835
Smith Barney Pacific Portfolio A	Pacific	−46.80	−15.39		5	4	5	1.31	800 544-7835
Smith Barney Pacific Portfolio B	Pacific	−47.19	−15.99		5	4	0	4.08	800 544-7835
Smith Barney Pacific Portfolio L	Pacific	−42.50	−13.64		5	4	0	4.23	800 544-7835
Smith Barney Premium Tot Ret A	Growth/Inc	17.94	20.94	16.80	2	1	5	1.11	800 544-7835
Smith Barney Premium Tot Ret B	Growth/Inc	17.23	20.50	16.31	2	1	0	1.60	800 544-7835
Smith Barney Premium Tot Ret O	Growth/Inc	17.31	20.06	16.23	2	2	0	1.56	800 544-7835
Smith Barney Special Equities A	Small Co	7.90	10.14	11.51	4	5	5	1.20	800 544-7835
Smith Barney Special Equities B	Small Co	7.10	9.34	10.70	5	5	0	1.91	800 544-7835
Smith Barney Special Equities L	Small Co	7.05	9.35		5	5		1.96	800 544-7835
Smith Barney Telecom Income	Utilities	28.98	23.91	16.96	3	4	0	0.92	800 544-7835
Smith Breeden Equity Plus Fund	Growth/Inc	28.09	30.52	23.24	1	3	0	0.88	800 221-3138
SoGen Gold Fund	Gold	−28.93	−13.96		5	5	3.75	1.60	800 334-2143
SoGen International Fund	Global	4.72	11.68	11.66	3	1	3.75	1.19	800 334-2143
SoGen Overseas Fund	Foreign	2.15	11.62		4	1	3.75	1.19	800 334-2143
Sound Shore Fund	Growth	20.54	28.23	21.48	1	3	0	1.10	800 551-1980
SouthTrust Vulcan Stock Fund	Growth/Inc	19.94	25.32	18.84	2	3	4.5	0.95	800 843-8618
Spectra Fund	Agg Growth	32.28	26.39	29.29	3	4	0	2.12	800 711-6141
SSgA Active International Fund	Foreign	−2.90	6.46		5	3	0	1.40	800 997-7327
SSgA Emerging Markets Fund	Foreign	−32.77	−3.58		5	4	0	1.51	800 997-7327
SSgA Growth & Income Fund	Growth/Inc	34.34	29.18		2	3	0	0.95	800 997-7327
SSgA Matrix Equity Fund	Growth	31.07	27.52		2	3	0	0.96	800 997-7327
SSgA S&P 500 Index Fund	Growth	29.92	29.62		1	3	0	0.26	800 997-7327
SSgA Small Cap Fd	Small Co	17.40	27.75	21.10	3	4	0	1.00	800 997-7327
Stagecoach Asset Allocation A	AssetAlloc	27.96	19.68	15.54	3	2	4.5	0.94	800 222-8222
Stagecoach Balanced Fund A	Balanced	15.85	16.38	12.31	3	1	5.25	1.05	800 222-8222
Stagecoach Balanced Fund B	Balanced	15.06						0.66	800 222-8222
Stagecoach Diversified Eq Inc A	Income	18.68	21.88	17.25	2	3	5.25	1.26	800 222-8222
Stagecoach Diversified Eq Inc B	Income	17.84	18.83		3	3	0	2.08	800 222-8222
Stagecoach Equity Index A	Growth/Inc	28.97	28.92	21.83	1	3	0	0.98	800 222-8222
Stagecoach Equity Value A	Growth	19.24	24.97	19.22	3	3	5.25	1.05	800 222-8222
Stagecoach Equity Value B	Growth	18.43	16.58	14.33	3	4	0	0.00	800 222-8222
Stagecoach Equity Value Instl	Growth	19.40					0		800 222-8222
Stagecoach Growth Fund A	Growth/Inc	23.01	23.10	18.72	3	3	5.25	1.13	800 222-8222
Stagecoach Growth Fund B	Growth/Inc	22.27	22.43		2	3	0	2.03	800 222-8222
Stagecoach Index Allocation A	AssetAlloc	28.51	24.69	19.08	1	2	4.5	1.26	800 222-8222
Stagecoach Lifepath 2010 A	AssetAlloc	15.40	15.07		3	1	4.5	1.20	800 222-8222
Stagecoach Lifepath 2010 B	AssetAlloc	14.83							800 222-8222
Stagecoach Lifepath 2020 A	AssetAlloc	19.92	18.94		3	2	4.5	1.20	800 222-8222
Stagecoach Lifepath 2020 B	AssetAlloc	19.41					0		800 222-8222
Stagecoach Lifepath 2030 A	AssetAlloc	23.36	22.03		1	2	4.5	1.20	800 222-8222
Stagecoach Lifepath 2030 B	AssetAlloc	22.69					0		800 222-8222
Stagecoach Lifepath 2040 A	AssetAlloc	25.10	24.89		1	3	4.5	1.20	800 222-8222
Stagecoach Lifepath 2040 B	AssetAlloc	24.50					0		800 222-8222
Stagecoach Lifepath Opportunity A	AssetAlloc	10.47	9.32		3	1	0	1.20	800 222-8222
Stagecoach Small Cap A	Small Co	11.59	24.65		4	5	5.25	1.10	800 222-8222
Stagecoach Small Cap B	Small Co	10.85	24.38		4	5	0	0.00	800 222-8222
Stagecoach Small Cap Instl	Small Co	12.17	24.88		4	5	0		800 222-8222
Stagecoach Strategic Growth A	Agg Growth	16.77					5.25	1.23	800 222-8222
Stagecoach Strategic Growth B	Agg Growth	16.04					0	1.91	800 222-8222
Standish Ayer & Wood Equity Fund	Growth	26.58	29.55	22.51	1	3	0	0.72	800 221-4795

Stock Fund Name	Objective	Annualized Return for			Rank		Max Load	Expense Ratio	Toll-Free Telephone
		1 Year	3 Years	5 Years	Overall	Risk			
Standish Ayer & Wood Intl Equity Fd	Foreign	11.60	11.40	9.37	4	3	0	1.48	800 221-4795
Standish Ayer & Wood Sm Cap T S Eq	Small Co	21.25					0	1.51	800 221-4795
Standish Ayer & Wood Small Cap Eq	Small Co	14.55	19.38	17.03	4	5	0	0.74	800 221-4795
Standish Ayer & Wood Tax Sens Eq	Growth	30.05					0	2.19	800 221-4795
Star Capital Appreciation	Growth	21.00	12.92		4	4	4.5	1.28	800 677-3863
Star Growth Equity	Growth	25.98	26.26		1	3	0	1.11	800 677-3863
Star Relative Value Fund	Growth/Inc	23.78	27.80	21.83	2	3	4.5	1.01	800 677-3863
Star Select REIT Plus Fund	Real Est	4.28					0		800 677-3863
Star Stellar Fund Investment Class	Flexible	11.28	13.65	10.38	3	1	4.5	1.59	800 677-3863
Star Stellar Fund Trust Class	Flexible	11.59	13.92		3	1	0	1.34	800 677-3863
State Street Rsch Alpha Fund A	Income	27.81	25.98	19.36	1	2	4.5	1.23	800 562-0032
State Street Rsch Alpha Fund B	Income	27.24	25.07	18.73	1	2	0	2.00	800 562-0032
State Street Rsch Alpha Fund C	Income	27.24	25.09	19.00	1	2	0	1.00	800 562-0032
State Street Rsch Alpha Fund S	Income	28.45	26.32	19.93	1	2	0	2.00	800 562-0032
State Street Rsch Aurora Fund A	Small Co	21.49	38.10		2	4	4.5	1.45	800 562-0032
State Street Rsch Aurora Fund B	Small Co	20.59	37.05		3	4	0	2.20	800 562-0032
State Street Rsch Aurora Fund C	Small Co	20.53	37.02		3	4	0	1.20	800 562-0032
State Street Rsch Aurora Fund S	Small Co	21.66	38.42		3	4	0	1.20	800 562-0032
State Street Rsch Capital A	Agg Growth	20.73	12.56	14.71	4	4	4.5	1.21	800 562-0032
State Street Rsch Capital B	Agg Growth	19.71	11.66	14.05	4	4	0	2.01	800 562-0032
State Street Rsch Capital C	Agg Growth	19.76	11.67	14.07	4	4	0	2.01	800 562-0032
State Street Rsch Capital S	Agg Growth	21.06	12.84	15.21	4	4	0	1.01	800 562-0032
State Street Rsch Emerging Growth A	Small Co	16.50	21.82		4	5	4.5	1.35	800 562-0032
State Street Rsch Emerging Growth B	Small Co	15.61	20.92		4	5	0	1.35	800 562-0032
State Street Rsch Emerging Growth C	Small Co	15.71	20.96		4	5	0	1.10	800 562-0032
State Street Rsch Emerging Growth S	Small Co	16.90	22.13		4	5	0	2.10	800 562-0032
State Street Rsch Equity Inv A	Growth/Inc	27.62	27.94	20.12	2	3	4.5	1.25	800 562-0032
State Street Rsch Equity Inv B	Growth/Inc	26.67	26.97	15.91	2	3	0	2.00	800 562-0032
State Street Rsch Equity Inv C	Growth/Inc	26.80	27.02	19.33	2	3	0	1.00	800 562-0032
State Street Rsch Equity Inv S	Growth/Inc	27.90	28.24	20.51	2	3	0	2.00	800 562-0032
State Street Rsch Exchange Fund	Growth/Inc	26.52	30.59	22.40	1	3	0	0.56	800 562-0032
State Street Rsch Global Res A	Energy/Res	−14.28	17.80	8.00	3	5	4.5	1.75	800 562-0032
State Street Rsch Global Res B	Energy/Res	−14.94	16.90	7.31	4	5	0	2.17	800 562-0032
State Street Rsch Global Res C	Energy/Res	−14.97	16.85	7.26	4	5	0		800 562-0032
State Street Rsch Global Res S	Energy/Res	−14.11	18.08	8.36	4	5	0	2.17	800 562-0032
State Street Rsch Growth A	Growth/Inc	21.43	15.41	14.52	4	4	4.5	0.88	800 562-0032
State Street Rsch Growth B	Growth/Inc	20.60	14.54	13.59	4	4	0		800 562-0032
State Street Rsch Growth C	Growth/Inc	20.47	14.51	13.58	4	4	0		800 562-0032
State Street Rsch Intl Equity A	Foreign	4.04	5.75		4	3	4.5	1.90	800 562-0032
State Street Rsch Intl Equity B	Foreign	3.37	4.96		4	3	0	2.65	800 562-0032
State Street Rsch Intl Equity C	Foreign	3.28	4.93		4	3	0	2.65	800 562-0032
State Street Rsch Intl Equity S	Foreign	4.28	5.97	7.40	4	3	0	1.65	800 562-0032
State Street Rsch Invest Trust A	Growth	29.63	28.46	20.39	2	3	4.5	0.75	800 562-0032
State Street Rsch Invest Trust B	Growth	28.66	27.50	19.48	2	3	0	1.50	800 562-0032
State Street Rsch Invest Trust C	Growth	28.75	27.51	19.49	2	3	0	1.50	800 562-0032
State Street Rsch Invest Trust S	Growth	29.91	28.77	20.68	2	3	0	0.45	800 562-0032
State Street Rsch Mgd Assets A	AssetAlloc	18.12	18.42	13.92	2	2	4.5	1.25	800 562-0032
State Street Rsch Mgd Assets B	AssetAlloc	17.29	17.56	13.26	3	2	0	2.00	800 562-0032
State Street Rsch Mgd Assets C	AssetAlloc	17.25	17.56	13.76	3	2	0	2.00	800 562-0032
State Street Rsch Mgd Assets S	AssetAlloc	18.41	18.71	14.96	3	2	0	1.00	800 562-0032
State Street Rsch Strat Aggress S	AssetAlloc	20.43	19.74		2	2	0		800 562-0032
State Street Rsch Strat Consv S	AssetAlloc	14.61	12.66		3	1	0		800 562-0032
State Street Rsch Strat Mod S	AssetAlloc	17.34	15.83		3	1	0		800 562-0032
Stein Roe Adv Tax-Managed Growth A	Growth	24.89					5.75	1.50	800 338-2550
Stein Roe Adv Tax-Managed Growth B	Growth	23.92					0	2.25	800 338-2550
Stein Roe Adv Tax-Managed Growth C	Growth	23.83					1	2.25	800 338-2550
Stein Roe Adv Tax-Managed Growth E	Growth	24.62					5	1.60	800 338-2550
Stein Roe Adv Tax-Managed Growth F	Growth	23.89					0	2.25	800 338-2550

353

Stock Fund Name	Objective	Annualized Return for			Rank		Max Load	Expense Ratio	Toll-Free Telephone
		1 Year	3 Years	5 Years	Overall	Risk			
Stein Roe Adv Tax-Managed Growth G	Growth	24.69					4.5	1.60	800 338-2550
Stein Roe Adv Tax-Managed Growth H	Growth	23.92					0	2.25	800 338-2550
Stein Roe Balanced Fund	Balanced	13.51	16.99	12.74	3	1	0	0.87	800 338-2550
Stein Roe Capital Opportunities	Agg Growth	21.11	22.58	20.96	3	5	0	1.04	800 338-2550
Stein Roe Emerging Markets Fund	Foreign	−51.75					0		800 338-2550
Stein Roe Growth & Income Fund	Growth/Inc	25.09	26.42	20.08	1	2	0	1.13	800 338-2550
Stein Roe Growth Stock Fund	Growth	30.13	29.80	21.49	2	3	0	1.07	800 338-2550
Stein Roe International Fund	Foreign	−3.53	7.65		5	3	0	1.50	800 338-2550
Stein Roe Special Fund	Growth	12.86	18.51	14.01	4	3	0	1.14	800 338-2550
Stein Roe Young Investor Fund	Growth	31.16	32.84		2	3	0	1.43	800 338-2550
STI Classic Balanced Flex	Balanced	20.47	17.84		3	1	0	2.45	800 428-6970
STI Classic Balanced Inv	Balanced	21.34	18.73		3	1	3.75	1.64	800 428-6970
STI Classic Balanced Tr	Balanced	21.70	19.04		3	1	0	1.08	800 428-6970
STI Classic Capital Growth Flex	Growth	27.00	26.57		1	3	0	2.43	800 428-6970
STI Classic Capital Growth Inv	Growth	27.47	27.18	17.59	2	3	3.75	2.02	800 428-6970
STI Classic Capital Growth Tr A	Growth	31.34	28.97	18.87	2	3	0	1.25	800 428-6970
STI Classic Emrg Mkt Equity Trust	Foreign	−24.79					0	2.04	800 428-6970
STI Classic Intl Equity Flex	Foreign	11.77					0	3.03	800 428-6970
STI Classic Intl Equity Index Flex	Foreign	18.32	13.52		3	3	0	3.69	800 428-6970
STI Classic Intl Equity Index Inv	Foreign	18.38	14.05		4	3	3.75	1.88	800 428-6970
STI Classic Intl Equity Index Tr	Foreign	19.52	14.69		3	3	0	1.15	800 428-6970
STI Classic Intl Equity Inv	Foreign	12.58					3.75	2.05	800 428-6970
STI Classic Intl Equity Trust	Foreign	13.05					0	1.51	800 428-6970
STI Classic Mid-Cap Equity Flex	Agg Growth	17.82	16.99		4	3	0	2.58	800 428-6970
STI Classic Mid-Cap Equity Inv	Agg Growth	18.50	17.78		3	3	3.75	1.85	800 428-6970
STI Classic Mid-Cap Equity Trust	Agg Growth	19.07	18.24		3	3	0	1.15	800 428-6970
STI Classic Small Cap Equity Flex	Small Co	9.10					0		800 428-6970
STI Classic Small Cap Equity Trust	Small Co	10.01					0	1.37	800 428-6970
STI Classic Sunbelt Equity Flex	Growth	16.26	18.45		4	4	0	2.69	800 428-6970
STI Classic Sunbelt Equity Inv	Growth	17.02	19.17		4	4	3.75	1.60	800 428-6970
STI Classic Sunbelt Equity Tr	Growth	17.53	19.68		4	4	0	1.26	800 428-6970
STI Classic Value Income Stock Flex	Income	17.22	22.28		2	2	0	2.03	800 428-6970
STI Classic Value Income Stock Inv	Income	18.04	23.15	18.71	2	2	3.75	0.91	800 428-6970
STI Classic Value Income Stock Tr	Income	18.48	23.61		2	2	0	0.91	800 428-6970
StoneBridge Growth Fund	Growth/Inc	10.73	18.42	14.48	2	2	0	0.68	800 639-3935
Stratton Growth Fund	Growth/Inc	27.39	26.18	20.90	1	2	0	1.11	800 634-5726
Stratton Monthly Dividend REIT Shs	Real Est	9.47	12.06	5.67	3	1	0	1.02	800 634-5726
Stratton Small Cap Yield Fund	Small Co	21.48	22.49	15.77	3	3	0	1.62	800 634-5726
Strong American Utilities Fund	Utilities	22.82	20.59	15.18	3	3	0	1.20	800 368-1030
Strong Asia Pacific Fund	Pacific	−45.74	−15.20		5	4	0	2.00	800 368-1030
Strong Asset Allocation Fund	AssetAlloc	23.75	17.50	13.50	3	2	0	1.10	800 368-1030
Strong Bluechip 100	Growth	32.33					0		800 368-1030
Strong Common Stock Fund	Growth	16.85	22.27	19.14	3	3	0	1.20	800 368-1030
Strong Discovery Fund	Agg Growth	14.85	11.90	12.76	4	4	0	1.40	800 368-1030
Strong Equity Income Fund	Income	27.78					0	1.30	800 368-1030
Strong Growth & Income Fund	Growth/Inc	32.25					0	1.90	800 368-1030
Strong Growth 20	Growth	35.58					0		800 368-1030
Strong Growth Fund	Growth	26.27	25.06		3	4	0	1.30	800 368-1030
Strong Index 500	Growth/Inc	29.76					0		800 368-1030
Strong International Stock Fund	Foreign	−18.58	1.86	6.12	5	3	0	1.60	800 368-1030
Strong Mid-Cap Fund	Growth	30.60					0	1.60	800 368-1030
Strong Opportunity Fund	Agg Growth	28.85	22.89	19.34	2	3	0	1.20	800 368-1030
Strong Schafer Value Fund	Growth	14.72	22.18	18.97	3	3	0	1.20	800 368-1030
Strong Small Cap Fund	Small Co	13.14					0	1.40	800 368-1030
Strong Total Return Fund	Growth/Inc	28.62	22.54	18.12	3	3	0	1.10	800 368-1030
Strong Value Fund	Growth	25.25					0	1.40	800 368-1030
Style Select Aggressive Growth A	Agg Growth	32.63					5.75	1.90	800 858-8850
Style Select Aggressive Growth B	Agg Growth	31.62					0	2.55	800 858-8850

Stock Fund Name	Objective	Annualized Return for			Rank		Max Load	Expense Ratio	Toll-Free Telephone
		1 Year	3 Years	5 Years	Overall	Risk			
Style Select Aggressive Growth C	Agg Growth	31.69					0	1.84	800 858-8850
Style Select International Equity A	Foreign	1.21					5.75	2.15	800 858-8850
Style Select International Equity B	Foreign	0.55					0	2.80	800 858-8850
Style Select International Equity C	Foreign	0.55					0	2.80	800 858-8850
Style Select Midcap A	Growth	28.58					5.75	1.90	800 858-8850
Style Select Midcap B	Growth	27.75					0	2.55	800 858-8850
Style Select Midcap C	Growth	28.08					0	2.55	800 858-8850
Style Select Value A	Growth	16.86					5.75	1.90	800 858-8850
Style Select Value B	Growth	16.10					0	2.55	800 858-8850
Style Select Value C	Growth	16.10					0	2.55	800 858-8850
SunAmerica Balanced Assets Fund A	Balanced	26.15	20.11		3	2	5.75	1.50	800 858-8850
SunAmerica Balanced Assets Fund B	Balanced	24.59	19.13	14.36	3	2	0	2.11	800 858-8850
SunAmerica Blue Chip Growth Fund A	Growth	31.53	25.83		2	3	5.75	1.53	800 858-8850
SunAmerica Blue Chip Growth Fund B	Growth	30.58	24.99	17.08	3	3	0	2.22	800 858-8850
SunAmerica Growth and Income A	Growth/Inc	25.97	31.08		1	3	5.75	1.38	800 858-8850
SunAmerica Growth and Income B	Growth/Inc	25.19	28.68		1	2	0	1.94	800 858-8850
SunAmerica Mid-Cap Growth A	Growth	21.48	17.55	12.96	4	4	5.75	1.64	800 858-8850
SunAmerica Mid-Cap Growth B	Growth	20.51	16.68		4	4	0	2.34	800 858-8850
SunAmerica Small Company Growth A	Small Co	17.75	15.56	15.69	4	5	5.75	1.72	800 858-8850
SunAmerica Small Company Growth B	Small Co	16.99	14.81		4	5	0	2.34	800 858-8850
Swisskey Global Equity Fund	Global	8.06	17.51		3	2	0	1.75	800 448-2430
Swisskey Global Fund	Global	7.60	13.72	10.78	3	1	0	1.64	800 448-2430
Swisskey Non US Equity Fund	Foreign	5.25	15.51		3	3	0	1.81	800 448-2430
Swisskey US Balanced Fund	Balanced	12.61	13.53		3	1	0	1.38	800 448-2430
Swisskey US Equity Fund	Growth/Inc	20.80	27.33		2	3	0	1.41	800 448-2430
T Rowe Price Balanced Fund	Balanced	18.41	18.20	14.65	3	1	0	0.81	800 638-5660
T Rowe Price Blue Chip Growth Fund	Growth	29.75	30.06	24.92	1	3	0	1.01	800 638-5660
T Rowe Price Capital Appreciation	Growth	13.07	15.95	14.51	3	1	0	0.64	800 638-5660
T Rowe Price Capital Opportunity	Growth	27.92	21.35		3	3	0	1.35	800 638-5660
T Rowe Price Div Small Cap Growth	Small Co	13.91					0	1.25	800 638-5660
T Rowe Price Dividend Growth	Growth/Inc	24.31	27.42	21.27	1	2	0	0.80	800 638-5660
T Rowe Price Emrg Markets Stock	Foreign	−27.32	−2.54		5	5	0	1.75	800 638-5660
T Rowe Price Equity Income	Income	19.39	23.96	19.59	2	2	0	0.79	800 638-5660
T Rowe Price Equity Index 500	Growth/Inc	29.71	29.83	22.54	1	3	0	0.40	800 638-5660
T Rowe Price European Stock	European	30.80	25.74	22.64	1	2	0	1.06	800 638-5660
T Rowe Price Financial Service Fund	Financial	35.31					0	1.25	800 638-5660
T Rowe Price Global Stock Fund	Global	14.65					0	1.30	800 638-5660
T Rowe Price Growth & Income	Growth/Inc	18.84	24.13	18.17	2	2	0	0.78	800 638-5660
T Rowe Price Growth Stock Fund	Growth	28.75	26.55	21.44	1	3	0	0.75	800 638-5660
T Rowe Price Health Sciences	Health	17.75					0	1.29	800 638-5660
T Rowe Price International Discover	Foreign	0.29	8.18	7.01	4	3	0	1.41	800 638-5660
T Rowe Price International Stock Fd	Foreign	4.38	13.34	13.19	4	3	0	0.85	800 638-5660
T Rowe Price Japan Fund	Pacific	−32.25	−9.84	−6.64	5	4	0	1.24	800 638-5660
T Rowe Price Latin America Fund	Foreign	−20.53	11.80		5	5	0	1.48	800 638-5660
T Rowe Price Media & Telecom Fund	Technology	47.13	23.95		3	4	0		800 638-5660
T Rowe Price Mid-Cap Growth Fund	Growth	29.90	26.98	22.83	2	3	0	0.95	800 638-5660
T Rowe Price Mid-Cap Value	Growth	21.21					0	1.25	800 638-5660
T Rowe Price New America Growth	Growth	30.82	27.14	20.89	3	4	0	0.96	800 638-5660
T Rowe Price New Asia Fund	Pacific	−50.61	−17.80	−6.25	5	5	0	1.10	800 638-5660
T Rowe Price New Era Fund	Energy/Res	3.70	15.17	13.97	4	3	0	0.74	800 638-5660
T Rowe Price New Horizons	Small Co	17.10	20.21	20.54	3	4	0	0.88	800 638-5660
T Rowe Price Personal Strat Balance	AssetAlloc	17.59	17.74		3	1	0	1.05	800 638-5660
T Rowe Price Personal Strat Growth	AssetAlloc	20.28	21.49		2	2	0	1.10	800 638-5660
T Rowe Price Personal Strat Income	AssetAlloc	13.43	14.28		3	1	0	0.95	800 638-5660
T Rowe Price Science & Tech	Technology	15.36	16.97	22.72	4	5	0	0.94	800 638-5660
T Rowe Price Small-Cap Stock Fund	Small Co	20.89	23.93	19.51	3	3	0	1.02	800 638-5660
T Rowe Price Small-Cap Value	Small Co	17.93	22.04	18.13	3	2	0	0.87	800 638-5660
T Rowe Price Spectrum Growth	Growth	16.94	21.24	18.38	1	2	0	0.00	800 638-5660

355

Stock Fund Name	Objective	Annualized Return for			Rank		Max Load	Expense Ratio	Toll-Free Telephone
		1 Year	3 Years	5 Years	Overall	Risk			
T Rowe Price Spectrum International	Foreign	1.37					0	0.00	800 638-5660
T Rowe Price Tax-Efficient Balanced	Balanced	20.83					0	1.00	800 638-5660
T Rowe Price Value	Growth	19.69	26.88		1	2	0	1.10	800 638-5660
Target International Equity	Foreign	17.00	18.25	16.57	3	3	0	0.93	800 225-1852
Target Large Cap Growth	Growth	32.94	25.50	19.24	3	4	0	0.73	800 225-1852
Target Large Cap Value	Growth	20.85	23.84	18.46	2	3	0	0.72	800 225-1852
Target Small Cap Growth	Small Co	20.18	20.98	16.10	3	4	0	0.79	800 225-1852
Target Small Cap Value	Small Co	13.98	20.67	12.94	3	3	0	0.81	800 225-1852
TCW/DW Global Telecom Trust Class B	Technology	26.56					0	2.38	800 869-6397
TCW/DW Income and Growth Class C	Flexible	21.17	15.72	12.21	3	1	0	1.97	800 869-6397
TCW/DW Latin America Growth Class B	Foreign	−25.10	8.91	3.08	5	5	0	2.81	800 869-6397
TCW/DW Mid-Cap Equity Trust Class B	Growth	41.92					0	2.28	800 869-6397
TCW/DW Small Cap Growth Class B	Small Co	28.78	23.68		3	5	0	2.27	800 869-6397
TCW/DW Total Return Trust Class B	Growth/Inc	22.03	22.58		3	3	0	2.12	800 869-6397
Templeton American Trust II	Flexible	17.25	18.30	15.26	3	2	1	2.17	800 237-0738
Templeton Capital Accumulator I	Growth	8.96	17.22	16.80	3	3	0	1.00	800 237-0738
Templeton Developing Markets I	Foreign	−37.87	−3.43	2.76	5	5	5.75	1.96	800 237-0738
Templeton Developing Markets II	Foreign	−38.22	−4.11		5	5	1	2.69	800 237-0738
Templeton Foreign Fund I	Foreign	−1.60	10.39	11.77	4	2	5.75	1.08	800 237-0738
Templeton Foreign Fund II	Foreign	−2.30	9.58		3	2	1	1.83	800 237-0738
Templeton Foreign Smaller Co	Foreign	−0.96	11.17	13.15	4	2	4.5	1.60	800 237-0738
Templeton Global Opportunities I	Global	1.74	14.65	14.48	4	3	5.75	1.37	800 237-0738
Templeton Global Opportunities II	Global	0.00	9.62	7.20	5	3	0	2.12	800 237-0738
Templeton Global Real Estate I	Real Est	−4.09	7.85	6.76	5	2	5.75	1.45	800 237-0738
Templeton Global Smaller Co I	Global	−0.37	12.44	12.15	4	2	5.75	1.30	800 237-0738
Templeton Growth Fund I	Global	5.83	15.94	15.90	4	2	5.75	1.08	800 237-0738
Templeton Growth Fund II	Global	5.00	10.77		4	3	0	1.84	800 237-0738
Templeton Pacific Growth Fund	Pacific	−51.73	−16.84	−6.33	5	5	5.75	1.63	800 237-0738
Templeton World Fund I	Global	8.55	18.34	17.69	2	3	5.75	1.03	800 237-0738
Texas Capital Value and Growth	Growth/Inc	42.92					4.5	1.83	888 839-4769
The Osterweis Fund	Growth	27.04	21.01		3	2		1.75	
Third Avenue Small-Cap Value Fund	Small Co	5.83					0	2.71	800 443-1021
Third Avenue Value Fund	Agg Growth	11.17	20.21	16.89	3	2	0	1.08	800 443-1021
Thomas White World Fund	Global	14.67	16.61		3	2	0	1.47	800 811-0535
Thompson Plumb Balanced Fund	Balanced	21.16	21.05	16.43	3	2	0	1.45	800-499-0079
Thompson Plumb Growth Fund	Growth	27.81	28.47	22.16	2	3	0	1.54	800-499-0079
Thornburg Value Fund A	Growth	37.40					4.5	1.61	800 847-0200
Thornburg Value Fund C	Growth	36.25					0	1.73	800 847-0200
Time Horizon Fund 1A (2005)	Income	13.66					0	1.67	800 737-5438
Time Horizon Fund 1B (2005)	Income	12.12					0	2.43	800 737-5438
Time Horizon Fund 2A (2015)	Growth/Inc	15.77					0	1.63	800 737-5438
Time Horizon Fund 2B (2015)	Growth/Inc	14.33					0	2.39	800 737-5438
Time Horizon Fund 3A (2030)	Growth	20.06					0	1.66	800 737-5438
Time Horizon Fund 3B (2030)	Growth	18.28					0	2.40	800 737-5438
Timothy Plan A	Growth	8.62	11.42		4	2	5.5	2.75	800 441-6580
Timothy Plan B	Growth	7.15					0	3.48	800 441-6580
TIP Clover Equity Value Fund	Growth/Inc	19.53	17.74	19.67	3	3	0	1.10	800 224-6312
TIP Clover Small Cap Value Fund	Small Co	16.36					0	1.40	800 224-6312
TIP Turner Growth Equity	Growth	39.55	29.60	20.13	2	4	0	1.05	800 224-6312
TIP Turner Small Cap Fund	Small Co	28.22	32.03		3	5	0	1.24	800 224-6312
TIP Turner Ultra Large Cap Fund	Income	37.35					0	1.00	800 224-6312
Titan Financial Services Fund	Financial	37.11					0	2.49	888 448-4826
Tocqueville Fund	Flexible	15.01	21.44	18.28	3	3	4	1.40	800 697-3863
Tocqueville International Value	Global	−43.12	−8.66		5	5	4	1.91	800 697-3863
Tocqueville Small Cap Value Fund	Small Co	21.91	22.11		2	4	4	1.75	800 697-3863
Torray Fund	Growth/Inc	37.16	35.42	26.45	1	3	0	1.13	
Touchstone Balanced Fund A	Balanced	16.07	16.89		3	2	4.75	0.90	800 669-2796
Touchstone Balanced Fund C	Balanced	15.13	16.03		3	2	0	2.10	800 669-2796

| Stock Fund Name | Objective | Annualized Return for | | | Rank | | Max Load | Expense Ratio | Toll-Free Telephone |
		1 Year	3 Years	5 Years	Overall	Risk			
Touchstone Emerging Growth A	Small Co	23.10	19.29		3	4	4.75	1.50	800 669-2796
Touchstone Emerging Growth C	Small Co	21.69	18.17		4	4	0	2.25	800 669-2796
Touchstone Growth & Income A	Growth/Inc	23.95	21.07		3	3	4.75	1.30	800 669-2796
Touchstone Growth & Income C	Growth/Inc	22.19	20.00		3	3	0	2.05	800 669-2796
Touchstone International Equity A	Foreign	25.23	18.61		3	3	4.75	1.60	800 669-2796
Touchstone International Equity C	Foreign	24.30	17.72		3	3	0	2.34	800 669-2796
Tower Capital Appreciation Fund A	Growth/Inc	29.17	29.45	21.97	2	3	4.5	1.24	800 999-0124
Tower Capital Appreciation Fund B	Growth/Inc	28.07					0	2.03	800 999-0124
Trent Equity Fund	Growth	28.94	20.81	15.02	3	3	0	2.00	800 282-2340
Triflex Fund	Balanced	15.83	15.30	12.95	3	1	5.75	1.36	800 231-4639
Tweedy Browne American Value Fund	Growth	30.25	29.07		1	2	0	1.39	800 873-8242
Tweedy Browne Global Value Fund	Global	21.33	22.94	18.07	2	2	0	1.43	800 873-8242
UAM Acadian Asset Mgmt Emrg Market	Foreign	−39.35	−9.61	−2.20	5	5	0	1.60	800 638-7983
UAM Acadian Asset Mgmt Intl Equity	Foreign	−8.36	1.75	3.65	5	3	0	1.00	800 638-7983
UAM C&B Balanced	Balanced	12.40	16.31	12.98	3	1	0	1.00	800 638-7983
UAM C&B Equity	Growth	15.62	23.55	18.56	1	3	0	0.84	800 638-7983
UAM C&B Equity for Taxable Investor	Growth	13.05					0	1.00	800 638-7983
UAM Chicago Asset Mgmt Val/Con Port	Growth	14.13	13.32		4	2	0	0.95	800 638-7983
UAM DSI Disciplined Value A	Growth	18.29	24.29	14.72	3	3	0	1.06	800 638-7983
UAM DSI Disciplined Value B	Growth	17.65					0		800 638-7983
UAM FMA Small Company A	Small Co	23.60	26.19	16.10	3	3	0	1.03	800 638-7983
UAM FPA Crescent A	Financial	17.20	21.40	18.11	2	1	0	1.60	800 638-7983
UAM FPA Crescent B	Financial	16.83					0	1.85	800 638-7983
UAM ICM Equity	Growth	13.25	23.04		2	3	0	0.90	800 638-7983
UAM ICM Small Company	Small Co	22.51	23.11	18.83	3	3	0	0.89	800 638-7983
UAM Jacobs International Octagon	Foreign	3.47					0	1.75	800 638-7983
UAM McKee Domestic Equity Portfolio	Growth	17.01	20.91		2	3	0	1.00	800 638-7983
UAM McKee International Equity	Foreign	1.60	17.15		3	4	0	0.99	800 638-7983
UAM MJI International Equity Port A	Foreign	6.08	10.63		4	3	0	1.50	800 638-7983
UAM MJI International Equity Port B	Foreign	5.92					0	1.76	800 638-7983
UAM NWQ Balanced Portfolio A	Balanced	15.56					0	1.00	800 638-7983
UAM NWQ Balanced Portfolio B	Balanced	15.31					0		800 638-7983
UAM NWQ Value Equity Portfolio A	Growth	16.71	21.38		3	5	0	1.00	800 638-7983
UAM NWQ Value Equity Portfolio B	Growth	15.69					0	1.40	800 638-7983
UAM Rice Hall James Small Cap Port	Small Co	0.09	17.95		4	5	0	1.40	800 638-7983
UAM Rice Hall James Small/Mid Cap	Small Co	28.42					0	2.07	800 638-7983
UAM Sami Preferred Stock Inc Port	Growth/Inc	7.53	8.07	5.73	3	1	0	2.07	800 638-7983
UAM Sirach Growth Portfolio A	Growth	7.16	19.09		4	4	0	0.90	800 638-7983
UAM Sirach Special Equity A	Small Co	22.35	19.33	11.96	4	5	0	0.92	800 638-7983
UAM Sirach Special Equity B	Small Co	22.12					0	1.17	800 638-7983
UAM Sirach Strategic Bal Port A	Balanced	23.53	18.92		3	1	0	0.96	800 638-7983
UAM Sirach Strategic Bal Port B	Balanced	22.71					0	1.21	800 638-7983
UAM Sterling Partners' Bal Port	Balanced	17.27	18.23	13.53	3	1	0	1.04	800 638-7983
UAM Sterling Partners' Equity Port	Growth	21.88					0	0.99	800 638-7983
UAM Sterling Partners' Small Cap	Small Co	16.63					0	1.25	800 638-7983
UAM TJ Core Equity Portfolio	Growth	25.81					0	1.26	800 638-7983
UAM TS&W Equity Portfolio	Growth	16.38	21.95		3	2	0	0.99	800 638-7983
UAM TS&W International Equity Port	Foreign	6.42	10.87	12.69	4	3	0	1.30	800 638-7983
UBS Equity Fund	Growth	21.83					0	0.90	888 827-3863
UBS International Equity Fund	Foreign	−0.25					0	1.39	888 827-3863
Undiscovered Mgrs Behavioral Growth	Growth	15.62					0		888 242-3514
United Accumulative Fund Class A	Growth	26.87	24.74	18.80	2	3	5.75	0.82	800 366-5465
United Asset Strategy Fund A	AssetAlloc	17.67	10.92		3	2	5.75	1.74	800 366-5465
United Continental Income Fund A	Balanced	−23.19	0.84	3.86	5	5	5.75	0.91	800 366-5465
United Continental Income Fund Y	Balanced	−23.07					0	0.75	800 366-5465
United Gold & Government Fund A	Gold	−17.67	−7.41	−4.60	5	4	5.75	2.04	800 366-5465
United Gold & Government Fund Y	Gold	−17.37					0	1.50	800 366-5465
United Income Fund A	Income	25.13	24.81	20.05	3	3	5.75	0.84	800 366-5465

357

Stock Fund Name	Objective	Annualized Return for			Rank		Max Load	Expense Ratio	Toll-Free Telephone
		1 Year	3 Years	5 Years	Overall	Risk			
United International Growth Fund A	Foreign	34.49	22.72	21.62	3	3	5.75	1.24	800 366-5465
United New Concepts Fund A	Agg Growth	36.94	21.11	19.77	3	4	5.75	1.25	800 366-5465
United Retirement Shares A	Growth/Inc	14.45	15.36	13.13	3	1	5.75	0.93	800 366-5465
United Retirement Shares Y	Growth/Inc	14.62					0	0.78	800 366-5465
United Science & Tech Fund A	Technology	38.89	22.49	22.94	3	5	5.75	1.02	800 366-5465
United Science & Tech Fund Y	Technology	39.07					0	0.88	800 366-5465
United Vanguard Fund A	Growth	21.49	17.12	17.38	3	3	5.75	1.09	800 366-5465
Universal Capital Growth Fund	Growth	31.75	24.31	22.85	3	4	5.5	2.00	800 223-9100
US Global Invs All Amer Equity	Growth/Inc	27.28	28.37	19.66	2	3	0	0.67	800 426-6635
US Global Invs Bonnel Growth Fund	Growth	22.19	23.52		4	5	0	1.77	800 426-6635
US Global Invs China Region Opport	Pacific	−52.06	−14.23		5	5	0	2.49	800 426-6635
US Global Invs Global Resources	Energy/Res	−29.89	0.85	0.90	5	4	0	2.30	800 426-6635
US Global Invs Gold Shares	Gold	−58.72	−42.02	−29.33	5	5	0	1.80	800 426-6635
US Global Invs Income	Income	23.84	18.61	11.43	3	2	0	2.19	800 426-6635
US Global Invs Real Estate	Real Est	1.39	16.37	8.01	4	3	0	1.80	800 426-6635
US Global Invs Regent Eastern Euro	European	−12.25					0	3.25	800 426-6635
US Global Invs World Gold	Gold	−37.45	−12.58	−6.22	5	5	0	1.78	800 426-6635
US Global Leaders Growth Fund	Growth	37.20					0	1.48	800 282-2340
USAA Aggressive Growth	Agg Growth	18.57	21.72	19.10	4	5	0	0.72	800 382-8722
USAA Balanced Strategy	Balanced	13.79					0		800 382-8722
USAA Cornerstone Strategy Fund	AssetAlloc	12.42	16.64	12.95	3	1	0	1.02	800 382-8722
USAA Emerging Markets Fund	Foreign	−31.76	−3.78		5	5	0	1.81	800 382-8722
USAA Gold	Gold	−28.90	−15.98	−10.27	5	5	0	1.37	800 382-8722
USAA Growth & Income	Growth/Inc	18.74	24.55	18.88	1	2	0	0.89	800 382-8722
USAA Growth & Tax Strategy	Balanced	13.98	15.04	11.56	3	1	0	0.72	800 382-8722
USAA Growth Fund	Growth	7.93	17.03	15.10	4	4	0	0.97	800 382-8722
USAA Income Fund	Flexible	12.87	9.03	7.03	3	1	0	0.38	800 382-8722
USAA Income Stock	Income	23.73	21.23	16.01	2	2	0	0.68	800 382-8722
USAA Income Strategy	Income	15.85					0	1.00	800 382-8722
USAA International	Foreign	5.39	15.37	14.72	4	4	0	1.01	800 382-8722
USAA S&P 500 Index Fund	Growth/Inc	29.82					0	0.18	800 382-8722
USAA World Growth	Global	10.72	17.46	14.85	3	3	0	1.20	800 382-8722
Valley Forge Fund	Growth	0.27	6.31	6.39	3	1	0	1.30	800-548-1942
Value Line Asset Allocation Fund	AssetAlloc	28.28	27.55		1	2	0	1.16	800 223-0818
Value Line Convertible Fund	Converts	13.54	16.79	12.37	3	1	0	0.99	800 223-0818
Value Line Fund	Growth/Inc	21.55	23.57	16.28	3	3	0	0.78	800 223-0818
Value Line Income Fund	Income	19.29	19.70	13.49	3	2	0	0.87	800 223-0818
Value Line Leverage Growth Invest	Agg Growth	36.89	27.83	21.47	3	4	0	0.86	800 223-0818
Value Line Small-Cap Growth Fund	Small Co	1.74	10.51	12.98	5	4	0	1.76	800 223-0818
Value Line Special Situations Fund	Growth	41.80	23.51	20.00	3	4	0	1.08	800 223-0818
Value Line US Multinational Co	Growth	21.52					0	1.75	800 223-0818
Van Eck Asia Dynasty A	Pacific	−47.09	−17.03	−7.37	5	4	4.75	2.42	800 826-2333
Van Eck Asia Dynasty B	Pacific	−47.59	−17.57		5	4	0	2.86	800 826-2333
Van Eck Chubb Growth & Income	Growth/Inc	19.05	24.06	19.50	3	3	5	1.25	800 826-2333
Van Eck Chubb Total Return Fund	Growth/Inc	17.44	19.82	15.94	3	2	5	1.25	800 826-2333
Van Eck Global Balanced A	Balanced	17.82	15.97		3	2	4.75	2.00	800 826-2333
Van Eck Global Balanced B	Balanced	17.24	15.15		3	2	0	2.51	800 826-2333
Van Eck Global Hard Assets A	Other	−10.73	15.25		4	4	4.75	2.00	800 826-2333
Van Eck Gold/Resources Fund A	Gold	−31.05	−15.78	−11.20	5	5	5.75	1.85	800 826-2333
Van Eck Intl Investors Gold Fund A	Gold	−30.59	−19.14	−11.37	5	5	5.75	1.61	800 826-2333
Van Kampen Am Cap Aggressive Gr A	Agg Growth	37.76					5.75	1.29	800 421-5666
Van Kampen Am Cap Aggressive Gr B	Agg Growth	36.79						2.05	800 421-5666
Van Kampen Am Cap Aggressive Gr C	Agg Growth	36.75						2.05	800 421-5666
Van Kampen Am Cap Emerging Gr A	Small Co	35.60	27.51	20.61	3	4	5.75	1.05	800 421-5666
Van Kampen Am Cap Emerging Gr B	Small Co	33.74	26.28	19.51	3	4	0	1.90	800 421-5666
Van Kampen Am Cap Emerging Gr C	Small Co	33.75	26.29		3	4	0	1.89	800 421-5666
Van Kampen Amer Cap Comstock A	Growth/Inc	28.85	26.14	19.41	1	2	5.75	0.94	800 421-5666
Van Kampen Amer Cap Comstock B	Growth/Inc	27.89	25.13	18.50	1	2	0	1.80	800 421-5666

Stock Fund Name	Objective	Annualized Return for			Rank		Max Load	Expense Ratio	Toll-Free Telephone
		1 Year	3 Years	5 Years	Overall	Risk			
Van Kampen Amer Cap Comstock C	Growth/Inc	27.89	25.14		1	2	0	1.80	800 421-5666
Van Kampen Amer Cap Enterprise A	Growth	28.90	27.12	21.22	2	4	5.75	0.93	800 421-5666
Van Kampen Amer Cap Enterprise B	Growth	27.57	25.96	20.17	2	4	0	1.82	800 421-5666
Van Kampen Amer Cap Enterprise C	Growth	27.61	26.00		2	4	0	1.82	800 421-5666
Van Kampen Amer Cap Equity Inc A	Income	22.35	22.38	17.78	2	2	5.75	0.86	800 421-5666
Van Kampen Amer Cap Equity Inc B	Income	21.33	21.37	16.19	2	2	0	1.74	800 421-5666
Van Kampen Amer Cap Equity Inc C	Income	20.72	21.17		2	2	0	1.74	800 421-5666
Van Kampen Amer Cap Exchange Fund	Growth	16.72	24.37	21.40	3	4	0	0.93	800 421-5666
Van Kampen Amer Cap Gbl Mgd Asset A	Balanced	11.79	13.10		3	1	4.75	3.75	800 421-5666
Van Kampen Amer Cap Gbl Mgd Asset B	Balanced	11.33	12.37		3	1	0	4.52	800 421-5666
Van Kampen Amer Cap Gbl Mgd Asset C	Balanced	11.40	12.30		3	1	0	4.56	800 421-5666
Van Kampen Amer Cap Growth & Inc A	Growth/Inc	23.69	24.55	19.76	1	3	5.75	0.94	800 421-5666
Van Kampen Amer Cap Growth & Inc B	Growth/Inc	22.68	23.54		2	3	0	1.69	800 421-5666
Van Kampen Amer Cap Growth & Inc C	Growth/Inc	22.59	23.52		2	3	0	1.69	800 421-5666
Van Kampen Amer Cap Harbor A	Converts	14.21	14.98	10.84	4	2	5.75	1.04	800 421-5666
Van Kampen Amer Cap Harbor B	Converts	13.37	14.08	9.99	4	2	0	1.82	800 421-5666
Van Kampen Amer Cap Harbor C	Converts	13.35	14.11		4	2	0	1.82	800 421-5666
Van Kampen Amer Cap Pace A	Growth	29.89	26.73	19.46	2	3	5.75	0.97	800 421-5666
Van Kampen Amer Cap Pace B	Growth	28.92	25.73	18.53	2	3	0	1.98	800 421-5666
Van Kampen Amer Cap Pace C	Growth	28.88	25.81		2	3	0	1.74	800 421-5666
Van Kampen Amer Cap RE Secs A	Real Est	8.02	20.82		3	3	4.75	2.60	800 421-5666
Van Kampen Amer Cap RE Secs B	Real Est	7.20	19.92		3	3	0	3.37	800 421-5666
Van Kampen Amer Cap RE Secs C	Real Est	7.20	19.89		3	3	0	3.54	800 421-5666
Van Kampen Amer Cap Utility A	Utilities	28.17	20.24		3	2	5.75	1.38	800 421-5666
Van Kampen Amer Cap Utility B	Utilities	27.20	19.34		3	2	0	2.13	800 421-5666
Van Kampen Amer Cap Utility C	Utilities	27.14	19.58		3	2	0	2.13	800 421-5666
Van Wagoner Emerging Growth Fund	Agg Growth	−10.27					0	1.95	800 228-2121
Van Wagoner Micro Cap Fund	Small Co	−8.27					0	1.95	800 228-2121
Van Wagoner Mid Cap Fund	Agg Growth	0.35					0	1.95	800 228-2121
Van Wagoner Post-Venture Fund	Agg Growth	9.20					0	1.95	800 228-2121
Vance Sanders Exchange Fund	Growth/Inc	28.80	29.47	23.13	1	3	4.5	0.69	800 225-6265
Vanguard Asset Allocation Fund	AssetAlloc	28.46	24.26	18.67	2	2	0	0.49	800 662-7447
Vanguard Balanced Index Fund	Balanced	21.29	19.66	15.33	2	1	0	0.20	800 662-7447
Vanguard Convertible Securities	Converts	14.25	14.71	11.09	4	2	0	0.67	800 662-7447
Vanguard Equity Income Fund	Income	24.36	25.85	18.84	2	2	0	0.45	800 662-7447
Vanguard Explorer Fund	Small Co	11.63	14.82	14.35	4	4	0	0.62	800 662-7447
Vanguard Growth and Income Port	Growth/Inc	34.61	30.90	22.91	1	3	0	0.36	800 662-7447
Vanguard Index 500 Portfolio	Growth/Inc	30.07	30.13	22.94	1	3	0	0.19	800 662-7447
Vanguard Index Extended Market	Growth	23.76	22.96	18.35	3	3	0	0.23	800 662-7447
Vanguard Index Growth	Growth	34.73	33.26	25.18	1	3	0	0.20	800 662-7447
Vanguard Index Small Cap Stock Fund	Small Co	16.94	20.07	17.04	3	4	0	0.23	800 662-7447
Vanguard Index Value	Growth	24.94	26.76	20.51	1	3	0	0.20	800 662-7447
Vanguard International Value Port	Foreign	−0.20	9.43	9.57	4	3	0	0.49	800 662-7447
Vanguard Intl Eq Index Emrg Markets	Foreign	−37.90	−6.77		5	5	0	0.57	800 662-7447
Vanguard Intl Eq Index European	European	37.43	27.14	23.22	2	3	0	0.31	800 662-7447
Vanguard Intl Eq Index Pacific	Pacific	−35.22	−11.19	−5.94	5	4	0	0.35	800 662-7447
Vanguard Intl Eq Index Total Intl	Foreign	−0.32					0	0.00	800 662-7447
Vanguard Intl Growth Portfolio	Foreign	1.65	13.57	14.51	3	3	0	0.57	800 662-7447
Vanguard LIFEStrategy Conserv Gr	AssetAlloc	17.15	15.47		3	1	0	0.00	800 662-7447
Vanguard LIFEStrategy Growth	Growth	21.88	21.47		1	2	0	0.00	800 662-7447
Vanguard LIFEStrategy Moderate Gr	Growth	19.86	18.65		3	1	0	0.00	800 662-7447
Vanguard Morgan Growth	Growth	32.17	28.20	21.29	2	3	0	0.48	800 662-7447
Vanguard Preferred Stk Fund	Income	13.89	11.27	9.31	3	1	0	0.37	800 662-7447
Vanguard PRIMECAP Fund	Growth	26.47	25.13	24.51	3	4	0	0.51	800 662-7447
Vanguard REIT Index Port	Real Est	7.75					0	0.36	800 662-7447
Vanguard Specialized Energy	Energy/Res	6.49	19.16	12.67	4	4	0	0.38	800 662-7447
Vanguard Specialized Gold & Prec	Gold	−33.02	−16.30	−9.49	5	5	0	0.24	800 662-7447
Vanguard Specialized Health	Health	27.77	32.83	28.11	1	2	0	0.40	800 662-7447

| Stock Fund Name | Objective | Annualized Return for | | | Rank | | Max Load | Expense Ratio | Toll-Free Telephone |
		1 Year	3 Years	5 Years	Overall	Risk			
Vanguard Specialized Utilities Inc	Utilities	26.42	18.06	11.88	3	2	0	0.44	800 662-7447
Vanguard STAR Fund	Balanced	19.93	19.74	15.68	2	1	0	0.00	800 662-7447
Vanguard Tax-Managed Balanced	Balanced	17.30	16.05		3	1	0	0.20	800 662-7447
Vanguard Tax-Managed Cap Apprec	Growth	28.14	26.42		2	3	0	0.20	800 662-7447
Vanguard Tax-Managed Growth & Inc	Growth/Inc	30.19	30.23		1	3	0	0.17	800 662-7447
Vanguard Total Stock Market	Growth/Inc	28.54	27.69	21.22	1	3	0	0.20	800 662-7447
Vanguard Trustees' Equity US Port	Growth/Inc	26.92	27.38	19.69	2	3	0	0.53	800 662-7447
Vanguard US Growth Portfolio	Growth	32.91	31.13	24.08	1	3	0	0.42	800 662-7447
Vanguard Wellesley Income Fund	Flexible	20.34	15.85	12.47	3	1	0	0.31	800 662-7447
Vanguard Wellington Fund	Balanced	19.06	20.75	16.70	2	2	0	0.29	800 662-7447
Vanguard Windsor Fund	Growth/Inc	17.01	22.35	19.03	3	3	0	0.27	800 662-7447
Vanguard Windsor II	Growth/Inc	30.43	30.18	22.29	1	3	0	0.37	800 662-7447
Victory Balanced Fund A	Balanced	18.77	17.25		3	1	5.75	1.23	800 539-3863
Victory Balanced Fund B	Balanced	17.38					0	2.55	800 539-3863
Victory Diversified Stock Fund A	Growth	25.79	27.30	22.24	1	3	5.75	1.03	800 539-3863
Victory Diversified Stock Fund B	Growth	26.03					0	2.12	800 539-3863
Victory Growth Stock Fund	Growth	30.88	28.61		2	3	5.75	1.35	800 539-3863
Victory International Growth A	Foreign	9.33	8.31	9.30	4	2	5.75	1.69	800 539-3863
Victory International Growth B	Foreign	8.01					0	3.00	800 539-3863
Victory Lakefront Fund	Growth	17.37					5.75	0.00	800 539-3863
Victory OH Regional Stock Fund A	Growth	16.10	20.25	17.48	3	3	5.75	1.26	800 539-3863
Victory OH Regional Stock Fund B	Growth	15.23					0	2.67	800 539-3863
Victory Real Estate Investment Fund	Real Est	11.79					5.75	0.00	800 539-3863
Victory Special Growth Fund	Growth	10.78	13.72		4	5	5.75	1.42	800 539-3863
Victory Special Value Fund A	Growth	12.70	16.67		3	3	5.75	1.36	800 539-3863
Victory Special Value Fund B	Growth	11.18					0	2.65	800 539-3863
Victory Stock Index Fund	Growth	29.15	28.30		1	3	5.75	0.57	800 539-3863
Victory Value Fund	Growth/Inc	26.96	27.18		1	3	5.75	1.32	800 539-3863
Vintage Aggressive Growth	Agg Growth	25.72					0	1.59	800 438-6375
Vintage Balanced Fund	Balanced	20.92	18.76		3	2	0	1.55	800 438-6375
Vintage Equity Fund	Growth	20.63	26.36	20.47	2	3	0	1.30	800 438-6375
Volumetric Fund	Growth	18.33	17.25	11.48	3	2	0	1.96	800 541-3863
Vontobel Eastern European Equity	European	−28.16					0	2.18	800 527-9500
Vontobel International Equity	Foreign	14.33	19.01	14.80	3	3	0	1.56	800 527-9500
Vontobel US Value	Growth/Inc	30.41	28.36	21.23	1	1	0	1.56	800 527-9500
Voyageur Aggressive Growth A	Agg Growth	57.96	34.18		3	5	4.75	1.75	800 553-2143
Voyageur Aggressive Growth C	Agg Growth	54.37	32.35		3	5	0	2.50	800 553-2143
Wachovia Balanced Fund A	Balanced	17.36	18.31		3	2	4.5	0.97	800 462-7538
Wachovia Balanced Fund B	Balanced	16.56					0	1.76	800 462-7538
Wachovia Balanced Fund Y	Balanced	17.71					0	0.76	800 462-7538
Wachovia Emerging Markets Fund A	Foreign	−30.13	−3.71		5	4	4.5	1.72	800 462-7538
Wachovia Emerging Markets Fund Y	Foreign	−30.01					0	1.51	800 462-7538
Wachovia Equity Fund A	Growth	22.05	24.09	18.42	2	3	4.5	1.11	800 462-7538
Wachovia Equity Fund B	Growth	21.16					0	1.90	800 462-7538
Wachovia Equity Fund Y	Growth	22.34					0	0.90	800 462-7538
Wachovia Equity Index Fund A	Growth	29.14	29.43		1	3	4.5	0.70	800 462-7538
Wachovia Equity Index Fund Y	Growth	29.56					0	0.46	800 462-7538
Wachovia Growth & Income Fund	Growth/Inc	24.22	28.78	20.16	2	3	4.5	1.31	800 462-7538
Wachovia Quantitative Equity Fund A	Growth	27.19	28.30		1	3	4.5	1.11	800 462-7538
Wachovia Quantitative Equity Fund B	Growth	26.24					0	1.81	800 462-7538
Wachovia Quantitative Equity Fund Y	Growth	27.47					0	0.87	800 462-7538
Wachovia Special Values A	Small Co	20.78	31.08	21.55	3	3	4.5	1.35	800 462-7538
Wachovia Special Values Y	Small Co	21.07					0	1.12	800 462-7538
Waddell & Reed Asset Strategy B	Growth/Inc	16.59	9.59		3	1	0		800 366-5465
Waddell & Reed Asset Strategy Y	Growth/Inc	17.57					0		800 366-5465
Waddell & Reed Growth Fund B	Growth	48.10	22.86	22.77	3	4	0	2.18	800 366-5465
Waddell & Reed Growth Fund Y	Growth	49.25					0		800 366-5465
Waddell & Reed Intl Growth Fund B	Foreign	37.03	24.33	15.95	3	3	0		800 366-5465

Stock Fund Name	Objective	Annualized Return for			Rank		Max Load	Expense Ratio	Toll-Free Telephone
		1 Year	3 Years	5 Years	Overall	Risk			
Waddell & Reed Intl Growth Fund Y	Foreign	38.18					0		800 366-5465
Waddell & Reed Total Return Fund B	Growth/Inc	21.77	22.25	18.19	2	3	0		800 366-5465
Waddell & Reed Total Return Fund Y	Growth/Inc	22.60					0		800 366-5465
Wall Street Fund	Growth	10.02	13.80	14.40	4	4	4	1.82	800-625-5759
Warburg Pincus Balanced A	Balanced	16.52	18.12	15.23	3	2	0	1.60	800 888-6878
Warburg Pincus Balanced Advisor	Balanced	16.01					0	1.60	800 888-6878
Warburg Pincus Capital Apprec Adv	Growth	32.60	29.49	21.63	1	3	0	1.49	800 888-6878
Warburg Pincus Capital Appreciation	Growth	33.18	30.04	22.22	1	3	0	1.01	800 888-6878
Warburg Pincus Emerging Growth	Small Co	24.07	21.62	18.82	3	4	0	1.22	800 888-6878
Warburg Pincus Emerging Growth Adv	Small Co	23.57	21.10	18.26	3	4	0	1.63	800 888-6878
Warburg Pincus Emerging Mkts Adv	Foreign	−42.12	−6.74		5	5	0	1.90	800 888-6878
Warburg Pincus Emerging Mkts Fund A	Foreign	−41.93	−6.72		5	5	0	1.65	800 888-6878
Warburg Pincus Gl Post Venture	Global	26.38					0	1.67	800 888-6878
Warburg Pincus Gl Post Venture Adv	Global	25.90					0	1.90	800 888-6878
Warburg Pincus Growth & Income	Growth/Inc	26.29	16.14	14.37	3	3	0	1.18	800 888-6878
Warburg Pincus Growth & Income Adv	Growth/Inc	25.82	15.69		3	3	0	1.57	800 888-6878
Warburg Pincus Health Sciences	Health	37.15					0	1.59	800 888-6878
Warburg Pincus Instl Emrg Markets	Foreign	−38.37					0	1.90	800 888-6878
Warburg Pincus Instl Sm Co Growth	Small Co	16.75					0	1.40	800 888-6878
Warburg Pincus Instl-Intl Equity	Foreign	−3.26	11.37	11.83	4	3	0	1.79	800 888-6878
Warburg Pincus Intl Equity	Foreign	−5.46	10.45	11.15	4	3	0	1.33	800 888-6878
Warburg Pincus Intl Equity Adv	Foreign	−5.88	9.97	10.77	4	3	0	1.79	800 888-6878
Warburg Pincus Japan Growth	Pacific	−9.15					0	2.00	800 888-6878
Warburg Pincus Japan Growth Adv	Pacific	−10.47					0	2.00	800 888-6878
Warburg Pincus Japan OTC	Pacific	−18.35	−2.33		5	4	0	1.75	800 888-6878
Warburg Pincus Japan OTC Adv	Pacific	−17.91	−2.67		5	4	0	2.00	800 888-6878
Warburg Pincus Major Foreign Mkts	Growth/Inc	8.35					0		800 888-6878
Warburg Pincus Post-Venture Cap Adv	Growth	21.44					0	1.90	800 888-6878
Warburg Pincus Post-Venture Cap Com	Growth	21.67					0	1.66	800 888-6878
Warburg Pincus Sm Co Value	Small Co	15.09					0	1.68	800 888-6878
Warburg Pincus Sm Co Value Adv	Small Co	13.79					0	1.92	800 888-6878
Warburg Pincus Small Company Growth	Small Co	16.15					0	1.41	800 888-6878
Warburg Pincus Strategic Value	Growth	16.03					0	1.45	800 888-6878
Warburg Pincus Strategic Value Adv	Growth	14.79					0	1.70	800 888-6878
Warburg Pincus Tr Post Venture Cap	Growth	24.10					0	1.66	800 888-6878
Warburg Pincus Trust Intl Equity	Foreign	−3.73					0	1.79	800 888-6878
Warburg Pincus Trust Sm Co Growth	Small Co	18.13					0	1.40	800 888-6878
Wasatch Aggressive Equity	Small Co	18.06	15.16	16.52	4	4	0	1.50	800 551-1700
Wasatch Growth	Growth	21.21	22.89	20.80	3	3	0	1.50	800 551-1700
Wasatch Micro-Cap Fund	Small Co	37.44	34.60		3	4	0	2.50	800 551-1700
Wasatch Mid Cap Fund	Agg Growth	9.98	10.13	15.31	4	5	0	1.75	800 551-1700
Washington Mutual Investors Fund	Growth/Inc	27.24	29.16	21.50	1	2	5.75	0.32	800 421-0180
Wayne Hummer Growth Fund	Growth	22.77	21.13	15.70	3	2	0	0.97	800 621-4477
Weiss Peck & Greer International	Foreign	8.92	10.17	10.01	4	3	0	1.95	800 223-3332
Weitz Hickory Fd	Growth	61.99	44.62	29.94	1	4	0	1.50	800 232-4161
Weitz Partners Value Fund	Growth	49.31	33.42		1	3	0	1.23	800 232-4161
Weitz Series Value Fund	Growth	47.81	33.04	23.03	1	3	0	1.27	800 232-4161
Westcore Blue Chip Fund	Growth/Inc	28.15	28.46	21.19	1	3	0	1.21	800 392-2673
Westcore Growth & Income Fund	Growth/Inc	16.35	22.54	14.28	3	3	0	1.15	800 392-2673
Westcore Midco Growth Fund	Agg Growth	14.65	17.67	15.86	4	4	4.5	1.11	800 392-2673
Westcore Small Cap Opport Fund	Small Co	24.22	26.74		2	3	0	1.30	800 392-2673
White Oak Growth Stock Fund	Growth	31.38	34.93	28.45	3	4	0	0.98	888 462-5386
William Blair Growth Fund	Growth	28.10	22.28	21.23	3	4	0	0.84	800 742-7272
William Blair Intl Growth Fund	Foreign	7.79	14.36	11.89	4	3	0	1.43	800 742-7272
William Blair Value Discovery Fund	Small Co	31.73					0	1.50	800 742-7272
Wilshire Target Large Co Gr Instl	Agg Growth	32.32					0	0.78	888-200-6796
Wilshire Target Large Co Gr Retail	Agg Growth	32.09	31.95	24.19	2	3	0	0.61	888-200-6796
Wilshire Target Large Co Val Instl	Agg Growth	26.31					0	0.91	888-200-6796

Stock Fund Name	Objective	Annualized Return for			Rank		Max Load	Expense Ratio	Toll-Free Telephone
		1 Year	3 Years	5 Years	Overall	Risk			
Wilshire Target Large Co Val Inv	Agg Growth	26.14	25.81	17.88	2	3	0	0.78	888-200-6796
Wilshire Target Sm Co Growth Instl	Small Co	9.62					0	1.22	888-200-6796
Wilshire Target Sm Co Growth Retail	Small Co	9.55	13.96	13.49	4	4	0	1.22	888-200-6796
Wilshire Target Small Co Val Instl	Small Co	19.18					0	0.86	888-200-6796
Wilshire Target Small Co Val Inv	Small Co	19.13	19.80	13.78	3	2	0	0.86	888-200-6796
Winthrop Focus Growth & Income A	Growth/Inc	27.90	27.94	20.09	2	3	0	1.22	800 494-6847
Winthrop Focus Growth & Income B	Growth/Inc	26.99					0	1.92	800 494-6847
Winthrop Focus Growth A	Growth	27.12	29.29	20.18	3	4	4.75	1.40	800 494-6847
Winthrop Focus Growth B	Growth	26.18					0	2.10	800 494-6847
Winthrop Focus Small Company Val A	Small Co	13.11	16.80	14.95	4	3		1.35	800 494-6847
Winthrop Focus Small Company Val B	Small Co	12.30					0	2.09	800 494-6847
WM Bond & Stock Fund A	Balanced	13.43	17.55	14.03	3	1	4.5	0.99	800 531-6466
WM Bond & Stock Fund B	Balanced	12.65	16.58		3	1	0	1.83	800 531-6466
WM Emerging Growth Fund A	Small Co	12.95	14.78	13.70	4	4	5.75	1.72	800 531-6466
WM Emerging Growth Fund B	Small Co	12.05	13.92		4	4	0	2.39	800 531-6466
WM Emerging Growth Fund S	Small Co	12.05	13.91		4	4	0	2.39	800 531-6466
WM Growth & Income Fund A	Growth/Inc	20.88	26.21	20.08	2	3	4.5	1.05	800 531-6466
WM Growth & Income Fund B	Growth/Inc	20.08	25.11		2	3	0	1.93	800 531-6466
WM Growth Fund A	Growth	35.43	23.53	20.06	3	4	5.75	1.70	800 531-6466
WM Growth Fund B	Growth	34.43	22.58		3	4	0	2.45	800 531-6466
WM Growth Fund S	Growth	34.40	22.59		3	4	0	2.45	800 531-6466
WM International Growth A	Foreign	−4.19	7.79	6.29	5	3	5.75	1.69	800 531-6466
WM International Growth B	Foreign	−4.95	6.98		5	3	0	2.40	800 531-6466
WM International Growth S	Foreign	−4.37	7.74		5	3	0	2.40	800 531-6466
WM Northwest Fund A	Growth	12.44	22.37	16.95	3	4	4.5	1.05	800 531-6466
WM Northwest Fund B	Growth	11.50	21.31		3	4	0	1.93	800 531-6466
Women's Equity Fund	Growth	32.46	24.69		3	3	0	1.50	
WPG Growth & Income	Growth/Inc	33.14	31.83	21.14	1	3	0	1.06	800 223-3332
WPG Growth Fund	Small Co	7.07	15.16	11.04	4	4	0	1.09	800 223-3332
WPG Quantitative Equity Fund	Growth/Inc	24.88	24.83	19.17	2	3	0	1.05	800 223-3332
WPG Tudor Fund	Agg Growth	9.57	17.70	13.20	4	4	0	1.25	800 223-3332
Wright EquiFund Belgian Luxembourg	European	33.50	22.96		3	3	0	2.15	800 232-0013
Wright EquiFund Hong Kong Fund	Pacific	−54.52	−13.97	−9.69	5	5	0	1.85	800 232-0013
Wright EquiFund Japanese Fund	Pacific	−28.33	−9.54		5	4	0	2.01	800 232-0013
Wright EquiFund Mexico Fund	Foreign	−10.93	10.08		3	5	0	1.66	800 232-0013
Wright EquiFund Netherland Fund	European	24.99	25.14	24.45	2	3	0	2.17	800 232-0013
Wright EquiFund Nordic Fund	European	14.47	21.39		3	3	0	2.17	800 232-0013
Wright International Blue Chip	Foreign	4.01	11.00	12.07	4	2	0	1.31	800 232-0013
Wright Jr Blue Chip Equities	Small Co	12.54	18.62	14.25	3	3	0	1.18	800 232-0013
Wright Major Blue Chip Equities	Growth/Inc	27.01	26.59	19.08	2	3	0	1.08	800 232-0013
Wright Selected Blue Chip Equities	Growth/Inc	19.76	22.99	16.63	2	2	0	1.08	800 232-0013
Yacktman Focused Fund	Growth	14.04					0	1.25	800 525-8258
Yacktman Fund	Growth	8.59	20.37	18.00	3	2	0	0.91	800 525-8258
ZSA Asset Allocation	AssetAlloc	11.34	14.23	8.99	3	1	0	1.95	800 525-3863
Zweig Appreciation A	Small Co	24.05	19.95	14.93	3	2	5.5	1.52	800 272-2700
Zweig Appreciation B	Small Co	23.16					0	2.26	800 272-2700
Zweig Appreciation C	Small Co	23.13	19.10	14.01	3	2	0	2.26	800 272-2700
Zweig Managed Assets A	AssetAlloc	16.91	14.37	10.77	3	1	5.5	1.63	800 272-2700
Zweig Managed Assets B	AssetAlloc	16.07					0	2.33	800 272-2700
Zweig Managed Assets C	AssetAlloc	16.11	13.58	10.10	3	1	0	2.29	800 272-2700
Zweig Strategy A	Growth	20.65	15.78	13.73	3	2	5.5	1.25	800 272-2700
Zweig Strategy B	Growth	19.82					0	1.95	800 272-2700
Zweig Strategy C	Growth	20.14	15.08	12.78	3	2	0	1.95	800 272-2700

Bond Fund Name	Objective	Annualized Return for			Rank		Max Load	Expense Ratio	Toll-Free Telephone
		1 Year	3 Years	5 Years	Overall	Risk			
BOND FUNDS									
AAL Bond Fund A	Corp-Inv	9.40	6.73	5.28	3	3	4.75	0.75	800 553-6319
AAL Bond Fund B	Corp-Inv	8.48					0	1.86	800 553-6319
AAL High Yield Bond Fund A	Corp-HY	10.25					4	1.00	800 553-6319
AAL High Yield Bond Fund B	Corp-HY	9.33					0	1.75	800 553-6319
AAL Municipal Bond Fund A	Muni Natl	10.00	8.42	6.64	3	4	4	0.86	800 553-6319
AAL Municipal Bond Fund B	Muni Natl	8.97					0	1.69	800 553-6319
AARP Bond Fund for Income	Corp-Inv	9.05					0	6.75	800 253-2277
AARP GNMA & US Treasury Fund	Govt-Mtg	7.92	6.84	5.50	3	2	0	0.65	800 253-2277
AARP High Quality ST Bond Funds	Corp-Inv	7.74	6.51	5.58	4	3	0	0.93	800 253-2277
AARP Insured TF General Bond	Muni Natl	7.66	7.19	5.55	4	3	0	0.63	800 253-2277
ABN AMRO Fixed Income Fund Comn Shs	Corp-Inv	10.12	7.68	6.44	3	4	0	0.71	800 443-4725
ABN AMRO Fixed Income Fund Inv Shs	Corp-Inv	9.93	7.42	5.68	3	4	4.5	0.96	800 443-4725
ABN AMRO Intl Fixed Income Comn Shs	Intl Bond	0.41	0.92	4.54	5	5	0	1.22	800 443-4725
ABN AMRO Intl Fixed Income Inv Shs	Intl Bond	0.31	0.69	4.24	5	5	4.5	1.37	800 443-4725
ABN AMRO Sht-Intmed Govt Comn Shs	Government	7.75	6.46	5.15	4	2	0	0.71	800 443-4725
ABN AMRO Sht-Intmed Govt Inv Shs	Government	7.83	6.38	5.09	4	2	0	0.96	800 443-4725
ABN AMRO Tax-Exempt Fxd Inc Cmn Shs	Muni Natl	8.94	7.39	5.23	3	3	0	0.72	800 443-4725
ABN AMRO Tax-Exempt Fxd Inc Inv Shs	Muni Natl	8.59	7.10	5.41	3	3	0	0.97	800 443-4725
Accessor Intermediate Fixed Income	Corp-Inv	10.04	7.20		3	4	0	0.84	800 759-3504
Accessor Mortgage Securities	Govt-Mtg	8.96	7.66	6.58	1	2	0	0.84	800 759-3504
Accessor Short/Intmed Fixed Income	Corp-Inv	6.57	5.56	4.75	4	1	0	0.84	800 759-3504
Achievement Idaho Muni Bond Instl	Muni State	7.37	6.67		4	3	4	0.75	800 472-0577
Achievement Idaho Muni Bond Retail	Muni State	7.17	6.45		4	3	4	1.00	800 472-0577
Achievement Intmed Term Bond Instl	Corp-Inv	8.65	6.24		4	3	3.5	0.75	800 472-0577
Achievement Intmed Term Bond Retail	Corp-Inv	8.26	5.98		3	3	3.5	1.00	800 472-0577
Achievement Muni Bond Fund Instl	Muni Natl	9.04					0	0.75	800 472-0577
Achievement Muni Bond Fund Retail	Muni Natl	8.79					4	1.00	800 472-0577
Achievement ST Bond Fund Instl	Corp-Inv	5.96	5.49		4	1	1.5	0.75	800 472-0577
Achievement ST Bond Fund Retail	Corp-Inv	5.64	5.28		4	1	4	1.00	800 472-0577
Achievement ST Muni Bond Instl	Muni Natl	4.29	4.11		3	1	1.5	0.75	800 472-0577
Achievement ST Muni Bond Retail	Muni Natl	4.07	3.92		4	1	1.5	1.00	800 472-0577
Advantus Bond Fund A	Corp-Inv	10.18	7.70	6.83	2	4	5	1.00	800 665-6005
Advantus Bond Fund B	Corp-Inv	9.52	6.86		3	4	0	1.90	800 665-6005
Advantus Bond Fund C	Corp-Inv	9.28	6.77		4	4	0	1.90	800 665-6005
Advantus Mortgage Secs Income A	Govt-Mtg	9.39	7.67	6.39	2	3	5	0.95	800 665-6005
Advantus Mortgage Secs Income B	Govt-Mtg	8.70	6.95		3	3	0	1.70	800 665-6005
Advantus Mortgage Secs Income C	Govt-Mtg	8.60	6.81		3	3	0	1.70	800 665-6005
Aetna Bond Fund A	Corp-Inv	8.31	6.48	5.63	3	3	0	1.50	800 238-6263
Aetna Bond Fund I	Corp-Inv	9.34	7.33	6.34	3	3	0	0.75	800 238-6263
Aetna Government Fund A	Government	9.48	6.23		3	3	0	1.45	800 238-6263
Aetna Government Fund I	Government	10.00	6.93		3	3	0	0.70	800 238-6263
AHA Investment Full Maturity	Corp-Inv	10.77	7.80	6.73	2	4	0	0.21	800 332-2111
AHA Investment Limited Maturity I	Corp-Inv	6.59	6.11	5.52	3	1	0	0.12	800 332-2111
AIM Global Government Income A	Intl Bond	6.70	5.66	4.52	5	4	4.75	1.34	800 347-4246
AIM Global Government Income B	Intl Bond	6.16	4.97	3.84	4	4	0	2.06	800 347-4246
AIM Global High Income A	Intl Bond	−4.39	18.14	12.06	4	5	4.75	1.61	800 347-4246
AIM Global High Income B	Intl Bond	−5.01	17.41	11.03	4	5	0	2.18	800 347-4246
AIM Global Income A	Intl Bond	10.07	10.13		1	3	4.75	1.25	800 347-4246
AIM Global Income B	Intl Bond	9.48	9.56		1	3	0	1.75	800 347-4246
AIM High Yield Fund A	Corp-HY	11.21	12.43	10.35	1	4	4.75	0.90	800 347-4246
AIM High Yield Fund B	Corp-HY	10.32	11.60		1	4	0	1.64	800 347-4246
AIM Income Fund A	Dvsfd Bond	12.91	11.35	8.46	2	5	4.75	0.94	800 347-4246
AIM Income Fund B	Dvsfd Bond	12.00	10.45		2	5	0	1.75	800 347-4246
AIM Interm Government Fund A	Government	9.55	7.01	5.73	3	3	4.75	1.00	800 347-4246
AIM Interm Government Fund B	Government	8.77	6.21		4	3	0	1.77	800 347-4246
AIM Limited Maturity Treas A	Government	5.99	5.65	5.06	3	1	1	0.54	800 347-4246
AIM Municipal Bond A	Muni Natl	6.75	6.30	5.32	3	2	4.75	0.90	800 347-4246

363

Bond Fund Name	Objective	Annualized Return for			Rank		Max Load	Expense Ratio	Toll-Free Telephone
		1 Year	3 Years	5 Years	Overall	Risk			
AIM Municipal Bond B	Muni Natl	6.12	5.48		4	2	0	1.68	800 347-4246
AIM Strategic Income Fund A	Intl Bond	2.91	12.69	7.83	4	5	4.75	1.35	800 347-4246
AIM Strategic Income Fund B	Intl Bond	2.25	11.93	7.15	4	5	0	2.05	800 347-4246
AIM Tax Free Intermediate A	Muni Natl	6.34	5.72	5.05	3	2	1	0.48	800 347-4246
AIM TE Bond Fund CT	Muni State	6.47	6.05	5.24	3	2	4.75	0.84	800 347-4246
Alabama Tax Free Bond Fund	Muni State	6.12	5.55	4.91	3	2	0	0.66	800 543-8721
Alliance Bond US Government A	Government	10.00	6.02	5.22	4	4	4.25	0.29	800 221-5672
Alliance Bond US Government B	Government	9.18	5.25	4.45	5	4	0	1.74	800 221-5672
Alliance Bond US Government C	Government	9.18	5.25	4.45	5	4	0	1.74	800 221-5672
Alliance Corporate Bond A	Corp-Inv	8.69	12.43	9.42	3	5	4.25	1.06	800 221-5672
Alliance Corporate Bond B	Corp-Inv	7.98	11.68	8.33	4	5	0	1.76	800 221-5672
Alliance Corporate Bond C	Corp-Inv	7.98	11.65	8.33	4	5	0	1.76	800 221-5672
Alliance Global Dollar Govt Fund A	Intl Bond	−6.34	19.24		4	5	4.25	1.55	800 221-5672
Alliance Global Dollar Govt Fund B	Intl Bond	−7.03	18.34		4	5	0	2.26	800 221-5672
Alliance Global Dollar Govt Fund C	Intl Bond	−7.00	18.38		4	5	0	2.25	800 221-5672
Alliance Global Strategic Inc A	Intl Bond	9.75					4.25	1.90	800 221-5672
Alliance Global Strategic Inc B	Intl Bond	8.99					0	2.60	800 221-5672
Alliance Global Strategic Inc C	Intl Bond	8.99					0	2.60	800 221-5672
Alliance High Yield Fund A	Corp-HY	20.12					4.25	1.40	800 221-5672
Alliance High Yield Fund Adv	Corp-HY	20.42					0	1.12	800 221-5672
Alliance High Yield Fund B	Corp-HY	19.31					0	2.11	800 221-5672
Alliance High Yield Fund C	Corp-HY	19.31					0	2.11	800 221-5672
Alliance Limited Maturity Govt A	Govt-Mtg	7.22	5.79		4	2	4.25	1.65	800 221-5672
Alliance Limited Maturity Govt B	Govt-Mtg	6.46	5.00	3.84	4	2	0	2.39	800 221-5672
Alliance Limited Maturity Govt C	Govt-Mtg	6.47	5.01	3.76	4	2	0	2.37	800 221-5672
Alliance Mortgage Secs Income A	Govt-Mtg	8.17	7.12	5.31	3	2	4.25	1.41	800 221-5672
Alliance Mortgage Secs Income B	Govt-Mtg	7.37	6.28	4.53	5	2	0	2.14	800 221-5672
Alliance Mortgage Secs Income C	Govt-Mtg	7.37	6.29	4.54	4	2	0	2.12	800 221-5672
Alliance Multi Market Strategy A	Intl Bond	7.03	11.28	4.28	2	2	4.44	1.58	800 221-5672
Alliance Multi Market Strategy B	Intl Bond	6.08	10.36	3.44	3	2	0	2.29	800 221-5672
Alliance Multi Market Strategy C	Intl Bond	6.10	10.47	3.53	3	3	0	2.28	800 221-5672
Alliance Muni Income CA A	Muni CA	10.51	9.42	6.44	2	4	4.25	0.78	800 221-5672
Alliance Muni Income CA B	Muni CA	9.75	8.65	6.20	3	4	0	1.48	800 221-5672
Alliance Muni Income CA C	Muni CA	9.75	8.65	6.17	3	4	0	1.48	800 221-5672
Alliance Muni Income II AZ A	Muni State	9.99	8.85		1	3	4.25	0.78	800 221-5672
Alliance Muni Income II AZ B	Muni State	9.28	8.15		2	3	0	1.48	800 221-5672
Alliance Muni Income II AZ C	Muni State	9.28	8.11		2	3	0	1.48	800 221-5672
Alliance Muni Income II FL A	Muni State	10.27	9.32	6.68	1	3	4.25	0.73	800 221-5672
Alliance Muni Income II FL B	Muni State	9.39	8.49	5.89	2	3	0	1.43	800 221-5672
Alliance Muni Income II FL C	Muni State	9.39	8.54	5.94	2	3	0	1.43	800 221-5672
Alliance Muni Income II MA A	Muni State	10.59	10.29		2	4	4.25	0.72	800 221-5672
Alliance Muni Income II MA B	Muni State	9.80	9.55		2	4	0	1.42	800 221-5672
Alliance Muni Income II MA C	Muni State	9.90	9.55		2	4	0	1.42	800 221-5672
Alliance Muni Income II MI A	Muni State	10.48	9.34		2	4	4.25	0.96	800 221-5672
Alliance Muni Income II MI B	Muni State	9.75	8.60		2	4	0	1.66	800 221-5672
Alliance Muni Income II MI C	Muni State	9.75	8.60		2	4	0	1.66	800 221-5672
Alliance Muni Income II MN A	Muni State	9.40	8.30	6.11	2	4	4.25	0.75	800 221-5672
Alliance Muni Income II MN B	Muni State	8.63	7.50	5.33	3	4	0	1.46	800 221-5672
Alliance Muni Income II MN C	Muni State	8.63	7.46	5.33	3	4	0	1.45	800 221-5672
Alliance Muni Income II NJ A	Muni State	9.09	8.45	6.38	2	3	4.25	0.82	800 221-5672
Alliance Muni Income II NJ B	Muni State	8.32	7.62		3	4	0	1.53	800 221-5672
Alliance Muni Income II NJ C	Muni State	8.31	7.62	5.53	3	4	0	1.52	800 221-5672
Alliance Muni Income II OH A	Muni State	10.01	8.99	6.55	1	3	4.25	0.75	800 221-5672
Alliance Muni Income II OH B	Muni State	9.25	8.20	5.77	2	3	0	1.46	800 221-5672
Alliance Muni Income II OH C	Muni State	9.25	8.20		1	3	0	1.45	800 221-5672
Alliance Muni Income II PA A	Muni State	9.64	9.19	6.92	2	3	4.25	0.95	800 221-5672
Alliance Muni Income II PA B	Muni State	8.89	8.41	6.17	2	3	0	1.66	800 221-5672
Alliance Muni Income II PA C	Muni State	8.89	8.40	6.14	2	3	0	1.65	800 221-5672

Bond Fund Name	Objective	Annualized Return for			Rank		Max Load	Expense Ratio	Toll-Free Telephone
		1 Year	3 Years	5 Years	Overall	Risk			
Alliance Muni Income II VA A	Muni State	12.88	10.50		1	3	4.25	0.67	800 221-5672
Alliance Muni Income II VA B	Muni State	12.17	9.77		1	3	0	1.37	800 221-5672
Alliance Muni Income II VA C	Muni State	12.07	9.74		1	3	0	1.37	800 221-5672
Alliance Muni Income Ins CA A	Muni CA	8.76	8.31	6.14	3	5	4.25	1.11	800 221-5672
Alliance Muni Income Ins CA B	Muni CA	7.90	7.51	4.64	4	5	0	1.81	800 221-5672
Alliance Muni Income Ins CA C	Muni CA	7.90	7.51	5.34	4	5	0	1.81	800 221-5672
Alliance Muni Income Ins Ntl A	Muni Natl	9.44	8.70	6.56	2	4	4.25	1.02	800 221-5672
Alliance Muni Income Ins Ntl B	Muni Natl	8.75	8.01	5.86	3	4	0	1.75	800 221-5672
Alliance Muni Income Ins Ntl C	Muni Natl	8.75	7.97	5.86	3	4	0	1.72	800 221-5672
Alliance Muni Income Natl A	Muni Natl	9.23	8.79	6.51	3	4	4.25	0.69	800 221-5672
Alliance Muni Income Natl B	Muni Natl	8.43	8.05	5.87	3	4	0	1.40	800 221-5672
Alliance Muni Income Natl C	Muni Natl	8.45	8.06	5.89	3	4	0	1.39	800 221-5672
Alliance Muni Income NY A	Muni NY	9.42	8.99	6.50	2	4	4.25	0.65	800 221-5672
Alliance Muni Income NY B	Muni NY	8.66	7.92	5.53	3	4	0	1.35	800 221-5672
Alliance Muni Income NY C	Muni NY	8.67	7.92	5.53	3	4	0	1.35	800 221-5672
Alliance North American Govt Inc A	Intl Bond	9.44	19.82		4	5	4.25	1.38	800 221-5672
Alliance North American Govt Inc B	Intl Bond	8.65	18.78	7.03	4	5	0	2.09	800 221-5672
Alliance North American Govt Inc C	Intl Bond	8.65	18.78	7.04	4	5	0	2.08	800 221-5672
Alliance Short Term Multi Market A	Intl Bond	5.91	9.22	3.95	3	2	4.25	1.28	800 221-5672
Alliance Short Term Multi Market B	Intl Bond	5.09	8.44	3.19	3	2	0	1.99	800 221-5672
Alliance Short Term Multi Market C	Intl Bond	5.23	8.45	3.20	3	2	0	1.99	800 221-5672
Alliance Short Term US Govt A	Government	4.24	4.70	3.71	4	1	4.25	2.42	800 221-5672
Alliance Short Term US Govt B	Government	3.53	3.95	3.00	3	1	0	2.10	800 221-5672
Alliance Short Term US Govt C	Government	3.53	3.95		4	1	0	2.10	800 221-5672
Alliance World Income Trust	Intl Bond	4.00	5.17	2.24	3	1	0	2.25	800 221-5672
Amer Cent-Benham AZ Muni Intmed	Muni State	6.43	5.92		4	2	0	0.79	800 345-2021
Amer Cent-Benham Bond Fund	Corp-Inv	9.81	7.25	6.45	3	4	0	0.80	800 345-2021
Amer Cent-Benham CA Intmed-Term TF	Muni CA	6.49	6.42	5.41	3	3	0	0.52	800 345-2021
Amer Cent-Benham CA Long-Term TF	Muni CA	8.98	8.54	7.28	3	4	0	0.52	800 345-2021
Amer Cent-Benham CA Ltd-Term TF	Muni CA	4.95	4.77	4.26	3	1	0	0.49	800 345-2021
Amer Cent-Benham CA Muni High-Yield	Muni CA	9.52	9.22	7.20	1	3	0	0.50	800 345-2021
Amer Cent-Benham CA TF Insured	Muni CA	8.86	8.13	6.25	3	5	0	0.48	800 345-2021
Amer Cent-Benham FL Intmed Term TF	Muni State	7.20	6.39		3	2	0	0.65	800 345-2021
Amer Cent-Benham GNMA Income Fund	Govt-Mtg	8.12	7.49	6.45	2	2	0	0.57	800 345-2021
Amer Cent-Benham International Bond	Intl Bond	3.57	2.89	6.83	3	5	0	0.84	800 345-2021
Amer Cent-Benham Intmed Term TF	Muni Natl	2.59	4.63	4.31	5	5	0	0.60	800 345-2021
Amer Cent-Benham Intmed-Term Bond	Corp-Inv	8.56	6.84		4	3	0	0.75	800 345-2021
Amer Cent-Benham Intmed-Term Treas	Government	9.40	6.92	5.72	3	3	0	0.51	800 345-2021
Amer Cent-Benham Limited-Term Bond	Corp-Inv	6.23	5.96		3	1	0	0.69	800 345-2021
Amer Cent-Benham LT Tax-Free Fund	Muni Natl	8.79	7.87	6.16	3	5	0	0.58	800 345-2021
Amer Cent-Benham LT Treas & Agency	Government	19.10	9.77	8.08	3	5	0	0.57	800 345-2021
Amer Cent-Benham Ltd-Term TF	Muni Natl	4.46	4.57	4.36	3	1	0	0.60	800 345-2021
Amer Cent-Benham Premium Bond	Corp-Inv	9.91	7.44	6.53	3	4	0	0.45	800 345-2021
Amer Cent-Benham Short-Term Govt	Government	6.16	5.58	4.78	3	1	0	0.68	800 345-2021
Amer Cent-Benham ST Treas & Agency	Government	6.20	5.53	4.89	3	1	0	0.58	800 345-2021
Amer Cent-Benham Target Mat 2000	Government	7.92	6.01	5.43	4	3	0	0.56	800 345-2021
Amer Cent-Benham Target Mat 2005	Government	14.81	8.34	7.77	3	5	0	0.57	800 345-2021
Amer Cent-Benham Target Mat 2010	Government	22.50	11.03	9.91	3	5	0	0.62	800 345-2021
Amer Cent-Benham Target Mat 2015	Government	31.62	14.13	12.39	3	5	0	0.61	800 345-2021
Amer Cent-Benham Target Mat 2020	Government	39.95	16.51	14.08	3	5	0	0.53	800 345-2021
American AAdvantage Ltd Tm Inc Inst	Corp-Inv	6.84	5.83	5.21	3	1	0	0.50	800 231-4252
American AAdvantage Ltd Tm Inc Mlge	Corp-Inv	6.56	5.68		3	2	0	0.31	800 231-4252
American AAdvantage Ltd Tm Inc Pl A	Corp-Inv	6.59	5.78		4	1	0	0.85	800 231-4252
American High-Income Muni Bond	Muni Natl	9.29	9.14		1	2	4.75	0.90	800 421-0180
American High-Income Trust	Corp-HY	10.71	12.66	10.23	1	3	4.75	0.82	800 421-0180
American National Govt Income	Government	8.28	6.61	5.99	3	3	4.5	0.97	800 231-4639
American National Tax Free Fund	Muni Natl	8.49	7.63		1	3	4.5	0.32	800 231-4639
American Performance Bond	Corp-Inv	11.48	7.57	6.17	3	4	4	0.94	800 762-7085

Bond Fund Name	Objective	Annualized Return for			Rank		Max Load	Expense Ratio	Toll-Free Telephone
		1 Year	3 Years	5 Years	Overall	Risk			
American Performance Intermed Bond	Corp-Inv	8.34	6.47	5.17	3	2	3	0.93	800 762-7085
American Performance Intmed TF Bond	Muni Natl	6.81	6.02	5.51	3	2	3	0.76	800 762-7085
Ameristar Limited Duration Inc A	Corp-Inv	6.71	5.90		4	1	3	1.08	800-852-0045
Ameristar Ltd Dur Tennessee A	Muni State	5.10					3	1.57	800-852-0045
Ameristar Ltd Dur US Govt Fund A	Government	6.65					3	1.62	800-852-0045
Ameristar Tennessee Tax-Exempt A	Muni State	6.68	5.12		5	3	3	1.08	800-852-0045
AMF Adjustable Rate Mortgage Port	Govt-Mtg	5.58	6.16	5.54	3	1	0	0.49	800 527-3713
AMF Intermediate Mortgage Secs Port	Govt-Mtg	8.27	6.62	5.66	3	2	0	0.49	800 527-3713
AMF Short US Govt Secs Port	Government	6.59	5.70	5.21	3	1	0	0.50	800 527-3713
AMF US Govt Mort Secs Port	Govt-Mtg	9.21	7.48	5.93	2	3	0	0.53	800 527-3713
AmSouth Bond Fund	Corp-Inv	10.90	7.24	6.39	3	4	3	0.71	800 451-8382
AmSouth FL Tax Free Fund	Muni State	6.37	5.38		3	2	3	0.54	800 451-8382
AmSouth Government Income	Government	9.60	7.43		2	3	3	0.72	800 451-8382
AmSouth Limited Maturity	Corp-Inv	7.50	5.95	5.23	3	2	3	0.77	800 451-8382
Anchor International Bond Trust	Intl Bond	−0.13	−4.52	2.14	4	5	0	1.28	
Aon Government Securities Fund	Government	12.28					0	0.67	800 266-3637
Aquinas Fixed Income	Corp-Inv	9.39	6.88		3	3	0	1.00	800 423-6369
Arch Missouri Tax Ex Bond Inv	Muni State	7.63	6.75	5.61	4	5	4.5	0.86	800 452-2724
Arch Missouri Tax Ex Bond Trust	Muni State	7.51	6.72	5.67	3	3	0	0.66	800 452-2724
Arch Short-Intmed Muni A	Muni Natl	4.93					2.5	0.61	800 452-2724
Arch Short-Intmed Muni Trust	Muni Natl	5.04					0	0.36	800 452-2724
Arch US Government Secs B	Government	6.15	4.88	4.52	4	2	0	1.66	800 452-2724
Arch US Government Secs Instl	Government	7.10	5.69	5.22	3	2	0	0.96	800 452-2724
Arch US Government Secs Inv	Government	6.84	5.59	5.21	3	2	2.5	0.97	800 452-2724
Arch US Government Secs Trust	Government	7.13	5.91	5.54	3	2	0	0.66	800 452-2724
Ariel Premier Bond Fund Instl	Corp-Inv	9.93					0	0.45	800 292-7435
Ark Income Instl	Corp-Inv	10.47	7.52		2	3	0	0.68	888 427-5386
Ark Income Retail	Corp-Inv	10.24	7.25		2	3	4.5	0.89	888 427-5386
Ark Intermediate Fixed Income Instl	Corp-Inv	8.32					0	0.68	888 427-5386
Ark MD Tax-Free Instl	Muni State	7.52					0	0.67	888 427-5386
Ark MD Tax-Free Retail	Muni State	7.30					4.5	0.91	888 427-5386
Ark PA Tax-Free Instl	Muni State	6.64					0	0.63	888 427-5386
Ark PA Tax-Free Retail	Muni State	6.57					4.5	0.87	888 427-5386
Ark Short-Term Treasury Instl	Government	6.12					0	0.55	888 427-5386
Ark Short-Term Treasury Retail	Government	5.96					0	0.67	888 427-5386
Armada Enhanced Income Fund Instl	Dvsfd Bond	6.50	6.08		4	1	2.75	0.21	800 622-3863
Armada Enhanced Income Fund Retail	Dvsfd Bond	6.39	5.93		4	1	2.75	0.31	800 622-3863
Armada GNMA Instl	Govt-Mtg	8.32	7.54		2	2	0	1.12	800 622-3863
Armada GNMA Retail Class	Govt-Mtg	7.63					3.75	1.12	800 622-3863
Armada Intermediate Bond Instl	Corp-Inv	7.75	6.18	5.04	3	2	0	0.66	800 622-3863
Armada Intermediate Bond Retail	Corp-Inv	7.68	5.88	4.80	4	2	3.75	0.96	800 622-3863
Armada Intermediate Govt Instl	Government	8.60	6.62		3	2	3.75	0.83	800 622-3863
Armada Intermediate Govt Retail	Government	7.51					3.75	1.07	800 622-3863
Armada OH Tax Exempt Instl	Muni State	6.84	6.21	5.17	3	2	0	0.24	800 622-3863
Armada OH Tax Exempt Retail	Muni State	6.83	6.23		4	2	3	0.24	800 622-3863
Armada PA Municipal Bond Instl	Muni State	6.43	5.66		4	2	0	0.87	800 622-3863
Armada PA Municipal Bond Retail	Muni State	5.90					3	0.99	800 622-3863
Armada Total Return Advanced Instl	Corp-Inv	9.79	7.73		3	4	0	0.16	800 622-3863
Armada Total Return Advanced Retail	Corp-Inv	9.40	7.46		3	5	0	0.41	800 622-3863
Atlas California Municipal Bond A	Muni CA	8.01	6.94	5.44	4	3	3	0.95	800 933-2852
Atlas California Municipal Bond B	Muni CA	7.38	6.43		5	3	0	1.45	800 933-2852
Atlas National Municipal Bond A	Muni Natl	8.18	7.12	5.63	3	3	3	1.00	800 933-2852
Atlas National Municipal Bond B	Muni Natl	7.54	6.38		4	3	0	1.50	800 933-2852
Atlas Strategic Income Fund A	Dvsfd Bond	9.33					3	0.30	800 933-2852
Atlas Strategic Income Fund B	Dvsfd Bond	7.85					0	1.04	800 933-2852
Atlas US Govt & Mortgage Sec A	Govt-Mtg	7.64	7.02	5.83	3	2	0	1.03	800 933-2852
Atlas US Govt & Mortgage Sec B	Govt-Mtg	7.09	6.48		4	2	0	1.53	800 933-2852
Babson Bond Trust Long	Corp-Inv	10.45	7.24	6.28	2	3	0	0.97	800 422-2766

Bond Fund Name	Objective	Annualized Return for			Rank		Max Load	Expense Ratio	Toll-Free Telephone
		1 Year	3 Years	5 Years	Overall	Risk			
Babson Bond Trust Short	Corp-Inv	8.77	6.97	5.92	2	2	0	0.67	800 422-2766
Babson TF Income Long Term	Muni Natl	7.78	7.02	5.94	3	3	0	1.01	800 422-2766
Babson TF Income Short Term	Muni Natl	4.89	4.77	4.06	3	1	0	1.01	800 422-2766
BB&K International Bond Fund	Intl Bond	4.82	6.57	3.29	3	3	0	1.33	800 882-8383
BB&T Intmed US Government Bond A	Government	10.15	6.45	5.43	3	4	4.5	1.13	800 228-1872
BB&T Intmed US Government Bond Tr	Government	10.54	6.74	6.14	3	4	0	0.86	800 228-1872
BB&T NC Intermediate TF A	Muni State	5.60	5.01	4.22	4	2	2	1.06	800 228-1872
BB&T NC Intermediate TF Trust	Muni State	5.76	5.19	4.35	4	2	0	0.87	800 228-1872
BB&T Short Intmed US Govt Bond A	Government	6.81	5.38	4.73	4	2	2	1.13	800 228-1872
BB&T Short Intmed US Govt Bond Tr	Government	7.08	5.64		4	2	0	0.86	800 228-1872
BEA Global Fixed Income Port	Intl Bond	3.31	5.76		5	4	0	0.75	800 401-2230
BEA High Yield Portfolio	Corp-HY	14.22	12.03	7.85	2	4	0		800 401-2230
BEA High Yield Portfolio Adv	Corp-HY	13.82					0	0.95	800 401-2230
BEA Municipal Bond Portfolio	Muni Natl	8.20	6.55		4	4	0	1.00	800 401-2230
BEA US Core Fixed Income	Government	9.81	8.53		1	3	0	0.50	800 401-2230
Bear Stearns Emrg Markets Debt A	Intl Bond	2.49	23.29	12.30	3	5	3.75	1.75	800 766-4111
Bear Stearns Emrg Markets Debt C	Intl Bond	1.87					0	2.40	800 766-4111
Bear Stearns Total Return Bond A	Corp-Inv	7.19	7.55		5	5	3.75	0.80	800 766-4111
Bear Stearns Total Return Bond C	Corp-Inv	6.70	5.81		5	3	0	1.20	800 766-4111
Bear Stearns Total Return Bond Y	Corp-Inv	6.41	5.53		5	4	0	0.80	800 766-4111
Benchmark Bond A	Corp-Inv	11.81	8.80	7.65	2	4	0	0.36	800 637-1380
Benchmark Bond C	Corp-Inv	11.55					0	0.60	800 637-1380
Benchmark Bond D	Corp-Inv	10.99	8.22		2	4	0	0.75	800 637-1380
Benchmark International Bond A	Intl Bond	2.49	3.41		5	5	0	0.96	800 637-1380
Benchmark International Bond D	Intl Bond	2.10					0	1.35	800 637-1380
Benchmark Short/Intermediate Bond A	Corp-Inv	7.49	6.37	5.91	3	1	0	0.36	800 637-1380
Benchmark Short/Intermediate Bond D	Corp-Inv	6.94	5.90		4	1	0	0.75	800 637-1380
Benchmark US Govt Securities A	Government	7.37	6.22	5.39	3	1	0	0.36	800 637-1380
Benchmark US Govt Securities C	Government	7.06					0	0.60	800 637-1380
Benchmark US Govt Securities D	Government	12.26	7.51		4	3	0	0.75	800 637-1380
Benchmark US Treasury D	Government	11.12	7.14		3	4	0	0.65	800 637-1380
Benchmark US Treasury Index A	Government	11.57	7.59	6.60	2	4	0	0.26	800 637-1380
Bernstein California Municipal	Muni CA	6.17	5.93	5.04	3	2	0	0.68	
Bernstein Diversified Municipal	Muni Natl	6.18	5.85	5.10	3	2	0	0.64	
Bernstein Government Short Duration	Government	5.51	5.31	4.79	4	1	0	0.69	
Bernstein Intermediate Duration	Government	7.79	6.74	6.02	3	3	0	0.62	
Bernstein New York Municipal	Muni NY	6.35	5.80	5.06	3	2	0	0.65	
Bernstein Short Duration Plus	Government	4.76	5.55	4.91	3	1	0	0.65	
Bishop High Grade Income Instl	Corp-HY	9.57					0	0.80	800 262-9565
Bishop Street HI Muni Instl	Muni State	8.02	7.17		3	3	0	0.25	800 262-9565
BJB Global Income A	Intl Bond	5.46	4.78	4.32	4	3	0	1.99	800 435-4659
BlackRock Core Bond Blackrock Cl	Corp-Inv	10.22					0	0.40	800 388-8734
BlackRock Core Bond Instl	Corp-Inv	10.54	7.91	7.00	2	3	0	0.55	800 388-8734
BlackRock Core Bond Inv A	Corp-Inv	9.93					4.5	1.01	800 388-8734
BlackRock Core Bond Inv B	Corp-Inv	8.74					0	1.75	800 388-8734
BlackRock Core Bond Inv C	Corp-Inv	8.74					0	1.74	800 388-8734
BlackRock Core Bond Svc	Corp-Inv	9.53					0	0.85	800 388-8734
BlackRock Govt Income Inv A	Government	11.02	7.99		2	4	4.5	1.02	800 388-8734
BlackRock Govt Income Inv B	Government	10.20	7.21		3	4	0	1.77	800 388-8734
BlackRock Govt Income Inv C	Government	10.22					0	1.70	800 388-8734
BlackRock Intl Bond Instl	Intl Bond	10.25					0	0.98	800 388-8734
BlackRock Intl Bond Inv A	Intl Bond	−3.79					5	1.42	800 388-8734
BlackRock Intl Bond Inv B	Intl Bond	8.95					0	2.12	800 388-8734
BlackRock Intl Bond Inv C	Intl Bond	8.95					0	2.11	800 388-8734
BlackRock Intl Bond Service	Intl Bond	9.79	10.38	9.71	1	2	5	1.29	800 388-8734
BlackRock Intmed Govt Instl	Government	8.42	6.73	5.56	3	2	0	0.55	800 388-8734
BlackRock Intmed Govt Invest A	Government	7.92	6.25	5.19	3	2	4	1.02	800 388-8734
BlackRock Intmed Govt Invest B	Government	7.12					0	1.77	800 388-8734

Bond Fund Name	Objective	Annualized Return for			Rank		Max Load	Expense Ratio	Toll-Free Telephone
		1 Year	3 Years	5 Years	Overall	Risk			
BlackRock Intmed Govt Invest C	Government	7.12					0	1.71	800 388-8734
BlackRock Intmed Govt Service	Government	8.10	6.40		3	2	0	0.85	800 388-8734
BlackRock Intmed Term Bond Instl	Government	8.69	7.04		3	2	0	0.53	800 388-8734
BlackRock Intmed Term Bond Inv A	Government	7.56	6.25		4	2	4	1.00	800 388-8734
BlackRock Intmed Term Bond Svc	Government	7.23	6.24		4	2	0	0.83	800 388-8734
BlackRock Low Duration A	Corp-Inv	6.22					3	1.02	800 388-8734
BlackRock Low Duration B	Corp-Inv	5.46					0	1.73	800 388-8734
BlackRock Low Duration C	Corp-Inv	5.46					0	1.72	800 388-8734
BlackRock Low Duration Instl	Corp-Inv	6.73	6.12	5.63	2	1		0.55	800 388-8734
BlackRock Low Duration Svc	Corp-Inv	6.40					0	0.85	800 388-8734
BlackRock Managed Inc Instl	Corp-Inv	10.87	7.91	6.44	2	3	0	0.58	800 388-8734
BlackRock Managed Inc Inv A	Corp-Inv	10.34	7.25	5.99	3	3	4.5	1.05	800 388-8734
BlackRock Managed Inc Service	Corp-Inv	10.42	7.56		2	3	0	0.88	800 388-8734
BlackRock NJ TF Inc Inv A	Muni State	7.84					4	1.02	800 388-8734
BlackRock NJ TF Inc Inv B	Muni State	7.00					0	1.74	800 388-8734
BlackRock NJ TF Inc Service	Muni State	8.03	6.80	5.54	3	3	0	0.86	800 388-8734
BlackRock OH TF Income Instl	Muni State	8.33	7.63	5.90	2	3	0	0.55	800 388-8734
BlackRock OH TF Income Invest A	Muni State	7.83	7.15	5.60	3	3	4	1.02	800 388-8734
BlackRock OH TF Income Invest B	Muni State	7.02	6.35		5	3	0	1.75	800 388-8734
BlackRock OH TF Income Service	Muni State	8.44	7.45		3	3	0	0.85	800 388-8734
BlackRock PA TF Income Instl	Muni State	8.86	9.25		2	4	4	0.86	800 388-8734
BlackRock PA TF Income Invest A	Muni State	8.38	7.47	5.63	3	4	4.5	1.30	800 388-8734
BlackRock PA TF Income Invest B	Muni State	7.74	6.72	4.27	3	3	0	1.76	800 388-8734
BlackRock PA TF Income Service	Muni State	8.52	7.60		1	3	0	0.85	800 388-8734
BlackRock Tax Free Income Instl	Muni Natl	9.40	8.33	6.95	1	3	0	0.55	800 388-8734
BlackRock Tax Free Income Inv A	Muni Natl	8.85	9.35	6.36	2	3	4.5	1.02	800 388-8734
BlackRock Tax Free Income Inv B	Muni Natl	8.01					0	1.75	800 388-8734
BlackRock Tax Free Income Inv C	Muni Natl	8.01					0	1.70	800 388-8734
BlackRock Tax Free Income Service	Muni Natl	9.02	8.01		1	3	0	0.85	800 388-8734
BNY Hamilton Intmed Govt Instl	Government	8.56					0	0.90	800 426-9363
BNY Hamilton Intmed Govt Investor	Government	8.86	6.41	4.99	3	2	0	1.06	800 426-9363
BNY Hamilton Intmed NY TE Instl	Muni NY	5.70					0	0.90	800 426-9363
BNY Hamilton Intmed NY TE Inv	Muni NY	5.76	5.14	4.40	4	2	0	0.96	800 426-9363
BNY Hamilton Intmed TE Instl	Muni Natl	5.41					0	0.82	800 426-9363
BNY Hamilton Intmed TE Inv	Muni Natl	5.55					0	1.11	800 426-9363
BNY Hamilton Invest Grade Bd Instl	Corp-Inv	9.35					0	0.81	800 426-9363
BNY Hamilton Invest Grade Bd Inv	Corp-Inv	9.71					0	1.04	800 426-9363
Bond Fund of America	Corp-Inv	9.01	8.93	7.21	1	2	4.75	0.68	800 421-0180
Bond Portfolio for Endowments	Corp-Inv	9.02	7.79	6.12	2	3	0	0.74	800 421-0180
Boston 1784 CT Tax Exempt Fund A	Muni State	8.60	7.25		2	2	0	0.80	800 252-1784
Boston 1784 Income Fund	Corp-Inv	8.25	6.63		5	4	0	1.11	800 252-1784
Boston 1784 MA Tax-Exempt Income	Muni State	8.14	6.93	5.44	2	2	0	0.80	800 252-1784
Boston 1784 RI Tax-Exempt Fund	Muni State	7.68	7.20		2	2	0	0.80	800 252-1784
Boston 1784 Short Term Income Fund	Government	6.67	6.07		4	1	0	0.65	800 252-1784
Boston 1784 Tax-Exempt Medium Inc	Muni Natl	8.68	7.45	6.27	1	3	0	0.80	800 252-1784
Boston 1784 US Govt Medium Term Inc	Government	8.52	6.29	5.28	3	3	0	1.12	800 252-1784
Bremer Bond Fund	Dvsfd Bond	7.72					0	1.01	800-595-5552
Brinson Global Bond Fund	Intl Bond	2.70	7.24		4	4	0	0.90	800 448-2430
Brinson US Bond Fund	Corp-Inv	10.60					0	1.65	800 448-2430
Brundage Story & Rose Sh/Int Fixed	Corp-Inv	8.49	6.80	6.05	2	2	0	0.65	800 320-2212
BT Investment Global HY Securities	Corp-HY	4.98	15.88		3	5	0		800 730-1313
BT Investment Intermediate Tax Free	Muni Natl	6.96	6.04	5.23	4	3	0	0.85	800 730-1313
BT Investment Ltd Term US Govt Sec	Government	6.87	5.77	5.16	3	1	0	0.60	800 730-1313
Buffalo High Yield Fund	Corp-HY	10.18	13.88		1	3	0	1.13	800 492-8332
California Insured CA Intermediate	Muni CA	6.26	6.07	5.07	4	3	0	0.55	800 225-8778
California Invest Tr TF Income	Muni CA	8.69	7.82	6.02	3	5	0	0.60	800 225-8778
California Invest Tr US Govt Sec	Government	12.91	8.04	6.85	3	5	0	0.65	800 225-8778
Calvert Income Fund A	Corp-Inv	13.89	8.63	6.85	2	4	3.75	1.26	800 368-2745

Bond Fund Name	Objective	Annualized Return for			Rank		Max Load	Expense Ratio	Toll-Free Telephone
		1 Year	3 Years	5 Years	Overall	Risk			
Calvert MD Muni Intmed Fund A	Muni State	6.49	6.09		3	2	2.75	0.93	800 368-2745
Calvert National Intmed Muni A	Muni Natl	6.53	6.30	6.04	3	2	2.75	0.97	800 368-2745
Calvert Social Bond Portfolio A	Corp-Inv	10.47	7.41	6.15	2	3	3.75	1.23	800 368-2745
Calvert TF Reserve Limited Term A	Muni Natl	3.88	4.04	3.95	3	1	2	0.70	800 368-2745
Calvert TF Reserve Long Term A	Muni Natl	7.64	6.75	6.12	3	3	3.75	0.85	800 368-2745
Calvert TF Reserve Vermont Muni A	Muni State	6.92	6.66	5.72	2	3	3.75	0.75	800 368-2745
Calvert VA Muni Intmed Fund A	Muni State	5.68	5.53		3	2	2.75	0.89	800 368-2745
Canandaigua National Bond	Muni Natl	9.20	6.68	6.62	3	3	0	0.52	303 572-5401
Capital World Bond Fund	Intl Bond	3.28	5.42	6.92	3	3	4.75	1.08	800 421-0180
Capstone Government Income Fund	Government	4.66	4.36	3.76	4	1	0	0.88	800 262-6631
Cardinal Government Obligations	Govt-Mtg	7.44	7.49	6.20	2	2	4.5	1.01	800 848-7734
Carnegie Ohio General Muni Fund	Muni State	6.74	6.04	5.06	3	2	4.5	0.91	800 321-2322
CGCM International Fixed Income	Intl Bond	4.26	5.43	7.66	3	5	0	0.96	800-544-7835
CGCM Intmed Fixed Income	Corp-Inv	7.65	6.42	5.57	4	2	0	0.73	800-544-7835
CGCM Long Term Bond Fund	Corp-Inv	16.05	9.24	7.04	3	5	0	0.78	800-544-7835
CGCM Mortgaged Backed Investments	Govt-Mtg	8.60	7.35	6.22	2	2	0	0.80	800-544-7835
CGCM Municipal Bond Investments	Muni Natl	8.47	7.32	5.19	3	4	0	0.80	800-544-7835
CGM American Tax Free Fund	Muni Natl	8.72	7.74		2	3	0	2.14	800 345-4048
CGM Fixed Income Fund	Corp-HY	2.17	9.29	8.20	5	5	0	0.85	800 345-4048
Chase Income Fund	Corp-Inv	10.84	7.48	6.02	3	4	0	0.75	800 34-VISTA
Chase Intermediate Term Bond Fund	Corp-Inv	8.76	6.02		4	3	0	0.75	800 34-VISTA
Chase Short Intmed US Govt Fund	Government	6.68	5.27	4.75	4	2	0	0.75	800 34-VISTA
Chase US Govt Securities Fund	Government	12.40	7.43	6.71	3	5	0	0.75	800 34-VISTA
Chase Vista Bond Fund A	Corp-Inv	10.32					4.5	0.90	800 34-VISTA
Chase Vista Bond Fund B	Corp-Inv	9.41					0	1.64	800 34-VISTA
Chase Vista Bond Fund I	Corp-Inv	10.73	7.72	6.75	3	4	0	0.50	800 34-VISTA
Chase Vista CA Interm Tax Free Inc	Muni CA	7.48	6.85		3	3	4.75	0.60	800 34-VISTA
Chase Vista NY TF Income Fund A	Muni NY	8.67	7.38	5.70	3	3	4.5	0.85	800 34-VISTA
Chase Vista NY TF Income Fund B	Muni NY	7.08	6.33		5	3	0	1.64	800 34-VISTA
Chase Vista Select Bond Fund	Dvsfd Bond	9.56					0		800 34-VISTA
Chase Vista Select Intmed Bond	Dvsfd Bond	7.84					0		800 34-VISTA
Chase Vista Select Intmed Tax Free	Muni Natl	7.53					0		800 34-VISTA
Chase Vista Select NJ Tax Free	Muni State	7.14					0		800 34-VISTA
Chase Vista Select NY Tax Free	Muni NY	7.57					0		800 34-VISTA
Chase Vista Select Short Term Bond	Corp-Inv	6.54					0		800 34-VISTA
Chase Vista Select Tax Free Fund	Muni Natl	8.67					0		800 34-VISTA
Chase Vista Short-Term Bond Fund A	Corp-Inv	5.82					1.5	0.75	800 34-VISTA
Chase Vista Short-Term Bond Fund I	Corp-Inv	6.28	6.07	5.42	3	1	4.5	0.42	800 34-VISTA
Chase Vista Tax Free Income Fund A	Muni Natl	8.64	7.70	5.69	3	3	4.5	0.85	800 34-VISTA
Chase Vista Tax Free Income Fund B	Muni Natl	7.84	6.82		4	3	0	1.64	800 34-VISTA
Chase Vista US Government Secs A	Government	9.28					4.5	1.05	800 34-VISTA
Chase Vista US Government Secs I	Government	9.57	6.66	6.41	2	4	0	0.85	800 34-VISTA
Chase Vista US Treasury Income A	Government	9.95	6.42	5.54	4	4	4.5	0.90	800 34-VISTA
Chase Vista US Treasury Income B	Government	9.26	5.69		5	5	0	1.64	800 34-VISTA
Chicago Trust Bond Fund	Corp-Inv	9.90	7.68		2	3	0	1.00	800 992-8151
Chicago Trust Municipal Bond Fund	Muni Natl	5.54	5.10		3	2	0	1.62	800 992-8151
Churchill Tax Free Fund of KY A	Muni State	7.91	6.85	5.71	2	2	4	0.71	800 228-4227
Churchill Tax Free Fund of KY C	Muni State	6.90					0	1.56	800 228-4227
Churchill Tax Free Fund of KY Y	Muni State	8.00					0	0.56	800 228-4227
CitiFunds Intermediate Income	Corp-Inv	9.98	6.63	5.84	3	3	4	0.90	800 721-1899
CitiFunds NY Tax Free Income	Muni NY	8.81	7.69	5.72	3	4	4	0.80	800 721-1899
CitiFunds Short Term US Govt Inc	Government	6.18	5.21	4.61	3	1	1.5	0.80	800 721-1899
Citizens Income Portfolio	Corp-Inv	10.59	8.51	7.13	1	3	0	1.52	800 223-7010
Colonial California Tax-Exempt A	Muni CA	9.08	8.30	6.05	3	4	4.75	0.88	800 345-6611
Colonial California Tax-Exempt B	Muni CA	8.27	7.50	5.27	3	4	0	1.62	800 345-6611
Colonial Connecticut Tax-Exempt A	Muni State	8.21	7.72	5.66	2	3	4.75	0.61	800 345-6611
Colonial Connecticut Tax-Exempt B	Muni State	7.41	6.93	4.91	4	3	0	1.36	800 345-6611
Colonial Federal Securities A	Government	11.07	7.23	6.04	3	5	4.75	1.15	800 345-6611

Bond Fund Name	Objective	Annualized Return for			Rank		Max Load	Expense Ratio	Toll-Free Telephone
		1 Year	3 Years	5 Years	Overall	Risk			
Colonial Federal Securities B	Government	10.25	6.44	5.26	4	5	0	1.95	800 345-6611
Colonial Florida Tax-Exempt A	Muni State	8.61	7.55	5.54	3	4	4.75	0.57	800 345-6611
Colonial Florida Tax-Exempt B	Muni State	7.81	6.78	4.77	5	4	0	1.32	800 345-6611
Colonial High Yield Municipal A	Muni Natl	9.97	8.45		1	2	4.75	1.86	800 345-6611
Colonial High Yield Municipal B	Muni Natl	9.15	7.67	6.27	1	2	0	1.11	800 345-6611
Colonial High Yield Securities A	Corp-HY	12.32	12.80	10.91	1	3	4.75	1.20	800 345-6611
Colonial High Yield Securities B	Corp-HY	11.49	11.96	10.09	1	3	0	1.96	800 345-6611
Colonial High Yield Securities C	Corp-HY	11.64					0	1.96	800 345-6611
Colonial Income Fund A	Corp-Inv	10.24	8.26	6.96	2	4	4.75	1.11	800 345-6611
Colonial Income Fund B	Corp-Inv	9.43	7.24	6.16	3	4	0	1.10	800 345-6611
Colonial Intermediate Tax-Exempt A	Muni Natl	7.57	6.94	5.70	3	2	3.25	0.77	800 345-6611
Colonial Intermediate Tax-Exempt B	Muni Natl	6.88	6.27	5.04	4	2	0	0.77	800 345-6611
Colonial Intermediate US Govt A	Govt-Mtg	8.90	6.78	5.71	3	3	4.75	1.14	800 345-6611
Colonial Intermediate US Govt B	Govt-Mtg	8.10	5.99	4.92	4	3	0	1.88	800 345-6611
Colonial Massachusetts TE A	Muni State	8.34	7.74	6.03	3	3	4.75	0.90	800 345-6611
Colonial Massachusetts TE B	Muni State	7.54	6.95	5.27	5	3	0	1.65	800 345-6611
Colonial Michigan Tax-Exempt A	Muni State	9.40	7.95	5.87	3	4	4.75	0.90	800 345-6611
Colonial Michigan Tax-Exempt B	Muni State	8.59	7.17	5.09	5	4	0	1.65	800 345-6611
Colonial Minnesota Tax-Exempt A	Muni State	8.94	7.91	6.01	3	4	4.75	0.91	800 345-6611
Colonial Minnesota Tax-Exempt B	Muni State	8.13	7.13	5.23	5	4	0	1.66	800 345-6611
Colonial NC Tax-Exempt A	Muni State	8.66	7.86		2	3	4.75	0.66	800 345-6611
Colonial NC Tax-Exempt B	Muni State	7.86	7.11		4	3	0	0.66	800 345-6611
Colonial NY Tax-Exempt A	Muni NY	8.90	8.00	5.78	3	4	4.75	0.67	800 345-6611
Colonial NY Tax-Exempt B	Muni NY	8.09	7.20	5.00	4	4	0	1.41	800 345-6611
Colonial OH Tax Exempt A	Muni State	8.82	7.91	5.77	3	4	4.75	0.89	800 345-6611
Colonial OH Tax Exempt B	Muni State	8.01	7.11	4.99	5	4	0	1.64	800 345-6611
Colonial Short Duration US Govt A	Government	6.39	6.12	5.28	3	1	3.25	0.50	800 345-6611
Colonial Short Duration US Govt B	Government	5.70	5.45	4.62	3	1	0	1.15	800 345-6611
Colonial Short Duration US Govt C	Government	6.17	5.92		3	1	0	1.75	800 345-6611
Colonial Strategic Income A	Dvsfd Bond	9.27	10.28	8.71	1	3	4.75	1.18	800 345-6611
Colonial Strategic Income B	Dvsfd Bond	8.46	9.47		2	3	0	1.93	800 345-6611
Colonial Tax Exempt Fund A	Muni Natl	9.56	7.57	5.89	3	4	4.75	0.98	800 345-6611
Colonial Tax Exempt Fund B	Muni Natl	8.75	6.75	5.09	4	4	0	1.72	800 345-6611
Colonial Tax Exempt Insured A	Muni Natl	8.79	7.36	5.53	4	5	4.75	1.07	800 345-6611
Colonial Tax Exempt Insured B	Muni Natl	7.98	6.57	4.75	5	5	0	1.83	800 345-6611
Colorado Bondshares	Muni State	7.95	8.46	7.96	1	1	4.75	0.66	800 572-0069
Columbia Fixed Income Securities	Corp-Inv	9.82	7.67	6.65	2	3	0	0.66	800 547-1707
Columbia High Yield Fund	Corp-HY	11.23	11.44		1	3	0	1.00	800 547-1707
Columbia Municipal Bond Fund	Muni Natl	7.08	6.59	5.22	3	2	0	0.58	800 547-1707
Columbia US Government Securities	Government	5.90	5.45	4.79	4	1	0	0.87	800 547-1707
Commerce Bond Fund I	Corp-Inv	9.99	7.19		2	4	3.5	0.87	800 305-2140
Commerce MO Tax-Free Bond Fund	Muni State	6.59	5.59		3	2	3.5	0.65	800 305-2140
Commerce National Tax-Free Bond	Muni Natl	6.24	5.58		4	2	3.5	0.85	800 305-2140
Commerce Short-Term Government I	Govt-Mtg	7.57	6.06		3	2	3.5	0.68	800 305-2140
Comstock Partners Strategy A	Intl Bond	−17.36	−6.75	−2.47	5	5	4.5	1.43	800-645-6561
Comstock Partners Strategy C	Intl Bond	−18.05					0	2.14	800-645-6561
Comstock Partners Strategy O	Intl Bond	−17.13	−6.52	−2.21	5	5	0	1.18	800-645-6561
Concert Invmt Series Government 1	Government	9.81	6.88	5.53	3	3	6.75	0.95	800 221-3627
Concert Invmt Series Government A	Government	9.45	5.90		4	3	4.75	1.19	800 221-3627
Concert Invmt Series Government B	Government	9.02	5.27		5	3	0	1.94	800 221-3627
Concert Invmt Series Muni Bond Fund	Muni Natl	8.49	7.48	6.09	2	3	4.75	1.09	800 221-3627
Conseco Fixed Income Fund A	Corp-Inv	9.31					5	1.25	800 986-3384
Conseco Fixed Income Fund Y	Corp-Inv	10.34					0	0.60	800 986-3384
CoreFund Bond A	Dvsfd Bond	9.76	6.95	5.68	3	5	4.75	0.93	800 355-2673
CoreFund Bond Y	Dvsfd Bond	9.98	7.24		3	3	0	0.68	800 355-2673
CoreFund Global Bond A	Intl Bond	4.38	6.01		3	2	4.75	1.10	800 355-2673
CoreFund Global Bond Y	Intl Bond	4.42	6.22		3	2	0	0.85	800 355-2673
CoreFund Government Income A	Government	9.76	6.91	5.65	3	3	3.25	0.95	800 355-2673

Bond Fund Name	Objective	Annualized Return for			Rank		Max Load	Expense Ratio	Toll-Free Telephone
		1 Year	3 Years	5 Years	Overall	Risk			
CoreFund Government Income Y	Government	9.99	7.19	5.86	2	3	0	0.70	800 355-2673
CoreFund Intermediate Municipal A	Muni Natl	5.72	5.09	4.01	4	2	3.25	0.80	800 355-2673
CoreFund Intermediate Municipal Y	Muni Natl	6.07	5.37	4.26	4	2	0	0.55	800 355-2673
CoreFund NJ Muni Bond A	Muni State	8.04	6.37		3	3	4.5	0.21	800 355-2673
CoreFund NJ Muni Bond Y	Muni State	8.28	6.62		3	3	0	0.96	800 355-2673
CoreFund PA Muni Bond A	Muni State	7.64	6.90		4	3	3.25	0.33	800 355-2673
CoreFund PA Muni Bond Y	Muni State	7.88	7.15		2	3	0	0.08	800 355-2673
CoreFund Short-Intmed Term Bond A	Corp-Inv	7.20	6.23	5.17	4	2	3.25	0.74	800 355-2673
CoreFund Short-Intmed Term Bond Y	Corp-Inv	7.57	6.51	5.48	3	2	0	0.49	800 355-2673
CoreFund Short-Term Income A	Dvsfd Bond	5.58	5.24		4	1	3.25	0.74	800 355-2673
CoreFund Short-Term Income Y	Dvsfd Bond	5.83	5.50		3	1		0.49	800 355-2673
Countrywide Adj Rate US Govt Sec A	Govt-Mtg	4.27	5.63	4.78	3	1	2	1.05	800 543-8721
Countrywide Intermediate Bond	Dvsfd Bond	9.36					4.5	0.85	800 543-8721
Countrywide Intmed Term Govt Inc A	Government	8.55	6.05	4.84	4	3	2	0.99	800 543-8721
Countrywide KY Tax-Free Fund	Muni State	7.62					4.5	0.85	800 543-8721
Countrywide OH Insured Tax Free A	Muni State	7.04	6.42	5.28	4	3	4	0.73	800 543-8721
Countrywide OH Insured Tax Free C	Muni State	6.32	5.78		5	3	0	1.42	800 543-8721
Countrywide Tax-Free Intmed-Term A	Muni Natl	5.62	5.43	4.85	3	2	2	0.99	800 543-8721
Countrywide Tax-Free Intmed-Term C	Muni Natl	4.86	4.77		4	2	0	1.65	800 543-8721
Cowen Government Securities Fund	Government	7.52	6.37	5.40	4	3	4.75	0.20	800 221-5616
Cowen Intermediate Fixed Income	Corp-Inv	8.25	6.58	5.66	3	2	2.35		800 221-5616
Crabbe Huson Income Fund	Corp-Inv	13.71	8.93	6.58	3	5	0	0.80	800 541-9732
Crabbe Huson OR Tax-Free Fund	Muni State	6.38	5.65	4.82	4	2	0	0.98	800 541-9732
Crabbe Huson US Government Income	Government	7.79	6.10	4.81	4	2	0	1.78	800 541-9732
CrestFunds Government Bond Inv B	Government	8.94	5.48		5	4	0	1.53	800 451-5435
CrestFunds Government Bond Trust	Government	10.02	6.33		3	4	0	0.67	800 451-5435
CrestFunds Intmed Bond Fund Inv A	Corp-Inv	9.41	6.54	5.59	3	3	3	0.89	800 451-5435
CrestFunds Intmed Bond Fund Tr Cl	Corp-Inv	9.54	6.56	5.45	3	3	0	0.87	800 451-5435
CrestFunds Ltd Term Bond Fund Trust	Corp-Inv	7.30	5.80	4.97	4	2	0	0.75	800 451-5435
CrestFunds MD Muni Bond Inv B	Muni State	7.20					0	1.53	800 451-5435
CrestFunds MD Muni Bond Trust	Muni State	8.07					0	0.67	800 451-5435
CrestFunds VA Intmed Muni Bond Inv	Muni State	6.72	5.92	4.65	4	2	3.5	0.79	800 451-5435
CrestFunds VA Intmed Muni Bond Tr	Muni State	6.73	5.93	4.66	4	2	0	0.78	800 451-5435
CrestFunds VA Muni Bond Inv B	Muni State	7.48	5.76		5	3	0	1.57	800 451-5435
CrestFunds VA Muni Bond Trust	Muni State	8.33	6.62		3	4	0	0.71	800 451-5435
CUFund Adjustable Rate Portfolio	Govt-Mtg	5.76	6.01	5.42	3	1	0	0.39	800 538-9683
CUFund Short-Term Maturity Port	Government	6.15	5.95	4.90	3	2	0	0.39	800 538-9683
Davis Government Bond Fund A	Govt-Mtg	8.01	6.20		4	3	0	1.68	800 279-0279
Davis Government Bond Fund B	Govt-Mtg	7.23	5.35	4.44	4	2	0	2.01	800 279-0279
Davis High Income Fund A	Corp-HY	7.37	7.88	7.68	2	2	4.75	1.48	800 279-0279
Davis High Income Fund B	Corp-HY	6.33	6.65		3	3	0	2.13	800 279-0279
Davis Tax-Free High Income Fund A	Muni Natl	6.61	6.59		2	1	4.75	1.40	800 279-0279
Davis Tax-Free High Income Fund B	Muni Natl	5.78	5.82	5.56	3	1	0	1.86	800 279-0279
Delaware Grp Delchester A	Corp-HY	12.35	12.29	9.14	1	3	4.75	1.05	800 523-4640
Delaware Grp Delchester B	Corp-HY	11.59	11.48		1	3	0	1.79	800 523-4640
Delaware Grp Delchester C	Corp-HY	11.58					0	1.79	800 523-4640
Delaware Grp Delchester Instl	Corp-HY	13.00	12.69	8.55	1	3	0	0.86	800 523-4640
Delaware Grp Global Bond A	Intl Bond	2.04	8.20		3	5	4.75	1.25	800 523-4640
Delaware Grp Global Bond B	Intl Bond	1.22	7.39		5	5	0	1.95	800 523-4640
Delaware Grp Global Bond C	Intl Bond	1.23					0	1.95	800 523-4640
Delaware Grp Global Bond Instl	Intl Bond	2.42	8.51		4	5	0		800 523-4640
Delaware Grp High Yld Opportunity A	Corp-HY	15.41					4.75	0.74	800 523-4640
Delaware Grp Ltd-Term Govt Fund A	Govt-Mtg	4.69	4.76	3.84	3	1	2.75	0.98	800 523-4640
Delaware Grp Ltd-Term Govt Fund B	Govt-Mtg	3.79	3.87		5	1	0	1.78	800 523-4640
Delaware Grp Ltd-Term Govt Fund C	Govt-Mtg	3.78					0	1.78	800 523-4640
Delaware Grp Ltd-Term Govt Instl	Govt-Mtg	4.84	4.91	3.98	4	1	0	0.78	800 523-4640
Delaware Grp Natl High Yld Muni B	Muni Natl	8.22					0	1.56	800 523-4640
Delaware Grp Natl High Yld Muni C	Muni Natl	8.38					0	1.62	800 523-4640

Bond Fund Name	Objective	Annualized Return for			Rank		Max Load	Expense Ratio	Toll-Free Telephone
		1 Year	3 Years	5 Years	Overall	Risk			
Delaware Grp Tax-Free Insured A	Muni Natl	7.83	6.49	5.31	3	3	3.75	0.94	800 523-4640
Delaware Grp Tax-Free Insured B	Muni Natl	7.00	5.73		5	3	0	1.83	800 523-4640
Delaware Grp Tax-Free Insured C	Muni Natl	7.00					0	1.83	800 523-4640
Delaware Grp Tax-Free PA Fund A	Muni State	7.79	6.60	5.57	3	3	4.75	0.94	800 523-4640
Delaware Grp Tax-Free PA Fund B	Muni State	6.80	5.71		4	3	0	1.71	800 523-4640
Delaware Grp Tax-Free USA A	Muni Natl	8.04	5.93	5.27	3	3	3.75	0.94	800 523-4640
Delaware Grp Tax-Free USA B	Muni Natl	7.22	5.10		5	3	0	1.75	800 523-4640
Delaware Grp Tax-Free USA C	Muni Natl	7.22					0	1.75	800 523-4640
Delaware Grp Tax-Free USA Intmed A	Muni Natl	6.76	6.29	5.65	3	2	2.75	0.25	800 523-4640
Delaware Grp Tax-Free USA Intmed B	Muni Natl	5.94	5.42		3	2	0	1.19	800 523-4640
Delaware Grp Tax-Free USA Intmed C	Muni Natl	5.88					0	1.19	800 523-4640
Delaware Grp US Govt A	Govt-Mtg	9.37	6.78	4.71	3	3	4.75	1.23	800 523-4640
Delaware Grp US Govt B	Govt-Mtg	8.61	6.06		4	3	0	1.88	800 523-4640
Delaware Grp US Govt C	Govt-Mtg	8.50					0	1.88	800 523-4640
Delaware Grp US Govt Instl	Govt-Mtg	9.47	6.99	4.96	3	3	0	0.97	800 523-4640
Delaware-Voyageur Natl HY Muni Bd A	Muni Natl	8.49	8.64	7.10	1	2	3.75	0.84	800 523-4640
Delaware-Voyageur Tax-Free CO A	Muni State	10.66	8.67	6.68	1	3	3.75	0.81	800 523-4640
Delaware-Voyageur Tax-Free CO C	Muni State	9.96	7.81		2	3	0	1.66	800 523-4640
Delaware-Voyageur Tax-Free MN A	Muni State	9.00	7.63	5.99	2	3	3.75	0.91	800 523-4640
Delaware-Voyageur Tax-Free MN C	Muni State	8.35	6.88		3	3	0	1.67	800 523-4640
Delaware-Voyageur US Govt Secs A	Government	9.98	6.83	6.02	3	4	4.75	0.93	800 523-4640
Delaware-Voyageur US Govt Secs B	Government	9.19	6.42		3	4	0		800 523-4640
DFA Five-Year Government	Government	6.60	5.30	4.13	3	2	0	0.30	888-326-5327
DFA Global Fixed Income	Intl Bond	8.01	10.08	7.90	1	2	0	0.44	888-326-5327
DFA Intermediate Govt Fixed Income	Government	10.91	7.25	6.09	3	4	0	0.25	888-326-5327
DFA One-Year Fixed Income	Corp-Inv	5.93	5.85	5.37	3	1	0	0.21	888-326-5327
DFA Two-Year Global Fixed Inc Port	Intl Bond	5.82					0	0.33	888-326-5327
DG Government Income Fund	Government	10.28	6.84	5.97	3	3	3.5	0.80	800 530-7377
DG Limited Term Govt Income	Government	5.86	5.39		4	1	2	0.68	800 530-7377
DG Municipal Income Fund	Muni Natl	7.05	6.58	5.32	3	3	2	0.70	800 530-7377
Dodge & Cox Income Fund	Corp-Inv	11.05	8.03	7.31	2	4	0	0.49	800 621-3979
Dreyfus A Bonds Plus Fund	Corp-Inv	10.88	7.54	6.60	2	4	0	0.97	800 645-6561
Dreyfus Basic GNMA Fund	Govt-Mtg	10.12	8.22	7.15	1	3	0	0.65	800 645-6561
Dreyfus Basic Intmed Muni Bond	Muni Natl	7.88	7.23		2	3	0	0.24	800 645-6561
Dreyfus Basic Muni Bond	Muni Natl	9.42	8.88		2	4	0	0.26	800 645-6561
Dreyfus Bond Market Index Fund Inv	Corp-Inv	10.67	7.16		3	4	0	0.60	800 645-6561
Dreyfus Bond Market Index Fund R	Corp-Inv	10.86	7.45		2	4	0	0.35	800 645-6561
Dreyfus CA Intermediate Muni Bond	Muni CA	7.01	6.20	5.26	4	3	0	0.79	800 645-6561
Dreyfus CA Tax-Exempt Bond Fund	Muni CA	8.26	6.70	4.83	3	3	0	0.73	800 645-6561
Dreyfus CT Intermediate Muni Bond	Muni State	6.75	6.12	5.44	4	2	0	0.75	800 645-6561
Dreyfus Disciplined Intmed Bond Inv	Corp-Inv	10.25					0	0.80	800 645-6561
Dreyfus Disciplined Intmed Bond R	Corp-Inv	10.41					0	0.55	800 645-6561
Dreyfus FL Intermediate Municipal	Muni State	5.86	5.54	5.00	3	3	0	0.80	800 645-6561
Dreyfus Global Bond Fund	Intl Bond	7.57	6.20		4	5	0	1.35	800 645-6561
Dreyfus GNMA Fund	Govt-Mtg	9.54	7.46	6.18	1	2	0	0.99	800 645-6561
Dreyfus High Yield Securities	Corp-HY	20.38					0	0.71	800 645-6561
Dreyfus Insured Municipal Bond Fund	Muni Natl	8.04	6.38	4.50	5	4	0	0.85	800 645-6561
Dreyfus Intermediate Municipal Bond	Muni Natl	7.50	6.35	5.49	3	2	0	0.73	800 645-6561
Dreyfus Invmt Grade Bond Intmed Inc	Corp-Inv	15.23					0	0.52	800 645-6561
Dreyfus MA Intermediate Muni Bond	Muni State	6.94	5.97	5.05	4	3	0	0.80	800 645-6561
Dreyfus MA Tax-Exempt Bond Fund	Muni State	8.98	7.49	5.76	2	3	0	0.78	800 645-6561
Dreyfus Municipal Bond Fund	Muni Natl	8.06	6.82	5.33	3	3	0	0.72	800 645-6561
Dreyfus NJ Intermediate Muni Bond	Muni State	6.54	5.82	5.05	4	2	0	0.77	800 645-6561
Dreyfus NJ Municipal Bond Fund	Muni State	8.77	7.02	5.53	3	3	0	0.80	800 645-6561
Dreyfus NY Insured Tax-Exempt Bond	Muni NY	7.63	6.09	4.60	5	4	0	0.99	800 645-6561
Dreyfus NY Tax-Exempt Bond	Muni NY	8.77	7.16	5.34	4	4	0	0.70	800 645-6561
Dreyfus NY Tax-Exempt Intermediate	Muni NY	7.42	6.61	5.50	4	3	0	0.80	800 645-6561
Dreyfus PA Intermed Muni Bond Fund	Muni State	7.23	6.71		3	2	0	0.80	800 645-6561

Bond Fund Name	Objective	Annualized Return for			Rank		Max Load	Expense Ratio	Toll-Free Telephone
		1 Year	3 Years	5 Years	Overall	Risk			
Dreyfus Prem CA Muni Bond Fund A	Muni CA	7.95	7.24	5.77	3	4	4.5	0.95	800 334-6899
Dreyfus Prem CA Muni Bond Fund B	Muni CA	7.38	6.59	5.07	5	4	0	1.46	800 334-6899
Dreyfus Prem CA Muni Bond Fund C	Muni CA	7.18	6.48		5	3	0	1.68	800 334-6899
Dreyfus Prem State Muni Bd CT Ser A	Muni State	8.90	7.53	5.85	1	3	4.5	0.91	800 334-6899
Dreyfus Prem State Muni Bd CT Ser B	Muni State	8.34	6.94	5.27	2	3	0	1.45	800 334-6899
Dreyfus Prem State Muni Bd CT Ser C	Muni State	8.07					0	1.70	800 334-6899
Dreyfus Prem State Muni Bd FL Ser A	Muni State	6.66	5.77	5.22	3	3	4.5	0.92	800 334-6899
Dreyfus Prem State Muni Bd FL Ser B	Muni State	6.13	5.26	4.67	4	3	0	1.42	800 334-6899
Dreyfus Prem State Muni Bd FL Ser C	Muni State	5.90					0	1.97	800 334-6899
Dreyfus Prem State Muni Bd GA Ser A	Muni State	7.71	6.96	5.65	4	4	4.5	0.98	800 334-6899
Dreyfus Prem State Muni Bd GA Ser B	Muni State	7.11	6.50	5.15	5	4	0	1.47	800 334-6899
Dreyfus Prem State Muni Bd GA Ser C	Muni State	6.56					0	1.80	800 334-6899
Dreyfus Prem State Muni Bd MD Ser A	Muni State	8.74	7.58	6.04	1	2	4.5	0.91	800 334-6899
Dreyfus Prem State Muni Bd MD Ser B	Muni State	8.17	7.03	5.48	2	2	0	1.43	800 334-6899
Dreyfus Prem State Muni Bd MD Ser C	Muni State	7.90					0	1.64	800 334-6899
Dreyfus Prem State Muni Bd MI Ser A	Muni State	8.33	7.47	6.31	1	3	4.5	0.92	800 334-6899
Dreyfus Prem State Muni Bd MI Ser B	Muni State	7.78	6.90	5.81	3	3	0	1.42	800 334-6899
Dreyfus Prem State Muni Bd MI Ser C	Muni State	7.49					0	1.72	800 334-6899
Dreyfus Prem State Muni Bd MN Ser A	Muni State	7.23	6.49	5.61	3	2	4.5	0.91	800 334-6899
Dreyfus Prem State Muni Bd MN Ser B	Muni State	6.68	5.94	5.04	3	2	0	1.44	800 334-6899
Dreyfus Prem State Muni Bd MN Ser C	Muni State	6.32					0	1.67	800 334-6899
Dreyfus Prem State Muni Bd NC Ser A	Muni State	9.61	8.25	5.94	2	3	4.5	0.87	800 334-6899
Dreyfus Prem State Muni Bd NC Ser B	Muni State	9.07	7.71	5.40	3	3	0	1.37	800 334-6899
Dreyfus Prem State Muni Bd NC Ser C	Muni State	8.80					0	1.60	800 334-6899
Dreyfus Prem State Muni Bd NJ Ser A	Muni State	9.96	6.93		3	4	4.5	0.93	800 334-6899
Dreyfus Prem State Muni Bd NJ Ser B	Muni State	9.44	6.45		3	4	0	1.44	800 334-6899
Dreyfus Prem State Muni Bd NJ Ser C	Muni State	9.10					0	1.90	800 334-6899
Dreyfus Prem State Muni Bd OH Ser A	Muni State	7.74	7.21	5.87	2	3	4.5	0.90	800 334-6899
Dreyfus Prem State Muni Bd OH Ser B	Muni State	7.07	6.63	5.31	4	3	0	1.42	800 334-6899
Dreyfus Prem State Muni Bd OH Ser C	Muni State	6.89					0	1.64	800 334-6899
Dreyfus Prem State Muni Bd PA Ser A	Muni State	8.83	7.89	6.36	1	3	4.5	0.92	800 334-6899
Dreyfus Prem State Muni Bd PA Ser B	Muni State	8.22	7.32	5.79	2	3	0	1.44	800 334-6899
Dreyfus Prem State Muni Bd PA Ser C	Muni State	7.80					0	1.68	800 334-6899
Dreyfus Prem State Muni Bd TX Ser A	Muni State	9.03	8.39	6.95	1	3	4.5	0.58	800 334-6899
Dreyfus Prem State Muni Bd TX Ser B	Muni State	8.49	7.85	6.40	2	3	0	0.88	800 334-6899
Dreyfus Prem State Muni Bd TX Ser C	Muni State	8.20					0	1.19	800 334-6899
Dreyfus Prem State Muni Bd VA Ser A	Muni State	9.51	8.21	6.35	2	4	4.5	0.59	800 334-6899
Dreyfus Prem State Muni Bd VA Ser B	Muni State	8.92	7.64	5.79	3	4	0	1.10	800 334-6899
Dreyfus Prem State Muni Bd VA Ser C	Muni State	8.59					0	1.36	800 334-6899
Dreyfus Premier GNMA Fund A	Govt-Mtg	9.26	7.36	6.07	2	2	4.5	1.55	800 334-6899
Dreyfus Premier GNMA Fund B	Govt-Mtg	8.71	6.81	5.50	3	2	0	1.58	800 334-6899
Dreyfus Premier GNMA Fund C	Govt-Mtg	8.40					0	1.83	800 334-6899
Dreyfus Premier Ltd CA Muni A	Muni CA	6.23	6.13	5.34	4	3	3	0.75	800 334-6899
Dreyfus Premier Ltd CA Muni B	Muni CA	5.33	5.49		4	2	0	1.25	800 334-6899
Dreyfus Premier Ltd CA Muni C	Muni CA	5.67	5.70		4	2	0	1.23	800 334-6899
Dreyfus Premier Ltd CA Muni R	Muni CA	6.49	6.41	5.50	3	2	0	0.50	800 334-6899
Dreyfus Premier Ltd MA Muni A	Muni State	6.41	6.26	5.17	4	3	3	0.75	800 334-6899
Dreyfus Premier Ltd MA Muni B	Muni State	5.87	5.55		4	2	0	1.25	800 334-6899
Dreyfus Premier Ltd MA Muni C	Muni State	6.19	5.58		4	2	0	1.25	800 334-6899
Dreyfus Premier Ltd MA Muni R	Muni State	6.58	6.19	5.38	2	2	0	0.50	800 334-6899
Dreyfus Premier Ltd Municipal A	Muni Natl	6.52	6.18	5.15	4	2	3	0.75	800 334-6899
Dreyfus Premier Ltd Municipal B	Muni Natl	5.89	5.70		4	2	0	1.25	800 334-6899
Dreyfus Premier Ltd Municipal C	Muni Natl	6.02	5.77		4	2	0	1.24	800 334-6899
Dreyfus Premier Ltd Municipal R	Muni Natl	6.69	6.46		4	2	0	0.50	800 334-6899
Dreyfus Premier Ltd NY Muni A	Muni NY	6.33	5.56	4.85	5	5	3	0.75	800 334-6899
Dreyfus Premier Ltd NY Muni B	Muni NY	5.80	5.12		4	2	0	1.25	800 334-6899
Dreyfus Premier Ltd NY Muni C	Muni NY	5.79	5.26		5	3	0	1.25	800 334-6899
Dreyfus Premier Ltd NY Muni R	Muni NY	6.60	5.81	5.08	4	2	0	0.50	800 334-6899

Bond Fund Name	Objective	Annualized Return for			Rank		Max Load	Expense Ratio	Toll-Free Telephone
		1 Year	3 Years	5 Years	Overall	Risk			
Dreyfus Premier Ltd Term High Inc A	Corp-HY	10.17					4.5		800 334-6899
Dreyfus Premier Ltd Term High Inc B	Corp-HY	9.64					0		800 334-6899
Dreyfus Premier Ltd Term High Inc C	Corp-HY	9.44					0		800 334-6899
Dreyfus Premier Ltd Term High Inc R	Corp-HY	10.40					0		800 334-6899
Dreyfus Premier Ltd Term Income A	Corp-Inv	9.04	6.68		3	3	3	0.85	800 334-6899
Dreyfus Premier Ltd Term Income B	Corp-Inv	8.77	6.23	5.32	4	3	0	1.35	800 334-6899
Dreyfus Premier Ltd Term Income C	Corp-Inv	7.66	5.71		5	3	0	1.35	800 334-6899
Dreyfus Premier Ltd Term Income R	Corp-Inv	9.33	6.96	5.90	3	3	0	0.60	800 334-6899
Dreyfus Premier MA Municipal Bond A	Muni State	8.85	7.18	5.82	2	3	4.5	0.92	800 334-6899
Dreyfus Premier MA Municipal Bond B	Muni State	8.28	6.62	5.24	3	5	0	1.43	800 334-6899
Dreyfus Premier MA Municipal Bond C	Muni State	8.02					0	1.65	800 334-6899
Dreyfus Premier Managed Income A	Dvsfd Bond	10.42	7.90	6.80	2	3	4.5	0.95	800 334-6899
Dreyfus Premier Managed Income B	Dvsfd Bond	9.58	7.10		3	3	0	1.70	800 334-6899
Dreyfus Premier Managed Income C	Dvsfd Bond	9.48	7.06		2	3	0	1.70	800 334-6899
Dreyfus Premier Managed Income R	Dvsfd Bond	10.69	8.17	7.07	1	3	0	0.70	800 334-6899
Dreyfus Premier Municipal Bond A	Muni Natl	9.01	7.72	6.34	1	3	4.5	0.92	800 334-6899
Dreyfus Premier Municipal Bond B	Muni Natl	8.44	7.15	5.77	3	3	0	1.43	800 334-6899
Dreyfus Premier Municipal Bond C	Muni Natl	8.22					0	1.66	800 334-6899
Dreyfus Premier Natl Ins Muni Bd A	Muni Natl	8.30	6.80		3	4	4.5	1.25	800 334-6899
Dreyfus Premier Natl Ins Muni Bd B	Muni Natl	7.75	6.27		4	4	0	1.75	800 334-6899
Dreyfus Premier Natl Ins Muni Bd C	Muni Natl	7.57					0	2.00	800 334-6899
Dreyfus Premier NY Municipal Bond A	Muni NY	9.32	7.81	6.12	3	4	4.5	0.92	800 334-6899
Dreyfus Premier NY Municipal Bond B	Muni NY	8.63	7.23	5.54	4	4	0	1.44	800 334-6899
Dreyfus Premier NY Municipal Bond C	Muni NY	8.41					0	1.69	800 334-6899
Dreyfus Short Term High Yield Fund	Corp-HY	11.02					0	1.09	800 645-6561
Dreyfus Short-Intermediate Govt	Government	7.11	5.74	5.29	3	1	0	0.74	800 645-6561
Dreyfus Short-Intermediate Muni	Muni Natl	5.00	4.73	4.17	3	1	0	0.76	800 645-6561
Dreyfus Short-Term Income	Corp-Inv	8.72	7.65	6.54	1	1	0	0.80	800 645-6561
Dreyfus Strategic Income	Dvsfd Bond	12.39	9.88	7.99	1	3	0	1.03	800 645-6561
Dreyfus US Treasury Intmed Term Bd	Government	8.99	6.22	5.32	3	3	0	0.80	800 645-6561
Dreyfus US Treasury Long Term Bond	Government	16.70	8.52	6.86	3	5	0	0.80	800 645-6561
Dreyfus US Treasury Short Term Bond	Government	6.56	5.61	5.14	3	1	0	0.70	800 645-6561
Dupree Intermediate Government	Government	9.47	7.18	6.10	2	3	0	0.28	800 866-0614
Dupree KY Tax-Free Income Fund	Muni State	7.80	7.11	5.90	2	2	0	0.32	800 866-0614
Dupree KY Tax-Free Short-to-Medium	Muni State	5.12	4.70	4.05	3	1	0	0.37	800 866-0614
Dupree NC Tax-Free Income	Muni State	10.02					0	0.16	800 866-0614
Dupree NC Tax-Free Short-to-Medium	Muni State	5.20					0	0.20	800 866-0614
Dupree TN Tax-Free Income	Muni State	9.60	8.42		1	3	0	0.22	800 866-0614
Dupree TN Tax-Free Short-to-Medium	Muni State	5.26	4.91		3	2	0	0.26	800 866-0614
Eaton Vance AL Municipals Fund A	Muni State	6.91	7.12		4	5	3.75	0.91	800 225-6265
Eaton Vance AL Municipals Fund B	Muni State	6.25	6.58	5.00	4	3	0	1.60	800 225-6265
Eaton Vance AR Municipals Fund A	Muni State	8.10	7.13		2	3	3.75	0.95	800 225-6265
Eaton Vance AR Municipals Fund B	Muni State	7.19	6.48	4.83	4	3	0	1.63	800 225-6265
Eaton Vance AZ Municipals Fund A	Muni State	9.13	7.86		2	3	4.75	0.69	800 225-6265
Eaton Vance AZ Municipals Fund B	Muni State	8.32	7.30	5.47	3	3	0	1.57	800 225-6265
Eaton Vance CA Ltd Maturity Muni B	Muni CA	5.76	5.03	3.88	5	2	0	1.70	800 225-6265
Eaton Vance CA Municipals Fund A	Muni CA	9.73	9.06		2	4	4.75	0.72	800 225-6265
Eaton Vance CA Municipals Fund B	Muni CA	8.32	7.74	5.33	3	4	0	1.63	800 225-6265
Eaton Vance CO Municipals Fund A	Muni State	8.56	8.16		2	3	4.75	0.76	800 225-6265
Eaton Vance CO Municipals Fund B	Muni State	7.82	7.60	5.35	3	3	0	1.59	800 225-6265
Eaton Vance CT Ltd Maturity Muni B	Muni State	5.33	4.94	4.10	4	2	0	1.68	800 225-6265
Eaton Vance CT Municipals Fund A	Muni State	8.65	7.79		2	3	4.75	0.67	800 225-6265
Eaton Vance CT Municipals Fund B	Muni State	7.73	7.04	4.62	3	3	0	1.61	800 225-6265
Eaton Vance FL Insured Muni Fund A	Muni State	9.02	7.57		3	4	4.75	0.62	800 225-6265
Eaton Vance FL Insured Muni Fund B	Muni State	8.85	7.09		4	4	0	1.21	800 225-6265
Eaton Vance FL Ltd Maturity Muni B	Muni State	5.27	4.28	3.75	4	2	0	1.63	800 225-6265
Eaton Vance FL Ltd Maturity Muni C	Muni State	5.21	4.19		4	2	2.25	1.68	800 225-6265
Eaton Vance FL Municipals Fund A	Muni State	9.58	7.79		3	4	4.75	0.52	800 225-6265

374

Bond Fund Name	Objective	Annualized Return for			Rank		Max Load	Expense Ratio	Toll-Free Telephone
		1 Year	3 Years	5 Years	Overall	Risk			
Eaton Vance FL Municipals Fund B	Muni State	8.77	6.92	4.86	4	4	0	1.54	800 225-6265
Eaton Vance GA Municipals Fund A	Muni State	7.90	7.33		3	3	3.75	0.83	800 225-6265
Eaton Vance GA Municipals Fund B	Muni State	7.31	6.73	4.43	4	3	0	1.58	800 225-6265
Eaton Vance Govt Obligations Fund A	Govt-Mtg	6.51	6.28	5.78	3	2	4.75	1.97	800 225-6265
Eaton Vance Govt Obligations Fund B	Govt-Mtg	5.67	5.56		5	2	0	1.95	800 225-6265
Eaton Vance Govt Obligations Fund C	Govt-Mtg	5.62	5.34		5	2	0	2.22	800 225-6265
Eaton Vance HI Municipals Fund A	Muni State	7.24	6.83		5	4	4.75	0.72	800 225-6265
Eaton Vance HI Municipals Fund B	Muni State	7.31	6.86		5	5	0	1.20	800 225-6265
Eaton Vance High Income Fund B	Corp-HY	14.28	13.08	10.32	1	3	4.75	1.70	800 225-6265
Eaton Vance Income Fund of Boston	Corp-HY	14.42	13.63	11.05	1	4	4.75	1.05	800 225-6265
Eaton Vance KS Municipals Fund A	Muni State	7.54	7.12		2	3	4.75	0.72	800 225-6265
Eaton Vance KS Municipals Fund B	Muni State	6.92	6.71		5	3	0	1.25	800 225-6265
Eaton Vance KY Municipals Fund A	Muni State	8.23	7.62		2	3	4.75	0.71	800 225-6265
Eaton Vance KY Municipals Fund B	Muni State	7.58	7.04	4.89	3	3	0	1.56	800 225-6265
Eaton Vance LA Municipals Fund A	Muni State	8.17	7.55		3	3	4.75	0.54	800 225-6265
Eaton Vance LA Municipals Fund B	Muni State	7.37	6.86	4.51	4	3	0	1.49	800 225-6265
Eaton Vance MA Ltd Maturity Muni B	Muni State	5.29	4.75	3.99	4	2	0	1.66	800 225-6265
Eaton Vance MA Municipals Fund A	Muni State	9.85	8.16		2	3	4.75	0.60	800 225-6265
Eaton Vance MA Municipals Fund B	Muni State	8.67	7.29	4.93	3	3	0	1.50	800 225-6265
Eaton Vance MD Municipals Fund A	Muni State	8.37	7.88		2	3	4.75	0.60	800 225-6265
Eaton Vance MD Municipals Fund B	Muni State	7.58	7.29	4.97	3	3	0	1.58	800 225-6265
Eaton Vance MI Ltd Maturity Muni B	Muni State	5.42	5.16	4.09	4	3	0	1.96	800 225-6265
Eaton Vance MI Municipals Fund A	Muni State	8.01	7.36		3	5	4.75	0.70	800 225-6265
Eaton Vance MI Municipals Fund B	Muni State	7.78	7.02	4.97	3	3	0	1.58	800 225-6265
Eaton Vance MN Municipals Fund A	Muni State	9.16	7.48		3	3	4.75	0.69	800 225-6265
Eaton Vance MN Municipals Fund B	Muni State	8.17	6.81	4.57	4	3	0	1.61	800 225-6265
Eaton Vance MO Municipals Fund A	Muni State	9.21	7.98		2	3	4.75	1.11	800 225-6265
Eaton Vance MO Municipals Fund B	Muni State	8.41	7.36	5.31	3	3	0	1.59	800 225-6265
Eaton Vance MS Municipals Fund A	Muni State	8.06	7.73		2	3	4.75	0.91	800 225-6265
Eaton Vance MS Municipals Fund B	Muni State	7.40	7.25	5.13	3	3	0	1.66	800 225-6265
Eaton Vance Muni Bond Fund I	Muni Natl	12.33	9.84	7.14	2	4	3.75	0.77	800 225-6265
Eaton Vance National Ltd Mat Muni B	Muni Natl	7.74	5.67	4.49	3	2	0	1.67	800 225-6265
Eaton Vance National Ltd Mat Muni C	Muni Natl	7.25	5.30		3	2	0	2.07	800 225-6265
Eaton Vance National Municipals A	Muni Natl	11.43	9.65		2	5	4.75	1.04	800 225-6265
Eaton Vance National Municipals B	Muni Natl	11.15	9.08	6.88	3	5	0	1.52	800 225-6265
Eaton Vance NC Municipals Fund A	Muni State	8.49	7.37		4	5	4.75	0.84	800 225-6265
Eaton Vance NC Municipals Fund B	Muni State	7.64	6.72	4.49	5	3	0	1.57	800 225-6265
Eaton Vance NJ Ltd Maturity Muni B	Muni State	5.24	4.87	3.86	5	2	0	1.66	800 225-6265
Eaton Vance NJ Municipals Fund A	Muni State	9.55	8.08		1	3	4.75	0.64	800 225-6265
Eaton Vance NJ Municipals Fund B	Muni State	8.68	7.12	4.94	3	3	0	1.48	800 225-6265
Eaton Vance NY Ltd Maturity Muni B	Muni NY	6.49	5.21	4.15	5	2	0	1.61	800 225-6265
Eaton Vance NY Municipals Fund A	Muni NY	9.42	8.27		2	3	4.75	0.76	800 225-6265
Eaton Vance NY Municipals Fund B	Muni NY	8.48	7.39	5.26	3	4	0	1.55	800 225-6265
Eaton Vance OH Ltd Maturity Muni B	Muni State	5.67	5.29	4.27	4	2	0	1.81	800 225-6265
Eaton Vance OH Municipals Fund A	Muni State	9.05	7.80		1	3	4.75	0.79	800 225-6265
Eaton Vance OH Municipals Fund B	Muni State	7.98	7.02	5.14	3	3	0	1.59	800 225-6265
Eaton Vance OR Municipals Fund A	Muni State	8.71	6.77		3	3	3.75	0.89	800 225-6265
Eaton Vance OR Municipals Fund B	Muni State	7.85	6.19	4.49	3	3	0	1.69	800 225-6265
Eaton Vance PA Ltd Maturity Muni B	Muni State	6.61	5.24	4.24	4	2	0	1.67	800 225-6265
Eaton Vance PA Ltd Maturity Muni C	Muni State	6.39	5.14		4	2	2.25	1.79	800 225-6265
Eaton Vance PA Municipals Fund B	Muni State	7.60	7.12	5.06	3	3	0	1.56	800 225-6265
Eaton Vance RI Municipals Fund A	Muni State	8.40	7.67		3	3	4.75	0.90	800 225-6265
Eaton Vance RI Municipals Fund B	Muni State	7.62	7.37	4.96	3	3	0	1.42	800 225-6265
Eaton Vance SC Municipals Fund B	Muni State	7.76	7.04	4.83	3	3	0	1.58	800 225-6265
Eaton Vance Short Term Treasury	Government	4.96	5.04	4.71	2	1	0	0.60	800 225-6265
Eaton Vance Strategic Income Fund B	Intl Bond	6.25	12.72	8.30	3	4	0	2.08	800 225-6265
Eaton Vance TN Municipals Fund A	Muni State	8.22	7.86		2	3	3.75	0.62	800 225-6265
Eaton Vance TN Municipals Fund B	Muni State	7.28	7.17	4.97	4	3	0	1.51	800 225-6265

Bond Fund Name	Objective	Annualized Return for			Rank		Max Load	Expense Ratio	Toll-Free Telephone
		1 Year	3 Years	5 Years	Overall	Risk			
Eaton Vance TX Municipals Fund A	Muni State	9.34	8.05		1	3	2.75	0.72	800 225-6265
Eaton Vance TX Municipals Fund B	Muni State	8.30	7.51	5.64	2	3	0	1.52	800 225-6265
Eaton Vance VA Municipals Fund A	Muni State	8.45	7.41		3	3	0	0.81	800 225-6265
Eaton Vance VA Municipals Fund B	Muni State	7.57	6.80	4.84	4	3	0	1.53	800 225-6265
Eaton Vance WV Municipals Fund A	Muni State	9.12	7.96		2	3	0	0.45	800 225-6265
Eaton Vance WV Municipals Fund B	Muni State	8.14	7.27	5.16	3	3	0	1.54	800 225-6265
Eclipse Ultra ST Income Fund	Government	6.33	6.17		3	1	0	0.71	800 872-2710
Elfun Income Fund	Corp-Inv	10.35	8.08	7.01	1	3	0	0.24	800 242-0134
Elfun Tax Exempt Income Fund	Muni Natl	8.98	7.69	6.03	2	3	0	0.13	800 242-0134
Empire Builder Tax Free (NY)	Muni NY	6.95	6.08	5.16	5	3	0	0.98	800 662-8417
Enterprise Government Securities	Govt-Mtg	8.39	7.89	6.16	2	3	4.75	1.30	800 432-4320
Enterprise High Yield Bond	Corp-HY	11.81	12.05	10.42	1	4	4.75	1.30	800 432-4320
Enterprise Tax Exempt Income	Muni Natl	7.39	6.32	5.05	3	2	4.75	1.25	800 432-4320
Evergreen CA Tax Free A	Muni CA	8.00	7.45		4	5	4.75	0.77	800 343-2898
Evergreen CA Tax Free B	Muni CA	7.39	6.73		5	5	0	1.52	800 343-2898
Evergreen CA Tax Free C	Muni CA	7.39	6.74		5	5	0	1.52	800 343-2898
Evergreen Capital Pres and Inc A	Govt-Mtg	5.09	6.06	5.17	3	1	3.25	0.90	800 343-2898
Evergreen Capital Pres and Inc B	Govt-Mtg	4.48	5.35	4.42	4	1	0	1.50	800 343-2898
Evergreen Capital Pres and Inc C	Govt-Mtg	4.59	5.39	4.34	4	1		1.67	800 343-2898
Evergreen Diversified Bond Fund B	Dvsfd Bond	11.48	8.62	6.36	3	4	0	1.92	800 343-2898
Evergreen FL High Income Muni Bd A	Muni State	10.01	8.90		1	2	4.75	0.87	800 343-2898
Evergreen FL High Income Muni Bd B	Muni State	9.24					0	1.62	800 343-2898
Evergreen FL High Income Muni Bd Y	Muni State	10.34					0	0.62	800 343-2898
Evergreen FL Muni Bond Fund A	Muni State	8.83	7.58	6.18	2	3	4.75	0.82	800 343-2898
Evergreen FL Muni Bond Fund B	Muni State	7.84			4	3	4.75	1.65	800 343-2898
Evergreen FL Muni Bond Fund Y	Muni State	8.91	7.67		2	3	0	0.65	800 343-2898
Evergreen GA Muni Bond Fund A	Muni State	9.81	8.16		3	3	4.75	0.94	800 343-2898
Evergreen GA Muni Bond Fund B	Muni State	8.75	7.27		3	3	0	1.69	800 343-2898
Evergreen GA Muni Bond Fund Y	Muni State	10.15	8.49		2	3	0	0.69	800 343-2898
Evergreen High Grade TF A	Muni Natl	8.10	7.20		4	5	4.75	1.11	800 343-2898
Evergreen High Grade TF B	Muni Natl	7.32	6.40		5	5	0	1.86	800 343-2898
Evergreen High Grade TF Y	Muni Natl	8.36	7.48		3	5	0	1.00	800 343-2898
Evergreen High Yield Bond Fund B	Corp-HY	12.59	9.91	6.32	3	5	0	1.93	800 343-2898
Evergreen Intermediate Term Bond A	Corp-Inv	8.37	7.15	5.88	3	3	4.75	1.80	800 343-2898
Evergreen Intermediate Term Bond B	Corp-Inv	7.96	6.53	5.18	5	3	0	1.81	800 343-2898
Evergreen Intermediate Term Bond C	Corp-Inv	8.06	6.52	5.19	5	3	0	1.80	800 343-2898
Evergreen Intermediate Term Bond Y	Corp-Inv	8.67	6.43	5.64	4	4	0	0.73	800 343-2898
Evergreen Intmed Term Govt Sec A	Government	7.55	5.82		4	2	3.25	0.86	800 343-2898
Evergreen Intmed Term Govt Sec B	Government	6.57					0	1.81	800 343-2898
Evergreen Intmed Term Govt Sec C	Government	6.57					0	1.81	800 343-2898
Evergreen Intmed Term Govt Sec Y	Government	7.64	5.87	5.08	3	2	0	0.81	800 343-2898
Evergreen MA Tax Free A	Muni State	7.76	7.03		3	4	4.75	1.58	800 343-2898
Evergreen MA Tax Free B	Muni State	7.08	6.28		5	4	0	1.51	800 343-2898
Evergreen MA Tax Free C	Muni State	7.20	6.30		5	4	0	1.51	800 343-2898
Evergreen MD Muni A	Muni State	6.11	5.15	4.26	5	3	0	1.57	800 343-2898
Evergreen MD Muni Y	Muni State	6.37	5.31		5	3		1.32	800 343-2898
Evergreen MO Tax Free A	Muni State	8.07	7.55		3	4	4.75	0.76	800 343-2898
Evergreen MO Tax Free B	Muni State	7.52	6.88		4	4	0	1.51	800 343-2898
Evergreen MO Tax Free C	Muni State	7.62	6.88		4	4	0	1.51	800 343-2898
Evergreen NC Muni Bond A	Muni State	9.95	7.93	5.88	3	4	4.75	1.10	800 343-2898
Evergreen NC Muni Bond B	Muni State	9.14	7.12		3	4	0	1.85	800 343-2898
Evergreen NC Muni Bond Y	Muni State	10.23	8.13		3	4	0	0.85	800 343-2898
Evergreen NJ Tax Free Income Fund A	Muni State	7.74	6.85	5.58	3	3	4.75	0.43	800 343-2898
Evergreen NJ Tax Free Income Fund B	Muni State	6.77					0	1.35	800 343-2898
Evergreen NJ Tax Free Income Fund Y	Muni State	7.84					0	0.35	800 343-2898
Evergreen NY Tax Free A	Muni NY	8.17	7.41		3	4	4.75	0.76	800 343-2898
Evergreen NY Tax Free B	Muni NY	7.40	6.70		5	4	0	1.51	800 343-2898
Evergreen NY Tax Free C	Muni NY	7.39	6.65		5	4	0	1.51	800 343-2898

Bond Fund Name	Objective	Annualized Return for			Rank		Max Load	Expense Ratio	Toll-Free Telephone
		1 Year	3 Years	5 Years	Overall	Risk			
Evergreen PA Tax Free A	Muni State	8.02	7.25	5.69	3	3	4.75	0.70	800 343-2898
Evergreen PA Tax Free B	Muni State	7.39	6.53	4.94	5	3	0	1.51	800 343-2898
Evergreen PA Tax Free C	Muni State	7.38	6.51	4.82	4	3	0	1.51	800 343-2898
Evergreen SC Muni Bond A	Muni State	8.26	7.93		1	3	4.75	0.97	800 343-2898
Evergreen SC Muni Bond Y	Muni State	8.44	8.16		2	3	0	0.72	800 343-2898
Evergreen Select Adj Rate I	Govt-Mtg	5.65	6.43		3	1	0	0.90	800 343-2898
Evergreen Select Adj Rate IS	Govt-Mtg	5.71	6.58	5.53	3	1	0	0.30	800 343-2898
Evergreen Short Interm Bond Fund A	Corp-Inv	7.10	6.10		4	3	3.25	0.72	800 343-2898
Evergreen Short Interm Bond Fund B	Corp-Inv	6.14	5.17	4.41	5	2	0	1.62	800 343-2898
Evergreen Short Interm Bond Fund C	Corp-Inv	6.14	5.13		5	2	0	1.62	800 343-2898
Evergreen Short Interm Bond Fund Y	Corp-Inv	7.21	6.22	5.38	3	2	0	0.67	800 343-2898
Evergreen Short Intermediate Muni A	Muni Natl	4.84	4.33		3	1	3.25	0.96	800 343-2898
Evergreen Short Intermediate Muni B	Muni Natl	3.80	3.43		4	1	0	1.86	800 343-2898
Evergreen Short Intermediate Muni Y	Muni Natl	4.80	4.39	0.46	3	1	0	0.55	800 343-2898
Evergreen Strategic Income A	Dvsfd Bond	9.78	9.60	6.58	2	3	4.75	1.31	800 343-2898
Evergreen Strategic Income B	Dvsfd Bond	8.93	8.73	5.78	2	3	0	2.04	800 343-2898
Evergreen Strategic Income C	Dvsfd Bond	8.93	8.73	5.76	3	3	0	2.04	800 343-2898
Evergreen Tax Free Fund B	Muni Natl	7.02	6.51	4.95	5	3	0	0.96	800 343-2898
Evergreen US Government A	Government	9.66	7.04	6.02	2	3	4.75	1.02	800 343-2898
Evergreen US Government B	Government	8.85	6.24	5.18	3	3	0	1.73	800 343-2898
Evergreen US Government C	Government	8.85	6.23	5.07	3	3	0	1.73	800 343-2898
Evergreen US Government Y	Government	9.93	7.31		2	3	0	0.73	800 343-2898
Evergreen VA Muni Bond Fund A	Muni State	8.82	7.69		2	3	4.75	1.03	800 343-2898
Evergreen VA Muni Bond Fund B	Muni State	8.04	6.90		3	3	0	1.78	800 343-2898
Evergreen VA Muni Bond Fund Y	Muni State	9.14	7.97		1	3	4.75	0.78	800 343-2898
Excelsior CA Tax Exempt Income	Muni CA	5.69					0	1.53	800 446-1012
Excelsior Instl Total Return Bond	Corp-Inv	10.87	7.81		2	4	0	0.50	800 446-1012
Excelsior Intermed-Term Managed Inc	Muni Natl	9.65	6.85		3	4	0	0.68	800 446-1012
Excelsior Intermed-Term Tax-Exempt	Muni Natl	6.81	6.41	5.80	3	2	0	0.58	800 446-1012
Excelsior Long-Term Tax-Exempt	Muni Natl	8.59	8.50	7.57	3	5	0	0.66	800 446-1012
Excelsior Managed Income	Corp-Inv	11.46	7.27	6.37	3	5	0	1.04	800 446-1012
Excelsior NY Interm Tax Exempt	Muni NY	6.51	5.93	5.32	2	2	0	0.71	800 446-1012
Excelsior Short-Term Govt Secs	Government	6.05	5.48	5.05	3	1	0	0.62	800 446-1012
Excelsior Short-Term Tax-Ex Secs	Muni Natl	4.52	4.35	3.89	3	1	0	0.65	800 446-1012
Executive Investors High Yield	Corp-HY	10.99	12.31	10.23	1	3	4.75	1.22	800 423-4026
Executive Investors Insured TE Fund	Muni Natl	10.34	10.21		3	5	4.75	0.50	800 423-4026
Expedition Bond Fund Institutional	Government	7.94					0	1.10	800 992-2085
Expedition Bond Fund Investment Cl	Government	7.83	5.54	4.70	4	2	2.5	1.15	800 992-2085
Fairport Govt Securities Fund	Government	8.23	6.11		4	3	0	2.61	800 332-6459
FBL High Grade Bond	Corp-Inv	9.20	7.24	6.41	2	2	0	1.84	800 247-4170
FBL High Yield Bond	Corp-HY	9.04	9.50	8.00	2	2	0	1.97	800 247-4170
Federated Adj Rate US Govt Fund F	Govt-Mtg	4.84	5.67	4.58	3	1	0	1.10	800 245-5051
Federated ARMs Fund (IS)	Govt-Mtg	5.37	6.23	5.14	3	1	0	0.55	800 245-5051
Federated ARMs Fund (ISS)	Govt-Mtg	5.11	5.97	4.88	3	1	0	0.80	800 245-5051
Federated Bond Fund A	Dvsfd Bond	11.39					4.5	1.05	800 245-5051
Federated Bond Fund B	Dvsfd Bond	10.46	8.58		2	4	0	1.85	800 245-5051
Federated Bond Fund C	Dvsfd Bond	10.47	8.58		2	4	0	1.85	800 245-5051
Federated Bond Fund F	Dvsfd Bond	11.41	9.41	8.15	1	4	1	1.08	800 245-5051
Federated Bond Index (IS)	Corp-Inv	9.98	7.05		2	3	0		800 245-5051
Federated Bond Index (ISS)	Corp-Inv	9.73	6.87		3	3	0		800 245-5051
Federated Fund for US Govt Sec A	Govt-Mtg	8.08	6.98	5.55	3	2	4.5	0.93	800 245-5051
Federated Fund for US Govt Sec B	Govt-Mtg	7.05	6.08		5	2	0	1.80	800 245-5051
Federated Fund for US Govt Sec C	Govt-Mtg	7.08	6.09	4.80	5	2	0	1.80	800 245-5051
Federated GNMA (IS)	Govt-Mtg	8.27	7.45	6.20	2	2	0	0.61	800 245-5051
Federated GNMA (ISS)	Govt-Mtg	8.06	7.21	5.97	2	2	0	0.80	800 245-5051
Federated Govt Income Securities A	Govt-Mtg	10.61					4.5	0.95	800 245-5051
Federated Govt Income Securities B	Govt-Mtg	9.62					0	1.80	800 245-5051
Federated Govt Income Securities C	Govt-Mtg	9.72					0	1.80	800 245-5051

Bond Fund Name	Objective	Annualized Return for			Rank		Max Load	Expense Ratio	Toll-Free Telephone
		1 Year	3 Years	5 Years	Overall	Risk			
Federated Govt Income Securities F	Govt-Mtg	10.52	7.51	6.04	2	3	1	0.96	800 245-5051
Federated High Income Bond A	Corp-HY	11.02	12.74	10.61	1	3	4.5	1.22	800 245-5051
Federated High Income Bond B	Corp-HY	10.20					0	1.99	800 245-5051
Federated High Income Bond C	Corp-HY	10.19	11.87	7.75	1	3	0	1.99	800 245-5051
Federated High Yield Trust	Corp-HY	11.01	12.58	10.21	1	3	0	0.88	800 245-5051
Federated Income Trust (IS)	Govt-Mtg	8.25	7.36	6.28	2	2	0	0.58	800 245-5051
Federated Income Trust (ISS)	Govt-Mtg	8.07	7.13	6.04	3	2	0	0.80	800 245-5051
Federated Intermediate Income Instl	Corp-Inv	10.22	7.73		2	4	0	0.55	800 245-5051
Federated Intl High Income Fund A	Intl Bond	−1.90					4.5	0.75	800 245-5051
Federated Intl High Income Fund B	Intl Bond	−2.66					0	1.50	800 245-5051
Federated Intl High Income Fund C	Intl Bond	−2.66					0	1.50	800 245-5051
Federated Intl Income Fund A	Intl Bond	1.19	4.69	6.78	5	5	4.5	1.30	800 245-5051
Federated Intl Income Fund B	Intl Bond	0.46					0	2.10	800 245-5051
Federated Intl Income Fund C	Intl Bond	0.40	3.88	4.85	5	5	0	2.06	800 245-5051
Federated Intmed Municipal Tr (IS)	Muni Natl	6.46	5.78	4.78	3	2	0	0.57	800 245-5051
Federated Limited Duration (IS)	Dvsfd Bond	7.87					0	0.00	800 245-5051
Federated Limited Duration (ISS)	Dvsfd Bond	7.55					0	0.30	800 245-5051
Federated Limited Term Fund A	Corp-Inv	6.92	6.38	5.50	3	1	1	1.10	800 245-5051
Federated Limited Term Fund F	Corp-Inv	6.97					1	1.01	800 245-5051
Federated Managed Income (IS)	Dvsfd Bond	12.14	8.85		1	2	0	0.79	800 245-5051
Federated Managed Income (Select)	Dvsfd Bond	11.38	8.09		1	2	0	1.50	800 245-5051
Federated MI Intmed Muni Trust	Muni State	6.61	6.07	5.28	3	2	3	0.51	800 245-5051
Federated Muni Opportunities Fund A	Muni Natl	8.89					4.5	1.09	800 245-5051
Federated Muni Opportunities Fund B	Muni Natl	7.95					0	1.84	800 245-5051
Federated Muni Opportunities Fund C	Muni Natl	8.09					0	1.86	800 245-5051
Federated Muni Opportunities Fund F	Muni Natl	8.89	6.77	5.42	2	3	0	1.08	800 245-5051
Federated Muni Securities A	Muni Natl	8.93	5.78	4.86	3	3	4.5	0.92	800 245-5051
Federated Muni Securities B	Muni Natl	7.90						1.81	800 245-5051
Federated Muni Securities C	Muni Natl	7.91	4.84	3.94	4	3	0	1.80	800 245-5051
Federated NY Muni Income Fund F	Muni NY	9.09	8.27	5.92	2	3	1	0.62	800 245-5051
Federated OH Muni Income Fund F	Muni State	8.34	7.33	5.89	2	3	0	0.91	800 245-5051
Federated PA Muni Income Fund A	Muni State	8.44	8.21	6.44	1	3	4.5	0.75	800 245-5051
Federated Short-Term Income (IS)	Corp-Inv	6.47	6.32	5.36	3	1	0	0.56	800 245-5051
Federated Short-Term Income (ISS)	Corp-Inv	6.20	6.07	5.12	3	1	0		800 245-5051
Federated ST Municipal Tr (IS)	Muni Natl	4.68	4.36	3.99	3	2	0	0.46	800 245-5051
Federated ST Municipal Tr (ISS)	Muni Natl	4.41	4.10		5	3	0		800 245-5051
Federated Strategic Income A	Dvsfd Bond	6.31	10.35		2	3	4.5	1.10	800 245-5051
Federated Strategic Income B	Dvsfd Bond	5.49					0	1.85	800 245-5051
Federated Strategic Income C	Dvsfd Bond	5.42	9.50		3	3	0	1.85	800 245-5051
Federated Strategic Income F	Dvsfd Bond	6.31	10.25		2	3	1	1.10	800 245-5051
Federated Total Return Bond (IS)	Corp-Inv	11.00					0	0.03	800 245-5051
Federated Total Return Bond (ISS)	Corp-Inv	10.66					0	0.30	800 245-5051
Federated US Government Bond Fund	Government	14.76	8.34	7.29	3	5	0	0.86	800 245-5051
Federated US Govt Secs:1-3 Yrs(IS)	Government	6.13	5.67	5.04	3	1	0	0.54	800 245-5051
Federated US Govt Secs:1-3 Yrs(ISS)	Government	5.85	5.41	4.79	3	1	0	0.79	800 245-5051
Federated US Govt Secs:2-5 Yrs(IS)	Government	7.74	6.13	5.35	3	2	0	0.54	800 245-5051
Federated US Govt Secs:2-5 Yrs(ISS)	Government	7.47	5.90	5.11	3	2	0	0.79	800 245-5051
Federated US Govt Secs:5-10 Yrs ISS	Government	11.12					0	0.60	800 245-5051
Federated US Govt Secs:5-10 Yrs(IS)	Government	11.40					0	0.30	800 245-5051
FFTW US Short Term Fixed Income	Corp-Inv	5.26	5.36	4.94	3	1	0	0.25	800 762-4848
FFTW Worldwide Fixed Income	Intl Bond	6.85	5.53	5.84	4	5	0	0.60	800 762-4848
FFTW Worldwide Fixed Income Hedged	Intl Bond	12.99	11.43	10.14	1	3	0	0.26	800 762-4848
Fidelity Adv Emerging Markets Inc A	Intl Bond	1.04					4.25	1.40	800 522-7297
Fidelity Adv Emerging Markets Inc B	Intl Bond	0.09	22.01		4	5	0	2.15	800 522-7297
Fidelity Adv Emerging Markets Inc I	Intl Bond	1.02					0	1.25	800 522-7297
Fidelity Adv Emerging Markets Inc T	Intl Bond	0.64	22.79		3	5	3.5	1.49	800 522-7297
Fidelity Adv Govt Investment A	Government	10.44					4.25	0.90	800 522-7297
Fidelity Adv Govt Investment B	Government	9.67	6.28		3	3	0	1.67	800 522-7297

Bond Fund Name	Objective	Annualized Return for			Rank		Max Load	Expense Ratio	Toll-Free Telephone
		1 Year	3 Years	5 Years	Overall	Risk			
Fidelity Adv Govt Investment Instl	Government	10.37					0		800 522-7297
Fidelity Adv Govt Investment T	Government	9.72	6.76	5.75	3	3	3.5	0.89	800 522-7297
Fidelity Adv High Yield Fund A	Corp-HY	14.76					4.25	1.25	800 522-7297
Fidelity Adv High Yield Fund B	Corp-HY	14.21	13.27		2	5	0	1.79	800 522-7297
Fidelity Adv High Yield Fund Instl	Corp-HY	14.92					0		800 522-7297
Fidelity Adv High Yield Fund T	Corp-HY	14.69	13.98	11.63	2	5	3.5	1.09	800 522-7297
Fidelity Adv Intmed Bond A	Corp-Inv	7.90					3.25	0.90	800 522-7297
Fidelity Adv Intmed Bond B	Corp-Inv	7.22	5.47		5	2	0	1.65	800 522-7297
Fidelity Adv Intmed Bond Instl	Corp-Inv	8.10	6.45	5.67	3	2	0	0.65	800 522-7297
Fidelity Adv Intmed Bond T	Corp-Inv	7.78	6.16		4	2	2.75	1.06	800 522-7297
Fidelity Adv Intmed Muni Inc A	Muni Natl	7.37					3.25	0.90	800 522-7297
Fidelity Adv Intmed Muni Inc B	Muni Natl	6.79	5.90		4	2	0	1.66	800 522-7297
Fidelity Adv Intmed Muni Inc Instl	Muni Natl	7.42	6.76	5.29	3	2	0	0.75	800 522-7297
Fidelity Adv Intmed Muni Inc T	Muni Natl	7.19	6.51		4	2	3.25	1.00	800 522-7297
Fidelity Adv Mortgage Securities A	Govt-Mtg	7.52					4.25	0.90	800 522-7297
Fidelity Adv Mortgage Securities B	Govt-Mtg	6.75					0	1.65	800 522-7297
Fidelity Adv Mortgage Securities I	Govt-Mtg	7.65					0	0.73	800 522-7297
Fidelity Adv Mortgage Securities T	Govt-Mtg	7.48					3.5	1.00	800 522-7297
Fidelity Adv Muni Bond B	Muni Natl	6.70					0	1.65	800 522-7297
Fidelity Adv Muni Bond I	Muni Natl	7.65					0	0.56	800 522-7297
Fidelity Adv Muni Bond Initial	Muni Natl	7.57	7.33	5.56	3	3	0	0.55	800 522-7297
Fidelity Adv Muni Bond T	Muni Natl	7.69					3.5	1.00	800 522-7297
Fidelity Adv Municipal Income A	Muni Natl	9.08					4.25	0.90	800 522-7297
Fidelity Adv Municipal Income B	Muni Natl	8.46	6.69		3	3	0	1.58	800 522-7297
Fidelity Adv Municipal Income Instl	Muni Natl	9.12					0	0.75	800 522-7297
Fidelity Adv Municipal Income T	Muni Natl	8.34	7.15	5.52	3	3	3.5	0.96	800 522-7297
Fidelity Adv Short Fixed-Income A	Corp-Inv	6.68					1.5	0.90	800 522-7297
Fidelity Adv Short Fixed-Income I	Corp-Inv	6.54					0	0.80	800 522-7297
Fidelity Adv Short Fixed-Income T	Corp-Inv	5.92	5.71	4.62	3	1	1.5	0.89	800 522-7297
Fidelity Adv Strategic Income A	Corp-Inv	7.77					4.25	1.25	800 522-7297
Fidelity Adv Strategic Income B	Corp-Inv	7.11	10.28		2	4	0	1.88	800 522-7297
Fidelity Adv Strategic Income I	Corp-Inv	7.94					0	1.09	800 522-7297
Fidelity Adv Strategic Income T	Corp-Inv	7.72	10.93		2	4	3.5	1.18	800 522-7297
Fidelity Capital & Income Fund	Corp-HY	17.63	13.27	10.34	2	5	0	0.83	800 544-8888
Fidelity Freedom Income	Corp-HY	11.42					0	0.08	800 544-8888
Fidelity Ginnie Mae	Govt-Mtg	8.72	7.59	6.46	2	2	0	0.74	800 544-8888
Fidelity Government Securities Fund	Government	11.17	7.24	6.09	3	4	0	0.73	800 544-8888
Fidelity High Income Fund	Corp-HY	14.73	14.52	13.01	1	5	0	0.80	800 544-6666
Fidelity Inst US Bond Index	Corp-Inv	11.15	7.95	6.93	2	3	0	0.32	800 544-8888
Fidelity Instl ST Govt	Government	7.10	6.38	5.56	3	1	0	0.81	800 544-8888
Fidelity Intermediate Bond Fund	Corp-Inv	9.01	6.75	5.89	3	2	0	0.65	800 544-8888
Fidelity Intermediate Government	Government	8.93	7.08	5.99	2	2	0	0.38	800 544-6666
Fidelity International Bond Fund	Intl Bond	1.41	1.41	0.33	5	5	0	1.14	800 544-8888
Fidelity Investment Grade Bond	Corp-Inv	10.63	7.60	6.26	3	3	0	0.70	800 544-8888
Fidelity Mortgage Securities	Govt-Mtg	9.19	8.18	7.75	1	2	0	0.72	800 544-8888
Fidelity New Markets Income Fund	Intl Bond	1.57	24.16	13.70	3	5	0	1.08	800 544-8888
Fidelity Short Interm Government	Government	6.81	5.80	5.00	4	1	0	0.65	800 544-8888
Fidelity Short-Term Bond	Corp-Inv	6.57	5.91	4.62	4	1	0	0.71	800 544-8888
Fidelity Spartan Aggress Muni Inc	Muni Natl	9.62	7.74	6.05	2	3	0	0.56	800 544-8888
Fidelity Spartan AZ Muni Income Fd	Muni State	7.16	6.43		4	3	0	0.55	800 544-6666
Fidelity Spartan CA Muni Income	Muni CA	9.25	8.53	6.19	2	3	0	0.53	800 544-8888
Fidelity Spartan CT Muni Income	Muni State	8.39	7.44	5.89	2	3	0	0.55	800 544-6666
Fidelity Spartan FL Muni Income	Muni State	8.11	7.54	6.24	2	3	0	0.55	800 544-6666
Fidelity Spartan GNMA	Govt-Mtg	8.45	7.58	6.56	2	2	0	0.51	800 544-6666
Fidelity Spartan Government Income	Government	10.83	7.43	6.17	2	3	0	0.60	800 544-6666
Fidelity Spartan Insured Muni Inc	Muni Natl	9.38	7.89	6.11	2	3	0	0.57	800 544-8888
Fidelity Spartan Intmed Muni Inc	Muni Natl	7.59	7.09	5.86	2	2	0	0.55	800 544-8888
Fidelity Spartan Investment Grade	Corp-Inv	10.49	7.61	6.64	2	3	0	0.61	800 544-6666

| Bond Fund Name | Objective | Annualized Return for | | | Rank | | Max Load | Expense Ratio | Toll-Free Telephone |
		1 Year	3 Years	5 Years	Overall	Risk			
Fidelity Spartan MA Muni Income	Muni State	8.83	7.81	6.30	1	3	0	0.53	800 544-6666
Fidelity Spartan MD Muni Income	Muni State	8.19	7.39	5.74	2	3	0	0.55	800 544-6666
Fidelity Spartan MI Muni Income	Muni State	8.76	7.54	5.44	3	3	0	0.56	800 544-6666
Fidelity Spartan MN Muni Income	Muni State	8.34	7.19	5.82	2	3	0	0.57	800 544-6666
Fidelity Spartan Municipal Income	Muni Natl	8.86	8.11	5.45	2	3	0	0.55	800 544-8888
Fidelity Spartan NJ Muni Income	Muni State	7.76	6.95	5.62	2	3	0	0.55	800 544-6666
Fidelity Spartan NY Muni Income	Muni NY	9.24	8.05	6.11	3	4	0	0.55	800 544-8888
Fidelity Spartan OH Muni Income	Muni State	8.26	7.30	6.08	2	3	0	0.56	800 544-6666
Fidelity Spartan PA Muni Income	Muni State	8.17	7.30	6.27	2	3	0	0.55	800 544-6666
Fidelity Spartan Short-Intmed Govt	Government	7.38	6.16	5.58	3	1	0	0.55	800 544-6666
Fidelity Spartan Short-Intmed Muni	Muni Natl	5.10	4.96	4.48	3	1	0	0.55	800 544-6666
Fidelity Spartan Short-Term Bond	Corp-Inv	7.44	6.48	4.74	3	1	0	0.61	800 544-6666
Fidelity Target Timeline 1999	Corp-Inv	7.70					0	0.34	800 544-8888
Fidelity Target Timeline 2001	Corp-Inv	9.74					0	0.34	800 544-8888
Fidelity Target Timeline 2003	Corp-Inv	12.30					0	0.34	800 544-8888
59 Wall St TF Fixed Income	Muni Natl	4.22	4.02	3.80	3	1	0	0.70	800 625-5759
First American CO Intmed TF A	Muni State	6.70	6.02		3	2	3	0.70	800 637-2548
First American CO Intmed TF Instl	Muni State	6.60	5.99		4	2	0	0.70	800 637-2548
First American Fixed Income A	Corp-Inv	10.66	7.11	6.49	3	4	3.75	0.95	800 637-2548
First American Fixed Income B	Corp-Inv	9.80	6.28		4	4	0	1.70	800 637-2548
First American Fixed Income Instl	Corp-Inv	10.93	7.38		3	3	0	0.70	800 637-2548
First American Intmed Tax Free A	Muni Natl	6.38	5.91	5.12	3	2	3	0.67	800 637-2548
First American Intmed Tax Free I	Muni Natl	6.39	5.89		4	2	0	0.67	800 637-2548
First American Intmed Term Govt A	Government	7.69	6.19	5.44	3	2	3	0.70	800 637-2548
First American Intmed Term Govt I	Government	7.70	6.20		4	2	0	0.70	800 637-2548
First American Intmed Term Inc A	Corp-Inv	8.37	6.57	5.68	3	2	3.75	0.70	800 637-2548
First American Intmed Term Inc I	Corp-Inv	8.20	6.52		3	2	0	0.70	800 637-2548
First American Limited Term Inc A	Corp-Inv	6.04	5.90	5.22	3	1	2	1.15	800 637-2548
First American Limited Term Inc I	Corp-Inv	5.93	5.87		3	1	0	0.60	800 637-2548
First American MN Intmed Tax-Free A	Muni State	6.41	5.87		3	2	3	0.70	800 637-2548
First American MN Intmed Tax-Free I	Muni State	6.39	5.97		3	2	0	0.70	800 637-2548
First Funds Bond Fund I	Corp-Inv	11.04	7.58		3	4	0	0.49	800 442-1941
First Funds Bond Fund II	Corp-Inv	10.74		.			3.75	0.90	800 442-1941
First Funds Bond Fund III	Corp-Inv	9.74	6.38		4	4	0	1.63	800 442-1941
First Funds TN Tax-Free I	Muni State	8.18					0	0.07	800 442-1941
First Funds TN Tax-Free II	Muni State	8.24					3.75	0.12	800 442-1941
First Funds TN Tax-Free III	Muni State	7.86					0	0.23	800 442-1941
First Hawaii Intmed Muni Fund	Muni State	4.20	4.29		4	1	0	1.07	
First Hawaii Municipal Bond	Muni State	6.72	6.14	4.99	3	2	0	0.97	
First Idaho Tax-Free Fund	Muni State	7.05					2.75	1.59	
First Investors CA Insured Tax Free	Muni CA	9.30	8.09	6.25	3	4	6.25	0.89	800 423-4026
First Investors CO Insured Tax Free	Muni State	9.09	8.11	6.64	1	3	6.25	0.40	800 423-4026
First Investors CT Insured Tax Free	Muni State	8.34	7.27	5.61	3	3	6.25	0.80	800 423-4026
First Investors FL Insured Tax Free	Muni State	8.10	7.49	6.32	3	4	6.25	0.80	800 423-4026
First Investors Fund for Income A	Corp-HY	11.26	12.68	11.01	1	3	6.25	1.15	800 423-4026
First Investors GA Insured Tax Free	Muni State	9.40	8.22	6.91	3	4	6.25	0.40	800 423-4026
First Investors Government Fund A	Govt-Mtg	8.38	6.75	5.42	3	3	6.25	1.34	800 423-4026
First Investors High Yield A	Corp-HY	10.72	11.74	10.68	1	3	6.25	1.29	800 423-4026
First Investors Ins Tax Exempt A	Muni Natl	8.03	6.85	5.29	4	3	4.75	1.14	800 423-4026
First Investors Investment Grade A	Corp-Inv	10.66	7.34	6.49	3	4	6.25	1.10	800 423-4026
First Investors MA Insured TF A	Muni State	7.52	6.96	5.61	3	3	6.25	0.80	800 423-4026
First Investors MD Insured Tax Free	Muni State	9.14	7.77	6.24	2	3	6.25	0.50	800 423-4026
First Investors MI Insured TF A	Muni State	8.74	7.27	5.94	3	4	6.25	0.88	800 423-4026
First Investors MN Insured Tax Free	Muni State	8.15	7.02	5.39	3	3	6.25	0.17	800 423-4026
First Investors MO Insured Tax Free	Muni State	8.80	7.93	6.27	1	3	6.25	0.40	800 423-4026
First Investors NC Insured Tax Free	Muni State	9.21	8.22	6.40	1	4	6.25	0.40	800 423-4026
First Investors NJ Insured TF A	Muni State	7.75	6.89	5.43	4	3	6.25	0.96	800 423-4026
First Investors NY Insured Tax Free	Muni NY	7.49	6.34	5.14	5	3	6.25	1.90	800 423-4026

380

Bond Fund Name	Objective	Annualized Return for			Rank		Max Load	Expense Ratio	Toll-Free Telephone
		1 Year	3 Years	5 Years	Overall	Risk			
First Investors OH Insured Tax Free	Muni State	7.90	7.46	5.97	2	3	6.25	0.80	800 423-4026
First Investors OR Insured Tax Free	Muni State	9.20	7.92	6.26	2	3	6.25	1.76	800 423-4026
First Investors PA Insured TF A	Muni State	8.69	7.57	6.19	1	3	6.25	0.86	800 423-4026
First Investors US Govt Plus I	Government	12.27	6.53	5.50	3	5	0	1.60	800 423-4026
First Investors VA Insured Tax Free	Muni State	8.57	7.35	5.94	3	3	6.25	0.80	800 423-4026
First Omaha Fixed Income	Corp-Inv	11.09	7.05	6.25	3	5	0	0.90	800 662-4203
First Omaha Sh/Intmed Fixed Income	Corp-Inv	7.46	5.87		4	2	0	0.97	800 662-4203
First Source Mono Income	Corp-Inv	8.25					4	1.05	800 554-3862
Firstar Bond IMMDEX Instl Fund	Corp-Inv	10.91	7.83	6.97	2	4	0	0.42	800 982-8909
Firstar Bond IMMDEX Retail Fund	Corp-Inv	10.65	7.57	6.79	2	4	2	0.67	800 982-8909
Firstar Intmed Bond Mkt Instl	Corp-Inv	8.06	6.70	6.03	3	2	0	0.50	800 982-8909
Firstar Intmed Bond Mkt Retail	Corp-Inv	7.79	6.46	6.00	3	2	2	0.75	800 982-8909
Firstar Short-Term Bond Mkt Instl	Corp-Inv	6.64	6.17	5.63	3	1	0	0.50	800 982-8909
Firstar Short-Term Bond Mkt Retail	Corp-Inv	6.38	5.94	5.46	3	1	2	0.75	800 982-8909
Firstar TE Intmed Bond Instl	Muni Natl	5.76	5.26	4.89	3	1	0	0.50	800 982-8909
Firstar TE Intmed Bond Retail	Muni Natl	5.40	4.99	4.71	3	1	2	0.75	800 982-8909
Flag Investors Managed Muni Fund A	Muni Natl	7.44	6.74		4	4	4.5	0.90	800 767-3524
Flag Investors MD Int TF Inc	Muni State	6.37	5.92		3	2	1.5	0.70	800 767-3524
Flag Investors Sht Intmed Inc Instl	Corp-Inv	8.57					0	0.45	800 767-3524
Flag Investors Sht Intmed Inc Inv	Corp-Inv	7.18	6.71	5.42	4	2	1.5	0.70	800 767-3524
Flag Investors Tot Ret US Treas A	Government	13.44	7.57	5.75	3	5	4.5	1.18	800 767-3524
Flex Funds US Govt Bond Fund	Government	10.25	5.63	6.08	3	4	0	1.00	800 325-3539
Fortis High Yield Fund A	Corp-HY	6.98	8.56	7.91	4	5	4.5	1.18	800 800-2638
Fortis High Yield Fund B	Corp-HY	6.32	7.92		3	5	0	1.88	800 800-2638
Fortis High Yield Fund C	Corp-HY	6.33	7.89		4	5	0	1.88	800 800-2638
Fortis High Yield Fund H	Corp-HY	6.32	7.88		3	5	0	1.88	800 800-2638
Fortis MN Tax Free Portfolio A	Muni State	6.90	6.09		5	3	4.5	1.21	800 800-2638
Fortis MN Tax Free Portfolio B	Muni State	6.15	5.28		5	3	0	1.96	800 800-2638
Fortis MN Tax Free Portfolio C	Muni State	5.84	5.21		5	3	0	1.96	800 800-2638
Fortis MN Tax Free Portfolio E	Muni State	7.12	6.31	5.27	4	3	4.5	0.96	800 800-2638
Fortis MN Tax Free Portfolio H	Muni State	6.24	5.30		5	3	0	1.96	800 800-2638
Fortis National Tax Free Port A	Muni Natl	7.64	6.85		5	4	4.5	1.17	800 800-2638
Fortis National Tax Free Port B	Muni Natl	6.84	6.03		5	4	0	1.92	800 800-2638
Fortis National Tax Free Port C	Muni Natl	6.84	5.97		5	4	0	1.92	800 800-2638
Fortis National Tax Free Port E	Muni Natl	7.86	7.05	5.55	4	4	4.5	0.95	800 800-2638
Fortis National Tax Free Port H	Muni Natl	6.64	5.93		5	4	0	1.93	800 800-2638
Fortis US Government Securities A	Government	9.84	7.13		3	3	4.5	1.06	800 800-2638
Fortis US Government Securities B	Government	8.98	6.30		4	3	0	1.81	800 800-2638
Fortis US Government Securities C	Government	8.99	6.32		4	3	0	1.81	800 800-2638
Fortis US Government Securities E	Government	10.01	7.38	5.47	3	3	4.5	0.80	800 800-2638
Fortis US Government Securities H	Government	8.98	6.32		4	3	0	1.81	800 800-2638
Forum Investors Bond	Corp-Inv	10.18	8.72	7.24	1	2	3.75	0.70	800 551-1980
Forum ME Muni Bond	Muni State	6.71	6.22	5.63	3	2	2.5	0.60	800 551-1980
Forum NH Bond Fund	Muni State	7.03	6.15	5.68	3	3	2.5	0.60	800 551-1980
Forum Tax Saver Bond Fund	Muni Natl	6.70	6.47	6.03	3	2	3.75	0.60	800 551-1980
Founders Government Securities	Government	10.11	6.22	3.95	4	3	0	1.26	800 525-2440
Fountain Square Bond Fund for Inc A	Corp-Inv	8.17					4.5	0.75	888 799-5353
Fountain Square Bond Fund for Inc C	Corp-Inv	7.44					0	1.50	888 799-5353
Fountain Square Muni Bond Fund A	Muni Natl	6.44					4.5	0.75	888 799-5353
Fountain Square Ohio Tax Free Bd C	Muni State	5.65					0	1.50	888 799-5353
Fountain Square Quality Bond A	Corp-Inv	9.38	6.35		3	3	4.5	0.75	888 799-5353
Fountain Square Quality Bond C	Corp-Inv	8.59					0	1.49	888 799-5353
Fountain Square US Govt Sec Fund A	Government	7.76	5.69		4	2	4.5	0.75	888 799-5353
Fountain Square US Govt Sec Fund C	Government	6.65					0	1.50	888 799-5353
FPA New Income	Corp-Inv	7.45	7.74	7.37	2	1	4.5	0.59	800 982-4372
Franklin Adjustable Rate Securities	Govt-Mtg	5.99	6.41		3	1	2.25	0.81	800 342-5236
Franklin Adjustable US Govt Sec	Govt-Mtg	5.59	6.43	4.34	4	1	2.25	0.75	800 342-5236
Franklin AGE High Income Fund Adv	Corp-HY	10.32					0	0.60	800 342-5236

381

Bond Fund Name	Objective	Annualized Return for			Rank		Max Load	Expense Ratio	Toll-Free Telephone
		1 Year	3 Years	5 Years	Overall	Risk			
Franklin AGE High Income Fund I	Corp-HY	10.33	12.07	10.63	1	3	4.25	0.72	800 342-5236
Franklin AGE High Income Fund II	Corp-HY	9.79	11.44		1	4	1	1.25	800 342-5236
Franklin AL Tax-Free Income I	Muni State	6.20	6.82	5.89	2	2	4.25	0.72	800 342-5236
Franklin AL Tax-Free Income II	Muni State	5.68	6.30		3	2	1	1.28	800 342-5236
Franklin AR Municipal Bond	Muni State	9.70	8.45		2	4	4.25	0.10	800 342-5236
Franklin AZ Insured Tax-Free Income	Muni State	8.86	8.18	6.41	2	4	4.25	0.40	800 342-5236
Franklin AZ Tax-Free Income I	Muni State	7.69	6.92	5.84	2	2	4.25	0.63	800 342-5236
Franklin AZ Tax-Free Income II	Muni State	7.22	6.44		3	2	1	1.20	800 342-5236
Franklin CA High Yield Muni Fund I	Muni CA	10.90	9.50	7.52	1	3	4.25	0.42	800 342-5236
Franklin CA High Yield Muni Fund II	Muni CA	10.49			1			0.90	800 342-5236
Franklin CA Insured TF Income I	Muni CA	8.77	7.45	6.14	1	3	4.25	0.60	800 342-5236
Franklin CA Insured TF Income II	Muni CA	8.20	6.92		3	3	1	1.16	800 342-5236
Franklin CA Intermediate TF Income	Muni CA	7.80	7.78	6.40	1	2	2.25	0.50	800 342-5236
Franklin CA Tax-Free Income I	Muni CA	8.53	7.53	6.23	1	2	4.25	0.56	800 342-5236
Franklin CA Tax-Free Income II	Muni CA	7.92	6.93		2	2	1	1.14	800 342-5236
Franklin CO Tax-Free Income I	Muni State	8.75	7.64	6.27	1	2	4.25	0.71	800 342-5236
Franklin CO Tax-Free Income II	Muni State	8.11	7.13		1	3	1	1.30	800 342-5236
Franklin CT Tax-Free Income I	Muni State	8.36	7.45	5.80	2	2	4.25	0.74	800 342-5236
Franklin CT Tax-Free Income II	Muni State	7.73	6.86		2	2	1	1.28	800 342-5236
Franklin Federal Intmed Tax-Free	Muni Natl	7.87	7.07	6.27	2	2	2.25	0.75	800 342-5236
Franklin Federal Tax-Free Income I	Muni Natl	8.37	7.59	6.28	1	2	4.25	0.60	800 342-5236
Franklin Federal Tax-Free Income II	Muni Natl	7.77	6.97		2	2	1	1.18	800 342-5236
Franklin FL Insured Tax-Free Income	Muni State	9.60	8.10	6.02	3	4	4.25	0.35	800 342-5236
Franklin FL Tax-Free Income I	Muni State	8.05	6.98	6.12	2	2	4.25	0.61	800 342-5236
Franklin FL Tax-Free Income II	Muni State	7.55	6.45		3	2	1	1.18	800 342-5236
Franklin GA Tax-Free Income I	Muni State	7.62	6.85	5.85	2	2	4.25	0.77	800 342-5236
Franklin GA Tax-Free Income II	Muni State	7.08	6.32		3	2	1	1.33	800 342-5236
Franklin Global Govt Income Adv	Intl Bond	5.19					0	0.82	800 342-5236
Franklin Global Govt Income I	Intl Bond	5.10	8.21	6.13	3	3	4.25	0.82	800 342-5236
Franklin Global Govt Income II	Intl Bond	4.45	7.60		3	4	1	1.46	800 342-5236
Franklin HI Municipal Bond Fund	Muni State	8.50	7.99	6.16	1	3	4.25	0.40	800 342-5236
Franklin High-Yield TF Income I	Muni Natl	9.98	8.72	7.69	1	2	4.25	0.61	800 342-5236
Franklin High-Yield TF Income II	Muni Natl	9.40	8.18		1	2	1	1.20	800 342-5236
Franklin IN Tax-Free Income	Muni State	8.06	7.35	5.92	1	2	4.25	0.82	800 342-5236
Franklin Institutional Adj Rt Sec	Govt-Mtg	6.32	6.79	5.66	3	1	0	0.37	800 342-5236
Franklin Institutional Adj US Govt	Govt-Mtg	5.85	6.69		4	1	0	0.54	800 342-5236
Franklin Insured TF Income I	Muni Natl	8.06	6.83	5.83	2	2	4	0.61	800 342-5236
Franklin Insured TF Income II	Muni Natl	7.51	6.31		3	2	1	1.24	800 342-5236
Franklin Investment Grade Inc Adv	Corp-Inv	6.15					0	0.85	800 342-5236
Franklin Investment Grade Income I	Corp-Inv	5.92	5.17	4.70	4	1	4.25	1.05	800 342-5236
Franklin KY Tax-Free Income	Muni State	9.26	8.16	6.34	1	3	4.25	0.35	800 342-5236
Franklin LA Tax-Free Income I	Muni State	8.05	7.39	5.80	1	2	4.25	0.77	800 342-5236
Franklin LA Tax-Free Income II	Muni State	7.52	6.89		3	2	1	1.33	800 342-5236
Franklin MA Insured Tax-Free Inc I	Muni State	8.33	7.02	5.88	2	2	4.25	0.68	800 342-5236
Franklin MA Insured Tax-Free Inc II	Muni State	7.66	6.44		3	3	1	1.24	800 342-5236
Franklin MD Tax-Free Income I	Muni State	8.34	7.52	6.21	2	3	4.25	0.74	800 342-5236
Franklin MD Tax-Free Income II	Muni State	7.78	6.80		3	3	1	1.31	800 342-5236
Franklin MI Insured Tax-Free Inc I	Muni State	8.70	7.07	5.89	2	3	4.25	0.63	800 342-5236
Franklin MI Insured Tax-Free Inc II	Muni State	8.09	6.52		3	3	1	1.21	800 342-5236
Franklin MI Tax-Free Income	Muni State	11.09					0	0.25	800 342-5236
Franklin MN Insured Tax-Free Inc I	Muni State	7.59	6.42	5.38	3	2	4.25	0.69	800 342-5236
Franklin MN Insured Tax-Free Inc II	Muni State	6.96	5.87		4	3	1	1.26	800 342-5236
Franklin MO Tax-Free Income I	Muni State	8.68	7.61	6.42	1	2	4.25	0.70	800 342-5236
Franklin MO Tax-Free Income II	Muni State	8.23	7.07		1	3	1	1.27	800 342-5236
Franklin NC Tax-Free Income I	Muni State	8.35	7.30	5.90	1	2	4.25	0.71	800 342-5236
Franklin NC Tax-Free Income II	Muni State	7.89	6.80		3	3	1	1.27	800 342-5236
Franklin NJ Tax-Free Income I	Muni State	8.34	7.17	5.78	1	2	4.25	0.66	800 342-5236
Franklin NJ Tax-Free Income II	Muni State	7.71	6.62		3	2	1	1.23	800 342-5236

Bond Fund Name	Objective	Annualized Return for			Rank		Max Load	Expense Ratio	Toll-Free Telephone
		1 Year	3 Years	5 Years	Overall	Risk			
Franklin NY Insured Tax-Free Inc I	Muni NY	8.59	7.46	6.13	2	3	4.25	0.71	800 342-5236
Franklin NY Insured Tax-Free Inc II	Muni NY	8.09	7.02		2	3	0	1.27	800 342-5236
Franklin NY Tax-Free Income I	Muni NY	9.52	7.67	6.15	1	2	4.25	0.60	800 342-5236
Franklin NY Tax-Free Income II	Muni NY	8.80	7.05		1	2	1	1.18	800 342-5236
Franklin NY Tax-Free Intmed Term	Muni NY	8.48	7.46	5.63	2	2	2.25	0.45	800 342-5236
Franklin OH Insured Tax-Free Inc I	Muni State	8.00	6.98	5.74	2	3	4.25	0.64	800 342-5236
Franklin OH Insured Tax-Free Inc II	Muni State	7.54	6.53		3	3	0	1.22	800 342-5236
Franklin OR Tax-Free Income I	Muni State	7.89	7.01	5.70	2	2	4.25	0.68	800 342-5236
Franklin OR Tax-Free Income II	Muni State	7.35	7.47		3	2	1	1.24	800 342-5236
Franklin PA Tax-Free Income I	Muni State	8.42	7.30	6.18	1	2	4.25	0.65	800 342-5236
Franklin PA Tax-Free Income II	Muni State	7.88	6.76		2	2	1	1.22	800 342-5236
Franklin PR Tax-Free Income I	Muni State	8.51	7.58	6.15	1	2	4.25	0.78	800 342-5236
Franklin PR Tax-Free Income II	Muni State	7.90	6.91		2	2	1	1.34	800 342-5236
Franklin Short-Intmed US Govt Adv	Government	6.46					0	0.70	800 342-5236
Franklin Short-Intmed US Govt I	Government	6.37	5.55	4.48	4	1	2.25	0.78	800 342-5236
Franklin Strategic Income Fund	Dvsfd Bond	7.87	12.20		2	4	4.25	0.25	800 342-5236
Franklin Strategic Mortgage Fund	Govt-Mtg	8.43	7.73	6.03	2	2	4.25	0.82	800 342-5236
Franklin TN Municipal Fund	Muni State	10.21	8.60		1	5	4.25	0.40	800 342-5236
Franklin TX Tax-Free Income I	Muni State	8.25	7.34	6.28	1	2	4.25	0.76	800 342-5236
Franklin TX Tax-Free Income II	Muni State	7.65	7.16		2	2	1	1.31	800 342-5236
Franklin US Govt Securities Fd Adv	Govt-Mtg	7.84					0	0.56	800 342-5236
Franklin US Govt Securities Fd I	Govt-Mtg	8.37	7.62	6.40	1	2	4.25	0.66	800 342-5236
Franklin US Govt Securities Fd II	Govt-Mtg	7.65	8.87		2	4	1	1.20	800 342-5236
Franklin VA Tax-Free Income I	Muni State	8.43	7.12	6.02	1	2	4.25	0.70	800 342-5236
Franklin VA Tax-Free Income II	Muni State	7.96	6.67		2	2	1	1.26	800 342-5236
Franklin WA Municipal Bond Fund	Muni State	9.34	8.68	6.44	2	5	4.25	0.10	800 342-5236
Franklin/Temp German Govt Bond I	Intl Bond	1.34	−2.25	4.11	5	5	3	1.42	800 342-5236
Franklin/Temp Global Currency	Intl Bond	−1.51	−1.26	2.46	5	4	3	1.10	800 342-5236
Franklin/Temp Hard Currency Fd I	Intl Bond	−7.06	−8.49	−0.12	5	5	3	1.13	800 342-5236
Franklin/Temp High Income Currency	Intl Bond	−1.00	2.09	3.96	5	4	3	1.49	800 342-5236
Fremont Bond Fund	Corp-Inv	9.96	8.84	8.00	2	4	0	0.64	800 548-4539
Fremont CA Intermediate Tax Free	Muni CA	6.55	6.35	5.33	3	2	0	0.49	800 548-4539
Frontegra Total Return Bond Fund	Dvsfd Bond	8.34					0	0.50	888 825-2100
Fundamental New York Muni Fund	Muni NY	1.40	−0.79	−2.27	5	5	0	1.99	800 421-4120
Fundamental US Govt Strat Income	Government	−1.16	5.64	−0.96	4	5	0	5.85	800 421-4120
FundManager Bond Portfolio Adv	Corp-Inv	8.74	6.53	5.46	4	3	0	1.43	800 344-9033
Gabelli Westwood Intmed Bond Retail	Corp-Inv	10.48	8.05	6.08	3	4	0	6.71	800 937-8966
Galaxy CT Muni Bond Fund Instl	Muni State	8.32	7.27	5.60	3	3	0	1.19	800 628-0414
Galaxy CT Muni Bond Fund Retail A	Muni State	8.11	7.08	5.48	3	3	3.75	0.71	800 628-0414
Galaxy High Quality Bond Instl	Government	10.94	7.50	6.46	3	4	0	1.09	800 628-0414
Galaxy High Quality Bond Retail A	Government	10.80	7.34	6.24	3	4	3.75	1.01	800 628-0414
Galaxy High Quality Bond Retail B	Government	10.26					0	1.98	800 628-0414
Galaxy Intermediate Govt Instl	Government	8.77	6.34	4.95	3	2	0	0.93	800 628-0414
Galaxy Intermediate Govt Retail A	Government	8.46	6.07	4.64	3	2	3.75	1.02	800 628-0414
Galaxy MA Muni Bond Fund Retail A	Muni State	8.11	6.98	5.39	3	3	3.75	0.68	800 628-0414
Galaxy Municipal Bond Retail A	Muni Natl	10.46	7.39	6.02	3	3	3.75	0.60	800 628-0414
Galaxy NY Muni Bond Fund Instl	Muni NY	8.49	7.22	5.55	3	3	0	1.02	800 628-0414
Galaxy NY Muni Bond Fund Retail A	Muni NY	8.29	6.99	5.42	3	3	3.75	0.94	800 628-0414
Galaxy Short Term Bond Instl	Corp-Inv	6.12	5.65		4	1	0	1.08	800 628-0414
Galaxy Short Term Bond Retail A	Corp-Inv	5.90	5.41	4.67	3	1	0	1.00	800 628-0414
Galaxy Short Term Bond Retail B	Corp-Inv	5.21					0	1.89	800 628-0414
Galaxy TE Bond Fund Instl	Muni Natl	8.48	7.27	5.81	2	3	0	0.97	800 628-0414
Galaxy TE Bond Fund Retail A	Muni Natl	8.24	6.89	5.44	3	3	3.75	0.95	800 628-0414
Galaxy TE Bond Fund Retail B	Muni Natl	7.56					0	1.86	800 628-0414
Galaxy US Treasury Index Retail A	Government	11.04	7.27	7.02	3	4	0	0.40	800 628-0414
GE Fixed Income Fund A	Corp-Inv	9.44	6.98		3	3	4.25	1.10	800 242-0134
GE Fixed Income Fund B	Corp-Inv	8.80	6.45		3	3	0	1.60	800 242-0134
GE Fixed Income Fund C	Corp-Inv	9.71	7.20	6.29	2	3	0	0.85	800 242-0134

Bond Fund Name	Objective	Annualized Return for			Rank		Max Load	Expense Ratio	Toll-Free Telephone
		1 Year	3 Years	5 Years	Overall	Risk			
GE Fixed Income Fund D	Corp-Inv	9.88	7.48		2	3	0	0.60	800 242-0134
GE Government Securities Fund A	Government	10.25	7.14		3	3	4.25	0.88	800 242-0134
GE Government Securities Fund B	Government	9.72	6.43	3.76	4	3	0	1.63	800 242-0134
GE S&S Long A	Corp-Inv	10.50	8.19	7.11	1	3	0	0.13	800 242-0134
GE Short Term Government A	Government	5.78	5.43		4	1	2.5	0.95	800 242-0134
GE Short Term Government B	Government	5.42	5.01		5	1	0	1.30	800 242-0134
GE Short Term Government C	Government	6.03	5.70		4	1	0	0.70	800 242-0134
GE Short Term Government D	Government	6.31	5.96		4	1	0	0.45	800 242-0134
GE Tax Exempt Fund A	Muni Natl	3.16	4.51		5	4	4.25	0.75	800 242-0134
GE Tax Exempt Fund B	Muni Natl	2.55	3.99		5	4	0	1.25	800 242-0134
GE Tax Exempt Fund C	Muni Natl	6.94	5.95	4.71	5	3	0	0.50	800 242-0134
GE Tax Exempt Fund D	Muni Natl	7.79	6.41		4	3	0	0.25	800 242-0134
General CA Municipal Bond	Muni CA	8.73	7.25	6.12	3	4	0	0.76	800 645-6561
General Municipal Bond Fund	Muni Natl	8.10	6.86	5.39	3	3	0	0.87	800 645-6561
General NY Municipal Bond	Muni NY	9.36	7.62	5.64	3	4	0	0.91	800 645-6561
Glenmede Core Fixed Income	Government	10.16	7.70	6.21	2	3	0	0.16	800 442-8299
Glenmede Muni Intermediate	Muni Natl	6.14	5.90	5.09	3	2	0	0.50	800 442-8299
Glenmede NJ Municipal	Muni State	5.41	5.84		3	2	0	0.24	800 442-8299
Golden Oak Intmed-Term Income A	Corp-Inv	8.40	5.93	5.15	3	2	4.5	0.90	800 545-6331
Golden Oak Intmed-Term Income I	Corp-Inv	8.55	6.19	5.37	3	2	0	0.65	800 545-6331
Goldman Sachs Global Income A	Intl Bond	10.99	10.55	8.11	1	3	4.5	1.17	800 292-4726
Goldman Sachs Global Income B	Intl Bond	10.44					0	1.71	800 292-4726
Goldman Sachs Government Income A	Government	10.18	7.66	6.70	2	3	4.5	0.50	800 292-4726
Goldman Sachs Government Income B	Government	9.50					0	1.43	800 292-4726
Goldman Sachs Instl Adj Rate Govt	Govt-Mtg	5.16	6.68	5.51	3	1	0	0.49	800 292-4726
Goldman Sachs Instl Short Dur TF	Muni Natl	5.25	5.03	4.09	3	1	0	0.45	800 292-4726
Goldman Sachs Muni Income Fund A	Muni Natl	9.18	8.41		2	4	4.5	0.85	800 292-4726
Goldman Sachs Muni Income Fund B	Muni Natl	8.37					0	1.60	800 292-4726
Goldman Sachs Short Dur Govt Instl	Govt-Mtg	6.39	6.81	5.43	3	1	0	0.45	800 292-4726
Government Street Bond Fund	Corp-Inv	8.50	6.69	5.85	3	2	0	0.75	800 543-8721
Govett Global Income Fund A	Intl Bond	7.00	2.77	3.09	5	5	4.95	1.75	800 225-2222
Gradison Government Income Fund	Government	8.52	6.87	5.87	2	3	2	0.90	800 869-5999
Gradison OH Tax Free Income Fund	Muni State	8.12	7.71	5.86	2	3	2	0.96	800 869-5999
Griffin Bond Fund A	Corp-Inv	10.18	7.07		3	4	4.5	0.59	800 676-4450
Griffin Bond Fund B	Corp-Inv	9.42	6.52		4	4	0	1.09	800 676-4450
Griffin CA Tax Free Fund A	Muni CA	8.10	7.62		3	4	4.5	0.50	800 676-4450
Griffin CA Tax Free Fund B	Muni CA	7.48	7.06		5	4	0	1.00	800 676-4450
Griffin Muni Bond Fund A	Muni Natl	8.33	7.16		3	4	4.5	0.50	800 676-4450
Griffin Muni Bond Fund B	Muni Natl	7.51	6.55		5	4	0	1.00	800 676-4450
Griffin US Govt Income Fund A	Government	10.00	7.15		2	3	4.5	0.59	800 676-4450
Griffin US Govt Income Fund B	Government	9.41	6.69		3	3	0	0.96	800 676-4450
Guardian Investment Quality Bond	Corp-Inv	9.14	6.98	5.64	3	3	4.5	0.75	800 221-3253
Guardian Tax Exempt Fund	Muni Natl	8.06	7.19	4.59	3	3	4.5	0.75	800 221-3253
Guinness Flight Global Govt Bond	Intl Bond	8.59	6.08		4	4	0	0.75	800 915-6565
Harbor Bond Fund	Corp-Inv	10.34	9.05	7.31	2	4	0	0.67	800 422-1050
Harbor Short Duration Fund	Corp-Inv	6.09	6.14	5.44	3	1	0	0.36	800 422-1050
Harris Insight Bond Fund A	Corp-Inv	10.16					4.5	0.85	800 982-8782
Harris Insight Bond Fund C	Corp-Inv	10.43					0	0.60	800 982-8782
Harris Insight Intmed Govt Bond A	Government	8.23					4.5	0.75	800 982-8782
Harris Insight Intmed Govt Bond C	Government	8.51					0	0.50	800 982-8782
Harris Insight Intmed T E Bond A	Muni Natl	5.76					4.5	1.05	800 982-8782
Harris Insight Intmed T E Bond C	Muni Natl	6.00					0	0.80	800 982-8782
Harris Insight Short Intmed Bond A	Corp-Inv	7.42	6.27	5.64	3	2	4.5	0.85	800 982-8782
Harris Insight Short Intmed Bond C	Corp-Inv	7.66					0	0.60	800 982-8782
Harris Insight Tax Exempt Bond A	Muni Natl	7.83					4.5	1.05	800 982-8782
Harris Insight Tax Exempt Bond C	Muni Natl	8.10					0	0.80	800 982-8782
Hartford Bond Income Strategy A	Corp-Inv	11.02					4.5	1.50	888 843-5517
Hartford Bond Income Strategy B	Corp-Inv	10.26					0	5.62	888 843-5517

Bond Fund Name	Objective	Annualized Return for			Rank		Max Load	Expense Ratio	Toll-Free Telephone
		1 Year	3 Years	5 Years	Overall	Risk			
Hawaiian Tax-Free Trust A	Muni State	7.33	6.67	5.50	3	3	4	0.72	800 228-4227
Hawaiian Tax-Free Trust C	Muni State	6.60					0	1.51	800 228-4227
Hawaiian Tax-Free Trust Y	Muni State	7.96					0	0.51	800 228-4227
Heartland US Govt Securities Fund	Government	10.84	7.70	5.58	3	5	0	0.87	800 432-7856
Heartland WI Tax Free	Muni State	7.44	7.41	5.72	2	3	0	0.81	800 432-7856
Heritage Income Trust-High Yield A	Corp-HY	9.62	10.76	8.00	1	3	3.75	1.21	800 421-4184
Heritage Income Trust-High Yield C	Corp-HY	9.12	10.30		1	3	0	1.70	800 421-4184
Heritage Income Trust-Intmed Govt A	Government	7.94	5.70	4.79	3	2	2	0.93	800 421-4184
Heritage Income Trust-Intmed Govt C	Government	7.81	5.46		4	2	0	1.20	800 421-4184
HGK Fixed Income Fund	Dvsfd Bond	9.80	5.68		4	4	0	1.00	800 932-7781
HighMark Bond Fund Institutional	Corp-Inv	10.55	7.36	5.82	3	4	0	0.80	800 433-6884
HighMark Bond Fund Retail	Corp-Inv	10.54	7.42	5.67	3	4	3	1.68	800 433-6884
HighMark CA Interm TF Bond Instl	Muni CA	7.28	6.90		3	3	0	0.21	800 433-6884
HighMark CA Interm TF Bond Retail	Muni CA	6.97	6.83		3	3	3	0.21	800 433-6884
HighMark Government Secs Instl	Government	10.03	6.28		4	4	0	0.73	800 433-6884
HighMark Interm Term Bond Instl	Corp-Inv	8.75	6.35	5.49	4	3	0	0.67	800 433-6884
HighMark Interm Term Bond Retail	Corp-Inv	8.87	6.56	5.19	4	3	3	0.69	800 433-6884
Homestead Short Term Bond	Corp-Inv	6.74	6.19	5.52	3	1	0	0.75	800 258-3030
Homestead ST Government Sec	Government	5.94	5.43		4	1	0	0.75	800 258-3030
Hotchkis & Wiley Low Duration Fund	Corp-Inv	7.03	7.43	8.31	2	1	0	0.58	800 796-5606
Hotchkis & Wiley ST Investment Fund	Corp-Inv	6.34	6.44	6.52	2	1	0	0.48	800 796-5606
Hotchkis & Wiley Total Return	Dvsfd Bond	10.44	9.30		2	3	0	0.65	800 796-5606
HSBC Fixed Income	Corp-Inv	9.68	6.67	6.25	2	3	4.75	0.84	800 634-2536
HSBC NY Tax Free Bond Fund	Muni NY	8.62	7.63	5.36	3	3	4.75	0.92	800 634-2536
IAA Long-Term Bond Series	Corp-Inv	10.01					0	0.78	800 245-2100
IAA Short-Term Govt Bond Series	Government	5.66					0	0.76	800 245-2100
IAA Tax Exempt Bond	Muni Natl	7.45	6.84	5.17	5	3	0	1.14	800 245-2100
IAI Bond Fund	Corp-Inv	10.86	8.27	6.48	2	4	0	1.10	800 945-3863
IAI Government Fund	Government	7.38	5.86	4.52	5	2	0	1.10	800 945-3863
IAI Institutional Bond Fund	Corp-Inv	11.85	8.26		2	4	0	0.50	800 945-3863
IAI Reserve Fund	Corp-Inv	5.32	4.95	4.61	3	1	0	0.85	800 945-3863
ICON ST Fixed Income	Corp-Inv	5.30					0	1.10	888 389-ICON
IDEX Flexible Income Portfolio A	Corp-HY	12.76	9.84	8.04	1	4	4.5	1.85	800 851-9777
IDEX Flexible Income Portfolio B	Corp-HY	12.04					0	2.50	800 851-9777
IDEX Flexible Income Portfolio C	Corp-HY	12.15	9.23		1	3	0	2.40	800 851-9777
IDEX Income Plus Portfolio A	Corp-HY	10.53	9.61	8.36	1	3	4.75	1.27	800 851-9777
IDEX Income Plus Portfolio B	Corp-HY	9.82					0	1.98	800 851-9777
IDEX Income Plus Portfolio C	Corp-HY	9.92	8.96		2	3	0	1.88	800 851-9777
IDEX Tax Exempt Portfolio A	Muni Natl	9.50	7.39	5.98	2	3	4.75	1.00	800 851-9777
IDEX Tax Exempt Portfolio B	Muni Natl	8.79					0	1.65	800 851-9777
IDEX Tax Exempt Portfolio C	Muni Natl	9.22	7.10		3	3	0	1.25	800 851-9777
IDS Bond Fund	Dvsfd Bond	10.12	8.97	8.04	1	3	5	0.83	800 328-8300
IDS CA Tax-Exempt Fund	Muni CA	7.58	7.08	5.62	3	3	5	0.76	800 328-8300
IDS Extra Income Fund	Corp-HY	10.63	12.83	10.08	1	3	5	0.91	800 328-8300
IDS Federal Income Fund	Government	8.03	7.17	6.01	2	2	5	0.87	800 328-8300
IDS Global Bond	Intl Bond	4.94	6.13	6.64	4	5	5	1.16	800 328-8300
IDS High-Yield Tax-Exempt Fund	Muni Natl	8.56	7.45	5.93	1	3	5	0.70	800 328-8300
IDS Insured Tax-Exempt Fund	Muni Natl	7.59	6.95	5.54	4	3	5	0.73	800 328-8300
IDS MA Tax-Exempt Fund	Muni State	8.01	7.28	5.79	3	3	5	0.83	800 328-8300
IDS MI Tax-Exempt Fund	Muni State	7.82	7.07	5.73	3	3	5	0.82	800 328-8300
IDS MN Tax-Exempt Fund	Muni State	7.93	7.35	5.83	2	3	5	0.75	800 328-8300
IDS NY Tax-Exempt Fund	Muni NY	8.20	6.96	5.26	4	3	5	0.80	800 328-8300
IDS OH Tax-Exempt Fund	Muni State	7.72	6.98	5.29	3	3	5	0.84	800 328-8300
IDS Selective Fund	Corp-Inv	9.53	7.44	6.76	3	4	5	0.85	800 328-8300
IDS Strategist Government Income Fd	Government	8.60						1.10	800 328-8300
IDS Strategist High Yield Fund	Government	10.63						1.20	800 328-8300
IDS Strategist TF High Yield Fund	Muni Natl	8.92						0.95	800 328-8300
IDS Strategist World Income Fund	Intl Bond	5.13						1.35	800 328-8300

385

Bond Fund Name	Objective	Annualized Return for			Rank		Max Load	Expense Ratio	Toll-Free Telephone
		1 Year	3 Years	5 Years	Overall	Risk			
IDS Tax-Exempt Bond Fund	Muni Natl	8.56	7.94	5.93	3	4	5	0.73	800 328-8300
Independence One Fixed Income Fd	Corp-Inv	8.21					0	0.55	800 245-0242
Independence One MI Muni Bd Fd	Muni State	6.74					0	0.70	800 245-0242
Independence One US Govt Sec	Government	10.78	7.21		3	4	0	0.57	800 245-0242
Integrity KS Insured Intmed Fund	Muni State	3.11	4.70	4.09	3	2	2.75	0.76	800 345-2363
Integrity KS Muni Fund	Muni State	3.65	5.46	3.45	4	3	4.25	0.85	800 345-2363
Intermediate Bond Fund of America	Corp-Inv	7.29	6.33	5.28	4	2	4.75	0.80	800 421-0180
Intrust Intmed Bond Fund Instl	Corp-Inv	8.08					0		888 266-8787
Intrust KS TE Bond Fund Instl	Muni State	7.46	6.27	5.45	4	5	0	0.51	888 266-8787
Intrust ST Bond Fund Instl	Corp-Inv	5.99					0		888 266-8787
INVESCO High-Yield	Corp-HY	16.02	14.75	10.78	2	5	0	0.88	800 525-8085
INVESCO Intermediate Government Bd	Government	6.98	5.33	5.51	3	2	0	1.07	800 525-8085
INVESCO Select Income	Dvsfd Bond	12.36	9.57	8.52	1	4	0	1.06	800 525-8085
INVESCO Short-Term Bond Fund	Corp-Inv	7.27	6.14		3	1	0	0.42	800 525-8085
INVESCO Tax-Free Long-Term Bond	Muni Natl	6.89	6.98	5.14	5	4	0	0.46	800 525-8085
INVESCO US Government Securities	Government	14.61	8.15	6.41	3	5	0	1.00	800 525-8085
Investek Fixed Income	Corp-Inv	8.32	7.17	6.16	3	3	0	0.90	800 525-3863
ISI North American Government Bond	Government	12.50	8.86	5.20	3	5	3	1.25	800 882-8585
ISI Total Return US Treasury	Government	13.52	7.60	6.97	3	5	4.45	0.83	800 882-8585
Ivy Bond Fund A	Corp-Inv	8.78	9.72	7.84	2	4	4.75	1.47	800 456-5111
Ivy Bond Fund B	Corp-Inv	8.15	8.92		2	4	0	2.23	800 456-5111
Ivy Bond Fund C	Corp-Inv	8.13					0	2.26	800 456-5111
Janus Federal Tax Exempt Fund	Muni Natl	7.88	7.69	5.51	3	3	0	0.65	800 525-3713
Janus Flexible Income Fund	Dvsfd Bond	13.24	10.84	9.32	1	4	0	0.86	800 525-3713
Janus High-Yield Fund	Corp-HY	15.25					0	1.00	800 525-3713
Janus Short Term Bond Fund	Corp-Inv	6.30	6.69	5.32	3	1	0	0.67	800 525-3713
John Hancock CA Tax-Free Income A	Muni CA	9.42	8.84	6.50	2	4	4.5	0.76	800 225-5291
John Hancock CA Tax-Free Income B	Muni CA	8.60	8.02	5.71	3	4	0	1.59	800 225-5291
John Hancock Government Income A	Government	10.44	7.24		3	4	4.5	1.14	800 225-5291
John Hancock Government Income B	Government	9.63	6.51	5.43	3	4	0	1.87	800 225-5291
John Hancock High Yield Bond Fund A	Corp-HY	14.32	15.75	10.98	2	5	4.5	1.04	800 225-5291
John Hancock High Yield Bond Fund B	Corp-HY	13.35	14.76	10.14	2	5	0	2.25	800 225-5291
John Hancock High Yield Tax-Free A	Muni Natl	10.35	7.20		2	3	4.5	1.07	800 225-5291
John Hancock High Yield Tax-Free B	Muni Natl	9.51	6.39	5.68	2	3	0	1.76	800 225-5291
John Hancock Intmed Maturity Govt A	Government	9.44	6.79	5.59	3	3	3	1.12	800 225-5291
John Hancock Intmed Maturity Govt B	Government	7.99	5.78	4.75	4	3	0	1.80	800 225-5291
John Hancock MA Tax-Free Income A	Muni State	9.84	8.14	6.29	1	3	4.5	0.71	800 225-5291
John Hancock MA Tax-Free Income B	Muni State	9.05						1.79	800 225-5291
John Hancock NY Tax-Free Income A	Muni NY	8.83	7.80	5.73	2	3	4.5	0.71	800 225-5291
John Hancock NY Tax-Free Income B	Muni NY	8.06						1.80	800 225-5291
John Hancock Sovereign Bond A	Corp-Inv	10.17	8.09	7.18	2	3	4.5	1.10	800 225-5291
John Hancock Sovereign Bond B	Corp-Inv	9.40	7.35		3	3	0	1.81	800 225-5291
John Hancock Sovereign US Govt A	Government	10.44	6.87		3	4	4.5	1.17	800 225-5291
John Hancock Sovereign US Govt B	Government	9.67	6.20	5.19	4	4	0	1.86	800 225-5291
John Hancock ST Strat Inc A	Intl Bond	3.66	6.64	5.95	3	2	3	1.00	800 225-5291
John Hancock ST Strat Inc B	Intl Bond	3.09	6.18	5.93	3	2	0	2.13	800 225-5291
John Hancock Strategic Income A	Dvsfd Bond	11.97	12.51	9.89	1	4	4.5	0.94	800 225-5291
John Hancock Strategic Income B	Dvsfd Bond	11.32	11.80		1	4	0	1.70	800 225-5291
John Hancock Tax-Free Bond A	Muni Natl	9.18	8.47	6.07	3	4	4.5	0.85	800 225-5291
John Hancock Tax-Free Bond B	Muni Natl	8.36	7.72	5.32	3	4	0	1.60	800 225-5291
John Hancock World Bond Fund A	Intl Bond	1.72	4.34	4.94	5	4	4.5	1.71	800 225-5291
John Hancock World Bond Fund B	Intl Bond	1.02	3.65	4.28	4	4	0	2.38	800 225-5291
JP Morgan Bond Fund	Corp-Inv	9.69	7.43	6.39	2	3	0	0.68	800 766-7722
JP Morgan CA Bond Fund Instl Shs	Muni CA	6.68					0	0.45	800 766-7722
JP Morgan CA Bond Fund Select Shs	Muni CA	6.52					0	0.65	800 766-7722
JP Morgan Emerging Mkts Debt	Intl Bond	−5.32					0	1.25	800 766-7722
JP Morgan Instl Bond Fund	Corp-Inv	9.86	7.61		1	3	0	0.50	800 766-7722
JP Morgan Instl NY Tot Ret Bond	Muni NY	6.88	6.38		4	3	0	0.50	800 766-7722

| Bond Fund Name | Objective | Annualized Return for | | | Rank | | Max Load | Expense Ratio | Toll-Free Telephone |
		1 Year	3 Years	5 Years	Overall	Risk			
JP Morgan Instl Short Term Bond	Corp-Inv	6.66	6.23	4.04	4	1	0	0.25	800 766-7722
JP Morgan Instl Tax Exempt Bond	Muni Natl	6.89	6.25		4	2	0	0.50	800 766-7722
JP Morgan NY Total Return Bond	Muni NY	6.77	6.15		5	3	0	0.72	800 766-7722
JP Morgan Short Term Bond Fund	Dvsfd Bond	6.39	6.01		3	1	0	0.50	800 766-7722
JP Morgan Tax Exempt Bond Fund	Muni Natl	6.72	6.08	5.01	4	2	0	0.64	800 766-7722
Kemper Adjustable Rate US Govt A	Govt-Mtg	4.26	5.16	4.34	4	1	3.5	1.28	800 621-1048
Kemper Adjustable Rate US Govt B	Govt-Mtg	3.51	4.43		5	1		1.89	800 621-1048
Kemper Adjustable Rate US Govt C	Govt-Mtg	3.67	4.37		4	1	0	1.84	800 621-1048
Kemper CA Tax-Free Income Fund A	Muni CA	8.05	7.55	6.04	3	4	4.5	0.73	800 621-1048
Kemper CA Tax-Free Income Fund B	Muni CA	7.28	6.72		5	4	0	1.64	800 621-1048
Kemper CA Tax-Free Income Fund C	Muni CA	6.68	6.26		5	4	0	1.62	800 621-1048
Kemper Diversified Income Fund A	Dvsfd Bond	9.14	9.12	8.44	2	4	4.5	1.03	800 621-1048
Kemper Diversified Income Fund B	Dvsfd Bond	7.94	8.07		2	3	0	1.94	800 621-1048
Kemper Diversified Income Fund C	Dvsfd Bond	8.20	8.05		2	3	0	1.85	800 621-1048
Kemper FL Tax-Free Income Fund AZ	Muni State	7.81	7.26	6.01	3	4	4.5	0.83	800 621-1048
Kemper FL Tax-Free Income Fund B	Muni State	6.92	6.44		4	4	0	1.68	800 621-1048
Kemper FL Tax-Free Income Fund C	Muni State	6.92	6.35		5	4	0	1.68	800 621-1048
Kemper Global Income Fund A	Intl Bond	4.49	4.42	6.48	5	4	4.5	1.32	800 621-1048
Kemper Global Income Fund B	Intl Bond	3.60	3.62		5	4	0	2.24	800 621-1048
Kemper Global Income Fund C	Intl Bond	3.66	3.73		4	4	0	2.06	800 621-1048
Kemper High-Yield Fund A	Corp-HY	10.68	12.12	10.49	1	3	4.5	0.88	800 621-1048
Kemper High-Yield Fund B	Corp-HY	9.73	11.16		1	3	0	1.77	800 621-1048
Kemper High-Yield Fund C	Corp-HY	9.88	10.96		1	3	0	1.72	800 621-1048
Kemper Income & Cap Preservation A	Corp-Inv	9.51	7.41	6.84	2	4	4.5	0.97	800 621-1048
Kemper Income & Cap Preservation B	Corp-Inv	8.54	6.37		4	4	0	1.94	800 621-1048
Kemper Income & Cap Preservation C	Corp-Inv	8.55	8.00		3	5	0	1.89	800 621-1048
Kemper MI Tax-Free Income A	Muni State	8.32	7.84		2	3	4.5	1.27	800 621-1048
Kemper MI Tax-Free Income B	Muni State	7.59	6.63		5	4	0	2.16	800 621-1048
Kemper MI Tax-Free Income C	Muni State	7.78	6.63		4	4	0	2.03	800 621-1048
Kemper Municipal Bond Fund A	Muni Natl	8.72	7.85	6.31	2	3	4.5	0.66	800 621-1048
Kemper Municipal Bond Fund B	Muni Natl	7.88	8.93		4	5	0	1.56	800 621-1048
Kemper Municipal Bond Fund C	Muni Natl	7.80	6.47		4	4	0	1.53	800 621-1048
Kemper NJ Tax-Free Income Fund A	Muni State	7.30	5.67		4	4	4.5	1.25	800 621-1048
Kemper NJ Tax-Free Income Fund B	Muni State	7.22	6.21		4	4	0	2.01	800 621-1048
Kemper NJ Tax-Free Income Fund C	Muni State	8.00	6.56		5	4	0	2.01	800 621-1048
Kemper NY Tax-Free Income Fund A	Muni NY	8.29	7.45	6.04	3	4	4.5	0.82	800 621-1048
Kemper NY Tax-Free Income Fund B	Muni NY	7.41	6.33		4	3	0	1.70	800 621-1048
Kemper NY Tax-Free Income Fund C	Muni NY	7.30	6.26		5	4	0	1.68	800 621-1048
Kemper OH Tax-Free Income Fund A	Muni State	8.15	7.49	6.51	3	4	4.5	0.89	800 621-1048
Kemper OH Tax-Free Income Fund B	Muni State	7.39	6.68		4	3	0	1.72	800 621-1048
Kemper OH Tax-Free Income Fund C	Muni State	7.60	6.73		4	3	0	1.70	800 621-1048
Kemper PA Tax-Free Income Fund A	Muni State	8.32	8.03		2	3	4.5	1.19	800 621-1048
Kemper PA Tax-Free Income Fund B	Muni State	7.93	7.31		3	4	0	1.19	800 621-1048
Kemper PA Tax-Tree Income Fund C	Muni State	7.86	7.32		4	4	0	1.93	800 621-1048
Kemper Short Intermediate Govt A	Government	6.07	4.87	4.34	4	1	3.5	1.18	800 621-1048
Kemper Short Intermediate Govt B	Government	4.91	4.20	3.58	5	1	0	1.97	800 621-1048
Kemper Short Intermediate Govt C	Government	5.31	4.43		5	5	0	1.83	800 621-1048
Kemper TX Tax-Free Income Fund A	Muni State	8.38	7.95	6.08	2	3	0	0.95	800 621-1048
Kemper TX Tax-Free Income Fund B	Muni State	7.51	7.03		3	3	0	1.76	800 621-1048
Kemper TX Tax-free Income Fund C	Muni State	7.62	6.18		4	4	0	1.75	800 621-1048
Kemper US Government Securities A	Govt-Mtg	8.77	7.17	6.29	2	3	4.5	0.78	800 621-1048
Kemper US Government Securities B	Govt-Mtg	7.37	5.89		5	3		1.72	800 621-1048
Kemper US Mortgage Cl A	Govt-Mtg	8.67	7.00	5.97	2	3	4.5	0.94	800 621-1048
Kemper US Mortgage Cl B	Govt-Mtg	7.88	6.16	5.12	4	3	0	1.80	800 621-1048
Kemper US Mortgage Cl C	Govt-Mtg	7.99	6.26		4	3	0	1.70	800 621-1048
Kent Income Fund Instl	Corp-Inv	12.35	8.17		3	5	0	0.82	800 633-5368
Kent Income Fund Invest	Corp-Inv	11.99	7.30		3	5	0	1.07	800 633-5368
Kent Intermediate Instl	Corp-Inv	8.72	6.46	5.45	3	3	0	0.75	800 633-5368

Bond Fund Name	Objective	Annualized Return for			Rank		Max Load	Expense Ratio	Toll-Free Telephone
		1 Year	3 Years	5 Years	Overall	Risk			
Kent Intermediate Invest	Corp-Inv	8.43	6.19	6.43	3	3	4	1.00	800 633-5368
Kent Intermediate Tax Free Instl	Muni Natl	6.47	5.85		4	2	0	0.72	800 633-5368
Kent Intermediate Tax Free Invest	Muni Natl	6.30	5.63	4.94	4	2	4	0.97	800 633-5368
Kent Ltd Term Tax Free Instl	Muni Natl	4.17	4.40		3	1	0	0.76	800 633-5368
Kent Ltd Term Tax Free Invest	Muni Natl	3.99	4.29		3	1	0	0.93	800 633-5368
Kent MI Municipal Ltd Mat Invest	Muni State	5.14	4.62	4.17	3	1	4	0.84	800 633-5368
Kent Short Term Bd Instl	Corp-Inv	6.58	5.77	5.28	3	1	0	0.72	800 633-5368
Kent Short Term Bd Invest	Corp-Inv	6.46	5.59	5.09	4	1	4	0.88	800 633-5368
Kent Tax-Free Income Instl	Muni Natl	7.38	6.71		2	3	0	0.79	800 633-5368
Kent Tax-Free Income Invest	Muni Natl	7.04	6.40		4	3	0	1.04	800 633-5368
KeyPremier Intmed Income Fund	Corp-Inv	9.95					4.5	0.37	800 766-3960
KeyPremier Ltd Dur Govt Secs Fund	Government	5.50					3	0.54	800 766-3960
KeyPremier PA Municipal Bond Fund	Muni State	5.89					3	0.37	800 766-3960
Kiewit Intermediate-Term Bond Port	Corp-Inv	8.70	6.68		3	3	0	0.50	800 254-3948
Kiewit Short-Term Govt Portfolio	Government	6.30	5.63		4	1	0	0.30	800 254-3948
Lazard Bond Portfolio	Corp-Inv	8.01	6.92	5.75	3	2	0	0.80	800 823-6300
Lazard International Fixed Income	Intl Bond	−0.74	0.22	5.70	5	5	0	1.06	800 823-6300
Lazard Strategic Yield Portfolio	Corp-HY	4.34	9.71	7.36	2	2	0	1.08	800 823-6300
Lebenthal NJ Muni Bond	Muni State	9.83	8.76		1	3	4.5	0.70	800 221-5822
Lebenthal NY Muni Bond A	Muni NY	10.18	8.50	6.66	2	3	4.5	0.89	800 221-5822
Lebenthal Taxable Muni Bond	Muni Natl	16.12	10.95		3	5	4.5	0.79	800 221-5822
Legg Mason Global Govt	Intl Bond	0.58	4.33	6.57	5	5	0	1.86	800 822-5544
Legg Mason Invest Grade Income	Corp-Inv	10.27	8.29	6.71	2	4	0	1.00	800 822-5544
Legg Mason MD Tax Free	Muni State	7.62	6.59	5.65	3	3	2.75	0.70	800 822-5544
Legg Mason PA Tax Free Fund	Muni State	7.98	6.74	5.72	2	3	2.75	0.67	800 822-5544
Legg Mason TF Intmd Income Tr	Muni Natl	5.91	5.29	4.99	3	2	2	0.67	800 822-5544
Legg Mason US Government Intmed	Government	7.92	6.44	5.52	3	2	0	1.00	800 822-5544
Lexington GNMA Income Fund	Govt-Mtg	10.13	8.28	6.93	1	2	0	1.01	800 526-0056
Lexington Ramirez Global Income	Intl Bond	5.94	10.86	7.30	3	4	0	1.50	800 526-0056
LifeUSA Income Fund	Corp-Inv	9.65					5.75	0.50	800 864-4725
Loomis Sayles Bond Fund Instl	Corp-Inv	11.31	12.90	12.08	3	5	0	0.75	800 626-9390
Loomis Sayles Bond Fund Retail	Corp-Inv	10.94					0		800 626-9390
Loomis Sayles Global Bond Fund I	Intl Bond	0.63	11.79	8.13	4	5	0	0.90	800 626-9390
Loomis Sayles Global Bond Retail	Intl Bond	0.36					0		800 626-9390
Loomis Sayles High Yield Fund Instl	Corp-HY	7.05					0		800 626-9390
Loomis Sayles High Yield Retail	Corp-HY	6.79					0		800 626-9390
Loomis Sayles Intmed Mat Bond Instl	Dvsfd Bond	6.73					0		800 626-9390
Loomis Sayles Intmed Mat Bond Ret	Dvsfd Bond	6.46					0		800 626-9390
Loomis Sayles Inv Grade Bond Instl	Corp-Inv	11.71					0		800 626-9390
Loomis Sayles Inv Grade Bond Retail	Corp-Inv	11.45					0		800 626-9390
Loomis Sayles Muni Bond Fund	Muni Natl	8.05	7.21	5.67	3	4	0	0.60	800 626-9390
Loomis Sayles Short Term Bond	Corp-Inv	6.82	6.12	5.89	3	1	0	0.50	800 626-9390
Loomis Sayles ST Bond Retail	Corp-Inv	6.66					0		800 626-9390
Loomis Sayles US Govt Sec Fund	Government	14.68	8.99	7.20	3	5	0	0.60	800 626-9390
Lord Abbett Bond Debenture Fund A	Corp-HY	11.02	11.92	9.45	1	3	4.75	0.89	800 426-1130
Lord Abbett Bond Debenture Fund B	Corp-HY	10.21					0	0.81	800 426-1130
Lord Abbett Bond Debenture Fund C	Corp-HY	10.19					0	0.77	800 426-1130
Lord Abbett Global Income Series A	Intl Bond	7.07	6.32	6.10	3	4	4.75	1.10	800 426-1130
Lord Abbett Global Income Series B	Intl Bond	6.33					0	0.85	800 426-1130
Lord Abbett Global Income Series C	Intl Bond	6.46					0	0.84	800 426-1130
Lord Abbett Natl Tax-Free Income B	Muni Natl	9.21					0	0.69	800 426-1130
Lord Abbett Natl Tax-Free Income C	Muni Natl	9.11					0	0.78	800 426-1130
Lord Abbett Natl Tax-Free Income Fd	Muni Natl	9.80	8.20	5.83	2	3	4.75	0.88	800 426-1130
Lord Abbett Tax-Free Income CA A	Muni CA	8.98	7.14	4.89	3	3	4.75	0.72	800 426-1130
Lord Abbett Tax-Free Income CA C	Muni CA	8.08					0	0.79	800 426-1130
Lord Abbett Tax-Free Income CT	Muni State	8.54	7.42	5.36	2	3	4.75	0.59	800 426-1130
Lord Abbett Tax-Free Income FL A	Muni State	8.13	6.47	4.53	4	3	4.75	0.82	800 426-1130
Lord Abbett Tax-Free Income FL C	Muni State	7.34					0	0.44	800 426-1130

388

Bond Fund Name	Objective	Annualized Return for			Rank		Max Load	Expense Ratio	Toll-Free Telephone
		1 Year	3 Years	5 Years	Overall	Risk			
Lord Abbett Tax-Free Income GA	Muni State	10.43					4.75	0.40	800 426-1130
Lord Abbett Tax-Free Income HI	Muni State	8.78	7.31	5.42	3	3	4.75	0.58	800 426-1130
Lord Abbett Tax-Free Income MI	Muni State	8.40	7.52	5.76	2	3	4.75	0.36	800 426-1130
Lord Abbett Tax-Free Income MN	Muni State	8.26					4.75	0.44	800 426-1130
Lord Abbett Tax-Free Income MO	Muni State	8.08	6.92	5.05	3	3	4.75	0.70	800 426-1130
Lord Abbett Tax-Free Income NJ	Muni State	9.46	7.72	5.71	1	3	4.75	0.82	800 426-1130
Lord Abbett Tax-Free Income NY A	Muni NY	8.47	6.88	5.02	3	3	4.75	0.84	800 426-1130
Lord Abbett Tax-Free Income NY C	Muni NY	7.79					0	0.78	800 426-1130
Lord Abbett Tax-Free Income PA	Muni State	9.15	7.58	5.83	1	3	4.75	0.68	800 426-1130
Lord Abbett Tax-Free Income TX	Muni State	8.97	7.94	5.89	3	3	4.75	0.90	800 426-1130
Lord Abbett Tax-Free Income WA	Muni State	9.47	8.51	5.90	1	3	4.75	0.57	800 426-1130
Lord Abbett US Government Secs A	Government	10.52	6.78	5.32	3	4	4.75	0.92	800 426-1130
Lord Abbett US Government Secs B	Government	10.14					0	0.46	800 426-1130
Lord Abbett US Government Secs C	Government	9.69					0	0.82	800 426-1130
Lutheran Brotherhood Hi Yld	Corp-HY	11.78	12.31	9.69	2	5	5	0.84	800 328-4552
Lutheran Brotherhood Income Fund	Corp-Inv	10.02	7.08	6.05	3	4	5	0.80	800 328-4552
Lutheran Brotherhood Municipal Bond	Muni Natl	8.97	7.69	6.13	2	3	5	0.70	800 328-4552
MainStay CA Tax Free Fund A	Muni CA	6.17	6.57	5.08	5	4	4.5	1.24	800 624-6782
MainStay CA Tax Free Fund B	Muni CA	6.00	6.06		4	4	0	1.49	800 624-6782
MainStay Government Fund A	Government	10.81	6.71		2	4	4.5	1.00	800 624-6782
MainStay Government Fund B	Government	10.09	6.26	5.41	3	4	0	1.65	800 624-6782
MainStay Hi Yd Corporate Bd Fund A	Corp-HY	11.40	14.03		1	2	4.5	1.00	800 624-6782
MainStay Hi Yd Corporate Bd Fund B	Corp-HY	10.77	13.44	12.53	1	2	0	1.62	800 624-6782
MainStay Institutional Bond Fund	Corp-Inv	9.59	7.20	6.28	3	4	0	0.75	800 695-2126
MainStay Institutional Index Bd	Corp-Inv	10.04	7.20	6.04	2	3	0	0.50	800 695-2126
MainStay Institutional ST Bond	Corp-Inv	6.16	5.85	5.09	3	1	0	0.60	800 695-2126
MainStay International Bond Fund A	Intl Bond	5.06	7.94		3	4	4.5	1.49	800 624-6782
MainStay NY Tax Free Fund Bond A	Muni NY	6.46	6.74	5.36	4	4	4.5	1.24	800 624-6782
MainStay NY Tax Free Fund Bond B	Muni NY	6.14	6.24		5	3	0	1.49	800 624-6782
MainStay Strategic Income A	Dvsfd Bond	6.11					4.5	1.15	800 624-6782
MainStay Strategic Income B	Dvsfd Bond	5.31						1.90	800 624-6782
MainStay Tax Free Bond Fund A	Muni Natl	7.99	7.14		3	4	4.5	1.01	800 624-6782
MainStay Tax Free Bond Fund B	Muni Natl	7.77	6.92	5.04	4	4	0	1.22	800 624-6782
Managed Municipal Fund ISI Shares	Muni Natl	7.91	6.83	5.43	4	4	4.45	0.90	800 882-8585
Managers Bond	Corp-Inv	11.34	9.82	8.77	2	5	0	1.31	800 835-3879
Managers Global Bond Fund	Intl Bond	4.55	2.89		5	5	0	1.63	800 835-3879
Managers Intermediate Mortgage	Govt-Mtg	7.93	6.55	0.39	4	2	0	1.24	800 835-3879
Managers Short & Interm Bond	Corp-Inv	6.02	6.23	4.34	4	1	0	1.40	800 835-3879
Managers Short Government	Government	5.27	5.01	3.24	5	1	0	1.13	800 835-3879
Marquis Government Securities A	Government	8.86	6.62		3	2	3.5	0.70	800-480-4111
Marquis Government Securities B	Government	8.02	6.19		3	2	0	1.45	800-480-4111
Marquis LA Tax Free Income A	Muni State	6.62	6.42		4	3	3.5	0.65	800-480-4111
Marquis LA Tax Free Income B	Muni State	5.87	5.61		5	3	0	1.40	800-480-4111
Marshall Govt Inc Fund	Government	8.49	7.13		2	3	0	0.86	800 236-8560
Marshall Intermediate Bond Fund	Corp-Inv	8.08	6.44	5.01	3	3	0	0.72	800 236-8560
Marshall Intermediate Tax Free Fund	Muni Natl	6.82	5.79		4	2	0	0.61	800 236-8560
Marshall Short Term Income Fund	Corp-Inv	6.23	6.02	5.09	3	1	0	0.51	800 236-8560
MAS Funds Domestic Fixed Income	Corp-Inv	9.94	7.78	7.12	2	3	0	0.51	800 354-8185
MAS Funds Fixed Income	Corp-Inv	8.97	9.27	7.47	2	3	0	0.47	800 354-8185
MAS Funds Fixed Income II	Corp-Inv	9.28	8.34	6.92	2	3	0	0.50	800 354-8185
MAS Funds Global Fixed Income	Intl Bond	4.61	4.73		5	4	0	0.57	800 354-8185
MAS Funds High Yield	Corp-HY	11.90	14.54	11.82	2	5	0	0.51	800 354-8185
MAS Funds International Fixed Inc	Intl Bond	1.84	2.23		5	5	0	0.53	800 354-8185
MAS Funds Intmed Duration Port	Dvsfd Bond	8.31	7.67		2	2	0	0.54	800 354-8185
MAS Funds Limited Duration Port	Corp-Inv	6.13	6.06	5.24	3	1	0	0.42	800 354-8185
MAS Funds Mortgage Backed Sec Port	Govt-Mtg	7.93	8.25	6.65	2	3	0	0.50	800 354-8185
MAS Funds Muni Fixed Income	Muni Natl	7.90	9.28	6.72	3	4	0	0.51	800 354-8185
MAS Funds PA Muni Fixed Income	Muni State	7.31	8.90		3	3	0	0.50	800 354-8185

Bond Fund Name	Objective	Annualized Return for			Rank		Max Load	Expense Ratio	Toll-Free Telephone
		1 Year	3 Years	5 Years	Overall	Risk			
MAS Funds Special Purpose Fixed Inc	Corp-HY	9.02	8.87	7.43	2	3	0	0.49	800 354-8185
Mason Street High Yield Bond A	Corp-HY	13.72					4.75	1.30	888 627-6678
Mason Street High Yield Bond B	Corp-HY	12.93					0	1.95	888 627-6678
Mason Street Muni Bond A	Muni Natl	9.13					4.75	0.85	888 627-6678
Mason Street Muni Bond B	Muni Natl	8.10					0	1.50	888 627-6678
Mason Street Select Bond A	Dvsfd Bond	9.47					4.75	0.85	888 627-6678
Mason Street Select Bond B	Dvsfd Bond	6.88					0	1.50	888 627-6678
MassMutual Instl Core Bond S	Dvsfd Bond	11.16	7.78		2	4	0	0.53	
MassMutual Instl Prime Fund S	Corp-Inv	5.42	5.38		3	1	0	0.53	
MassMutual Instl Short Term Bond S	Dvsfd Bond	7.30	5.99		5	2	0	0.53	
MasterWorks Bond Index Fund	Corp-Inv	11.16	7.44		2	4	0	0.32	800 776-0179
MasterWorks US Treasury Allocation	Government	7.74	6.23		4	3	0	0.71	800 776-0179
McM Fixed Income Fund	Dvsfd Bond	10.24	7.34		3	4	0	0.50	800 788-9485
McM Intermediate Fixed Income Fund	Dvsfd Bond	8.75	6.69		3	2	0	0.50	800 788-9485
Mentor Municipal Income A	Muni Natl	8.28	7.68	5.96	2	3	4.75	1.17	800 382-0016
Mentor Municipal Income B	Muni Natl	7.83	7.11	5.40	3	3	0	1.69	800 382-0016
Mentor Quality Income A	Government	8.54	6.87	5.54	3	4	4.75	1.05	800 382-0016
Mentor Quality Income B	Government	8.07	6.34	5.01	5	4	0	1.55	800 382-0016
Mentor Short Duration Income Port A	Corp-Inv	5.84	5.87		5	2	1	0.84	800 382-0016
Mentor Short Duration Income Port B	Corp-Inv	5.56	5.34		4	2	0	1.16	800 382-0016
Merrill Lynch Adjustable Rate Sec B	Govt-Mtg	4.69	5.58	4.51	4	1	0	1.71	800 637-3863
Merrill Lynch Adjustable Rate Sec D	Govt-Mtg	5.24	6.09	5.00	3	1	3	1.13	800 637-3863
Merrill Lynch AZ Muni Bond A	Muni State	7.80	6.91	5.60	3	3	5.25	0.79	800 637-3863
Merrill Lynch AZ Muni Bond B	Muni State	7.27	6.37	5.07	5	3	0	1.30	800 637-3863
Merrill Lynch CA Insured Muni A	Muni CA	7.78	8.19	6.26	3	4	4	0.63	800 637-3863
Merrill Lynch CA Insured Muni B	Muni CA	7.24	7.66	6.65	4	4	0	1.14	800 637-3863
Merrill Lynch CA Muni Bond A	Muni CA	8.01	7.58	5.84	3	3	4	0.63	800 637-3863
Merrill Lynch CA Muni Bond B	Muni CA	7.47	7.07	5.30	4	3	0	1.14	800 637-3863
Merrill Lynch Corp Bd High Income A	Corp-HY	8.71	11.21	9.58	2	3	4	0.51	800 637-3863
Merrill Lynch Corp Bd High Income B	Corp-HY	7.89	10.36	8.77	2	3	0	1.27	800 637-3863
Merrill Lynch Corp Bd High Income C	Corp-HY	7.84	10.26		2	3	0	1.31	800 637-3863
Merrill Lynch Corp Bd High Income D	Corp-HY	8.44	10.88		1	3	4	0.75	800 637-3863
Merrill Lynch Corp Bd Intmed Term A	Corp-Inv	8.85	6.94	6.26	3	3	5.25	0.65	800 637-3863
Merrill Lynch Corp Bd Intmed Term B	Corp-Inv	8.29	6.39	5.66	3	3	0	1.14	800 637-3863
Merrill Lynch Corp Bd Inv Grade A	Corp-Inv	9.88	7.17	6.75	3	4	5.25		800 637-3863
Merrill Lynch Corp Bd Inv Grade B	Corp-Inv	9.05	6.36	5.89	3	4	0	1.34	800 637-3863
Merrill Lynch Federal Securities A	Govt-Mtg	8.46	7.32		3	2	5.25	0.65	800 637-3863
Merrill Lynch Federal Securities B	Govt-Mtg	7.52	6.47	4.97	4	2	0	1.42	800 637-3863
Merrill Lynch Federal Securities C	Govt-Mtg	7.47	6.42		5	2	0	1.47	800 637-3863
Merrill Lynch Federal Securities D	Govt-Mtg	8.08	7.02	5.75	3	2	4	0.92	800 637-3863
Merrill Lynch FL Muni Bond A	Muni State	8.29	7.30	5.85	3	3	5.25	0.70	800 637-3863
Merrill Lynch FL Muni Bond B	Muni State	7.74	6.76	5.32	4	3	0	1.20	800 637-3863
Merrill Lynch Global Bond Fund A	Intl Bond	9.26	5.65	4.31	4	5	5.25	0.99	800 637-3863
Merrill Lynch Global Bond Fund B	Intl Bond	8.42	4.84	4.13	5	5	0	1.73	800 637-3863
Merrill Lynch Global Bond Fund C	Intl Bond	8.25	4.73		5	5	0	1.86	800 637-3863
Merrill Lynch Global Bond Fund D	Intl Bond	8.88	5.35		4	5	4	1.25	800 637-3863
Merrill Lynch Intmed Govt Bond D	Government	9.27	5.97	4.97	3	3	1	1.32	800 637-3863
Merrill Lynch MA Muni Bond A	Muni State	8.54	7.61	5.68	3	4	5.25	0.83	800 637-3863
Merrill Lynch MA Muni Bond B	Muni State	7.99	7.07	5.23	3	3	0	1.34	800 637-3863
Merrill Lynch MI Muni Bond B	Muni State	6.90	6.51	4.93	5	3	0	1.08	800 637-3863
Merrill Lynch MN Muni Bond A	Muni State	8.34	6.91	5.69	3	3	5.25	0.92	800 637-3863
Merrill Lynch MN Muni Bond B	Muni State	7.80	6.37	5.05	3	3	0	1.43	800 637-3863
Merrill Lynch Muni Insured Port A	Muni Natl	8.03	7.09	5.64	3	4	5.25	0.43	800 637-3863
Merrill Lynch Muni Insured Port B	Muni Natl	7.22	6.23	4.87	5	4	0	1.19	800 637-3863
Merrill Lynch Muni Insured Port C	Muni Natl	7.03	6.19		5	4	0	1.25	800 637-3863
Merrill Lynch Muni Insured Port D	Muni Natl	7.63	6.78		3	4	4	0.69	800 637-3863
Merrill Lynch Muni Intmed Term A	Muni Natl	7.93	6.67	5.34	3	3	5.25	0.81	800 637-3863
Merrill Lynch Muni Intmed Term B	Muni Natl	7.60	6.34	5.00	4	3	0	1.11	800 637-3863

Bond Fund Name	Objective	Annualized Return for			Rank		Max Load	Expense Ratio	Toll-Free Telephone
		1 Year	3 Years	5 Years	Overall	Risk			
Merrill Lynch Muni Ltd Maturity A	Muni Natl	4.26	4.15	3.78	3	1	5.25	0.41	800 637-3863
Merrill Lynch Muni Ltd Maturity B	Muni Natl	3.88	3.80	3.47	3	1	0	0.75	800 637-3863
Merrill Lynch Muni National A	Muni Natl	8.35	8.05	6.25	2	3	5.25	0.56	800 637-3863
Merrill Lynch Muni National B	Muni Natl	7.54	7.21	5.43	2	3	0	1.31	800 637-3863
Merrill Lynch Muni National C	Muni Natl	7.49	7.15		3	3	0	1.36	800 637-3863
Merrill Lynch Muni National D	Muni Natl	7.98	7.75		2	3	4	0.80	800 637-3863
Merrill Lynch NC Muni Bond B	Muni State	8.31	6.91	5.34	4	4	0	1.31	800 637-3863
Merrill Lynch NJ Muni Bond A	Muni State	8.58	7.04	5.41	3	3	4	0.70	800 637-3863
Merrill Lynch NJ Muni Bond B	Muni State	8.03	6.50	4.88	5	3	0	1.21	800 637-3863
Merrill Lynch NY Muni Bond A	Muni NY	8.97	7.64	5.15	4	4	4	0.65	800 637-3863
Merrill Lynch NY Muni Bond B	Muni NY	9.05	7.30	4.73	4	4	0	1.16	800 637-3863
Merrill Lynch OH Muni Bond A	Muni State	7.99	7.46	5.81	2	3	5.25	0.80	800 637-3863
Merrill Lynch OH Muni Bond B	Muni State	7.44	6.92	5.36	4	3	0	1.31	800 637-3863
Merrill Lynch PA Muni Bond A	Muni State	8.71	7.43	6.15	1	3	5.25	0.74	800 637-3863
Merrill Lynch PA Muni Bond B	Muni State	8.17	6.89	6.58	3	3	0	1.25	800 637-3863
Merrill Lynch ST Global Income B	Intl Bond	3.44	4.29	2.88	4	1	0	1.74	800 637-3863
Merrill Lynch ST Global Income D	Intl Bond	4.00	4.85	3.42	4	1	3	1.20	800 637-3863
Merrill Lynch TX Muni Bond A	Muni State	7.34	6.61	5.63	4	3	5.25	0.83	800 637-3863
Merrill Lynch TX Muni Bond B	Muni State	6.80	6.07	5.10	5	3	0	1.34	800 637-3863
Merrill Lynch World Income A	Intl Bond	1.79	7.24	6.13	3	5	4	0.76	800 637-3863
Merrill Lynch World Income B	Intl Bond	0.89	6.44	5.30	2	5	0	1.54	800 637-3863
Merriman Flexible Bond Fund	Corp-Inv	5.74	6.62	6.49	3	3	0	1.46	800 423-4893
MFR Global High Yield A	Intl Bond	4.80	8.78		3	4	4.75	1.90	888 743-6432
MFR Global High Yield B	Intl Bond	3.89	7.91		3	4	0	1.96	888 743-6432
MFS AL Municipal Bond A	Muni State	7.74	7.23	6.14	1	3	4.75	1.14	800 343-2829
MFS AR Municipal Bond A	Muni State	8.06	7.04	5.49	2	3	4.75	0.67	800 343-2829
MFS Bond Fund A	Corp-Inv	9.98	8.23	7.39	3	4	4.75	1.00	800 343-2829
MFS Bond Fund B	Corp-Inv	9.15	7.43		3	4	0	1.76	800 343-2829
MFS Bond Fund C	Corp-Inv	19.11	7.47		4	5	0	1.74	800 343-2829
MFS CA Municipal Bond A	Muni CA	9.26	7.81	5.84	3	4	4.75	0.64	800 343-2829
MFS FL Municipal Bond A	Muni State	8.33	6.81	5.07	4	3	4.75	0.78	800 343-2829
MFS GA Municipal Bond A	Muni State	8.16	7.11	5.58	3	3	4.75	1.17	800 343-2829
MFS Government Limited Maturity A	Government	6.07	5.54	4.19	4	1	2.5	0.96	800 343-2829
MFS Government Mortgage A	Govt-Mtg	7.79	6.66	6.12	3	2	4.75	0.98	800 343-2829
MFS Government Mortgage B	Govt-Mtg	7.00	5.92	4.55	4	2	0	1.94	800 343-2829
MFS Government Securities A	Government	10.14	6.99	6.17	3	4	4.75	0.94	800 343-2829
MFS Government Securities B	Government	9.50	6.28	4.59	3	4	0	2.10	800 343-2829
MFS Government Securities C	Government	9.47					0		800 343-2829
MFS High Income Fund A	Corp-HY	13.03	12.74	10.59	1	3	4.75	1.01	800 343-2829
MFS High Income Fund B	Corp-HY	12.17	11.88		1	3	0	2.11	800 343-2829
MFS High Income Fund C	Corp-HY	12.21	11.91		1	3	0	1.72	800 343-2829
MFS Intermediate Income Fund A	Dvsfd Bond	6.47	6.47		4	2	4.75	1.16	800 343-2829
MFS Intermediate Income Fund B	Dvsfd Bond	5.38	5.38	4.34	5	2	0	1.16	800 343-2829
MFS Limited Maturity A	Corp-Inv	5.86	5.92	5.79	3	1	2.5	0.95	800 343-2829
MFS Limited Maturity B	Corp-Inv	4.94	4.95		4	1	0	1.78	800 343-2829
MFS Limited Maturity C	Corp-Inv	4.86	4.98		5	1	0	1.80	800 343-2829
MFS MA Municipal Bond A	Muni State	7.58	6.81	5.28	4	3	4.75	1.06	800 343-2829
MFS MD Municipal Bond A	Muni State	8.52	7.13	5.18	3	3	4.75	1.20	800 343-2829
MFS MS Municipal Bond A	Muni State	9.15	7.98	6.00	1	3	4.75	0.87	800 343-2829
MFS MS Municipal Bond B	Muni State	8.28	7.08		3	3	0	1.72	800 343-2829
MFS Municipal Bond Fund A	Muni Natl	7.56	6.72	5.34	4	4	4.75	0.57	800 343-2829
MFS Municipal Bond Fund B	Muni Natl	6.78	5.81		5	4	0	1.55	800 343-2829
MFS Municipal High-Income A	Muni Natl	9.69	7.15	6.25	2	3	4.75	0.89	800 343-2829
MFS Municipal High-Income B	Muni Natl	8.75	6.22		3	3	0	2.10	800 343-2829
MFS Municipal Income A	Muni Natl	9.12	7.13		2	3	4.75	1.28	800 343-2829
MFS Municipal Income B	Muni Natl	8.29	6.29	5.13	3	3	0	1.98	800 343-2829
MFS Municipal Income C	Muni Natl	8.28	6.36		3	3	0	2.05	800 343-2829
MFS Municipal Limited Maturity A	Muni Natl	4.87	4.42	3.61	3	1	4.75	0.95	800 343-2829

Bond Fund Name	Objective	Annualized Return for			Rank		Max Load	Expense Ratio	Toll-Free Telephone
		1 Year	3 Years	5 Years	Overall	Risk			
MFS Municipal Limited Maturity B	Muni Natl	3.82	3.52		4	1	0	1.75	800 343-2829
MFS Municipal Limited Maturity C	Muni Natl	3.99	3.53		4	1	0	1.80	800 343-2829
MFS NC Municipal Bond A	Muni State	8.15	7.11	5.47	3	3	4.75	1.17	800 343-2829
MFS NY Municipal Bond A	Muni NY	8.71	7.49	5.75	3	4	4.75	1.09	800 343-2829
MFS PA Municipal Bond A	Muni State	9.28	7.83	6.09	2	3	4.75	0.00	800 343-2829
MFS SC Municipal Bond A	Muni State	8.31	7.02	5.71	3	3	4.75	1.17	800 343-2829
MFS Strategic Income Fund A	Dvsfd Bond	5.00	8.91	7.97	3	4	4.75	0.79	800 343-2829
MFS TN Municipal Bond A	Muni State	8.69	7.31	5.94	3	3	4.75	1.21	800 343-2829
MFS VA Municipal Bond A	Muni State	8.00	6.61	5.12	4	3	4.75	1.04	800 343-2829
MFS World Governments A	Intl Bond	5.49	3.79	4.87	4	4	4.75	1.35	800 343-2829
MFS World Governments B	Intl Bond	4.62	2.95		5	4	0	2.15	800 343-2829
MFS World Governments C	Intl Bond	4.63	3.00		4	4	0	2.14	800 343-2829
MFS WV Municipal Bond A	Muni State	7.80	6.77	5.46	3	3	4.75	0.86	800 343-2829
MMA Praxis Intermediate Income Fund	Corp-Inv	8.99	6.28		3	3	0	1.10	800 977-2947
Monetta Intermediate Bond Fund	Corp-Inv	9.37	7.56	7.26	1	2	0	0.87	800 666-3882
Monitor Fixed Income Secs Fund Inv	Corp-Inv	9.94	8.80	6.31	3	5	2	0.96	800 253-0412
Monitor Fixed Income Secs Fund Tr	Corp-Inv	10.30	7.08	5.94	3	4	0	0.70	800 253-0412
Monitor Intmed Govt Inc Instl Shs	Government	7.61	6.27	5.39	3	2	0	0.79	800 845-8406
Monitor Intmed Govt Inc Inv Shs	Government	7.50	6.09		3	2	4.75	1.14	800 845-8406
Monitor MI Tax-Free Bond Instl Shs	Muni State	6.63	6.06	5.43	3	2	0	1.01	800 845-8406
Monitor MI Tax-Free Bond Inv Shs	Muni State	6.41	5.91		3	2	4.75	1.36	800 845-8406
Monitor Mortgage Sec Invest Shares	Govt-Mtg	8.29	8.63	4.70	3	3	2	0.95	800 253-0412
Monitor Mortgage Sec Trust Shares	Govt-Mtg	8.44	8.81		2	2	0	0.70	800 253-0412
Monitor OH TF Investment Shs	Muni State	5.78	4.91		3	2	2	1.00	800 253-0412
Monitor OH TF Trust Shares	Muni State	6.07	5.28	4.28	3	2	0	0.75	800 253-0412
Monitor Short/Intmed FI Secs Trust	Corp-Inv	7.04	6.05	5.41	3	2	0	0.70	800 253-0412
Monterey Camborne Government Income	Government	10.78	7.47	6.31	3	4	4.5	1.10	800 628-9403
Monterey PIA Global Bond Fund	Intl Bond	3.70					0	0.51	800 628-9403
Monterey PIA Short-Term Govt Fund	Government	6.32	6.61		3	1	0	0.30	800 628-9403
Montgomery CA TF Short/Intmed Fd	Muni CA	6.87	6.60		3	2	0	1.18	800 572-3863
Montgomery Short Govt Bond Fund	Government	7.52	6.71	6.16	2	1	0	1.55	800 572-3863
Montgomery Total Return Bond Fund	Dvsfd Bond	10.90					0		800 572-3863
Morg Stan Dean Witter CA TF Inc B	Muni CA	7.34	6.54	4.96	5	3	0	1.32	800 869-6397
Morg Stan Dean Witter Diver Inc B	Dvsfd Bond	6.80	7.18	6.08	2	2	0	1.40	800 869-6397
Morg Stan Dean Witter Fed Secs B	Government	10.42	6.80	5.53	3	4	0	1.53	800 869-6397
Morg Stan Dean Witter Gl Sh-Trm Inc	Intl Bond	4.01	6.70	5.57	2	2	0	1.79	800 869-6397
Morg Stan Dean Witter HI Muni Trust	Muni State	5.60	7.37		3	4	3	0.35	800 869-6397
Morg Stan Dean Witter HY Secs D	Corp-HY	9.39	11.75	9.75	1	3	5.5	0.56	800 869-6397
Morg Stan Dean Witter Intmed Inc B	Corp-Inv	7.24	5.73	5.01	5	3	0	1.74	800 869-6397
Morg Stan Dean Witter IT US Treas	Government	9.29					0	0.35	800 869-6397
Morg Stan Dean Witter Ltd Trm Treas	Muni Natl	6.16	5.87		4	2	0	1.60	800 869-6397
Morg Stan Dean Witter MS Muni AZ	Muni State	7.02	6.66	5.30	3	3	4	1.50	800 869-6397
Morg Stan Dean Witter MS Muni CA	Muni CA	8.41	8.09	5.84	2	3	4	0.59	800 869-6397
Morg Stan Dean Witter MS Muni FL	Muni State	8.37	7.25	5.77	3	3	4	0.62	800 869-6397
Morg Stan Dean Witter MS Muni MA	Muni State	8.27	7.35	5.93	3	5	4	0.75	800 869-6397
Morg Stan Dean Witter MS Muni MI	Muni State	8.14	7.58	5.89	2	3	4	0.50	800 869-6397
Morg Stan Dean Witter MS Muni MN	Muni State	6.56	6.81	5.44	3	2	4	0.50	800 869-6397
Morg Stan Dean Witter MS Muni NJ	Muni State	8.31	7.35	5.62	2	3	4	1.00	800 869-6397
Morg Stan Dean Witter MS Muni NY	Muni NY	9.15	8.08	5.88	3	5	4	0.50	800 869-6397
Morg Stan Dean Witter MS Muni OH	Muni State	7.57	7.35	5.77	3	3	4	0.70	800 869-6397
Morg Stan Dean Witter MS Muni PA	Muni State	7.86	7.23	5.59	3	3	4	1.20	800 869-6397
Morg Stan Dean Witter NY TF Inc B	Muni NY	8.10	6.78	4.92	5	3	0	1.42	800 869-6397
Morg Stan Dean Witter Select Muni	Muni Natl	7.51	6.88	5.40	4	3	0	0.94	800 869-6397
Morg Stan Dean Witter Short Term Bd	Corp-Inv	6.81	6.20		3	1	0	1.20	800 869-6397
Morg Stan Dean Witter ST US Treas	Government	6.48	5.41	4.48	4	1	0	0.83	800 869-6397
Morg Stan Dean Witter Tax-Exempt D	Muni Natl	8.36	7.47	5.91	1	3	4	0.49	800 869-6397
Morg Stan Dean Witter US Govt Sec B	Govt-Mtg	8.63	6.82	5.75	3	3	0	1.26	800 869-6397
Morg Stan Dean Witter WrldWde Inc B	Intl Bond	5.41	7.83	6.52	4	4	0	2.02	800 869-6397

Bond Fund Name	Objective	Annualized Return for			Rank		Max Load	Expense Ratio	Toll-Free Telephone
		1 Year	3 Years	5 Years	Overall	Risk			
Morgan Grenfell Emrg Markets Debt	Intl Bond	−3.68	17.85		3	5	0	1.25	800 550-6426
Morgan Grenfell Fixed Income	Corp-Inv	10.69	8.46	7.59	2	3	0	0.55	800 550-6426
Morgan Grenfell Global Fixed Income	Intl Bond	5.01	4.19		5	4	0	0.65	800 550-6426
Morgan Grenfell Intnl Fixed Income	Intl Bond	2.45	3.44		5	5	0	0.65	800 550-6426
Morgan Grenfell Muni Bond Instl	Muni Natl	7.64	7.42	6.55	2	2	0	0.54	800 550-6426
Morgan Grenfell ST Fixed Income	Corp-Inv	6.63	6.36		3	1	0	0.52	800 550-6426
Morgan Grenfell ST Muni Bond Instl	Muni Natl	5.93	6.26		3	1	0	0.52	800 550-6426
Morgan Stanley Emrg Market Debt A	Intl Bond	−2.95	25.42		2	5	0	1.60	800 548-7786
Morgan Stanley Emrg Market Debt B	Intl Bond	−3.06					0	2.06	800 548-7786
Morgan Stanley Fixed Income A	Corp-Inv	9.51	7.88	7.44	2	3	0	0.45	800 548-7786
Morgan Stanley Fixed Income B	Corp-Inv	9.36					0	0.60	800 548-7786
Morgan Stanley Gl Fixed Inc Instl A	Intl Bond	6.12	5.81	5.94	4	4	0	0.50	800 548-7786
Morgan Stanley Gl Fixed Inc Instl B	Intl Bond	5.91					0	0.65	800 548-7786
Morgan Stanley Gl Fixed Inc Ret A	Intl Bond	5.34	4.93	5.27	4	4	4.75	1.45	800 548-7786
Morgan Stanley Gl Fixed Inc Ret B	Intl Bond	4.63	4.09		4	4	0	2.20	800 548-7786
Morgan Stanley Gl Fixed Inc Ret C	Intl Bond	4.63	4.19	4.46	5	4	0	2.20	800 548-7786
Morgan Stanley High Yield A	Corp-HY	10.81					4.75	1.25	800 548-7786
Morgan Stanley High Yield B	Corp-HY	9.26					0	2.00	800 548-7786
Morgan Stanley High Yield C	Corp-HY	9.85					0	2.00	800 548-7786
Morgan Stanley High Yield Instl A	Corp-HY	11.38	14.10	12.47	1	5	0	0.69	800 548-7786
Morgan Stanley High Yield Instl B	Corp-HY	11.08					0	1.00	800 548-7786
Morgan Stanley Muni Bond Instl A	Muni Natl	6.61	5.70		3	2	0	0.45	800 548-7786
Morgan Stanley Worldwide High Inc A	Intl Bond	3.40	17.56		2	5	4.75	1.52	800 548-7786
Morgan Stanley Worldwide High Inc B	Intl Bond	2.63	15.97		3	5	0	2.27	800 548-7786
Morgan Stanley Worldwide High Inc C	Intl Bond	2.55	16.31		2	5	0	2.27	800 548-7786
Mosaic Bond Fund	Corp-Inv	5.92	4.93	4.64	5	2	0	1.61	888 670-3600
Mosaic Government Fund	Government	8.30	5.14	4.43	5	4	0	1.43	888 670-3600
Mosaic High Yield Fund	Corp-HY	8.38	8.47	7.29	2	3	0	1.22	888 670-3600
Mosaic Tax-Free AZ Fund	Muni State	6.43	6.15	4.37	5	3	0	1.16	888 670-3600
Mosaic Tax-Free MD Fund	Muni State	6.58	5.89	4.35	5	3	0	1.20	888 670-3600
Mosaic Tax-Free MO Fund	Muni State	7.07	6.31	4.54	5	3	0	1.17	888 670-3600
Mosaic Tax-Free National Fund	Muni Natl	6.91	6.29	4.43	5	3	0	1.05	888 670-3600
Mosaic Tax-Free VA Fund	Muni State	7.02	6.77	4.85	5	3	0	1.14	888 670-3600
Munder All Season Conservative Y	Corp-Inv	6.32					0	0.55	800 438-5789
Munder Bond Fund A	Corp-Inv	10.45	7.16	6.06	3	3	4	0.96	800 438-5789
Munder Bond Fund B	Corp-Inv	9.76					0	1.71	800 438-5789
Munder Bond Fund K	Corp-Inv	10.56	7.21	5.80	3	3	0	0.96	800 438-5789
Munder Bond Fund Y	Corp-Inv	10.83	7.41	6.29	3	4	0	0.71	800 438-5789
Munder Intermediate Bond A	Corp-Inv	7.84	6.02	5.01	4	2	4	0.93	800 438-5789
Munder Intermediate Bond B	Corp-Inv	6.94	5.24		5	4	0	1.68	800 438-5789
Munder Intermediate Bond K	Corp-Inv	7.73	6.02	5.28	3	2	0	0.93	800 438-5789
Munder Intermediate Bond Y	Corp-Inv	7.99	6.28	5.21	3	2	0	0.68	800 438-5789
Munder International Bond K	Intl Bond	0.70					0		800 438-5789
Munder Michigan Triple Tax-Free A	Muni State	9.02	7.37		3	4	4	0.88	800 438-5789
Munder Michigan Triple Tax-Free B	Muni State	8.23	6.58		4	4	0	1.63	800 438-5789
Munder Michigan Triple Tax-Free K	Muni State	9.02	7.38		3	4	0	0.88	800 438-5789
Munder Michigan Triple Tax-Free Y	Muni State	9.18	7.64		3	4	0	0.63	800 438-5789
Munder Short Term Treasury Fund B	Government	4.78					0	1.52	800 438-5789
Munder Short Term Treasury Fund Y	Government	5.78					0	0.52	800 438-5789
Munder Tax-Free Bond Fund A	Muni Natl	8.55					4	0.95	800 438-5789
Munder Tax-Free Bond Fund B	Muni Natl	7.65	6.12		5	4	0	1.70	800 438-5789
Munder Tax-Free Bond Fund K	Muni Natl	8.43	6.86		4	4	0	0.95	800 438-5789
Munder Tax-Free Bond Fund Y	Muni Natl	8.70	7.12		4	4	0	0.70	800 438-5789
Munder Tax-Free Intmed Bond A	Muni Natl	5.44	4.75	4.49	3	2	4	0.93	800 438-5789
Munder Tax-Free Intmed Bond B	Muni Natl	4.68					0	1.68	800 438-5789
Munder Tax-Free Intmed Bond K	Muni Natl	5.44	4.71	4.11	4	2	0	0.93	800 438-5789
Munder Tax-Free Intmed Bond Y	Muni Natl	5.70	4.98	4.52	3	2	0	0.68	800 438-5789
Munder US Govt Income Bond Fund A	Government	9.71	7.13		3	3	4	0.96	800 438-5789

Bond Fund Name	Objective	Annualized Return for			Rank		Max Load	Expense Ratio	Toll-Free Telephone
		1 Year	3 Years	5 Years	Overall	Risk			
Munder US Govt Income Bond Fund B	Government	8.89					0	1.71	800 438-5789
Munder US Govt Income Bond Fund C	Government	8.82					0	1.71	800 438-5789
Munder US Govt Income Bond Fund K	Government	9.70	7.14		3	3	0	0.91	800 438-5789
Munder US Govt Income Bond Fund Y	Government	9.97	7.39		3	3	0	0.71	800 438-5789
Narragansett Insured TF Income A	Muni Natl	7.98	7.55	6.20	2	3	4	0.21	800 228-4227
Narragansett Insured TF Income C	Muni Natl	6.90					0	1.06	800 228-4227
Narragansett Insured TF Income Y	Muni Natl	8.80					0	0.06	800 228-4227
Nations Divers Income Invest A	Dvsfd Bond	9.82	7.13	7.13	3	4	0	1.00	800 321-7854
Nations Divers Income Invest B	Dvsfd Bond	9.15	6.56	6.56	3	4	0	1.57	800 321-7854
Nations Divers Income Invest C	Dvsfd Bond	9.20	6.71	6.65	3	4	0	1.25	800 321-7854
Nations Divers Income Primary A	Dvsfd Bond	10.09	7.40	7.38	2	4	0	0.75	800 321-7854
Nations FL Intmed Muni Inv A	Muni State	6.64	5.98	5.19	3	2	0	0.70	800 321-7854
Nations FL Intmed Muni Inv B	Muni State	6.09	5.59	4.83	4	2	0	1.00	800 321-7854
Nations FL Intmed Muni Inv C	Muni State	6.09	5.58	4.79	4	2	0	1.00	800 321-7854
Nations FL Intmed Muni Pr A	Muni State	6.91	6.20	5.40	3	2	0	0.50	800 321-7854
Nations FL Municipal Bond Inv A	Muni State	8.08	7.25		3	3	0	0.80	800 321-7854
Nations FL Municipal Bond Inv B	Muni State	7.37	6.62		4	3	0	1.35	800 321-7854
Nations FL Municipal Bond Inv C	Muni State	7.41	6.78		4	3	0	1.10	800 321-7854
Nations FL Municipal Bond Pr A	Muni State	8.27	7.45		2	3	0	0.60	800 321-7854
Nations GA Intmed Muni Inv A	Muni State	6.61	5.95	4.97	4	2	0	0.70	800 321-7854
Nations GA Intmed Muni Inv B	Muni State	6.00	5.55	4.66	4	2	0	1.00	800 321-7854
Nations GA Intmed Muni Inv C	Muni State	6.04	5.55	4.62	4	2	0	1.00	800 321-7854
Nations GA Intmed Muni Pr A	Muni State	6.82	6.17		4	2	0	0.50	800 321-7854
Nations GA Municipal Bond Inv A	Muni State	8.11	7.43		2	3	0	0.80	800 321-7854
Nations GA Municipal Bond Inv B	Muni State	7.42	6.89		3	3	0	1.35	800 321-7854
Nations GA Municipal Bond Inv C	Muni State	7.43	7.02		3	3	0	1.10	800 321-7854
Nations GA Municipal Bond Pr A	Muni State	8.32	7.72		2	3	0	0.60	800 321-7854
Nations Global Govt Inc Fund Inv B	Intl Bond	2.68	4.02		5	4	0	2.26	800 321-7854
Nations Global Govt Inc Fund Inv C	Intl Bond	2.71	4.29		5	4	0	1.76	800 321-7854
Nations Global Govt Inc Fund Pr A	Intl Bond	3.57	4.98		5	4	0	1.26	800 321-7854
Nations Government Sec Inv A	Government	10.39	6.44	5.11	3	3	0	0.85	800 321-7854
Nations Government Sec Inv B	Government	9.75	5.94	4.62	4	3	0	1.45	800 321-7854
Nations Government Sec Inv C	Government	9.76	6.02	4.64	3	3	0	1.30	800 321-7854
Nations Government Sec Pr A	Government	10.66	6.70	5.34	3	3	0	0.80	800 321-7854
Nations Intmed Muni Bond Invest A	Muni Natl	6.34	6.16		4	2	0	0.70	800 321-7854
Nations Intmed Muni Bond Invest B	Muni Natl	5.79	5.79		4	2	0	1.00	800 321-7854
Nations Intmed Muni Bond Invest C	Muni Natl	5.98	5.81		4	2	0	1.00	800 321-7854
Nations Intmed Muni Bond Pr A	Muni Natl	6.55	6.35		3	2	0	0.50	800 321-7854
Nations MD Intmed Muni Invest A	Muni State	6.08	5.53	4.79	4	2	0	0.70	800 321-7854
Nations MD Intmed Muni Invest B	Muni State	5.47	5.13	4.42	4	2	0	1.00	800 321-7854
Nations MD Intmed Muni Invest C	Muni State	5.47	5.11	4.38	4	2	0	1.00	800 321-7854
Nations MD Intmed Muni Pr A	Muni State	6.30	5.71		4	2	0	0.50	800 321-7854
Nations MD Muni Bond Invest A	Muni State	8.45	7.34		2	3	0	0.80	800 321-7854
Nations MD Muni Bond Invest B	Muni State	7.76	6.72		4	3	0	1.35	800 321-7854
Nations MD Muni Bond Invest C	Muni State	7.83	6.89		4	3	0	1.10	800 321-7854
Nations MD Muni Bond Pr A	Muni State	8.66	7.55		2	3	0	0.60	800 321-7854
Nations Muni Income Invest A	Muni Natl	8.60	8.04	6.20	2	3	0	0.60	800 321-7854
Nations Muni Income Invest B	Muni Natl	7.93	7.43	5.60	3	3	0	1.35	800 321-7854
Nations Muni Income Invest C	Muni Natl	8.02	7.59	5.70	3	3	0	1.10	800 321-7854
Nations Muni Income Pr A	Muni Natl	8.82	8.25	6.41	1	3	0	0.60	800 321-7854
Nations NC Intmed Muni Invest A	Muni State	5.99	5.80	4.94	3	2	0	0.70	800 321-7854
Nations NC Intmed Muni Invest B	Muni State	5.82	5.54	4.67	4	2	0	1.00	800 321-7854
Nations NC Intmed Muni Invest C	Muni State	5.77	5.53	4.62	4	2	0	1.00	800 321-7854
Nations NC Intmed Muni Pr A	Muni State	6.59	6.13	5.20	3	2	0	0.50	800 321-7854
Nations NC Muni Bd Invest A	Muni State	8.62	7.42		2	3	0	0.80	800 321-7854
Nations NC Muni Bd Invest B	Muni State	7.93	6.81		3	3	0	1.35	800 321-7854
Nations NC Muni Bd Invest C	Muni State	7.97	6.96		3	3	0	1.10	800 321-7854
Nations NC Muni Bd Pr A	Muni State	8.84	7.64		2	3	0	0.60	800 321-7854

Bond Fund Name	Objective	Annualized Return for			Rank		Max Load	Expense Ratio	Toll-Free Telephone
		1 Year	3 Years	5 Years	Overall	Risk			
Nations SC Intmed Muni Invest A	Muni State	6.37	5.96	5.22	3	2	0	0.70	800 321-7854
Nations SC Intmed Muni Invest B	Muni State	5.77	5.53	4.84	4	2	0	1.00	800 321-7854
Nations SC Intmed Muni Invest C	Muni State	5.77	5.54	4.80	4	2	0	1.00	800 321-7854
Nations SC Intmed Muni Pr A	Muni State	6.59	6.16	5.42	3	2	0	0.50	800 321-7854
Nations SC Muni Bd Invest A	Muni State	8.09	7.44	4.55	2	3	0	0.80	800 321-7854
Nations SC Muni Bd Invest B	Muni State	7.40	6.85		3	3	0	1.00	800 321-7854
Nations SC Muni Bd Invest C	Muni State	7.48	6.97		3	3	0	1.10	800 321-7854
Nations SC Muni Bd Pr A	Muni State	8.31	7.65		2	3	0	0.60	800 321-7854
Nations Short-Intmed Govt Invest A	Government	7.56	5.77	4.88	4	2	0	0.83	800 321-7854
Nations Short-Intmed Govt Invest B	Government	6.94	5.30		4	2	0	1.23	800 321-7854
Nations Short-Intmed Govt Invest C	Government	7.08	5.40	4.40	4	2	0	1.13	800 321-7854
Nations Short-Intmed Govt Pr A	Government	7.77	5.97	5.00	3	2	0	0.63	800 321-7854
Nations Short-Term Inc Invest A	Corp-Inv	6.33	5.89	5.23	3	1	0	0.76	800 321-7854
Nations Short-Term Inc Invest B	Corp-Inv	6.19	5.72		3	1	0	0.90	800 321-7854
Nations Short-Term Inc Invest C	Corp-Inv	6.19	5.73	5.06	3	1	0	0.90	800 321-7854
Nations Short-Term Inc Pr A	Corp-Inv	6.56	6.26	5.53	3	1	0	0.55	800 321-7854
Nations Short-Term Muni Inc Inv A	Muni Natl	4.77	4.49		3	1	0	0.60	800 321-7854
Nations Short-Term Muni Inc Inv B	Muni Natl	4.61	4.34		3	1	0	0.75	800 321-7854
Nations Short-Term Muni Inc Inv C	Muni Natl	4.62	4.35		3	1	0	0.75	800 321-7854
Nations Short-Term Muni Inc Pr A	Muni Natl	4.97	4.71		3	1	0	0.40	800 321-7854
Nations Strategic FI Invest A	Dvsfd Bond	9.08	6.53		3	3	0	0.91	800 321-7854
Nations Strategic FI Invest B	Dvsfd Bond	8.47	5.91	5.29	4	3	0	1.36	800 321-7854
Nations Strategic FI Invest C	Dvsfd Bond	8.60	6.16		4	3	0	1.21	800 321-7854
Nations Strategic FI Pr A	Dvsfd Bond	9.31	6.60	5.96	3	3	0	0.71	800 321-7854
Nations TN Intmed Muni Invest A	Muni State	6.29	5.91	5.04	3	2	0	0.70	800 321-7854
Nations TN Intmed Muni Invest B	Muni State	5.68	5.50	4.66	4	2	0	1.00	800 321-7854
Nations TN Intmed Muni Invest C	Muni State	5.69	5.54		4	2	0	1.00	800 321-7854
Nations TN Intmed Muni Pr A	Muni State	6.50	6.13	5.26	3	2	0	0.50	800 321-7854
Nations TN Muni Bd Invest A	Muni State	8.16	7.61		3	3	0	0.80	800 321-7854
Nations TN Muni Bd Invest B	Muni State	7.47	8.21		5	4	0	1.35	800 321-7854
Nations TN Muni Bd Invest C	Muni State	7.50	7.16		3	3	0	1.10	800 321-7854
Nations TN Muni Bd Pr A	Muni State	8.38	7.84		2	3	0	0.60	800 321-7854
Nations TX Intmed Muni Invest A	Muni State	6.33	5.88	5.54	3	2	0	0.70	800 321-7854
Nations TX Intmed Muni Invest B	Muni State	5.73	5.46	4.74	4	2	0	1.00	800 321-7854
Nations TX Intmed Muni Invest C	Muni State	5.73	5.48		4	2	0	1.00	800 321-7854
Nations TX Intmed Muni Pr A	Muni State	6.55	6.08	5.11	3	2	0	0.50	800 321-7854
Nations TX Municipal Bond Inv A	Muni State	8.75	7.65		2	4	0	0.80	800 321-7854
Nations TX Municipal Bond Inv B	Muni State	8.06	7.04		4	4	0	1.35	800 321-7854
Nations TX Municipal Bond Inv C	Muni State	7.75	7.07		4	4	0	1.10	800 321-7854
Nations TX Municipal Bond Pr A	Muni State	8.96	7.93		2	4	0	0.60	800 321-7854
Nations US Govt Bond Fund Inv C	Government	8.38					0	1.77	800 321-7854
Nations US Govt Bond Fund Pr B	Government	8.87					0		800 321-7854
Nations VA Intmed Muni Invest A	Muni State	6.37	5.57	4.67	4	2	0	0.70	800 321-7854
Nations VA Intmed Muni Invest B	Muni State	5.75	5.28		4	2	0	1.00	800 321-7854
Nations VA Intmed Muni Invest C	Muni State	5.75	5.28		4	2	0	1.00	800 321-7854
Nations VA Intmed Muni Pr A	Muni State	6.57	5.91	5.00	3	2	0	0.50	800 321-7854
Nations VA Municipal Bond Inv A	Muni State	8.81	7.81		2	3	0	0.70	800 321-7854
Nations VA Municipal Bond Inv B	Muni State	8.12	7.19		3	3	0	1.35	800 321-7854
Nations VA Municipal Bond Inv C	Muni State	8.13	7.34		3	3	0	1.10	800 321-7854
Nations VA Municipal Bond Pr A	Muni State	9.03	8.02		2	3	0	0.60	800 321-7854
Nationwide Bond Fund D	Corp-Inv	11.29	7.81	6.31	3	5	4.5	0.72	800 848-0920
Nationwide Intmed US Govt Bond D	Government	10.42	7.39	6.42	3	3	0	1.07	800 848-0920
Nationwide Long-Term US Govt Bond D	Government	11.34	7.75	6.60	2	4	0	1.60	800 848-0920
Nationwide Tax-Free Income Fund D	Muni Natl	8.13	7.19	5.37	2	3	0	0.96	800 848-0920
ND Tax-Free Fund	Muni State	2.42	5.77	4.16	3	2	0	1.30	800 345-2363
Neuberger&Berman Ltd Mat Bond Fd	Corp-Inv	6.45	6.16	5.22	4	1	0	0.70	800 877-9700
Neuberger&Berman Ltd Mat Bond Tr	Corp-Inv	6.24	6.05		4	4	0	0.70	800 877-9700
Neuberger&Berman Muni Secs	Muni Natl	6.87	6.04	4.92	3	2	0	0.62	800 877-9700

Bond Fund Name	Objective	Annualized Return for			Rank		Max Load	Expense Ratio	Toll-Free Telephone
		1 Year	3 Years	5 Years	Overall	Risk			
New England Adjust Rate US Govt A	Govt-Mtg	5.28	5.75	4.90	3	1	1	0.70	800 225-5478
New England Adjust Rate US Govt B	Govt-Mtg	4.50	5.01		4	1	0	1.45	800 225-5478
New England Bond Income A	Corp-Inv	11.33	9.00	7.70	2	5	5.75	1.04	800 225-5478
New England Bond Income B	Corp-Inv	10.51	8.19		2	5	0	1.83	800 225-5478
New England Bond Income C	Corp-Inv	10.24	8.09		2	5	0	1.83	800 225-5478
New England Bond Income Y	Corp-Inv	11.59	9.26		1	5	0	0.83	800 225-5478
New England Govt Securities Fund A	Government	12.17	7.37	6.10	3	5	4.5	1.36	800 225-5478
New England Govt Securities Fund B	Government	11.34	6.61		4	5	0	2.07	800 225-5478
New England Govt Securities Fund Y	Government	12.47	7.63		3	5	0		800 225-5478
New England High-Income Fund A	Corp-HY	11.24	12.27	9.22	2	4	4.5	1.36	800 225-5478
New England High-Income Fund B	Corp-HY	10.42	11.51		2	4	0	2.15	800 225-5478
New England Intmed Term CA TF A	Muni CA	6.65	7.38	5.81	3	2	2.5	0.85	800 225-5478
New England Intmed Term CA TF B	Muni CA	5.87	6.62		3	2	0	1.60	800 225-5478
New England Limited Term US Govt A	Government	7.53	5.91	4.91	4	2	3	1.28	800 225-5478
New England Limited Term US Govt B	Government	6.85	5.19		4	2	0	1.93	800 225-5478
New England Limited Term US Govt C	Government	6.85	5.18		5	2	0	1.93	800 225-5478
New England Limited Term US Govt Y	Government	7.98	6.24		4	2	0	0.93	800 225-5478
New England MA Tax Free Income A	Muni State	7.86	7.40	5.54	3	3	4.25	1.00	800 225-5478
New England MA Tax Free Income B	Muni State	7.18	6.70		4	3	0	1.65	800 225-5478
New England Municipal Income A	Muni Natl	8.18	7.39	5.67	2	3	4.5	0.93	800 225-5478
New England Municipal Income B	Muni Natl	7.38	6.65		3	3	0	1.69	800 225-5478
New England Strategic Income A	Dvsfd Bond	5.73	12.18		2	5	4.5	1.18	800 225-5478
New England Strategic Income B	Dvsfd Bond	4.87	11.33		3	5	0	1.97	800 225-5478
New England Strategic Income C	Dvsfd Bond	4.87	11.30		3	5	0	1.97	800 225-5478
New England Tax Free Fund of NY A	Muni NY	6.91	7.35	5.79	2	3	2.5	0.85	800 225-5478
New England Tax Free Fund of NY B	Muni NY	6.13	6.59		3	3	0	1.60	800 225-5478
Nicholas Income Fund	Corp-HY	9.60	11.48	9.62	1	3	0	0.50	800 227-5987
Nicholas-Applegate Fully Dis FI	Corp-Inv	10.42					0	0.45	800 551-8045
Nicholas-Applegate Govt Income A	Government	11.78	7.11	6.61	3	5	4.75	0.90	800 551-8045
Nicholas-Applegate Govt Income B	Government	11.14	6.76	6.04	3	5	0	1.29	800 551-8045
Nicholas-Applegate Govt Income C	Government	11.08	6.67	5.99	3	5	0	1.30	800 551-8045
Nicholas-Applegate Govt Income Q	Government	11.45	4.35	6.59	3	5	0	0.88	800 551-8045
Nicholas-Applegate High Yield Bd I	Corp-HY	18.79					0	0.75	800 551-8045
Nicholas-Applegate Sh-Int Instl FI	Corp-Inv	6.95					0	0.35	800 551-8045
Nicholas-Applegate Strategic Inc I	Corp-HY	9.68					0	0.77	800 551-8045
North American Invest Quality Bd A	Corp-Inv	10.50	7.45	5.84	2	4	4.75	1.25	800 872-8037
North American Invest Quality Bd B	Corp-Inv	9.77	6.81		3	4	0	1.90	800 872-8037
North American Invest Quality Bd C	Corp-Inv	9.78	6.83		3	4	0	1.90	800 872-8037
North American National Muni A	Muni Natl	8.79	8.00		2	3	4.75	0.99	800 872-8037
North American National Muni B	Muni Natl	7.89	7.12		3	3	0	1.84	800 872-8037
North American National Muni C	Muni Natl	7.89	7.12		3	3	0	1.84	800 872-8037
North American Strategic Income A	Dvsfd Bond	7.76	11.64		2	4	4.75	1.50	800 872-8037
North American Strategic Income B	Dvsfd Bond	7.03	10.73		2	5	0	2.15	800 872-8037
North American Strategic Income C	Dvsfd Bond	7.50	11.10		3	4	0	2.15	800 872-8037
North American US Govt Secs A	Govt-Mtg	8.35	6.17	5.70	3	3	4.75	1.25	800 872-8037
North American US Govt Secs B	Govt-Mtg	7.41	5.46		5	3	0	1.90	800 872-8037
North American US Govt Secs C	Govt-Mtg	7.42	5.64		5	2	0	1.90	800 872-8037
Northeast Investors Trust	Corp-HY	12.63	15.24	13.55	1	3	0	0.64	800 225-6704
Northern Fixed Income Fund	Corp-Inv	10.31	7.64		3	4	0	0.90	800 595-9111
Northern Florida Intmed TE Fund	Muni State	6.64					0	2.31	800 595-9111
Northern Intermediate Tax Exempt Fd	Muni Natl	5.57	5.07		4	2	0	1.07	800 595-9111
Northern Intl Fixed Income Fund	Intl Bond	3.46	3.54		5	5	0	1.96	800 595-9111
Northern Tax Exempt Fund	Muni Natl	8.14	7.21		3	4	0	1.10	800 595-9111
Northern US Government Fund	Government	7.42	5.93		4	2	0	1.09	800 595-9111
Northstar Government Secs A	Government	9.01	7.68		4	5	4.75	1.13	800 595-7827
Northstar Government Secs B	Government	9.01	6.79		5	5	0	1.84	800 595-7827
Northstar Government Secs C	Government	8.26	6.95		5	5	0	1.80	800 595-7827
Northstar Government Secs T	Government	8.68	7.44	5.25	5	5	0	0.20	800 595-7827

Bond Fund Name	Objective	Annualized Return for			Rank		Max Load	Expense Ratio	Toll-Free Telephone
		1 Year	3 Years	5 Years	Overall	Risk			
Northstar High Total Return A	Corp-HY	10.28	13.91		2	5	4.75	1.11	800 595-7827
Northstar High Total Return B	Corp-HY	9.49	13.42		3	5	0	2.05	800 595-7827
Northstar High Total Return C	Corp-HY	9.49	13.08		2	5	0	1.86	800 595-7827
Northstar High Yield Fund A	Corp-HY	10.13	11.80		1	3	4.75	1.08	800 595-7827
Northstar High Yield Fund B	Corp-HY	9.45	11.05		1	3	0	1.78	800 595-7827
Northstar High Yield Fund C	Corp-HY	9.33	11.01		1	3	0	1.66	800 595-7827
Northstar High Yield Fund T	Corp-HY	9.79	11.50	9.43	2	3	0	1.47	800 595-7827
Northstar Strategic Income A	Corp-Inv	−0.47	6.64		5	5	4.75	1.41	800 595-7827
Northstar Strategic Income B	Corp-Inv	−1.29	5.88		5	5	0	2.12	800 595-7827
Northstar Strategic Income C	Corp-Inv	−1.22	5.82		5	5	0	2.12	800 595-7827
Northstar Strategic Income T	Corp-Inv	−1.10	6.03		4	5	0	1.93	800 595-7827
Northwest ID Tax Exempt	Muni State	6.90	6.01	5.58	3	2	0	0.40	800 728-8762
Norwest CO Tax Free A	Muni State	9.31	8.49		2	3	3.75	1.14	800 338-1348
Norwest CO Tax Free B	Muni State	8.49	7.69		3	3	0	2.15	800 338-1348
Norwest CO Tax Free I	Muni State	9.34	8.52		2	3	0	1.13	800 338-1348
Norwest Diversified Bond Fund I	Dvsfd Bond	12.62	7.43	6.08	3	4	0	0.77	800 338-1348
Norwest Intmed Government Income A	Government	10.06			4	3	3.25	0.80	800 338-1348
Norwest Intmed Government Income B	Government	8.68					0	1.85	800 338-1348
Norwest Intmed Government Income I	Government	9.43	6.50		4	3	0	0.72	800 338-1348
Norwest MN Tax Free A	Muni State	9.03	7.65	6.14	2	3	3.75	1.21	800 338-1348
Norwest MN Tax Free B	Muni State	8.18	6.84		4	3	0	2.21	800 338-1348
Norwest MN Tax Free I	Muni State	9.10	7.82		2	3		1.23	800 338-1348
Norwest Stable Income Fund A	Corp-Inv	6.28	6.04		4	1	1.5	0.87	800 338-1348
Norwest Stable Income Fund B	Corp-Inv	4.98					0	2.89	800 338-1348
Norwest Stable Income Fund I	Corp-Inv	5.80	5.88		4	1	0	0.79	800 338-1348
Norwest Strategic Income Fund	Dvsfd Bond	13.72	11.41		2	4	0	0.98	800 338-1348
Norwest TF Income Bond A	Muni Natl	9.67	8.49		2	3	3.25	1.06	800 338-1348
Norwest TF Income Bond B	Muni Natl	8.85	7.67		3	3	0	2.15	800 338-1348
Norwest TF Income Bond I	Muni Natl	9.57	8.48		2	3	0	1.03	800 338-1348
Norwest Total Return Bond A	Dvsfd Bond	9.31	6.53		3	3	3.75	1.31	800 338-1348
Norwest Total Return Bond B	Dvsfd Bond	8.49	5.75		4	3	0	2.37	800 338-1348
Norwest Total Return Bond I	Dvsfd Bond	9.31	6.53		3	3	0	1.05	800 338-1348
Nuveen CA Insured Municipal Bond A	Muni CA	8.06	7.49		3	4	4.5	0.95	800 621-7227
Nuveen CA Insured Municipal Bond C	Muni CA	7.56	6.91		4	4	0	1.70	800 621-7227
Nuveen CA Insured Municipal Bond R	Muni CA	8.25	7.75	5.99	3	4	0	0.70	800 621-7227
Nuveen CA Municipal Bond Fund A	Muni CA	8.30	7.82		2	3	4.5	0.95	800 621-7227
Nuveen CA Municipal Bond Fund C	Muni CA	7.70	7.14		3	3	0	1.70	800 621-7227
Nuveen CA Municipal Bond Fund R	Muni CA	8.52	8.12	6.12	1	3	0	0.70	800 621-7227
Nuveen Flagship All-American Muni A	Muni Natl	8.98	8.45	6.60	2	3	4.2	0.80	800 621-7227
Nuveen Flagship All-American Muni C	Muni Natl	8.32	7.82	6.00	3	3		1.53	800 621-7227
Nuveen Flagship AZ Municipal Bond A	Muni State	8.70	7.93	6.31	3	4	4.2	0.44	800 621-7227
Nuveen Flagship AZ Municipal Bond C	Muni State	8.13	7.18		4	4		1.97	800 621-7227
Nuveen Flagship AZ Municipal Bond R	Muni State	8.93	7.54	6.21	2	3	0	0.75	800 621-7227
Nuveen Flagship CO Municipal Bond A	Muni State	10.01	8.81	6.97	3	4	4.2	0.49	800 621-7227
Nuveen Flagship CT Municipal Bond A	Muni State	8.34	7.50	5.87	1	3	4.2	0.66	800 621-7227
Nuveen Flagship CT Municipal Bond C	Muni State	7.65	6.84		3	3	0		800 621-7227
Nuveen Flagship FL Intmed Muni Bd A	Muni State	7.80	6.47		4	3	4.2	1.18	800 621-7227
Nuveen Flagship FL Intmed Muni Bd C	Muni State	7.25	5.85		5	3	0	1.71	800 621-7227
Nuveen Flagship FL Municipal Bond A	Muni State	8.08	6.93	5.62	3	3	4.2	0.84	800 621-7227
Nuveen Flagship FL Municipal Bond C	Muni State	7.40	7.20		4	4	0	1.79	800 621-7227
Nuveen Flagship FL Municipal Bond R	Muni State	8.12	7.20	5.84	2	3	0	0.81	800 621-7227
Nuveen Flagship GA Municipal Bond A	Muni State	9.12	8.23	6.32	3	4	4.2	0.62	800 621-7227
Nuveen Flagship GA Municipal Bond C	Muni State	8.55	7.67		3	4	0		800 621-7227
Nuveen Flagship Intmed Muni Bond A	Muni Natl	8.35	7.73	6.32	2	3	3		800 621-7227
Nuveen Flagship KS Municipal Bond A	Muni State	8.91	7.86	5.67	2	3	4.2	0.63	800 621-7227
Nuveen Flagship KY Municipal Bond A	Muni State	7.93	7.28	5.99	2	3	4.2	0.67	800 621-7227
Nuveen Flagship KY Municipal Bond C	Muni State	7.36	6.69		3	3	0	1.90	800 621-7227
Nuveen Flagship LA Municipal Bond A	Muni State	8.65	8.40	6.50	2	3	4.2	0.61	800 621-7227

Bond Fund Name	Objective	Annualized Return for			Rank		Max Load	Expense Ratio	Toll-Free Telephone
		1 Year	3 Years	5 Years	Overall	Risk			
Nuveen Flagship LA Municipal Bond C	Muni State	7.99	7.77		3	3	0		800 621-7227
Nuveen Flagship Ltd-Term Muni Bd A	Muni Natl	6.37	5.72	5.01	3	2	2.5	0.80	800 621-7227
Nuveen Flagship MI Municipal Bond A	Muni State	8.05	7.43	5.88	1	3	4.2	0.84	800 621-7227
Nuveen Flagship MI Municipal Bond C	Muni State	7.38	6.82		4	3	0	1.52	800 621-7227
Nuveen Flagship MO Municipal Bond A	Muni State	8.62	7.56	5.96	2	3	4.2	0.55	800 621-7227
Nuveen Flagship MO Municipal Bond C	Muni State	7.94	7.02		3	3	0		800 621-7227
Nuveen Flagship NC Municipal Bond A	Muni State	8.06	7.21	5.44	3	3	4.2	0.95	800 621-7227
Nuveen Flagship NC Municipal Bond C	Muni State	7.45	6.58		5	3	0		800 621-7227
Nuveen Flagship NJ Intmed Muni Bd A	Muni Natl	6.66	6.13	5.24	3	2	3	0.89	800 621-7227
Nuveen Flagship NJ Municipal Bond A	Muni State	8.03	7.08		2	2	4.5	1.01	800 621-7227
Nuveen Flagship NJ Municipal Bond C	Muni State	7.38	6.42		3	2	0	1.56	800 621-7227
Nuveen Flagship NJ Municipal Bond R	Muni State	8.17	7.32	6.30	1	2	0	0.75	800 621-7227
Nuveen Flagship NM Municipal Bond A	Muni State	9.54	8.12	6.28	2	4	4.2	1.30	800 621-7227
Nuveen Flagship NY Municipal Bond A	Muni NY	8.98	7.87		2	3	4.5	0.92	800 621-7227
Nuveen Flagship NY Municipal Bond C	Muni NY	8.45	7.35		3	3	0	1.67	800 621-7227
Nuveen Flagship NY Municipal Bond R	Muni NY	9.23	8.13	6.51	1	3	0	0.71	800 621-7227
Nuveen Flagship OH Municipal Bond A	Muni State	7.64	6.84	5.54	2	3	4.2	0.85	800 621-7227
Nuveen Flagship OH Municipal Bond C	Muni State	7.09	6.34		4	3	0	1.51	800 621-7227
Nuveen Flagship OH Municipal Bond R	Muni State	7.87	7.05	5.89	2	3	0	0.65	800 621-7227
Nuveen Flagship PA Municipal Bond A	Muni State	9.20	7.86	6.19	1	3	4.2	0.63	800 621-7227
Nuveen Flagship PA Municipal Bond C	Muni State	8.55	7.28		3	3	0	1.87	800 621-7227
Nuveen Flagship PA Municipal Bond R	Muni State	9.46	8.38	6.54	1	3	0	0.75	800 621-7227
Nuveen Flagship SC Municipal Bond A	Muni State	9.16	7.75		1	4	4.2		800 621-7227
Nuveen Flagship TN Municipal Bond A	Muni State	8.04	7.17	5.65	3	3	4.2	0.88	800 621-7227
Nuveen Flagship TN Municipal Bond C	Muni State	7.51	6.58		4	3	0	2.30	800 621-7227
Nuveen Flagship VA Municipal Bond A	Muni State	8.80	7.66	6.07	1	3	4.2	0.68	800 621-7227
Nuveen Flagship VA Municipal Bond C	Muni State	8.11	7.21	5.81	1	3	0	1.84	800 621-7227
Nuveen Flagship VA Municipal Bond R	Muni State	8.94	8.04	6.41	1	3	0	0.75	800 621-7227
Nuveen Flagship WI Municipal Bond A	Muni State	9.64	7.57		3	3	4.2		800 621-7227
Nuveen Insured Muni Bond Fund A	Muni Natl	8.03	7.23		3	4	4.5	0.84	800 621-7227
Nuveen Insured Muni Bond Fund C	Muni Natl	7.36	6.72		5	4	0	1.39	800 621-7227
Nuveen Insured Muni Bond Fund R	Muni Natl	8.27	7.53	6.10	3	4	0	0.65	800 621-7227
Nuveen MA Insured Municipal Bond A	Muni State	7.20	6.28		4	3	4.5		800 621-7227
Nuveen MA Insured Municipal Bond C	Muni State	6.61	5.61		4	3	0		800 621-7227
Nuveen MA Insured Municipal Bond R	Muni State	7.39	6.54	5.57	3	3	0	0.83	800 621-7227
Nuveen MA Municipal Bond Fund A	Muni State	7.27	6.70		3	2	4.5	1.01	800 621-7227
Nuveen MA Municipal Bond Fund C	Muni State	6.74	5.99		3	2	0	1.74	800 621-7227
Nuveen MA Municipal Bond Fund R	Muni State	7.49	6.91	5.81	2	2	0	0.75	800 621-7227
Nuveen MD Municipal Bond Fund A	Muni State	7.53	6.55		3	2	4.5	1.12	800 621-7227
Nuveen MD Municipal Bond Fund C	Muni State	6.92	5.81		3	2	0	1.87	800 621-7227
Nuveen MD Municipal Bond Fund R	Muni State	7.70	6.74	5.60	2	2	0	0.75	800 621-7227
Nuveen Municipal Bond Fund A	Muni Natl	8.10	7.30		3	3	4.5	0.77	800 621-7227
Nuveen Municipal Bond Fund C	Muni Natl	7.51	6.75		3	3	0	1.32	800 621-7227
Nuveen Municipal Bond Fund R	Muni Natl	8.31	7.55	6.37	2	3	0	0.58	800 621-7227
Nuveen NY Insured Municipal Bond A	Muni NY	7.51	6.72		4	3	4.5		800 621-7227
Nuveen NY Insured Municipal Bond C	Muni NY	6.91	5.98		5	3	0		800 621-7227
Nuveen NY Insured Municipal Bond R	Muni NY	7.69	6.91	5.63	3	3	0	0.68	800 621-7227
Ocean State Tax Ex (RI)	Muni State	6.30	6.43	5.41	3	2	4	0.98	800 992-2207
One Group Income Bond Fid	Corp-Inv	7.99	6.91	5.86	4	3	0	0.61	800 480-4111
One Group LA Tax Free Fund	Muni State	6.00	6.00	5.08	3	2	4.5	0.87	800 480-4111
One Group Ltd Volatility Fid	Government	6.65	6.17	5.44	3	2	3	0.53	800 480-4111
One Group Ltd Volatility Inv A	Government	6.38	5.89	5.20	3	2	3	0.76	800 480-4111
One Group OH Muni Fund Inv A	Muni State	7.12	6.64	5.05	3	2	4.5	0.79	800 480-4111
Oppenheimer Bond Fund A	Corp-Inv	10.34	7.99	6.71	2	3	4.75	1.27	800 525-7048
Oppenheimer Bond Fund B	Corp-Inv	9.50	7.14	5.89	3	3	0	2.02	800 525-7048
Oppenheimer Bond Fund C	Corp-Inv	9.49					0	2.02	800 525-7048
Oppenheimer CA Municipal Fund A	Muni CA	8.75	8.05	6.22	3	4	4.75	0.94	800 525-7048
Oppenheimer CA Municipal Fund B	Muni CA	7.83	7.25	5.36	3	3	0	1.70	800 525-7048

Bond Fund Name	Objective	Annualized Return for			Rank		Max Load	Expense Ratio	Toll-Free Telephone
		1 Year	3 Years	5 Years	Overall	Risk			
Oppenheimer CA Municipal Fund C	Muni CA	8.14	6.21	4.88	4	4	0	1.70	800 525-7048
Oppenheimer Champion Income A	Corp-HY	11.30	12.11	10.17	1	3	4.75	1.10	800 525-7048
Oppenheimer Champion Income B	Corp-HY	10.47					0	1.86	800 525-7048
Oppenheimer Champion Income C	Corp-HY	10.46	11.19		1	3	0	1.84	800 525-7048
Oppenheimer FL Municipal Fund A	Muni State	8.56	7.59		1	3	4.75	1.15	800 525-7048
Oppenheimer FL Municipal Fund B	Muni State	7.63	6.77		3	3	0	1.89	800 525-7048
Oppenheimer High Yield Fund A	Corp-HY	12.34	12.58	10.18	1	3	4.75	1.01	800 525-7048
Oppenheimer High Yield Fund B	Corp-HY	11.49	11.69	8.25	1	3	0	1.80	800 525-7048
Oppenheimer High Yield Fund C	Corp-HY	11.39					0	1.82	800 525-7048
Oppenheimer Insured Municipal A	Muni Natl	8.76	7.90	5.84	3	3	4.75	0.96	800 525-7048
Oppenheimer Insured Municipal B	Muni Natl	7.95	7.07	4.99	4	4	0	1.72	800 525-7048
Oppenheimer International Bond A	Intl Bond	−0.64	10.17		4	4	4.75	1.81	800 525-7048
Oppenheimer International Bond B	Intl Bond	−1.39	9.60		4	5	0	2.36	800 525-7048
Oppenheimer International Bond C	Intl Bond	−1.28	9.64		4	4	0	2.36	800 525-7048
Oppenheimer Intmed Muni Fund A	Muni Natl	7.82	7.32	5.73	1	2	3.5	0.97	800 525-7048
Oppenheimer Intmed Muni Fund C	Muni Natl	6.95	6.49		3	2	0	1.75	800 525-7048
Oppenheimer Limited Term Govt A	Government	6.70	6.52	5.59	3	1	3.75	0.87	800 525-7048
Oppenheimer Limited Term Govt B	Government	5.91	5.75	4.79	4	1	0	1.64	800 525-7048
Oppenheimer Limited Term Govt C	Government	5.81	5.67		5	1	0	1.63	800 525-7048
Oppenheimer Limited Term NY Muni B	Muni NY	6.18					0	1.53	800 525-7048
Oppenheimer Limited Term NY Muni C	Muni NY	6.92					0	1.51	800 525-7048
Oppenheimer Main Street CA TE A	Muni CA	9.49	8.43	6.68	2	3	4.75	0.53	800 525-7048
Oppenheimer Main Street CA TE B	Muni CA	8.31	7.37		3	4	0	1.57	800 525-7048
Oppenheimer Municipal Bond Fund A	Muni Natl	8.42	8.03	6.01	2	3	4.75	0.88	800 525-7048
Oppenheimer Municipal Bond Fund B	Muni Natl	7.50	7.17	4.73	3	3	0	1.65	800 525-7048
Oppenheimer Municipal Bond Fund C	Muni Natl	7.50					4.75	1.67	800 525-7048
Oppenheimer NJ Municipal Fund A	Muni State	8.83	7.53		2	3	4.75	1.24	800 525-7048
Oppenheimer NJ Municipal Fund B	Muni State	8.02	6.69		3	3	0	2.00	800 525-7048
Oppenheimer NJ Municipal Fund C	Muni State	8.02					0	1.98	800 525-7048
Oppenheimer NY Municipal Fund A	Muni NY	8.11	7.57	5.49	2	3	4.75	5.01	800 525-7048
Oppenheimer NY Municipal Fund B	Muni NY	7.38	6.77	4.88	4	3	0	1.64	800 525-7048
Oppenheimer NY Municipal Fund C	Muni NY	7.38					0	1.66	800 525-7048
Oppenheimer PA Municipal Fund A	Muni State	7.82	7.32	5.63	2	3	4.75	0.90	800 525-7048
Oppenheimer PA Municipal Fund B	Muni State	7.10	6.50	4.82	3	3	0	1.65	800 525-7048
Oppenheimer PA Municipal Fund C	Muni State	7.02					0	1.66	800 525-7048
Oppenheimer Strat Income A	Dvsfd Bond	7.88	10.65	8.39	2	2	4.75	0.93	800 525-7048
Oppenheimer Strat Income B	Dvsfd Bond	7.06	9.82	7.64	2	2	0	1.72	800 525-7048
Oppenheimer US Government Trust A	Government	8.64	7.51	6.49	2	3	4.75	1.05	800 525-7048
Oppenheimer US Government Trust B	Government	7.89					0	1.84	800 525-7048
Oppenheimer US Government Trust C	Government	7.90	6.74		3	3	0	1.81	800 525-7048
OVB Government Securities A	Government	10.74	7.39		3	4	0	1.11	800 545-6331
OVB Government Securities B	Government	10.35	7.13		3	4	0	1.36	800 545-6331
OVB West Virginia Tax Exempt A	Muni State	8.01	7.14		3	3	0	0.78	800 545-6331
OVB West Virginia Tax Exempt B	Muni State	7.84	6.90		3	3	0	1.03	800 545-6331
Pacific Advisors Govt Securities	Government	19.72	8.42	7.21	3	5	4.75	1.65	800 282-6693
Pacific Horizon CA Tax Ex Bond	Muni CA	8.77	7.43	5.64	3	4	4.5	0.91	800 332-3863
Pacific Horizon Corporate Bond Fund	Corp-Inv	11.38	7.61	6.99	3	5	4.5	0.85	800 332-3863
Pacific Horizon Intmed Bond SRF Cl	Corp-Inv	7.53	5.54	5.04	4	3	0	0.90	800 332-3863
Pacific Horizon US Govt Securities	Govt-Mtg	8.39	7.01	5.18	3	2	4.5	0.75	800 332-3863
PaineWebber CA Tax-Free Income A	Muni CA	8.84	10.25	7.06	3	5	4	1.00	800 647-1568
PaineWebber CA Tax-Free Income B	Muni CA	7.96	6.45	4.38	5	4	0	1.77	800 647-1568
PaineWebber CA Tax-Free Income C	Muni CA	8.16	6.67	4.53	4	4	0	1.51	800 647-1568
PaineWebber Global Income A	Intl Bond	6.02	6.66	5.82	3	2	4	1.21	800 647-1568
PaineWebber Global Income B	Intl Bond	5.19	5.85	5.37	2	2	0	1.99	800 647-1568
PaineWebber Global Income C	Intl Bond	5.45	6.16	5.31	2	2	0	1.69	800 647-1568
PaineWebber Global Income Y	Intl Bond	6.26	6.47	4.03	4	2	0	0.94	800 647-1568
PaineWebber High Income A	Corp-HY	11.74	12.88	8.06	2	5	4	0.98	800 647-1568
PaineWebber High Income B	Corp-HY	10.75	12.06	7.36	2	5	0	1.75	800 647-1568

Bond Fund Name	Objective	Annualized Return for			Rank		Max Load	Expense Ratio	Toll-Free Telephone
		1 Year	3 Years	5 Years	Overall	Risk			
PaineWebber High Income C	Corp-HY	11.18	12.16	7.42	2	5	0	1.48	800 647-1568
PaineWebber Invest Grade Inc A	Corp-Inv	12.96	9.38	7.51	2	4	4.5	1.03	800 647-1568
PaineWebber Invest Grade Inc B	Corp-Inv	11.68	8.53	6.70	2	4	0	1.78	800 647-1568
PaineWebber Invest Grade Inc C	Corp-Inv	12.08	8.75	6.91	2	4	0	1.53	800 647-1568
PaineWebber Low Dur US Govt Inc A	Government	7.67	6.99	4.73	3	1	3	1.04	800 647-1568
PaineWebber Low Dur US Govt Inc B	Government	6.67	6.08		3	1	0	1.87	800 647-1568
PaineWebber Low Dur US Govt Inc C	Government	7.00	6.34		4	1	0	1.64	800 647-1568
PaineWebber Municipal High Income A	Muni Natl	10.22	8.79	6.20	1	2	4	1.22	800 647-1568
PaineWebber Municipal High Income B	Muni Natl	9.34	8.00	5.33	1	2	0	1.96	800 647-1568
PaineWebber Municipal High Income C	Muni Natl	9.64	8.32		1	2	0	1.70	800 647-1568
PaineWebber National Tax-Free Inc A	Muni Natl	8.64	6.96	5.18	3	4	4	0.94	800 647-1568
PaineWebber National Tax-Free Inc B	Muni Natl	7.77	6.12	4.32	5	4	0	1.70	800 647-1568
PaineWebber National Tax-Free Inc C	Muni Natl	8.06	6.39	4.59	5	4	0	1.45	800 647-1568
PaineWebber NY Tax-Free Income A	Muni NY	9.28	7.73	5.54	3	3	4	1.02	800 647-1568
PaineWebber NY Tax-Free Income B	Muni NY	8.56	6.98	4.72	4	3	0	1.77	800 647-1568
PaineWebber NY Tax-Free Income C	Muni NY	8.72	7.17	4.92	3	3	0	1.52	800 647-1568
PaineWebber PACE Global Fxd Inc	Intl Bond	5.58					0	0.95	800 647-1568
PaineWebber PACE Gov Sec Fxd Inc	Government	8.99					0	0.85	800 647-1568
PaineWebber PACE Intmed Fxd Inc	Corp-Inv	8.09					0	0.84	800 647-1568
PaineWebber PACE Muni Fixed Inc	Muni Natl	6.94					0	0.85	800 647-1568
PaineWebber PACE Strategic Fxd Inc	Corp-Inv	11.72					0	0.85	800 647-1568
PaineWebber Strategic Income B	Dvsfd Bond	8.40	10.01		2	3	0	2.43	800 647-1568
PaineWebber Strategic Income C	Dvsfd Bond	8.68	10.32		2	3	0	2.17	800 647-1568
PaineWebber US Government Income A	Govt-Mtg	10.40	6.56	4.19	4	4	4	0.94	800 647-1568
PaineWebber US Government Income B	Govt-Mtg	9.52	5.78	3.28	5	4	0	1.69	800 647-1568
PaineWebber US Government Income C	Govt-Mtg	9.83	6.06	3.61	5	4	0	1.44	800 647-1568
Parkstone Bond Fund Institutional	Corp-Inv	10.10	7.57	6.44	2	3	0	0.48	800 451-8377
Parkstone Bond Fund Investor A	Corp-Inv	9.87	7.20	6.01	3	4	4.5	0.60	800 451-8377
Parkstone Bond Fund Investor B	Corp-Inv	9.15	6.55		4	3	0	0.98	800 451-8377
Parkstone Bond Fund Investor C	Corp-Inv	9.09	6.56	5.25	4	3	0	0.98	800 451-8377
Parkstone Government Income Instl	Government	8.56	7.32	6.32	1	2	0	0.38	800 451-8377
Parkstone Government Income Inv A	Government	8.30	7.05		2	2	4.5	0.51	800 451-8377
Parkstone Government Income Inv B	Government	7.41	6.23		3	2	0	0.89	800 451-8377
Parkstone Government Income Inv C	Government	7.46	6.26	4.89	3	2	0	0.89	800 451-8377
Parkstone Intmed Govt Instl	Government	7.50	5.84	4.60	4	2	0	0.49	800 451-8377
Parkstone Intmed Govt Inv A	Government	7.22	5.60	4.86	4	2	4.5	0.62	800 451-8377
Parkstone Intmed Govt Inv B	Government	6.44	4.83		5	2	0	1.00	800 451-8377
Parkstone Intmed Govt Inv C	Government	6.47	4.77	3.96	5	3	0	1.00	800 451-8377
Parkstone Ltd Maturity Instl	Corp-Inv	5.92	5.66	4.91	4	1	0	0.42	800 451-8377
Parkstone Ltd Maturity Inv A	Corp-Inv	5.66	5.36	4.75	4	1	4.5	0.55	800 451-8377
Parkstone Ltd Maturity Inv B	Corp-Inv	4.87	4.56		5	1	0	0.92	800 451-8377
Parkstone Ltd Maturity Inv C	Corp-Inv	4.85	4.60	3.55	5	1	0	0.92	800 451-8377
Parkstone MI Muni Bond Instl	Muni State	6.49	5.90	5.00	4	2	0	0.38	800 451-8377
Parkstone MI Muni Bond Inv A	Muni State	6.22	5.66	4.96	4	2	4.5	0.50	800 451-8377
Parkstone MI Muni Bond Inv B	Muni State	5.33	5.13		5	2	0	0.88	800 451-8377
Parkstone Municipal Bond Instl	Muni Natl	5.83	5.42	4.72	4	2	0	0.40	800 451-8377
Parkstone Municipal Bond Inv A	Muni Natl	5.67	5.28	4.68	4	3	4	0.52	800 451-8377
Parkstone Municipal Bond Inv B	Muni Natl	4.79	4.36		5	3	0	0.90	800 451-8377
Parnassus Income-CA Tax Exempt	Muni CA	8.44	8.11	6.49	2	3	0	0.35	800 999-3505
Parnassus Income-Fixed Port	Corp-Inv	10.64	7.89	6.75	3	5	0	0.82	800 999-3505
Pauze US Govt Total Return Bond	Government	15.65	7.91		3	5	0	1.40	800 327-7170
Payden & Rygel Global Fixed Inc R	Intl Bond	11.08	8.78	8.00	1	3	0	0.49	800 572-9336
Payden & Rygel Global Short Bond R	Intl Bond	6.71					0	0.45	800 572-9336
Payden & Rygel Intmed Bond Fund R	Corp-Inv	7.83	6.12		4	2	0	0.62	800 572-9336
Payden & Rygel Invmt Quality Bond R	Corp-Inv	9.83	7.28		3	4	0	0.58	800 572-9336
Payden & Rygel Limited Maturity R	Corp-Inv	5.67	5.54		3	1	0	0.51	800 572-9336
Payden & Rygel Short Bond Fund R	Corp-Inv	5.96	5.52		3	1	0	0.50	800 572-9336
Payden & Rygel Short Duration TE R	Muni Natl	4.25	4.13		3	1	0	0.66	800 572-9336

Bond Fund Name	Objective	Annualized Return for			Rank		Max Load	Expense Ratio	Toll-Free Telephone
		1 Year	3 Years	5 Years	Overall	Risk			
Payden & Rygel Tax Exempt Bond R	Muni Natl	6.71	6.36		5	3	0	0.60	800 572-9336
Payden & Rygel Total Return Fund R	Dvsfd Bond	9.25					0	0.45	800 572-9336
Payden & Rygel US Government R	Government	8.15	6.34		3	3	0	0.63	800 572-9336
Pegasus Bond Fund A	Corp-Inv	10.41	8.80	7.16	2	3	4.5	0.86	800 688-3350
Pegasus Bond Fund B	Corp-Inv	9.54					0	1.60	800 688-3350
Pegasus Bond Fund I	Corp-Inv	10.58	8.73	7.26	2	4	0	0.60	800 688-3350
Pegasus Intermediate Bond Fund A	Corp-Inv	8.27	7.82	6.14	2	2	3	0.85	800 688-3350
Pegasus Intermediate Bond Fund B	Corp-Inv	7.47					0	1.60	800 688-3350
Pegasus Intermediate Bond Fund I	Corp-Inv	8.52	8.04	6.29	2	2	0	0.60	800 688-3350
Pegasus Intermediate Muni Bond A	Muni Natl	6.64	5.78	5.35	3	2	3	0.85	800 688-3350
Pegasus Intermediate Muni Bond B	Muni Natl	5.86	4.91		5	2	0	1.58	800 688-3350
Pegasus Intermediate Muni Bond I	Muni Natl	6.84	6.04		4	2	0	0.60	800 688-3350
Pegasus International Bond Fund A	Intl Bond	0.46	2.13		5	5	4.5	1.11	800 688-3350
Pegasus International Bond Fund B	Intl Bond	−0.29	1.44		5	5	0	1.86	800 688-3350
Pegasus International Bond Fund I	Intl Bond	0.69	2.43		5	5	0	0.86	800 688-3350
Pegasus MI Municipal Bond Fund A	Muni State	8.36	7.27	5.97	1	3	4.5	0.95	800 688-3350
Pegasus MI Municipal Bond Fund B	Muni State	7.76					0	1.70	800 688-3350
Pegasus MI Municipal Bond Fund I	Muni State	8.74	7.48	6.10	1	3	0	0.70	800 688-3350
Pegasus Multi-Sector Bond Fund A	Corp-Inv	10.20	7.18	6.59	3	3	3	0.87	800 688-3350
Pegasus Multi-Sector Bond Fund B	Corp-Inv	9.55	7.59		3	4	0	1.62	800 688-3350
Pegasus Multi-Sector Bond Fund I	Corp-Inv	10.44	7.46	6.79	2	3	0	0.62	800 688-3350
Pegasus Municipal Bond Fund A	Muni Natl	8.22	6.55	6.11	3	3	4.5	0.85	800 688-3350
Pegasus Municipal Bond Fund B	Muni Natl	7.44	6.11		4	3	0	1.60	800 688-3350
Pegasus Municipal Bond Fund I	Muni Natl	8.58	7.26		3	3	0	0.60	800 688-3350
Pegasus Short Bond Fund A	Corp-Inv	5.96	5.62		4	1	3	0.82	800 688-3350
Pegasus Short Bond Fund B	Corp-Inv	5.23					0	1.57	800 688-3350
Pegasus Short Bond Fund I	Corp-Inv	6.28	5.81		4	1	0	0.57	800 688-3350
Performance Intmed Term Govt Cons	Government	9.99	6.59	5.38	3	4	2	1.03	800 737-3676
Performance Intmed Term Govt Instl	Government	10.36	6.88	5.66	3	4	0	0.76	800 737-3676
Performance ST Govt Inc Consumer	Government	6.27	5.46	4.67	4	1	2	0.87	800 737-3676
Performance ST Govt Inc Instl	Government	6.63	5.75	4.95	3	1	0	0.66	800 737-3676
Permanent Treasury Bill Portfolio	Government	4.11	4.26	3.98	4	1	0	1.20	800 531-5142
Permanent Versatile Bond Portfolio	Corp-Inv	5.02	5.06	4.78	3	1	0	0.98	800 531-5142
Phoenix CA TE Bond Fund A	Muni CA	7.98	7.11	5.86	3	4	4.75	1.00	800 243-4361
Phoenix CA TE Bond Fund B	Muni CA	7.25	6.32		5	4	0	0.93	800 243-4361
Phoenix Emerging Markets Bond A	Intl Bond	−11.95					4.75	2.50	800 243-4361
Phoenix Emerging Markets Bond B	Intl Bond	−12.56					0	2.20	800 243-4361
Phoenix High-Yield Fund A	Corp-HY	9.31	13.71	10.22	2	5	4.75	1.11	800 243-4361
Phoenix High-Yield Fund B	Corp-HY	8.49	12.87		2	5	0		800 243-4361
Phoenix Instl Managed Bond Port X	Corp-Inv	8.53	9.41	7.74	2	3	0		800 243-4361
Phoenix Instl Managed Bond Port Y	Corp-Inv	8.26	9.15	7.47	2	3	0		800 243-4361
Phoenix Instl US Govt Secs Port X	Government	6.75	6.34	5.71	3	1	0		800 243-4361
Phoenix Instl US Govt Secs Port Y	Government	6.49	6.01	5.42	3	1	0		800 243-4361
Phoenix Multi-Sector Fixed Inc A	Dvsfd Bond	3.65	10.17	7.58	3	5	4.75	1.04	800 243-4361
Phoenix Multi-Sector Fixed Inc B	Dvsfd Bond	2.85	9.33	6.79	4	5	0	1.78	800 243-4361
Phoenix Multi-Sector Short Term A	Corp-Inv	6.44	9.54	7.62	2	3	2.25	1.00	800 243-4361
Phoenix Multi-Sector Short Term B	Corp-Inv	5.88	8.99	7.09	2	2	0		800 243-4361
Phoenix Tax-Exempt Bond A	Muni Natl	7.95	6.76	5.54	3	3	4.75	0.96	800 243-4361
Phoenix Tax-Exempt Bond B	Muni Natl	7.20	5.97		4	3	0		800 243-4361
Phoenix US Govt Secs Fund A	Government	10.19	6.77	5.82	3	4	4.75	0.98	800 243-4361
Phoenix US Govt Secs Fund B	Government	9.37	5.96		4	4	0		800 243-4361
Pilgrim America High Yield Fund A	Corp-HY	11.68	13.81	11.01	1	4	4.75	1.00	800 334-3444
Pilgrim America High Yield Fund B	Corp-HY	10.95					0	1.75	800 334-3444
Pilgrim America High Yield Fund M	Corp-HY	11.20					3.25	1.50	800 334-3444
Pilgrim Government Secs Income A	Govt-Mtg	7.57	6.06	4.85	4	2	4.75	1.41	800 334-3444
Pilgrim Government Secs Income B	Govt-Mtg	6.33					0	2.16	800 334-3444
Pilgrim Government Secs Income M	Govt-Mtg	6.92					3.25	1.91	800 334-3444
Pillar Fixed Income A	Corp-Inv	8.29	6.19	5.04	4	3	0	1.05	800 932-7782

401

Bond Fund Name	Objective	Annualized Return for			Rank		Max Load	Expense Ratio	Toll-Free Telephone
		1 Year	3 Years	5 Years	Overall	Risk			
Pillar Fixed Income B	Corp-Inv	7.46					0	1.80	800 932-7782
Pillar Fixed Income I	Corp-Inv	8.43	6.52	5.34	3	3	0	0.80	800 932-7782
Pillar GNMA Fund A	Govt-Mtg	8.73	6.87	5.66	3	4	3	1.05	800 932-7782
Pillar GNMA Fund I	Govt-Mtg	8.87	7.10	5.92	3	4	0	0.80	800 932-7782
Pillar Intermediate Govt Sec A	Government	6.78	5.64	4.49	5	2	4	1.05	800 932-7782
Pillar Intermediate Govt Sec I	Government	6.91	5.88	4.74	4	2	0	0.80	800 932-7782
Pillar NJ Muni Sec Trust A	Muni State	5.58	5.40	4.59	3	2		1.05	800 932-7782
Pillar NJ Muni Sec Trust I	Muni State	5.88	5.76	4.89	3	2	0		800 932-7782
Pillar PA Muni Sec Trust A	Muni State	6.23	5.46	4.59	4	2	0	1.05	800 932-7782
Pillar PA Muni Sec Trust I	Muni State	6.53	5.83	4.89	4	2	0	0.80	800 932-7782
Pillar Short Term Investment A	Corp-Inv	5.04	4.78	4.42	3	1	1	1.05	800 932-7782
Pillar Short Term Investment I	Corp-Inv	5.17	5.00		4	1	0	0.80	800 932-7782
PIMCO Foreign Bond A	Intl Bond	10.20					5.5	0.97	800 426-0107
PIMCO Foreign Bond Admin	Intl Bond	10.42					0	0.79	800 426-0107
PIMCO Foreign Bond B	Intl Bond	9.44					0	1.75	800 426-0107
PIMCO Foreign Bond C	Intl Bond	9.49					0	1.76	800 426-0107
PIMCO Foreign Bond Fund Instl	Intl Bond	10.70	15.83	10.20	1	4	0	0.50	800 426-0107
PIMCO Global Bond Fund Admin	Intl Bond	3.96					0	0.78	800 426-0107
PIMCO Global Bond Fund Instl	Intl Bond	4.24	6.89		4	5	0	0.55	800 426-0107
PIMCO Global Bond II Fund A	Intl Bond	8.73					4.5	2.05	800 426-0107
PIMCO Global Bond II Fund B	Intl Bond	7.94					0	2.57	800 426-0107
PIMCO Global Bond II Fund C	Intl Bond	7.87					0	2.43	800 426-0107
PIMCO High Yield A	Corp-HY	11.13					4.5	0.92	800 426-0107
PIMCO High Yield Administrative	Corp-HY	11.26	12.41		1	3	0	0.76	800 426-0107
PIMCO High Yield B	Corp-HY	10.26					0	1.67	800 426-0107
PIMCO High Yield C	Corp-HY	10.26					0	1.68	800 426-0107
PIMCO High Yield Instl	Corp-HY	11.45	12.68	11.78	1	3	0	0.50	800 426-0107
PIMCO Long Term US Govt A	Government	19.11					5.5	1.12	800 426-0107
PIMCO Long Term US Govt B	Government	18.28					0	1.87	800 426-0107
PIMCO Long Term US Govt C	Government	18.21					0		800 426-0107
PIMCO Long Term US Govt Instl	Government	19.58	11.00	9.41	2	5	0	0.50	800 426-0107
PIMCO Low Duration A	Dvsfd Bond	7.00					3	0.91	800 426-0107
PIMCO Low Duration Administrative	Dvsfd Bond	7.19	7.32		3	2	0	0.68	800 426-0107
PIMCO Low Duration B	Dvsfd Bond	6.17					0	1.67	800 426-0107
PIMCO Low Duration C	Dvsfd Bond	6.47					0	1.42	800 426-0107
PIMCO Low Duration II Instl	Dvsfd Bond	7.39	6.93	5.95	3	1	0	0.50	800 426-0107
PIMCO Low Duration III Instl	Dvsfd Bond	6.72					0	0.51	800 426-0107
PIMCO Low Duration Instl	Dvsfd Bond	7.47	7.59	6.50	2	2	0	0.43	800 426-0107
PIMCO Moderate Duration Instl	Dvsfd Bond	8.42					0	0.44	800 426-0107
PIMCO Real Return Bond A	Corp-Inv	4.48					5.5	0.90	800 426-0107
PIMCO Real Return Bond B	Corp-Inv	3.80					0	1.59	800 426-0107
PIMCO Real Return Bond C	Corp-Inv	4.11					0	1.62	800 426-0107
PIMCO Real Return Bond Instl	Corp-Inv	5.03					0	0.51	800 426-0107
PIMCO Short Term Fund A	Corp-Inv	6.04					5.5	0.86	800 426-0107
PIMCO Short Term Fund Admin	Corp-Inv	6.10					0	0.72	800 426-0107
PIMCO Short Term Fund B	Corp-Inv	5.10					0	1.62	800 426-0107
PIMCO Short Term Fund C	Corp-Inv	5.59					0	1.14	800 426-0107
PIMCO Short Term Fund Instl	Corp-Inv	6.30	7.13	6.25	1	1	0	0.45	800 426-0107
PIMCO Total Return A	Corp-Inv	10.42					4.5	0.91	800 426-0107
PIMCO Total Return Administrative	Corp-Inv	10.73	9.04		2	4	0	0.68	800 426-0107
PIMCO Total Return B	Corp-Inv	9.66					0	1.67	800 426-0107
PIMCO Total Return C	Corp-Inv	9.67					0	1.67	800 426-0107
PIMCO Total Return II Admin	Corp-Inv	10.65	8.29		3	4	0	0.75	800 426-0107
PIMCO Total Return II Instl	Corp-Inv	10.93	8.62	7.03	2	4	0	0.50	800 426-0107
PIMCO Total Return III Admin	Corp-Inv	10.52					0		800 426-0107
PIMCO Total Return III Instl	Corp-Inv	10.80	8.94	7.65	2	4	0	0.50	800 426-0107
PIMCO Total Return Instl	Corp-Inv	11.01	9.29	7.61	2	4	0	0.43	800 426-0107
Pioneer America Income A	Government	9.12	6.65	5.48	3	3	4.5	1.14	800 225-6292

| Bond Fund Name | Objective | Annualized Return for | | | Rank | | Max Load | Expense Ratio | Toll-Free Telephone |
		1 Year	3 Years	5 Years	Overall	Risk			
Pioneer America Income B	Government	8.45	6.02		4	3	0	1.77	800 225-6292
Pioneer America Income C	Government	8.34					0	1.74	800 225-6292
Pioneer Bond Fund A	Corp-Inv	10.09	7.04	6.18	3	4	4.5	1.17	800 225-6292
Pioneer Bond Fund B	Corp-Inv	9.23	6.18		4	4	0	1.97	800 225-6292
Pioneer Bond Fund C	Corp-Inv	9.15					0	2.05	800 225-6292
Pioneer Intermediate Tax Free A	Muni Natl	6.56	5.50	4.54	5	3	3.5	1.02	800 225-6292
Pioneer Intermediate Tax Free B	Muni Natl	5.74	4.71		5	3	0	1.78	800 225-6292
Pioneer Intermediate Tax Free C	Muni Natl	5.63					0	1.84	800 225-6292
Pioneer Short Term Income A	Government	6.25	5.66	5.23	3	1	2.5	0.85	800 225-6292
Pioneer Short Term Income B	Government	5.31	4.89		5	1	0	0.88	800 225-6292
Pioneer Tax Free Income A	Muni Natl	8.53	7.26	5.80	3	3	4.5	0.93	800 225-6292
Pioneer Tax Free Income B	Muni Natl	7.69	6.43		4	3	0	1.67	800 225-6292
Pioneer Tax Free Income C	Muni Natl	7.68					0	1.66	800 225-6292
Piper Adjustable Rate Mortgage Sec	Govt-Mtg	5.57					1.5	0.82	800 866-7778
Piper Government Income	Govt-Mtg	10.43	7.94	5.77	3	4	4	1.05	800 866-7778
Piper Intermediate Bond Fund A	Corp-Inv	7.22	7.65	1.23	3	3	2	0.85	800 866-7778
Piper Intermediate Bond Fund Y	Corp-Inv	7.73					0	0.72	800 866-7778
Piper MN Tax Exempt	Muni State	8.16	7.34	6.21	2	3	2	0.93	800 866-7778
Piper National Tax-Exempt	Muni Natl	8.42	7.63	5.74	3	3	4	1.09	800 866-7778
Preferred Fixed Income Fund	Corp-Inv	9.32	7.26	5.88	2	3	0	0.74	800 662-4769
Preferred ST Government Securities	Government	5.72	5.48	4.49	4	1	0	0.63	800 662-4769
Primary US Government Fund	Government	6.20	5.68	4.94	4	2	0	2.84	800 443-6544
Principal Bond Fund A	Corp-Inv	12.18	8.12	7.64	2	5	4.75	0.95	800 247-4123
Principal Bond Fund B	Corp-Inv	11.33	7.33		3	5		1.45	800 247-4123
Principal Government Secs Income A	Govt-Mtg	9.63	7.71	6.43	2	4	4.75	0.84	800 247-4123
Principal Government Secs Income B	Govt-Mtg	9.09	6.98		3	4		1.39	800 247-4123
Principal Government Secs Income R	Govt-Mtg	8.95					0	1.79	800 247-4123
Principal High Yield Fund A	Corp-HY	7.75	10.14	8.42	1	3	4.75	1.22	800 247-4123
Principal High Yield Fund B	Corp-HY	6.95	9.09		2	3	0	2.13	800 247-4123
Principal Limited-Term Bond Fund A	Corp-Inv	3.76					1.5	0.90	800 247-4123
Principal Limited-Term Bond Fund B	Corp-Inv	3.76					0	1.24	800 247-4123
Principal Pres Government Portfolio	Government	9.38	6.36	5.07	4	3	3.5	1.10	800 826-4600
Principal Pres TE Portfolio	Muni Natl	8.27	7.27	6.03	3	4	3.5	1.10	800 826-4600
Principal Pres WI Tax Exempt	Muni State	7.98	6.84		2	3	2.5	0.50	800 826-4600
Principal Tax-Exempt Bond A	Muni Natl	8.07	7.97	6.01	2	3	4.75	0.79	800 247-4123
Principal Tax-Exempt Bond B	Muni Natl	7.30	7.20		3	3	0	1.45	800 247-4123
Prudential Diversified Bond A	Dvsfd Bond	7.35	8.40		3	4	4	0.67	800 225-1852
Prudential Diversified Bond B	Dvsfd Bond	6.72	7.90		3	4	0	0.67	800 225-1852
Prudential Diversified Bond C	Dvsfd Bond	6.71	7.90		3	4	0	0.67	800 225-1852
Prudential Diversified Bond Z	Dvsfd Bond	7.51					0	0.67	800 225-1852
Prudential Global Ltd Maturity A	Intl Bond	5.15	8.32	4.88	3	2	3	1.13	800 225-1852
Prudential Global Ltd Maturity B	Intl Bond	4.59	7.70	4.30	3	2	0	1.17	800 225-1852
Prudential Global Total Return A	Intl Bond	7.09	9.96	8.94	2	3	4	1.24	800 225-1852
Prudential Global Total Return B	Intl Bond	6.34					0	1.24	800 225-1852
Prudential Global Total Return C	Intl Bond	6.34					0	1.24	800 225-1852
Prudential Global Total Return Z	Intl Bond	7.12					0	1.24	800 225-1852
Prudential Government Income Fund A	Government	10.41	7.09	6.04	3	4	4	0.90	800 225-1852
Prudential Government Income Fund B	Government	9.79	6.40	5.35	3	4	0	1.53	800 225-1852
Prudential Govt Sec Sht-Intmed Sr	Government	6.43	5.97	5.04	4	2	0	0.97	800 225-1852
Prudential High Yield A	Corp-HY	11.14	12.28	9.92	1	4	4	0.53	800 225-1852
Prudential High Yield B	Corp-HY	10.43	11.67	9.33	2	4	0	1.29	800 225-1852
Prudential High Yield C	Corp-HY	10.43	11.62		2	4	0	0.53	800 225-1852
Prudential Interm Global Income A	Intl Bond	6.93	9.21	7.80	2	3	3	1.41	800 225-1852
Prudential Interm Global Income B	Intl Bond	6.17	8.56	7.09	3	3	0	1.90	800 225-1852
Prudential International Bond A	Intl Bond	6.01	9.77	8.91	2	3	4	1.52	800 225-1852
Prudential International Bond B	Intl Bond	5.33					0	1.52	800 225-1852
Prudential International Bond C	Intl Bond	5.33					0	1.52	800 225-1852
Prudential International Bond Z	Intl Bond	6.16					0	1.52	800 225-1852

Bond Fund Name	Objective	Annualized Return for			Rank		Max Load	Expense Ratio	Toll-Free Telephone
		1 Year	3 Years	5 Years	Overall	Risk			
Prudential Mortgage Income A	Govt-Mtg	7.16	6.42	5.56	3	3	4		800 225-1852
Prudential Mortgage Income B	Govt-Mtg	6.14	5.80	4.97	4	3	0	1.56	800 225-1852
Prudential Muni Intermediate B	Muni Natl	6.18	5.20	4.08	5	3	0	1.40	800 225-1852
Prudential Municipal CA A	Muni CA	8.68	7.63	5.99	3	4	3	0.72	800 225-1852
Prudential Municipal CA B	Muni CA	8.34	7.18	5.58	4	4	0	0.76	800 225-1852
Prudential Municipal CA Income A	Muni CA	10.10	8.72	7.39	2	4	3	0.69	800 225-1852
Prudential Municipal FL Series A	Muni State	8.32	7.62	5.91	3	4	3	0.47	800 225-1852
Prudential Municipal FL Series B	Muni State	7.89	7.21		4	4	0	0.97	800 225-1852
Prudential Municipal High-Yield A	Muni Natl	10.38	8.48	6.90	1	3	3	0.74	800 225-1852
Prudential Municipal High-Yield B	Muni Natl	9.85	8.02	6.45	1	3	0	1.03	800 225-1852
Prudential Municipal Insured A	Muni Natl	8.51	7.17	5.32	4	4	3	0.62	800 225-1852
Prudential Municipal Insured B	Muni Natl	8.09	6.75	4.90	5	4	0	1.09	800 225-1852
Prudential Municipal MA Series A	Muni State	8.06	7.15	5.84	3	3	3		800 225-1852
Prudential Municipal MA Series B	Muni State	7.63	6.69	5.38	3	3	0		800 225-1852
Prudential Municipal MD Series A	Muni State	8.26	7.35	5.31	4	3	3		800 225-1852
Prudential Municipal MD Series B	Muni State	8.03	6.98	4.91	5	3	0		800 225-1852
Prudential Municipal MI Series B	Muni State	8.25	6.97	5.28	3	4	0	1.37	800 225-1852
Prudential Municipal NC Series A	Muni State	8.72	7.38	5.49	3	4	3		800 225-1852
Prudential Municipal NC Series B	Muni State	8.19	6.95	5.05	4	4	0	1.34	800 225-1852
Prudential Municipal NJ Series A	Muni State	8.18	7.02	5.46	4	3	3		800 225-1852
Prudential Municipal NJ Series B	Muni State	7.65	6.60	5.04	5	3	0	0.97	800 225-1852
Prudential Municipal NJ Series C	Muni State	7.38	6.34		4	3	0		800 225-1852
Prudential Municipal NY Series A	Muni NY	8.51	7.29	5.70	3	4	3	0.74	800 225-1852
Prudential Municipal NY Series B	Muni NY	7.99	6.88	5.28	4	4	0	1.15	800 225-1852
Prudential Municipal OH Series A	Muni State	8.38	7.02	5.65	3	3	3		800 225-1852
Prudential Municipal OH Series B	Muni State	7.85	6.52	5.21	4	4	0	1.20	800 225-1852
Prudential Municipal OH Series C	Muni State	7.56	6.24		4	5	0		800 225-1852
Prudential Municipal PA Series B	Muni State	7.89	7.08	5.40	3	3	0	1.17	800 225-1852
Prudential National Municipals A	Muni Natl	8.75	7.44	5.72	3	4	3	0.75	800 225-1852
Prudential National Municipals B	Muni Natl	8.38	7.05	5.32	4	4	0	0.60	800 225-1852
Prudential Structured Maturity A	Corp-Inv	6.81	6.55	5.45	3	2	3.25	0.94	800 225-1852
Prudential Structured Maturity B	Corp-Inv	6.20	5.89		3	2	0	1.56	800 225-1852
Prudential Structured Maturity C	Corp-Inv	6.20	5.89		4	2	0	0.81	800 225-1852
Putnam American Govt Income Fund A	Government	10.48	7.54	6.13	2	4	4.75	0.97	800 225-1581
Putnam American Govt Income Fund B	Government	9.84	6.78		3	4	0	0.85	800 225-1581
Putnam American Govt Income Fund M	Government	10.29	7.34		2	4	3.25	1.22	800 225-1581
Putnam AZ Tax Exempt Income A	Muni State	7.18	6.85	5.22	4	3	4.75	0.98	800 225-1581
Putnam AZ Tax Exempt Income B	Muni State	6.63	6.08		5	3	0	1.63	800 225-1581
Putnam AZ Tax Exempt Income M	Muni State	6.60					3.25	1.28	800 225-1581
Putnam CA Tax Exempt Income A	Muni CA	8.22	7.57	5.96	2	3	4.75	0.76	800 225-1581
Putnam CA Tax Exempt Income B	Muni CA	7.56	6.76	5.03	5	4	0	0.69	800 225-1581
Putnam CA Tax Exempt Income M	Muni CA	7.90	7.09		4	4	3.25	0.52	800 225-1581
Putnam Diversified Income A	Dvsfd Bond	8.48	9.19	7.71	1	3	4.75	0.99	800 225-1581
Putnam Diversified Income B	Dvsfd Bond	7.62	8.34	6.88	2	3	0	0.86	800 225-1581
Putnam Diversified Income M	Dvsfd Bond	8.21	8.93		2	3	3.25	0.61	800 225-1581
Putnam Diversified Income Y	Dvsfd Bond	8.69					0	0.19	800 225-1581
Putnam FL TE Income A	Muni State	7.84	7.21	5.48	3	3	4.75	0.48	800 225-1581
Putnam FL TE Income B	Muni State	7.03	6.48	4.55	5	3	0	1.61	800 225-1581
Putnam FL TE Income M	Muni State	7.52	6.89		3	4	3.25	1.26	800 225-1581
Putnam Global Govt Income Trust A	Intl Bond	−1.26	5.08	3.55	4	5	4.75	1.29	800 225-1581
Putnam Global Govt Income Trust B	Intl Bond	−2.08	3.80		5	5	0	1.02	800 225-1581
Putnam High Quality Bond Fund A	Government	8.73	6.99	5.72	3	4	4.75	1.15	800 225-1581
Putnam High Quality Bond Fund B	Government	7.98	6.21		5	4	0	0.93	800 225-1581
Putnam High Quality Bond Fund M	Government	8.57	6.77		5	4	3.25	0.68	800 225-1581
Putnam High Yield Advantage Fund A	Corp-HY	11.72	11.93	9.60	2	4	4.75	0.97	800 225-1581
Putnam High Yield Advantage Fund B	Corp-HY	10.96	11.11		2	4	0	0.87	800 225-1581
Putnam High Yield Advantage Fund M	Corp-HY	11.46	11.64		1	4	3.25	0.62	800 225-1581
Putnam High Yield Tr A	Corp-HY	12.09	12.92	10.03	1	4	4.75	0.98	800 225-1581

404

Bond Fund Name	Objective	Annualized Return for			Rank		Max Load	Expense Ratio	Toll-Free Telephone
		1 Year	3 Years	5 Years	Overall	Risk			
Putnam High Yield Tr B	Corp-HY	11.30	12.11	9.21	2	4	0	0.86	800 225-1581
Putnam Income Fund A	Corp-Inv	8.93	7.74	6.89	3	4	4.75	1.17	800 225-1581
Putnam Income Fund B	Corp-Inv	8.04	6.87	6.05	4	4	0	0.95	800 225-1581
Putnam Income Fund M	Corp-Inv	8.64	7.49		4	4	3.25	0.70	800 225-1581
Putnam Intmed US Government Inc A	Government	7.85	6.76	5.41	3	2	3.25	0.59	800 225-1581
Putnam Intmed US Government Inc B	Government	7.44	6.08	4.79	4	2	0	0.89	800 225-1581
Putnam Intmed US Government Inc M	Government	7.67	6.72		3	2	2	0.67	800 225-1581
Putnam MA Tax Exempt Income A	Muni State	7.87	7.75	5.77	3	3	4.75	0.95	800 225-1581
Putnam MA Tax Exempt Income B	Muni State	7.18	6.72	5.23	4	3		1.63	800 225-1581
Putnam MA Tax Exempt Income M	Muni State	7.56	7.15		3	5	3.25	1.28	800 225-1581
Putnam MI Tax Exempt Income A	Muni State	7.40	7.42	5.52	3	3	4.75	0.49	800 225-1581
Putnam MI Tax Exempt Income B	Muni State	6.64	6.61	4.84	5	3	0	1.63	800 225-1581
Putnam MI Tax Exempt Income M	Muni State	6.99	6.60		4	5	3.25	1.28	800 225-1581
Putnam MN Tax Exempt Income A	Muni State	7.23	6.85	5.59	3	3	4.75	0.95	800 225-1581
Putnam MN Tax Exempt Income B	Muni State	6.54	6.12	4.76	5	3	0	1.68	800 225-1581
Putnam MN Tax Exempt Income M	Muni State	7.03	6.29		5	4	3.25	1.33	800 225-1581
Putnam Municipal Income A	Muni Natl	8.65	7.80	6.02	1	3	4.75	0.95	800 225-1581
Putnam Municipal Income B	Muni Natl	8.00	7.05	5.33	3	3	0	1.56	800 225-1581
Putnam Municipal Income M	Muni Natl	8.03	7.41		3	3	3.25	1.21	800 225-1581
Putnam NJ Tax Exempt Income A	Muni State	7.49	6.73	5.12	3	3	4.75	0.48	800 225-1581
Putnam NJ Tax Exempt Income B	Muni State	6.81	6.44	4.43	5	3	0	1.61	800 225-1581
Putnam NJ Tax Exempt Income M	Muni State	7.17	6.84		3	3	3.25	1.26	800 225-1581
Putnam NY Tax Exempt Income A	Muni NY	7.65	7.03	4.86	4	3	4.75	0.79	800 225-1581
Putnam NY Tax Exempt Income B	Muni NY	7.08	6.37	4.18	5	3	0	0.73	800 225-1581
Putnam NY Tax Exempt Income M	Muni NY	6.18	6.39		4	4	3.25	0.55	800 225-1581
Putnam NY Tax Exempt Opport A	Muni NY	8.06	7.43	6.19	2	3	4.75	0.96	800 225-1581
Putnam NY Tax Exempt Opport B	Muni NY	7.75	6.98		3	3		0.81	800 225-1581
Putnam NY Tax Exempt Opport M	Muni NY	7.74	7.15		3	3	3.25	0.64	800 225-1581
Putnam OH Tax Exempt Income A	Muni State	7.37	7.01	5.35	3	3	4.75	0.98	800 225-1581
Putnam OH Tax Exempt Income B	Muni State	6.67	6.32	4.82	5	3		1.63	800 225-1581
Putnam OH Tax Exempt Income M	Muni State	7.05	6.22		5	5	3.25	1.28	800 225-1581
Putnam PA Tax Exempt Income A	Muni State	7.52	7.19	6.05	2	3	4.75	0.49	800 225-1581
Putnam PA Tax Exempt Income B	Muni State	6.82	6.20		4	3	0	1.63	800 225-1581
Putnam PA Tax Exempt Income M	Muni State	7.19					3.25	1.28	800 225-1581
Putnam Strategic Income A	Dvsfd Bond	8.36					4.75	1.25	800 225-1581
Putnam Strategic Income B	Dvsfd Bond	7.67					0	2.00	800 225-1581
Putnam Strategic Income M	Dvsfd Bond	7.86					3.25	1.50	800 225-1581
Putnam Tax Exempt Income A	Muni Natl	8.26	7.67	5.19	3	3	4.75	0.80	800 225-1581
Putnam Tax Exempt Income B	Muni Natl	7.55	6.97	4.81	5	4		0.71	800 225-1581
Putnam Tax Exempt Income M	Muni Natl	7.93	7.37		3	3		0.54	800 225-1581
Putnam Tax-Free High Yield A	Muni Natl	8.43	7.33		2	3	4.75	0.85	800 225-1581
Putnam Tax-Free High Yield B	Muni Natl	7.87	6.92	5.30	3	3	0	1.52	800 225-1581
Putnam Tax-Free High Yield M	Muni Natl	8.18	7.01		3	4	3.25	1.15	800 225-1581
Putnam Tax-Free Insured Fund A	Muni Natl	7.19	6.70		5	4	4.75	0.92	800 225-1581
Putnam Tax-Free Insured Fund B	Muni Natl	7.40	6.66	4.97	5	4	0	0.92	800 225-1581
Putnam Tax-Free Insured Fund M	Muni Natl	6.87	7.10		5	5	3.25	1.22	800 225-1581
Putnam US Government Income Trust A	Govt-Mtg	8.47	7.33	6.01	2	3	4.75	0.88	800 225-1581
Putnam US Government Income Trust B	Govt-Mtg	7.52	6.48	5.20	3	3	0	0.81	800 225-1581
Putnam US Government Income Trust M	Govt-Mtg	8.10	7.01		3	3	3.25	0.56	800 225-1581
Quaker Fixed Income Fund	Corp-Inv	9.97					0	0.90	800 355-3553
Rainier Intermediate Fixed Income	Corp-Inv	8.50	6.11		3	2	0	0.95	800 248-6314
RBB Government Securities Port	Government	10.12	6.55	5.07	4	4	4.75	0.64	800 401-2230
Regions Fixed Income B	Corp-Inv	8.20	6.38		3	3	0	1.02	800 433-2829
Republic Bank NY TF Bond Retail A	Muni NY	8.25	7.06		2	3	0		800 782-8183
Republic Bank Taxable Bond Retail A	Corp-Inv	7.68					0		800 782-8183
Reynolds US Government Bond Fund	Corp-Inv	5.69	5.14	5.40	2	2	0	0.90	800 773-9665
RIMCO Monument Bond Fund	Corp-Inv	10.33	6.72	6.78	3	4	4.75	0.90	800 934-3883
Riverfront US Government Income A	Government	7.48	5.93	4.80	4	2	4.5	1.11	800 424-2295

Bond Fund Name	Objective	Annualized Return for			Rank		Max Load	Expense Ratio	Toll-Free Telephone
		1 Year	3 Years	5 Years	Overall	Risk			
Riverfront US Government Income B	Government	6.58	5.03	6.55	3	2	0	1.96	800 424-2295
Rochester Fund Municipals A	Muni NY	9.69	8.44	6.38	1	3	4.75	0.75	800 525-7048
Rochester Fund Municipals B	Muni NY	8.72					0		800 525-7048
Rochester Fund Municipals C	Muni NY	8.79					0		800 525-7048
Rochester Limited Term NY Muni A	Muni NY	7.63	6.72	5.79	2	1	3.5	0.81	800 525-7048
Rodney Square Diversified Income	Corp-Inv	8.52	6.53	5.76	3	2	3.5	0.65	800 336-9970
RSI Retirement Active Mortgage Bond	Govt-Mtg	11.53	7.73	6.45	3	4	0	0.40	800 368-3527
RSI Retirement Intermediate Bond	Corp-Inv	7.80	6.32	5.39	3	2	0	1.04	800 368-3527
RSI Retirement Short Term Invest	Corp-Inv	5.01	4.91	4.42	3	1	0	1.00	800 368-3527
Rushmore MD Tax Free Investors	Muni State	7.63	6.47	5.21	3	2	0	0.93	800 343-3355
Rushmore US Government Bond	Government	17.85	8.90	7.35	3	5	0	0.80	800 343-3355
Rushmore VA Tax Free Investors	Muni State	7.94	6.81	5.43	3	3	0	0.93	800 343-3355
RYDEX US Government Bond Fund	Government	23.32	8.36		3	5	0	1.49	800 820-0888
SAFECO Adv Intmed Term US Treas A	Government	9.63					0.55	1.07	800 426-6730
SAFECO Adv Intmed Term US Treas B	Government	8.77					0	1.72	800 426-6730
SAFECO Advisor CA Tax-Free Income A	Muni CA	10.73					0.55	0.91	800 426-6730
SAFECO Advisor CA Tax-Free Income B	Muni CA	10.10					0	1.63	800 426-6730
SAFECO Advisor High Yield A	Corp-HY	11.10					0.65	1.10	800 426-6730
SAFECO Advisor High Yield B	Corp-HY	10.30					0	1.81	800 426-6730
SAFECO Advisor Managed Bond A	Dvsfd Bond	10.14					0.5	1.45	800 426-6730
SAFECO Advisor Managed Bond B	Dvsfd Bond	8.97					0	2.23	800 426-6730
SAFECO Advisor Municipal Bond A	Muni Natl	10.48					0.55	0.95	800 426-6730
SAFECO Advisor Municipal Bond B	Muni Natl	9.26					0	1.53	800 426-6730
SAFECO Advisor WA Municipal Bond A	Muni State	8.44					0.65	1.32	800 426-6730
SAFECO Advisor WA Municipal Bond B	Muni State	7.82					0	2.13	800 426-6730
SAFECO CA Tax Free Income Fund	Muni CA	11.16	9.29	6.76	3	5	0	0.68	800 426-6730
SAFECO GNMA Fund	Govt-Mtg	8.73	7.85	5.62	2	3	0	0.93	800 426-6730
SAFECO High Yield Bond Fund	Corp-HY	11.38	11.10	9.10	1	3	0	0.73	800 426-6730
SAFECO Insured Muni Bd	Muni Natl	10.14	8.78	6.24	3	5	0	0.86	800 426-6730
SAFECO Intermediate Muni Bd	Muni Natl	6.72	6.15	5.29	4	3	0	0.83	800 426-6730
SAFECO Intmed Term US Treas Bond	Government	9.95	6.38	5.37	3	4	0	0.92	800 426-6730
SAFECO Managed Bond Fund	Dvsfd Bond	10.40	6.47		3	4	0	1.15	800 426-6730
SAFECO Municipal Bond Fund	Muni Natl	10.51	8.65	6.45	3	5	0	0.51	800 426-6730
SAFECO WA Muni Bd	Muni State	8.93	7.63	5.58	3	4	0	1.02	800 426-6730
Salomon Brothers High Yield Bond A	Corp-HY	7.11	15.72		3	5	4.75	1.24	800 725-6666
Salomon Brothers High Yield Bond B	Corp-HY	6.35	14.83		3	5	0	1.99	800 725-6666
Salomon Brothers High Yield Bond C	Corp-HY	6.26	14.80		2	5	0	1.99	800 725-6666
Salomon Brothers High Yield Bond O	Corp-HY	7.37	15.96		3	5	0	0.99	800 725-6666
Salomon Brothers Natl Int Muni Bd A	Muni Natl	6.76	5.85		4	2	4.75	0.75	800 725-6666
Salomon Brothers Natl Int Muni Bd B	Muni Natl	5.87	4.95		4	2	0	1.50	800 725-6666
Salomon Brothers Natl Int Muni Bd C	Muni Natl	5.77	4.96		4	2	0	1.50	800 725-6666
Salomon Brothers Natl Int Muni Bd O	Muni Natl	6.97	6.06		3	2	0	0.50	800 725-6666
Salomon Brothers Strategic Bond A	Dvsfd Bond	8.02	11.12		2	3	4.75	1.24	800 725-6666
Salomon Brothers Strategic Bond B	Dvsfd Bond	7.05	10.23		2	3	0	1.99	800 725-6666
Salomon Brothers Strategic Bond C	Dvsfd Bond	7.15	10.23		2	3	0	1.99	800 725-6666
Salomon Brothers Strategic Bond O	Dvsfd Bond	8.05	11.33		2	3	0	0.96	800 725-6666
Salomon Brothers US Govt Income A	Government	8.47	6.50		3	2	4.75	0.85	800 725-6666
Salomon Brothers US Govt Income B	Government	7.58	5.67		4	2	0	1.60	800 725-6666
Salomon Brothers US Govt Income C	Government	7.58	5.95		4	2	0	1.59	800 725-6666
Salomon Brothers US Govt Income O	Government	8.79	6.73		2	2	0	0.60	800 725-6666
Schroder Investment Grade Inc	Corp-Inv	9.58	6.55		3	3	0	1.12	800 344-8332
Schroder ST Investment Fund	Corp-Inv	4.42	4.57		4	1	0	1.03	800 344-8332
Schwab CA Long Term TF Bond	Muni CA	9.66	8.53	6.15	3	4	0	0.49	800 266-5623
Schwab CA Short/Intmed TF Bd	Muni CA	4.81	5.15		3	1	0	0.49	800 266-5623
Schwab LT TF Bond Fund	Muni Natl	9.66	8.05	6.39	2	4	0	0.49	800 266-5623
Schwab Short/Intmed Government Bond	Government	7.04	6.04	4.73	4	1	0	0.82	800 266-5623
Schwab Short/Intmed TF Bd	Muni Natl	5.07	4.84		3	1	0	0.49	800 266-5623
Schwab Total Bond Market Index	Government	10.42	7.59	6.68	3	5	0	0.20	800 266-5623

406

Bond Fund Name	Objective	Annualized Return for			Rank		Max Load	Expense Ratio	Toll-Free Telephone
		1 Year	3 Years	5 Years	Overall	Risk			
Scout Bond Fund	Corp-Inv	7.99	6.14	5.22	3	2	0	0.87	800 422-2766
Scudder CA Tax Free	Muni CA	8.95	8.00	6.08	2	4	0	0.78	800 225-2470
Scudder Emerging Mkts Income	Intl Bond	−2.82	18.96		3	5	0	1.49	800 225-2470
Scudder Global Bond Fund	Intl Bond	4.39	3.73	2.61	4	4	0	1.00	800 225-2470
Scudder GNMA Fund	Govt-Mtg	8.50	7.30	5.78	2	3	0	1.02	800 225-2470
Scudder High Yield Bond Fund	Corp-HY	10.66					0	1.35	800 225-2470
Scudder High-Yield Tax Free	Muni Natl	10.15	8.60	6.58	1	3	0	0.90	800 225-2470
Scudder Income Fund	Corp-Inv	8.99	7.45	6.45	2	3	0	1.18	800 225-2470
Scudder International Bond Fund	Intl Bond	0.09	1.20	0.91	4	5	0	1.61	800 225-2470
Scudder Limited Term Tax Free	Muni Natl	5.31	5.05		3	1	0	0.83	800 225-2470
Scudder MA Ltd Term Tax Free	Muni State	5.48	5.00		3	1	0	0.75	800 225-2470
Scudder MA Tax Free	Muni State	8.16	7.52	6.23	1	3	0	0.76	800 225-2470
Scudder Managed Municipal Bonds	Muni Natl	8.36	7.86	6.12	3	3	0	0.64	800 225-2470
Scudder Medium-Term Tax Free	Muni Natl	6.62	6.22	5.50	2	2	0	0.74	800 225-2470
Scudder NY Tax Free	Muni NY	8.51	7.52	5.72	3	4	0	0.84	800 225-2470
Scudder OH Tax Free	Muni State	7.65	7.37	5.93	3	3	0	0.25	800 225-2470
Scudder PA Tax Free	Muni State	7.74	7.07	5.84	3	3	0	0.25	800 225-2470
Scudder Short Term Bond Fund	Corp-Inv	5.23	5.49	4.43	4	1	0	0.86	800 225-2470
Scudder Zero Coupon 2000	Government	7.63	5.38	4.52	5	3	0	0.94	800 225-2470
Security Income Corp Bond A	Corp-Inv	10.93	6.58	4.83	4	5	4.75	1.07	800 888-2461
Security Income Corp Bond B	Corp-Inv	10.08	5.72		5	5		1.08	800 888-2461
Security Income US Government A	Govt-Mtg	10.88	7.75	6.15	3	4	4.75	0.55	800 888-2461
Security Income US Government B	Govt-Mtg	9.29	6.39		4	4		1.52	800 888-2461
Security Tax Exempt A	Muni Natl	7.67	6.62	4.72	4	3	4.75	0.82	800 888-2461
Security Tax Exempt B	Muni Natl	6.42	5.28		5	4		2.01	800 888-2461
Sefton CA TF Bond Fund	Muni CA	8.08	7.81		1	3	0	1.17	
Sefton US Govt Bond Fund	Govt-Mtg	9.77	6.56		3	4	0	1.39	
SEI Bond Index A	Corp-Inv	10.66	7.55	6.54	2	3	0	0.71	800 342-5734
SEI Daily Inc GNMA A	Govt-Mtg	8.90	7.60	6.20	1	2	0	0.60	800 342-5734
SEI Daily Inc Intmed-Dur Govt A	Government	8.84	6.77	5.78	2	2	0	0.50	800 342-5734
SEI Daily Inc Short Duration Govt A	Government	6.80	6.19	5.42	3	1	0	0.45	800 342-5734
SEI Daily Inc Short Duration Govt B	Government	6.00	5.71	5.00	4	2	0	0.75	800 342-5734
SEI Emerging Markets Debt Port	Intl Bond	−1.33					0		800 342-5734
SEI Instl Mgd Core Fixed Income A	Corp-Inv	10.77	7.84	6.60	2	3	0	0.60	800 342-5734
SEI Instl Mgd Tr High Yield Bond A	Corp-HY	13.64	14.04		1	3		0.87	800 342-5734
SEI Intermediate-Term Municipal A	Muni Natl	7.34	6.54	5.45	3	2	0	0.60	800 342-5734
SEI International Fixed Income	Intl Bond	2.82	2.11		5	5	0	1.00	800 342-5734
SEI Tax-Exempt PA Municipal	Muni State	7.08	6.57	5.42	3	2	0	0.48	800 342-5734
Selected US Government Income	Government	7.74	6.02	5.46	3	3	0	1.34	800 279-0279
Seligman High-Yield Bond A	Corp-HY	14.53	14.44	12.51	1	5	4.75	2.00	800 221-2783
Seligman High-Yield Bond B	Corp-HY	13.69					0	1.90	800 221-2783
Seligman High-Yield Bond D	Corp-HY	13.84	13.59		1	5	0	1.90	800 221-2783
Seligman Muni Series Tr CA Qual A	Muni CA	8.65	7.96	5.85	3	3	4.75	0.82	800 221-2783
Seligman Muni Series Tr CA Qual D	Muni CA	7.68	6.92		4	3	0	1.72	800 221-2783
Seligman Muni Series Trust CA HY A	Muni CA	8.77	7.67	6.45	1	2	4.75	0.87	800 221-2783
Seligman Muni Series Trust CA HY D	Muni CA	7.61	6.67		3	2	0	1.77	800 221-2783
Seligman Municipal Series CO A	Muni State	7.55	6.30	5.13	3	2	4.75	0.89	800 221-2783
Seligman Municipal Series CO D	Muni State	6.59	5.31		4	3	0	1.80	800 221-2783
Seligman Municipal Series GA A	Muni State	8.82	7.73	6.21	2	3	4.75	0.88	800 221-2783
Seligman Municipal Series GA D	Muni State	7.97	6.86		4	4	0	1.79	800 221-2783
Seligman Municipal Series LA A	Muni State	7.53	7.35	5.69	2	3	4.75	0.86	800 221-2783
Seligman Municipal Series LA D	Muni State	6.60	6.42		5	3	0	1.76	800 221-2783
Seligman Municipal Series MA A	Muni State	9.02	7.45	5.91	2	3	4.75	0.83	800 221-2783
Seligman Municipal Series MA D	Muni State	8.04	6.54		3	3	0	1.74	800 221-2783
Seligman Municipal Series MD A	Muni State	8.20	7.11	5.79	2	3	4.75	0.89	800 221-2783
Seligman Municipal Series MD D	Muni State	7.16	6.14		5	3	0	1.80	800 221-2783
Seligman Municipal Series MI A	Muni State	8.37	7.38	5.85	2	3	4.75	0.81	800 221-2783
Seligman Municipal Series MI D	Muni State	7.28	6.40		4	3	0	1.72	800 221-2783

Bond Fund Name	Objective	Annualized Return for			Rank		Max Load	Expense Ratio	Toll-Free Telephone
		1 Year	3 Years	5 Years	Overall	Risk			
Seligman Municipal Series MN A	Muni State	7.00	5.65	5.24	3	2	4.75	0.85	800 221-2783
Seligman Municipal Series MN D	Muni State	6.01	4.73		4	2	0	1.75	800 221-2783
Seligman Municipal Series MO A	Muni State	8.31	7.21	5.60	3	3	4.75	0.90	800 221-2783
Seligman Municipal Series MO D	Muni State	7.34	6.26		4	3	0	1.80	800 221-2783
Seligman Municipal Series Natl A	Muni Natl	9.80	8.21	5.77	2	4	4.75	0.81	800 221-2783
Seligman Municipal Series Natl D	Muni Natl	8.82	7.18		3	4	0	1.74	800 221-2783
Seligman Municipal Series NY A	Muni NY	10.24	8.32	6.16	3	4	4.75	0.82	800 221-2783
Seligman Municipal Series NY D	Muni NY	9.21	7.34		4	4	0	1.73	800 221-2783
Seligman Municipal Series OH A	Muni State	8.26	6.89	5.58	2	3	4.75	0.81	800 221-2783
Seligman Municipal Series OH D	Muni State	7.24	6.02		5	3	0	1.71	800 221-2783
Seligman Municipal Series OR A	Muni State	8.90	7.15	5.78	2	3	4.75	0.90	800 221-2783
Seligman Municipal Series OR D	Muni State	7.78	6.17		4	3	0	1.80	800 221-2783
Seligman Municipal Series SC A	Muni State	8.53	7.57	5.85	2	3	4.75	0.82	800 221-2783
Seligman Municipal Series SC D	Muni State	7.68	6.66		5	4	0	1.72	800 221-2783
Seligman Municipal Series Tr FL A	Muni State	9.30	7.33	5.90	3	4	4.75	1.04	800 221-2783
Seligman Municipal Series Tr FL D	Muni State	8.67	6.55		4	5	0	1.78	800 221-2783
Seligman Municipal Series Tr NC A	Muni State	8.46	7.38	5.86	3	4	4.75		800 221-2783
Seligman Municipal Series Tr NC D	Muni State	7.63	6.55		5	4	0	1.83	800 221-2783
Seligman NJ Municipal Fund A	Muni State	9.01	7.08	5.49	2	3	4.75	1.06	800 221-2783
Seligman NJ Municipal Fund D	Muni State	8.11	6.29		4	3	0	1.79	800 221-2783
Seligman PA Municipal Fund A	Muni State	8.96	7.48	5.86	2	3	4.75	1.19	800 221-2783
Seligman PA Municipal Fund D	Muni State	8.20	7.00		4	3	0	1.88	800 221-2783
Seligman US Government Securities A	Government	10.08	6.32	5.38	4	5	4.75	1.23	800 221-2783
Seligman US Government Securities B	Government	9.39					0	2.01	800 221-2783
Seligman US Government Securities D	Government	9.38	5.38		5	5	0	2.00	800 221-2783
Seneca Bond Fund	Dvsfd Bond	12.38					0	1.09	800 990-9331
Sentinel Bond Fund A	Corp-Inv	10.72	7.22	6.23	3	4	4	0.97	800 282-3863
Sentinel Bond Fund B	Corp-Inv	9.72					4	1.87	800 282-3863
Sentinel Government Securities A	Government	10.74	7.11	5.88	3	4	4	0.98	800 282-3863
Sentinel High Yield Bond A	Corp-HY	14.45					0	1.20	800 282-3863
Sentinel High Yield Bond B	Corp-HY	14.19					4	1.30	800 282-3863
Sentinel NY Tax-Free A	Muni NY	9.84	7.76		3	4	4	1.09	800 282-3863
Sentinel PA Tax-Free A	Muni State	7.78	6.96	5.22	4	3	4	0.85	800 282-3863
Sentinel Short Maturity Government	Govt-Mtg	7.21	6.28		3	1		1.00	800 282-3863
Sentinel Tax-Free Income Fund A	Muni Natl	8.48	7.12	5.47	4	4	4	0.91	800 282-3863
Sit Bond	Dvsfd Bond	9.25	7.60		2	3	0	0.80	800 332-5580
Sit Minnesota Tax Free Income	Muni State	7.79	7.25		1	1		0.80	800 332-5580
Sit Tax Free Income Fund	Muni Natl	8.91	8.05	6.74	1	2	0	0.76	800 332-5580
Sit US Government Securities Fund	Government	8.33	7.14	6.28	2	1	0	0.80	800 332-5580
Smith Barney Adj Rt Govt Inc A	Govt-Mtg	5.46	5.63		3	1	0	1.57	800 544-7835
Smith Barney Adj Rt Govt Inc B	Govt-Mtg	5.39	5.59	4.89	3	1		1.59	800 544-7835
Smith Barney AZ Municipal A	Muni State	8.13	7.44	5.95	1	3	4.5	1.26	800 544-7835
Smith Barney AZ Municipal B	Muni State	11.23	8.08	6.14	3	3	0	1.39	800 544-7835
Smith Barney CA Municipals A	Muni CA	10.03	9.13	7.45	3	5	4	1.21	800 544-7835
Smith Barney CA Municipals B	Muni CA	9.49	8.55	6.85	3	5	0	1.23	800 544-7835
Smith Barney CA Municipals L	Muni CA	8.86	8.24		3	5	0	1.29	800 544-7835
Smith Barney Diver Strat Inc A	Dvsfd Bond	8.49	9.47	7.69	1	2	4.5	1.03	800 544-7835
Smith Barney Diver Strat Inc B	Dvsfd Bond	7.94	8.95	7.19	1	2	0	1.50	800 544-7835
Smith Barney Diver Strat Inc L	Dvsfd Bond	8.23	9.09	6.94	1	2	0	1.46	800 544-7835
Smith Barney Diver Strat Inc Y	Dvsfd Bond	8.86					0	0.70	800 544-7835
Smith Barney Global Govt Bond A	Intl Bond	9.08	9.06	7.52	1	3	4.5	1.26	800 451-2010
Smith Barney Global Govt Bond B	Intl Bond	8.45	8.33		2	3	0	1.79	800 451-2010
Smith Barney Global Govt Bond L	Intl Bond	8.59	8.56		2	5	0	1.69	800 451-2010
Smith Barney Global Govt Bond Y	Intl Bond	8.81	9.12	7.39	2	3	0	0.89	800 451-2010
Smith Barney Government Secs A	Government	11.21	7.46	6.13	4	5	4.5	0.92	800 544-7835
Smith Barney Government Secs B	Government	10.69	6.61	5.42	5	5	0	0.72	800 544-7835
Smith Barney High Income A	Corp-HY	10.82	12.49	9.60	1	3	4.5	1.06	800 544-7835
Smith Barney High Income B	Corp-HY	10.21	11.91	9.05	1	3	0	1.54	800 544-7835

408

Bond Fund Name	Objective	Annualized Return for			Rank		Max Load	Expense Ratio	Toll-Free Telephone
		1 Year	3 Years	5 Years	Overall	Risk			
Smith Barney High Income L	Corp-HY	10.34	12.03		1	3	0	1.48	800 544-7835
Smith Barney High Income Y	Corp-HY	11.07					0	0.73	800 544-7835
Smith Barney Inter Mat CA Muni A	Muni CA	6.85	6.67	4.97	3	2	2	0.77	800 451-2010
Smith Barney Inter Mat NY Muni A	Muni NY	7.59	6.64	5.31	3	3	2	0.65	800 451-2010
Smith Barney Inv Grade Bond A	Corp-Inv	21.02	11.20	9.88	2	5	4.5	1.02	800 544-7835
Smith Barney Inv Grade Bond B	Corp-Inv	20.44	10.65	9.37	3	5	0	1.51	800 544-7835
Smith Barney Inv Grade Bond L	Corp-Inv	20.57	10.72	9.38	3	5	0	1.47	800 544-7835
Smith Barney Ltd Term Muni A	Muni Natl	7.31	6.32	5.51	3	2	0	0.74	800 451-2010
Smith Barney Ltd Term Muni L	Muni Natl	7.73	6.26	5.36	2	2	0	0.97	800 451-2010
Smith Barney MA Municipal A	Muni State	9.03	8.09	5.86	2	3	4	2.15	800 544-7835
Smith Barney MA Municipal B	Muni State	8.50	7.53	5.26	3	3	0	2.12	800 544-7835
Smith Barney Managed Govt A	Govt-Mtg	8.92	6.98	5.95	3	3	4.5	1.03	800 544-7835
Smith Barney Managed Govt B	Govt-Mtg	8.38	6.45	5.35	4	3	0	1.56	800 544-7835
Smith Barney Managed Govt L	Govt-Mtg	8.54	6.37	5.26	5	4	0	1.49	800 544-7835
Smith Barney Managed Muni A	Muni Natl	10.21	8.43	7.48	3	5	4	0.68	800 544-7835
Smith Barney Managed Muni B	Muni Natl	9.59	8.69	7.39	3	5	0	1.19	800 544-7835
Smith Barney Muni FL A	Muni State	9.06	8.15	6.56	1	3	4	0.85	800 451-2010
Smith Barney Muni FL B	Muni State	8.52	7.54		2	3	0	1.35	800 451-2010
Smith Barney Muni FL L	Muni State	8.48	7.46	5.89	2	3	0	1.40	800 451-2010
Smith Barney Muni High Income A	Muni Natl	9.15	7.86		1	4	4	0.83	800 544-7835
Smith Barney Muni High Income B	Muni Natl	8.60	7.34	5.60	2	3	0	1.32	800 544-7835
Smith Barney Muni National A	Muni Natl	9.17	8.22	6.72	1	3	4	0.66	800 451-2010
Smith Barney Muni National B	Muni Natl	8.54	7.46	5.22	3	3	0	1.20	800 451-2010
Smith Barney Muni National L	Muni Natl	8.47	7.48	5.91	3	3		1.27	800 451-2010
Smith Barney Muni NY A	Muni NY	9.30	8.23	6.55	2	3	4	0.71	800 451-2010
Smith Barney Muni NY B	Muni NY	8.73	7.66		2	3	0	1.27	800 451-2010
Smith Barney Muni NY L	Muni NY	8.71	7.63	5.89	2	3	0	1.32	800 451-2010
Smith Barney NJ Muni A	Muni State	8.79	7.58	5.90	1	3	4	0.75	800 544-7835
Smith Barney NJ Muni B	Muni State	8.26	7.06	5.37	2	3	0	1.28	800 544-7835
Smith Barney NJ Muni L	Muni State	8.16	6.24		3	4	0	1.32	800 544-7835
Smith Barney Principal 1998	Corp-Inv	12.42	12.17	9.66	2	5	5	1.04	800 544-7835
Smith Barney Principal 2000	Corp-Inv	6.38	6.61	8.41	3	5	5	1.16	800 544-7835
Smith Barney Short Term US Treas	Government	7.22	5.37	4.75	5	3	0	0.98	800 451-2010
Smith Barney US Govt Securities A	Govt-Mtg	9.23	7.33	6.41	3	4	4.5	0.80	800 451-2010
Smith Barney US Govt Securities B	Govt-Mtg	8.63	6.79		3	4		1.31	800 451-2010
Smith Barney US Govt Securities L	Govt-Mtg	7.66	6.53	5.69	3	4	0	1.27	800 451-2010
Smith Breeden Interm Dur US Govt	Government	6.74	6.77	6.35	1	2	0	0.88	800 221-3138
Smith Breeden Sh Dur US Govt Series	Government	5.70	6.01	5.54	3	1	0	0.78	800 221-3138
SouthTrust Vulcan Bond Fund	Corp-Inv	10.98	7.14	5.79	3	4	3.5	0.86	800 843-8618
SSgA Bond Market Fund	Corp-Inv	9.92					0	0.74	800 997-7327
SSgA Intermediate Fund	Government	8.12	6.55		3	2	0	1.30	800 997-7327
SSgA Yield Plus Fund	Corp-Inv	5.62	5.69	5.33	3	1	0	0.38	800 997-7327
Stagecoach AZ Tax-Free Fund A	Muni State	7.60	6.41	5.59	4	3	4.5	1.46	800 222-8222
Stagecoach CA TF Bond Fund A	Muni CA	8.90	7.87	5.94	2	3	4.5	0.73	800 222-8222
Stagecoach CA TF Bond Fund B	Muni CA	8.19	7.22		2	3	0	1.73	800 222-8222
Stagecoach CA TF Income A	Muni CA	4.89	4.92	4.37	3	1	3	1.14	800 222-8222
Stagecoach National Tax Free A	Muni Natl	8.33					4.5	1.42	800 222-8222
Stagecoach National Tax Free B	Muni Natl	7.69	5.48	4.57	4	3	0	0.00	800 222-8222
Stagecoach National Tax Free Instl	Muni Natl	8.33	6.80	5.66	3	3	0	1.45	800 222-8222
Stagecoach OR Tax-Free A	Muni State	7.81	6.68	5.45	4	3	4.5	1.15	800 222-8222
Stagecoach OR Tax-Free B	Muni State	7.05	5.63	4.53	5	3	0	0.00	800 222-8222
Stagecoach Sht-Int US Govt Inc A	Government	7.53	6.23	3.81	4	2	3	1.21	800 222-8222
Stagecoach ST Govt Corp Inc	Government	5.55	5.60		4	1	3	0.37	800 222-8222
Stagecoach US Government Inc A	Government	15.05	7.89	6.65	4	5	4.5	0.88	800 222-8222
Stagecoach US Government Instl	Govt-Mtg	8.15	8.24	6.68	3	4	0	0.92	800 222-8222
Stagecoach US Govt Allocation A	Government	7.15	5.68	4.96	4	3	4.5	1.14	800 222-8222
Stagecoach US Govt Allocation B	Government	6.46	5.04		5	3	0	2.21	800 222-8222
Stagecoach Variable Rate Govt A	Govt-Mtg	4.20	5.10	3.45	3	1	4.5	0.83	800 222-8222

Bond Fund Name	Objective	Annualized Return for			Rank		Max Load	Expense Ratio	Toll-Free Telephone
		1 Year	3 Years	5 Years	Overall	Risk			
Standish Ayer & Wood Controlled Mat	Corp-Inv	6.87					0	1.16	800 221-4795
Standish Ayer & Wood Fixed Inc	Corp-Inv	9.78	8.75	6.60	2	3	0	0.38	800 221-4795
Standish Ayer & Wood Fixed Inc II	Corp-Inv	9.05					0	0.73	800 221-4795
Standish Ayer & Wood Glbl Fixed Inc	Intl Bond	10.63	12.73		1	3	0	0.63	800 221-4795
Standish Ayer & Wood Intl Fixed Inc	Intl Bond	10.88	13.95	9.80	1	3	0	0.53	800 221-4795
Standish Ayer & Wood Intmed TE	Muni Natl	7.34	6.92	5.55	3	2	0	0.76	800 221-4795
Standish Ayer & Wood MA Intmed TE	Muni State	7.17	6.39	5.26	3	2	0	0.73	800 221-4795
Standish Ayer & Wood Securitized Fd	Govt-Mtg	10.49	7.84	6.84	2	3	0	0.56	800 221-4795
Standish Ayer & Wood ST Asset Res	Corp-Inv	6.03	6.00	5.30	3	1	0	0.37	800 221-4795
Star Stellar Insured TF Bond Fund	Muni Natl	7.60					4.5		800 677-3863
Star Strategic Income	Dvsfd Bond	6.00	6.53		3	4	0	1.27	800 677-3863
Star US Govt Income Fund	Government	10.31	6.86		3	4	3.5	0.90	800 677-3863
State Street Rsch Govt Income A	Government	10.63	7.52	6.64	2	3	4.5	1.08	800 562-0032
State Street Rsch Govt Income B	Government	9.85	6.69		3	3	0	1.84	800 562-0032
State Street Rsch Govt Income C	Government	9.84	6.99	5.82	3	3	0	1.84	800 562-0032
State Street Rsch Govt Income S	Government	10.92	8.09	6.90	2	3	0	0.84	800 562-0032
State Street Rsch High Income A	Corp-HY	17.51	14.19	11.19	1	5	4.5	1.09	800 562-0032
State Street Rsch High Income B	Corp-HY	16.54	13.35	10.34	2	5	0	2.10	800 562-0032
State Street Rsch High Income C	Corp-HY	16.70	13.35	10.72	2	5	0	2.10	800 562-0032
State Street Rsch High Income S	Corp-HY	17.90	14.49	11.44	2	5	0	1.35	800 562-0032
State Street Rsch Int Bond S	Intl Bond	8.54	6.62		3	3	0		800 562-0032
State Street Rsch NY TF A	Muni NY	8.64	7.49	5.54	2	3	4.5	1.10	800 562-0032
State Street Rsch NY TF B	Muni NY	7.84	6.69	4.76	4	3	0	1.85	800 562-0032
State Street Rsch NY TF C	Muni NY	7.83	6.69	4.75	4	3	0	1.85	800 562-0032
State Street Rsch NY TF S	Muni NY	8.90	7.75	5.82	3	3	0	0.85	800 562-0032
State Street Rsch Strat Inc Fund A	Dvsfd Bond	11.01					4.5	1.35	800 562-0032
State Street Rsch Strat Inc Fund B	Dvsfd Bond	10.21					0	2.10	800 562-0032
State Street Rsch Strat Inc Fund C	Dvsfd Bond	10.36					0	1.10	800 562-0032
State Street Rsch Strat Inc Fund S	Dvsfd Bond	11.29					0		800 562-0032
State Street Rsch Tax-Exempt A	Muni Natl	9.31	7.94	5.58	3	4	4.5	1.08	800 562-0032
State Street Rsch Tax-Exempt B	Muni Natl	8.37	7.14	4.75	4	4	0	1.83	800 562-0032
State Street Rsch Tax-Exempt C	Muni Natl	8.38	7.14	4.78	3	4	0	0.83	800 562-0032
State Street Rsch Tax-Exempt S	Muni Natl	9.47	8.22	5.83	3	4	0		800 562-0032
Stein Roe High Yield Fund	Corp-HY	14.47					0		800 338-2550
Stein Roe High-Yield Municipals	Muni Natl	8.37	8.04	6.61	1	2	0	0.76	800 338-2550
Stein Roe Income Fund	Dvsfd Bond	8.77	8.19	7.22	2	3	0	0.83	800 338-2550
Stein Roe Intermediate Bond Fund	Corp-Inv	9.58	8.14	6.68	1	3	0	0.73	800 338-2550
Stein Roe Intermediate Municipals	Muni Natl	6.61	6.34	5.30	4	2	0	0.70	800 338-2550
Stein Roe Managed Municipals	Muni Natl	8.47	7.70	5.87	3	3	0	0.72	800 338-2550
STI Classic FL Tax Exempt Bond Flex	Muni State	7.19	6.31		5	3	0	2.28	800 428-6970
STI Classic FL Tax Exempt Inv	Muni State	7.71	6.84		3	3	3.75	1.31	800 428-6970
STI Classic FL Tax Exempt Tr	Muni State	7.92	7.01		3	3	0	0.80	800 428-6970
STI Classic GA Tax Exempt Bond Flex	Muni State	6.75	5.80		5	3	0	2.07	800 428-6970
STI Classic GA Tax Exempt Inv	Muni State	7.37	6.33		5	3	3.75	2.33	800 428-6970
STI Classic GA Tax Exempt Tr	Muni State	7.94	6.66		4	3	0	0.81	800 428-6970
STI Classic Inv Grade TE Bond Flex	Muni Natl	0.39	4.34		5	5	0	2.15	800 428-6970
STI Classic Invest Grade Bond Flex	Corp-Inv	16.75	8.60		4	5	0	2.20	800 428-6970
STI Classic Invest Grade Bond Inv	Corp-Inv	10.33	6.97	6.07	3	3	3.75	1.41	800 428-6970
STI Classic Invest Grade Bond Tr	Corp-Inv	10.74	7.39	6.41	2	3	0	0.85	800 428-6970
STI Classic Invest Grade TE Bd Inv	Muni Natl	7.11	6.86	6.64	2	2	3.75	1.44	800 428-6970
STI Classic Invest Grade TE Bond Tr	Muni Natl	7.71	7.35		1	2	3.75	0.86	800 428-6970
STI Classic Ltd Term Fed Mtg Sec Fl	Govt-Mtg	6.23	5.54		5	1	0	2.66	800 428-6970
STI Classic Ltd Term Fed Mtg Sec In	Govt-Mtg	6.69	5.87		5	3	2.5	1.48	800 428-6970
STI Classic Ltd Term Fed Mtg Sec Tr	Govt-Mtg	6.85	6.09		4	1	0	0.78	800 428-6970
STI Classic Short Term Bond Flex	Corp-Inv	6.62	5.53		5	2	0	1.20	800 428-6970
STI Classic Short Term Bond Inv	Corp-Inv	7.07	5.82	5.19	3	2	2	1.58	800 428-6970
STI Classic Short Term Bond Trust	Corp-Inv	7.25	6.03	5.39	3	2	0	0.78	800 428-6970
STI Classic Short Term US Treas Inv	Government	5.92	5.41	4.70	4	1	1	1.35	800 428-6970

410

Bond Fund Name	Objective	Annualized Return for			Rank		Max Load	Expense Ratio	Toll-Free Telephone
		1 Year	3 Years	5 Years	Overall	Risk			
STI Classic Short Term US Treas Tr	Government	6.08	5.55	5.02	3	1	0	0.92	800 428-6970
STI Classic ST US Treas Flex	Government	5.66	5.02		4	1	0	2.51	800 428-6970
STI Classic US Govt Secs Flex	Government	9.29	6.11		4	4	0	2.42	800 428-6970
STI Classic US Govt Secs Inv	Government	9.85	6.65		3	4	3.75	1.79	800 428-6970
STI Classic US Govt Secs Tr	Government	10.27	7.02		3	4	0	1.02	800 428-6970
Strong Advantage Fund	Corp-Inv	6.31	6.65	6.17	1	1	0	0.80	800 368-1030
Strong Corporate Bond Fund	Corp-Inv	12.58	10.62	10.27	1	5	0	1.00	800 368-1030
Strong Govt Securities Fund	Govt-Mtg	10.13	7.55	6.94	2	3	0	0.80	800 368-1030
Strong High Yield Bond Fund	Corp-HY	15.03					0	0.00	800 368-1030
Strong High Yield Municipal Bond Fd	Muni Natl	12.06	9.55		1	3	0	0.70	800 368-1030
Strong International Bond	Intl Bond	−3.01	0.80		5	5	0	1.50	800 368-1030
Strong Muni Advantage Fund	Muni Natl	4.89					0	0.40	800 368-1030
Strong Municipal Bond Fund	Muni Natl	10.78	7.78	5.63	3	3	0	0.80	800 368-1030
Strong Short-Term Bond Fund	Corp-Inv	6.89	7.44	6.15	2	1	0	0.90	800 368-1030
Strong Short-Term Global Bond Fund	Intl Bond	4.59	8.08		3	1	0	0.70	800 368-1030
Strong Short-term High Yield Bond	Corp-HY	13.27					0		800 368-1030
Strong Short-Term Municipal Bond	Muni Natl	6.46	6.05	4.16	3	1	0	0.60	800 368-1030
Summit High Yield Fund	Corp-HY	13.73	18.02		1	4	4.5	1.60	800 272-3442
SunAmerica Diversified Income A	Dvsfd Bond	7.15	10.99		3	5	4.75	1.42	800 858-8850
SunAmerica Diversified Income B	Dvsfd Bond	6.94	10.32	6.14	3	5	0	2.04	800 858-8850
SunAmerica Federal Securities A	Govt-Mtg	10.34	8.04		2	3	4.75	1.41	800 858-8850
SunAmerica Federal Securities B	Govt-Mtg	9.71	7.30	5.90	2	3	0	2.10	800 858-8850
SunAmerica High Income Fund A	Corp-HY	15.61	13.52	8.58	2	5	4.75	1.51	800 858-8850
SunAmerica High Income Fund B	Corp-HY	14.88	12.58		2	5	0	2.14	800 858-8850
SunAmerica Tax-Exempt Insured A	Muni Natl	8.31	7.12	5.61	2	3	4.75	1.24	800 858-8850
SunAmerica Tax-Exempt Insured B	Muni Natl	7.57	6.40		4	3	0	1.88	800 858-8850
SunAmerica US Government Secs A	Government	8.80	6.73	5.96	3	3	4.75	1.61	800 858-8850
SunAmerica US Government Secs B	Government	8.08	6.12	5.26	3	3	0	2.25	800 858-8850
Swisskey Global Bond Fund	Intl Bond	2.66	6.88		5	5	0	1.90	800 448-2430
Swisskey US Bond Fund	Corp-Inv	10.12					0	2.12	800 448-2430
T Rowe Price CA Tax-Free Bond	Muni CA	8.45	8.05	6.20	2	3	0	0.59	800 638-5660
T Rowe Price Corporate Income Fund	Corp-Inv	12.37					0	0.80	800 638-5660
T Rowe Price Emrg Markets Bond	Intl Bond	0.07	21.12		3	5	0	1.25	800 638-5660
T Rowe Price FL Tax-Free Ins Intmed	Muni State	6.49	5.88	5.40	3	2	0	0.60	800 638-5660
T Rowe Price GA Tax-Free Bond	Muni State	8.99	8.06	6.48	2	3	0	0.65	800 638-5660
T Rowe Price Global Government Bond	Intl Bond	5.11	5.56	5.68	4	4	0	1.20	800 638-5660
T Rowe Price GNMA Fund	Govt-Mtg	9.13	7.39	6.50	2	3	0	0.70	800 638-5660
T Rowe Price High-Yield Fund	Corp-HY	13.04	12.36	8.83	1	3	0	0.80	800 638-5660
T Rowe Price International Bond Fd	Intl Bond	1.98	3.16	6.38	5	5	0	0.86	800 638-5660
T Rowe Price MD Short-Term Tax-Free	Muni State	4.35	4.16	4.02	3	1	0		800 638-5660
T Rowe Price MD Tax-Free Bond	Muni State	8.10	7.31	5.91	1	3	0	0.51	800 638-5660
T Rowe Price New Income Fund	Corp-Inv	10.20	7.30	6.63	2	4	0	0.71	800 638-5660
T Rowe Price NJ Tax-Free Bond	Muni State	8.84	7.57	5.77	2	3	0	0.65	800 638-5660
T Rowe Price NY Tax-Free Bond	Muni NY	9.23	7.87	6.13	2	4	0	0.63	800 638-5660
T Rowe Price Short-Term Bond	Corp-Inv	6.63	5.87	4.34	4	1	0	0.72	800 638-5660
T Rowe Price Spectrum Income	Dvsfd Bond	11.22	10.40	9.00	1	3	0	0.00	800 638-5660
T Rowe Price ST US Government	Government	6.70	6.02	5.12	4	1	0	0.70	800 638-5660
T Rowe Price Summit GNMA Fd	Govt-Mtg	9.98	7.81		2	3	0	0.60	800 638-5660
T Rowe Price Summit Ltd Term Bd Fd	Dvsfd Bond	7.50	6.19		4	2	0	0.55	800 638-5660
T Rowe Price Summit Muni Inc	Muni Natl	10.49	9.06		1	3	0	0.50	800 638-5660
T Rowe Price Summit Muni Intmed Fd	Muni Natl	7.57	6.84		4	4	0	0.50	800 638-5660
T Rowe Price Tax-Free High-Yield	Muni Natl	9.40	8.36	6.80	1	3	0	0.72	800 638-5660
T Rowe Price Tax-Free Income	Muni Natl	8.74	7.65	6.11	2	3	0	0.55	800 638-5660
T Rowe Price Tax-Free Short-Intmed	Muni Natl	5.24	4.87	4.48	3	1	0	0.54	800 638-5660
T Rowe Price TF Insured Intmed Bond	Muni Natl	6.82	6.12	5.63	3	2	0	0.65	800 638-5660
T Rowe Price US Treasury Intmed	Government	9.73	6.59	5.78	3	3	0	0.61	800 638-5660
T Rowe Price US Treasury Long-Term	Government	19.16	9.51	8.17	3	5	0	0.80	800 638-5660
T Rowe Price VA Short-Term TF Bond	Muni State	4.42	4.11		3	1	0	0.65	800 638-5660

411

Bond Fund Name	Objective	Annualized Return for			Rank		Max Load	Expense Ratio	Toll-Free Telephone
		1 Year	3 Years	5 Years	Overall	Risk			
T Rowe Price VA Tax-Free Bond	Muni State	8.44	7.78	6.03	1	3	0	0.59	800 638-5660
Target Intermediate Bond	Corp-Inv	8.43	7.66	6.72	2	3	0	0.71	800 225-1852
Target International Bond	Intl Bond	−1.53	−0.41		5	5	0	1.35	800 225-1852
Target Mortgage Backed Securities	Govt-Mtg	8.59	7.96	6.95	1	2	0	0.88	800 225-1852
Target Total Return Bond	Dvsfd Bond	10.55	8.52	7.30	2	4	0	0.91	800 225-1852
Tax Exempt Bond Fund of America	Muni Natl	8.52	7.83	6.42	1	3	4.75	0.66	800 421-0180
Tax Exempt Fund of California	Muni CA	7.99	7.45	6.26	2	3	4.75	0.74	800 421-0180
Tax Exempt Fund of Maryland	Muni State	8.43	7.35	5.98	1	3	4.75	0.82	800 421-0180
Tax Exempt Fund of Virginia	Muni State	7.69	6.75	5.71	3	3	4.75	0.80	800 421-0180
Tax-Free Fund for Utah A	Muni State	8.37	7.75	6.20	1	3	4	0.27	800 228-4227
Tax-Free Fund for Utah C	Muni State	7.16					0	1.07	800 228-4227
Tax-Free Fund for Utah Y	Muni State	8.36					0	0.07	800 228-4227
Tax-Free Fund of Colorado A	Muni State	6.53	6.08	5.20	3	2	4	0.75	800 228-4227
Tax-Free Fund of Colorado C	Muni State	5.43					0	1.65	800 228-4227
Tax-Free Fund of Colorado Y	Muni State	6.57					0	0.68	800 228-4227
Tax-Free Trust of Arizona A	Muni State	7.79	6.87	5.60	2	3	4	0.72	800 228-4227
Tax-Free Trust of Arizona C	Muni State	6.85					0	1.57	800 228-4227
Tax-Free Trust of Arizona Y	Muni State	8.25					0	0.57	800 228-4227
Tax-Free Trust of Oregon A	Muni State	6.91	6.34	5.32	3	2	4	0.72	800 228-4227
Tax-Free Trust of Oregon C	Muni State	6.01					0	1.57	800 228-4227
Tax-Free Trust of Oregon Y	Muni State	7.05					0	0.57	800 228-4227
TCW/DW North Amer Govt Inc	Intl Bond	8.29	7.41	3.33	5	4	0	1.65	800 869-6397
Templeton Global Bond Fund I	Intl Bond	3.68	7.75	6.35	3	3	4.25	1.14	800 237-0738
Thompson Plumb Bond Fund	Corp-Inv	9.31	5.91	5.20	4	4	0	1.13	800-499-0079
Thornburg FL Intermediate Muni A	Muni State	6.85	6.25		3	1	3.5	0.61	800 847-0200
Thornburg Intermediate Muni Fund A	Muni Natl	6.69	6.45	5.87	3	2	3.5	1.00	800 847-0200
Thornburg Intermediate Muni Fund C	Muni Natl	6.25	5.99		3	2	0	1.64	800 847-0200
Thornburg Intermediate Muni Fund I	Muni Natl	6.93					0	2.71	800 847-0200
Thornburg Ltd Term Income Fund A	Corp-Inv	6.10	7.22	6.12	3	2	2.5	1.00	800 847-0200
Thornburg Ltd Term Income Fund C	Corp-Inv	5.62	6.80		3	2	0	1.40	800 847-0200
Thornburg Ltd Term Income Fund I	Corp-Inv	6.25					0	0.69	800 847-0200
Thornburg Ltd Term Muni Fund CA A	Muni CA	5.57	5.33	4.69	3	1	2.5	1.00	800 847-0200
Thornburg Ltd Term Muni Fund CA C	Muni CA	5.14	4.89		3	1	0	1.43	800 847-0200
Thornburg Ltd Term Muni Fund Natl A	Muni Natl	5.05	5.04	4.62	3	1	2.5	0.97	800 847-0200
Thornburg Ltd Term Muni Fund Natl C	Muni Natl	4.70	4.59		4	1	0	1.41	800 847-0200
Thornburg Ltd Term Muni Fund Natl I	Muni Natl	5.52					0	0.79	800 847-0200
Thornburg Ltd Term US Govt Fund A	Government	7.00	6.18	5.17	3	1	2.5	0.97	800 847-0200
Thornburg Ltd Term US Govt Fund C	Government	6.54	5.73		5	1	0	1.74	800 847-0200
Thornburg Ltd Term US Govt Fund I	Government	7.32					0	0.59	800 847-0200
Thornburg NM Intermediate Muni A	Muni State	6.28	5.74	5.14	3	1	3.5	1.06	800 847-0200
TIP Clover Fixed Income Fund	Corp-Inv	10.18	7.77	7.06	2	3	0	0.75	800 224-6312
Tocqueville Government Fund	Government	5.27					4	1.00	800 697-3863
Touchstone Bond Fund A	Dvsfd Bond	8.75	6.73		4	3	4.75	0.90	800 669-2796
Touchstone Bond Fund C	Dvsfd Bond	7.44	5.62		4	3	0	1.65	800 669-2796
Touchstone Income Opportunity A	Corp-HY	1.31	15.99		3	5	4.75	1.20	800 669-2796
Touchstone Income Opportunity C	Corp-HY	0.21	15.08		3	5		1.95	800 669-2796
Touchstone Standby Income Ultra ST	Corp-Inv	5.31	5.18		4	1	0		800 669-2796
Tower LA Muni Income Fund	Muni State	7.86	7.04	5.69	2	3	4.5	0.73	800 999-0124
Tower Total Return Bd Fund	Corp-Inv	8.86	6.44		4	4	3	1.30	800 999-0124
Tower US Government Income Fund	Government	9.12	6.82	5.80	3	2	3	0.95	800 999-0124
Trust For Cr Unions Government	Govt-Mtg	5.82	5.48	3.42	3	1	0	0.34	
Trust For Cr Unions Mort Secs	Govt-Mtg	7.49	6.91	6.00	2	1	0	0.30	
UAM BHM&S Total Return Bond Port A	Corp-Inv	10.05					0	0.57	800 638-7983
UAM BHM&S Total Return Bond Port B	Corp-Inv	9.74					0	0.82	800 638-7983
UAM Chicago Asset Mgmt Interm Bond	Corp-Inv	7.81	5.34		5	3	0	0.80	800 638-7983
UAM DSI Limited Maturity Portfolio	Corp-Inv	6.67	6.19	4.99	3	1	0	0.96	800 638-7983
UAM ICM Fixed Income	Corp-Inv	9.40	7.32	6.30	3	3	0	0.50	800 638-7983
UAM McKee US Government Portfolio	Government	10.09	6.20		3	5	0	1.02	800 638-7983

Bond Fund Name	Objective	Annualized Return for			Rank		Max Load	Expense Ratio	Toll-Free Telephone
		1 Year	3 Years	5 Years	Overall	Risk			
UAM TS&W Fixed Income	Corp-Inv	10.11	6.93	5.70	3	4	0	0.72	800 638-7983
UBS Bond Fund	Dvsfd Bond	7.84					0	0.80	888 827-3863
United Bond Fund Class A	Corp-Inv	10.50	8.03	6.66	2	4	5.75	0.77	800 366-5465
United Government Securities Fund A	Government	10.24	7.27	6.29	2	3	4.25	0.93	800 366-5465
United High-Income Fund A	Corp-HY	13.35	13.01	10.32	1	3	5.75	0.84	800 366-5465
United High-Income Fund II A	Corp-HY	12.96	12.72	10.08	1	3	5.75	0.93	800 366-5465
United High-Income Fund II Y	Corp-HY	13.10					0	0.77	800 366-5465
United Municipal Bond Fund A	Muni Natl	8.73	8.33	6.59	2	3	4.25	0.68	800 366-5465
United Municipal High Income A	Muni Natl	11.17	9.62	8.14	1	2	4.25	0.81	800 366-5465
US Global Invs Near Term Tax Free	Muni Natl	6.06	5.19	4.28	4	5	0	1.92	800 426-6635
US Global Invs US Tax Free Fund	Muni Natl	7.71	6.96	5.79	3	2	0	0.40	800 426-6635
US Government Securities Fund	Government	8.99	6.78	5.37	3	3	4.75	0.80	800 421-0180
USAA CA Bond Fund	Muni CA	10.03	9.09	6.58	1	3	0	0.41	800 382-8722
USAA FL Tax-Free Income	Muni State	9.92	8.72		2	3	0	0.57	800 382-8722
USAA GNMA Trust	Govt-Mtg	10.17	7.88	6.79	1	3	0	0.30	800 382-8722
USAA NY Bond Fund	Muni NY	10.19	8.40	6.53	1	3	0	0.50	800 382-8722
USAA ST Bond Fund	Corp-HY	7.18	6.80	5.89	3	1	0	0.50	800 382-8722
USAA Tax Exempt Intermed-Term Fund	Muni Natl	8.81	7.73	6.34	1	2	0	0.37	800 382-8722
USAA Tax Exempt Long-Term Fund	Muni Natl	9.70	8.54	6.23	1	3	0	0.36	800 382-8722
USAA Tax Exempt Short-Term Fund	Muni Natl	5.64	5.44	4.77	3	1	0	0.39	800 382-8722
USAA TX Tax-Free Income	Muni State	10.47	9.68		2	4	0	1.35	800 382-8722
USAA VA Bond Fund	Muni State	8.85	7.96	6.58	1	3	0	0.47	800 382-8722
Value Line Aggress Income	Corp-HY	12.53	16.36	11.85	1	4	0	1.10	800 223-0818
Value Line NY Tax Exempt Fund	Muni NY	8.39	7.16	5.36	4	4	0	0.92	800 223-0818
Value Line TE High Yield	Muni Natl	8.05	7.13	5.45	3	3	0	0.60	800 223-0818
Value Line US Government Securities	Government	9.66	6.93	4.27	4	3	0	0.66	800 223-0818
Van Eck Chubb Government Securities	Government	8.59	6.87	6.13	2	3	4.75	1.00	800 826-2333
Van Eck Chubb Tax Exempt Fund	Muni Natl	8.31	7.01	5.63	1	2	3	1.00	800 826-2333
Van Kampen Am Cap Corporate Bond A	Corp-Inv	11.24	8.35	7.23	3	5	4.75	1.09	800 421-5666
Van Kampen Am Cap Corporate Bond B	Corp-Inv	10.43	7.56		3	5	0	1.33	800 421-5666
Van Kampen Am Cap Corporate Bond C	Corp-Inv	10.43	7.51		3	5	0	1.94	800 421-5666
Van Kampen Am Cap High Inc Corp A	Corp-HY	12.02	13.07	9.99	1	3	4.75	1.00	800 421-5666
Van Kampen Am Cap High Inc Corp B	Corp-HY	11.20	12.20	9.14	1	3	0	1.87	800 421-5666
Van Kampen Am Cap High Inc Corp C	Corp-HY	11.26	12.21		1	3	0	1.87	800 421-5666
Van Kampen Am Cap US Govt Tr Inc A	Government	8.40	6.25	5.25	3	3	4.75	1.13	800 421-5666
Van Kampen Am Cap US Govt Tr Inc B	Government	7.63	5.47	4.24	5	3	0	1.94	800 421-5666
Van Kampen Am Cap US Govt Tr Inc C	Government	7.63	5.46		5	3	0	1.89	800 421-5666
Van Kampen Amer Cap CA Ins TF A	Muni CA	8.63	7.95	5.72	3	4	3.25	0.96	800 421-5666
Van Kampen Amer Cap CA Ins TF B	Muni CA	7.79	7.13	4.90	4	4	0	1.79	800 421-5666
Van Kampen Amer Cap CA Ins TF C	Muni CA	7.79	7.14		4	4	0	1.80	800 421-5666
Van Kampen Amer Cap Fl Ins TF Inc A	Muni State	8.48	7.80		3	4	4.75	0.28	800 421-5666
Van Kampen Amer Cap Fl Ins TF Inc B	Muni State	7.68	7.02		3	4	0	1.03	800 421-5666
Van Kampen Amer Cap Fl Ins TF Inc C	Muni State	7.67	7.06		4	4	0	1.03	800 421-5666
Van Kampen Amer Cap Global Govt A	Intl Bond	5.06	3.87	3.78	5	4	4.75	1.52	800 421-5666
Van Kampen Amer Cap Global Govt B	Intl Bond	4.21	3.09	2.99	5	4	0	1.45	800 421-5666
Van Kampen Amer Cap Global Govt C	Intl Bond	4.25	3.11	3.03	5	5	0	2.63	800 421-5666
Van Kampen Amer Cap Govt Secs A	Government	9.76	6.73	5.54	3	4	4.75	1.03	800 421-5666
Van Kampen Amer Cap Govt Secs B	Government	8.94	5.91	4.75	4	4	0	1.82	800 421-5666
Van Kampen Amer Cap Govt Secs C	Government	8.97	5.92	4.73	4	4	0	1.82	800 421-5666
Van Kampen Amer Cap High Yield A	Corp-HY	9.36	11.40	9.09	1	2	4.75	1.14	800 421-5666
Van Kampen Amer Cap High Yield B	Corp-HY	8.58	10.58	8.04	1	2	0	1.90	800 421-5666
Van Kampen Amer Cap High Yield C	Corp-HY	8.47	10.54		1	2	0	1.90	800 421-5666
Van Kampen Amer Cap HY Muni A	Muni Natl	10.67	9.02	7.64	1	2	4.75	0.95	800 421-5666
Van Kampen Amer Cap HY Muni B	Muni Natl	9.78	8.18		1	2	0	0.86	800 421-5666
Van Kampen Amer Cap HY Muni C	Muni Natl	9.79	8.18		1	2	0	1.77	800 421-5666
Van Kampen Amer Cap Ins TF Inc A	Muni Natl	8.12	7.19	5.70	3	4	4.75	0.92	800 421-5666
Van Kampen Amer Cap Ins TF Inc B	Muni Natl	7.31	6.40	4.87	5	4	0	1.74	800 421-5666
Van Kampen Amer Cap Ins TF Inc C	Muni Natl	7.31	6.38		5	4	0	1.74	800 421-5666

Bond Fund Name	Objective	Annualized Return for			Rank		Max Load	Expense Ratio	Toll-Free Telephone
		1 Year	3 Years	5 Years	Overall	Risk			
Van Kampen Amer Cap Int Muni Inc A	Muni Natl	8.14	6.97	6.49	2	2	3.25	1.56	800 421-5666
Van Kampen Amer Cap Int Muni Inc B	Muni Natl	7.31	6.24	5.72	3	2	0	2.32	800 421-5666
Van Kampen Amer Cap Int Muni Inc C	Muni Natl	7.41	6.27		3	2	0	2.32	800 421-5666
Van Kampen Amer Cap Ltd Mat Govt A	Govt-Mtg	5.82	5.21	4.45	4	1	3.25	1.31	800 421-5666
Van Kampen Amer Cap Ltd Mat Govt B	Govt-Mtg	5.06	4.39	3.73	4	1	0	2.11	800 421-5666
Van Kampen Amer Cap Ltd Mat Govt C	Govt-Mtg	5.07	4.45		5	1	0	2.20	800 421-5666
Van Kampen Amer Cap Muni Inc A	Muni Natl	8.22	7.61	5.63	3	3	4.75	0.89	800 421-5666
Van Kampen Amer Cap Muni Inc B	Muni Natl	7.37	6.79	4.88	3	3	0	1.49	800 421-5666
Van Kampen Amer Cap NY TF Inc A	Muni NY	10.63	9.22		2	4	4.75	0.64	800 421-5666
Van Kampen Amer Cap NY TF Inc B	Muni NY	9.80	8.42		1	4	0	1.07	800 421-5666
Van Kampen Amer Cap NY TF Inc C	Muni NY	9.80	8.42		1	4	0	1.08	800 421-5666
Van Kampen Amer Cap PA TF Inc A	Muni State	8.52	7.68	5.88	1	3	4.75	1.04	800 421-5666
Van Kampen Amer Cap PA TF Inc B	Muni State	7.67	6.87	5.19	4	3	0	1.85	800 421-5666
Van Kampen Amer Cap PA TF Inc C	Muni State	7.73	6.87		4	3	0	1.85	800 421-5666
Van Kampen Amer Cap ST Global Inc A	Intl Bond	3.46	6.08	2.99	5	2	3.25	1.18	800 421-5666
Van Kampen Amer Cap ST Global Inc B	Intl Bond	2.66	5.29	2.23	5	2	0	2.01	800 421-5666
Van Kampen Amer Cap ST Global Inc C	Intl Bond	2.67	5.29		5	2	0	2.09	800 421-5666
Van Kampen Amer Cap Strategic Inc A	Dvsfd Bond	3.89	10.47		3	5	4.75	1.75	800 421-5666
Van Kampen Amer Cap Strategic Inc B	Dvsfd Bond	3.11	9.61		3	5	0	2.57	800 421-5666
Van Kampen Amer Cap Strategic Inc C	Dvsfd Bond	3.03	9.59		4	5	0	2.56	800 421-5666
Van Kampen Amer Cap TF High Inc A	Muni Natl	8.71	7.46	6.72	2	3	4.75	0.94	800 421-5666
Van Kampen Amer Cap TF High Inc B	Muni Natl	7.90	6.64	5.98	3	3	0	1.75	800 421-5666
Van Kampen Amer Cap TF High Inc C	Muni Natl	7.83	6.62		3	3	0	1.75	800 421-5666
Van Kampen Amer Cap US Govt A	Govt-Mtg	8.35	6.98	5.68	3	3	4.75	0.90	800 421-5666
Van Kampen Amer Cap US Govt B	Govt-Mtg	7.42	6.11	4.82	4	3	0	1.72	800 421-5666
Van Kampen Amer Cap US Govt C	Govt-Mtg	7.42	6.11		4	3	0	1.72	800 421-5666
Van Kampen Explorer Active Core	Corp-Inv	8.36					0	2.01	800 421-5666
Van Kampen Explorer Ltd Duration	Corp-Inv	6.32					0	1.86	800 421-5666
Vanguard Admiral Intmed US Treas	Government	10.90	7.37	6.49	3	4	0	0.15	800 662-7447
Vanguard Admiral LT US Treas	Government	18.53	9.82	8.62	3	5	0	0.15	800 662-7447
Vanguard Admiral ST US Treas	Government	6.84	6.11	5.52	3	1	0	0.15	800 662-7447
Vanguard Bond Index Intermed Term	Corp-Inv	10.88	7.68		3	4	0	0.20	800 662-7447
Vanguard Bond Index Long Term	Corp-Inv	17.46	9.85		3	5	0	0.20	800 662-7447
Vanguard Bond Index Short Term	Corp-Inv	7.31	6.42		4	1	0	0.20	800 662-7447
Vanguard Bond Index Total Bond Mkt	Corp-Inv	10.54	7.82	6.81	2	3	0	0.20	800 662-7447
Vanguard CA Tax-Free Ins Intermed	Muni CA	6.70	6.99		3	2	0	0.19	800 662-7447
Vanguard CA Tax-Free Ins Long-Term	Muni CA	8.39	8.25	6.49	3	4	0	0.16	800 662-7447
Vanguard F/I GNMA Portfolio	Govt-Mtg	8.92	8.01	6.96	1	3	0	0.31	800 662-7447
Vanguard F/I High-Yield Corporate	Corp-HY	11.25	11.21	9.72	1	3	0	0.28	800 662-7447
Vanguard F/I Intmed-Term Corporate	Corp-Inv	10.09	7.63		2	4	0	0.25	800 662-7447
Vanguard F/I Intmed-Term US Treas	Government	10.19	7.06	6.28	3	4	0	0.27	800 662-7447
Vanguard F/I Long Term Corporate	Corp-Inv	16.43	9.92	8.53	2	5	0	0.32	800 662-7447
Vanguard F/I Long-Term US Treasury	Government	18.41	9.73	8.49	3	5	0	0.27	800 662-7447
Vanguard F/I Short-Term Corporate	Corp-Inv	7.33	6.59	5.92	3	1	0	0.28	800 662-7447
Vanguard F/I Short-Term Federal	Government	6.83	6.27	5.58	3	1	0	0.27	800 662-7447
Vanguard FL Tax-Free Ins Long-Term	Muni State	8.38	7.95	6.46	3	4	0	0.19	800 662-7447
Vanguard LIFEStrategy Income	Corp-Inv	13.87	12.21		1	5	0	0.00	800 662-7447
Vanguard Municipal High-Yield	Muni Natl	8.84	7.99	6.55	1	3	0	0.19	800 662-7447
Vanguard Municipal Insured LT	Muni Natl	8.18	7.70	6.28	3	4	0	0.18	800 662-7447
Vanguard Municipal Intermed-Term	Muni Natl	6.61	6.41	5.80	3	2	0	0.18	800 662-7447
Vanguard Municipal Limited-Term	Muni Natl	5.19	4.82	4.52	3	1	0	0.18	800 662-7447
Vanguard Municipal Long-Term	Muni Natl	8.48	8.11	6.53	2	3	0	0.18	800 662-7447
Vanguard Municipal Short-Term	Muni Natl	4.16	4.02	3.81	3	1	0	0.18	800 662-7447
Vanguard NJ TF Insured Long-Term	Muni State	8.08	7.03	5.81	2	3	0	0.18	800 662-7447
Vanguard NY Insured Long-Term	Muni NY	8.41	7.63	6.15	2	3	0	0.20	800 662-7447
Vanguard OH TF Insured Long-Term	Muni State	8.09	7.47	6.12	2	3	0	0.19	800 662-7447
Vanguard PA TF Insured Long-Term	Muni State	8.17	7.48	6.15	2	3	0	0.18	800 662-7447
Vanguard ST US Treasury Portfolio	Government	6.81	6.05	5.31	3	1	0	0.25	800 662-7447

Bond Fund Name	Objective	Annualized Return for			Rank		Max Load	Expense Ratio	Toll-Free Telephone
		1 Year	3 Years	5 Years	Overall	Risk			
Victory Fund for Income	Govt-Mtg	7.45	6.80	5.93	3	2	2	0.99	800 539-3863
Victory Govt Mortgage Fund	Govt-Mtg	8.57	7.12	6.21	2	2	5.75	0.85	800 539-3863
Victory Intermediate Income Fund	Corp-Inv	8.15	6.11		3	2	5.75	0.96	800 539-3863
Victory Investment Quality Bd Fund	Corp-Inv	9.70	6.81		3	3	5.75	1.02	800 539-3863
Victory Limited Term Income Fund	Corp-Inv	6.00	5.44	4.79	4	1	2	0.85	800 539-3863
Victory National Muni Bd A	Muni Natl	8.20	7.64		2	3	5.75	0.30	800 539-3863
Victory National Muni Bd B	Muni Natl	6.96	6.66		4	3	0	1.55	800 539-3863
Victory NY Tax-Free Fund	Muni NY	5.93	5.61	4.85	3	2	5.75	0.94	800 539-3863
Victory NY Tax-Free Fund B	Muni NY	4.84	4.76		5	4	0	1.76	800 539-3863
Victory OH Municipal Bond Fund	Muni State	8.47	7.58	6.42	2	3	5.75	0.89	800 539-3863
Vintage Income Fund	Corp-Inv	8.42	6.09	5.32	3	2	0	1.20	800 438-6375
Vintage Limited Term Bond Fund	Corp-Inv	7.40	5.50		5	3	0	1.40	800 438-6375
Vintage Muni Bond Fund	Muni Natl	6.10	5.54	4.86	4	3	0	1.28	800 438-6375
Vontobel Intl Bond	Intl Bond	3.54	3.36		4	5	0	1.48	800 527-9500
Voyageur AZ Insured Tax-Free A	Muni State	8.25	7.51	5.95	2	3	3.75	0.59	800 553-2143
Voyageur AZ Insured Tax-Free C	Muni State	7.42	6.61		4	3	0	1.70	800 553-2143
Voyageur CA Insured Tax-Free A	Muni CA	10.18	8.34	5.82	2	4	3.75	0.82	800 553-2143
Voyageur CA Insured Tax-Free B	Muni CA	9.53	7.83		3	4	0	1.21	800 553-2143
Voyageur FL Insured Tax-Free A	Muni State	9.90	8.08	6.09	2	4	3.75	0.73	800 553-2143
Voyageur FL Insured Tax-Free B	Muni State	9.22	7.47		3	4	0	1.24	800 553-2143
Voyageur FL Ltd-Term TF A	Muni State	6.88	6.02		3	2	2.75		800 553-2143
Voyageur FL Ltd-Term TF C	Muni State	5.83	4.99		3	2	0		800 553-2143
Voyageur IA Tax-Free Fund	Muni State	8.20	7.64		4	4	3.75	0.92	800 553-2143
Voyageur KS Tax-Free	Muni State	9.67	8.01	6.38	2	3	3.75	0.83	800 553-2143
Voyageur MN Insured Tax-Free Fund A	Muni State	8.34	7.06	5.67	2	3	3.75	0.70	800 553-2143
Voyageur MN Insured Tax-Free Fund C	Muni State	7.50	6.25		5	3	0	1.68	800 553-2143
Voyageur MN Ltd Term Tax-Free Fd A	Muni State	6.36	5.41	4.90	3	2	2.75	0.92	800 553-2143
Voyageur MN Ltd Term Tax-Free Fd C	Muni State	5.56	4.62		4	2	0		800 553-2143
Voyageur MO Insured Tax-Free A	Muni State	8.37	7.56	5.96	2	3	3.75	0.71	800 553-2143
Voyageur MO Insured Tax-Free B	Muni State	7.68	6.90		2	3	0	1.29	800 553-2143
Voyageur ND Tax-Free Fund A	Muni State	8.72	7.91	6.24	1	3	3.75	0.34	800 553-2143
Voyageur ND Tax-Free Fund B	Muni State	7.96	7.31		2	3	0	1.36	800 553-2143
Voyageur NM Tax-Free Fund A	Muni State	9.81	8.32	6.59	1	3	3.75	0.88	800 553-2143
Voyageur NM Tax-Free Fund B	Muni State	9.02	8.42		2	3	0	1.61	800 553-2143
Voyageur NY Tax Free Fund A	Muni NY	7.11	5.50	4.66	3	2	3.75	0.99	800 553-2143
Voyageur NY Tax Free Fund B	Muni NY	6.26	4.56		4	2	0	1.87	800 553-2143
Voyageur NY Tax Free Fund C	Muni NY	6.26	4.49		4	2	0	1.84	800 553-2143
Voyageur OR Ins Tax-Free Fund A	Muni State	9.43	7.80		2	3	3.75	0.71	800 553-2143
Voyageur OR Ins Tax-Free Fund B	Muni State	8.77	7.19		3	3	0	1.25	800 553-2143
Voyageur UT Tax-Free Fund	Muni State	9.56	8.11	6.61	1	3	3.75	0.68	800 553-2143
Voyageur WA Ins Tax-Free Fd	Muni State	9.55	8.25		1	3	3.75	0.44	800 553-2143
Voyageur WI Tax-Free Fd	Muni State	8.16	7.26		2	3	3.75	0.98	800 553-2143
Wachovia Fixed Income Fund A	Corp-Inv	9.70	7.05	5.92	3	4	4.5	0.95	800 462-7538
Wachovia Fixed Income Fund B	Corp-Inv	8.89					0	1.76	800 462-7538
Wachovia Fixed Income Fund Y	Corp-Inv	9.96					0	0.74	800 462-7538
Wachovia GA Muni Bond Fund A	Muni State	6.44					4.5	1.12	800 462-7538
Wachovia GA Muni Bond Fund Y	Muni State	6.64					0	0.92	800 462-7538
Wachovia Intmed Fixed Income	Corp-Inv	11.14	6.85		3	4	4.5	1.05	800 462-7538
Wachovia NC Muni Bond Fund A	Muni State	6.40	6.47		5	3	4.5	1.05	800 462-7538
Wachovia NC Muni Bond Fund Y	Muni State	6.79					0	0.85	800 462-7538
Wachovia SC Muni Bond Fund A	Muni State	7.35	6.93	5.95	3	3	4.5	0.79	800 462-7538
Wachovia SC Muni Bond Fund Y	Muni State	7.68					0	0.58	800 462-7538
Wachovia ST Fixed Income Fund A	Corp-Inv	6.17	5.61	4.97	3	1	2.5	0.84	800 462-7538
Wachovia ST Fixed Income Fund Y	Corp-Inv	6.40					0	0.63	800 462-7538
Wachovia VA Muni Bond	Muni State	7.66	6.38		5	3	4.5	0.96	800 462-7538
Waddell & Reed Ltd Term Bd Fund B	Corp-Inv	5.95	4.94	4.35	5	2	0		800 366-5465
Waddell & Reed Ltd Term Bd Fund Y	Corp-Inv	6.71					0		800 366-5465
Waddell & Reed Muni Bd Fund B	Muni Natl	8.94	7.89		2	3	0		800 366-5465

415

Bond Fund Name	Objective	Annualized Return for			Rank		Max Load	Expense Ratio	Toll-Free Telephone
		1 Year	3 Years	5 Years	Overall	Risk			
Warburg Pincus Fixed Income A	Corp-Inv	8.67	8.35	7.14	2	2	0	0.75	800 888-6878
Warburg Pincus Fixed Income Adv	Corp-Inv	7.15					0	1.00	800 888-6878
Warburg Pincus Global FI	Intl Bond	1.12	7.88	6.20	2	3	0	0.96	800 888-6878
Warburg Pincus Global FI Adv	Intl Bond	0.54					0	1.45	800 888-6878
Warburg Pincus Intmed Mat Govt	Government	8.42	6.71	5.73	3	3	0	0.61	800 888-6878
Warburg Pincus NY Intmed Muni Bd Ad	Muni NY	5.27					0	0.83	800 888-6878
Warburg Pincus NY Intmed Muni Bond	Muni NY	5.61	5.44	4.96	3	2	0	0.60	800 888-6878
Warburg Pincus Tr II-Fixed Income	Corp-Inv	8.97					0		800 888-6878
Warburg Pincus Tr II-Global Fxd Inc	Intl Bond	3.75					0		800 888-6878
Wasatch-Hoisington US Treasury Fund	Government	21.37	10.96	7.70	3	5	0	0.75	800 551-1700
Wayne Hummer Income Fund	Corp-Inv	9.57	7.15	6.24	3	3	0	1.01	800 621-4477
Weitz Series Fixed Income	Corp-Inv	9.21	7.23	6.25	2	3	0	0.75	800 232-4161
Westcore CO Tax Exempt Bond	Muni State	6.65	6.04	5.35	2	2	0	1.21	800 392-2673
Westcore Intmed-Term Bond Fund	Corp-Inv	8.48	6.87	5.69	3	2	0	0.85	800 392-2673
Westcore Long Term Bond	Corp-Inv	16.64	9.95	8.18	2	5	0	0.95	800 392-2673
Western Asset Core Portfolio	Corp-Inv	11.64	8.22	7.47	2	4	0	0.50	800 822-5544
Western Asset Intermediate Port	Corp-Inv	8.78	7.41		2	2	0		800 822-5544
Western Asset Limited Duration Port	Corp-Inv	7.12					0		800 822-5544
William Blair Income Fund	Corp-Inv	8.27	6.56	5.85	2	2	0	0.68	800 742-7272
Winthrop Focus Fixed Income A	Corp-Inv	8.32	6.01	5.17	3	3	4.75	1.00	800 494-6847
Winthrop Focus Fixed Income B	Corp-Inv	7.63					0	1.70	800 494-6847
Winthrop Focus Municipal Trust A	Muni Natl	6.93	6.07		3	3	4.75	0.50	800 494-6847
Winthrop Focus Municipal Trust B	Muni Natl	6.19					0	1.20	800 494-6847
WM CA Insured Intmed Muni A	Muni CA	6.26	6.49		4	2	4.5	0.82	800 531-6466
WM CA Insured Intmed Muni B	Muni CA	5.47	5.70		4	2	0	1.57	800 531-6466
WM CA Insured Intmed Muni S	Muni CA	5.48	5.70		4	2	0	1.57	800 531-6466
WM CA Municipal Fund A	Muni CA	9.25	8.13	5.88	1	3	4.5	0.80	800 531-6466
WM CA Municipal Fund B	Muni CA	8.03	7.21		3	3	0	1.72	800 531-6466
WM FL Municipal Fund A	Muni State	9.36	8.44	6.00	3	4	4.5	0.82	800 531-6466
WM FL Municipal Fund B	Muni State	8.53	7.63		3	4	0	1.57	800 531-6466
WM FL Municipal Fund S	Muni State	8.51	7.63		3	4	0	1.57	800 531-6466
WM Income Fund A	Corp-Inv	10.88	8.39	7.30	3	5	4	1.06	800 531-6466
WM Income Fund B	Corp-Inv	9.95	7.53		3	5	0	1.88	800 531-6466
WM ST High Quality Bond A	Corp-Inv	5.99	5.73		4	1	3.5	0.82	800 531-6466
WM ST High Quality Bond B	Corp-Inv	5.25	4.96		5	1	0	1.57	800 531-6466
WM ST High Quality Bond S	Corp-Inv	5.25	4.96		5	1	0	1.57	800 531-6466
WM Tax Exempt Bond Fund A	Muni Natl	7.58	6.78	5.53	4	3	4	0.80	800 531-6466
WM Tax Exempt Bond Fund B	Muni Natl	6.76	6.05		5	3	0	1.63	800 531-6466
WM US Government Securities A	Govt-Mtg	10.37	7.28	6.14	3	4	5.5	1.05	800 531-6466
WM US Government Securities B	Govt-Mtg	9.57	6.41		4	4	0	1.85	800 531-6466
WPG Core Bond Fund	Government	9.42	6.83	4.26	3	2	0	0.86	800 223-3332
WPG Intermediate Municipal Bond	Muni Natl	7.10	6.52		3	2	0	0.85	800 223-3332
Wright Current Income Fund	Govt-Mtg	8.09	7.16	5.93	2	3	0	0.48	800 232-0013
Wright Total Return Bond Fund	Corp-Inv	11.33	7.16	5.98	3	5	0	0.90	800 232-0013
Wright US Treasury Fund	Government	11.20	7.06	6.24	3	5	0	0.90	800 232-0013
Wright US Treasury Near Term Fund	Government	6.11	5.49	4.43	4	1	0	0.87	800 232-0013
Zweig Government Fund A	Government	10.28	5.88	5.14	5	4	4.75	1.36	800 272-2700
Zweig Government Fund B	Government	9.58					0	2.09	800 272-2700
Zweig Government Fund C	Government	9.79	5.39	4.57	5	4	0	1.84	800 272-2700

GLOSSARY OF
FUND INVESTMENT TERMS

Adviser. Organization or person hired by a mutual fund to provide professional management and guidance.

Aggressive Growth Fund. Mutual fund that seeks high growth by employing aggressive investment strategies. Such funds typically own shares of small, emerging companies that offer the potential for rapid growth.

Alpha. Excess return provided by an investment that is uncorrelated with the general stock market.

Annual Report. Yearly summary sent by mutual funds to shareholders, showing which securities are owned and discussing performance over the period under review.

Ask or Offer Price. Lowest amount a seller is willing to take for shares of a stock or closed-end fund. In the case of no-load funds, it represents the net asset value plus any sales charges.

Asset Allocation. Act of spreading an investment portfolio across various categories, such as stocks, bonds, and money market funds.

Assets. Investment holdings owned by a fund.

Automatic Reinvestment. Shareholder-authorized purchase of additional shares using fund dividends and capital gains distributions.

Average Maturity. Length of time before a bond issuer must return the holder's principal. Bonds are issued for a variety of maturities, from 30 days to more than 30 years. Bond mutual funds attempt to maintain a portfolio of securities with different maturities. When taken together, the overall fund's average maturity can then be measured.

Balanced Fund. Mutual fund that invests in a blended portfolio of stocks, bonds, and cash.

Bear Market. Period of time in which prices on the stock market are generally falling.

Beta. Coefficient measure of a stock's or mutual fund's relative volatility in relation to the Standard & Poor's 500 Index, which has a beta of 1.

Bid Price.   Highest amount a buyer is willing to pay for shares of a stock or mutual fund. Also referred to as the *redemption price.* This is the same as *net asset value,* except for funds with back-end sales loads.

Blue Chip.   Common stock of a nationally known company with a long record of profit growth and dividend payments, and a reputation for quality products and services.

Blue-Sky Laws.   State laws governing the registration and distribution of mutual fund shares. All 50 states and the District of Columbia regulate mutual funds.

Bond.   Any interest-bearing or discounted government or corporate obligation to pay a specified sum of money, usually at regular intervals.

Bond Fund.   Mutual fund that holds bonds of various maturities and safety ratings.

Book Value.   What a company would be worth if all assets were sold (assets minus liability). Also, the price at which an asset is carried on a balance sheet.

Bottom-Up Investing.   Process used to search for individual stocks without regard for overall economic trends.

Broker.   Person who acts as an intermediary between a buyer and seller.

Bull Market.   Period of time in which security prices are generally rising.

Buy-and-Hold Strategy.   Technique that calls for accumulating and keeping shares of a mutual fund for many years, regardless of price swings.

Call.   Option contract giving the holder the right to purchase a specified security at a stated price during a specific time period.

Capital Appreciation.   Increase in the market value of a mutual fund's securities. This is reflected in the increased net asset value of a fund's shares.

Capital Depreciation.   Decline in the value of a given investment, including the net asset value of a fund's shares.

Capital Gains Distribution.   Payment to fund shareholders of profits realized for securities sold at a premium to their original cost. For tax purposes, shares held more than 18 months are treated as long-term capital gains, with a maximum tax rate of 20 percent. However, gains from securities held less than 18 months are taxed as ordinary income by the Internal Revenue Service.

Cash Equivalent.   Investment that can easily be turned into cash. Examples include certificates of deposit and money market funds.

Cash Position.   Percentage of a fund's portfolio invested in cash and cash equivalents, minus current liabilities.

Certificate of Deposit.   Instrument issued by a bank or savings and loan that pays a specific amount of interest for a set time period. If you take your money out before the maturity date, you must pay an early-withdrawal penalty.

Check-Writing Privilege.   Service offered by most discount brokers and large fund families allowing shareholders to write checks against their money market fund holdings. This cash continues to earn interest until a check clears.

Classes of Shares (i.e., Class A, Class B).   Trend among fund organizations to provide multiple purchase options for the same fund. This is a way of disguising sales load in various ways. Class A shares, for example, might require payment of an up-front load. Class B shares, on the other hand, might impose a 12b-1 fee and redemption fee instead.

Closed-End Fund. Investment company that issues a limited number of shares and is traded on a stock exchange. The value of such funds is determined by market supply and demand; shares are not necessarily traded at net asset value.

Commercial Paper. Short-term, unsecured promissory notes issued by corporations to finance immediate credit needs.

Commission. Fee paid by investors to a broker or other sales agent for the purchase of investment products. Also referred to as a *sales load*.

Common Stock. Security representing ownership of a corporation's assets that generally carries voting rights. Common stock dividends, however, are always paid after the company has met its obligations for bonds, debentures, and preferred stock.

Compounding. Earnings on top of earnings.

Contractual Plan. Program for the accumulation of mutual fund shares in which an investor agrees to invest a fixed amount on a regular basis for a specific number of years.

Contrarian. Investor who does the opposite of the majority at any particular time.

Convertible Securities. Securities that can be exchanged for other securities of the issuer under certain conditions; usually, the exchange is from preferred stock or bonds into common stock.

Corporate Bond Fund. Mutual fund that holds bonds of various maturities and safety ratings issued by a private or publicly traded company.

Credit Risk. Possibility that a bond issuer will default on the payment of interest and return of principal. Risk is minimized by investing in bonds issued by large blue-chip corporations or government agencies.

Current Assets. In a mutual fund, cash plus cash equivalents, minus current liabilities.

Current Liabilities. Obligations due within one year or sooner.

Custodian. Person or organization (usually a bank or trust company) that holds the securities and other assets of a mutual fund.

Debenture. Bond secured only by the general credit of a corporation.

Distribution. Dividends paid from net investment income plus realized capital gains.

Diversification. Act of spreading risk by putting assets into several different investment categories (i.e., stocks, bonds, and cash).

Diversified Investment Company. Under the Investment Company Act, a company (or fund) that, with respect to 75 percent of total assets, has not invested more than 5 percent nor holds more than 10 percent of the outstanding voting securities of any one company.

Dividend. Distribution of earnings to shareholders.

Dividend Yield. Cash dividend paid per share each year, divided by the current share price.

Dollar-Cost Averaging. Process of accumulating positions in mutual funds over time by investing a set amount of money on a regular basis. This allows the investor to buy more shares when prices are down and fewer when they are up.

Dow Jones Industrial Average. Oldest and most widely quoted stock market indicator. It represents the price direction of 30 blue-chip stocks on the New York Stock Exchange. However, it doesn't always give an accurate view of what's happening with the market as a whole, because it completely ignores small-cap and mid-cap stocks.

Earnings. Net income after all charges, divided by the number of outstanding shares.

Equity Income Fund. Mutual fund that seeks to produce a high level of income without undue risk by investing primarily in a combination of dividend-paying stocks, corporate bonds, and convertibles.

Exchange Privilege. Option enabling fund shareholders to shift investments from one fund to another, usually at no cost.

Ex-Dividend Date. Day on which a mutual fund's declared distributions are deducted from the fund's net asset value and distributed to shareholders.

Expense Ratio. Percent of assets taken from a fund to cover all operating costs.

Family of Funds. Group of mutual funds managed and distributed by the same company; each fund typically has its own investment objective.

Fixed-Income Security. Preferred stock or debt instrument, such as a bond, with a stated percentage or dollar amount of income paid at regular intervals.

401(k) Plan. Employer-sponsored retirement plan enabling employees to defer taxes on a portion of their salaries by making a contribution. In some cases, employers will match part or all of an employee's contribution.

403(b) Plan. Employer-sponsored retirement plan enabling employees of universities, public schools, and nonprofit organizations to defer taxes on a portion of their salaries by earmarking it for the retirement plan.

Front-End Load. Sales fee charged to investors of some funds at the time shares are purchased.

Fund Family. Group of mutual funds managed and distributed by the same company.

Fund Symbol. Letter code used to identify a fund on the exchange.

General Government Bond (Short/Intermediate Term). Mutual fund that seeks to provide current income and stability of principal by investing in a blend of U.S. government-backed securities. The average maturity of bonds in this type of portfolio is usually ten years or less.

Global Stock Fund. Mutual fund that seeks growth by investing primarily in stocks of companies located around the world, including the United States.

Government Agency Issues. Debt securities issued by governmental enterprises, federal agencies, and international institutions.

Growth Fund. Mutual fund that seeks long-term growth without undue risk by investing in the stocks of solid U.S.-based companies.

Growth and Income Fund. Mutual fund that seeks both growth of capital and current income by investing in dividend-paying stocks with the potential for growth.

Growth Stock. Stock of a corporation that shows greater-than-average gains in earnings.

Hedge Fund. Mutual fund that hedges its market commitments by holding securities likely to increase in value, while *selling short* other securities likely to decrease. The sole objective is capital appreciation.

High-Yield Bond Fund.   Mutual fund that invests in corporate bonds that pay high interest and typically have low credit ratings. Such securities are also known as junk bonds.

Income.   Dividends, interest, and/or short-term capital gains paid to a mutual fund's shareholders.

Income Fund.   Mutual fund for which the primary objective is to generate current income.

Index Fund.   Mutual fund that seeks to match the returns of a particular market index, such as the Standard & Poor's 500 or Russell 2000. These funds essentially allow investors to "buy the market" but never outperform it.

Individual Retirement Account (IRA).   Tax-deferred account established to hold funds until retirement.

Inflation.   Persistent upward movement in the general price level of goods and services; its effect is to reduce the purchasing power of money.

Institutional Investor.   Organization (a mutual fund, bank, or insurance company) that trades a large volume of securities.

Interest Rate Risk.   Chance that market rates will rise above the fixed rate of a bond, thus reducing the bond's principal value and total return. (The opposite is also true. If rates fall, the principal value of the bond will rise.) Interest rate risk can be minimized by investing in short-term bond funds.

International Equity Fund.   Mutual fund that seeks growth by investing in securities of companies located in developing markets outside of the United States, such as in Japan, New Zealand, Australia, Canada, and Western Europe. International equity funds entail an added degree of risk because of political instability, currency fluctuations, foreign taxes, and differences in financial reporting standards.

Investment Company.   Corporation, trust, or partnership that invests pooled shareholder dollars in securities, in line with the organization's objective. Mutual funds, also known as "open-end" investment companies, are the most popular type of investment company.

Investment Company Act of 1940.   Federal statute enacted by Congress in 1940, requiring the registration and regulation of investment companies (mutual funds).

Investment Management Company.   Organization hired to advise the directors and trustees of a mutual fund in selecting and supervising assets in the fund's portfolio.

Investment Objective.   Investors' long-term goal; the reason for placing money in a mutual fund in the first place.

Keogh Plan.   Tax-favored retirement program for the self-employed and their employees.

Large-Cap Growth Fund.   Mutual fund that invests in established, growing companies with market capitalizations of $5 billion or more.

Large-Cap Value Fund.   Mutual fund that invests in established companies with market capitalizations of $5 billion or more, when their securities are available at what the manager deems to be bargain prices.

Liquidity.   Ability to redeem all or part of mutual fund shares, on any business day, for the closing net asset value.

Load. Sales commission assessed by some mutual funds to compensate the person who sells them (usually a stockbroker or financial planner). There are two types of loads: (1) front-end loads are taken at the time of the initial purchase; (2) back-end loads are collected when fund shares are redeemed. Loads typically range from 2 to 8 percent.

Long-Term Funds. Mutual fund designed for capital appreciation over an extended period of time.

Management Fee. Amount paid by a mutual fund for the services of an investment adviser.

Market Capitalization. Calculated by multiplying the number of shares outstanding by the per-share price of a stock. Equities can be categorized into several different classes, including micro cap, small cap, mid cap, and large cap. The general guidelines for these classifications are as follows:

- **Micro Cap**—stock market capitalizations of $0 to $300 million.
- **Small Cap**—stock market capitalizations of $300 million to $1 billion.
- **Mid Cap**—stock market capitalizations of $1 billion to $5 billion.
- **Large Cap**—stock market capitalizations of $5 billion or more.

Market Order. Order to buy or sell a security at the best available price.

Mid-Cap Growth Fund. Mutual fund that invests in growing medium-size companies with market capitalizations generally between $1 billion and $5 billion.

Mid-Cap Value Fund. Mutual fund that invests in medium-size companies with market capitalizations generally between $1 billion and $5 billion, when securities are available at what the manager deems to be bargain prices.

Money Market Fund. Highly liquid mutual fund that invests in short-term securities and seeks to maintain a stable net asset value of $1 per share (although this is not guaranteed).

Mortgage-Backed Securities Fund. Mutual fund that invests in mortgage pass-through instruments, such as those issued by the Government National Mortgage Association (GNMA).

Municipal Fund. Fund that deals in bonds issued by a state, city, municipality, or revenue district. Municipal bonds, also known as *munis,* are exempt from federal and, in some cases, state and local income taxes.

Mutual Fund. Investment company that raises money from shareholders and puts it to work in stocks, options, bonds, or money market securities. Offers investors diversification, professional management, liquidity, and convenience.

NASDAQ Composite. An index (formerly National Association of Securities Dealers Automated Quotation System) weighted by market value and representing domestic companies that are sold over-the-counter.

National Association of Securities Dealers (NASD). Self-regulatory organization with authority over firms that distribute mutual fund shares and other securities.

Net Asset Value (NAV). Market worth of one share of a mutual fund. Calculated by adding up the fund's total assets, subtracting any liabilities, and dividing the resulting figure by the number of shares outstanding.

No-Load Fund. Mutual fund for which shares are bought and sold at the prevailing net asset value, without any sales charges or commissions.

Open-End Fund. Mutual fund that stands ready to issue and redeem an unlimited number of shares as requested by investors.

Operating Expenses. Costs paid from a fund's assets, before earnings are distributed to shareholders, to cover overhead and operations.

Over-the-Counter Market. Universe of securities, both stocks and bonds, not listed on a national or regional exchange (like the New York Stock Exchange or NASDAQ stock market). Over-the-counter transactions are primarily conducted through an informal network or by auction.

Payroll Deduction Plan. Arrangement that some employers offer employees to accumulate mutual fund shares. Employees authorize their employer to deduct a specified amount from their salaries at stated times, and to transfer the proceeds to a fund.

Pension Plan. Retirement program based on a defined formula providing employees with benefits paid during the remainder of their lifetime, upon reaching a stated age.

Pension Rollover. Opportunity to take distributions from a qualified pension or profit-sharing plan and reinvest the proceeds in an individual retirement account (IRA) within 60 days from the date of distribution.

Performance Record. Statistical record of the returns a fund and/or fund manager has produced over a stated period of time.

Pooling. Concept behind mutual funds; the assets of various investors with common goals are brought together and invested in a single diversified portfolio.

Portfolio. Collection of investment securities owned by an individual or institution—perhaps including stocks, bonds, and money market instruments.

Portfolio Manager. Person responsible for investing a fund's pool of assets in accordance with the provisions set forth in the prospectus.

Portfolio Turnover. Measure of trading activity in a fund. Shows how frequently a manager buys and sells securities in the portfolio.

Preferred Stock. Equity instrument that generally carries a fixed dividend that must be satisfied before dividends are paid to holders of common shares.

Price-to-Earnings Ratio. Price of a stock divided by its earnings per share.

Principal. Initial amount of money invested in a fund.

Professional Management. Ability to hire an experienced professional to decide which securities in the fund's portfolio should be bought and sold. A major advantage to mutual fund investing.

Prospectus. Official document describing a mutual fund's investment objectives, policies, services, fees, and past performance history.

Proxy Statement. Information about fund matters, sent to shareholders of record annually for a vote. (Sadly, many fund investors don't even bother to vote. Fund trustees can then get their way on such matters as raising operating expenses and changing investment policies, when these outcomes may not be in the best interest of shareholders.)

Prudent Man Rule. Law governing the investment of trust funds in states that give broad discretion to trustees.

Qualified Plans. Retirement plans that meet the requirements of Sections 401(k), 403(a), or 403(b) of the Internal Revenue Code and/or the Self-Employed Individuals Tax Retirement Act.

Record Date. Date by which shareholder must own shares in a fund in order to receive the announced distribution.

Redemption. Act of selling shares in a mutual fund.

Redemption-In-Kind. Redemption of investment company shares for which payment is made in portfolio securities rather than cash.

Registered Investment Company. Investment company that has filed a registration statement with the Securities and Exchange Commission (SEC) under the requirements of the Investment Company Act of 1940.

Reinvestment. Process of using mutual fund dividends and capital gains distributions to automatically buy additional shares, thus increasing overall holdings.

Return on Investment. Amount of money an investment earns over a given period of time. This figure is often expressed as a percentage.

Risk. Accepted possibility that an investment will fluctuate in value.

Risk/Reward Tradeoff. Principle stating that an investment must offer higher potential returns to compensate for the likelihood of increased volatility. Investors are normally willing to accept higher risk on long-term investments, because the effects of price volatility generally diminish over time. Conversely, they seek lower risk with short-term investments, where accessibility and preservation of principal override the need for maximum return.

Rollover. Shifting of assets from one qualified retirement plan to another without incurring a penalty.

Roth IRA. Tax-deferred account in which contributions are nondeductible, but earnings grow tax-free. Eligibility for the Roth IRA gradually phases out at income levels of $95,000 to $110,000 for individuals, and $150,000 to $160,000 for married couples.

Sales Load. Amount charged for the sale of mutual fund shares by a stockbroker or other financial professional. The cost is usually added to the fund's net asset value.

Sector Fund. Mutual fund that invests in the securities of a single industry or country-specific region.

Securities and Exchange Commission (SEC). Federal agency charged with regulating the registration and distribution of mutual fund shares.

Senior Securities. Notes, bonds, debentures, or preferred stocks that have a claim to assets and earnings that supercedes claims by holders of common stock.

Series Funds. Funds organized with separate portfolios of securities, each with its own unique investment objective.

Shareholder. Investor who owns shares in a mutual fund.

Short Sale. Sale of a security that is borrowed, not owned, in the hope that the price will go down so it can be repurchased at a lower price, therefore generating a profit through the underlying spread.

Short-Term Funds.   Mutual funds that invest in securities with the intention of holding them for one year or less (i.e., money market funds).

Small-Cap Growth Fund.   Mutual fund that invests in small, fast-growing companies with market capitalizations generally under $1 billion.

Small-Cap Value Fund.   Mutual fund that invests in small, growing companies with market capitalizations generally under $1 billion, whose securities are available at what the manager deems to be bargain prices.

Small-Company or Small-Cap Fund.   Mutual fund that seeks capital appreciation by investing in the stocks of small, fast-growing companies.

Standard & Poor's Composite Index of 500 Stocks (S&P 500).   Index that tracks the performance of 500 widely held common stocks, weighted by market value. It includes mostly blue-chip names and represents some two-thirds of the U.S. stock market's total value.

Statement of Additional Information (SAI).   Supplement to a prospectus; contains updated and more complete information about a mutual fund. (Also referred to as "Part B" of the registration statement.)

Stock.   Representation of ownership in a corporation. Usually issued in terms of shares.

Systematic Withdrawal Plan.   Program in which fund shareholders receive regular automatic distributions from their investments. Shares are redeemed to meet the shareholders' income needs, and payments are sent out monthly, quarterly, or annually, as specified.

Tax-Deferred Income.   Dividends, interest, and capital gains received from investments held in qualified retirement plans, such as IRAs, Keoghs, 401(k)s, and 403(b)s. This income is not subject to current taxation. Instead, it is taxed upon withdrawal.

Time Horizon.   Length of time money is to be invested in a fund. Time horizon helps to pinpoint the types of investments that should be included in a portfolio mix. The longer the time horizon, the more risk one can afford to take, because of the ability to weather any short-term declines in the market.

Total Return.   Measure of a fund's overall performance during a given period of time. Encompasses all aspects affecting return, including dividends, capital gains distributions, and changes in net asset value.

Transfer Agent.   Organization or person hired by a mutual fund to prepare and maintain records on shareholders' accounts.

Treasury Bill.   Non-interest-bearing security issued at a discount to its value by the U.S. Treasury. Maturity is one year or less.

Turnover Ratio.   Measure of how frequently a manager buys and sells securities in the portfolio. The higher the number, the more trading that occurs.

12b-1 Fee.   Mutual fund expense used to pay for marketing and distribution costs.

Underwriter.   Organization or person acting as the distributor of a mutual fund's shares to broker/dealers and investors.

U.S. Government Bond.   Bond issued by the U.S. Treasury or other government agency. Considered among the safest investments available, because they are backed by the full faith and credit of the U.S. government.

U.S. Government Securities. Various types of marketable securities, including bills, notes, and bonds, issued by the U.S. Treasury.

Value Fund. Mutual fund with the objective of buying stocks in companies whose shares are considered to be undervalued, as measured by price-to-earnings ratio, book value, or other valuation benchmark.

Variable Annuity. Investment contract sold by an insurance company. Accumulates capital, often through mutual fund investments, which is later converted to an income stream, often at retirement.

Volatility. Measure of risk that refers to how a fund's share price moves up or down compared to its underlying index.

Warrant. Option to buy a specific number of shares of stock at a stated price during a limited time period.

Wash Sale. Purchase and sale of a security either simultaneously or within a short time period. Wash sales that take place within 30 days of the underlying purchase do not quality for a tax loss deduction under rules set forth by the Internal Revenue Service.

Withdrawal Plan. Program in which shareholders receive income on principal payments at regular intervals from their mutual fund investments.

Yield. Measure of the net income (dividends and interest minus expenses) earned by the securities in a fund's portfolio during a specific period of time.

Yield to Maturity. The rate of return offered on a debt security if held to maturity.

INDEX

Now that you're ready to start investing in mutual funds,
keep track of your investments with the best
mutual fund research tools available anywhere.

**Be sure to check out these special offers
available only to investors
who have purchased the**
NYIF Guide to Mutual Funds 1999...

Value Line Publishing, Inc.
220 E. 42nd St.
New York, NY 10017
www.valueline.com

The Most Trusted Name for Investment Advice

Analyze and Track

The Value Line No-Load Analyzer *for Windows*® focuses exclusively on no-load and low-load funds. It includes sophisticated sorting, screening, filtering, portfolio analysis, and graphics capabilities. Subscribers can receive either monthly or quarterly updates, and update weekly data by accessing the **Data Updates** section of our web site: *www.value-line.com.*

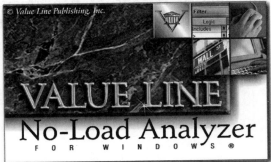

Highlights of this service include:

- Coverage of over 4,000 no-load and low-load funds.
- Over 170 data fields.
- 20-year performance data.
- Investor Profile Questionnaire with sample portfolio allocations.
- Financial calculators, including college and retirement calculators.
- Portfolio tracking with *Stress Tester* and *Rebalance* features.
- Style attribution analysis.
- Analyst commentaries.
- Over two dozen reports and graphs, including risk-reward, performance, holdings, asset allocation, and more.
- Manager bios and photos.